VOICES OF WISDOM
A Multicultural Philosophy Reader
Second Edition

Gary E. Kessler
California State University, Bakersfield

Wadsworth Publishing Company
Belmont, California
A Division of Wadsworth, Inc.

For my daughters Amy and Sara
From whose voices I have learned much

Philosophy Editor: Tammy Goldfeld
Editorial Assistant: Kelly Zavislak
Production Services Coordinator: Debby Kramer
Production: Julie Kranhold and Dianne Rhudy/Ex Libris
Print Buyer: Karen Hunt
Permissions Editor: Bob Kauser
Designer: Polly Christensen
Copy Editor: Lisa Watson
Cover Design: Laurie Anderson
Cover Art: Piet Mondrian, *Trees* c. 1912, oil on canvas, 37 x 27 ⅞″ (94 x 70.8 cm).
    The Carnegie Museum of Art; Patrons Art Fund, 61.1.
Compositor: G & S Typesetters, Inc.
Printer: Malloy Lithographing, Inc.

*This book is printed on
acid-free recycled paper.*

I T P™

International Thomson Publishing
The trademark ITP is used under license.

Printed in the United States of America

1 2 3 4 5 6 7 8 9 10—99 98 97 96 95

Library of Congress Cataloging-in-Publication Data

Voices of wisdom: a multicultural philosophy reader/[edited by]
    Gary E. Kessler.—2nd ed.
        p.   cm.
    ISBN 0-534-21630-7
    1. Philosophy—Introductions.   I. Kessler, Gary E.
BD41.V65   1994
100—dc20   94-542

Contents

Preface

The unique feature of this introductory reader is its multicultural character. Practically all of the introductory readers available today treat philosophy as if it were entirely an Anglo-European male phenomenon. Little or no attention is given to Hindu, Buddhist, Chinese, African, Native American, Latin American, and feminist philosophy. This text remedies that situation, offering to those who wish it the possibility of assigning significant readings that represent the global nature of philosophizing.

It is often said that philosophizing is a natural human activity. If we are reflective at all, we cannot help but wonder about issues fundamental to human existence. And yet, beginning philosophy courses often appear far removed from the concerns of students and, by the very material excluded, strongly imply that only European and North American answers to fundamental questions are worth studying. This textbook covers some of the philosophical problems beginning students often find stimulating and provides an opportunity for them to see that at least some of these problems are indeed universal and fundamental to *all* of humanity. They will also learn that ideas from other cultures are worth pondering and that these ideas make important contributions to human understanding.

Pedagogical Features

I agree with John Dewey's often-repeated comment that we learn by doing. In my experience, the more I can get my students to do for themselves, the more they learn. Thus, rather than providing summaries of the selections (which discourage careful reading by the students), I provide instead the background information needed to understand the selections, and I supply questions that are designed to guide the students' reading *prior* to the selections. This approach encourages students to formulate their own analytical and critical questions about the material. It also gives instructors an opportunity to require the students to answer the questions in a philosophical "notebook" before class meetings. The questions and the students' responses can then be used as the basis for class discussion. This requires students to become actively engaged in the process of figuring out what a text means and allows instructors to correct students' misunderstandings, to clarify particularly difficult points, and to provide alternative interpretations in class.

I have written the introductory material in an informal, engaging, and, I trust, clear manner. I hope to engage students in the thinking process by connecting the selections to questions and issues the students have already begun to encounter. The selections themselves have been classroom-tested and represent different degrees of difficulty. Most will challenge beginning students to think in more depth and in a more precise way.

Topics

Voices of Wisdom includes much philosophical material that has come to be regarded as "classic" in the West. This material is included for two reasons. First, most students take an introductory philosophy course in conjunction with general education and, as part of that experience, it is important that they read philosophical writing significant to the Western cultural tradition. Second, this writing is good philosophy (that is why it has become "classic"), and students should experience the ideas of profound philosophical minds. But profound philosophical minds exist all over the world, and, while other styles of thinking and other traditions may be very different, they are no less important.

I begin with a **Prelude** that sets the tone of philosophical wonder which I sustain throughout the book. In **Chapter 1,** I discuss the nature of philosophy, the meaning of rationality, and how to read philosophy. The section on the meaning of rationality has been completely revised in this second edition. Some basic principles of critical reasoning and a glossary of technical terms are provided in two appendixes. The appendix on critical thinking provides students with the minimal tools of logic necessary for them to engage in critical analysis of different sorts of arguments. I have placed this material in an appendix so that instructors may assign it at the points in their courses where they think it is most appropriate. I recommend assigning it near the beginning because so much of what is included in the text requires students to use analytical and critical skills.

In most chapters the material is arranged chronologically. Sometimes, however, another sort of arrangement is more pedagogically useful, and so I have not restricted myself to the chronological pattern in all cases.

Some critics of the first edition have argued that one should begin with epistemology or metaphysics rather than with moral issues, because so many ethical theories presuppose metaphysical and epistemological views. This is a strong argument. However, I have decided to retain the order of the chapters from the first edition because it is, in my experience, more pedagogically effective. Of course instructors can order the chapters any way they think best. I have begun with the questions "How should one live?" and "How can we know what is right?" (**Chapters 2** and **3**) because these are fundamental questions that have received much global attention. Further, these are questions with which students can connect existentially, thereby allowing for immediate values clarification. I have shortened some of the selections, rewritten the introductions to some, used some new translations, and replaced an old selection with a new one. **Chapter 4** "What Makes a Society Just?" is now totally devoted to political philosophy with four new selections; and a new **Chapter 5** "Is Justice for All Possible?" has been created to deal with applied ethics and social issues in a pro/con format. **Chapter 6** "Are We Free or Determined?" has been completely revised and forms a transition from moral issues of responsibility to metaphysical concerns.

I take up ontological and epistemological questions directly in **Chapter 7,** "What Is Really Real?" and **Chapter 8,** "Is Knowledge Possible?" because the answers to moral problems reflect views on what is real and how we might know it is. The division between moral, metaphysical, and epistemological issues may be useful for purposes of organization, but the problems and questions are logically connected. Questions about how we distinguish appearance from reality lead naturally into questions about how we distinguish error from truth. Both chapters have been revised with the addition of new materials.

Religious issues come next. **Chapter 9** "Is There a God?" and **Chapter 10** "Why Evil?" have been partially revised. I construe the question about the existence of God as, in part, a question about what (who) caused the universe. Hence, issues of science and its relationship to religion are discussed. Since the problem of evil is one of the most serious challenges to the assertion that an all-powerful and perfectly good God exists, I take it up next. Unfortunately, space constraints have forced me to drop the chapter from the first edition dealing with the problem of faith and/or reason. Many users reported not covering this topic and wanted coverage of other topics.

The mind-body problem is closely related to issues of personal identity and life after death; thus I have placed these issues together in an extensively revised **Chapter 11** "Who Am I and Can I Survive Death?" Although the issue of immortality might be treated as a separate religious problem, it presupposes a number of important philosophical ideas relating to dualism and personal identity.

I close with a completely new **Postscript** that addresses the issue of multicultural education, its justification, and value. In it, students are invited to stand back from their experience and reflect on the issue of multiculturalism. A number of issues addressed in the book (such as relativism and comparative cultural evaluation) arise again here. Hence this postscript can be used to draw together various concerns and problems that have surfaced in the other parts of the book.

Philosophy in a Multicultural Perspective

Although I wish to stress the universal nature of philosophizing, I am well aware of the dangers of anachronism. A text of this sort not only faces the problems associated with anachronism in the historical sense, but also with what we might term "cultural" anachronism. The writings of ancient philosophers mingle with modern texts, and thinkers from alien cultures are brought together. The student may get the impression that Plato, Buddha, Mill, Confucius, Descartes, and Aristotle are all contemporaries discussing the same issues with the same concepts in English! There *are* similarities. But there are also vast differences. Where appropriate, the important differences are stressed in my introductory remarks.

Historical and cultural comparisons are inevitable, and I encourage them. However, I wish to stress that this reader is not meant primarily to be an exercise in comparative philosophy. It is meant to serve a course that introduces students to "doing" philosophy by drawing on *multicultural* resources. The students who read this text should be impressed with the rich diversity that comprises global philosophizing and should learn the art of philosophizing in a broader and more inclusive context than is usual.

I do wish to stress that it is *global* philosophizing with which I am concerned. Some associate the word "multicultural" almost exclusively with "multiethnic" and "minorities." Those who do so will expect more African American, Latin American, Native American, and feminist philosophers than I have included. These voices also need to be heard, and I have included some. But my primary concern has been to provide sources that promote an *international* perspective. I believe it is important to educate students for a new century in which an understanding of the interconnectedness of all peoples will be increasingly important in determining the policies and practices of nations.

My selection of issues betrays my own Anglo-European perspective. While many of the topics are fundamental and universal (How should one live? What is really real? What is good?), their importance and centrality differ from tradition to tradition. The mind-body problem, the puzzle of freedom and determinism, the problem of evil—these are not necessarily the central problems that gripped the minds of Chinese or Hindu philosophers. Just as Anglo-European philosophers have not had much to say about Karma, Buddhist thinkers have not been overly concerned with reconciling the existence of evil with an all-good creator God.

However, I do believe this Western way of organizing the material is justified in this instance. Even though the significance of the problems and the way they are formulated differ from culture to culture, many of the underlying issues are the same. One cannot reflect for long on Karma and reincarnation without addressing issues relating to freedom and human identity. Furthermore, I think it best, for introductory and practical purposes, to organize the material around traditional Anglo-European philosophical themes. Many students already have some concern with these issues (e.g., the existence of God). In addition, most introductory courses deal with these themes, and this book allows instructors to continue that practice; but some new and different voices are added, thereby enriching philosophical thinking.

It should be noted that there exists no culturally neutral set of categories for organizing the material. If I had used the dominant concerns of, let us say, the Hindu tradition (concerns such as release from suffering, duty and the stages of life, the nature of bondage) to organize the selections, I would not have thereby escaped a cultural perspective. Perhaps, as a multicultural approach becomes more commonplace in introductory courses and as Western philosophy becomes more open and diverse, new categories will emerge. However, until that day, the sources need to be organized in some fashion. What is important is that we are aware of the limitations of our categories and that we continually remind ourselves of the diverse and subtle ways long-held biases influence our thinking as well as the way we select and organize materials.

John Stuart Mill in his essay *On Liberty* spoke of how the European family of nations had benefited from the interaction of a variety of ideas:

> What has made the European family of nations an improving, instead of a stationary, portion of mankind? Not any superior excellence in them which, when it exists, exists as the effect, not as the cause, but their remarkable diversity of character and culture. Individuals, classes, nations have been extremely unlike one another: they have struck out a great variety of paths, each leading to something valuable; and although at every period those who travelled in different paths have been intolerant of one another, and each would have thought it an excellent thing if all the rest would have been compelled to travel his road, their attempts to thwart each other's development have rarely had any permanent success, and each has in time endured to receive the good which the others have offered. Europe is, in my judgement, wholly indebted to this plurality of paths for its progressive and many sided development.

And so too, I might add, is the United States indebted to cultural plurality.

Acknowledgments

A book like this is written, edited, and revised by many people. The reviewers of my first edition were particularly helpful in the selection of topics and suggestions of readings. I wish it were possible to follow all of their valuable suggestions. Tammy Goldfeld's enthusiasm, suggestions, and support have been immensely valuable. The staff at Wadsworth has been most accommodating and patient. They have kept me from many errors. Whatever errors remain are of my own doing.

I would like to thank the following reviewers for their helpful suggestions and comments: Kostas Bagakis, San Francisco State University; James F. Doyle, University of Missouri, St. Louis; Marie Friquegnon, William Paterson College of New Jersey; Richard Gull, University of Michigan, Flint; Steve S. Infantino, College of Lake County; Michael Neville, Washington State University; and Susan Rouse, Kennesaw State College.

A very special thanks goes to my wife Katy, whose ideas, critical insights, and loving support made this book possible.

I also wish to thank all of you who used the first edition. Your responses have been gratifying and reinforce my hope that one day a multicultural approach to the study, teaching, and doing of philosophy will be commonplace. I hope this second edition (which includes over 23 new selections based on careful consideration of the advice of those of you who have used the first edition) proves more useful than the first, and I would appreciate hearing your responses to this new edition—about how it works and how it can be improved.

Gary E. Kessler

Prelude

HAVE YOU EVER WONDERED whether you are awake or dreaming you are awake? Have you ever wondered whether there was any truly objective perspective from which all arguments could be definitely settled? Have you ever thought that perhaps all views of the world, even those that seem to contradict each other, might somehow be in harmony with one another? If you have, you are not alone.

Zhuangzi lived in China somewhere between 399 and 295 B.C.E. You might have heard of him under the name of Chuang-Tzu or Chuang Chou (I'm using the Pinyin spelling of his name, the spelling used in China, and I will be using the Pinyin spelling of Chinese words in the rest of this book). If you have heard of him, you might also know he was a Daoist philosopher. Daoist philosophers are very much interested in nature and in the **Dao** (you may have encountered this word spelled *Tao,* which is in accord with the Wade-Giles system, a system named after its inventors and used in many of the translations I have selected). The *Dao* is the Way of nature (for more on the *Dao* see Section 7.1). Zhuangzi viewed nature as a universal process of constant change, binding all things together into a vast, natural harmony. He taught that we should live freely, naturally, and spontaneously in accord with the *Dao*.

Some of Zhuangzi's writings were collected in a book that bears his name. The selection that follows comes from a section of that book entitled "The Equality of Things." In this section he is concerned with whether there might be some absolutely objective point of view from which we might firmly and finally distinguish right from wrong, truth from error, reality from appearance. He suggests that if we look at things from the point of view of nature they appear equal or relative to one another—relative in the sense that they depend on one another. Further, our views are relative in the sense that every view reflects some particular and limited perspective. This insight does not lead Zhuangzi to despair, however, because once we realize the relativity and equality of things we can forget about distinctions and "relax in the realm of the infinite." In other words, we can realize harmony with the *Dao*.

Before you read this selection think about how you might answer this question: How do you *know* you are not now dreaming?

The Equality of Things

ZHUANGZI

"How do I know that the love of life is not a delusion? And how do I know that the hate of death is not like a man who lost his home when young and does not know where his home is to return to? Li Chi was the daughter of the border warden of Ai. When the Duke of Chin first got her, she wept until the bosom of her dress was drenched with tears. But when she came to the royal residence, shared with the Duke his luxurious couch and ate delicate food, she regretted that she had wept. How do I know that the dead will not repent having previously craved for life?

"Those who dream of the banquet may weep the next morning, and those who dream of weeping may go out to hunt after dawn. When we dream, we do not know that we are dreaming. In our dreams we may even interpret our dreams. Only after we are awake do we know we have dreamed. Finally there comes a great awakening, and then we know life is a great dream. But the stupid think they are awake all the time and believe they know it distinctly. Are we (honorable) rulers? Are we (humble) shepherds? How vulgar! Both Confucius and you were dreaming. When I say you were dreaming, I am also dreaming. This way of talking may be called perfectly strange. If after ten thousand generations we could meet one great sage who can explain this, it would be like meeting him in as short a time as in a single morning or evening.

"Suppose you and I argue. If you beat me instead of my beating you, are you really right and am I really wrong? If I beat you instead of your beating me, am I really right and are you really wrong? Or are we both partly right and partly wrong? Or are we both wholly right and wholly wrong? Since between us neither you nor I know which is right, others are naturally in the dark. Whom shall we ask to arbitrate? If we ask someone who agrees with you, since he has already agreed with you, how can he arbitrate? If we ask someone who agrees with me, since he has already agreed with me, how can he arbitrate? If we ask someone who disagrees with both you and me to arbitrate, since he has already disagreed with you and me, how can he arbitrate? If we ask someone who agrees with both you and me to arbitrate, since he has already agreed with you and me, how can he arbitrate? Thus among you, me, and others, none knows which is right. Shall we wait for still others? The great variety of sounds are relative to each other just as much as they are not relative to each other. To harmonize them in the functioning of Nature and leave them in the process of infinite evolution is the way to complete our lifetime."

"What is meant by harmonizing them with the functioning of Nature?"

"We say this is right or wrong, and is so or is not so. If the right is really right, then the fact that it is different from the wrong leaves no room for argument. If what is so is really so, then the fact that it is different from what is not so leaves no room for argument. Forget the passage of time (life and death) and forget the distinction of right and wrong. Relax in the realm of the infinite and thus abide in the realm of the infinite."

The Shade asks the Shadow, "A little while ago you moved, and now you stop. A little while ago you sat down and now you stand up. Why this instability of purpose?"

"Do I depend on something else to be this way?" answered the Shadow. "Does that something on which I depend also depend on something else? Do I depend on anything any more than a snake depends on its discarded scale or a

From Chan, W., editor, A Source Book in Chinese Philosophy. *Copyright © 1963 by Princeton University Press. Excerpt, pp. 189–190. Reprinted with permission of Princeton University Press. Footnotes deleted.*

cicada on its new wings? How can I tell why I am so or why I am not so?"

Once I, Chuang Chou, dreamed that I was a butterfly and was happy as a butterfly. I was conscious that I was quite pleased with myself, but I did not know that I was Chou. Suddenly I awoke, and there I was, visibly Chou. I do not know whether it was Chou dreaming that he was a butterfly or the butterfly dreaming that it was Chou. Between Chou and the butterfly there must be some distinction. [But one may be the other.] This is called the transformation of things.

Chapter 1

What Is Philosophy?

"*. . . those who are eager to learn because they wonder at things are lovers of wisdom* (philosophoi)."

ALEXANDER OF APHRODISIAS

1.1. A Definition of Philosophy

Have you ever wondered about why you are here? Have you ever been curious about what you can believe? Have you ever marveled at the beauty of nature or been puzzled and upset by the suffering of good people? Have you ever thought about what you can know or what you ought to do or whether there is any point to life? When you hear the word "philosophy," what do you think it means? Think about it awhile and write down your answer.

Aristotle (384–322 B.C.E.) was a Greek philosopher and a contemporary of Zhuangzi. While Zhuangzi was wondering about dreaming, Aristotle was claiming that philosophy begins in wonder. Aristotle was impressed by the ability of human beings to think. In fact he defined humans as "rational animals." Aristotle claimed that from this ability to reflect on our experiences, to wonder and be curious about what happens to us and our environment, philosophy arises.

Of course this is not the sole cause of philosophizing. Sufficient leisure must be available to engage in reflection, and hence economic and cultural factors play an important role in promoting and influencing human curiosity. But without the human capacity to wonder and be curious, it is doubtful that philosophical thinking would occur. I hope that this text will stimulate your natural ability to wonder, teach you something of the art of wondering, and help you learn how to live in wonder. Cultivating the art of wondering is important, Aristotle believed, because such an art leads us along the path toward wisdom.

The word "philosophy" comes from a combination of two Greek words—*philos* meaning "love" and *sophia* meaning "wisdom." Etymologically "philosophy" means the love of wisdom. The sort of love indicated by the word *philos* is the kind of love that exists between close friends. So the philosopher is the lover of or the close friend of wisdom. The historical origin of a word, however, often does not help us very much when we are searching for an adequate definition today. The meanings of words sometimes change. Also, meanings derived etymologically are sometimes unclear. If the philosopher is the lover of wisdom, then what is wisdom? About that, philosophers, even Greek philosophers, disagree.

Philosophy in Western culture was born in the sixth century B.C.E. among a group of thinkers called the Pre-Socratics. According to tradition, one of these thinkers, Pythagoras (about 570 B.C.E.), coined the word "philosophy." Along with other Pre-Socratics, he was intensely interested in nature, in knowing how the universe or cosmic order developed, and in figuring out what things were made of. These thinkers disagreed about the stuff of which things are made (some said earth, some air, others fire, still others water or some combination of these elements), but many of them did think that wisdom consisted of knowledge about nature. To love wisdom, as far as they were concerned, is to search for knowledge about the universe.

A century later, another group of thinkers in Athens offered their services as teachers to those who could afford them. They claimed to teach virtue. The Greek word for virtue (*arete*) means "excellence or power." So to possess virtue is to possess power. Wisdom, they taught, is the possession of virtue. It is to have certain powers or abilities, especially in the social and political realm, to influence people and be successful. Since these teachers claimed to possess this wisdom, they came to be called "Sophists" or "The Wise Ones." For them, philosophy is not the search for knowledge about the universe nor the *search* for wisdom. Rather, philosophy is the *possession* of wisdom and hence the possession of virtue or excellence, especially in the social and political dimensions of life.

Socrates (470–399 B.C.E.) lived in Athens at the same time as the Sophists. He spent his days wandering around the marketplace asking people questions about all kinds of things. He found himself perplexed by things other people claimed to know. For example, people claimed to know what knowledge, justice, virtue, and the right way to live are. The Sophists, for instance, claimed to teach these things. But under Socrates' relentless critical questioning, the definitions and grand theories that people held about these sorts of things collapsed. The oracle at Delphi, a well-respected source of divine truth in the ancient world, said that Socrates was the wisest man in Athens. When word of this got to Socrates, he was greatly puzzled. How could he, who knew next to nothing and spent his days asking others, be the wisest? What about the Sophists, the teachers of wisdom? Were not they the wisest? Socrates did believe he knew what virtue is; it is knowledge. But what on earth is knowledge? He had to confess he did not know. So how could he be wise? And yet, he reasoned, the oracle of Delphi could not be lying. It was, after all, the voice of the god Apollo. But the oracle was tricky. You had to figure out what it meant.

Finally Socrates understood. Wisdom, the oracle was telling him, is knowing that he did not know! Wisdom is the awareness of our ignorance, an awareness of the limitations of knowledge. Let the Sophists claim to be wise; the best Socrates could do was to claim he was the lover of wisdom. He lived his life in the pursuit of wisdom as lovers live their lives in pursuit of the beloved. For him philosophy was a critical examination of our pretensions to knowledge and the constant search for that final truth that always seems to be just beyond our grasp.

Of course the Greeks were not the only ones to philosophize. The pursuit of wisdom is common to all cultures. Nor were the Greeks the only ones to disagree about the nature of wisdom. For example, in South Asia some philosophical traditions claimed that wisdom is to come to know one's true self as an eternal essence of pure consciousness. But other traditions (most notably the Buddhist) claimed that there is no such thing as a true essential self, and wisdom consists, at least in part, in coming to understand this fact.

There are different understandings of what wisdom is, what philosophy is all about, and hence there is a wide variety of definitions. No single definition could possibly capture all the nuances of the art of wondering. But this does not mean that we can define philosophy any way we wish. And it does not mean that some definitions are not better than others. Let me offer my definition, which, I think, states something important about philosophizing and helps us distinguish it from other types of thinking. **Philosophy is the rational attempt to formulate, understand, and answer fundamental questions.**

Many people think that philosophy is a body of doctrines and that philosophers are people who have answers to difficult questions about the meaning of life. My definition stresses that philosophy is an activity rather than a body of set teachings and that philosophers are as concerned with formulating and understanding questions as they are with finding answers.

Formulating questions is very important. What we ask and how we ask it determine, in large part, where we look for answers and the kinds of answers we get. Progress in many fields consists, in part, of an ever greater refinement of our questions and more precision and sophistication in our methods of interrogation. You won't get good answers if you don't ask the right questions.

Understanding what we are after when we ask questions is as important as formulating questions. Words are often ambiguous and vague; we must be as clear as possible about what they mean. If I ask, "What is the meaning of life?" what do I mean? What am I looking for? Is this the best way to put it? What might count as a helpful answer? Where should I look for an answer? Am I asking about the purpose of life? Is life the sort of thing that has a purpose? Or am I interested in what makes life worthwhile? Is the purpose of life (if there is one) the same as what makes life valuable or worthwhile?

Of course the purpose of formulating and understanding questions as precisely as we can is to find answers. But often our answers lead to further questions. Why assume some answer is final? Or why assume all questions we can ask have answers? Also, what counts as an answer? How do I know when I have a good one?

Jane: What is the meaning of life?

José: What do you mean by that question?

Jane: I mean, what is the purpose of life?

José: Oh, that's easy, its purpose is reproduction. That's what my biology text says.

Is José's answer a good one? Is it the sort of answer Jane is after? Can this question be answered with factual information, or is it about values? When Jane asks, "What is the meaning of life?" is she asking, "What makes life ultimately valuable?" And if she is asking that, then the answer José gives may well miss the mark (unless, of course, Jane thinks reproduction is more valuable than anything else).

Bertrand Russell (1872–1970), a leading British philosopher, remarked:

Philosophy is to be studied, not so much for the sake of any definite answers to its questions, since no definite answers can, as a rule, be known to be true; but rather for the sake of the questions themselves; because these questions enlarge our conception of what is possible, enrich our intellectual imagination, and diminish the dogmatic assurance which closes the mind against speculation; but above all because, through the greatness of the universe which philosophy contemplates, the mind also is rendered great, and becomes capable of that union with the universe which constitutes its highest good. (1959, pp. 93–94)

I said in my definition that philosophers are concerned with not just any sort of question, but with *fundamental* questions. The word "fundamental" means "basic" and has to do with what is primary. Hence fundamental questions are radical questions in the sense of pertaining to roots. They are the most basic questions we can ask. Therefore they are often *abstract* questions that have to do with a wide area of human experience. But even though these sorts of questions are abstract, they are about concepts we employ every day. We are constantly making judgments about good and bad, right and wrong, true and false, reality and fiction, beautiful and ugly, just and unjust. But what is good? By what norms can we distinguish right behavior from wrong? What is truth? How can I distinguish appearance from reality? Is beauty only in the eye of the beholder? What is justice, and is it ever possible to achieve it?

Some of the main branches of Western philosophy are distinguished by the kinds of fundamental questions they ask. Many philosophers have regarded "What is truly real?" as a fundamental question. Note the word "truly." I did not ask, "What is real?" but "What is *truly* real?" In other words, I am assuming that not everything that appears to be real is real. Or, to put that another way, by asking, "What is truly real?" I am asking how we might distinguish appearance from reality. The branch of philosophy called **metaphysics** deals with this and related issues. One of its purposes, some philosophers have claimed, is to develop a theory of reality or a theory of what is genuinely real. It is also concerned with what might be the most fundamental question we can think of, "Why is there something rather than nothing?"

What is knowledge and what is truth? These seem to be good candidates for fundamental questions. The branch of Western philosophy known as **epistemology** concerns itself with the issues of knowledge and truth. Epistemologists search for a theory of what knowledge is and how it might be distinguished from opinion. They look for a definition of truth and wonder how we might correctly distinguish truth from error.

Axiology is a third main branch of Western philosophy. It has to do with the study of value and the distinction between value and fact. Traditionally it is divided into two main subdivisions: **aesthetics** and **ethics.** Aesthetics deals with such questions as: Is beauty a matter of taste or is it something objective? What standards should be used to judge artistic work? Can we define art? Ethics attempts to decide what values and principles we should use to judge human action as morally right or wrong. What is the greatest good? How should one live? Applied ethics applies these values and principles to such social concerns as abortion, capital punishment, discrimination, and euthanasia in order to determine what would be the right or wrong thing to do in each case.

Fundamental questions, it is said by some, are not just basic and abstract, they are also *universal* questions. They are the sorts of questions any thinking person anywhere and at any time might ask. They arise out of our capacity to wonder about ourselves and the world in which we live.

Although fundamental questions are universal, or nearly so, it should be noted that the way I have described the organization of the field of philosophy (metaphysics, epistemology, axiology) is decidedly Western. Different societies organize knowledge in different ways. Also, what may seem fundamental in one society may seem far less important in another. For example, some Buddhist philosophers have been suspicious of intellectual speculation about metaphysical matters, especially questions like "Does God exist?" This question, so important to many people, excites little interest among these Buddhist thinkers.

It should also be noted that each of the three main branches of Western philosophy deals with important distinctions that all of us learn to make based on the standards our society teaches us. Hence, metaphysics is concerned with the distinction between *appearance and reality,* epistemology with the distinction between *knowledge and opinion,* and axiology with the distinction between *fact and value.* One important question is whether we can discover criteria for making these distinctions that are universal and not merely relative to our own particular time in history and our own particular cultural view. Fundamental and abstract questions about reality, knowledge, and value and the distinctions these questions imply, may be universal in the sense that most cultures have developed intellectual traditions concerned with these issues. But the concrete way the questions are asked, understood, and answered varies a great deal from one tradition of reflection to another.

For example, Plato (428–348 B.C.E.) made the distinction between knowledge and opinion, at least in part, by claiming that opinion has to do with beliefs about the world which are based on our sensations, but knowledge has to do with the reality we discover through our reason. For him logic and mathematics constituted examples of knowledge, but information about physical objects based on sensation did not. Under the influence of physical science, many people today would be inclined to say almost the opposite of what Plato said. For instance, many of my students have maintained that knowledge is what empirical science provides, and opinion is a product of abstract speculation.

As twentieth-century students living in a highly technological and pluralistic society, we live in a very different world from the ancient Greeks or Chinese or Indians. Yet we, like them, wonder about life and ask basic questions about what is real, what is true, what is good, and what is beautiful. This is not to say that there are not vast differences among philosophies. There are. Something of this variety you are about to experience firsthand as you read different philosophers from different cultures and different eras.

In sum, I think philosophy is the activity of rationally attempting to formulate, understand, and answer fundamental questions. I have discussed most of the parts of that definition except the word "rational." Why must it be a rational attempt? And what is it to be rational, anyway? If we cannot agree on what rationality is, how can we know what constitutes a rational attempt to formulate and answer basic questions?

1.2. What Is Rationality?

This fundamental question is one of the most hotly debated issues in philosophy today, and I cannot hope to settle the issue here. The most I can do is give you some idea about what the issues are, describe some of the different views, and offer a few thoughts of my own.

William James (1842–1910), a great American philosopher, said that "philosophy is the unusually stubborn attempt to think clearly." Now "thinking" is a word with a much broader meaning than the word "rational." To be rational is to think, but all thinking is not necessarily rational thinking. James does add the qualification "clearly." That narrows the field somewhat. But what is clear thinking, and how do we know it when we see it?

Reread that paragraph in the Prelude where Zhuangzi talks about two people arguing. It begins, "Suppose you and I argue." Zhuangzi wonders how we might decide who is right and who is wrong. You and I are not in a good position to make such a decision, at least not an objective one, because the fact that we are arguing about who is right and who is wrong shows we disagree. To bring in a third party to settle the dispute does not seem to help much because he or she will either disagree with you or with me or with both of us and what was a two-person argument now becomes a three-person argument.

Zhuangzi is wondering how we might proceed to settle an argument. What procedures do we have that will eventuate in agreement? Should we appeal to authority? Perhaps some divine revelation? A long-standing tradition? Common sense? Force? Rationality? You might be tempted to say that we should settle it by applying rational standards. That way, we can decide which argument is the most rational. But are there objective and universal standards of rationality? Or is rationality something entirely subjective or, at the very least, relative to particular historical periods and cultural communities?

Fundamental disagreements about the nature of rationality are very difficult to settle because in initially proceeding to approach the topic we have already made assumptions about what is a rational way to proceed. I believe this is one of the points Zhuangzi was making. Rationality has to do with the way we proceed to investigate matters, settle disputes, evaluate evidence, assess people's behaviors, practices, and beliefs. If we could get agreement about the standards of rationality, then the only thing left to argue about is whether or not these standards were fairly and accurately applied.

One view of rationality which does hold that there are objective and universal standards of rationality has been called **foundationalism.** Generally (there are many different varieties of foundationalism), foundationalists hold that we can decide what is rational by appealing to principles which are undeniable to any rational person. For example, if I maintain that my belief about extraterrestrials visiting Peru is rational, I, according to this view, should be able to present good reasons in support of my belief. The reasons I present will be good ones insofar as they ultimately rest on a set of ideas that are self-evidently true for any person who can properly understand them.

What are these foundational principles? Many philosophers have maintained that they are the basic laws of logic and the rules and procedures deducible from those laws (see Appendix A for more on the nature of logic and the procedures of logical reasoning). Aristotle, for example, claims that the **law of noncontradiction** (a statement cannot be both true and false at the same time and in the same respect) stands at the foundation of all rational reasoning. You cannot rationally assert p (where "p" stands for any statement) *and* not p. If you claim p is true, you cannot also claim it is false and be rational. Furthermore, he argues, anyone who denies this law and who is prepared to defend that denial will be unable to advance her or his argument without relying upon the very law supposedly rejected.

I must confess that people who argued that they could picture a square circle, I would think either perverse or irrational. A square circle is a contradiction in terms.

Being logical and correctly applying the laws of logic is, however, at best a necessary condition of rationality. It is not sufficient. I can imagine someone applying logical procedures to arrive at the most absurd conclusions. If I were clever enough, I could justify my belief in extraterrestrials visiting Peru without violating any logical laws, but is that enough for you to conclude my belief is rational?

So it would seem we need some fundamental principles in addition to the laws of logic in order to know both the necessary and sufficient conditions of rationality. And here is where the fight really breaks out among foundationalists. Some claim that these principles amount to "clear and distinct ideas" that can be logically deduced from a critical examination of our beliefs. Others argue that the foundations of knowledge and rationality are the immediate impressions made on our senses. Still others have maintained that the experimental procedures of science provide such a foundation. You will encounter something of this debate as you read this book, so I will not belabor the point here. I only wish you to understand that much philosophical energy in the modern Western world has been extended in a search of these fundamental principles. If we can find them, then we would have agreed upon procedures for shifting through the many different answers to what is real, what is knowledge, what is value, what is good, and settling on those which prove most rational.

I think you can see the attractiveness of the foundationalist position, especially if you have ever been in one of those arguments where someone keeps asking you, "How do you know that?" At first you are patient and display your reasons. But she or he persists, "How do you know those are good reasons?" You explain why. Again, "Well, how can you be so sure?" About now your blood pressure is rising because you are beginning to see an infinite, bottomless abyss opening up. This could go on forever! But have no fear. Foundationalism can ride to your rescue because foundationalism maintains the regress is not infinite, the pit is not bottomless, there is a sure foundation of first principles which your questioner will recognize to be rational.

However, the foundation you reach on your descent may turn out to be a ledge which gives way under your weight. Why? Because all the energy that has been spent on the search for fundamental principles has ended in disagreement. Thus many philosophers have declared the modern search for fundamental rational principles bankrupt. Welcome to the postmodern age of anti-foundationalism.

Just as there are many varieties of foundationalism, there are also many varieties of anti-foundationalism. Some critics of foundationalism point to the failure of agreement as proof that the search is fruitless. Others argue that these so-called objective, universal, ahistorical, transcultural foundations have been shown again and again to be little more than the elevation of the prejudices of an elite class, or of males, or of white culture, or of Western civilization to the honorific title of "fundamental and universal rational principles." What is "rational" it turns out, is what Anglo-American European white males value. Foundationalism, this criticism maintains, is just a variety of ethnocentric imperialism disguised with a mask of rationality. Still others argue that we are all so embedded in our cultures, our traditions, our religions, our historical situations that we can never find some neutral point, some god's eye view from which to pass judgment. Not one of our limited viewpoints is privileged. We are hopelessly culture bound. Still others point out that foundationalism is fatally flawed because it is itself based on a contradiction. It claims that a rational belief is one supported by good reasons. But it turns out that these "good" reasons rest on principles which we are asked to accept as self-evidently true and in need of no further support. Such principles would be irrational given that criterion initially assumed to be the hallmark of a rational belief, that is, a belief supported by good reasons.

To display the evidence and explore the subtleties and shifts of arguments supporting the anti-foundationalist stance would take us too far afield. But I should mention one major issue that this debate has engendered because it is particularly relevant to what this book is about. That is the issue of **relativism.** The foundationalists charge the anti-foundationalists with relativism. If you deny, they claim, that there are any transcultural, universal, objective standards of rationality, then what you are claiming amounts to the view that there is no such thing as rationality; all there are, are rationalities. Your culture, your society, your religious tradition, your morality, your philosophic stance, your beliefs, your science, your magic, your truth, your revelation is just as good or just as rational as anyone else's. But this is self-defeating. If your view is no better nor worse than my view, then all views are of equal merit. Therefore, you have no justification to support your claim that foundationalism is wrong.

This is a powerful response. Few of us would argue with others if we thought that all views of morality or all views of truth were of equal worth. Yet we do argue. Few of us would be willing to maintain that programs of "ethnic cleansing" which lamentably characterize so much of human practice in our century are just as rational as programs which aim at getting human beings to live in peace with one another.

We seem to be caught on the horns of a dilemma. Few of us would opt for either ethnocentric imperialism or a kind of relativism which advocates "anything goes." Is there a way out of this predicament? Much contemporary philosophy is presently concerned with finding a way out, a sort of middle ground, which allows us to assert that some answers to fundamental questions are better than others, but stops short of imposing on others our own local views of what is rational. Zhuangzi appears to be looking for just such a middle ground when he writes, "The great variety of sounds are relative to each other just as much as they are not relative to each other. To harmonize them in the functioning of Nature and leave them in the process of infinite evolution is the way to complete our lifetime." He goes on to explain that if something is *really* right, then there is no room for argument. So forget the distinction between right and wrong and "relax in the realm of the infinite." But what does this mean, and how can we forget such distinctions? Perhaps he is counseling us to stop worrying about what is rational and what is not and have confidence that in the end the rational will prevail. That is certainly one option. But there are others.

Another option is to distinguish carefully between different kinds of relativism. Not all relativism may be self-defeating, contrary to what some foundationalists believe. Zhuangzi may be hinting at this sort of possibility when he claims sounds are relative and not relative. Unless this is a genuine contradiction, the word "relative" must mean two different things. It seems obvious that standards of rationality are relative to historical and cultural conditions in the sense that they are related to such conditions. Standards of rationality don't float in some timeless, nonhuman space. But to conclude from this that all standards of rationality are of equal value or are equally true (the sort of self-defeating relativism the foundationalists charge the anti-foundationalist with) requires a big leap. Why not conclude instead that the historically and culturally conditioned criteria we use for determining which reasons are good ones appear to be good criteria *to us,* but may not so appear to someone else because of a different set of historically and culturally conditioned criteria? It does not follow from the fact that there exist different understandings of rationality, that all understandings are of equal value.

But, you might argue, if there are no objective standards of rationality or, at the very least, if we must admit we don't know what they might be, then all we are left with are rationalities bound to historical conditions and local cultural communities, and we have no way of determining which are better. Perhaps. But we do have some options. We can remain convinced that our community has the last word on the subject and all others are wrong. Or, as we encounter other communities, other cultures, we can listen to them (and they to us) and try to discover together ways of settling our disputes. We can expand our dialogue, listen to other voices, and together with them ask What is real? What is knowledge? What is good? As we listen, as we dialogue, yes, and even as we argue, our standards of rationality will grow and, while in the end we may still disagree, at least we can say we have understood.

This book is an attempt to expand the dialogue. A wide variety of sounds will be heard—African American, Latino, Native American, feminist and yes, Anglo-American European white males—and hopefully these sounds will turn into meaningful voices of wisdom. We will not agree with all these voices, but we can learn from each. And we may discover wider areas of agreement than we thought possible.

My claim that agreement about what is rational can emerge out of dialogue and expanded cultural communication rests on the assumption that we can understand philosophical views held by people who live in times and places very different from our own and on the hope that learning about ourselves and others is a worthwhile enterprise. Some might argue that we can never understand what others who are very different from us are saying and that my hope is naive. I do not have the space to defend my assumption and my hope, but I do believe that good reasons can be given. In any case, we will never find out if we do not try.

Recall, I have characterized philosophy as a rational activity of formulating, understanding, and answering fundamental questions. This activity, I wish to stress, relies heavily on the logical skills of analyzing, criticizing, and developing arguments. But it is more than this. If the goal of philosophy is to formulate, understand, and answer fundamental questions on both an intellectual and practical level, then we can only determine how rational this activity is by assessing how successfully this goal is achieved by all those who participate in this sort of activity. I do not believe we can rule out any of the profound thinking about fundamental problems that the many peoples of the world have to offer by imposing some predetermined model of rationality. Hence the very process of assessment is something we must learn as we go.

The Jains of India have a teaching called *syad-vada* which might be translated as the "perhaps method." This teaching holds that 353 different viewpoints can be held on any question. Hence dogmatic closed-mindedness is inappropriate. To any perspective or any issue, the thoughtful will reply, "Perhaps."

There are times, I think, when we can be a bit more definite than "perhaps," but the flexibility and openness this method recommends is a virtue we all need to practice when we have no privileged viewpoint from which we might settle a matter once and for all. Not all answers are rational. Some are better than others. But the range of rational responses may be far broader than we realize.

1.3. How to Read Philosophy

Reading philosophy can be both exciting and rewarding. Philosophy provides intellectual stimulation: the pleasure of discovering new ideas, the fascination of following the thread of a provocative argument, the challenge of rethinking unexamined assumptions.

Reading philosophy can be enjoyable, but it is not easy. Much philosophical writing presents trains of reasoning. To fully appreciate such writing, you must learn to think along with the author. This requires concentration, and so it is best to read philosophy when you are refreshed and alert.

Philosophical texts come in a wide variety of styles, from different cultures and different historical periods, and they are written in different languages. It is not easy to adjust to this variety. It takes practice to appreciate and understand ancient Greek dialogues, Buddhist fables, seventeenth-century French essays, and Chinese poetry.

Most of us are used to reading secondary sources that explain the ideas of others. We are assigned textbooks that digest what others say, explain it to us, underline the important points for us, present summaries, and define the words we don't know. We are not used to wrestling with primary sources, the original texts and words. Since we are not used to digesting material on our own, explaining it to ourselves, learning how to do our own summaries, and looking up words and references we don't understand, we will find it difficult at first to read primary sources. Like anything else, it will take some practice.

This book is a secondary source that collects and presents to you primary sources. I will explain some things, provide background information, highlight key points. I will also ask a lot of questions in the hope of arousing your curiosity and provoking you to think for yourself. But in the end, you must read the texts, grapple with the style, struggle with the ideas, and figure out what is being said. Here are some suggestions that will help you do this.

1. Read the material at least twice. First, skim it very rapidly to get the lay of the land. Pick out the main points to determine what the author is concerned with and what the overall point of the writing is. Then reread more carefully, looking for answers to particular questions and noting the details.

2. Read actively and with a purpose. Engage the text in a conversation. Imagine the author is speaking directly to you and, as in any conversation, respond to what is being said. Ask questions, look for answers, evaluate, and seek more information about puzzling ideas.

3. Take notes as you read. This will help you concentrate on the text and aid you in actively engaging what the author has to say. Your notes will also prove valuable when you review the material. In my introductions to the sources, I have placed some of the technical terms in bold type the first time they occur. These words are defined in the glossary in Appendix B. But before you look at the glossary, write your own definition in your own words based on your understanding of the text. Then you can check your definition by turning to the glossary. You should also make a list of authors, their dates, their works, and a brief identifying description.

4. Read analytically and sympathetically. Your first task in reading is to analyze and comprehend what the author is saying. Make a list in your own words of

the main ideas. Try to understand the author's viewpoint and the goal he or she is attempting to accomplish. Don't expect to understand everything. Make an "I don't understand" list and discuss it with others. It is no sin not to understand. Here are some analytical questions that you can ask and answer as you read which will help you understand the selections: (a) What is the thesis (the central idea or main point)? (b) What are the major points made in developing and supporting the thesis? (c) How are key terms defined? (d) What are the basic assumptions made by the author? (e) What are the important implications of the author's position?

5. On a second reading, read critically. Don't believe everything you read. If something seems wrong, say so. But also go on to formulate, as best you can, why something seems wrong to you. If possible, figure out what could be changed to improve the idea or the argument. Make an "I don't agree, and this is why" list. Here are some critical questions that will help you evaluate the strengths and weaknesses of the selections: (a) Is what is said clear? If not, how is it unclear? (b) Are adequate definitions given for important concepts? Can you think of counterexamples? (c) Are the arguments adequate to support the claims, e.g., are the premises true? the assumptions dubious? (d) Do the implications of the text lead to absurd or false consequences? (e) Are important aspects of the issue overlooked? (f) How well did the author accomplish his or her goal?

6. After you have finished, review what you have read. Don't get lost in the trees. Stand back and try to see the forest. Can you summarize what you have read in your own words in a single paragraph? If you cannot, then restudy the material until you can.

I will provide you with reading questions in my introductions to the primary sources. These questions get at some of the things I think are important. Keep these questions in mind as you read and answer them. Also, create questions of your own as you go along. Some things that will seem important to you I have overlooked, and ideas that you will want to ponder I have ignored. As you gain practice reading primary sources, I will be asking you to assume more of the responsibility for creating the reading questions. It is a good idea to keep a notebook in which you write your answers to these questions.

I will also provide suggestions for further reading which you can pursue if you desire more information about the topic or further clarification and development of key ideas. Becoming an independent thinker requires that you learn to interrogate the texts, to enjoy their insights, and to search for more information, thereby coming to appreciate the stimulation and challenge of reading philosophy.

Suggestions for Further Reading and References

John Passmore's article on "Philosophy" in Volume 6 of *The Encyclopedia of Philosophy* (New York: Macmillan and The Free Press, 1967) is a good place to start for an overview of different conceptions of what philosophy is. It is a good idea to get used to using this valuable resource, since it will aid you with the other topics and readings in this book. Arthur C. Danto's little book *What Philosophy Is: A Guide to the Elements* (New York: Harper & Row, 1968) will take you deeper into the discussion. He stresses that philosophy should be thought of as an activity rather than a set of doctrines or ideas. Bertrand Russell's *The Problems of Philosophy*, 2d ed. (Oxford: Oxford University Press, 1959) will also give you a feel for philosophizing.

Danto, Passmore, and Russell approach philosophy from a Western perspective. For a discussion of philosophy and philosophizing in a global context see the essays in *Interpreting Across Boundaries: New Essays in Comparative Philosophy*, edited by Gerald James Larson and Eliot Deutsch (Princeton: Princeton University Press, 1988) and *Philosophy East/Philosophy West: A Critical Comparison of Indian, Chinese, Islamic, and European Philosophy* by Ben-Ami Scharfstein, et al. (Oxford: Basil Blackwell, 1978). See *From Africa to Zen: An Invitation to World Philosophy*, edited by Robert C. Solomon and Kathleen M. Higgins (Lanham, MA: Rowman & Littlefield, 1993) for a collection of essays that summarize the philosophic activity in diverse cultures.

It is difficult to know where to send a beginning student for a discussion of the nature of rationality and relativism. You may find some manageable material in *Farewell to Reason* by Paul Feyerabend (New York: Verso, 1987); see especially the last essay. Also see *After Philosophy: End or Transformation?* edited by Kenneth Baynes, et al. (Cambridge, MA: MIT Press, 1987), for a good collection of essays. More manageable is Genevieve Lloyd's *The Man of Reason: "Male" and "Female" in Western Philosophy* (Minneapolis: University of Minnesota Press, 1984). Janice Moulton's "A Paradigm of Philosophy: The Adversary Method," in *Discovering Reality*, edited by Sandra Harding and Merill B. Hintikka (D. Reidel Publishing, 1983), pp. 149–164, is quite valuable in stimulating you to think about reasoning in a different way. Richard Foley's "Some Different Conceptions of Rationality," in *Construction and Constraint: The Shaping of Scientific Rationality*, edited by Ernan McMullin (Notre Dame, IN: University of Notre Dame Press, 1988), pp.123–152, advocates and develops the idea of rationality as a goal-oriented activity. See William James' "The Sentiment of Rationality," in *Essays on Faith and Morals* (New York: World Publishing, 1962), pp. 63–110, for views on the feeling of rationality and what sort of philosophy might create those feelings. *Relativism: Interpretation and Confrontation*, edited by Michael Krauz (Notre Dame, IN: University of Notre Dame Press, 1989) provides an excellent collection of first rate articles. Also see *Rationality and Relativism*, edited by M. Hollis and S. Lukes (Cambridge, MA: MIT Press, 1982). The opening chapter of *Whose Justice? Which Rationality?* by Alasdair MacIntyre (Notre Dame, IN: University of Notre Dame Press, 1988) is also useful in stimulating you to think about the importance of tradition in providing a context for agreement.

Video

The Gods Must Be Crazy (109 minutes, produced by CBS/Fox) compares an encounter between modern technological society and a society of hunter/gatherers in South Africa. Within the first 15 to 20 minutes you will be able to see how what appears rational to one kind of society appears to be quite "crazy" from the point of view of a very different kind of society. See your Media Services Catalogue for more information.

Chapter 2

How Should One Live?

HAVE YOU EVER WONDERED about how one should live? Should we live compassionately, pursuing a wisdom that will free us from suffering? Or should we live a virtuous and sincere life of balance, harmony, and family loyalty? Perhaps we should live a life of critical reflection, searching for truth, and following an argument wherever it may lead. Should we live in pursuit of happiness? But what exactly is happiness? How can we attain it? Perhaps we must unselfishly do what duty demands in devotion to God. But we must not lose sight of the fact that we are connected to this earth. We are all related and this relatedness demands that we live peacefully and with ecological awareness.

The question of how one should live is fundamental to human existence. It is a question that has concerned ancient and modern peoples, Eastern and Western cultures. What do you understand by the question? If you had to write an essay on the topic, how would you begin? "One should live the good life," you might say. That seems a sensible way to start. But what is the good life? Well, what is most important to you? What sorts of things do you value the most? Health? Wealth? Pleasure? But just because you desire certain things, does that mean you *ought* to desire them? To desire something is one thing; to claim you ought to desire it is something else.

But what does "ought" have to do with this question about conducting one's life? "How *should* one live?" is not the same question as "How *ought* one to live?" You might say "I should go to the store" but that does not mean that you "ought" to in the sense that you are morally obligated to do so. Yet your sense of what you are morally obligated to do, often grows out of your sense of what you should do.

And who is the "one" whom this question addresses? It is an impersonal one. "How should *one* live?" is not the same question as "How should *I* live?" So does your answer hold good for you alone? What about others? Is there one way we all ought to live? Writing an essay about how you think you should live is one thing. Writing an essay about how you think everyone ought to live is another matter. For one thing, the latter essay is a lot more difficult to write.

If you have ever wondered about how you or anyone else ought to live, you have been concerned with what philosophers call "ethics" or "moral philosophy." Ethics comes from the Greek word *ethos,* which means "character." For the Greeks, ethics had to do with developing a virtuous or moral character. They believed that if you develop such a character you not only will know the right thing to do, you will do it.

Today we use the word "ethics" in many different ways. Sometimes it refers to moral rules or a way of life based on a religiously inspired moral code. We speak of "Christian ethics" or "Buddhist ethics." But sometimes it refers to the secular study of moral values and a search for the principles of right moral action. As a branch of philosophy, "ethics" is used in this latter sense to refer to reflection on or study of moral issues. It is concerned with such questions as: What is the morally right way to live? How can I know what is morally right? How can I decide morally difficult cases? What makes a society just?

We can answer moral questions in different ways. One way is **descriptive.** We might describe the kinds of values people have and the sorts of principles they use in making moral judgments. Another way is **normative.** Normative reflection has to do with trying to discover norms or principles by which we *ought* to live. Many philosophers maintain that ethics is primarily a normative study. It is not merely a description of what people find morally good and morally bad, but it seeks to discover norms that ought to guide our actions.

While we can distinguish the kinds of questions moral philosophers ask, the answers often blend into one another. An answer to the question about how one should live will sooner or later have to address such issues as how we can know what is right, whether justice is possible, does God exist, is there life after death, and many more. While the readings in this chapter directly address the question of how one should live, in a broad sense, this same question is addressed one way or another by the other readings included in this book.

2.1. The Buddha and the Middle Way

The word "Buddha," which means "The Enlightened One," is the title bestowed on Siddhartha Gautama, who was born into a royal family in Nepal around 563 B.C.E. He lived a life of luxury in the palace. On a trip outside the palace he became aware of the suffering (*dukkha*) of humans. He witnessed people experiencing disease, old age, and death. At the age of twenty-nine he left his life of comfort and became an ascetic in search of the solution to the problem of suffering.

Siddhartha studied with the sages of his day and practiced extreme austerities. He nearly starved himself to death. But he found no satisfactory answer either from his teachers or from his extreme ascetic practices. Eventually he went his own way. One evening, he seated himself under a tree (later called the Bo-tree or Tree of Enlightenment) and resolved not to stir from meditation until he discovered how to overcome suffering. He attained enlightenment and henceforth was called the Buddha.

After his enlightenment he preached the wisdom he had realized and the practice for attaining that wisdom because he wished to help others gain **nirvana,** the release or freedom from suffering. He was convinced, based on his experience, that human beings should live free from suffering and that such a life was possible. He taught for forty-five years and founded an order of monks. He died at the age of eighty, in 483 B.C.E., thirteen years before Socrates was born. From his teachings a religion called Buddhism has grown and spread throughout Asia and much of the rest of the world. It is divided into several groups, two of which, the Theravada (Way of the Elders) and the Mahayana (Greater Vehicle), have had widespread influence. His teachings also inspired philosophical reflection, and various philosophical schools have also developed.

What follows is one selection from the "Long Discourses" (*Digha Nikaya*, Sutta 22 : 18–22), attributed to the Buddha himself, concerning the "**Four Noble Truths.**" These constitute the heart of his message and express, in condensed form, what he learned under the Bo-tree. The second selection is a commentary, from a Theravadan viewpoint, on "The Fourth Noble Truth" (also called the **Middle Way** or the **Eightfold Path**) by a contemporary Sri Lankan Buddhist scholar, Rev. Dr. Walpola Rahula.

Reading Questions

As you read the first selection see if you can answer these questions:

1. What is suffering?
2. What is the relationship between craving and pleasure?
3. Why does the Buddha teach that the cessation of suffering (Third Noble Truth) is the extinction of craving?

As you read the commentary by Rahula, see if you can answer these questions:

4. Why is the Fourth Noble Truth called the Middle Path?
5. What is the relationship between compassion and wisdom?
6. What is the difference between "knowing accordingly" and "penetration?" Can you give an example of each from your own experience?
7. What is the good life, according to the Buddha, and how would he answer the question, "How should one live?" Do you agree? Why or why not?

The Four Noble Truths

THE BUDDHA

17. "Again, monks, a monk abides contemplating mind-objects as mind-objects in respect of the Four Noble Truths. How does he do so? Here, a monk knows as it really is: 'This is suffering'; he knows as it really is: 'This is the origin of suffering'; he knows as it really is: 'This is the cessation of suffering'; he knows as it really is: 'This is the way of practice leading to the cessation of suffering.'

18. "And what, monks, is the Noble Truth of Suffering? Birth is suffering, ageing is suffering, death is suffering, sorrow, lamentation, pain, sadness and distress are suffering. Being attached to the unloved is suffering, being separated from the loved is suffering, not getting what one wants is suffering. In short, the five aggregates of grasping are suffering. . . .

"And how, monks, in short, are the five aggregates of grasping suffering? They are as follows: the aggregate of grasping that is form, the aggre-

Thus Have I Heard: The Long Discourses of the Buddha: Digha Nikaya, translated by Maurice Walshe, 1987, pp. 344–349. Reprinted by permission of Wisdom Publications, Boston. Footnotes deleted.

gate of grasping that is feeling, the aggregate of grasping that is perception, the aggregate of grasping that is the mental formations, the aggregate of grasping that is consciousness. These are, in short, the five aggregates of grasping that are suffering.[1] And that, monks, is called the Noble Truth of Suffering.

19. "And what, monks, is the Noble Truth of the Origin of Suffering? It is that craving which gives rise to rebirth, bound up with pleasure and lust, finding fresh delight now here, now there: that is to say sensual craving, craving for existence, and craving for non-existence.

"And where does this craving arise and establish itself? Wherever in the world there is anything agreeable and pleasurable, there this craving arises and establishes itself.

"And what is there in the world that is agreeable and pleasurable? The eye in the world is agreeable and pleasurable, the ear . . . , the nose . . . , the tongue . . . , the body . . . , the mind in the world is agreeable and pleasurable, and there this craving arises and establishes itself. Sights, sounds, smells, tastes, tangibles, mind-objects in the world are agreeable and pleasurable, and there this craving arises and establishes itself.

"The craving for sights, sounds, smells, tastes, tangibles, mind-objects in the world is agreeable and pleasurable, and there this craving arises and establishes itself.[2]

"Thinking of sights, sounds, smells, tastes, tangibles, mind-objects in the world is agreeable and pleasurable, and there this craving arises and establishes itself.

"Pondering on sights, sounds, smells, tastes, tangibles and mind-objects in the world is agreeable and pleasurable, and there this craving arises and establishes itself. And that, monks, is called the Noble Truth of the Origin of Suffering.

20. "And what, monks, is the Noble Truth of the Cessation of Suffering? It is the complete fading-away and extinction of this craving, its forsaking and abandonment, liberation from it, detachment from it. And how does this craving come to be abandoned, how does its cessation come about? . . .

21. "And what, monks, is the Noble Truth of the Way of Practice Leading to the Cessation of Suffering? It is just this Noble Eightfold Path, namely:—Right View, Right Thought; Right Speech, Right Action, Right Livelihood; Right Effort, Right Mindfulness, Right Concentration.

"And what, monks, is Right View? It is, monks, the knowledge of suffering, the knowledge of the origin of suffering, the knowledge of the cessation of suffering, and the knowledge of the way of practice leading to the cessation of suffering. This is called Right View.

"And what, monks, is Right Thought? The thought of renunciation, the thought of non-ill-will, the thought of harmlessness. This, monks, is called Right Thought.

"And what, monks, is Right Speech? Refraining from lying, refraining from slander, refraining from harsh speech, refraining from frivolous speech. This is called Right Speech.

"And what, monks, is Right Action? Refraining from taking life, refraining from taking what is not given, refraining from sexual misconduct. This is called Right Action.

"And what, monks, is Right Livelihood? Here, monks, the Ariyan disciple, having given up wrong livelihood, keeps himself by right livelihood.

"And what, monks, is Right Effort? Here, monks, a monk rouses his will, makes an effort, stirs up energy, exerts his mind and strives to prevent the arising of unarisen evil unwholesome mental states. He rouses his will . . . and strives to overcome evil unwholesome mental states that have arisen. He rouses his will . . . and strives to produce unarisen wholesome mental states.

1. [The five aggregates constitute the components of the individual human being. "Form" refers to the physical body, "feelings" to the sensations that arise from the operation of the senses, "perception" to the cognition or awareness of sensation, "mental formations" to the emotions and dispositions to act based on sensations, and "consciousness" to the product or result of the interaction of the other four aggregates.—Ed.]

2. [In the West, we classify the senses as five: sight, sound, smell, taste, and touch. Buddhism adds a sixth, the mind.—Ed.]

He rouses his will, makes an effort, stirs up energy, exerts his mind and strives to maintain wholesome mental states that have arisen, not to let them fade away, to bring them to greater growth, to the full perfection of development. This is called Right Effort.

"And what, monks, is Right Mindfulness? Here, monks, a monk abides contemplating body as body, ardent, clearly aware and mindful, having put aside hankering and fretting for the world; he abides contemplating feelings as feelings . . . ; he abides contemplating mind as mind . . . ; he abides contemplating mind-objects as mind-objects, ardent, clearly aware and mindful, having put aside hankering and fretting for the world. This is called Right Mindfulness.

"And what, monks, is Right Concentration? Here, a monk, detached from sense-desires, detached from unwholesome mental states, enters and remains in the first jhāna,[3] which is with thinking and pondering, born of detachment, filled with delight and joy. And with the subsiding of thinking and pondering, by gaining inner tranquillity and oneness of mind, he enters and remains in the second jhāna, which is without thinking and pondering, born of concentration, filled with delight and joy. And with the fading away of delight, remaining imperturbable, mindful and clearly aware, he experiences in himself the joy of which the Noble Ones say: 'Happy is he who dwells with equanimity and mindfulness,' he enters the third jhāna. And, having given up pleasure and pain, and with the disappearance of former gladness and sadness, he enters and remains in the fourth jhāna, which is beyond pleasure and pain, and purified by equanimity and mindfulness. This is called Right Concentration. And that, monks, is called the way of practice leading to the cessation of suffering."

3. [*Jhāna* (or *dhyana*) refers to altered states of consciousness that occur in meditation.—Ed.]

The Fourth Noble Truth

WALPOLA RAHULA

THE FOURTH NOBLE TRUTH is that of the Way leading to the Cessation of *Dukkha* [suffering] (*Dukkhanirodhagāminîpatipadāariyasacca*). This is known as the "Middle Path" (*Majjhimā Paṭipadā*), because it avoids two extremes: one extreme being the search for happiness through the pleasures of the senses, which is "low, common, unprofitable and the way of the ordinary people"; the other being the search for happiness through self-mortification in different forms of asceticism, which is "painful, unworthy and unprofitable." Having himself first tried these two extremes, and having found them to be useless, the Buddha discovered through personal experience the Middle Path "which gives vision and knowledge, which leads to Calm, Insight, Enlightenment, Niryāna." This Middle Path is generally referred to as the Noble Eightfold Path (*Ariya-Aṭṭhansgika-Magga*), because it is composed of eight categories or divisions: namely,

1. Right Understanding (*Sammā diṭṭhi*),
2. Right Thought (*Sammā sanskappa*),
3. Right Speech (*Sammā vācā*),
4. Right Action (*Sammā kammanta*),
5. Right Livelihood (*Sammā ājīva*),

6. Right Effort (*Sammā vāyāma*),
7. Right Mindfulness (*Sammā sati*),
8. Right Concentration (*Sammā samādhi*).

Practically the whole teaching of the Buddha, to which he devoted himself during 45 years, deals in some way or other with this Path. He explained it in different ways and in different words to different people, according to the stage of their development and their capacity to understand and follow him. But the essence of those many thousand discourses scattered in the Buddhist Scriptures is found in the Noble Eightfold Path.

It should not be thought that the eight categories or divisions of the Path should be followed and practised one after the other in the numerical order as given in the usual list above. But they are to be developed more or less simultaneously, as far as possible according to the capacity of each individual. They are all linked together and each helps the cultivation of the others.

These eight factors aim at promoting and perfecting the three essentials of Buddhist training and discipline: namely: (*a*) Ethical Conduct (*Sīla*), (*b*) Mental Discipline (*Samādhi*) and (*c*) Wisdom (*Paññā*). It will therefore be more helpful for a coherent and better understanding of the eight divisions of the Path, if we group them and explain them according to these three heads.

Ethical Conduct is built on the vast conception of universal love and compassion for all living beings, on which the Buddha's teaching is based. It is regrettable that many scholars forget this great ideal of the Buddha's teaching, and indulge in only dry philosophical and metaphysical divagations when they talk and write about Buddhism. The Buddha gave his teaching "for the good of the many, for the happiness of the many, out of compassion for the world" (*bahujanahitāya bahujanasukhāya lokānukampāya*).

According to Buddhism, for a man to be perfect there are two qualities that he should develop equally: compassion (*karuṅā*) on one side, and wisdom (*paññā*) on the other. Here compassion represents love, charity, kindness, toler-

ance and such noble qualities on the emotional side, or qualities of the heart, while wisdom would stand for the intellectual side or the qualities of the mind. If one develops only the emotional neglecting the intellectual, one may become a good-hearted fool; while to develop only the intellectual side neglecting the emotional may turn one into a hard-hearted intellect without feeling for others. Therefore, to be perfect one has to develop both equally. That is the aim of the Buddhist way of life: in it wisdom and compassion are inseparably linked together, as we shall see later.

Now, in Ethical Conduct (*Sīla*), based on love and compassion, are included three factors of the Noble Eightfold Path: namely, Right Speech, Right Action and Right Livelihood. (Nos. 3, 4 and 5 in the list).

Right speech means abstention (1) from telling lies, (2) from backbiting and slander and talk that may bring about hatred, enmity, disunity and disharmony among individuals or groups of people, (3) from harsh, rude, impolite, malicious and abusive language, and (4) from idle, useless and foolish babble and gossip. When one abstains from these forms of wrong and harmful speech one naturally has to speak the truth, has to use words that are friendly and benevolent, pleasant and gentle, meaningful and useful. One should not speak carelessly: speech should be at the right time and place. If one cannot say something useful, one should keep "noble silence."

Right Action aims at promoting moral, honourable and peaceful conduct. It admonishes us that we should abstain from destroying life, from stealing, from dishonest dealings, from illegitimate sexual intercourse, and that we should also help others to lead a peaceful and honourable life in the right way.

Right Livelihood means that one should abstain from making one's living through a profession that brings harm to others, such as trading in arms and lethal weapons, intoxicating drinks, poisons, killing animals, cheating, etc., and should live by a profession which is honourable, blameless and innocent of harm to others. One can clearly see here that Buddhism is strongly opposed to any kind of war, when it lays down that trade in arms and lethal weapons is an evil and unjust means of livelihood.

These three factors (Right Speech, Right Action and Right Livelihood) of the Eightfold Path constitute Ethical Conduct. It should be realized that the Buddhist ethical and moral conduct aims at promoting a happy and harmonious life both for the individual and for society. This moral conduct is considered as the indispensable foundation for all higher spiritual attainments. No spiritual development is possible without this moral basis.

Next comes Mental Discipline, in which are included three other factors of the Eightfold Path: namely, Right Effort, Right Mindfulness (or Attentiveness) and Right Concentration. (Nos. 6, 7 and 8 in the list).

Right Effort is the energetic will (1) to prevent evil and unwholesome states of mind from arising, and (2) to get rid of such evil and unwholesome states that have already arisen within a man, and also (3) to produce, to cause to arise, good and wholesome states of mind not yet arisen, and (4) to develop and bring to perfection the good and wholesome states of mind already present in a man.

Right Mindfulness (or Attentiveness) is to be diligently aware, mindful and attentive with regard to (1) the activities of the body (*kāya*), (2) sensations or feelings (*vedanā*), (3) the activities of the mind (*citta*) and (4) ideas, thoughts, conceptions and things (*dhamma*).

The practice of concentration on breathing (*ānāpānasati*) is one of the well-known exercises, connected with the body, for mental development. There are several other ways of developing attentiveness in relation to the body—as modes of meditation.

With regard to sensations and feelings, one should be clearly aware of all forms of feelings and sensations, pleasant, unpleasant and neutral, of how they appear and disappear within oneself.

Concerning the activities of mind, one should be aware whether one's mind is lustful or not, given to hatred or not, deluded or not, distracted or concentrated, etc. In this way one should be aware of all movements of mind, how they arise and disappear.

As regards ideas, thoughts, conceptions and things, one should know their nature, how they appear and disappear, how they are developed, how they are suppressed, and destroyed, and so on.

These four forms of mental culture or meditation are treated in detail in the *Satipaṭṭhāna-sutta* (Setting-up of Mindfulness).

The third and last factor of Mental Discipline is Right Concentration leading to the four stages of *Dhyāna*, generally called trance or *recueillement*. In the first stage of *Dhyāna*, passionate desires and certain unwholesome thoughts like sensuous lust, ill-will, languor, worry, restlessness, and sceptical doubt are discarded, and feelings of joy and happiness are maintained, along with certain mental activities. In the second stage, all intellectual activities are suppressed, tranquillity and "one-pointedness" of mind developed, and the feelings of joy and happiness are still retained. In the third stage, the feeling of joy, which is an active sensation, also disappears, while the disposition of happiness still remains in addition to mindful equanimity. In the fourth stage of *Dhyāna*, all sensations, even of happiness and unhappiness, of joy and sorrow, disappear, only pure equanimity and awareness remaining.

Thus the mind is trained and disciplined and developed through Right Effort, Right Mindfulness, and Right Concentration.

The remaining two factors, namely Right Thought and Right Understanding go to constitute Wisdom.

Right Thought denotes the thoughts of selfless renunciation or detachment, thoughts of love and thoughts of non-violence, which are extended to all beings. It is very interesting and important to note here that thoughts of selfless detachment, love and non-violence are grouped on the side of wisdom. This clearly shows that true wisdom is endowed with these noble qualities, and that all thoughts of selfish desire, ill-will, hatred and violence are the result of a lack of wisdom—in all spheres of life whether individual, social, or political.

Right Understanding is the understanding of things as they are, and it is the Four Noble Truths that explain things as they really are. Right Understanding, therefore, is ultimately reduced to the understanding of the Four Noble Truths. This understanding is the highest wisdom which sees the Ultimate Reality. According to Buddhism there are two sorts of understanding: What we generally call understanding is knowledge, an accumulated memory, an intellectual grasping of a subject according to certain given data. This is called "knowing accordingly" (*anubodha*). It is not very deep. Real deep understanding is called "penetration" (*paṭivedha*), seeing a thing in its true nature, without name and label. This penetration is possible only when the mind is free from all impurities and is fully developed through meditation.

From this brief account of the Path, one may see that it is a way of life to be followed, practised and developed by each individual. It is self-discipline in body, word and mind, self-development and self-purification. It has nothing to do with belief, prayer, worship or ceremony. In that sense, it has nothing which may popularly be called "religious." It is a Path leading to the realization of Ultimate Reality, to complete freedom, happiness and peace through moral, spiritual and intellectual perfection.

In Buddhist countries there are simple and beautiful customs and ceremonies on religious occasions. They have little to do with the real Path. But they have their value in satisfying certain religious emotions and the needs of those who are less advanced, and helping them gradually along the Path.

With regard to the Four Noble Truths we have four functions to perform:

The First Noble Truth is *Dukkha*, the nature of life, its suffering, its sorrows and joys, its imperfection and unsatisfactoriness, its impermanence and insubstantiality. With regard to this, our function is to understand it as a fact, clearly and completely (*pariññeyya*).

The Second Noble Truth is the Origin of *Dukkha*, which is desire, "thirst," accompanied by all other passions, defilements and impurities. A mere understanding of this fact is not sufficient. Here our function is to discard it, to eliminate, to destroy and eradicate it (*pahātabba*).

The Third Noble Truth is the Cessation of *Dukkha*, Niryāṇa, the Absolute Truth, the Ultimate Reality. Here our function is to realize it (*sacchikātabba*).

The Fourth Noble Truth is the Path leading to the realization of Nirvānya. A mere knowledge of the Path, however complete, will not do. In this case, our function is to follow it and keep to it (*bhāvetabba*).

Suggestions for Further Reading

For a general overview of Buddhism and a good bibliography, see Ninian Smart's article on "Buddhism" in *The Encyclopedia of Philosophy*.

Herman Hesse's *Siddhartha*, translated by Hilda Rosner (New York: New Directions Publishing, 1951), is an entertaining and thought-provoking fictional account of the Buddha's life. It promotes the values of self-realization and independence of thought.

Gunapala Dharmasiri's *Fundamentals of Buddhist Ethics* (Antioch, CA: Golden Leaves Publishing, 1988) provides an excellent introduction to Buddhist ideas in general and Buddhist ethics in particular. It is written from a Theravadan perspective.

Videos

Buddhism: The Path to Enlightenment (35 minutes) traces the life of the Buddha. *Buddhism, Man, and Nature* (14 minutes) attempts to capture the underlying philosophy of Buddhism as interpreted by Alan Watts. *Buddhism: Footprint of the Buddha—India* (52 minutes) documents the type of Buddhism practiced in Southeast Asia. *Buddhism: The Land of the Disappearing Buddha— Japan* (52 minutes) focuses on the type of Buddhism practiced in Japan. These videos are available from Insight Media, 121 West 85th Street, New York, N.Y. 10024.

2.2. Confucianism, The Great Learning, and The Mean

Twelve years after the Buddha was born in India, Confucius (551–479 B.C.E.) was born in the state of Lu in China. ("Confucius" is the latinization of Kong Fuzi, which means "Master Kong.") He lived at a time when Chinese society had disintegrated into social and political chaos. Because of these circumstances, he became interested in the question of how the well-being of society can best be achieved.

Biographical information is uncertain, but tradition tells us that Confucius was from the nobility. When he was three, his father died. At nineteen he married and sought a government career. Ultimately, however, he was to make his name as an educator, not as a politician. He provided what we today would call a "humanistic" education to commoner and noble alike, and he taught what might be termed a "humanistic social philosophy"—"social" because of his concern for achieving a good social order and "humanistic" because of his concern to cultivate humane qualities in the human spirit. His reputation in China became so immense that on the popular level he was deified, while among scholars he was venerated as a great sage.

Ren (the Pinyin [see Prelude] spelling for *jen*) is one of the central ideas of his thought. It has been translated in a variety of ways: "human excellence," "virtue," "humanity," "love," "benevolence," "humaneness," and "human heartedness," to name only a few. At times, the term is used to refer to what we might call "ideal human nature." It is humanity at its best, having realized its full positive potential. It is both the source of moral principles and, when embodied in the sage or superior person, represents the outcome of a life lived doing the right things. Viewed as love or benevolence, *ren* gives rise to the principles of conscientiousness (*zhong*) and altruism (*shu*), or "Do unto others as you would have them do unto you." Long before Judaism and Christianity, Confucius had articulated the "Golden Rule."

Li (pronounced "lee") is another central concept. It can mean order, ritual or rite, custom, manners, ceremony, appropriateness or propriety. Humans should behave appropriately. The models for appropriate behavior came, according to Confucius, from the traditional rites and customs handed down from the past Golden Age. He regarded himself as a traditionalist and spent much of his time teaching and interpreting the cultural classics (called the "Six Disciplines") from China's past. Tradition is important in his view because it provides an external check on what one may subjectively believe to be the right way to act.

One of the major traditional virtues in China is **xiao** (the Pinyin spelling of *hsiao,* pronounced "shee-ow"). *Xiao* is familial love and involves the practice of kindness, honor, respect, and loyalty among family members. Confucius believed that a strong family is the basis of a strong society. In fact, the family is the microcosmic version of society. Society ought to be one large family, and ultimately familial love should be extended to the whole human community.

Yi (pronounced "yee" and sometimes spelled "*i*") can be translated as "rightness." It is both a virtue and a principle of behavior. As a principle it states that one should do what is right just because it is right. In other words, your motive should be pure. You should not follow *li* because it is traditional to do so, or practice *xiao* because you will be rewarded, or seek to realize *ren* because it will make you happy or give you pleasure or make you wealthy. You should do what is right simply because it is the right thing to do. Doing good is *intrinsically* valuable. It is not *extrinsically* or instrumentally valuable (i.e., valuable as a means to something else like wealth or pleasure).

Although it is usual to interpret Confucius as primarily concerned with moral, social, and political values, the *aesthetic* dimension of his thought needs to be emphasized as well. Ethics has to do with moral value; aesthetics has to do with artistic value or beauty. The Confucian concern with balance, harmony, and appropriateness reflects aesthetic values. Indeed, the very division between moral and aesthetic value is something Confucius probably did not recognize. For him to call an action right was not merely to pass a moral judgment, but an aesthetic judgment as well. Moral order is aesthetic order. The good and the beautiful are one.

The two essays known as "The Great Learning" and "The Doctrine of the Mean" are two chapters from the Confucian classic *The Book of Rites*. They were not written by Confucius, but by his disciples some time after his death. In all likelihood they contain ideas of Confucius and were combined with the *Analects* and the *Mencius* to form the so-called *Four Books*. From 1313 to 1905 these texts served as the basis for the civil service examinations in China and were memorized by students.

"The Great Learning" has to do with higher or adult education; its central theme is self-cultivation. Because of present-day concerns with individual self-realization associated with the human potential movement, it is tempting to read this essay as if it were concerned exclusively with the self-improvement of the individual. However, the individual can never be abstracted from society. The text is addressed to the ruler and his officials. Self-cultivation must take place at all levels of society from the top down and the bottom up if the well-being of society is to be realized. "The Great Learning" sets forth an eight-point program for self-cultivation. The following selection deals with only two of the eight points.

"The Doctrine of the Mean" deals with moderation, which is portrayed as a universal harmony between humans and nature. Characteristic of much ethical thinking in the ancient world is the belief that there exists a cosmic order that dictates the place of the virtues in a harmonious scheme. The moral order and the cosmic or natural order are mutually reinforcing. The sincere practice of moderation not only expresses ideal human nature but reflects the "Way of Heaven," that is, the natural order, as well.

Reading Questions

As you study "The Great Learning" see if you can answer these questions:

1. In what does the "Way of the Great Learning" consist?

2. What is the root of good government?

3. Do you agree or not with the notion that the government of the state depends on the regulation of the family? Why?

4. What is the principle of measuring the square?

As you read "The Doctrine of the Mean" see if you can answer these questions:

5. What is the Mean?

6. Do you think the principle of conscientiousness and altruism (the Golden Rule) is a good guide for moral action? Why or why not?

7. What are the greatest applications of *ren* (*jen* in the text) and *Yi* (*i* in the text)?
8. What are the three universal virtues?
9. What is sincerity? Why is it important?
10. What are the five steps needed to develop sincerity?
11. How do you think the sort of Confucianism expressed in these texts (*The Great Learning* and *The Doctrine of the Mean*) would answer the question, "How should one live?"

The Great Learning

THE WAY OF THE GREAT LEARNING consists in clearly exemplifying illustrious virtue, in loving the people, and in resting in the highest good.

Only when one knows where one is to rest can one have a fixed purpose. Only with a fixed purpose can one achieve calmness of mind. Only with calmness of mind can one attain serene repose. Only in serene repose can one carry on careful deliberation. Only through careful deliberation can one have achievement. Things have their roots and branches; affairs have their beginning and end. He who knows what comes first and what comes last comes himself near the Way.

The ancients who wished clearly to exemplify illustrious virtue throughout the world would first set up good government in their states. Wishing to govern well their states, they would first regulate their families. Wishing to regulate their families, they would first cultivate their persons. Wishing to cultivate their persons, they would first rectify their minds. Wishing to rectify their minds, they would first seek sincerity in their thoughts. Wishing for sincerity in their thoughts, they would first extend their knowledge. The extension of knowledge lay in the investigation of things. For only when things are investigated is knowledge extended; only when knowledge is extended are thoughts sincere; only when thoughts are sincere are minds rectified; only when minds are rectified are our persons cultivated; only when our persons are cultivated are our families regulated; only when families are regulated are states well governed; and only when states are well governed is there peace in the world.

From the emperor down to the common people, all, without exception, must consider cultivation of the individual character as the root. If the root is in disorder, it is impossible for the branches to be in order. To treat the important as unimportant and to treat the unimportant as important—this should never be. This is called knowing the root; this is called the perfection of knowledge. . . .

What is meant by saying that "the cultivation of the person depends on the rectification of the mind" is this: When one is under the influence of anger, one's mind will not be correct; when one is under the influence of fear, it will not be correct; when one is under the influence of fond regard, it will not be correct; when one is under the influence of anxiety, it will not be correct. When the mind is not there, we gaze at things but do not see; we listen but do not hear; we eat but do not know the flavors. This is what is meant by saying that the cultivation of the person depends on the rectification of the mind. . . .

What is meant by saying that "the government of the state depends on the regulation of the family" is this: One can never teach outsiders if one cannot teach one's own family. Therefore the prince perfects the proper teaching for the

From Sources of Chinese Tradition. *Compiled by Wm. Theodore de Bary, et al., 1960, pp. 115–117. Reprinted by permission of Columbia University Press. Footnotes edited.*

whole country without going outside his family; the filial piety wherewith one serves his sovereign, the brotherly respect wherewith one treats his elders, the kindness wherewith one deals with the multitude. There is the saying in the "Announcement to K'ang" [in the *Book of History*]: "Act as if you were rearing an infant." If you set yourself to a task with heart and soul you will not go far wrong even if you do not hit the mark. No girl has ever learned to suckle an infant before she got married.

If one family exemplifies humanity, humanity will abound in the whole country. If one family exemplifies courtesy, courtesy will abound in the whole country. On the other hand, if one man exemplifies greed and wickedness, rebellious disorder will arise in the whole country.[1] Therein lies the secret. Hence the proverb: One word ruins an enterprise; one man determines the fate of an empire. Yao and Shun ruled the empire with humanity, and the people followed them. Chieh and Chou ruled the empire with cruelty, and the people only submitted to them. Since these last commanded actions that they themselves would not like to take, the people refused to follow them. Thus it is that what [virtues] a prince finds in himself he may expect in others, and what [vices] he himself is free from he may condemn in others. It is impossible that a man devoid of every virtue which he might wish to have in others could be able effectively to instruct them.

Thus we see why it is that "the government of the state depends on the regulation of the family." . . .

What is meant by saying that "the establishment of peace in the world depends on the government of the state" is this: When superiors accord to the aged their due, then the common people will be inspired to practice filial piety; when superiors accord to elders their due, then the common people will be inspired to practice brotherly respect; when superiors show compassion to the orphaned, then the common people do not do otherwise. Thus the gentleman has a principle with which, as with a measuring square, he may regulate his conduct.

What a man dislikes in his superiors let him not display in his treatment of his inferiors; what he dislikes in his inferiors let him not display in his service to his superiors; what he dislikes in those before him let him not set before those who are behind him; what he dislikes in those behind him let him not therewith follow those who are before him; what he dislikes from those on his right let him not bestow upon those on his left; what he dislikes from those on his left let him not bestow upon those on his right. This is called the regulating principle of the measuring square.

1. The "one family" and "one man" refer to the family and person of the ruler.

The Doctrine of the Mean

CHU HSI'S REMARK: "Master Ch'eng I (Ch'eng I-ch'uan, 1033–1107) said, 'By *chung* (central) is meant what is not one-sided, and by *yung* (ordinary) is meant what is unchangeable. *Chung* is the correct path of the world and *yung* is the definite principle of the world.' 'This work represents the central way in which the doctrines of the Confucian school have been transmitted.' Fearing that in time errors should arise, Tzu-ssu wrote it down and transmitted it to Mencius.

From Chan, W., editor, A Source Book in Chinese Philosophy. *Copyright © 1963 by Princeton University Press. Excerpt pp. 97–110. Reprinted with permission of Princeton University Press. Footnotes edited.*

The book 'first speaks of one principle, next it spreads out to cover the ten thousand things, and finally returns and gathers them all under the one principle.' Unroll it, and it reaches in all directions. Roll it up, and it withdraws and lies hidden in minuteness. 'Its meaning and interest are inexhaustible. The whole of it is solid learning. If the skillful reader will explore and brood over it and apprehend it, he may apply it throughout his life, and will find it inexhaustible."

What Heaven (*T'ien*, Nature) imparts to man is called human nature. To follow our nature is called the Way (Tao). Cultivating the Way is called education. The Way cannot be separated from us for a moment. What can be separated from us is not the Way. Therefore the superior man is cautious over what he does not see and apprehensive over what he does not hear. There is nothing more visible than what is hidden and nothing more manifest than what is subtle. Therefore the superior man is watchful over himself when he is alone.

Before the feelings of pleasure, anger, sorrow, and joy are aroused it is called equilibrium (*chung*, centrality, mean). When these feelings are aroused and each and all attain due measure and degree, it is called harmony. Equilibrium is the great foundation of the world, and harmony its universal path. When equilibrium and harmony are realized to the highest degree, heaven and earth will attain their proper order and all things will flourish.

Chu Hsi's Remark. In the above first chapter, Tzu-ssu relates the ideas which had been transmitted to him, as the basis of discourse. First, it shows clearly that the origin of the Way is traced to Heaven and is unchangeable, while its concrete substance is complete in ourselves and may not be departed from. Next, it speaks of the essentials of preserving, nourishing, and examining the mind. Finally, it speaks of the meritorious achievements and transforming influence of the sage and the spirit man in their highest degree. Tzu-ssu's hope was that the student should hereby return to search within himself to find these truths, so that he might remove his selfish desires aroused by external temptations, and realize in full measure the goodness which is natural to him. This is what scholar Yang meant when he said that this chapter is the quintessence of the whole work. In the following ten chapters, Tzu-ssu quotes Confucius in order fully to develop the meaning of this chapter.

Chung-ni (Confucius) said, "The superior man [exemplifies] the Mean (*chung-yung*).[1] The inferior man acts contrary to the Mean. The superior man [exemplifies] the Mean because, as a superior man, he can maintain the Mean at any time. The inferior man [acts contrary to] the Mean because, as an inferior man, he has no caution."

Confucius said, "Perfect is the Mean. For a long time few people have been able to follow it."

Confucius said, "I know why the Way is not pursued. The intelligent go beyond it and the stupid do not come up to it. I know why the Way is not understood. The worthy go beyond it and the unworthy do not come up to it. There is no one who does not eat and drink, but there are few who can really know flavor."

Confucius said, "Alas! How is the Way not being pursued!"

Confucius said, "Shun was indeed a man of great wisdom! He loved to question others and to examine their words, however ordinary. He concealed what was bad in them and displayed what was good. He took hold of their two extremes, took the mean between them, and applied it in his dealing with the people. This was how he became Shun (the sage-emperor)."

Confucius said, "Men all say, 'I am wise'; but when driven forward and taken in a net, a trap, or a pitfall, none knows how to escape. Men all say, 'I am wise'; but should they choose the course of the Mean, they are not able to keep it for a round month."

1. The term *chung-yung,* literally "centrality and universality," has been translated as moderation, the Mean, mean-in-action, normality, universal moral order, etc. According to Cheng Hsüan, *yung* means the ordinary and *chung-yung* means using the Mean as the ordinary way. According to Chu Hsi, it means neither one-sided nor extreme but the ordinary principle of the Mean. The Mean is the same as equilibrium and harmony in Chapter 1.

Confucius said, "Hui was a man who chose the course of the Mean, and when he got hold of one thing that was good, he clasped it firmly as if wearing it on his breast and never lost it."

Confucius said, "The empire, the states, and the families can be put in order. Ranks and emolument can be declined. A bare, naked weapon can be tramped upon. But the Mean cannot [easily] be attained."

Tzu-lu asked about strength. Confucius said, "Do you mean the strength of the South, the strength of the North, or the strength you should cultivate yourself? To be genial and gentle in teaching others and not to revenge unreasonable conduct—this is the strength of the people of the South. The superior man lives by it. To lie under arms and meet death without regret—this is the strength of the people of the North. The strong man lives by it. Therefore the superior man maintains harmony [in his nature and conduct] and does not waver. How unflinching is his strength! He stands in the middle position and does not lean to one side. How unflinching is his strength! When the Way prevails in the state, [if he enters public life], he does not change from what he was in private life. How unflinching is his strength! When the Way does not prevail in the state, he does not change even unto death. How unflinching is his strength!"

"There are men who seek for the abstruse, and practice wonders. Future generations may mention them. But that is what I will not do. There are superior men who act in accordance with the Way, but give up when they have gone half way. But I can never give up. There are superior men who are in accord with the Mean, retire from the world and are unknown to their age, but do not regret. It is only a sage who can do this."

"The Way of the superior man functions everywhere and yet is hidden. Men and women of simple intelligence can share its knowledge; and yet in its utmost reaches, there is something which even the sage does not know. Men and women of simple intelligence can put it into practice; and yet in its utmost reaches there is something which even the sage is not able to put into practice. Great as heaven and earth are, men still find something in them with which to be dissatisfied. Thus with [the Way of] the superior man, if one speaks of its greatness, nothing in the world can contain it, and if one speaks of its smallness, nothing in the world can split it. The *Book of Odes* says, 'The hawk flies up to heaven; the fishes leap in the deep.' This means that [the Way] is clearly seen above and below. The Way of the superior man has its simple beginnings in the relation between man and woman, but in its utmost reaches, it is clearly seen in heaven and on earth."

Chu Hsi's Remark. The above twelfth chapter contains the words of Tzu-ssu, which are meant to clarify and elaborate on the idea of chapter 1 that the Way cannot be departed from. In the following eight chapters, he quotes Confucius here and there to clarify it.

Confucius said, "The Way is not far from man. When a man pursues the Way and yet remains away from man, his course cannot be considered the Way. The *Book of Odes* says, 'In hewing an axe handle, the pattern is not far off.' If we take an axe handle to hew another axe handle and look askance from the one to the other, we may still think the pattern is far away. Therefore the superior man governs men as men, in accordance with human nature, and as soon as they change [what is wrong], he stops. Conscientiousness (*chung*) and altruism (*shu*) are not far from the Way. What you do not wish others to do to you, do not do to them.

"There are four things in the Way of the superior man, none of which I have been able to do. To serve my father as I would expect my son to serve me: that I have not been able to do. To serve my ruler as I would expect my ministers to serve me: that I have not been able to do. To serve my elder brothers as I would expect my younger brothers to serve me: that I have not been able to do. To be the first to treat friends as I would expect them to treat me: that I have not been able to do. In practicing the ordinary virtues and in the exercise of care in ordinary conversation, when there is deficiency, the superior man never fails to make further effort, and when there is excess, never dares to go to the limit. His words correspond to his actions and his actions correspond to his words. Isn't the superior man earnest and genuine?"

Comment. It is often said that Confucianism teaches only the "negative golden rule," not to do to others what one does not want them to do to him. However, the golden rule is here positively stated, that is, to do to others what one expects others to do to him. There is no question about the positive character of the Confucian doctrine which is clearly stated in terms of conscientiousness and altruism.

The superior man does what is proper to his position and does not want to go beyond this. If he is in a noble station, he does what is proper to a position of wealth and honorable station. If he is in a humble station, he does what is proper to a position of poverty and humble station. If he is in the midst of barbarian tribes, he does what is proper in the midst of barbarian tribes. In a position of difficulty and danger, he does what is proper to a position of difficulty and danger. He can find himself in no situation in which he is not at ease with himself. In a high position he does not treat his inferiors with contempt. In a low position he does not court the favor of his superiors. He rectifies himself and seeks nothing from others, hence he has no complaint to make. He does not complain against Heaven above or blame men below. Thus it is that the superior man lives peacefully and at ease and waits for his destiny (*ming*, Mandate of Heaven, fate), while the inferior man takes to dangerous courses and hopes for good luck. Confucius said, "In archery we have something resembling the Way of the superior man. When the archer misses the center of the target, he turns around and seeks for the cause of failure within himself." . . .

Duke Ai asked about government. Confucius said, "The governmental measures of King Wen and King Wu are spread out in the records. With their kind of men, government will flourish. When their kind of men are gone, their government will come to an end. When the right

principles of man operate, the growth of good government is rapid, and when the right principles of soil operate, the growth of vegetables is rapid. Indeed, government is comparable to a fast-growing plant. Therefore the conduct of government depends upon the men. The right men are obtained by the ruler's personal character. The cultivation of the person is to be done through the Way, and the cultivation of the Way is to be done through humanity. Humanity (*jen*) is [the distinguishing characteristic of] man, and the greatest application of it is in being affectionate toward relatives. Righteousness (*i*) is the principle of setting things right and proper, and the greatest application of it is in honoring the worthy. The relative degree of affection we ought to feel for our relatives and the relative grades in the honoring of the worthy give rise to the rules of propriety. [If those in inferior positions do not have the confidence of their superiors, they will not be able to govern the people].

Comment. The sentence "Humanity is [the distinguishing characteristic of] man" is perhaps the most often quoted on the subject of humanity (*jen*). In Chinese it is " *jen* is *jen*," the first *jen* meaning humanity and the second referring to man. It is not just a pun, but an important definition of the basic Confucian concept of humanity, for to Confucianists, the virtue of humanity is meaningless unless it is involved in actual human relationships. This is the reason Cheng Hsüan defined it as "people living together," the definition to which scholars of the Ch'ing dynasty (1644–1912) returned in their revolt against the Neo-Confucianists of the Sung dynasty who interpreted *jen* as a state of mind.

Therefore the ruler must not fail to cultivate his personal life. Wishing to cultivate his personal life, he must not fail to serve his parents. Wishing to serve his parents, he must not fail to know man. Wishing to know man, he must not fail to know Heaven.

There are five universal ways [in human relations], and the way by which they are practiced is three. The five are those governing the relationship between ruler and minister, between father and son, between husband and wife, between elder and younger brothers, and those in the intercourse between friends. These five are universal paths in the world. Wisdom, humanity, and courage, these three are the universal virtues. The way by which they are practiced is one.

Some are born with the knowledge [of these virtues]. Some learn it through study. Some learn it through hard work. But when the knowledge is acquired, it comes to the same thing. Some practice them naturally and easily. Some practice them for their advantage. Some practice them with effort and difficulty. But when the achievement is made, it comes to the same thing.

Confucius said, "Love of learning is akin to wisdom. To practice with vigor is akin to humanity. To know to be shameful is akin to courage. He who knows these three things knows how to cultivate his personal life. Knowing how to cultivate his personal life, he knows how to govern other men. And knowing how to govern other men, he knows how to govern the empire, its states, and the families."

There are nine standards by which to administer the empire, its states, and the families. They are: cultivating the personal life, honoring the worthy, being affectionate to relatives, being respectful toward the great ministers, identifying oneself with the welfare of the whole body of officers, treating the common people as one's own children, attracting the various artisans, showing tenderness to strangers from far countries, and extending kindly and awesome influence on the feudal lords. If the ruler cultivates his personal life, the Way will be established. If he honors the worthy, he will not be perplexed. If he is affectionate to his relatives, there will be no grumbling among his uncles and brothers. If he respects the great ministers, he will not be deceived. If he identifies himself with the welfare of the whole body of officers, then the officers will repay him heavily for his courtesies. If he treats the common people as his own children, then the masses will exhort one another [to do good]. If he attracts the various artisans, there will be sufficiency of wealth and resources in the country. If he shows tenderness to strangers from far countries, people from all quarters of the world

will flock to him. And if he extends kindly and awesome influence over the feudal lords, then the world will stand in awe of him.

To fast, to purify, and to be correct in dress [at the time of solemn sacrifice], and not to make any movement contrary to the rules of propriety—this is the way to cultivate the personal life. To avoid slanderers, keep away seductive beauties, regard wealth lightly, and honor virtue—this is the way to encourage the worthy. To give them honorable position, to bestow on them ample emoluments, and to share their likes and dislikes—this is the way to encourage affection for relatives. To allow them many officers to carry out their functions—this is the way to encourage the great ministers. To deal with them loyally and faithfully and to give them ample emoluments—this is the way to encourage the body of officers. To require them for service only at the proper time [without interfering with their farm work] and to tax them lightly—this is the way to encourage the common masses. To inspect them daily and examine them monthly and to reward them according to the degree of their workmanship—this is the way to encourage the various artisans. To welcome them when they come and send them off when they go and to commend the good among them and show compassion to the incompetent—this is the way to show tenderness to strangers from far countries. To restore lines of broken succession, to revive states that have been extinguished, to bring order to chaotic states, to support those states that are in danger, to have fixed times for their attendance at court, and to present them with generous gifts while expecting little when they come—this is the way to extend kindly and awesome influence on the feudal lords.

There are nine standards by which to govern the empire, its states, and the families, but the way by which they are followed is one. In all matters if there is preparation they will succeed; if there is no preparation, they will fail. If what is to be said is determined beforehand, there will be no stumbling. If the business to be done is determined beforehand, there will be no difficulty. If action to be taken is determined beforehand, there will be no trouble. And if the way to be pursued is determined beforehand, there will be no difficulties. If those in inferior positions do not have the confidence of their superiors, they will not be able to govern the people. There is a way to have the confidence of the superiors: If one is not trusted by his friends, he will not have the confidence of his superiors. There is a way to be trusted by one's friends: If one is not obedient to his parents, he will not be trusted by his friends. There is a way to obey one's parents: If one examines himself and finds himself to be insincere, he will not be obedient to his parents. There is a way to be sincere with oneself: If one does not understand what is good, he will not be sincere with himself. Sincerity is the Way of Heaven. To think how to be sincere is the way of man. He who is sincere is one who hits upon what is right without effort and apprehends without thinking. He is naturally and easily in harmony with the Way. Such a man is a sage. He who tries to be sincere is one who chooses the good and holds fast to it.

Study it (the way to be sincere) extensively, inquire into it accurately, think over it carefully, sift it clearly, and practice it earnestly. When there is anything not yet studied, or studied but not yet understood, do not give up. When there is any question not yet asked, or asked but its answer not yet known, do not give up. When there is anything not yet thought over, or thought over but not yet apprehended, do not give up. When there is anything not yet sifted, or sifted but not yet clear, do not give up. When there is anything not yet practiced, or practiced but not yet earnestly, do not give up. If another man succeed by one effort, you will use a hundred efforts. If another man succeed by ten efforts, you will use a thousand efforts. If one really follows this course, though stupid, he will surely become intelligent, and though weak, will surely become strong.

Comment. The five steps of study, inquiry, thinking, sifting, and practice could have come from John Dewey.

It is due to our nature that enlightenment results from sincerity. It is due to education that sincerity results from enlightenment. Given sincerity, there will be enlightenment, and given enlightenment, there will be sincerity.

Chu Hsi's Remark. In the above twenty-first chapter, Tzu-ssu continues Confucius' idea in the preceding chapter of the Way of Heaven and the way of man as a basis for discussion. In the following twelve chapters, Tzu-ssu reiterates and elaborates the idea of this chapter.

Only those who are absolutely sincere can fully develop their nature. If they can fully develop their nature, they can then fully develop the nature of others. If they can fully develop the nature of others, they can then fully develop the nature of things. If they can fully develop the nature of things, they can then assist in the transforming and nourishing process of Heaven and Earth. If they can assist in the transforming and nourishing process of Heaven and Earth, they can thus form a trinity with Heaven and Earth.

Comment. Whether this chapter refers to rulers, as Cheng Hsüan and other Han dynasty scholars contended, or to the sage, as Chu Hsi and other Sung scholars thought, is immaterial. The important point is the ultimate trinity with Heaven and Earth. It is of course another way of saying the unity of man and Heaven or Nature, a doctrine which eventually assumed the greatest importance in Neo-Confucianism.

The next in order are those who cultivate to the utmost a particular goodness. Having done this, they can attain to the possession of sincerity. As there is sincerity, there will be its expression. As it is expressed, it will become conspicuous. As it becomes conspicuous, it will become clear. As it becomes clear, it will move others. As it moves others, it changes them. As it changes them, it transforms them. Only those who are absolutely sincere can transform others.

It is characteristic of absolute sincerity to be able to foreknow. When a nation or family is about to flourish, there are sure to be lucky omens. When a nation or family is about to perish, there are sure to be unlucky omens. These omens are revealed in divination and in the movements of the four limbs. When calamity or blessing is about to come, it can surely know beforehand if it is good, and it can also surely know beforehand if it is evil. Therefore he who has absolute sincerity is like a spirit.

Sincerity means the completion of the self, and the Way is self-directing. Sincerity is the beginning and end of things. Without sincerity there would be nothing. Therefore the superior man values sincerity. Sincerity is not only the completion of one's own self, it is that by which all things are completed. The completion of the self means humanity. The completion of all things means wisdom. These are the character of the nature, and they are the Way in which the internal and the external are united. Therefore whenever it is employed, everything done is right.

Comment. In no other Confucian work is the Way (Tao) given such a central position. This self-directing Way seems to be the same as the Tao in Taoism. But the difference is great. As Ch'ien Mu has pointed out, when the Taoists talk about Tao as being natural, it means that Tao is void and empty, whereas when Confucianists talk about Tao as being natural, they describe it as sincerity. This, according to him, is a great contribution of the *Doctrine of the Mean*. It should also be pointed out that with Confucianists, "The Way is not far from man." Contrary to the Tao of Taoism, the Confucian Tao is strongly humanistic.

Therefore absolute sincerity is ceaseless. Being ceaseless, it is lasting. Being lasting, it is evident. Being evident, it is infinite. Being infinite, it is extensive and deep. Being extensive and deep, it is high and brilliant. It is because it is extensive and deep that it contains all things. It is because it is high and brilliant that it overshadows all

things. It is because it is infinite and lasting that it can complete all things. In being extensive and deep, it is a counterpart of Earth. In being high and brilliant, it is a counterpart of Heaven. In being infinite and lasting, it is unlimited. Such being its nature, it becomes prominent without any display, produces changes without motion, and accomplishes its ends without action.

The Way of Heaven and Earth may be completely described in one sentence: They are without any doubleness and so they produce things in an unfathomable way. The Way of Heaven and Earth is extensive, deep, high, brilliant, infinite, and lasting. The heaven now before us is only this bright, shining mass; but when viewed in its unlimited extent, the sun, moon, stars, and constellations are suspended in it and all things are covered by it. The earth before us is but a handful of soil; but in its breadth and depth, it sustains mountains like Hua and Yüeh without feeling their weight, contains the rivers and seas without letting them leak away, and sustains all things. The mountain before us is only a fistful of straw; but in all the vastness of its size, grass and trees grow upon it, birds and beasts dwell on it, and stores of precious things (minerals) are discovered in it. The water before us is but a spoonful of liquid, but in all its unfathomable depth, the monsters, dragons, fishes, and turtles are produced in them, and wealth becomes abundant because of it [as a result of transportation]. The *Book of Odes* says, "The Mandate of Heaven, how beautiful and unceasing." This is to say, this is what makes Heaven to be Heaven. Again, it says, "How shining is it, the purity of King Wen's virtue!" This is to say, this is what makes King Wen what he was. Purity likewise is unceasing. . . .

Suggestions for Further Reading

A good place to start is with John Koller's chapter on "Confucianism" (Chapter 18) in *Oriental Philosophies,* 2d ed. (New York: Charles Scribner's Sons, 1985). Dr. Koller includes an excellent beginning bibliography. I would only add to his list a recent work by David L. Hall and Roger T. Ames called *Thinking Through Confucius* (New York: State University of New York Press, 1987). This book is advanced and should only be read after working through some of the more elementary material suggested by Koller. *Thinking Through Confucius* brings out the philosophical importance of Confucius for our time. On Chinese thought in general see

Thome H. Fang's *The Chinese View of Life* (Hong Kong: The Union Press, 1956). See "*Jen and Li* in the *Analects*" by Kwong-loi Shun in *Philosophy East and West: A Quarterly of Comparative Philosophy.* Vol. 43, July, 1993, 457–479, for a detailed discussion of these central Confucian concepts.

2.3. Living the Examined Life

Socrates (470–399 B.C.E.) was born in Athens nine years after Confucius died. He lived during the golden era of Greek culture in a city that had become the intellectual and cultural center of the Mediterranean world. Many consider him the father of Western philosophy.

We have inherited contradictory pictures of him. Plato (see Section 7.2), his most famous student and author of the dialogues in which Socrates stars, portrays him as the ideal philosopher. Aristophanes, in his play *The Clouds,* pictures him as an intellectual buffoon. Unlike the Pre-Socratics, Socrates showed little interest in natural philosophy. Like the Sophists, he was intensely interested in ethical and political problems. To many, he appeared to be just another Sophist, teaching the youth virtue. But Plato contrasts him with the Sophists, claiming that he took no fee for his instruction and that his instruction was not a matter of *telling* others the truth, but more like the activity of a midwife. He helped others give birth to and critically examine their own ideas.

His method (the **Socratic method**) consisted of asking people questions about matters they presumably knew something about. Socrates would usually begin by asking for an essential or analytic definition (see Appendix A) of a concept like justice. Once a definition was offered, he analyzed its meaning and critically examined it. Some defect was found, and the definition was reformulated to avoid the defect. Then this new definition was critically examined until another defect appeared. The process went on as long as Socrates could keep the other parties talking.

As an example, let's take the dialogue called the *Euthyphro.* Socrates is at the courthouse in Athens because he has been charged with corrupting the youth and inventing new gods. The latter charge amounts to a charge of impiety and so he is anxious to talk with Euthyphro, who has appeared at the courthouse on his way to prosecute his own father for the impious act of murder. He asks Euthyphro, who claims to be something of an expert in these matters, to define piety. Euthyphro responds by offering his own action of prosecuting his father for murder as an example of piety.

Socrates points out that this is an *example* of piety, but it is not the sort of definition he is seeking. He wants to know the *essential* characteristics of piety. So Euthyphro tries again and defines piety as whatever is pleasing to the gods. This definition is soon found wanting when Socrates points out that the gods are often pleased by different things. What pleases Zeus does not always please his wife, Hera. So Euthyphro amends his definition. Piety is what is pleasing to *all* the gods. Socrates responds to this reformulation by asking, "Do the gods love piety because it is pious, or is it pious because the gods love it?" What is at issue is whether piety has some characteristic in itself which accounts for the fact that the gods love it, or whether the essential trait that determines piety is simply the fact that the gods love it. Euthyphro replies that the gods love piety because it is pious. Then Socrates shows him that he has not yet offered a good definition of piety itself, but only stated an effect of piety, namely that, whatever it is essentially, piety has the effect of pleasing all the gods. So Euthyphro, getting rather upset, offers another definition. This one, too, proves inadequate, but Euthyphro manages to make an excuse and leave before Socrates can drag yet another definition from him and demolish it. The dialogue ends, as so many do, with the issue of what piety is still up in the air. However, progress has been made. We now know more about what piety is not. But no positive, agreed-upon definition has been formulated.

This dialogue not only illustrates Socratic method, it probes the interesting and complex problem of the foundation of ethics. Is moral goodness an independent value, or is it something that depends on something else like the will or command of God? Some theologians have argued in favor of the **divine command theory of ethics** (see Section 3.3 for a more detailed discussion). According to this theory, God's command or will makes something morally right. Such a theory implies that the Ten Commandments are good only because God decreed them. Murder, for example, is not morally wrong in itself, but only if God should happen to forbid it. But this sort of theory appears to make morality a matter of divine whim. If God decides to command just the opposite of the Ten Commandments, then this new set of commandments would become morally right. Don't we want to say that there is something intrinsically wrong about certain actions like murder, no matter what God might happen to command?

Socrates got in trouble with the people of Athens and was brought to trial in 399 B.C.E. Three Athenians—Meletus, Anytus, and Lycon—brought charges. There were 501 citizens on the jury. *The Apology,* which you are about to read, is Plato's account of the trial and Socrates' defense. It provides a dramatic statement of why Socrates believes that the pursuit of truth by the critical methods of rational inquiry is the way human beings ought to live. However, we should be cautious about interpreting Socrates' views in a purely intellectual way. He is concerned with the pursuit of wisdom and truth through the critical use of reason, there can be no doubt about that. But this way of living is not unrelated to moral concerns. As he says at one point, his teaching has always been "not to take thought of yourself or your properties, but to care about the improvement of your soul." This "improvement of soul" is not acquired by money, but by the practice of virtue. Indeed, he claims that "from virtue come money and every other good of man, public as well as private."

Reading Questions

As you read *The Apology* (which in Greek means "Defense") answer these questions:

1. What is the main point Socrates makes by telling the story about the Oracle of Delphi?

2. How does Socrates defend himself against the charge of corrupting the youth and the charge of atheism?

3. At one point Socrates compares himself to a gadfly (horsefly) and the Athenians to a thoroughbred horse. What is the point of this comparison?

4. During the penalty phase of the trial, Socrates asserts that the unexamined life is not worth living. Do you agree or not and why?

5. Would you find Socrates guilty or not guilty? Why?

6. How do you think Socrates would answer the question, "How should one live?"

7. Formulate your own *analytical* question (see Section 1.3) about any part of the text and answer it.

The Apology

PLATO

Socrates: HOW YOU HAVE FELT, O men of Athens, hearing the speeches of my accusers, I cannot tell. I know their persuasive words almost made me forget who I was, such was their effect. Yet they hardly spoke a word of truth. But many as their falsehoods were, there was one of them which quite amazed me—I mean when they told you to be on your guard and not let yourselves be deceived by the force of my eloquence. They ought to have been ashamed of saying this, because they were sure to be detected as soon as I opened my lips and displayed my deficiency. They certainly did appear to be most shameless in saying this, unless by the force of eloquence they mean the force of truth; for then I do indeed admit that I am eloquent. But in how different a way from theirs!

Well, as I was saying, they have hardly uttered a word, or not more than a word, of truth. You shall hear from me the whole truth: not, however, delivered in their manner, in an oration ornamented with words and phrases. No, indeed! I shall use the words and arguments which occur to me at the moment. I am certain this is right, and at my time of life I should not appear before you, O men of Athens, in the character of a juvenile orator—let no one expect this of me. And I must beg you to grant me one favor, which is this—if you hear me using the same words in my defense which I have been in the habit of using, and which most of you may have heard in the agora, and at the tables of the money-changers, or anywhere else, I ask you not to be surprised at this, and not to interrupt me. I am more than 70 years of age and this is the first time I have ever appeared in a court of law, and I am a stranger to the ways of this place. Therefore I would have you regard me as if I was really a stranger whom you would excuse if he spoke in his native tongue and after the fashion of his country. That, I think, is not an unfair request. Never mind the way I speak, which may or may not be good, but think only of the justice of my cause, and give heed to that. Let the judge decide justly and the speaker speak truly.

First, I have to reply to the older charges and to my first accusers, and then I will go on to the later ones. I have had many accusers who accused me in the past and their false charges have continued during many years. I am more afraid of them than of Anytus and his associates, who are dangerous, too, in their own way. But far more dangerous are these, who began when you were children, and took possession of your minds with their falsehoods, telling of Socrates, a wise man, who speculated about the heavens above, and searched into the earth beneath, and made the worse argument defeat the better. These are the accusers whom I fear because they are the circulators of this rumor and their listeners are too likely to believe that speculators of this sort do not believe in the gods. My accusers are many and their charges against me are of ancient date. They made them in days when you were impressionable—in childhood, or perhaps in youth—and the charges went by unanswered for there was none to answer. Hardest of all, their names I do not know and cannot tell, unless in the chance case of a comic poet. But the main body of these slanderers who from envy and malice have convinced you—and there are some of them who are convinced themselves, and impart their convictions to others—all these, I say, are most difficult to deal with. I cannot have them up here and ex-

The translation is based upon Benjamin Jowett's nineteenth-century translation as updated and revised by Christopher Biffle, A Guided Tour of Five Works by Plato (Mountain View, CA: Mayfield, 1988), pp. 30–50. Reprinted by permission of Mayfield Publishing Company. Footnotes deleted.

amine them. Therefore, I must simply fight with shadows in my own defense and examine when there is no one who answers. I will ask you then to assume with me that my opponents are of two kinds: one more recent, the other from the past. I will answer the latter first, for these accusations you heard long before the others, and much more often.

Well, then, I will make my defense, and I will try in the short time allowed to do away with this evil opinion of me which you have held for such a long time. I hope I may succeed, if this be well for you and me, and that my words may find favor with you. But I know to accomplish this is not easy—I see the nature of the task. Let the event be as the gods will; in obedience to the law I make my defense.

I will begin at the beginning and ask what the accusation is which has given rise to this slander of me and which has encouraged Meletus to proceed against me. What do the slanderers say? They shall be my prosecutors and I will sum up their words in an affidavit. "Socrates is an evildoer and a curious person, who searches into things under the earth and in the heavens. He makes the weaker argument defeat the stronger and he teaches these doctrines to others." That is the nature of the accusation, and that is what you have seen in the comedy of Aristophanes. He introduced a man whom he calls Socrates, going about and saying he can walk in the air, and talking a lot of nonsense concerning matters which I do not pretend to know anything about—however, I mean to say nothing disparaging of anyone who is a student of such knowledge. I should be very sorry if Meletus could add that to my charge. But the simple truth is, O Athenians, I have nothing to do with these studies. Very many of those here are witnesses to the truth of this and to them I appeal. Speak then, you who have heard me, and tell your neighbors whether any of you ever heard me hold forth in few words or in many upon matters of this sort. . . . You hear their answer. And from what they say you will be able to judge the truth of the rest.

There is the same foundation for the report I am a teacher, and take money; that is no more true than the other. Although, if a man is able to teach, I honor him for being paid. There is Gorgias of Leontium, Prodicus of Ceos, and Hippias of Elis, who go round the cities and are able to persuade young men to leave their own citizens, by whom they might be taught for nothing, and come to them, whom they not only pay but are thankful if they may be allowed to pay them.

There is actually a Parian philosopher residing in Athens who charges fees. I came to hear of him in this way: I met a man who spent a world of money on the sophists, Callias, the son of Hipponicus, and knowing he had sons, I asked him: "Callias," I said, "if your two sons were foals or calves, there would be no difficulty in finding someone to raise them. We would hire a trainer of horses, or a farmer probably, who would improve and perfect them in their own proper virtue and excellence. But, as they are human beings, whom are you thinking of placing over them? Is there anyone who understands human and political virtue? You must have thought about this because you have sons. Is there anyone?"

"There is," he said.

"Who is he?" said I. "And of what country? And what does he charge?"

"Evenus the Parian," he replied. "He is the man and his charge is five minae."

Happy is Evenus, I said to myself, if he really has this wisdom and teaches at such a modest charge. Had I the same, I would have been very proud and conceited; but the truth is I have no knowledge like this, O Athenians.

I am sure someone will ask the question, "Why is this, Socrates, and what is the origin of these accusations of you: for there must have been something strange which you have been doing? All this great fame and talk about you would never have come up if you had been like other men. Tell us then, why this is, as we should be sorry to judge you too quickly."

I regard this as a fair challenge, and I will try to explain to you the origin of this name of "wise," and of this evil fame. Please attend then and although some of you may think I am joking, I declare I will tell you the entire truth. Men of Athens, this reputation of mine has come from a certain kind of wisdom which I possess. If you ask me what kind of wisdom, I reply, such wisdom as is attainable by man, for to that extent I am inclined to believe I am wise. Whereas, the persons of whom I was speaking have a superhuman wisdom which I may fail to describe, because I do not have it. He who says I have, speaks false, and slanders me.

O men of Athens, I must beg you not to interrupt me, even if I seem to say something extravagant. For the word which I will speak is not mine. I will refer you to a wisdom which is worthy of credit, and will tell you about my wisdom—whether I have any, and of what sort—and that witness shall be the god of Delphi. You must have known Chaerephon. He was a friend of mine and also a friend of yours, for he shared in the exile of the people and returned with you. Well, Chaerephon, as you know, was very impetuous in all his doings, and he went to Delphi and boldly asked the oracle to tell him whether—as I said, I must beg you not to interrupt—he asked the oracle to tell him whether there was anyone wiser than I was. The Pythian prophetess answered, there was no man wiser. Chaerephon is dead, himself, but his brother, who is in court, will confirm the truth of this story.

Why do I mention this? Because I am going to explain to you why I have such an evil name. When I heard the answer, I said to myself, "What can the god mean and what is the interpretation of this riddle? I know I have no wisdom, great or small. What can he mean when he says I am the wisest of men? And yet he is a god, and cannot lie; that would be against his nature." After long consideration, I at last thought of a method of answering the question.

I reflected if I could only find a man wiser than myself then I might go to the god with a refutation in my hand. I would say to him, "Here is a man who is wiser than I am, but you said I was the wisest." Accordingly I went to one who had the reputation of wisdom, and observed him—his name I need not mention; he was a politician whom I selected for examination. When I began to talk with him I could not help thinking he was not really wise, although he was thought wise by many, and wiser still by himself. I tried to explain to him that he thought himself wise, but was not really wise. The result was he hated me and his hatred was shared by several who were present who heard me. So I left him, saying to myself, as I went away: "Well, although I do not suppose either of us knows anything really beautiful and good, I am better off than he is—for he knows nothing and thinks that he knows. I neither know nor think that I know. In this latter, then, I seem to have an advantage over him." Then I went to another who had still higher philosophical pretensions and my conclusion was exactly the same. I made another enemy of him and of many others besides him.

After this I went to one man after another, being aware of the anger which I provoked and I lamented and feared this, but necessity was laid upon me. The word of the god, I thought, ought to be considered first. And I said to myself, "I must go to all who appear to know, and find out the meaning of the oracle." And I swear to you Athenians, by the dog, I swear!, the result of my mission was this: I found the men with the highest reputations were all nearly the most foolish and some inferior men were really wiser and better.

I will tell you the tale of my wanderings and of the Herculean labors, as I may call them, which I endured only to find at last the oracle was right. When I left the politicians, I went to the poets: tragic, dithyrambic, and all sorts. There, I said to myself, you will be detected. Now you will find out you are more ignorant than they are. Accordingly, I took them some of the most elaborate passages in their own writings, and asked what was the meaning of them— thinking the poets would teach me something. Will you believe me? I am almost ashamed to say this, but I must say there is hardly a person present who would not have talked better about their poetry than the poets did themselves. That quickly showed me poets do not write poetry by wisdom, but by a sort of inspiration. They are like soothsayers who also say many fine things, but do not understand the meaning of what they say. The poets appeared to me to be much the same and I further observed that upon the strength of their poetry they believed themselves to be the wisest of men in other things in which they were not wise. So I departed, conceiving myself to be superior to them for the same reason I was superior to the politicians.

At last I went to the artisans, because I was conscious I knew nothing at all and I was sure they knew many fine things. In this I was not mistaken, for they did know many things of which I was ignorant, and in this they certainly were wiser than I was. But I observed even the good artisans fell into the same error as the poets. Because they were good workmen, they thought they also knew all sorts of high matters and this defect in them overshadowed their wisdom. Therefore, I asked myself on behalf of the oracle whether I would like to be as I was, having neither their knowledge nor their ignorance, or like them in both. I answered myself and the oracle that I was better off as I was.

This investigation led to my having many enemies of the worst and most dangerous kind and has given rise also to many falsehoods. I am called wise because my listeners always imagine I possess the wisdom which I do not find in others. The truth is, O men of Athens, the gods only are wise and in this oracle they mean to say wisdom of men is little or nothing. They are not speaking of Socrates, only using my name as an illustration, as if they said, "He, O men, is the wisest who, like Socrates, knows his wisdom is in truth worth nothing." And so I go my way, obedient to the gods, and seek wisdom of anyone, whether citizen or stranger, who appears to be wise. If he is not wise, then in support of the oracle I show him he is not wise. This occupation quite absorbs me, and I have no time to give either to any public matter of interest or to any concern of my own, but I am in utter poverty by reason of my devotion to the gods.

There is another thing. Young men of the richer classes, who have little to do, gather around me of their own accord. They like to hear the pretenders examined. They often imitate me and examine others themselves. There are plenty of persons, as they soon enough discover, who think they know something, but really know little or nothing. Then those who are examined by the young men instead of being angry with themselves are angry with me. "This confounded Socrates," they say, "this villainous misleader of youth!" Then if somebody asks them, "Why, what evil does he practice or teach?," they do not know and cannot tell. But so they may not appear ignorant, they repeat the readymade charges which are used against all philosophers about teaching things up in the clouds and under the earth, and having no gods, and making the worse argument defeat the stronger. They do not like to confess their pretense to knowledge has been detected, which it has. They are numerous, ambitious, energetic and are all in battle array and have persuasive tongues. They have filled your ears with their loud and determined slanders. This is the reason why my three accusers, Meletus and Anytus and Lycon, have set upon me. Meletus has a quarrel with me on behalf of the poets, Anytus, on behalf of the craftsmen, Lycon, on behalf of the orators. As I said at the beginning, I cannot expect to get rid of this mass of slander all in a moment.

This, O men of Athens, is the truth and the whole truth. I have concealed nothing. And yet, I know this plainness of speech makes my accusers hate me and what is their hatred but a proof that I am speaking the truth? This is the reason for their slander of me, as you will find out either in this or in any future inquiry.

I have said enough in my defense against the first class of my accusers. I turn to the second class who are headed by Meletus, that good and patriotic man, as he calls himself. Now I will try to defend myself against them: These new accusers must also have their affidavit read. What do they say? Something of this sort: "Socrates is a doer of evil and corrupter of the youth, and he does not believe in the gods of the state. He has other new divinities of his own." That is their charge and now let us examine the particular counts. He says I am a doer of evil, who corrupts the youth but I say, O men of Athens, Meletus is a doer of evil and the evil is that he makes a joke of a serious matter. He is too ready to bring other men to trial from a pretended zeal and interest about matters in which he really never had the smallest interest. And the truth of this I will try to prove to you.

Come here, Meletus, and let me ask a question of you. You think a great deal about the improvement of youth?

Meletus: Yes I do.

Socrates: Tell the judges, then, who is their improver. You must know, as you have taken the pains to discover their corruptor and are accusing me before them. Speak then, and tell the judges who their improver is. Observe, Meletus, that you are silent and have nothing to say. But is this not rather disgraceful and a very great proof of what I was saying, that you have no interest in the matter? Speak up, friend, and tell us who their improver is.

Mel: The laws.

Soc: But that, my good sir, is not my meaning. I want to know who the person is, who, in the first place, knows the laws.

Mel: The jury, Socrates, who are present in court.

Soc: Do you mean to say, Meletus, they are able to instruct and improve youth?

Mel: Certainly they are.

Soc: All of them, or only some and not others?

Mel: All of them.

Soc: By the goddess Hera, that is good news! There are plenty of improvers, then. And what do you say of the audience—do they improve them?

Mel: Yes, they do.

Soc: And the senators?

Mel: Yes, the senators improve them.

Soc: But perhaps the members of the Assembly corrupt them? Or do they too improve them?

Mel: They improve them.

Soc: Then every Athenian improves and elevates them, all with the exception of myself. I alone am their corruptor? Is that what you say?

Mel: Most definitely.

Soc: I am very unfortunate if that is true. But suppose I ask you a question. Would you say that this also holds true in the case of horses? Does one man do them harm and everyone else good?

Is not the exact opposite of this true? One man is able to do them good and not the many. The trainer of horses, that is to say, does them good, and others who deal with horses injure them? Is that not true, Meletus, of horses or any other animals? Yes, certainly. Whether you and Anytus say yes or no, that is no matter. Fortunate indeed would be the condition of youth if they had one corruptor only and all the rest of the world were their improvers. You, Meletus, have sufficiently shown you never had a thought about the young. Your carelessness is seen in your not caring about the matters spoken of in this very indictment.

And now, Meletus, I must ask you another question: Which is better, to live among bad citizens or among good ones? Answer, friend, I say, for that is a question which may be easily answered. Do not the good do their neighbors good and the bad do them evil?

Mel: Certainly.

Soc: And is there anyone who would rather be injured than benefited by those who associate with him? Answer, my good friend, the law requires you to answer—does anyone like to be injured?

Mel: Certainly not.

Soc: And when you accuse me of corrupting the youth, do you charge I corrupt them intentionally or unintentionally?

Mel: Intentionally, I say.

Soc: But you just admitted that the good do their neighbors good, and the evil do them evil. Now, is that a truth which your superior wisdom has recognized thus early in life, and am I, at my age, in such ignorance as not to know if a man with whom I associate is corrupted by me, I am very likely to be harmed by him? Yet you say I corrupt him, and intentionally too; of that you will never persuade me or any other human being. But either I do not corrupt them, or I corrupt them unintentionally, so that on either view of the case you lie. If my offense is unintentional, the law does not mention unintentional offenses. You ought to have taken me aside and warned me, because if I had been better advised, I should have stopped doing what I only did unintentionally—no doubt I should. Instead, you hated to talk with me or teach me and you indicted me in this court, which is a place not of instruction, but of punishment.

I have shown, Athenians, as I was saying, Meletus has no care at all, great or small, about the matter. But still I should like to know, Meletus, in what way do I corrupt the young. I suppose you mean, as I infer from your indictment, I teach them not to acknowledge the gods which the state acknowledges, but some other new divinities or spiritual agencies instead. These are the lessons which corrupt the youth, as you say.

Mel: Yes, I say that emphatically.

Soc: Then, by the gods, Meletus, of whom we are speaking, tell me and the court, in somewhat plainer terms, what you mean! I do not understand whether you charge I teach others to acknowledge some gods, and therefore do believe in gods, and am not an entire atheist—but only that they are not the same gods which the city recognizes, or, do you mean to say that I am atheist simply, and a teacher of atheism?

Mel: I mean the latter—that you are a complete atheist.

Soc: That is an extraordinary statement, Meletus. Why do you say that? Do you mean that I do not believe the sun or moon are gods, which is the common belief of all men?

Mel: I assure you, jurymen, he does not believe in them. He says the sun is stone and the moon, earth.

Soc: Friend Meletus, you think you are accusing Anaxagoras and you have a bad opinion of the jury, if you believe they do not know these doctrines are found in the books of Anaxagoras the Clazomenian. These are the doctrines which the youth are said to learn from Socrates, when these doctrines can be bought in the marketplace. The youth might cheaply purchase them and laugh at Socrates if he pretends to father such eccentricities. And so, Meletus, you really think that I do not believe in any god?

Mel: I swear by Zeus that you absolutely believe in none at all.

Soc: You are a liar, Meletus, not believed even by yourself. I cannot help thinking, O men of Athens, Meletus is reckless and impudent and has written this indictment in a spirit of wantonness and youthful bravado. He has made a riddle, thinking to fool me. He said to himself: "I shall see whether this wise Socrates will discover my ingenious contradiction, or whether I shall be able to deceive him and the rest of them." For he certainly does appear to me to contradict himself in the indictment as much as if he said that Socrates is guilty of not believing in the gods, and yet of believing in them—but this surely is a piece of nonsense.

I should like you, O men of Athens, to join me in examining what I conceive to be his inconsistency and you, Meletus, answer. And I must remind you not to interrupt me if I speak in my accustomed manner.

Did any man, Meletus, ever believe in the existence of human things, and not human beings? . . . I wish, men of Athens, that he would answer and not be always trying to create an interruption. Did ever any man believe in horsemanship and not in horses? Or in flute playing and not in flute players? No, my friend, I will answer for you and to the court, as you refuse to answer for yourself. There is no man who ever did. But now, please answer the next question. Can a man believe in spiritual and divine activities and not in divine beings?

Mel: He cannot.

Soc: I am glad I have extracted that answer, by the assistance of the court. Nevertheless you swear in the indictment that I teach and believe in divine activities (new or old, no matter for that). At any rate, I believe in divine activities, as you swear in the affidavit, but if I believe in divine activities, I must believe in divine beings. Is that not true? Yes, that is true, for I may assume that your silence gives assent to that. Now what are divine beings? Are they not either gods or the sons of gods? Is that true?

Mel: Yes, that is true.

Soc: But this is just the ingenious riddle of which I was speaking. The divine beings are gods and you say first that I don't believe in gods, and then again that I do believe in gods; that is, if I believe in divine beings. For if the divine beings are the illegitimate sons of gods, whether by the nymphs or by any other mothers, as is thought, that, as all men will agree, necessarily implies the existence of their parents. You might as well affirm the existence of mules, and deny the existence of horses and donkeys. Such nonsense, Meletus, could only have been intended by you as a test of me. You have put this into the indictment because you have no real charge against me. But no one who has a particle of understanding will ever be convinced by you that the same men can believe in divine and superhuman activities, and yet not believe that there are gods and demigods.

I have said enough in answer to the charge of Meletus. Any elaborate defense is unnecessary but, as I was saying before, I certainly have many enemies and this will be my destruction if I am destroyed; of that I am certain—not Meletus, nor Anytus, but the envy and slander of the world, which has been the death of many good men and will probably be the death of many more. I will not be the last of them.

Someone will say: Are you not ashamed, Socrates, of a way of life which is likely to bring you to an untimely end? To him I answer: There you are mistaken, a man who is good for anything should not calculate the chance of living or dying. He should only consider whether in doing anything he is doing right or wrong and acting the part of a good man or of a bad. Whereas, according to your view, the heroes who fell at Troy were not good for much, and the son of Thetis above all, who altogether despised danger in comparison with disgrace. His goddess mother said to him, in his eagerness to slay Hector, that if he avenged his companion Patroclus, and slew Hector, he would die himself.

"Fate," as she said, "waits upon you next after Hector."

He, hearing this, utterly despised danger and death, and instead of fearing them, feared rather to live in dishonor and not to avenge his friend.

"Let me die next," he replied, "and be avenged of my enemy, rather than stay here by the beaked ships to be mocked and a burden on the earth."

Had Achilles any thought of death and danger? For wherever a man's place is, whether the place which he has chosen or that in which he has been placed by a commander, there he should remain in the hour of danger. He should not consider death or anything else but only disgrace. And this, O men of Athens, is a true saying.

My conduct would be strange, O men of Athens, if I, who was ordered by the generals you chose to command me at Potidaea, Amphipolis and Delium, remained where they placed me, like any other man facing death, should know when, as I believe, God orders me to fulfil the philosopher's mission of searching into myself and other men, desert my post through fear of death, or any other fear. That would indeed be strange, and I might be justly arraigned in court for denying the existence of the gods, if I disobeyed the oracle because I was afraid of death. Then I should be supposing I was wise when I was not wise.

This fear of death is indeed the imitation of wisdom, and not real wisdom, being the appearance of knowing the unknown. No one knows whether death, which they in their fear believe to be the greatest evil, may not be the greatest good. Is there not here the pretense of knowledge, which is a disgraceful sort of ignorance? This is the point that, as I think, I am superior to men in general and in which I might believe myself wiser than other men. Whereas I know little of the other world, I do not suppose that I know. But I do know that injustice and disobedience to a better, whether god or man, is evil and dishonorable, and I will never fear or avoid a possible good rather than a certain evil. Therefore if you let me go now, reject the advice of Anytus, who said if I were not put to death I should not have been prosecuted, and that if I escape now, your sons will all be utterly ruined by listening to my words. If you say to me, Socrates, this time we will not listen to Anytus and will let you off, but upon one condition, you are not to inquire and speculate in this way any more and if you are caught doing this again you shall die. If this was the condition on which you let me go, I would reply: Men of Athens, I honor and love you but I shall obey the god rather than you. While I have life and strength I shall never cease from practicing and teaching philosophy, exhorting anyone whom I meet in my usual way and convincing him, saying: O my friend, why do you, who are a citizen of the great and wise city of Athens, care so much about laying up the greatest amount of money, honor and reputation, and so little about wisdom, truth and the greatest improvement of the soul, which you never regard or heed at all? Are you not ashamed of this? If the person with whom I am arguing says: Yes, but I do care; I do not depart or let him go at once. I question, examine and cross-examine him, and if I think he has no virtue, but only says he has, I reproach him with undervaluing the greater, and overvaluing the lesser. This I would say to everyone I meet, young and old, citizen and alien, but especially to the citizens, inasmuch as they are my brethren. This is the command of the god, as I would have you know and I believe that to this day no greater good has ever happened in the state than my service to the god.

I do nothing but go about persuading you all, old and young alike, not to take thought of yourself or your properties, but to care about the improvement of your soul. I tell you virtue is not acquired with money, but that from virtue come money and every other good of man, public as well as private. This is my teaching, and if this is the doctrine which corrupts the young, my influence is certainly ruinous. If anyone says this is not my teaching, he is speaking a lie. Therefore, O men of Athens, I say to you, do as Anytus bids or not as Anytus bids, and either acquit me or not; but whatever you do, know that I shall never change my ways, not even if I have to die many times.

Men of Athens, do not interrupt, but hear me. There was an agreement between us that you should hear me out. I think what I am going to say will do you good: for I have something more to say, which you may be inclined to interrupt but I ask you not to do this.

I want you to know if you kill someone like me, you will injure yourselves more than you will injure me. Meletus and Anytus will not injure me. They cannot because it is not possible that a bad man should injure someone better than himself. I do not deny he may, perhaps, kill him, or drive him into exile, or deprive him of civil rights. He may imagine, and others may imagine, he is doing him a great injury but I do not agree with him. The evil of doing as Anytus is doing—of unjustly taking away another man's life is far greater.

Now, Athenians, I am not going to argue for my own sake, as you may think, but for yours, that you may not sin against the gods or lightly reject their favor by condemning me. If you kill me you will not easily find another like me, who, if I may use such a ludicrous figure of speech, am a sort of gadfly, given to the State by the gods. The State is like a great and noble steed who is slow in his motions owing to his very size and needs to be stirred into life. I am that gadfly which the gods have given the State and all day long and in all places am always fastening upon you, arousing, persuading, and reproaching you. As you will not easily find another like me, I would advise you to spare me. I believe you may feel irritated at being suddenly awakened when you are caught napping. You may think if you were to strike me dead, as Anytus advises, which you easily might, then you would sleep on for the remainder of your lives, unless the god in his care of you gives you another gadfly. That I am given to you by the god is proved by this: if I had been like other men, I should not have neglected my own concerns all these years, and been occupied with yours, coming to you individually like a father or elder brother, exhorting you to think about virtue. This, I say, would not be like human nature. If I had gained anything, or if my exhortations had been paid, there would be some sense in that; but now, as you see not even my accusers dare to say I have ever sought pay from anyone. They have no witnesses for that. I have a witness of the truth of what I say; my poverty is my witness.

Someone may wonder why I go about in private giving advice and busying myself with the concerns of others, but do not come forward in public and advise the state. I will tell you the reason for this. You have often heard me speak of an oracle or sign which comes to me and is the divinity which Meletus ridicules in the indictment. This sign I have had ever since I was a child. The sign is a voice which comes to me and always forbids me to do something which I am going to do, but never commands me to do anything. This is what stands in the way of my being a politician. And correctly I think. For I am certain, O men of Athens, if I had engaged in politics, I would have perished long ago, and done no good either to you or to myself. Do not be offended at my telling you the truth. The truth is no man who goes to war with you or any other multitude, honestly struggling against acts of unrighteousness in the state, will save his life. He who will really fight for the right, if he would live even for a little while, must have a private station and not a public one.

I can give you proofs of this, not words only, but deeds, which you value more than words. Let me tell you a part of my own life which will prove to you I would never have yielded to unjustice from any fear of death, and that if I had not yielded I should have died at once. I will tell you a story—tasteless perhaps and commonplace, but nevertheless true . . . .

The only office of state which I ever held, O men of Athens, was when I served on the council. The clan Antiochis, which is my clan, had the presidency at the trial of the generals who had not taken up the bodies of the slain after the battle of Arginusae. You proposed to try them all together, which was illegal, as you all thought afterwards, but at the time I was the only one of the committee who was opposed to the illegality. I gave my vote against you. When the orators threatened to impeach and arrest me and have me taken away, and you called and shouted, I made up my mind I would run the risk, having law and justice with me, rather than take part in your injustice because I feared imprisonment and death. This happened in the days of the democracy. But when the oligarchy of the Thirty was in power, they brought me and four others into the rotunda, and told us to bring in Leon from Salamis because they wanted to execute him. This was an example of the sort of commands which they were always giving in order to implicate as many as possible in their crimes. Then I showed, not in word only but in deed, if I may be allowed to use such an expression, I cared not a straw for death, and my only fear was the fear of doing an unrighteous or unholy thing. The strong arm of that oppressive power did not frighten me into doing wrong. When we came out of the rotunda the other four went to Salamis and fetched Leon, but I went quietly home. For this I might have lost my life, had not the power of the Thirty shortly afterwards come to an end. And to this many will witness.

Now do you really imagine I could have survived all these years if I had led a public life, supposing that like a good man I always supported the right and made justice, as I should, the first thing? No indeed, men of Athens, neither I nor any other. I have been always the same in all my actions, public as well as private, and never have yielded to any base agreement with those who are slanderously termed my disciples, or to any other. The truth is I have no regular disciples but if anyone likes to come and hear me while I am pursuing my mission, whether he be young or old, he may freely come. Nor do I converse with those who pay only, and not with those who do not pay; but anyone, whether he be rich or poor, may question and answer me and listen to my words. If he turns out to be a bad man or a good one, I am not responsible, as I never taught him anything. If anyone says he has ever learned or heard anything from me in private which all the world has not heard, I would like you to know that he is lying.

I will be asked, why do people delight in continually conversing with you? I have told you already, Athenians, the whole truth about this. They like to hear the cross-examination of the pretenders to wisdom; there is amusement in this. This is a duty which the gods have imposed upon me, as I am assured by oracles, visions, and in every sort of way which the will of divine power was ever made plain to anyone. This is true, O Athenians or, if not true, would be soon refuted. If I am really corrupting the youth and have corrupted some of them already, those who have grown up and are aware I gave them bad advice in the days of their youth should come forward as accusers and take their revenge. If they do not like to come themselves, some of their relatives, fathers, brothers, or other kinsmen, should say what evil their families suffered at my hands. Now is their time. I see many of them in the court.

There is Crito, who is of the same age and of the same township as myself, and there is Critobulus, his son, whom I also see. There is Lysanias of Sphettus, who is the father of Aeschines—he is present; and also there is Antiphon of Cephisus, who is the father of Epigenes; and there are the brothers of several who have associated with me. There is Nicostratus, the son of Theosdotides, and the brother of Theodotus (not Theodotus himself—he is dead, and therefore, he will not seek to stop him). There is Paralus, the son of Demodocus, who had a brother Theages; and Adeimantus, the son of Ariston, whose brother Plato is present; and Aeantodorus, who is the brother of Apollodorus, whom I also see. I might mention a great many others, any of whom Meletus could have produced as witnesses in the course of his speech. Let him still produce them, if he has forgotten—I will make way for him. Let him speak, if he has any testimony of this sort which he can produce. Nay, Athenians, the very opposite is the truth. For all these are ready to witness on behalf of the corruptor, of the destroyer of their kindred, as Meletus and Anytus call me; not the corrupted youth only—there might have been a motive for that—but their uncorrupted elder relatives. Why should they, too, support me with their testimony? Why indeed, except for the reason of truth and justice, and because they know I am speaking the truth and Meletus is lying.

Well, Athenians, this and similar to this is nearly all the defense I have to offer. Yet a word more. Perhaps there may be someone who is offended by me, when he calls to mind how he himself on a similar, or even a less serious occasion, had recourse to prayers and supplications with many tears, and how he produced his children in court, which was a moving spectacle, together with a group of his relations and friends. I, who am probably in danger of my life, will do none of these things. Perhaps this may come into his mind and he may be set against me, and vote in anger because he is displeased at this. Now if there is such a person among you I reply to him: My friend, I am a man, and like other men, a creature of flesh and blood and not of wood or stone, as Homer says. I have a family, yes, and sons, O Athenians, three in number, one of whom is growing up, and two others who are still young. Yet I will not bring any of them here in order to beg you for an acquittal. And why not? Not from any self-will or disregard of you. Whether I am, or am not, afraid of death is another question, of which I will not now speak. My reason is that I feel such conduct to be discreditable to myself, you and the whole state. One who has reached my years and who has a name for wisdom, whether deserved or not, should not lower himself. The world has decided that Socrates is in some way superior to other men. And if those among you who are said to be superior in wisdom, courage and any other virtue, lower themselves in this way, how shameful is their conduct!

I have seen men of reputation, when they have been condemned, behaving in the strangest manner. They seemed to believe they were going to suffer something dreadful if they died, and they could be immortal if you only allowed them to live. I think they were a dishonor to the state, and any stranger coming in would say the most eminent men of Athens, to whom the Athenians themselves give honor and command, are no better than women. I say these things ought not to be done by those of us who are of reputation; and if they are done, you ought not to permit them. You ought to show you are more inclined to condemn, not the man who is quiet, but the man who gets up a doleful scene and makes the city ridiculous.

Setting aside the question of dishonor, there seems to be something wrong in begging a judge and thus procuring an acquittal instead of informing and convincing him. For his duty is not to make a present of justice, but to give judgment. He has sworn he will judge according to the laws and not according to his own good pleasure. Neither he nor we should get into the habit of perjuring ourselves—there can be no piety in that. Do not require me to do what I consider dishonorable, impious and wrong, especially now, when I am being tried for impiety on the indictment of Meletus. For if, O men of Athens, by force of persuasion and entreaty, I could overpower your oaths, then I should be teaching you to believe there are no gods, and convict myself in my own defense of not believing in them. But that is not the case. I do believe there are gods and in a far higher sense than any of my accusers believe in them. To you and to the gods I commit my cause, to be determined by you as is best for you and me.

(The jury returns a guilty verdict and Meletus proposes death as a punishment.)

There are many reasons why I am not grieved, O men of Athens, at the vote of condemnation. I expected this and am only surprised the votes are so nearly equal. I thought the majority against me would have been far larger, but now, had thirty votes gone over to the other side, I would have been acquitted. And I may say I have escaped Meletus' charges. And I may say more; without the assistance of Anytus and Lycon, he would not have had a fifth part of the votes, as the law requires, in which case he would have incurred a fine of a thousand drachmae.

He proposes death as the penalty. What shall I propose on my part, O men of Athens? Clearly what is my due. What is that which I ought to pay or to receive? What shall be done to the man who has never been idle during his whole life, but has been careless of what the many care about—wealth, family interests, military offices and speaking in the Assembly, and courts, plots, and parties. Believing I was really too honest a man to follow in this way and live, I did not go where I could do no good to you or to myself. I went where I could do the greatest good privately to every one of you. I sought to persuade every man among you that he must look to himself and seek virtue and wisdom before he looks to his private interests, and look to the welfare of the State before he looks to the wealth of the State. This should be the order which he observes in all his actions. What shall be done to someone like me? Doubtless some good thing, O men of Athens, if he has his reward and the good should be suitable to him. What would be a reward suitable to a poor man who is your benefactor, who desires to instruct you? There can be no more fitting reward than maintenance in the Prytaneum, O men of Athens, a reward which he deserves far more than the citizen who wins the prize at Olympia in the horse or chariot race, whether the chariots were drawn by two horses or many. For I am in need and he has enough. He only gives you the appearance of happiness and I give you the reality. Thus, if I am to estimate the penalty justly, I say maintenance in the Prytaneum is just.

Perhaps you think I am mocking you in saying this, as in what I said before about the tears and prayers. But that is not the case. I speak because I am convinced I never intentionally wronged anyone, although I cannot convince you of that—for we have had a short conversation only. If there were a law at Athens, such as there is in other cities, that a case involving the death penalty should not be decided in one day, then I believe I would have convinced you. Now the time is too short. I cannot quickly refute great slanders and, as I am convinced that I never wronged another, I will assuredly not wrong myself. I will not say of myself that I deserve any evil, nor propose any penalty. Why should I? Because I am afraid of the penalty of death which Meletus proposes? When I do not know whether death is a good or an evil, why should I propose a penalty which would certainly be an evil? Shall I say imprisonment? And why should I live in prison, and be the slave of the judges of the year—of the Eleven? Or shall the penalty be a fine, and imprisonment until the fine is paid? There is the same objection. I should have to stay in prison for I have no money and cannot pay. And if I say exile, and this may be the penalty which you will affix, I must indeed be blinded by love of life, if I do not realize that you, who are my own citizens, cannot endure my words and have found them so hateful you want to silence them, others are likely to endure me. No indeed, men of Athens, that is not very likely. And what a life should I lead, at my age, wandering from city to city, living in ever-changing exile and always being driven out! For I am quite sure that whatever place I go, the young men will come to me. If I drive them away, their elders will drive me out. And, if I let them come, their fathers and friends will drive me out for their sakes.

Someone will say: Yes, Socrates, but can you not hold your tongue, and then go into a foreign city, and no one will interfere with you? Now I have great difficulty in making you understand my answer to this. If I tell you this would be a disobedience to a divine command, and therefore I cannot hold my tongue, you will not believe I am serious. If I say again that greatest good is daily to converse about virtue, and all that concerning which you hear me examining myself and others, and that the life which is unexamined is not worth living—that you are still less likely to believe. And yet what I say is true, although it is hard for me to persuade you. Moreover, I am not accustomed to thinking I deserve any punishment. Had I money I might have proposed to give you what I had and would have been none the worse. But you see I have none and can only ask you to proportion the fine to my means. However, I think I could afford a mina, and therefore I propose that penalty. Plato, Crito, Critobulus, and Apollodorus, my friends here, bid me say 30 minae and they will pay the fine. Well, then, say 30 minae, let that be the penalty for that they will be ample security to you.

(The jury votes again to decide between Socrates' proposal of a fine and Meletus' proposal of the death penalty. The verdict is death.)

Not much time will be gained, O Athenians, in return for the evil name you will get from the enemies of the city, who will say you killed Socrates, a wise man. They will call me wise even though I am not wise when they want to reproach you. If you waited a little while, your desire would have been fulfilled in the course of nature. I am far advanced in years, as you may

perceive, and not far from death. I am speaking now only to those of you who have condemned me to death. And I have another thing to say to them: You think I was convicted through deficiency of words—I mean, if I had thought fit to leave nothing undone, nothing unsaid, I might have gained an acquittal. Not so, the deficiency which led to my conviction was not of words—certainly not. I did not have the boldness or impudence or inclination to address you as you would have liked me to address you, weeping, wailing, and lamenting, and saying and doing many things which you have been accustomed to hear from others, and which, as I say, are unworthy of me. I believed I should not do anything common or cowardly in the hour of danger. I do not now repent the manner of my defense. I would rather die having spoken after my manner than speak in your manner and live. Neither in war nor yet at law ought any man to use every way of escaping death. Often in battle there is no doubt if a man will throw away his arms and fall on his knees before his pursuers, he may escape death. In other dangers there are other ways of escaping death, if a man is willing to say and do anything.

The difficulty, my friends, is not in avoiding death, but in avoiding evil; for evil runs faster than death. I am old and move slowly, and the slower runner has overtaken me, and my accusers are keen and quick, and the faster runner, who is evil, has overtaken them. And now I depart hence condemned by you to suffer the penalty of death, and they, too, go their ways condemned by the truth to suffer the penalty of wickedness. I must abide by my award—let them abide by theirs. I suppose these things may be regarded as fated—and I think things are as they should be.

And now, O men who have condemned me, I would prophesy to you. I am about to die and that is the hour in which men are gifted with prophetic power. I prophesy to you who are my murderers that, immediately after my death, punishment far heavier than you have inflicted on me will await you. You have killed me because you wanted to escape the accuser, and not to give an account of your lives. That will not be as you suppose. I say there will be more accusers of you than there are now, accusers I have restrained: and as they are younger they will be more severe with you and you will be more offended at them. For if you think that by killing men you can avoid the accuser censuring your lives, you are mistaken; that is not a way of escape which is either possible or honorable. The easiest, noblest way is not to be crushing others but to be improving yourselves. This is the prophecy which I utter before my departure to the members of the jury who have condemned me.

Friends, who have acquitted me, I would like also to talk with you about this thing which has happened, while the judges are busy, and before I go to the place where I must die. Stay awhile, for we may as well talk with one another while there is time. You are my friends and I would like to show you the meaning of this event which has happened to me. O my judges—for you I may truly call judges—I should like to tell you of a wonderful occurrence. Before this, the familiar oracle within me has constantly been in the habit of opposing me even about trifles, if I was going to make a slip or error about anything. Now, as you see there has come upon me that what may be thought, and is generally believed to be, the last and worst evil. But the oracle made no sign of opposition, either as I was leaving my house and going out in the morning, or when I was going up into this court, or while I was speaking at anything I was going to say. I have often been stopped in the middle of a speech, but now in nothing I either said or did has the oracle opposed me. Why is this? I will tell you. I regard this as a proof that what has happened to me is a good, and that those of us who think that death is an evil are in error. This is a great proof to me of what I am saying, for the customary sign would surely have opposed me had I been going to evil and not to good.

Let us reflect in another way, and we shall see there is great reason to hope that death is a good. Either death is a state of nothingness and utter unconsciousness, or, as men say, there is a change and migration of the soul from this world to another. Now if you suppose there is no consciousness, but a sleep like the sleep of him who is undisturbed even by the sight of dreams, death will be an unspeakable gain. If a person were to select the night in which his sleep was undisturbed even by dreams and were to compare this with the other days and nights of his life, and then were to tell us how many days and nights he passed in the course of his life better and more pleasantly than this one, I think any man, even a great king, will not find many such days or nights, when compared with the others. Now if death is like this, I say to die is to gain, for eternity is then only a single night. But if death is the journey to another place, and there, as men say, all the dead are, what good, O my friends and judges, can be greater than this? If indeed when the traveler arrives in the other world, he is delivered from the false judges in this world, and finds the true judges who are said to give judgment there, Minos, Rhadamanthus, Aeacus, and Triptolemus, and other sons of the gods who were righteous in their own life, that journey will be worth making. What would a man give if he might converse with Orpheus and Masaeus and Hesiod and Homer? Nay, if this is true, let me die again and again. I, too, shall have a wonderful interest in a place where I can converse with Palamedes, and Ajax, the son of Telamon, and other heroes of old who have suffered death through an unjust judgment. I think there will be pleasure, in comparing my own sufferings with theirs. Above all, I shall be able to continue my search into true and false knowledge. As in this world, so also in that; I shall find out who is wise, and who pretends to be wise but is not. What would a man give, O judges, to be able to examine the leader of the great Trojan expedition; or Odysseus or Sisyphus, or numberless others, men and women too! What infinite delight would there be in conversing with them and asking them questions! For in that world they do not put a man to death for such investigations, certainly not. For besides being happier in that world than in this, they will be immortal, if what is said is true.

Wherefore, O judges, be of good cheer about death, and know this truth—no evil can happen to a good man, either in life or after death. He and his are not neglected by the gods nor has my own approaching end happened by mere chance.

I see clearly that to die and be released was better for me and therefore the oracle gave no sign. Because of this also, I am not angry with my accusers or my condemners. They have done me no harm, although neither of them meant to do me any good; and for this I gently blame them.

Still I have a favor to ask of them. When my sons are grown up, I would ask you, O my friends, to punish them. I would have you trouble them, as I troubled you, if they seem to care about riches, or anything, more than virtue. Or, if they pretend to be something when they are really nothing, then chastise them, as I chastised you, for not caring about what they ought to care, and thinking they are something when they are really nothing. And if you do this, I and my sons will have received justice at your hands.

The hour of departure has arrived, and we go on our different ways—I to die, and you to live. Which is better only the god knows.

Suggestions for Further Reading

There is so much written on Socrates it is hard to know where to begin. Perhaps the best I can do is point you to the article "Socrates" in *The Encyclopedia of Philosophy*. The article provides an overview and the bibliography guides you to the primary and secondary sources.

You may have noticed that Plato does not give an account of the prosecution's case. If you are interested in a controversial reconstruction of the Athenian side by one of America's great journalists, try I. F. Stone's *The Trial of Socrates* (Boston: Little, Brown, 1988). Stone's footnotes will take you deep into the literature, and his intriguing account will puncture some of the most sacred and cherished myths about Socrates. Gregory Vlastos' *Socrates, Ironist and Moral Philosopher* (Ithaca, N.Y.: Cornell University Press, 1991) challenges some traditional views of Socrates, but is advanced.

Videos

In *Plato's Apology: The Life and Teachings of Socrates* (30 minutes), M. Adler explains his view of Socrates' method and teaching by examining key passages in the *Apology*. Available from Insight Media. Maxwell Anderson's *Barefoot in Athens* (76 minutes) is a play that centers on Socrates' trial. From films for the Humanities and Sciences.

2.4. Aristotle on Happiness and the Life of Moderation

Aristotle (384–322 B.C.E.) was a student of Plato and is recognized, along with Plato, as one of the greatest philosophic minds of the ancient Western world. He made significant contributions to all areas of philosophy and to the natural sciences as well, writing on biology, psychology, physics, logic, metaphysics, politics, ethics, literature—just to name a few of the subjects that interested him. He founded a school in Athens called the Lyceum. His students became known as the Peripatetics (which means "to walk around") because of his habit of strolling in the garden of the school while giving instruction.

Aristotle was from Macedonia and, while living there, tutored Alexander, the son of the king. Alexander the Great, as he was later called, established a vast empire. As he traveled toward India on his conquests, he sent plant and animal specimens back to Aristotle, his old teacher. Alexander's death in 323 B.C.E. triggered anti-Macedonian sentiment. Realizing that his life might be in danger, Aristotle left town in a hurry and, recalling what happened to Socrates, reputedly made the comment that he was leaving lest he provide an opportunity for the Athenians to "sin twice against philosophy."

Aristotle was a **teleologist.** He believed that all existing things have a purpose (in Greek the word for end, goal, or purpose is *telos*) and that their purpose constitutes their good. So Aristotle, when seeking to answer the question "How should one live?" naturally considers the issue of what is the good for humans. Notice he does not ask what is his good. He is not concerned with individual goods, but with the good for all humans. He calls this good **eudaimonia,** which is here translated as "happiness." This translation is somewhat misleading because in English happiness refers to a psychological feeling. For Aristotle happiness is more than a feeling, it is also a way of acting and living. Hence some have translated it as human "flourishing." Since many people have claimed the happy life is the virtuous life, any discussion of *eudaimonia* or human flourishing must sooner or later pay attention to the notion of virtue.

The word "virtue" (*arete* in Greek) is also a bit misleading. For Aristotle, a virtue is an excellence. The excellence of a thing is the full development of the potentials of its essential nature. Since the human animal is essentially a "rational" animal according to Aristotle, the good for humans must involve the realization of their rational natures. According to Aristotle, a life of moderation accords best with reason. He views moral virtue as a mean between extremes and vice as either a deficiency or an excess. For example, courage is the mean between rashness (the vice of excess in confidence) and cowardice (the vice of deficiency in confidence). However, Aristotle does recognize that some actions have no mean. For example, there is no mean for the act of murder.

The selection that follows is from the first two books of the *Nicomachean Ethics* which consists of lectures on *ethos* (character, habit) supposedly recorded by Aristotle's son, Nicomachus. In the first book, Aristotle presents an argument in support of his claim that happiness is the chief end of humans and searches for a precise definition. In the second, he examines the question of virtue and proposes a theory about the nature of moral virtue. He argues that living a morally virtuous life is essential to being happy. The third and fourth books continue the discussion of moral virtue and introduce the issue of whether humans are free to chose to live a virtuous life. Book five examines the virtue of justice. This is the highest social value and since, Aristotle argues, the good life cannot be lived apart from a good society, it is also essential to happiness or human flourishing. In book six, Aristotle shifts his attention from moral virtue to intellectual virtue. Humans are concerned with both theoretical and practical wisdom. Practical wisdom is essential to happiness because in order to live our lives well we must exercise good judgment. Books seven, eight, and nine deal with issues of moral strength and weakness, pleasure, and friendship. Pleasure is not the highest good, he argues, but it is part of the highest good. We also need good friends to be happy. In the final chapter Aristotle focuses on theoretical wisdom and argues that the highest human happiness is the contemplation of truth. Hence, only theoretical wisdom can lead to "primary" happiness while practical wisdom can lead to "secondary" happiness.

Reading Questions

1. What, according to Aristotle, has the good been declared to be?
2. Why must the chief good be desired for its own sake?

3. Aristotle says that on a very abstract level, happiness can be considered as "living well and doing well." If so, the next question becomes, in what specifically does this consist? Aristotle argues that whatever it is it must be something final, chosen for its own sake, self-sufficient, and an end of action. If this is so, why will not health or wealth or pleasure or honor (all of which are goods) count as the chief good or happiness?

4. How does Aristotle arrive at the conclusion that the human good (happiness) is an activity of soul in accordance with virtue? (Hint: his argument begins with the notion that human beings have a function.)

5. Given what Aristotle says in Book I, section 9 about how happiness is acquired, how do you think he would respond to the question, "Can someone be happy even if they suffer bad luck?"

6. What are the two kinds of virtue and do the moral virtues arise by nature or by learning and practice?

7. Why does Aristotle conclude that virtue must be a state of character?

8. State in your own words what Aristotle means when he claims, "Virtue, then, is a state of character concerned with choice, lying in a mean, i.e., the mean relative to us, this being determined by a rational principle, and by that principle by which the man of practical wisdom would determine it."

9. What are the excesses, deficiencies, and the means with respect to (a) feelings of fear and confidence, (b) giving and taking of money, (c) honour and dishonour, (d) anger?

10. In Book II, section 9, Aristotle gives some advice for those who wish to practice virtue (hit the mean). Summarize his advice.

11. What are the similarities, if any, between how a Confucian would answer the question, "How should one live?" and how Aristotle would answer it?

Nicomachean Ethics

ARISTOTLE

Book I

1.

EVERY ART AND EVERY INQUIRY, and similarly every action and pursuit, is thought to aim at some good; and for this reason the good has rightly been declared to be that at which all things aim. But a certain difference is found among ends; some are activities, others are products apart from the activities that produce them. Where there are ends apart from the actions, it is the nature of the products to be better than the activities. Now, as there are many actions, arts, and sciences, their ends also are many; the end of the medical art is health, that of shipbuilding a vessel, that of strategy victory, that of economics wealth. But where such arts fall under a single capacity—as bridle-making and the other arts concerned with the equipment of horses fall under the art of riding, and this and every military action under strategy, in the same way other arts fall under yet others—in all of these the ends of the master arts are to be preferred to all the subordinate ends; for it is for the sake of the former that the latter are

Reprinted from Aristotle: Nicomachean Ethics translated by W. D. Ross (1925), by permission of Oxford University Press. Footnotes deleted.

pursued. It makes no difference whether the activities themselves are the ends of the actions, or something else apart from the activities, as in the case of the sciences just mentioned.

2.

If, then, there is some end of the things we do, which we desire for its own sake (everything else being desired for the sake of this), and if we do not choose everything for the sake of something else (for at that rate the process would go on to infinity, so that our desire would be empty and vain), clearly this must be the good and the chief good. Will not the knowledge of it, then, have a great influence on life? Shall we not, like archers who have a mark to aim at, be more likely to hit upon what is right? If so, we must try, in outline at least to determine what it is, and of which of the sciences or capacities it is the object. . . .

4.

Let us resume our inquiry and state, in view of the fact that all knowledge and every pursuit aims at some good, . . . what is the highest of all goods achievable by action. Verbally there is very general agreement; for both the general run of men and people of superior refinement say that it is happiness, and identify living well and doing well with being happy; but with regard to what happiness is they differ, and the many do not give the same account as the wise. For the former think it is some plain and obvious thing, like pleasure, wealth, or honour; they differ, however, from one another—and often even the same man identifies it with different things, with health when he is ill, with wealth when he is poor; but, conscious of their ignorance, they admire those who proclaim some great ideal that is above their comprehension. Now some thought that apart from these many goods there is another which is self-subsistent and causes the goodness of all these as well. To examine all the opinions that have been held were perhaps somewhat fruitless; enough to examine those that are most prevalent or that seem to be arguable. . . .

5.

Let us, however, resume our discussion from the point at which we digressed. To judge from the lives that men lead, most men, and men of the most vulgar type, seem (not without some ground) to identify the good, or happiness, with pleasure; which is the reason why they love the life of enjoyment. For there are, we may say, three prominent types of life—that just mentioned, the political, and thirdly the contemplative life. Now the mass of mankind are evidently quite slavish in their tastes, preferring a life suitable to beasts, but they get some ground for their view from the fact that many of those in high places share the tastes of Sardanapallus. A consideration of the prominent types of life shows that people of superior refinement and of active disposition identify happiness with honour; for this is, roughly speaking, the end of the political life. But it seems too superficial to be what we are looking for, since it is thought to depend on those who bestow honour rather than on him who receives it, but the good we divine to be something proper to a man and not easily taken from him. Further, men seem to pursue honour in order that they may be assured of their goodness; at least it is by men of practical wisdom that they seek to be honoured, and among those who know them, and on the ground of their virtue; clearly, then, according to them, at any rate, virtue is better. And perhaps one might even suppose this to be, rather than honour, the end of the political life. But even this appears somewhat incomplete; for possession of virtue seems actually compatible with being asleep, or with life-long inactivity, and, further, with the greatest sufferings and misfortunes; but a man who was living so no one would call happy, unless he were maintaining a thesis at all costs. But enough of this; for the subject has been sufficiently treated even in the current discussions. Third comes the contemplative life, which we shall consider later.

The life of money-making is one undertaken under compulsion, and wealth is evidently not the good we are seeking; for it is merely useful and for the sake of something else. And so one might rather take the aforenamed objects to be ends; for they are loved for themselves. But it is evident that not even these are ends; yet many arguments have been thrown away in support of them. Let us leave this subject, then. . . .

7.

Let us again return to the good we are seeking, and ask what it can be. It seems different in different actions and arts; it is different in medicine, in strategy, and in the other arts likewise. What then is the good of each? Surely that for whose sake everything else is done. In medicine this is health, in strategy victory, in architecture a house, in any other sphere something else, and in every action and pursuit the end; for it is for the sake of this that all men do whatever else they do. Therefore, if there is an end for all that we do, this will be the good achievable by action, and if there are more than one, these will be the goods achievable by action.

So the argument has by a different course reached the same point; but we must try to state this even more clearly. Since there are evidently more than one end, and we choose some of these (e.g., wealth, flutes, and in general instruments) for the sake of something else, clearly not all ends are final ends; but the chief good is evidently something final. Therefore, if there is only one final end, this will be what we are seeking, and if there are more than one, the most final of these will be what we are seeking. Now we call that which is in itself worthy of pursuit more final than that which is worthy of pursuit for the sake of something else, and that which is never desirable for the sake of something else more final than the things that are desirable both in themselves and for the sake of that other thing, and therefore we call final without qualification that which is always desirable in itself and never for the sake of something else.

Now such a thing happiness, above all else, is held to be; for this we choose always for itself and never for the sake of something else, but honour, pleasure, reason, and every virtue we choose indeed for themselves (for if nothing resulted from them we should still choose each of them), but we choose them also for the sake of happiness, judging that by means of them we shall be happy. Happiness, on the other hand, no one chooses for the sake of these, nor, in general, for anything other than itself.

From the point of view of self-sufficiency the same result seems to follow; for the final good is thought to be self-sufficient. Now by self-sufficient we do not mean that which is sufficient for a man by himself, for one who lives a solitary life, but also for parents, children, wife, and in general for his friends and fellow citizens, since man is born for citizenship. But some limit must be set to this; for if we extend our requirement to ancestors and descendants and friends' friends we are in for an infinite series. Let us examine this question, however, on another occasion; the self-sufficient we now define as that which when isolated makes life desirable and lacking in nothing; and such we think happiness to be; and further we think it most desirable of all things, without being counted as one good thing among others—if it were so counted it would clearly be made more desirable by the addition of even the least of goods; for that which is added becomes an excess of goods, and of goods the greater is always more desirable. Happiness, then, is something final and self-sufficient, and is the end of action.

Presumably, however, to say that happiness is the chief good seems a platitude, and a clearer account of what it is is still desired. This might perhaps be given, if we could first ascertain the function of man. For just as for a flute-player, a sculptor, or any artist, and, in general, for all things that have a function or activity, the good and the "well" is thought to reside in the function, so would it seem to be for man, if he has a function. Have the carpenter, then, and the tanner certain functions or activities, and has man none? Is he born without a function? Or as eye, hand, foot, and in general each of the parts evidently has a function, may one lay it down that man similarly has a function apart from all these? What then can this be? Life seems to be common even to plants, but we are seeking what is peculiar to man. Let us exclude, therefore, the life of nutrition and growth. Next there would be a life of perception, but it also seems to be common even to the horse, the ox, and every animal. There remains, then, an active life of the element that has a rational principle; of this, one part has such a principle in the sense of being obedient to one, the other in the sense of possessing one and exercising thought. And, as "life of the rational element" also has two meanings, we must state that life in the sense of activity is what we mean; for this seems to be the more proper sense of the term. Now if the function of man is an activity of soul which follows or implies a rational principle, and if we say "a so-and-so" and "a good so-and-so" have a function which is the same in kind, e.g., a lyre-player and a good lyre-player, and so without qualification in all cases, eminence in respect of goodness being added to the name of the function (for the function of a lyre-player is to play the lyre, and that of a good lyre-player is to do so well): if this is the case, [and we state the function of man to be a certain kind of life, and this to be an activity or actions of the soul implying a rational principle, and the function of a good man to be the good and noble performance of these, and if any action is well performed when it is performed in accordance with the appropriate excellence: if this is the case,] human good turns out to be activity of soul in accordance with virtue, and if there are more than one virtue, in accordance with the best and most complete.

But we must add "in a complete life." For one swallow does not make a summer, nor does one day; and so too one day, or a short time, does not make a man blessed and happy. . . .

[Editor's Note: In Section 8, here omitted, Aristotle compares his view of happiness as living well and doing well with what most people say. He finds that many who have expressed their views on this topic agree in general with his own views. He takes this as confirmation that he is on the right track. Many regard happiness as consisting of three kinds of goods: worldly goods, bodily goods, and goods of the soul. While Aristotle wishes to stress in his account that happiness resides primarily in goods of the soul (the

virtues), he acknowledges that we are not likely to call someone happy if they lack entirely worldly goods (wealth, friends, political influence) and bodily goods (noble family, handsome appearance, long life, and children.) But both worldly goods and bodily goods often depend on circumstances beyond one's control. Can one be happy, even if misfortune diminishes some worldly and bodily goods? Some would say that happiness depends on good fortune. Others that it is a matter of acquiring virtue or excellence.]

9.

For this reason also the question is asked, whether happiness is to be acquired by learning or by habituation or some other sort of training, or comes in virtue of some divine providence or again by chance. Now if there is any gift of the gods to men, it is reasonable that happiness should be god-given, and most surely god-given of all human things inasmuch as it is the best. But this question would perhaps be more appropriate to another inquiry; happiness seems, however, even if it is not god-sent but comes as a result of virtue and some process of learning or training, to be among the most god-like things; for that which is the prize and end of virtue seems to be the best thing in the world, and something godlike and blessed.

It will also on this view be very generally shared; for all who are not maimed as regards their potentiality for virtue may win it by a certain kind of study and care. But if it is better to be happy thus than by chance, it is reasonable that the facts should be so, since everything that depends on the action of nature is by nature as good as it can be, and similarly everything that depends on art or any rational cause, and especially if it depends on the best of all causes. To entrust to chance what is greatest and most noble would be a very defective arrangement.

The answer to the question we are asking is plain also from the definition of happiness; for it has been said to be a virtuous activity of soul, of a certain kind. Of the remaining goods, some must necessarily pre-exist as conditions of happiness, and others are naturally co-operative and useful as instruments. And this will be found to agree with what we said at the outset; for we stated the end of political science to be the best end, and political science spends most of its pains on making the citizens to be of a certain character, viz. good and capable of noble acts.

It is natural, then, that we call neither ox nor horse nor any other of the animals happy; for none of them is capable of sharing in such activity. For this reason also a boy is not happy; for he is not yet capable of such acts, owing to his age; and boys who are called happy are being congratulated by reason of the hopes we have for them. For there is required, as we said, not only complete virtue but also a complete life, since many changes occur in life, and all manner of chances, and the most prosperous may fall into great misfortunes in old age, as is told of Priam in the Trojan Cycle; and one who has experienced such chances and has ended wretchedly no one calls happy. . . .

13.

Since happiness is an activity of soul in accordance with perfect virtue, we must consider the nature of virtue; for perhaps we shall thus see better the nature of happiness. . . .

Book II

1.

Virtue, then, being of two kinds, intellectual and moral, intellectual virtue in the main owes both its birth and its growth to teaching (for which reason it requires experience and time), while moral virtue comes about as a result of habit, whence also its name *ethike* is one that is formed by a slight variation from the word *ethos* (habit). From this it is also plain that none of the moral virtues arises in us by nature; for nothing that exists by nature can form a habit contrary to its nature. For instance the stone which by nature moves downwards cannot be habituated to move upwards, not even if one tries to train it by throwing it up ten thousand times; nor can fire be ha-

bituated to move downwards, nor can anything else that by nature behaves in one way be trained to behave in another. Neither by nature, then, nor contrary to nature do the virtues arise in us; rather we are adapted by nature to receive them, and are made perfect by habit.

Again, of all the things that come to us by nature we first acquire the potentiality and later exhibit the activity (this is plain in the case of the senses; for it was not by often seeing or often hearing that we got these senses, but on the contrary we had them before we used them, and did not come to have them by using them); but the virtues we get by first exercising them, as also happens in the case of the arts as well. For the things we have to learn before we can do them, we learn by doing them, e.g., men become builders by building and lyre-players by playing the lyre; so too we become just by doing just acts, temperate by doing temperate acts, brave by doing brave acts.

This is confirmed by what happens in states; for legislators make the citizens good by forming habits in them, and this is the wish of every legislator, and those who do not effect it miss their mark, and it is in this that a good constitution differs from a bad one.

Again, it is from the same causes and by the same means that every virtue is both produced and destroyed, and similarly every art; for it is from playing the lyre that both good and bad lyre-players are produced. And the corresponding statement is true of builders and of all the rest; men will be good or bad builders as a result of building well or badly. For if this were not so, there would have been no need of a teacher, but all men would have been born good or bad at their craft. This, then, is the case with the virtues also; by doing the acts that we do in our transactions with other men we become just or unjust, and by doing the acts that we do in the presence of danger, and being habituated to feel fear or confidence, we become brave or cowardly. The same is true of appetites and feelings of anger; some men become temperate and good-tempered, others self-indulgent and irascible, by behaving in one way or the other in the appropriate circumstances. Thus, in one word, states of character arise out of like activities. This is why the activities we exhibit must be of a certain kind; it is because the states of character correspond to the differences between these. It makes no small difference, then, whether we form habits of one kind or of another from our very youth; it makes a very great difference, or rather *all* the difference. . . .

5.

Next we must consider what virtue is. Since things that are found in the soul are of three kinds—passions, faculties, states of character, virtue must be one of these. By passions I mean appetite, anger, fear, confidence, envy, joy, friendly feeling, hatred, longing, emulation, pity, and in general the feelings that are accompanied by pleasure or pain; by faculties the things in virtue of which we are said to be capable of feeling these, e.g., of becoming angry or being pained or feeling pity; by states of character the things in virtue of which we stand well or badly with reference to the passions, e.g., with reference to anger we stand badly if we feel it violently or too weakly, and well if we feel it moderately; and similarly with reference to the other passions.

Now neither the virtues nor the vices are *passions,* because we are not called good or bad on the ground of our passions, but are so called on the ground of our virtues and our vices, and because we are neither praised nor blamed for our passions (for the man who feels fear or anger is not praised, nor is the man who simply feels anger blamed, but the man who feels it in a certain way), but for our virtues and our vices we are praised or blamed.

Again, we feel anger and fear without choice, but the virtues are modes of choice or involve choice. Further, in respect of the passions we are said to be moved, but in respect of the virtues and the vices we are said not to be moved but to be disposed in a particular way.

For these reasons also they are not *faculties;* for we are neither called good nor bad, nor praised nor blamed, for the simple capacity of

feeling the passions; again, we have the faculties by nature, but we are not made good or bad by nature; we have spoken of this before.

If, then, the virtues are neither passions nor faculties, all that remains is that they should be *states of character.*

Thus we have stated what virtue is in respect of its genus.

6.

We must, however, not only describe virtue as a state of character, but also say what sort of state it is. We may remark, then, that every virtue or excellence both brings into good condition the thing of which it is the excellence and makes the work of that thing be done well; e.g., the excellence of the eye makes both the eye and its work good; for it is by the excellence of the eye that we see well. Similarly the excellence of the horse makes a horse both good in itself and good at running and at carrying its rider and at awaiting the attack of the enemy. Therefore, if this is true in every case, the virtue of man also will be the state of character which makes a man good and which makes him do his own work well.

How this is to happen we have stated already, but it will be made plain also by the following consideration of the specific nature of virtue. In everything that is continuous and divisible it is possible to take more, less, or an equal amount, and that either in terms of the thing itself or relative to us; and the equal is an intermediate between excess and defect. By the intermediate in the object I mean that which is equidistant from each of the extremes, which is one and the same for all men; by the intermediate relative to us that which is neither too much nor too little—and this is not one, nor the same for all. For instance, if ten is many and two is few, six is the intermediate, taken in terms of the object; for it exceeds and is exceeded by an equal amount; this is intermediate according to arithmetical proportion. But the intermediate relative to us is not to be taken so; if ten pounds are too much for a particular person to eat and two too little, it does not follow that the trainer will order six pounds;

for this also is perhaps too much for the person who is to take it, or too little—too little for Milo, too much for the beginner in athletic exercises. The same is true of running and wrestling. Thus a master of any art avoids excess and defect, but seeks the intermediate and chooses this—the intermediate not in the object but relative to us.

If it is thus, then, that every art does its work well—by looking to the intermediate and judging its works by this standard (so that we often say of good works of art that it is not possible either to take away or to add anything, implying that excess and defect destroy the goodness of works of art, while the mean preserves it; and good artists, as we say, look to this in their work), and if, further, virtue is more exact and better than any art, as nature also is, then virtue must have the quality of aiming at the intermediate. I mean moral virtue; for it is this that is concerned with passions and actions, and in these there is excess, defect, and the intermediate. For instance, both fear and confidence and appetite and anger and pity and in general pleasure and pain may be felt both too much and too little, and in both cases not well; but to feel them at the right times, with reference to the right objects, towards the right people, with the right motive, and in the right way, is what is both intermediate and best, and this is characteristic of virtue. Similarly with regard to actions also there is excess, defect, and the intermediate. Now virtue is concerned with passions and actions, in which excess is a form of failure, and so is defect, while the intermediate is praised and is a form of success; and being praised and being successful are both characteristics of virtue. Therefore virtue is a kind of mean, since, as we have seen, it aims at what is intermediate.

Again, it is possible to fail in many ways (for evil belongs to the class of the unlimited, as the Pythagoreans conjectured, and good to that of the limited), while to succeed is possible only in one way (for which reason also one is easy and the other difficult—to miss the mark easy, to hit it difficult); for these reasons also, then, excess and defect are characteristic of vice, and the mean of virtue;

For men are good in but one way, but bad in many.

Virtue, then, is a state of character concerned with choice, lying in a mean, i.e., the mean relative to us, this being determined by a rational principle, and by that principle by which the man of practical wisdom would determine it. Now it is a mean between two vices, that which depends on excess and that which depends on defect; and again it is a mean because the vices respectively fall short of or exceed what is right in both passions and actions, while virtue both finds and chooses that which is intermediate. Hence in respect of its substance and the definition which states its essence virtue is a mean, with regard to what is best and right an extreme.

But not every action nor every passion admits of a mean; for some have names that already imply badness, e.g., spite, shamelessness, envy, and in the case of actions adultery, theft, murder; for all of these and suchlike things imply by their names that they are themselves bad, and not the excesses or deficiencies of them. It is not possible, then, ever to be right with regard to them; one must always be wrong. Nor does goodness or badness with regard to such things depend on committing adultery with the right woman, at the right time, and in the right way, but simply to do any of them is to go wrong. It would be equally absurd, then, to expect that in unjust, cowardly, and voluptuous action there should be a mean, an excess, and a deficiency; for at that rate there would be a mean of excess and of deficiency, an excess of excess, and a deficiency of deficiency. But as there is no excess and deficiency of temperance and courage because what is intermediate is in a sense an extreme, so too of the actions we have mentioned there is no mean nor any excess and deficiency, but however they are done they are wrong; for in general there is neither a mean of excess and deficiency, nor excess and deficiency of a mean.

7.

We must, however, not only make this general statement, but also apply it to the individual facts. For among statements about conduct those which are general apply more widely, but those which are particular are more genuine, since conduct has to do with individual cases, and our statements must harmonize with the facts in these cases. We may take these cases from our table. With regard to feelings of fear and confidence courage is the mean; of the people who exceed, he who exceeds in fearlessness has no name (many of the states have no name), while the man who exceeds in confidence is rash, and he who exceeds in fear and falls short in confidence is a coward. With regard to pleasures and pains— not all of them, and not so much with regard to the pains—the mean is temperance, the excess self-indulgence. Persons deficient with regard to the pleasures are not often found; hence such persons also have received no name. But let us call them "insensible."

With regard to giving and taking of money, the mean is liberality, the excess and the defect prodigality and meanness. In these actions people exceed and fall short in contrary ways; the prodigal exceeds in spending and falls short in taking, while the mean man exceeds in taking and falls short in spending. (At present we are giving a mere outline or summary, and are satisfied with this; later these states will be more exactly determined.) With regard to money there are also other dispositions—a mean, magnificence (for the magnificent man differs from the liberal man; the former deals with large sums, the latter with small ones), and excess, tastelessness and vulgarity, and a deficiency, niggardliness; these differ from the states opposed to liberality, and the mode of their difference will be stated later.

With regard to honour and dishonour the mean is proper pride, the excess is known as a sort of "empty vanity," and the deficiency is undue humility; and as we said liberality was related to magnificence, differing from it by dealing with small sums, so there is a state similarly related to proper pride, being concerned with small honours while that is concerned with great. For it is possible to desire honour as one ought, and more than one ought, and less, and the man who exceeds in his desires is called ambitious, the man

who falls short unambitious, while the intermediate person has no name. The dispositions also are nameless, except that that of the ambitious man is called ambition. Hence the people who are at the extremes lay claim to the middle place; and we ourselves sometimes call the intermediate person ambitious and sometimes unambitious, and sometimes praise the ambitious man and sometimes the unambitious. The reason of our doing this will be stated in what follows; but now let us speak of the remaining states according to the method which has been indicated.

With regard to anger also there is an excess, a deficiency, and a mean. Although they can scarcely be said to have names, yet since we call the intermediate person good-tempered let us call the mean good temper; of the persons at the extremes let the one who exceeds be called irascible, and his vice irascibility, and the man who falls short an inirascible sort of person, and the deficiency inirascibility. . . .

9.

That moral virtue is a mean, then, and in what sense it is so, and that it is a mean between two vices, the one involving excess, the other deficiency, and that it is such because its character is to aim at what is intermediate in passions and in actions, has been sufficiently stated. Hence also it is no easy task to be good. For in everything it is no easy task to find the middle, e.g., to find the middle of a circle is not for everyone but for him who knows; so, too, any one can get angry—that is easy—or give or spend money; but to do this to the right person, to the right extent, at the right time, with the right motive, and in the right way, *that* is not for everyone, nor is it easy; wherefore goodness is both rare and laudable and noble. Hence he who aims at the intermediate must first depart from what is the more contrary to it, as Calypso advises—

Hold the ship out beyond that surf and spray.

For of the extremes one is more erroneous, one less so; therefore, since to hit the mean is hard in the extreme, we must as a second best, as people say, take the least of the evils; and this will be done best in the way we describe.

But we must consider the things towards which we ourselves also are easily carried away; for some of us tend to one thing, some to another; and this will be recognizable from the pleasure and the pain we feel. We must drag ourselves away to the contrary extreme; for we shall get into the intermediate state by drawing well away from error, as people do in straightening sticks that are bent.

Now in everything the pleasant or pleasure is most to be guarded against; for we do not judge it impartially. We ought, then, to feel towards pleasure as the elders of the people felt towards Helen, and in all circumstances repeat their saying; for if we dismiss pleasure thus we are less likely to go astray. It is by doing this, then, (to sum the matter up) that we shall best be able to hit the mean.

But this is no doubt difficult, and especially in individual cases; for it is not easy to determine both how and with whom and on what provocation and how long one should be angry; for we too sometimes praise those who fall short and call them good-tempered, but sometimes we praise those who get angry and call them manly. The man, however, who deviates little from goodness is not blamed, whether he do so in the direction of the more or of the less, but only the man who deviates more widely; for *he* does not fail to be noticed. But up to what point and to what extent a man must deviate before he becomes blameworthy it is not easy to determine by reasoning, any more than anything else that is perceived by the senses; such things depend on particular facts, and the decision rests with perception. So much, then, is plain, that the intermediate state is in all things to be praised, but that we must incline sometimes towards the excess, sometimes towards the deficiency; for so shall we most easily hit the mean and what is right.

Suggestions for Further Reading

Henry Veatch's *Aristotle* (Bloomington: Indiana University Press, 1974) provides a clearly written overview. The article on "Aristotle" by G. B. Kerferd in Volume 1 of *The Encyclopedia of Philosophy* provides a brief overview of Aristotle's thought, including a section on his ethical views.

For a summary of the *Nicomachean Ethics* see Marvin Easterling's essay in *World Philosophy* (Volume 1), edited by Frank N. Magill (Englewood Cliffs, NJ: Salem Press, 1961, 1982), pp. 369–380. Also see the chapter on ethics in W. D. Ross' *Aristotle* (New York: Barnes & Noble, 1964) which, though somewhat dated, remains one of the best brief commentaries. See Stephen A. White's *Sovereign Virtue: Aristotle on the Relation Between Happiness and Prosperity* (Stanford, CA: Stanford University Press, 1992) for a careful analysis of Aristotle's views on the good life and the conditions which make it possible.

Video

In *Aristotle's Ethics: The Theory of Happiness* (36 minutes), M. Adler concentrates on the first two books discussing his understanding of Aristotle's views on the good life. Available from Insight Media.

2.5. The Song of God

Have you ever faced a conflict of duties? For example, have you ever been torn between your duty to be loyal to a friend and your obligation to tell the truth? Have you ever confronted a situation in which, in order to do right, you had to do wrong? Have you ever been faced with options, neither of which were morally desirable? Have you ever felt sad because you live in a world where so often you must choose between doing the "lesser of two evils?"

And yet, in this same world, we are taught that we should strive for moral perfection. Reason demands that we should always do what is right and good, never what is wrong. Yes, we must face temptation and wrestle with evil, but in the end, are we not expected to triumph over sin? Jesus reportedly said, "Be perfect, as your Father in heaven is perfect." But moral perfection, be it demanded by reason or by God, is impossible. Try as we might, we cannot make this a black and white world. Too many choices are various shades of gray.

If you have ever faced moral conflicts or wondered how moral perfection in a morally imperfect world is possible, you ought to be able to identify with Arjuna, one of the main characters in the *Bhagavad-Gita* (*Song of God*). This Hindu poem forms part of India's greatest epic poem, *Mahabharata*. It was written sometime between the fourth and second centuries B.C.E. Much of the *Gita* is a conversation between Arjuna, who is a member of the warrior caste and a leader of the Pandava family, and Sri (Lord) Krishna, his cousin and the incarnation of the god Vishnu (Vishnu is the god responsible, according to traditional Hindu mythology, for sustaining the universe after it has been created by the god Brahman) which is narrated by Sanjaya, a poet and charioteer. This conversation takes place just before a horrendous battle, which is part of a civil war started by some of Arjuna's relatives. Krishna attempts to get Arjuna to do his duty, which, since he is a warrior and since he is on the side of right in this war, is to fight. But Arjuna is reluctant because those whom he must fight and kill are his relatives and friends. We can formulate Arjuna's conflict as a dilemma (see Appendix A for the dilemma form):

1. Either Arjuna must fight or he must not fight.
2. If he fights, he will violate his duty to protect his relatives.
3. If he does not fight, he will violate his duty as a warrior and his obligation to fight in a just war.
4. Therefore, either he violates one set of duties or he violates another set of duties.

To appreciate the depth of this dilemma in the Indian context, some background information on Hinduism is required. The word for duty is **dharma,** which means the pattern or law underlying the cosmos and embodied in social and ethical law codes. In this context, to violate one's duty is to violate *dharma* and thus to upset the natural, cosmic order. According to Hindu moral theory, there is a moral and natural law called the "law of **Karma.**" Karma comes from the Sanskrit word *karman,* which means "action" or "the consequences of action." The law of Karma states, "what you sow, so shall you reap." If you do good deeds you will experience good things sometime in this or a future life, and if you act wrongly, you will suffer accordingly (see Section 6.3 for a discussion of Karma and freedom). The ultimate goal in life is to escape **samsara,** the eternal round of rebirth and death. We are all trapped in this round of **reincarnation** because of Karma (see Section 11.7 for more information on reincarnation). If the full consequences of our Karma do not come in this life, we must live another life, and another, and another, and another, until there is no Karma left and we get it right.

But how can "getting it right" be possible? If, like Arjuna, we are faced with situations in which no matter what we do we will get bad Karma, there seems no hope of breaking the cycle. Arjuna is doomed if he fights and doomed if he doesn't. We live in a morally imperfect world, and we can never hope to achieve moral perfection. However, even if we could, even if all our actions produced good Karma, we would still be reborn. If we do evil, we are reborn to reap the bad consequences. If we do good, we are reborn to reap the good consequences.

We have now uncovered a more universal form of Arjuna's dilemma, what A. L. Herman (see suggested readings) calls the "dilemma of action." We can express it as follows:

1. Either you do good acts or bad acts.
2. If you do good acts, you are bound to be reborn to reap the good results.
3. If you do bad acts, you are bound to be reborn to reap the bad results.
4. Therefore, either you reap good results or bad results, but in either case you are reborn.

Now we may not believe that transgressions of moral codes violate the natural order of things, and we may not believe in the law of Karma or the idea of reincarnation. Nevertheless, each of us in our own way faces a form of Arjuna's dilemma—the conflict of duties, the necessity to do wrong in order to do right, the lack of moral perfection.

Is there a way out of these moral dilemmas? Krishna teaches that freedom from these dilemmas is found in the practice of disciplined action (*karmayoga*). All action is to be performed detached from the consequences of action. Or, to put it another way, act unselfishly. Do what is right, because it is right, not because the consequences will bring benefit or harm. How can this be done? One can do this by first gaining knowledge (*jnanayoga*) of our true natures (an eternal, unchanging Self), and by dedicating the fruits of our actions in devotion (*bhaktiyoga*) to the divine.

The first book describes Arjuna's state of mind and the dilemma he finds himself in. The second book states the assumptions on which Krishna's advice is based: (1) the self is eternal and survives bodily death and (2) one must do one's moral duty. While this selection ends with the second book, the rest of the Gita goes on to elaborate the themes found in the second book. The third and fourth books develop the relationship between sacrifice and action while the fifth and sixth examine the tension between a life of renunciation (withdrawal from action) and action. In the final six books, Krishna recapitulates his basic teaching and integrates it with the need for religious devotion. The climax comes with Krishna's awe-inspiring theophany (revelation of his divinity).

Reading Questions

1. Why does Arjuna declare, "We don't know which weight is worse to bear—our conquering them or their conquering us?"
2. What reasons does Krishna present to Arjuna in support of his advice to fight?
3. What is the method of "spiritual discipline" (*karmayoga*)?
4. What are the characteristics, according to Krishna, of a person "deep in contemplation whose insight and thought are sure?"
5. How would following Krishna's advice solve Arjuna's dilemma?
6. Do you think living the sort of life Krishna recommends (knowing the true nature of the

self, doing one's moral duty, being unconcerned about the results of one's action, devotion to the divine) would be a good way to live? Why or why not?

7. Try your own hand at formulating a *critical* question about any aspect of this selection and providing the answer. (If you have forgotten what a critical question is, reread Section 1.3.)

Bhagavad-Gita

I. The First Teaching: Arjuna's Dejection

Arjuna, his war flag a rampant monkey,
saw Dhritarashtra's sons assembled
as weapons were ready to clash,
and he lifted his bow.

He told his charioteer:
    "Krishna,
    halt my chariot
    between the armies!

    Far enough for me to see
    these men who lust for war,
    ready to fight with me
    in the strain of battle.

    I see men gathered here,
    eager to fight,
    bent on serving the folly
    of Dhritarashtra's son."

    When Arjuna had spoken,
    Krishna halted
    their splendid chariot
    between the armies.

    Facing Bhishma and Drona
    and all the great kings,
    he said, "Arjuna, see
    the Kuru men assembled here!"

Arjuna saw them standing there:
fathers, grandfathers, teachers,
uncles, brothers, sons,
grandsons, and friends.

He surveyed his elders
and companions in both armies,
all his kinsmen
assembled together.

The greed that distorts their reason
blinds them to the sin they commit
in ruining the family, blinds them
to the crime of betraying friends.

How can we ignore the wisdom
of turning from this evil
when we see the sin
of family destruction, Krishna?

When the family is ruined,
the timeless laws of family duty
perish; and when duty is lost,
chaos overwhelms the family.

In overwhelming chaos, Krishna,
women of the family are corrupted;
and when women are corrupted,
disorder is born in society.

This discord drags the violators
and the family itself to hell;

From The Bhagavad-gita: *by Barbara Stoler Miller, translation. Copyright © 1986 by Barbara Stoler Miller. Used by permission of Bantam Books, a division of Bantam Doubleday Dell Publishing Group, Inc. Pages 23–39.*

for ancestors fall when rites
of offering rice and water lapse.

The sins of men who violate
the family create disorder in society
that undermines the constant laws
of caste and family duty.

Krishna, we have heard
that a place in hell
is reserved for men
who undermine family duties.

I lament the great sin
we commit when our greed
for kingship and pleasures
drives us to kill our kinsmen.

Dejected, filled with strange pity,
he said this:

"Krishna, I see my kinsmen
gathered here, wanting war.

My limbs sink,
my mouth is parched,
my body trembles,
the hair bristles on my flesh.

The magic bow slips
from my hand, my skin burns,
I cannot stand still,
my mind reels.

I see omens of chaos,
Krishna; I see no good
in killing my kinsmen
in battle.

Krishna, I seek no victory,
or kingship or pleasures.
What use to us are kingship,
delights, or life itself?

We sought kingship, delights,
and pleasures for the sake of those
assembled to abandon their lives
and fortunes in battle.

They are teachers, fathers, sons,
and grandfathers, uncles, grandsons,
fathers and brothers of wives,

and other men of our family.

I do not want to kill them
even if I am killed, Krishna;
not for kingship of all three worlds,
much less for the earth!

What joy is there for us, Krishna,
in killing Dhritarashtra's sons?
Evil will haunt us if we kill them,
though their bows are drawn to kill.

Honor forbids us to kill
our cousins, Dhritarashtra's sons;
how can we know happiness
if we kill our own kinsmen?

If Dhritarashtra's armed sons
kill me in battle when I am unarmed
and offer no resistance,
it will be my reward."

Saying this in the time of war,
Arjuna slumped into the chariot
and laid down his bow and arrows,
his mind tormented by grief.

The Second Teaching

PHILOSOPHY AND SPIRITUAL DISCIPLINE

Sanjaya

Arjuna sat dejected,
filled with pity,
his sad eyes blurred by tears.
Krishna gave him counsel.

Lord Krishna

Why this cowardice
in time of crisis, Arjuna?
The coward is ignoble, shameful,
foreign to the ways of heaven.

Don't yield to impotence!
It is unnatural in you!
Banish this petty weakness from your heart.
Rise to the fight, Arjuna!

Arjuna

Krishna, how can I fight
against Bhishma and Drona
with arrows
when they deserve my worship?

It is better in this world
to beg for scraps of food
than to eat meals
smeared with the blood
of elders I killed
at the height of their power
while their goals
were still desires.

We don't know which weight
is worse to bear—
our conquering them
or their conquering us.
We will not want to live
if we kill
the sons of Dhritarashtra
assembled before us.

The flaw of pity
blights my very being;
conflicting sacred duties
confound my reason.
I ask you to tell me
decisively—Which is better?
I am your pupil.
Teach me what I seek!

I see nothing
that could drive away
the grief
that withers my senses;
even if I won kingdoms
of unrivaled wealth
on earth
and sovereignty over gods.

Sanjaya

Arjuna told this
to Krishna—then saying,
"I shall not fight,"
he fell silent.

Mocking him gently,
Krishna gave this counsel
as Arjuna sat dejected,
between the two armies.

Lord Krishna

You grieve for those beyond grief;
and you speak words of insight;
but learned men do not grieve
for the dead or the living.

Never have I not existed,
nor you, nor these kings;
and never in the future
shall we cease to exist.

Just as the embodied self
enters childhood, youth, and old age,
so does it enter another body;
this does not confound a steadfast man.

Contacts with matter make us feel
heat and cold, pleasure and pain.
Arjuna, you must learn to endure
fleeting things—they come and go!

When these cannot torment a man,
when suffering and joy are equal
for him and he has courage,
he is fit for immortality.

Nothing of nonbeing comes to be,
nor does being cease to exist;
the boundary between these two
is seen by men who see reality.

Indestructible is the presence
that pervades all this;
no one can destroy
this unchanging reality.

Our bodies are known to end,
but the embodied self is enduring,
indestructible, and immeasurable;
therefore, Arjuna, fight the battle!

He who thinks this self a killer
and he who thinks it killed,
both fail to understand;
it does not kill, nor is it killed.

It is not born,
it does not die;
having been,
it will never not be;
unborn, enduring,
constant, and primordial,
it is not killed
when the body is killed.

Arjuna, when a man knows the self
to be indestructible, enduring, unborn,
unchanging, how does he kill
or cause anyone to kill?

As a man discards
worn-out clothes
to put on new
and different ones,
so the embodied self
discards
its worn-out bodies
to take on other new ones.

Weapons do not cut it,
fire does not burn it,
waters do not wet it,
wind does not wither it.

It cannot be cut or burned;
it cannot be wet or withered;
it is enduring, all-pervasive,
fixed, immovable, and timeless.

It is called unmanifest,
inconceivable, and immutable;
since you know that to be so,
you should not grieve!

If you think of its birth
and death as ever-recurring,
then too, Great Warrior,
you have no cause to grieve!

Death is certain for anyone born,
and birth is certain for the dead;
since the cycle is inevitable,
you have no cause to grieve!

Creatures are unmanifest in origin,
manifest in the midst of life,

and unmanifest again in the end.
Since this is so, why do you lament?

Rarely someone
sees it,
rarely another
speaks it,
rarely anyone
hears it—
even hearing it,
no one really knows it.

The self embodied in the body
of every being is indestructible;
you have no cause to grieve
for all these creatures, Arjuna!

Look to your own duty;
do not tremble before it;
nothing is better for a warrior
than a battle of sacred duty.

The doors of heaven open
for warriors who rejoice
to have a battle like this
thrust on them by chance.

If you fail to wage this war
of sacred duty,
you will abandon your own duty
and fame only to gain evil.

People will tell
of your undying shame,
and for a man of honor
shame is worse than death.

The great chariot warriors will think
you deserted in fear of battle;
you will be despised
by those who held you in esteem.

Your enemies will slander you,
scorning your skill
in so many unspeakable ways—
could any suffering be worse?

If you are killed, you win heaven;
if you triumph, you enjoy the earth;
therefore, Arjuna, stand up
and resolve to fight the battle!

Impartial to joy and suffering,
gain and loss, victory and defeat,
arm yourself for the battle,
lest you fall into evil.

Understanding is defined in terms of
    philosophy;
now hear it in spiritual discipline.
Armed with this understanding, Arjuna,
you will escape the bondage of action.

No effort in this world
is lost or wasted;
a fragment of sacred duty
saves you from great fear.

This understanding is unique
in its inner core of resolve;
diffuse and pointless are the ways
irresolute men understand.

Undiscerning men who delight
in the tenets of ritual lore
utter florid speech, proclaiming,
"There is nothing else!"

Driven by desire, they strive after heaven
and contrive to win powers and delights,
but their intricate ritual language
bears only the fruit of action in rebirth.

Obsessed with powers and delights,
their reason lost in words,
they do not find in contemplation
this understanding of inner resolve.

Arjuna, the realm of sacred lore
is nature—beyond its triad of qualities,
dualities, and mundane rewards,
be forever lucid, alive to your self.

For the discerning priest,
all of sacred lore
has no more value than a well
when water flows everywhere.

Be intent on action,
not on the fruits of action;
avoid attraction to the fruits
and attachment to inaction!

Perform actions, firm in discipline,
relinquishing attachment;
be impartial to failure and success—
this equanimity is called discipline.

Arjuna, action is far inferior
to the discipline of understanding;
so seek refuge in understanding—pitiful
are men drawn by fruits of action.

Disciplined by understanding,
one abandons both good and evil deeds;
so arm yourself for discipline—
discipline is skill in actions.

Wise men disciplined by understanding
relinquish the fruit born of action;
freed from these bonds of rebirth,
they reach a place beyond decay.

When your understanding passes beyond
the swamp of delusion,
you will be indifferent to all
that is heard in sacred lore.

When your understanding turns
from sacred lore to stand fixed,
immovable in contemplation,
then you will reach discipline.

Arjuna

Krishna, what defines a man
deep in contemplation whose insight
and thought are sure? How would he speak?
How would he sit? How would he move?

Lord Krishna

When he gives up desires in his mind,
is content with the self within himself,
then he is said to be a man
whose insight is sure, Arjuna.

When suffering does not disturb his mind,
when his craving for pleasures has vanished,
when attraction, fear, and anger are gone,
he is called a sage whose thought is sure.

When he shows no preference
in fortune or misfortune

and neither exults nor hates,
his insight is sure.

When, like a tortoise retracting
its limbs, he withdraws his senses
completely from sensuous objects,
his insight is sure.

Sensuous objects fade
when the embodied self abstains from food;
the taste lingers, but it too fades
in the vision of higher truth.

Even when a man of wisdom
tries to control them, Arjuna,
the bewildering senses
attack his mind with violence.

Controlling them all,
with discipline he should focus on me;
when his senses are under control,
his insight is sure.

Brooding about sensuous objects
makes attachment to them grow;
from attachment desire arises,
from desire anger is born.

From anger comes confusion;
from confusion memory lapses;
from broken memory understanding is lost;
from loss of understanding, he is ruined.

But a man of inner strength
whose senses experience objects
without attraction and hatred,
in self-control, finds serenity.

In serenity, all his sorrows
dissolve;

his reason becomes serene,
his understanding sure.

Without discipline,
he has no understanding or inner power;
without inner power, he has no peace;
and without peace where is joy?

If his mind submits to the play
of the senses,
they drive away insight,
as wind drives a ship on water.

So, Great Warrior, when withdrawal
of the senses
from sense objects is complete,
discernment is firm.

When it is night for all creatures,
a master of restraint is awake;
when they are awake, it is night
for the sage who sees reality.

As the mountainous depths
of the ocean
are unmoved when waters
rush into it,
so the man unmoved
when desires enter him
attains a peace that eludes
the man of many desires.

When he renounces all desires
and acts without craving,
possessiveness,
or individuality, he finds peace.

This is the place of the infinite spirit;
achieving it, one is freed from delusion;
abiding in it even at the time of death,
one finds the pure calm of infinity.

Suggestions for Further Reading

If you want a general overview of Hinduism with essential background information, you can check any number of good texts on religion, such as John A. Hutchison, *Paths of Faith,* 3d ed. (New York: McGraw-Hill, [1969] 1981), p. 136ff.

For a careful philosophical analysis of the *Gita,* see A. L. Herman, *An Introduction to Indian Thought* (Englewood Cliffs, NJ: Prentice-Hall, 1976), p. 142ff. Herman focuses on the ethics of the *Gita,* beginning on page 223. Another helpful and philosophically sophisticated discussion can be found in Ronald M. Green, *Religious Reason* (New York: Oxford University Press, 1978), p. 238ff. See also the introduction to Miller's translation (the one I have used here) and the introduction found in *The Bhagavadgita in the Mahabharata: Text and Translation* (Chicago: The University of Chicago Press, 1981) by J.A. B. van Buitenen. Ramesh N. Patel's *Philosophy of the Gita* (New York: Peter Lang, 1991) provides a difficult but innovative treatment. See pp. 101–115 in particular.

Video

Hinduism and the Song of God: A modern Interpretation of the Bhagavad Gita" (30 minutes) is an award winning video that explains the four yoga, the four stages of life, Karma, and how the *Gita* describes the purpose of human life. Available from Insight Media.

2.6. Native Americans and Mother Earth

You may have heard that in one year an average American discards 84 pounds of plastic. You may also know that the U.S. has 5 percent of the earth's population, but uses 26 percent of the earth's oil, releases 26 percent of the world's nitrogen oxides and over 22 percent of the world's carbon dioxide, and disposes of 290 million tons of toxic waste (*Time,* Dec. 18, 1989). And did you know that cars, buses, trucks, and motorcycles create over 52 percent of the smog in Southern California? Have you heard that Los Angeles and Long Beach harbors have the highest levels of toxic copper waste ever recorded (*Los Angeles Times,* Dec. 10, 1989)? You have probably heard that we are rapidly running out of landfill space in which to dump our garbage, and that some people are eyeing the deserts and oceans as new places to create what the Environmental Protection Agency calls "resource recovery parks" (read "dumps").

Have you ever wondered why we pollute the place where we live? Of course, these wastes are by-products of our highly technological society. But why have we created such a society? What about our attitudes and values? Do they have anything to do with our messing up our home? How should we live on this earth? Native Americans have an answer to that question.

It is difficult to describe, in general, the worldview of the Native Americans because each tribe is different. However, many origin myths from different groups describe a primeval time when all beings on earth were more or less human. A change took place and many of these primeval beings became animals and birds. These stories reflect the close kinship between humans and animals that Native Americans feel. They tend to imitate animals and birds in dress and action, and they address them as "brothers" and "sisters." Animals are regarded as spirits that are both sacred and mysterious. Indeed, all of nature is potentially sacred; respect for the land and all the beings who share it is a fundamental value. Harmony with and appreciation of the world is central to the Native American worldview.

Many Native Americans believe that spiritual powers govern the universe. There are spirits of the winds and rains, fields and streams, bears and deer. These various powers are, however, also thought of as a unity, and so many tribes speak of a Supreme Being (usually identified with the sky) who embodies the quintessence of all spiritual powers. Among the Lakota Sioux this Supreme Being is called **Wakan Tanka.**

N. Scott Momaday, a Native American writer, tells a story that he believes accurately describes the view Native Americans have of their relationship to nature. The story centers on "appropriateness" as a basic value.

> There was a man living in a remote place on the Navajo reservation who had lost his job and was having a difficult time making ends meet. He had a wife and several children. As a matter of fact, his wife was expecting another child. One day a friend came to visit him and perceived that his situation was bad. The friend said to him, "Look, I see that you're in tight straits, I see you have many mouths to feed, that you have no wood and that there is very little food in your larder. But one thing puzzles me. I know you're a hunter, and I know, too, there are deer in the mountains very close at hand. Tell me, why don't you kill a deer so that you and your family might have fresh meat to eat?" And after a time the man replied, "No, it is inappropriate that I should take life just now when I am expecting the gift of life." (1976, pp. 81–82)

The following selection is by Ed McGaa (Eagle Man), an Oglala Sioux lawyer and writer. Like many contemporary Native Americans, Eagle Man subscribes to *Pan-Indianism*—the belief that all Native American tribes basically share the same culture, religion, and philosophy of life. Those who subscribe to this idea tend to de-emphasize past tribal conflicts and emphasize the best in the tradition, particularly the values of peace, harmony, and respect for nature. They draw on deep traditional values to forge an ethic for today; an ethic, they believe, all people must adopt if our environment is to be saved.

There is much more to Native American philosophy than concern with the environment. Native Americans developed a sophisticated and complex metaphysics and moral philosophy dealing with a wide variety of issues. I chose to emphasize their concern with the environment here, because when many of us think about answering the question, "How should one live?" we often do not think about how we should live with nature. Most of us have become so urbanized that we have lost touch with nature and do not see ourselves intimately connected to it any more. But any complete answer to the question of how we should live must deal with environmental issues.

Reading Questions

1. What are the four commandments?
2. What do you think is meant by the phrase "respect for Mother Earth?"
3. Do you agree that the "quest for peace can be more efficiently pursued through communication . . . than by stealth and unending superior weaponry?" Why or why not?
4. Given the values expressed by Eagle Man in this selection, how do you think he would answer the question, "How should one live?"
5. How does his answer compare with the answers given by the Buddha? by Socrates? by Confucianism? by Aristotle? by the *Gita*?

We Are All Related

EAGLE MAN

THE PLIGHT OF THE NON-INDIAN WORLD is that it has lost respect for Mother Earth, from whom and where we all come.

We all start out in this world as tiny seeds—no different from our animal brothers and sisters, the deer, the bear, the buffalo, or the trees, the flowers, the winged people. Every particle of our bodies comes from the good things Mother Earth has put forth. Mother Earth is our real mother, because every bit of us truly comes from her, and daily she takes care of us.

The tiny seed takes on the minerals and the waters of Mother Earth. It is fueled by *Wiyo*, the sun, and given a spirit by *Wakan Tanka*.

This morning at breakfast we took from Mother Earth to live, as we have done every day of our lives. But did we thank her for giving us the means to live? The old Indian did. When he drove his horse in close to a buffalo running at full speed across the prairie, he drew his bowstring back and said as he did so, "Forgive me, brother, but my people must live." After he butchered the buffalo, he took the skull and faced it toward the setting sun as a thanksgiving and an acknowledgment that all things come from Mother Earth. He brought the meat back to camp and gave it first to the old, the widowed, and the weak. For thousands of years great herds thrived across the continent because the Indian never took more than he needed. Today, the buffalo is gone.

You say *ecology*. We think the words *Mother Earth* have a deeper meaning. If we wish to survive, we must respect her. It is very late, but there is still time to revive and discover the old American Indian value of respect for Mother Earth. She is very beautiful, and already she is showing us signs that she may punish us for not respecting her. Also, we must remember she has been placed in this universe by the one who is the All Powerful, the Great Spirit Above, or *Wakan Tanka*— God. But a few years ago, there lived on the North American continent people, the American Indians, who knew a respect and value system that enabled them to live on their native grounds without having to migrate, in contrast to the white brothers and sisters who migrated by the thousands from their homelands because they had developed a value system different from that of the American Indian. There is no place now to which we can migrate, which means we can no longer ignore the red man's value system.

Carbon-dating techniques say that the American Indian has lived on the North American continent for thousands upon thousands of years. If we did migrate, it was because of a natural phenomenon—a glacier. We did not migrate because of a social system, value system, and spiritual system that neglected its responsibility to the land and all living things. We Indian people say we were always here.

We, the American Indian, had a way of living that enabled us to live within the great, complete beauty that only the natural environment can provide. The Indian tribes had a common value system and a commonality of religion, without religious animosity, that preserved that great beauty that the two-leggeds definitely need. Our four commandments from the Great Spirit are: (1) respect for Mother Earth, (2) respect for the Great Spirit, (3) respect for our fellow man and woman, and (4) respect for individual freedom (provided that individual freedom does not threaten the tribe or the people or Mother Earth).

We who respect the great vision of Black Elk see the four sacred colors as red, yellow, black, and white. They stand for the four directions—red for the east, yellow for the south, black for the west, and white for the north.

From the east comes the rising sun and new knowledge from a new day.

From the south will come the warming south winds that will cause our Mother to bring forth the good foods and grasses so that we may live.

To the west where the sun goes down, the day will end, and we will sleep; and we will hold our spirit ceremonies at night, from where we will communicate with the spirit world beyond. The sacred color of the west is black; it stands for the deep intellect that we will receive from the spirit ceremonies. From the west come the life-giving rains.

From the north will come the white winter snow that will cleanse Mother Earth and put her to sleep, so that she may rest and store up energy to provide the beauty and bounty of springtime. We will prepare for aging by learning to create, through our arts and crafts, during the long winter season. Truth, honesty, strength, endurance, and courage also are represented by the white of the north. Truth and honesty in our relationships bring forth harmony.

All good things come from these sacred directions. These sacred directions, or four sacred colors, also stand for the four races of humanity: red, yellow, black, and white. We cannot be a prejudiced people, because all men and women are brothers and sisters and because we all have the same mother—Mother Earth. One who is prejudiced, who hates another because of that person's color, hates what the Great Spirit has put here. Such a one hates that which is holy and will be punished, even during this lifetime, as humanity will be punished for violating Mother Earth. Worse, one's conscience will follow into the spirit world, where it will be discovered that all beings are equal. This is what we Indian people believe.

We, the Indian people, also believe that the Great Spirit placed many people throughout this planet: red, yellow, black, and white. What about the brown people? The brown people evolved from the sacred colors coming together. Look at our Mother Earth. She, too, is brown because the four directions have come together. After the Great Spirit, *Wakan Tanka*, placed them in their respective areas, the *Wakan Tanka* appeared to each people in a different manner and taught them ways so that they might live in harmony and true beauty. Some men, some tribes, some nations have still retained the teachings of the Great Spirit. Others have not. Unfortunately, many good and peaceful religions have been assailed by narrow-minded zealots. Our religious beliefs and our traditional Indian people have suffered the stereotype that we are pagans, savages, or heathens; but we do not believe that only one religion controls the way to the spirit world that lies beyond. We believe that *Wakan Tanka* loves all of its children equally, although the Great Spirit must be disturbed at times with those children who have destroyed proven value systems that practiced sharing and generosity and kept Mother Earth viable down through time. We kept Mother Earth viable because we did not sell her or our spirituality!

Brothers and sisters, we must go back to some of the old ways if we are going to truly save our Mother Earth and bring back the natural beauty that every person seriously needs, especially in this day of vanishing species, vanishing rain forests, overpopulation, poisoned waters, acid rain, a thinning ozone layer, drought, rising temperatures, and weapons of complete annihilation.

Weapons of complete annihilation? Yes, that is how far the obsession with war has taken us. These weapons are not only hydraheaded; they are hydroheaded as well, meaning that they are the ultimate in hydrogen bomb destruction. We will have to divert our obsessions with defense and wasteful, all-life-ending weapons of war to reviving our environment. If such weapons are ever fired, we will wind up destroying ourselves. The Armageddon of war is something that we have all been very close to and exposed to daily. However, ever since that day in August when people gathered in fields and cities all across the planet to beseech for peace and harmony, it appears that we are seeing some positive steps toward solving this horror. *Maybe some day two-leggeds will read this book and missiles will no longer be pointed at them.*

The quest for peace can be more efficiently pursued through communication and knowledge than by stealth and unending superior weaponry. If the nations of the world scale back their budgets for weaponry, we will have wealth to spend to solve our serious environmental problems. Our home planet is under attack. It is not an imagined problem. This calamity is upon us now. We are in a real war with the polluting, violating blue man of Black Elk's vision.

Chief Sitting Bull advised us to take the best of the white man's ways and to take the best of the old Indian ways. He also said, "When you find something that is bad, or turns out bad, drop it and leave it alone."

The fomenting of fear and hatred is something that has turned out very badly. This can continue no longer; it is a governmental luxury maintained in order to support pork-barrel appropriations to the Department of Defense, with its admirals and generals who have substituted their patriotism for a defense contractor paycheck after retirement. War has become a business for profit. In the last two wars, we frontline warriors—mostly poor whites and minorities—were never allowed to win our wars, which were endlessly prolonged by the politicians and profiteers, who had their warrior-aged sons hidden safely away or who used their powers, bordering on treason, to keep their offspring out of danger. The wrong was that the patriotic American or the poor had to be the replacement. The way to end wars in this day and age is to do like the Indian: put the chiefs and their sons on the front lines.

Sitting Bull answered a relative, "Go ahead and follow the white man's road and do whatever the [Indian] agent tells you. But I cannot so easily give up my old ways and Indian habits; they are too deeply ingrained in me."

My friends, I will never cease to be an Indian.

I will never cease respecting the old Indian values, especially our four cardinal commandments and our values of generosity and sharing. It is true that many who came to our shores brought a great amount of good to this world. Modern medicine, transportation, communication, and food production are but a few of the great achievements that we should all appreciate. But it is also true that too many of those who migrated to North America became so greedy and excessively materialistic that great harm has been caused. We have seen good ways and bad ways. The good way of the non-Indian way I am going to keep. The very fact that we can hold peace-seeking communication and that world leaders meet and communicate for peace shows the wisdom of the brothers and sisters of this time. By all means, good technology should not be curtailed, but care must be taken lest our water, air, and earth become irreparably harmed. The good ways I will always respect and support. But, my brothers and sisters, I say we must give up this obsession with excess consumption and materialism, especially when it causes the harming of the skies surrounding our Mother and the pollution of the waters upon her. *She is beginning to warn us!*

Keep those material goods that you need to exist, but be a more sharing and generous person. You will find that you can do with less. Replace this empty lifestyle of hollow impressing of the shallow ones with active participation for your Mother Earth. At least then, when you depart into the spirit world, you can look back with pride and fulfillment. Other spirit beings will gather around you, other spirits of your own higher consciousness will gather around you and share your satisfaction with you. The eternal satisfaction of knowing you did not overuse your Mother Earth and that you were here to protect her will be a powerful satisfaction when you reach the spirit world.

Indian people do not like to say that the Great Mystery is exactly this or exactly that, but we do know there is a spirit world that lies beyond. We are allowed to know that through our ceremonies. We know that we will go into a much higher plane beyond. We know nothing of hell-fire and eternal damnation from some kind of unloving power that placed us here as little children. None of that has ever been shown to us in our powerful ceremonies, conducted by kind, considerate, proven, and very nonmaterialistic leaders. We do know that everything the Great Mystery makes is in the form of a circle. Our Mother Earth is a very large, powerful circle.

Therefore, we conclude that our life does not end. A part of it is within that great eternal circle. If there is a hell, then our concept of hell would be an eternal knowing that one violated or took and robbed from Mother Earth and caused this suffering that is being bestowed upon the generations unborn. This then, if it were to be imprinted upon one's eternal conscience, this would surely be a terrible, spiritual, mental hell. Worse, to have harmed and hurt one's innocent fellow beings, and be unable to alter (or conceal) the harmful actions would also be a great hell. Truth in the spirit world will not be concealed, nor will it be for sale. Lastly, we must realize that the generations unborn will also come into the spirit world. Let us be the ones that they wish to thank and congratulate, rather than eternally scorn.

While we are shedding our overabundant possessions, and linking up with those of like minds, and advancing spiritual and environmental appreciations, we should develop a respect for the aged and for family-centered traditions, even those who are single warriors, fighting for the revitalization of our Mother on a lone, solitary, but vital front. We should have more respect for an extended family, which extends beyond a son or daughter, goes beyond to grandparents and aunts and uncles, goes beyond to brothers, sisters, aunts, and uncles that we have adopted or made as relatives—and further beyond, to the animal or plant world as our brothers and sisters, to Mother Earth and Father Sky and then above to *Wakan Tanka*, the *Unci/Tankashilah*, the Grandparent of us all. When we pray directly to the Great Spirit, we say *Unci* (Grandmother) or *Tankashilah* (Grandfather) because we are so family-minded that we think of the Great Power above as a grandparent, and we are the grandchildren. Of course, this is so because every particle of our being is from Mother Earth, and our energy and life force are fueled by Father Sky. This is a vital part of the great, deep feeling and spiritual psychology that we have as Indian people. It is why we preserved and respected our ecological environment for such a long period. *Mitakuye oyasin!* We are all related!

In conclusion, our survival is dependent on the realization that Mother Earth is a truly holy being, that all things in this world are holy and must not be violated, and that we must share and be generous with one another. You may call this thought by whatever fancy words you wish—psychology, theology, sociology, or philosophy—but you must think of Mother Earth as a living being. Think of your fellow men and women as holy people who were put here by the Great Spirit. Think of being related to all things! With this philosophy in mind as we go on with our environmental ecology efforts, our search for spirituality, and our quest for peace, we will be far more successful when we truly understand the Indians' respect for Mother Earth.

Suggestions for Further Reading

Paul Radin's *Primitive Man as Philosopher* (New York: Dover, 1927, 1957) is the classic place to start pursuing the argument about whether Native Americans philosophized. Radin argues they do have a tradition (albeit an oral tradition) of speculative inquiry.

Clyde Kluckhohn's "The Philosophy of the Navaho Indians," found in *Ideological Differences and World Order* edited by F. S. C. Northrop (New Haven: Yale University Press, 1949), pp. 356–384, supports Radin. But Kluckhohn does point out how very different Native American philosophy is from the Anglo-European tradition.

For a collection of essays on Native American religion and philosophy see *Teachings from the American Earth*, edited by Dennis Tedlock and Barbara Tedlock (New York: Liveright, 1975).

You will want to note Benjamin Lee Whorf's famous and influential essay on "An American Indian Model of the Universe." See Ake Hultkrantz's *Native Religions of North America: The Power of Visions and Fertility* (New York: Harper & Row, 1987) for an overview of Native American beliefs and practices.

Thomas W. Overholt and J. Baird Callicott, in *Clothed-in-Fur and Other Tales* (Washington, D.C.: University Press of America, 1982), provide a collection of primary sources and an analysis of the Ojibwa world view. They characterize their work as an exercise in "ethno-metaphysics." Also, by the same authors, see "Traditional American Indian Attitudes Toward Nature," in *From Africa to Zen: An Invitation to World Philosophy,* edited by Robert C. Solomon and Kathleen M. Higgins (Lanham, Maryland: Rowman & Littlefield, 1993.)

For a contrast between the Native American and Anglo-Euro-American views toward the land, see "The Artificial Universe" in *We Talk, You Listen: New Tribes, New Turf* by Vine Deloria, Jr. (New York: Macmillan, 1970), pp. 181–197. N. Scott Momaday's "Native American Attitudes to the Environment" in *Seeing With a Native Eye: Essays on Native American Religion,* edited by Walter Capps (New York: Harper & Row, 1976), is brief but insightful. Also see Momaday's essay "An American Land Ethic" in *Ecotactics: The Sierra Club Handbook for Environmental Activists,* edited by John G. Mitchell with Constance L. Stallings (New York: Simon & Schuster, 1970), pp. 97–105. Also Chapter 7 of *Lame Deer: Seeker of Visions* by John Fire Lame Deer and Richard Erodes (New York: Simon & Schuster, 1972) will provide a view of what the whites have done to the land from a Native American perspective. For a classic statement see *Black Elk Speaks* by John G. Neihardt first published in 1932.

Videos

The Peyote Road (60 minutes) describes the philosophy of the Native American Church (KIFARU Productions, San Francisco, CA). *Wiping the Tears of Seven Generations* (60 minutes) won many documentary awards for a careful examination of U.S. history through the eyes of the Lakota Sioux (KIFARU Productions, San Francisco, CA). *American Indian Influence on the U.S.* (20 minutes) shows how life today has been influenced in various ways by Native Americans. *American Indian Heritage* (audio only, 29 minutes) explores Native American history through legend and myth. Also see the *Indian View Point Series* (produced by Southwest Film Center, filmstrips and audio cassettes). *Geronimo and the Apache Resistance* (60 minutes, PBS) and *The Spirit of Crazy Horse* (60 minutes, PBS) provide further insights. See your Media Services Catalogue for further information.

Chapter 3

How Can I Know What Is Right?

HAVE YOU EVER WONDERED how you can know what is morally right? You have been told to do the right thing. But what is the "right thing?" Sometimes it is very hard to figure out. Sometimes our duties conflict. We know we should be loyal to our friends, but shouldn't we report them for cheating? Sometimes we must choose between alternatives both of which seem wrong. Rita thinks, "It seems wrong to get an abortion. It is not fair to the unborn child. Having an abortion goes against my religious training. Yet I don't want this baby. I can't afford to raise it. I didn't intend to get pregnant. It would be wrong of me to have this baby."

In order to know what is the right thing to do, we need to know what makes an action right. But how can we know that? Do my motives make my actions right? If I intend to do my moral duty as best I understand it, isn't that enough? But maybe a good will isn't enough. Maybe it is not my motives, but the consequences of what I do that count. If my actions result in good things for most people, isn't that sufficient to justify my actions? But what about the act itself. Surely it is either right or wrong in itself, no matter what my motives are or the consequences. Some things are just plain wrong because they go against what God has told us to do. It is not right to steal even if my motives are good or the consequences will benefit some. Stealing is just plain wrong.

We all know that people have different values and believe different things to be right. Are your moral beliefs any better than anyone else's? Some people are **moral skeptics.** They doubt whether there is any such thing as moral truth. How could you show them wrong? Some people are **moral relativists.** They say anyone's moral beliefs are as good as anyone else's. But isn't that itself a nonrelative judgment? Are there any absolute rights and wrongs? **Moral absolutists** claim there are. Moral values, they argue, are objective. They transcend time and place. What is right is right, regardless of what anyone may think. But if there are absolute moral values, what are they? If you have wondered about these things, you have been asking some important questions that have to do with the very foundations of morality. In this chapter we will explore some different answers to the question, "How we can know what is right?"

3.1. Kant and the Categorical Imperative

Immanuel Kant (1724–1804) was born, lived, and died in Koenigsberg, Prussia. He studied natural science, mathematics, history, and philosophy at the University of Koenigsberg. After graduation he worked for a while as a tutor to the children of Prussian aristocrats, eventually landing a job as *privatdozent* at the University. This meant that he was licensed by the University to offer lectures, but the University did not pay him. Rather, he was paid by the students who attended his lectures. For more than a dozen years Kant lectured on a wide variety of subjects for up to 21 hours a week in order to make enough money to live. I'm not sure what conclusion we can draw about his lectures from the fact that he was quite poor during this period.

Kant's monetary fortunes improved when he was finally appointed professor of logic and metaphysics in 1770 and was paid a decent wage by the University. In 1781 one of his many books appeared, *The Critique of Pure Reason,* which was destined to revolutionize Western philosophy. It earned Kant the reputation of being one of the greatest philosophical minds of the modern period. In this book Kant was concerned with epistemological as well as metaphysical issues. Does the world conform to our ideas, or do our ideas conform to the world? Most people thought that true ideas are those that conform to the world. But Kant argued just the opposite, namely, that the world conforms to our ideas. We do not have time to go into Kant's complex proof nor the radical implications of this contention. I note it in passing to indicate that Kant made contributions to philosophy in other areas besides moral philosophy even though we will be concerned here primarily with his ethical ideas.

What makes an action right? For example, do the consequences or the results of an action make it right? People who advocate the view that consequences determine the rightness of an action support what philosophers call **teleological ethical theories.**

But what about the motives for action? Surely people can do something that has good results, but for the wrong reasons? I may refrain from cheating on a test because I am afraid I will get caught. Not cheating has good consequences because it makes the test fair for all. But is it right to praise me for being morally good simply because I was afraid to cheat? Should I not do the right thing because it is the right thing? Moral theories that advocate doing what is good because it is good, regardless of the consequences, are called **deontological ethical theories** (from the Greek *deon,* meaning "duty" and *logos,* meaning "science").

Immanuel Kant wondered about the sorts of questions we have been discussing. His answers constitute a deontological theory. He argues that the only thing that is unconditionally good is a good will. What makes a good will good is not the consequences that result from its acts, nor the inclinations and desires that in fact influence it, but its freely willing to do what duty requires.

And what does duty require? It requires that we act in accord with the **categorical imperative,** which can be formulated, "Act only on that maxim through which you can at the same time will that it should become a universal law." For example, if you are wondering whether you should tell the truth, you should formulate a maxim, "Always tell the truth" and ask whether you can will that such a rule become a universal law, i.e., a law everyone ought to obey. Note that this imperative or command is *cate-*

gorical, that is, unconditional. It is not a *hypothetical* or conditional command. Kant does *not* say, "Act only on that maxim if . . . ." Kant believed that this imperative is equivalent to a rule that requires us always to treat persons as ends in themselves rather than as means to some other end, such as the production of pleasure, happiness, or wealth.

Thus an action is right, Kant argues, if it is done from a good will. And a will is good if it meets three conditions:

1. The maxim on which its action is based can be universalized.
2. It freely accepts its duty (what Kant called *autonomy*).
3. It treats people as ends, not means.

Kant was looking for a rational foundation for morality. He opposed ethical relativism and disagreed with those who were skeptical of moral truth. Kant was an ethical absolutist. Moral truth is objective, he contended, and there is a rational foundation to morality which reveals that some things are morally right no matter what anyone thinks or what any society claims.

The selection that follows is from *Groundwork of the Metaphysics of Morals,* which Kant published in 1785. He intended it to be a brief introduction to his theory, which he later elaborated in the *Critique of Practical Reason.* Even though this work is introductory, it is not easy to read. Take your time, think about what Kant is saying, and answer the following questions.

Reading Questions

1. What is good without qualification?
2. Do the consequences or results of a good will make it good?
3. According to Kant, a good will is manifested in acting for the sake of duty. He contends that "the worth of character begins to show" when a person "does good, not from inclination, but from duty." Why does Kant claim this? Do you agree or not? Why?
4. Where, according to Kant, does the moral value or worth of an action done from duty reside? In the results of the action? In the actual motive a person may in fact have ("the material principle")? If not in these, where?
5. What do you think Kant means when he says, "Duty is the necessity to act out of reverence for the law?"
6. What is the categorical imperative?
7. Kant claims we can will to lie, but we cannot will a universal law of lying. Do you agree or not? Why?
8. Kant says that if you want to know whether an action is morally right, determine the maxim or subjective principle on which it is based and then ask, "Can I also will that my maxim should become a universal law?" If the answer is "no," it is not the right thing to do. Apply Kant's advice to the following case: You are a bright individual who usually gets good grades. You want to go to law school, and you need good grades to get accepted at a good law school. You find yourself taking a philosophy test for which you are not well prepared, and you have the opportunity to cheat without being caught. By cheating, you will definitely improve your final grade for the course. *Should* you cheat? If you were a Kantian (a follower of Kant's theory), what would your answer be and what would your reasoning be like?
9. How does Kant answer the question, "How can I know what is right?"

Groundwork of the Metaphysics of Morals

IMMANUEL KANT

Chapter I
Passage from Ordinary Rational
Knowledge of Morality to Philosophical

THE GOOD WILL

IT IS IMPOSSIBLE to conceive anything at all in the world, or even out of it, which can be taken as good without qualification, except a *good will*. Intelligence, wit, judgment, and any other *talents* of the mind we may care to name, or courage, resolution, and constancy of purpose, as qualities of *temperament,* are without doubt good and desirable in many respects; but they can also be extremely bad and hurtful when the will is not good which has to make use of these gifts of nature, and which for this reason has the term "*character*" applied to its peculiar quality. It is exactly the same with *gifts of fortune.* Power, wealth, honour, even health and that complete well-being and contentment with one's state which goes by the name of "*happiness,*" produce boldness, and as a consequence often overboldness as well, unless a good will is present by which their influence on the mind—and so, too, the whole principle of action—may be corrected and adjusted to universal ends; not to mention that a rational and impartial spectator can never feel approval in contemplating the uninterrupted prosperity of a being graced by no touch of a pure and good will, and that consequently a good will seems to constitute the indispensable condition of our very worthiness to be happy.

Some qualities are even helpful to this good will itself and can make its task very much easier. They have none the less no inner unconditioned worth, but rather presuppose a good will which sets a limit to the esteem in which they are rightly held and does not permit us to regard them as absolutely good. Moderation in affections and passions, self-control, and sober reflexion are not only good in many respects: they may even seem to constitute part of the *inner* worth of a person. Yet they are far from being properly described as good without qualification (however unconditionally they have been commended by the ancients). For without the principles of a good will they may become exceedingly bad; and the very coolness of a scoundrel makes him, not merely more dangerous, but also immediately more abominable in our eyes than we should have taken him to be without it.

THE GOOD WILL AND ITS RESULTS

A good will is not good because of what it effects or accomplishes—because of its fitness for attaining some proposed end: it is good through its willing alone—that is, good in itself. Considered in itself it is to be esteemed beyond comparison as far higher than anything it could ever bring about merely in order to favour some inclination or, if you like, the sum total of inclinations. Even if, by some special disfavour of destiny or by the niggardly endowment of stepmotherly nature, this will is entirely lacking in power to carry out its intentions; if by its utmost effort it still accomplishes nothing, and only good will is left (not, admittedly, as a mere wish, but as the straining of every means so far as they are in our control); even then it would still shine like a jewel for its own sake as something which has its full value in itself. Its usefulness or fruitlessness can neither add to, nor subtract from, this value. Its usefulness would be merely, as it were, the setting which enables us to handle it better in our ordinary dealings or to attract the

From I. Kant, Groundwork of the Metaphysics of Morals, *translated by H. J. Paton (New York: Harper &*
Row, 1964), pp. 61–62; 64–71. Reprinted by permission of Unwin Hyman, Ltd. Translator's footnotes deleted.

attention of those not yet sufficiently expert, but not to commend it to experts or to determine its value. . . .

THE GOOD WILL AND DUTY

We have now to elucidate the concept of a will estimable in itself and good apart from any further end. This concept, which is already present in a sound natural understanding and requires not so much to be taught as merely to be clarified, always holds the highest place in estimating the total worth of our actions and constitutes the condition of all the rest. We will therefore take up the concept of *duty*, which includes that of a good will, exposed, however, to certain subjective limitations and obstacles. These, so far from hiding a good will or disguising it, rather bring it out by contrast and make it shine forth more brightly.

THE MOTIVE OF DUTY

I will here pass over all actions already recognized as contrary to duty, however useful they may be with a view to this or that end; for about these the question does not even arise whether they could have been done *for the sake of duty* inasmuch as they are directly opposed to it. I will also set aside actions which in fact accord with duty, yet for which men have *no immediate inclination,* but perform them because impelled to do so by some other inclination. For there it is easy to decide whether the action which accords with duty has been done *from duty* or from some purpose of self-interest. This distinction is far more difficult to perceive when the action accords with duty and the subject has in addition an *immediate* inclination to the action. For example, it certainly accords with duty that a grocer should not overcharge his inexperienced customer; and where there is much competition a sensible shopkeeper refrains from so doing and keeps to a fixed and general price for everybody so that a child can buy from him just as well as anyone else. Thus people are served *honestly;* but this is not nearly enough to justify us in believing that the shopkeeper has acted in this way from

duty or from principles of fair dealing; his interests required him to do so. We cannot assume him to have in addition an immediate inclination towards his customers, leading him, as it were out of love, to give no man preference over another in the matter of price. Thus the action was done neither from duty nor from immediate inclination, but solely from purposes of self-interest.

On the other hand, to preserve one's life is a duty, and besides this every one has also an immediate inclination to do so. But on account of this the often-anxious precautions taken by the greater part of mankind for this purpose have no inner worth, and the maxim of their action is without moral content. They do protect their lives *in conformity with duty,* but not *from the motive of duty.* When on the contrary, disappointments and hopeless misery have quite taken away the taste for life; when a wretched man, strong in soul and more angered at his fate than faint-hearted or cast down, longs for death and still preserves his life without loving it—not from inclination or fear but from duty; then indeed his maxim has a moral content.

To help others where one can is a duty, and besides this there are many spirits of so sympathetic a temper that, without any further motive of vanity or self-interest, they find an inner pleasure in spreading happiness around them and can take delight in the contentment of others as their own work. Yet I maintain that in such a case an action of this kind, however right and however amiable it may be, has still no genuinely moral worth. It stands on the same footing as other inclinations—for example, the inclination for honour, which if fortunate enough to hit on something beneficial and right and consequently honorable, deserves praise and encouragement, but not esteem; for its maxim lacks moral content, namely, the performance of such actions, not from inclination, but *from duty.* Suppose then that the mind of this friend of man were overclouded by sorrows of his own which extinguished all sympathy with the fate of others, but that he still had power to help those in distress, though no longer stirred by the need of others because sufficiently occupied with his own; and suppose that, when no longer moved by any in-clination, he tears himself out of this deadly insensibility and does the action without any in-clination for the sake of duty alone; then for the first time his action has its genuine moral worth. Still further: if nature had implanted little sym-pathy in this or that man's heart; if (being in other respects an honest fellow) he were cold in temperament and indifferent to the sufferings of others—perhaps because, being endowed with the special gift of patience and robust endurance in his own sufferings, he assumed the like in oth-ers or even demanded it; if such a man (who would in truth not be the worst product of na-ture) were not exactly fashioned by her to be a philanthropist, would he not still find in himself a source from which he might draw a worth far higher than any that a good-natured tempera-ment can have? Assuredly he would. It is pre-cisely in this that the worth of character begins to show—a moral worth and beyond all com-parison the highest—namely, that he does good, not from inclination, but from duty.

To assure one's own happiness is a duty (at least indirectly); for discontent with one's state, in a press of cares and amidst unsatisfied wants, might easily become a great *temptation to the transgression of duty*. But here also, apart from regard to duty, all men have already of them-selves the strongest and deepest inclination to-wards happiness, because precisely in this idea of happiness all inclinations are combined into a sum total. The prescription for happiness is, however, often so constituted as greatly to inter-fere with some inclinations, and yet men cannot form under the name of 'happiness' any deter-minate and assured conception of the satisfaction of all inclinations as a sum. Hence it is not to be wondered at that a single inclination which is de-terminate as to what it promises and as to the time of its satisfaction may outweigh a wavering idea; and that a man, for example, a sufferer from gout, may choose to enjoy what he fancies and put up with what he can—on the ground that on balance he has here at least not killed the enjoyment of the present moment because of some possibly groundless expectations of the good fortune supposed to attach to soundness of health. But in this case also, when the universal inclination towards happiness has failed to deter-mine his will, when good health, at least for him, has not entered into his calculations as so neces-sary, what remains over, here as in other cases, is a law—the law of furthering his happiness, not from inclination, but from duty; and in this for the first time his conduct has a real moral worth.

It is doubtless in this sense that we should understand too the passages from Scripture in which we are commanded to love our neighbour and even our enemy. For love out of inclination cannot be commanded; but kindness done from duty—although no inclination impels us, and even although natural and unconquerable disin-clination stands in our way—is *practical*, and not *pathological*, love, residing in the will and not in the propensions of feeling, in principles of action and not of melting compassion; and it is this practical love alone which can be an object of command.

THE FORMAL PRINCIPLE OF DUTY

Our second proposition is this: An action done from duty has its moral worth, *not in the purpose* to be attained by it, but in the maxim in accor-dance with which it is decided upon; it depends therefore, not on the realization of the object of the action, but solely on the *principle* of *volition* in accordance with which, irrespective of all ob-jects of the faculty of desire, the action has been performed. That the purposes we may have in our actions, and also their effects considered as ends and motives of the will, can give to actions no unconditioned and moral worth is clear from what has gone before. Where then can this worth be found if we are not to find it in the will's rela-tion to the effect hoped for from the action? It can be found nowhere but *in the principle of the will*, irrespective of the ends which can be brought about by such an action; for between its *a priori* principle, which is formal, and its *a pos-teriori* motive, which is material, the will stands, so to speak, at a parting of the ways; and since it must be determined by some principle, it will have to be determined by the formal principle of volition when an action is done from duty, where, as we have seen, every material principle is taken away from it.

REVERENCE FOR THE LAW

Our third proposition, as an inference from the two preceding, I would express thus: *Duty is the necessity to act out of reverence for the law.* For an object as the effect of my proposed action I can have an *inclination,* but *never reverence,* precisely because it is merely the effect, and not the activity, of a will. Similarly for inclination as such, whether my own or that of another, I cannot have reverence: I can at most in the first case approve, and in the second case sometimes even love—that is, regard it as favourable to my own advantage. Only something which is conjoined with my will solely as a ground and never as an effect—something which does not serve my inclination, but outweighs it or at least leaves it entirely out of account in my choice—and therefore only bare law for its own sake, can be an object of reverence and therewith a command. Now an action done from duty has to set aside altogether the influence of inclination, and along with inclination every object of the will; so there is nothing left able to determine the will except objectively the *law* and subjectively *pure reverence* for this practical law, and therefore the maxim[1] of obeying this law even to the detriment of all my inclinations.

Thus the moral worth of an action does not depend on the result expected from it, and so too does not depend on any principle of action that needs to borrow its motive from this expected result. For all these results (agreeable states and even the promotion of happiness in others) could have been brought about by other causes as well, and consequently their production did not require the will of a rational being, in which, however, the highest and unconditioned good can alone be found. Therefore nothing but the *idea of the law* in itself, *which admittedly is present only in a rational being*—so far as it, and not

an expected result, is the ground determining the will—can constitute that pre-eminent good which we call moral, a good which is already present in the person acting on this idea and has not to be awaited merely from the result.[2]

THE CATEGORICAL IMPERATIVE

But what kind of law can this be the thought of which, even without regard to the results expected from it, has to determine the will if this is to be called good absolutely and without qualification? Since I have robbed the will of every inducement that might arise for it as a consequence of obeying any particular law, nothing is left but the conformity of actions to universal law as such, and this alone must serve the will as its principle. That is to say, I ought never to act except in such a way *that I can also will that my maxim should become a universal law.* Here bare conformity to universal law as such (without hav-

---

1. A *maxim* is the subjective principle of a volition: an objective principle (that is, one which would also serve subjectively as a practical principle for all rational beings if reason had full control over the faculty of desire) is a practical *law.*

2. It might be urged against me that I have merely tried, under cover of the word "*reverence,*" to take refuge in an obscure feeling instead of giving a clearly articulated answer to the question by means of a concept of reason. Yet, although reverence is a feeling, it is not a feeling *received* through outside influence, but one *self-produced* by a rational concept, and therefore specifically distinct from feelings of the first kind, all of which can be reduced to inclination or fear. What I recognize immediately as law for me, I recognize with reverence, which means merely consciousness of the *subordination* of my will to a law without the mediation of external influences on my senses. Immediate determination of the will by the law and consciousness of this determination is called "*reverence,*" so that reverence is regarded as the *effect* of the law on the subject and not as the *cause* of the law. Reverence is properly awareness of a value which demolishes my self-love. Hence, there is something which is regarded neither as an object of inclination nor as an object of fear, though it has at the same time some analogy with both. The *object* of reverence is the *law* alone—that law which we impose *on ourselves* but yet as necessary in itself. Considered as a law, we are subject to it without any consultation of self-love; considered as self-imposed it is a consequence of our will. In the first respect it is analogous to fear, in the second to inclination. All reverence for a person is properly only reverence for the law (of honesty and so on) of which that person gives us an example. Because we regard the development of our talents as a duty, we see too in a man of talent a sort of *example of the law* (the law of becoming like him by practice), and this is what constitutes our reverence for him. All moral *interest,* so-called, consists solely in *reverence* for the law.

ing as its base any law prescribing particular actions) is what serves the will as its principle, and must so serve it if duty is not to be everywhere an empty delusion and a chimerical concept. The ordinary reason of mankind also agrees with this completely in its practical judgments and always has the aforesaid principle before its eyes.

Take this question, for example. May I not, when I am hard pressed, make a promise with the intention of not keeping it? Here I readily distinguish the two senses which the question can have—Is it prudent, or is it right, to make a false promise? The first no doubt can often be the case. I do indeed see that it is not enough for me to extricate myself from present embarrassment by this subterfuge: I have to consider whether from this lie there may not subsequently accrue to me much greater inconvenience than that from which I now escape, and also—since, with all my supposed *astuteness*, to foresee the consequences is not so easy that I can be sure there is no chance, once confidence in me is lost, of this proving far more disadvantageous than all the ills I now think to avoid—whether it may not be a *more prudent* action to proceed here on a general maxim and make it my habit not to give a promise except with the intention of keeping it. Yet it becomes clear to me at once that such a maxim is always founded solely on fear of consequences. To tell the truth for the sake of duty is something entirely different from doing so out of concern for inconvenient results; for in the first case the concept of the action already contains in itself a law for me, while in the second case I have first of all to look around elsewhere in order to see what effects may be bound up with it for me. When I deviate from the principle of duty, this is quite certainly bad; but if I desert my prudential maxim, this can often be greatly to my advantage, though it is admittedly safer to stick to it. Suppose I seek, however, to learn in the quickest

way and yet unerringly how to solve the problem "Does a lying promise accord with duty?" I have then to ask myself "Should I really be content that my maxim (the maxim of getting out of a difficulty by a false promise) should hold as a universal law (one valid both for myself and others)?" And could I really say to myself that everyone may make a false promise if he finds himself in a difficulty from which he can extricate himself in no other way? I then become aware at once that I can indeed will to lie, but I can by no means will a universal law of lying; for by such a law there could properly be no promises at all, since it would be futile to profess a will for future action to others who would not believe my profession or who, if they did so over-hastily, would pay me back in like coin; and consequently my maxim, as soon as it was made a universal law, would be bound to annul itself.

Thus I need no far-reaching ingenuity to find out what I have to do in order to possess a good will. Inexperienced in the course of world affairs and incapable of being prepared for all the chances that happen in it, I ask myself only "Can you also will that your maxim should become a universal law?" Where you cannot, it is to be rejected, and that not because of a prospective loss to you or even to others, but because it cannot fit as a principle into a possible enactment of universal law. For such an enactment reason compels my immediate reverence, into whose grounds (which the philosopher may investigate) I have as yet no *insight*, although I do at least understand this much: reverence is the assessment of a worth which far outweighs all the worth of what is commended by inclination, and the necessity for me to act out of *pure* reverence for the practical law is what constitutes duty, to which every other motive must give way because it is the condition of a will good *in itself*, whose value is above all else.

Suggestions for Further Reading

The article on Kant in *The Encyclopedia of Philosophy* will provide further information on Kant in general and on his ethical theory in particular. You may also want to refer to the article, "Ethics, History of," for more information on Kant (p. 95 of Volume 3).

H. J. Paton, in his translation of Kant's *Groundwork,* also provides a commentary on each major section of Kant's text. This commentary will help you figure out what Kant means. See Volume 3 of *World Philosophy* (p. 1131) for a summary of *Groundwork* and a bibliography. For an introductory explanation of Kant, see "Morality Depends on Motives" in David Stewart and H. Gene Blocker, *Fundamentals of Philosophy,* (New York: Macmillan, 1987).

3.2. Mill on Utilitarianism

John Stuart Mill was born in London in 1806, two years after Kant's death. He died in 1873 after a distinguished career. Unlike Kant, who was a professional philosopher, Mill was an administrator for the East India Company and eventually served in Parliament. He wrote on a wide range of topics including logic, economics, religion, and ethics. He addressed important social issues such as women's rights and became the most influential spokesman in the nineteenth century in support of a free society that granted all people equal rights.

Mill's ethical theory is called **utilitarianism.** It is classified as a teleological theory because it maintains that what makes an action right are its consequences. If the consequences are good, then the action is right. But what are good consequences? Mill answers that good consequences are those that result in the greatest amount of pleasure (happiness) for the greatest number of people. Because Mill believes the good is pleasure, his theory is also a variety of **hedonism,** a moral theory that claims the highest good is pleasure. However, this theory is not a variety of egoist or selfish hedonism because it stresses the need to produce pleasure for the greatest number of people (which, of course, would include oneself as well as others).

The following selection is from Chapters 2, 3, and 4 of Mill's work *Utilitarianism,* which was published in 1861. In the first chapter (not included here), Mill makes some general remarks about ethics and attacks Kant's theory. Kant believes that it is illogical and hence irrational to will universal immoral laws. Thus, while we can will to lie, we cannot will that everyone ought to lie. Mill says that Kant never proves that the adoption of immoral laws by all rational beings is illogical in the sense that it somehow involves a contradiction. All he ever shows is that the consequences of adopting immoral laws as universal would be so undesirable that no one would choose to do so. That is, we do not advocate that everyone should lie because it is irrational to do so; rather, we do not advocate it because we do not wish to live in societies where no one can be trusted. Thus Kant, in spite of his rejection of teleological ethical theories, ends up having to appeal to consequences but refusing to acknowledge it, or so Mill contends.

Ethicists who follow a Kantian deontological theory usually criticize Mill's utilitarianism, in turn, for its failure to provide an adequate theory of justice. For example, would not the greatest happiness principle justify the majority in denying the rights of the minority if that produced the greatest happiness for the greatest number? Or would it not be possible to justify slavery on utilitarian grounds? Kantians argue that it would be possible to deny people their rights given the utilitarian viewpoint. An adequate theory of justice, they claim, can only be based on the recognition that people have rights simply because they are people. That is, rights are intrinsic and Kant's categorical imperative acknowledges this. But utilitarianism does not hold that people have rights just because they are people. People have rights only if it produces greater happiness to a greater number to grant them rights.

In his last chapter (not included here) Mill turns to the issue of justice, acknowledging that providing an adequate theory of justice is one of the hardest problems for utilitarianism. Nevertheless, he argues that the fair treatment of all people in society can be justified on utilitarian grounds because it is in the best interest of all to promote the feeling of security. Fair treatment, extended to all, in fact promotes such a feeling.

But I am getting too far ahead. Before we can compare Kant's deontological theory with Mill's teleological theory, we need to learn more about Mill's theory. I think you will find Mill a lot easier to read than Kant, but answering the following questions will still prove helpful in understanding the main points of Mill's theory. The utilitarian viewpoint has sunk deeply into the value system of Western culture so most of us will have a social framework that makes it easier to understand and accept this moral theory.

Reading Questions

1. What is the "greatest happiness principle" (also called the "principle of utility")?
2. What does Mill mean by happiness?
3. What is the theory of life on which the utilitarian theory is based?
4. How does Mill answer the objection that Epicureanism (a variety of hedonism) is a "doctrine only worthy of swine?" Do you think his answer is a good one? Why?
5. According to Mill, how can we determine whether one pleasure is more valuable than another?
6. Mill claims it is "better to be Socrates dissatisfied than a fool satisfied." Do you agree or not? Why?
7. How does Mill answer the question, "Why am I bound to promote the general happiness?" If I asked you why be good, how would you respond?
8. Summarize Mill's proof for the principle of utility. Some philosophers have argued that Mill's proof is faulty because it confuses the descriptive (what people actually desire) with the normative (what people ought to desire). Do you agree with this criticism? Why?
9. Refer back to the case of potential cheating I recounted in question 8 in the section on Kant. If you were a utilitarian, how would you go about determining the right thing to do in this situation?
10. Some people have objected to utilitarianism on the grounds that it allows us to do things that are immoral. Can you think of an example of something that would be immoral, yet that utilitarian theory would say is good?
11. How does Mill answer the question, "How can I know what is right?"

What Utilitarianism Is

JOHN STUART MILL

THE CREED WHICH ACCEPTS as the foundation of morals "utility" or the "greatest happiness principle" holds that actions are right in proportion as they tend to promote happiness; wrong as they tend to produce the reverse of happiness. By "happiness" is intended pleasure and the absence of pain; by "unhappiness," pain and the privation of pleasure. To give a clear view

Excerpts from Chapters II, III, and IV of Utilitarianism *by J. S. Mill. (London:* Frasers Magazine, *1861).*

of the moral standard set up by the theory, much more requires to be said; in particular, what things it includes in the ideas of pain and pleasure, and to what extent this is left an open question. But these supplementary explanations do not affect the theory of life on which this theory of morality is grounded—namely, that pleasure and freedom from pain are the only things desirable as ends; and that all desirable things (which are as numerous in the utilitarian as in any other scheme) are desirable either for pleasure inherent in themselves or as means to the promotion of pleasure and the prevention of pain.

Now such a theory of life excites in many minds, and among them in some of the most estimable in feeling and purpose, inveterate dislike. To suppose that life has (as they express it) no higher end than pleasure—no better and nobler object of desire and pursuit—they designate as utterly mean and groveling, as a doctrine worthy only of swine, to whom the followers of Epicurus were, at a very early period, contemptuously likened; and modern holders of the doctrine are occasionally made the subject of equally polite comparisons by its German, French, and English assailants.

When thus attacked, the Epicureans have always answered that it is not they, but their accusers, who represent human nature in a degrading light, since the accusation supposes human beings to be capable of no pleasures except those of which swine are capable. If this supposition were true, the charge could not be gainsaid, but would then be no longer an imputation; for if the sources of pleasure were precisely the same to human beings and to swine, the rule of life which is good enough for the one would be good enough for the other. The comparison of the Epicurean life to that of beasts is felt as degrading, precisely because a beast's pleasures do not satisfy a human being's conceptions of happiness. Human beings have faculties more elevated than the animal appetites and, when once made conscious of them, do not regard anything as happiness which does not include their gratification. I do not, indeed, consider the Epicureans to have been by any means faultless in drawing

out their scheme of consequences from the utilitarian principle. To do this in any sufficient manner, many Stoic, as well as Christian elements require to be included. But there is no known Epicurean theory of life which does not assign to the pleasures of the intellect, of the feelings and imagination, and of the moral sentiments a much higher value as pleasures than to those of mere sensation. It must be admitted, however, that utilitarian writers in general have placed the superiority of mental over bodily pleasures chiefly in the greater permanency, safety, uncostliness, etc., of the former—that is, in their circumstantial advantages rather than in their intrinsic nature. And on all these points utilitarians have fully proved their case; but they might have taken the other and, as it may be called, higher ground with entire consistency. It is quite compatible with the principle of utility to recognize the fact that some kinds of pleasure are more desirable and more valuable than others. It would be absurd that, while in estimating all other things quality is considered as well as quantity, the estimation of pleasure should be supposed to depend on quantity alone.

If I am asked what I mean by difference of quality in pleasures, or what makes one pleasure more valuable than another, merely as a pleasure, except its being greater in amount, there is but one possible answer. Of two pleasures, if there be one to which all or almost all who have experience of both give a decided preference, irrespective of any feeling of moral obligation to prefer it, that is the more desirable pleasure. If one of the two is, by those who are competently acquainted with both, placed so far above the other that they prefer it, even though knowing it to be attended with a greater amount of discontent, and would not resign it for any quantity of the other pleasure which their nature is capable of, we are justified in ascribing to the preferred enjoyment a superiority in quality so far outweighing quantity as to render it, in comparison, of small account.

Now it is an unquestionable fact that those who are equally acquainted with and equally capable of appreciating and enjoying both do give a most marked preference to the manner of existence which employs their higher faculties. Few human creatures would consent to be changed into any of the lower animals for a promise of the fullest allowance of a beast's pleasures; no intelligent human being would consent to be a fool, no instructed person would be an ignoramus, no person of feeling and conscience would be selfish and base, even though they should be persuaded that the fool, the dunce, or the rascal is better satisfied with his lot than they are with theirs. They would not resign what they possess more than he for the most complete satisfaction of all the desires which they have in common with him. If they ever fancy they would, it is only in cases of unhappiness so extreme that to escape from it they would exchange their lot for almost any other, however undesirable in their own eyes. A being of higher faculties requires more to make him happy, is capable probably of more acute suffering, and certainly accessible to it at more points, than one of an inferior type; but in spite of these liabilities, he can never really wish to sink into what he feels to be a lower grade of existence. We may give what explanation we please of this unwillingness; we may attribute it to pride, a name which is given indiscriminately to some of the most and to some of the least estimable feelings of which mankind are capable; we may refer it to the love of liberty and personal independence, an appeal to which was with the Stoics one of the most effective means for the inculcation of it; to the love of power or to the love of excitement, both of which do really enter into and contribute to it; but its most appropriate appellation is a sense of dignity, which all human beings possess in one form or other, and in some, though by no means in exact, proportion to their higher faculties, and which is so essential a part of the happiness of those in whom it is strong that nothing which conflicts with it could be otherwise than momentarily an object of desire to them. Whoever supposes that this preference takes place at a sacrifice of happiness—that the superior being, in anything like equal circumstances, is not happier than the inferior—confounds the two very different ideas of happiness

and content. It is indisputable that the being whose capacities of enjoyment are low has the greatest chance of having them fully satisfied; and a highly endowed being will always feel that any happiness which he can look for, as the world is constituted, is imperfect. But he can learn to bear its imperfections, if they are at all bearable; and they will not make him envy the being who is indeed unconscious of the imperfections, but only because he feels not at all the good which those imperfections qualify. It is better to be a human being dissatisfied than a pig satisfied; better to be Socrates dissatisfied than a fool satisfied. And if the fool or the pig are of a different opinion, it is because they only know their own side of the question. The other party to the comparison knows both sides.

It may be objected that many who are capable of the higher pleasures occasionally, under the influence of temptation, postpone them to the lower. But this is quite compatible with a full appreciation of the intrinsic superiority of the higher. Men often, from infirmity of character, make their election for the nearer good, though they know it to be the less valuable; and this no less when the choice is between two bodily pleasures than when it is between bodily and mental. They pursue sensual indulgences to the injury of health, though perfectly aware that health is the greater good. It may be further objected that many who begin with youthful enthusiasm for everything noble, as they advance in years, sink into indolence and selfishness. But I do not believe that those who undergo this very common change voluntarily choose the lower description of pleasures in preference to the higher. I believe that, before they devote themselves exclusively to the one, they have already become incapable of the other. Capacity for the nobler feelings is in most natures a very tender plant, easily killed, not only by hostile influences, but by mere want of sustenance; and in the majority of young persons it speedily dies away if the occupations to which their position in life has devoted them, and the society into which it has thrown them, are not favorable to keeping that higher capacity in exercise. Men lose their high aspirations as they lose their intellectual tastes, because they have not time or opportunity for indulging them; and they addict themselves to inferior pleasures, not because they deliberately prefer them, but because they are either the only ones to which they have access or the only ones which they are any longer capable of enjoying. It may be questioned whether anyone who has remained equally susceptible to both classes of pleasures ever knowingly and calmly preferred the lower, though many, in all ages, have broken down in an ineffectual attempt to combine both.

From this verdict of the only competent judges, I apprehend there can be no appeal. On a question which is the best worth having of two pleasures, or which of two modes of existence is the most grateful to the feelings, apart from its moral attributes and from its consequences, the judgment of those who are qualified by knowledge of both, or, if they differ, that of the majority among them, must be admitted as final. And there needs be the less hesitation to accept this judgment respecting the quality of pleasures, since there is no other tribunal to be referred to even on the question of quantity. What means are there of determining which is the acutest of two pains, or the intensest of two pleasurable sensations, except the general suffrage of those who are familiar with both? Neither pains nor pleasures are homogeneous, and pain is always heterogeneous with pleasure. What is there to decide whether a particular pleasure is worth purchasing at the cost of a particular pain, except the feelings and judgment of the experienced? When, therefore, those feelings and judgment declare the pleasures derived from the higher faculties to be preferable *in kind,* apart from the question of intensity, to those of which the animal nature, disjoined from the higher faculties, is susceptible, they are entitled on this subject to the same regard. . . .

Of the Ultimate Sanction of the Principle of Utility

The question is often asked, and properly so, in regard to any supposed moral standard—What is its sanction? what are the motives to obey? or, more specifically, what is the source of its obligation? whence does it derive its binding force? It is a necessary part of moral philosophy to provide the answer to this question, which, though frequently assuming the shape of an objection to the utilitarian morality, as if it had some special applicability to that above others, really arises in regard to all standards. It arises, in fact, whenever a person is called on to *adopt* a standard, or refer morality to any basis on which he has not been accustomed to rest it. For the customary morality, that which education and opinion have consecrated, is the only one which presents itself to the mind with the feeling of being *in itself* obligatory; and when a person is asked to believe that this morality *derives* its obligation from some general principle round which custom has not thrown the same halo, the assertion is to him a paradox; the supposed corollaries seem to have a more binding force than the original theorem; the superstructure seems to stand better without than with what is represented as its foundation. He says to himself, I feel that I am bound not to rob or murder, betray or deceive; but why am I bound to promote the general happiness? If my own happiness lies in something else, why may I not give that the preference? . . .

The ultimate sanction, therefore, of all morality (external motives apart) being a subjective feeling in our own minds, I see nothing embarrassing to those whose standard is utility in the question, What is the sanction of that particular standard? We may answer, the same as of all other moral standards—the conscientious feelings of mankind. Undoubtedly this sanction has no binding efficacy on those who do not possess the feelings it appeals to; but neither will these persons be more obedient to any other moral principle than to the utilitarian one. On them morality of any kind has no hold but through the external sanctions. Meanwhile the feelings exist, a fact in human nature, the reality of which, and the great power with which they are capable of acting on those in whom they have been duly cultivated, are proved by experience. No reason has ever been shown why they may not be cultivated to as great intensity in connection with the utilitarian as with any other rule of morals.

There is, I am aware, a disposition to believe that a person who sees in moral obligation a transcendental fact, an objective reality belonging to the province of "things in themselves," is likely to be more obedient to it than one who believes it to be entirely subjective, having its seat in human consciousness only. But whatever a person's opinion may be on this point of ontology, the force he is really urged by is his own subjective feeling, and is exactly measured by its strength. No one's belief that duty is an objective reality is stronger than the belief that God is so; yet the belief in God, apart from the expectation of actual reward and punishment, only operates on conduct through, and in proportion to, the subjective religious feeling. The sanction, so far as it is disinterested, is always in the mind itself; and the notion, therefore, of the transcendental moralists must be that this sanction will not exist *in* the mind unless it is believed to have its root out of the mind; and that if a person is able to say to himself, "That which is restraining me and which is called my conscience is only a feeling in my own mind," he may possibly draw the conclusion that when the feeling ceases the obligation ceases, and that if he find the feeling inconvenient, he may disregard it and endeavor to get rid of it. But is this danger confined to the utilitarian morality? Does the belief that moral obligation has its seat outside the mind make the feeling of it too strong to be got rid of? The fact is so far otherwise that all moralists admit and lament the ease with which, in the generality of minds, conscience can be silenced or stifled. The question, "Need I obey my conscience?" is quite as often put to themselves by persons who never heard of the principle of utility as by its adherents. Those whose conscientious feelings are so weak as to allow of their asking this question, if they answer it affirmatively, will not do so because they believe in the transcendental theory, but because of the external sanctions. . . .

It is not necessary, for the present purpose, to decide whether the feeling of duty is innate or implanted. Assuming it to be innate, it is an open question to what objects it naturally attaches itself; for the philosophic supporters of that theory are now agreed that the intuitive perception is of principles of morality and not of the details. If there be anything innate in the matter, I see no reason why the feeling which is innate should not be that of regard to the pleasures and pains of others. If there is any principle of morals which is intuitively obligatory, I should say it must be that. If so, the intuitive ethics would coincide with the utilitarian, and there would be no further quarrel between them. Even as it is, the intuitive moralists, though they believe that there are other intuitive moral obligations, do already believe this to be one; for they unanimously hold that a large *portion* of morality turns upon the consideration due to the interests of our fellow creatures. Therefore, if the belief in the transcendental origin of moral obligation gives any additional efficacy to the internal sanction, it appears to me that the utilitarian principle has already the benefit of it.

On the other hand, if, as is my own belief, the moral feelings are not innate but acquired, they are not for that reason the less natural. It is natural to man to speak, to reason, to build cities, to cultivate the ground, though these are acquired faculties. The moral feelings are not indeed a part of our nature in the sense of being in any perceptible degree present in all of us; but this, unhappily, is a fact admitted by those who believe the most strenuously in their transcendental origin. Like the other acquired capacities above referred to, the moral faculty, if not a part of our nature, is a natural outgrowth from it; capable, like them, in a certain small degree, of springing up spontaneously; and susceptible of being brought by cultivation to a high degree of development. Unhappily it is also susceptible, by a sufficient use of the external sanctions and of the force of early impressions, of being cultivated in almost any direction, so that there is hardly anything so absurd or so mischievous that it may not, by means of these influences, be made to act on the human mind with all the authority of conscience. To doubt that the same potency might be given by the same means to the principle of utility, even if it had no foundation in human nature, would be flying in the face of all experience.

But moral associations which are wholly of artificial creation, when the intellectual culture goes on, yield by degrees to the dissolving force of analysis; and if the feeling of duty, when associated with utility, would appear equally arbitrary; if there were no leading department of our nature, no powerful class of sentiments, with which that association would harmonize, which would make us feel it congenial and incline us not only to foster it in others (for which we have abundant interested motives), but also to cherish it in ourselves—if there were not, in short, a natural basis of sentiment for utilitarian morality, it might well happen that this association also, even after it had been implanted by education, might be analyzed away.

But there *is* this basis of powerful natural sentiment; and this it is which, when once the general happiness is recognized as the ethical standard, will constitute the strength of the utilitarian morality. This firm foundation is that of the social feelings of mankind—the desire to be in unity with our fellow creatures, which is already a powerful principle in human nature, and happily one of those which tend to become stronger, even without express inculcation, from the influences of advancing civilization. The social state is at once so natural, so necessary, and so habitual to man, that, except in some unusual circumstances or by an effort of voluntary abstraction, he never conceives himself otherwise than as a member of a body; and this association is riveted more and more, as mankind are further removed from the state of savage independence. Any condition, therefore, which is essential to a state of society becomes more and more an inseparable part of every person's conception of the state of things which he is born into, and which is the destiny of a human being. Now society between human beings, except in the relation of master and slave, is manifestly impossible on any other footing than that the interests of all are to be consulted. Society between equals can only exist on the understanding that the interests of all are to be regarded equally. And since

in all states of civilization, every person, except an absolute monarch, has equals, everyone is obliged to live on these terms with somebody; and in every age some advance is made toward a state in which it will be impossible to live permanently on other terms with anybody. . . .

Of What Sort of Proof the Principle of Utility Is Susceptible

It has already been remarked that questions of ultimate ends do not admit of proof, in the ordinary acceptation of the term. To be incapable of proof by reasoning is common to all first principles, to the first premises of our knowledge, as well as to those of our conduct. But the former, being matters of fact, may be the subject of a direct appeal to the faculties which judge of fact—namely, our senses and our internal consciousness. Can an appeal be made to the same faculties on questions of practical ends? Or by what other faculty is cognizance taken of them?

Questions about ends are, in other words, questions about what things are desirable. The utilitarian doctrine is that happiness is desirable, and the only thing desirable, as an end; all other things being only desirable as means to that end. What ought to be required of this doctrine, what conditions is it requisite that the doctrine should fulfill—to make good its claim to be believed?

The only proof capable of being given that an object is visible is that people actually see it. The only proof that a sound is audible is that people hear it; and so of the other sources of our experience. In like manner, I apprehend, the sole evidence it is possible to produce that anything is desirable is that people do actually desire it. If the end which the utilitarian doctrine proposes to itself were not, in theory and in practice, acknowledged to be an end, nothing could ever convince any person that it was so. No reason can be given why the general happiness is desirable, except that each person, so far as he believes it to be attainable, desires his own happiness. This, however, being a fact, we have not only all the proof which the case admits of, but all which it is possible to require, that happiness is a good, that each person's happiness is a good to that person, and the general happiness, therefore, a good to the aggregate of all persons. Happiness has made out its title as *one* of the ends of conduct and, consequently, one of the criteria of morality.

But it has not, by this alone, proved itself to be the sole criterion. To do that, it would seem, by the same rule, necessary to show, not only that people desire happiness, but that they never desire anything else. Now it is palpable that they do desire things which, in common language, are decidedly distinguished from happiness. They desire, for example, virtue and the absence of vice no less really than pleasure and the absence of pain. The desire of virtue is not as universal, but it is as authentic a fact as the desire of happiness. And hence the opponents of the utilitarian standard deem that they have a right to infer that there are other ends of human action besides happiness, and that happiness is not the standard of approbation and disapprobation.

But does the utilitarian doctrine deny that people desire virtue, or maintain that virtue is not a thing to be desired? The very reverse. It maintains not only that virtue is to be desired, but that it is to be desired disinterestedly, for itself. Whatever may be the opinion of utilitarian moralists as to the original conditions by which virtue is made virtue, however they may believe (as they do) that actions and dispositions are only virtuous because they promote another end than virtue, yet this being granted, and it having been decided, from considerations of this description, what *is* virtuous, they not only place virtue at the very head of the things which are good as means to the ultimate end, but they also recognize as a psychological fact the possibility of its being, to the individual, a good in itself, without looking to any end beyond it; and hold that the mind is not in a right state, not in a state conformable to utility, not in the state most conducive to the general happiness, unless it does love virtue in this manner—as a thing desirable in itself, even although, in the individual instance, it should not produce those other desirable consequences which it tends to produce, and on account of which it is held to be virtue. This opinion is not,

in the smallest degree, a departure from the happiness principle. The ingredients of happiness are very various, and each of them is desirable in itself, and not merely when considered as swelling an aggregate. The principle of utility does not mean that any given pleasure, as music, for instance, or any given exemption from pain, as for example health, is to be looked upon as means to a collective something termed happiness, and to be desired on that account. They are desired and desirable in and for themselves; besides being means, they are a part of the end. Virtue, according to the utilitarian doctrine, is not naturally and originally part of the end, but it is capable of becoming so; and in those who live it disinterestedly it has become so, and is desired and cherished, not as a means to happiness, but as a part of their happiness. . . .

It results from the preceding considerations that there is in reality nothing desired except happiness. Whatever is desired otherwise than as a means to some end beyond itself, and ultimately to happiness, is desired as itself a part of happiness, and is not desired for itself until it has become so. Those who desire virtue for its own sake desire it either because the consciousness of it is a pleasure, or because the consciousness of being without it is a pain, or for both reasons united; as in truth the pleasure and pain seldom exist separately, but almost always together—the same person feeling pleasure in the degree of virtue attained, and pain in not having attained more. If one of these gave him no pleasure, and the other no pain, he would not love or desire virtue, or would desire it only for the other benefits which it might produce to himself or to persons whom he cared for.

We have now, then, an answer to the question, of what sort of proof the principle of utility is susceptible. If the opinion which I have now stated is psychologically true—if human nature is so constituted as to desire nothing which is not either a part of happiness or a means of happiness—we can have no other proof, and we require no other, that these are the only things desirable. If so, happiness is the sole end of human action, and the promotion of it the test by which to judge of all human conduct; from whence it necessarily follows that it must be the criterion of morality, since a part is included in the whole.

And now to decide whether this is really so, whether mankind does desire nothing for itself but that which is a pleasure to them, or of which the absence is a pain, we have evidently arrived at a question of fact and experience, dependent, like all similar questions, upon evidence. It can only be determined by practiced self-consciousness and self-observation, assisted by observation of others. I believe that these sources of evidence, impartially consulted, will declare that desiring a thing and finding it pleasant, aversion to it and thinking of it as painful, are phenomena entirely inseparable or, rather, two parts of the same phenomenon—in strictness of language, two different modes of naming the same psychological fact; that to think of an object as desirable (unless for the sake of its consequences) and to think of it as pleasant are one and the same thing; and that to desire anything except in proportion as the idea of it is pleasant is a physical and metaphysical impossibility. . . .

Suggestions for Further Reading

Once again, a good place to start is *The Encyclopedia of Philosophy.* J. B. Schneewind's article "Mill, John Stuart" will provide a brief summary of his life and writings. J. J. C. Smart's article on "Utilitarianism" will provide further information on the ethical aspects of Mill's philosophy.

For a summary of the main ideas of Mill's utilitarianism see Whitaker T. Deininger's "Utilitarianism" in Volume 3 of *World Philosophy.* Mill borrowed many of his ideas from his godfather Jeremy Bentham (1748–1832) who developed a "hedonistic calculus" which quantified pleasures and pains. Bentham believed this calculus made morality scientific because it provided a way to make objective moral decisions. See his *Introduction to the Principles of Morals and Legislation* (first printed in 1780, but not published until 1789).

For a collection of primary texts and the most important secondary comments see *Mill's Utilitarianism: Text and Criticism,* edited by James M. Smith and Ernest Sosa (Belmont, CA: Wadsworth Publishing Co., 1969), and *Utilitarianism and Its Critics,* edited by Jonathan Glover (New York: Macmillan Publishing Co., 1990). These volumes also provide an excellent bibliography.

3.3. Religion and Morality

You might be wondering by now why philosophers like Kant and Mill who are searching for the foundations of morality overlook what has been and remains so obvious to so many, namely, that God is the source of morality. Why all this talk of the categorical imperative (Kant), the principle of utility (Mill), when people from a variety of theistic religious traditions have been saying for centuries that God's will is the source of the moral laws that humans ought to obey?

That morality is dependent on religion is widely maintained by theologians and ministers who argue for the need to return to "the old-time religion" to save us from our present moral and social crisis. Moralists who seek to promote civic and personal virtue, educators who advocate the teaching of religion in the public schools, and politicians concerned with the "moral decay" of society all recognize some sort of essential link between religion and morality. Fundamentalists, be they Christian, Jewish, or Muslim, who propose the establishment of a **theocratic** state often make their case on moral grounds. How often have you been urged by parents, friends, or relatives to get your moral act together by "getting religion?" How many of you believe that being good is somehow involved with being godly? How many of you have been told that Jesus is the answer to all your problems?

We must be very careful about equating religion and God. Not only are some religions not theistic, even those religions that teach a doctrine of God should not be confused with the God about which they teach. To join a religion is not the same as becoming godly. Nevertheless, one common way of thinking about the connection between religion and morality is to assert that good is what God commands and evil is what God forbids. This is usually referred to as "the divine command theory of ethics." According to this theory, it is right to do X if God wills it, and it is wrong to do X if it is contrary to God's will. If this theory is true, then "right" means "divinely commanded," and a person's moral goodness consists of obedience to God's will. In other words, neither your motive nor the consequences make an action right. Conformity to God's law makes it right.

As you might guess, one major problem with this theory has to do with knowing what God's will is. You have probably read about parents having been prosecuted for murder because they let their child die, believing it was God's will. Wars have been fought with both sides claiming they were acting according to God's will.

But the divine command theory presents problems more serious than the problem of knowing for sure what God commands. The philosophical criticism of this theory is as old as Socrates' debate with Euthyphro (see Section 2.3). This deeper criticism can be stated as a dilemma.

1. Moral rightness is either the same as God's command or it is not.
2. If it is the same, then morality is arbitrary and moral goodness is merely obedience to power.
3. If it is not the same, then morality and religion are independent, and God is subject to an independent moral standard in terms of which even God is evaluated as good or not good.
4. Therefore, either morality is arbitrary and moral goodness merely obedience to power, or morality and religion are independent and God is subject to evaluation in terms of an independent moral standard.

I think it is clear that the conclusion to this argument presents two horns of a dilemma with which most **theists** (believers in God) would not be comfortable. They certainly would not want to conclude that morality is arbitrary and goodness mere obedience (the first horn). This would mean that if God decided to command the killing of innocent people, then such action would become, by definition, good. It would also mean that your motives and the consequences of what you do have nothing to do with being good. But we all take motives into account when judging someone, and Jesus in the "Sermon on the Mount" (Matt. 5) stressed love, not obedience, as the crucial moral factor.

The second horn of the dilemma might be more attractive. What is the problem with recognizing the independence of morality and religion? Of course this means that even **atheists** can be good, but isn't that, as a matter of fact, true? All good people are not necessarily believers, and many believers are not always good people. Yet many theists believe that God's will is supreme and absolute. It is God who judges, not humans. Doesn't this second horn require the theist to surrender belief in God's absolute will and view God as being under the same sort of moral obligations as the rest of us?

There have been many philosophical and theological attempts to respond to the various attacks on the divine command theory. In what follows we shall look at one such attempt by Tan Tai Wei, a professor at the Institute of Education in Singapore. If Professor Wei is right, it might still be possible to found morality on the principle of love and on the religious notion of God, insofar as God can be defined as love. Indeed, there have been important and influential attempts on the part of Christian theologians in this century to construct such a theory (see suggested readings). But Professor Wei is not nearly so ambitious here. He does not try to construct a complete moral theory founded on love, but he does try to clear the way for such a theory by suggesting a way to escape the dilemma of the divine command theory. Answer the following questions as you read and see if you think he succeeds.

Reading Questions

1. What is the "dilemma of ethical monotheism" according to Tan Tai Wei?
2. Why might a religious thinker say morality is based on God's absolute will?
3. What are some unacceptable implications of the view that the moral law is based on divine fiat (command)?
4. How are the notions that love fulfills the moral law and "God is love" supposed to provide a way out of the dilemma?
5. How does Tan Tai Wei's proposed solution account for our experience of the categorical imperative and our concept of worship?
6. Do you think Tan Tai Wei's proposed solution to the dilemma actually solves it? Why or why not?
7. How do you think Tan Tai Wei would define love?
8. Formulate an objection to Wei's argument.
9. How would Wei answer the question, "How can I know what is right?"

Morality and the God of Love

TAN TAI WEI

IF THE STATEMENT that God is good is to be morally and religiously meaningful and important, then God must be seen as being subject to the moral law in terms of which he is evaluated as good and worthy of our worship. Yet it is against the belief in God's supremacy and abso-luteness, and his being the creator of all, to conceive him as being under moral obligations and subject to logically autonomous precepts. This dilemma of ethical monotheism was posed by Plato in *Euthyphro* where he raised the question whether a thing can be good just because God

Tan Tai Wei, "Morality and the God of Love," Sophia: A Journal for Discussion of Philosophical Theology. *Vol. 26 (July, 1987), 20–25. Reprinted by permission of* Sophia *and the author. Footnotes deleted.*

wills it. If the divine goodwill is not to be reduced to divine fiat, there must be logically distinct and prior criteria in the light of which the
divine will is seen as good.

I think that the dilemma can be resolved
through an understanding of the nature of morality in relation to love, and the God of love.

We should first appreciate the sort of considerations that probably had led some religious
thinkers to say that since God is supreme, the
moral law must have arisen purely out of his
absolute will. The notion that God is subject to
the moral law has not only the implication that
God is no longer supreme, and creator of among
other things the moral law. This alone may not
worry the theist. I have heard it said that divine
supremacy in those respects is not crucial, since
the moral law is not of the same category of being as the personal God and therefore could not
affect his personal supremacy. What is probably
more worrying to the theist is that to conceive
God as being, like ordinary moral agents, impelled by the moral force or obligatoriness which
Kant tried to distinguish by the term "the categorical imperative." Call it conscience, the dictate of reason or what you will, we experience as
moral agents an imperatival force to be or do
what we are prepared to recognise as our moral
obligation to be or do. Explain it in terms of en-
culturalisation if you will, and then, perhaps like
some ethical emotivists, say that this culturally
acquired "conscience" issues in forceful ejacula-
tions of subjective preferences which are basically
what moral evaluations amount to. All such theories concede, even before attempting to explain
it away, that our moral experience includes this
feeling of our being imposed upon to abide by
objective moral dictates. Even if these dictates
are merely culturally acquired preferences, we experience them as being binding as against other
opposing inclinations we normally also have. It
would seem that, whatever it really means, the
experience of "the categorical imperative" is a
defining feature of moral agency. Therefore conceiving God as being under the moral law and
thereby a moral agent would mean seeing him as
being *impelled* by conscience, or *dictated* to by

the moral law. This means conceiving God as
sharing the related fact of our moral experience
that we have, as Kant reminded us, to exert a
deliberate act of will to obey the call of duty
(whether or not we also go along with him in his
further claim that the motive for this has to be
doing our duty for duty's sake). This implies that
even for God "the spirit indeed is willing but the
flesh is weak," so that temperance becomes for
him, as well as us, a virtue for keeping in check
what Plato called the appetitive part of the soul.
For an imperative or the imposing of force that
we act in certain ways would lose its point if not
to deter us from tendencies to act in contradictory or contrary ways.

It is clear now how unacceptably anthropo-
morphic is the conception of deity as moral agent
subject to independent moral constraints. However, is the only alternative to this the conception
of the moral law as representing divine fiat, a
view that has equally unacceptable implications
such as the reduction of the moral law to mere
"will-to-power," and theistic religion to mere
power worship? I think the way out of this dilemma is in Jesus' teaching that love fulfills the
moral law, and that "God is Love."

Jesus said that he had come not to destroy but
to fulfill the law. He had only one commandment to give which is that we should love one
another as he had loved us. We should love the
Lord our God with all our heart, soul and mind,
and our neighbors as ourselves. His saving work
includes showing us the way of love, by which he
would indeed be set free from the law. For love
would render the law redundant since it would
result in the spontaneous outflow of the sorts of
behaviour conscience would dictate. Paul's great
chapter on love in his first letter to the Corinthians (Chapter 13) surely is meant to say that love
expresses itself in being and doing all that the
moral law would dictate, the list of virtues provided in the chapter being only a sampling. And
it can indeed be shown, though there is space to
indicate this only schematically here, that love
does fulfill the moral law in the manner suggested. All of morality that has to do with right
interpersonal conduct must surely be acceptable

to any one who loves his fellow men. For example, can one love one's fellow men and not desire to be more than fair, more than truthful or more than honest towards them? If it is right that one should go one mile with one's beloved, would not one desire to go two, or more? Now, morality requires too that in our insistence on rightness, we should also temper justice with mercy and reason with compassion. Need love be reminded of this? For love is compassion, and forgiveness is its natural outcome. Forgiveness, though, does not overrule justice but presupposes it, since it implies some wrong to forgive. But it transforms the nature of justice under the perspective of love. The ultimate aim of justice, i.e., peace on earth and goodwill towards men, is best secured through love and forgiveness.

The significant difference love makes to one's living by the moral law is that it renders unnecessary the categorical imperative as a felt imposition. The man whom love has transformed is the man whose nature has become such that he is naturally inclined to doing right. He is not one who has to be impelled by a moral imperative to aim for the good. The latter man is only at most a second best on the moral path: even the Kantian moral man who is motivated to do his duty for duty's sake is still short of the moral best in that he needs a motive at all. Give me a man any time who does good to me because he loves me rather than one who does good to me in order to fulfill his moral duty even if it is done only for duty's sake! Which woman would believe a man who says he loves her, when this is only because he feels duty-bound to love?

We have then arrived at a conception of love that sees it as naturally translating itself into moral behavior without being tied up with the notion of obedience to the moral law. Now in the Judaeo-Christian traditions, and arguably also within schools of Hinduism and Buddhism that exhibit theistic tendencies, God is conceived as loving, indeed in Christianity as love itself. Do we not have here a notion of a God who is not subject to and needs no moral law and its demands, and yet who inspires moral conduct in his human creatures? The moral demands that arise would represent not arbitrary divine fiat but the proper way to live our lives both in relation to God and to our fellow men in view of and in response to God's love.

In elaborating upon and commending this resolution of the dilemma, let us see how the viewpoint would account for the experience of the categorical imperative which we saw to be basic to our moral awareness. Also, let us see how our resolution implies an improved concept of worship.

The viewpoint implies that the concept of morality and the moral law, with its imperatival force, has application only within the realm of human beings, or other possible rational beings who share with humans the character traits that give the categorical imperative its point and function. Such traits are summed up in Jesus' observation that "the spirit indeed is willing but the flesh is weak." The proper way to live, given a creator God of love to respond to, is the way of love exemplified in the life and death of Jesus. This way is the fulfillment of the moral law and more. But because man is still far from being "perfected in love" he has yet to realize the total spontaneity in loving and moral behavior vis-à-vis God and fellow men. The extent of his shortcomings in this regard determines the degree to which he still remains "under the curse of the law." He thus needs morality and the categorical imperative. Moral obligations are meaningful and functional for him, and he is thus appropriately described as a moral agent. That the concept of moral obligation has meaning and function only in this way is evident in the teaching of great moralists through the ages as to what constitutes moral perfection. Confucius, for instance, taught that self-cultivation is to aim at moral perfection, understood in terms of total spontaneity in good attitude and behavior. He said that at the age of seventy, (which he surely meant to be not autobiographical but representative of full developmental maturity) he could pursue all his heart naturally desired and yet not overstep the moral bound. The implication is that as long as we are not yet perfect we need the moral law and its imperatival force to keep us within the bound of the moral law. But morality is the ladder we can kick off once we have attained the height of sageliness.

It follows that the concept of morality does not apply to God, who by definition is perfect in love. "I am that I am": we are simply confronted by him who is, and he is love. He is under no moral obligation to be love, for the concept of moral obligation, as we analysed it, is derivative from the divine fact that he is love and arises only among humans who cannot as yet perfectly respond to him in love. We are being imposed upon to respond to him and we must do so in one way or another. The appropriate response is of course the agapeistic way of life as seen in Christ. In this sense he has created the way of love, which translated into practice among fallible beings like ourselves would call for the moral law. In this sense he is the author of the moral law, which is therefore not arbitrary divine fiat but the consistent outflow of an appropriate response to his nature. If we must say in worship and praise that God is good, we should mean by this merely that we see in his nature the perfection of everything the moral law requires of us, and more. For we saw that to mean by God's goodness that he is good in the way you and I can be said to be good, with the implication that he too has to obey the moral law, would be to misapply the concept of morality. This brings us naturally to our next and final observation that our thesis implies a religiously consistent conception of worship.

There is something fundamentally inappropriate in the claim made by many that if God is a being *worthy of our worship* then He must be morally good in the same sense that you and I may be evaluated to be morally good. Surely worship does not arise in the cool and calculated way implied, i.e., resulting from a prior examination and evaluation of the divine nature. Such has never been the manifestation of awe. And isn't it inconsistent with the humility and contrition implied in worship to presuppose that we are capable of judging God and this done by independent standards, as the logic of moral appraisal does insist? Isaiah's vision of God that left him humbled and awe-stricken in worship is rather his being immediately confronted by the very paradigm of goodness resulting in his realization of the utter incompatibility of his own being with the divine light. If anything resembling moral evaluation is at all implicit in this realization, it is certainly not done in terms of a standard independent of deity. In some sense, the realization is that he is the very standard: there can be no other. He is that he is and what he is is supremely worthy, and yet the worthiness is inherent in the fact that he is.

Nor does our account amount to the view that we worship God because of the mere fact that he is. Our point is that we respond to his love—"we love him because he first loved us." If he were other than love, creation would probably never be and the question of worship is rendered moot. In any case, Jesus also taught that no man can approach the Father unless the Father himself draws him: we worship him for he is love and draws us to himself, and not merely because he is.

Suggestions for Further Reading

There is much written on the divine command theory. Paul Helm edited a volume entitled *Divine Commands and Morality* (Oxford: Oxford University Press, 1981) that will provide you with a good sampling of the range of opinion. You will also find a good collection of essays on the topic in a volume edited by Gene Outka and J. P. Reeder, *Religion and Morality: A Collection of Essays* (New York: Anchor Books, 1973). A difficult but logically careful attempt to defend a divine command theory can be found in Philip Quinn's *Divine Commands and Moral Requirements* (Oxford: Clarendon Press, 1978).

Theologians who have attempted to develop moral theories based on the principle of love include Joseph Fletcher (see Part 1 of his *Moral Responsibility: Situation Ethics at Work*, published in 1967 by Westminster Press, Philadelphia, PA), and Paul Tillich (see *Morality and Beyond*, (New York: Harper & Row, 1963).

Kai Nielsen's *Ethics Without God* (New York: Prometheus Books, 1973) provides a clearly written critique of religious moral theories and an attempt to state a completely humanistic ethic.

3.4. Toward a Feminist Ethic

In 1982, Carol Gilligan, a developmental psychologist, published a book entitled *In a Different Voice*. She pointed out that empirical research into moral reasoning and moral development used samples consisting of mostly male subjects. Most of the major psychological theories of moral reasoning took male reasoning and male development as the norm.

Dr. Gilligan began to listen to women and discovered that their approach to moral issues was different from the male approach. The male perspective toward relationships tends to emphasize reciprocity. Equality, justice, rights, impartiality, objectivity, generalization, fair rules, and the importance of the authority of logical reasoning emerge as central concerns of males when dealing with moral dilemmas. For example, an eleven-year-old boy, Jake, is given the Heinz dilemma. A man named Heinz considers whether to steal a drug that he cannot afford to buy because the drug is essential for saving the life of his wife. Jake is confident that Heinz should steal the drug because this is a clear-cut case of a conflict between the values of property and life. Logically, he argues, life must be given greater priority than property since it is irreplaceable.

The female approach to moral problems, according to Gilligan, tends to be responsive. Care, love, trust, dealing with specific persons who have specific needs, compassion, mercy, forgiveness, the importance of not hurting anyone, and the authority of feeling in solving problems emerge as central concerns of females when dealing with moral issues. For example, Amy, also eleven, when given the Heinz dilemma, says she is not sure whether Heinz should steal the drug since that would harm the druggist. Also, Heinz might harm himself if he is caught and has to go to jail. That would also harm his wife who needs him to take care of her. Of course, she shouldn't be allowed to die either. Some other way needs to be found (borrow the money, work out installment payments) and she suggests they all get together, talk about the problem, and find a solution acceptable to all concerned.

Lawrence Kohlberg, who originally designed the study and developed the theory to which Gilligan is responding, construed the Heinz dilemma as a conflict between life and property and thus would regard Jake's response as indicative of a higher level of moral reasoning than Amy's. Gilligan remarks that one is not "higher" than the other—they are just different.

The major and most influential theories in moral philosophy have been developed by males. They reflect what Gilligan sees as the male concern with logical consistency, impartiality, rights, and obligations. Gilligan's work in descriptive psychology inspired the development of feminist ethical theories by philosophers. These feminist theories often began with a critique of the sexism hidden in traditional moral theories, and then go on to develop theories which take seriously caring and nurturing. However, some feminist philosophers have been critical of this development for several reasons. First, an ethics of care may itself be sexist by elevating to philosophic status gender stereotypes of women as more self-sacrificing and more nurturing than men. This can work against women by reinforcing the idea that women are best suited to raising children and working in the "caring" professions and thereby restricting their opportunities. Second, an ethics of care cannot be divorced from an ethics of justice without severe consequences. Justice demands that we treat people fairly, and this is an ethical notion that has played an important role in the women's movement for liberation. Whatever we may think about the ethical importance of caring for people, caring without justice leaves us with a very one-sided moral theory.

Rita Manning teaches philosophy at San Jose State University. She has written on the philosophy of mind and moral theory. In the essay that follows, she develops some central ideas in the ethics of care and shows how it relates to an ethics of justice.

Reading Questions

1. What are the two elements of an ethic of caring?
2. In what sort of situation am I obligated to care and in what situation can I choose when and how to care? Give an example of each.
3. Does the ethic of caring require feeling a particular emotion toward the one in need?
4. What is the difference between subsistence needs and psychological needs? Give an example of each.
5. If one's obligation to care arises from the existence of helplessness, why should I, according to Manning, care for values, institutions, and objects other than persons and animals?
6. Why is one obligated to respond with care just because someone else is in need?
7. What are the limits of our obligation to care?
8. What is the role of rules and rights in an ethic of care?
9. What is "caring burnout," and why are we obligated to avoid it if possible?
10. Formulate a critical question about Manning's essay and answer it.
11. Compare the answers of Kant, Mill, Tan Tai Wei, and Manning to the question, "How can I know what is right?"

Just Caring

RITA MANNING

IN THIS ESSAY, I shall sketch and provide a cursory defense of a model of ethical considerations which I shall call, following Nel Noddings, an ethic of caring.[1]

I shall confess at the outset that this model owes more to my experience as a woman, a teacher, and a mother than to my training and

1. I owe a special debt to Nel Noddings, whose powerful defense of caring inspired me to take caring seriously. *Caring: A Feminine Approach to Ethics and Moral Education* (Berkeley: University of California Press, 1984). I have also benefited from hearing talks given by Michelle Dumont, and by

my many conversations about feminist ethics with her over the years. A special thank you to Dianne Romain, who has encouraged me in this project and given me much food for thought. Melissa Burchard, Michael Katz, and William Shaw gave me very useful comments on an earlier version of this paper.

From Rita Manning, "Just Caring" in Explorations in Feminist Ethics: Theory and Practice, *edited by Eve Browning Cole and Susan Coultrap-McQuin. Copyright © 1992 by Indiana University Press. Reprinted by permission of Indiana University Press. Pages 45–54.*

experience in moral philosophy. Over the years, my students have convinced me of the barrenness of standard ethical theories. It has occurred to me only very recently that, in sketching a more adequate model, I might appeal to my own experience as a moral person. I credit Hume,[2] Annette Baier,[3] and Carol Gilligan[4] with waking me from my dogmatic slumber and Nel Noddings with allowing me to take caring, which is central to my moral experience, seriously.

An ethic of caring, as I shall defend it, includes two elements. First is a disposition to care. This is a willingness to receive others, a willingness to give the lucid attention to the needs of others which filling these needs appropriately requires. I see this disposition to care as nourished by a spiritual awareness similar to the awareness argued for by proponents of the women's spirituality movement. As Starhawk describes this awareness: "Immanent justice rests on the first principle of magic: all things are interconnected. All is relationship. Perhaps the ultimate ethic of immanence is to choose to make that relationship one of love . . . love for all the eternally self-creating world, love of the light and the mysterious darkness, and raging love against all that would diminish the unspeakable beauty of the world."[5]

In addition to being sensitive to my place in the world and to my general obligation to be a caring person, I am also obligated to care for. (I am following Noddings in using "care for" to indicate caring as expressed in action.) In the paradigm case, caring for involves acting in some appropriate way to respond to the needs of persons, and animals, but can also be extended to responding to the needs of communities, values, or objects. My obligation to care for is limited by a principle of supererogation, which is necessary to keep an ethic of caring from degenerating into an ethics of total self-sacrifice. I shall argue that we are obligated to adopt this model of caring as far as we can in our moral deliberations. We are morally permitted and sometimes morally obliged to appeal to rules and rights. In Gilligan's idiom, we are required to listen to the voices of both care and justice. In what follows, I shall first fill in some of the details of this model. Specifically, I shall discuss what it is to care for someone or something and when we are obligated to care for. Next, I shall say something about the role of rules and rights in this model.

Caring

I have often wondered if taking a class in moral philosophy was the best way for students to become sensitive to moral concerns. It seemed to me that a better way would be to have students work in soup kitchens or shelters for the homeless.[6] I am convinced that taking care of my children has made me more open to moral concerns. In taking care of the hungry, homeless, and helpless, we are engaged in caring for. In the standard case, caring for is immediate; it admits of no surrogates. When I directly care for some creature, I am in physical contact. Our eyes meet, our hands touch. Not every need can be met in this immediate way. In that case, I must accept a surrogate. Not every need can be met by individual action. In those cases, I must seek collective action.[7] But when I can do the caring for myself, I ought to do so, at least some of the time. The need of the other may sometimes require that I do the caring for. If my child needs my attention, I cannot meet this need by sending her to a

---

2. Hume argued that the task of moral philosophy ought to be to look reflectively at actual moral practice. This conception also can be seen, though to a lesser extent, in Aristotle, and in Alasdair MacIntyre, *After Virtue* (South Bend, Ind.: University of Notre Dame Press, 1981).

3. Annette Baier argues forcefully that we should pay exclusive attention to reforming current moral practices. See *Postures of the Mind: Essays on Mind and Morals,* especially Chapters 11–15 (Minneapolis: University of Minnesota Press, 1985).

4. Carol Gilligan, *In a Different Voice* (Cambridge, Mass.: Harvard University Press, 1982).

5. Starhawk, *Dreaming the Dark* (Boston: Beacon Press, 1988), 44.

6. Dick Schubert, one of my creative and courageous colleagues, makes such assignments.

7. See my "The Random Collective as a Moral Agent" for a further discussion of collective action and obligation. *Social Theory and Practice* 11, no. 1 (Spring 1985), 97–105.

therapist. Even when the needs of the other do not require my personal attention, I must provide some of the caring for directly in order to develop and sustain my ability to care.

My day-to-day interactions with other persons create a web of reciprocal caring. In these interactions, I am obliged to be a caring person. I am free, to a certain extent, to choose when and how to care for these others. My choice is limited by my relationships with these others and by their needs. A pressing need calls up an immediate obligation to care for; roles and responsibilities call up an obligation to respond in a caring manner. In the first case, I am obligated (though this obligation can be limited by a principle of supererogation) to respond; in the second, I can choose, within limits, when and how to care.

A creature in need who is unable to meet this need without help calls for a caring response on my part. This response needn't always be direct. Sometimes it is better to organize a political response. (Many, for example, who are confronted on the street by homeless people are unsure about how to respond, convinced that their immediate response will not be enough, might even be counterproductive.) Certain relationships obligate me to provide direct caring for. When my daughter falls and asks me to "kiss it and make it better," I can't send her to my neighbor for the kiss.

My roles as mother, as teacher, as volunteer, put me in particular relationships to others.[8] These roles require and sustain caring. My obligation to my infant children and my animals is to meet their basic needs for physical sustenance (food, shelter, clothing, health care) and for companionship and love. My obligation to my students is grounded on my roles as teacher and philosopher and their psychological needs to discover who they are and how they can live with integrity. Here I feel a connection with my students but also with teaching and philosophy. But

if one of my students comes to me needing another kind of care, I may be obligated to provide it, though I may not be obligated to do so single-handedly. My response depends on my ability to care for, my obligation to care for myself, and my sense of the appropriateness of the need and the best way to meet it.

In discharging obligations to care for that are based on role responsibility, I am conscious of my need to fill those roles conscientiously. The role of teacher, for example, requires a certain impartiality; the role of mother requires a fierce devotion to each particular child. But I am free, to a certain extent, to choose my roles. In adopting or reshaping roles, I should be sensitive to my need to be cared for as well as my capacity to care. In critiquing socially designed and assigned roles, we should aim for roles and divisions of roles that make caring more likely to occur.

Caring for can involve a measure of self-sacrifice. The rescuers of Jessica McClure who went without sleep for days, the parents of an infant who go without uninterrupted sleep for months, are involved in caring for. Caring for involves an openness to the one cared for. Caring for requires that I see the real need and that I satisfy it insofar as I am able. In satisfying it, I am sensitive not just to the need but to the feelings of those in need.

Caring for does not require that I feel any particular emotion toward the one cared for, but that I am open to the possibility that some emotional attachment may form in the caring for. Nor does it require that I have an ongoing relationship with the one cared for.[9] I may meet the one cared for as stranger, though the caring for will change that.

---

8. Alasdair MacIntyre, following Aristotle, made much of this notion of role-responsibility. See *After Virtue*. See also Virginia Held, *Rights and Goods* (New York: The Free Press, 1984).

9. Noddings makes much of the requirement that caring demands an on-going relationship. It is on this basis that she denies that we can have an obligation to care for the starving children in Africa and animals. In an October 1988 talk to the Society for Women in Philosophy, she allowed that caring for does not exhaust our obligations so we could have other obligations to the starving children in Africa. I would prefer to say that we have obligations to care for the starving children and animals, but that not all caring obligations require direct care.

Obviously, a model of caring along the lines I am defending must include an account of needs. I cannot offer a complete account here, but I would draw heavily from the biology, psychology, and other relevant social sciences in constructing such an account; there would be an essentially normative component as well. I want to begin by drawing a distinction between what I call subsistence needs and psychological needs. Subsistence needs will usually be needs that must be filled if physical existence is to continue. Psychological needs are needs that must be filled if human flourishing is to occur. Filling subsistence needs does not automatically benefit both the carer and the cared for. Rather, the carer is likely to feel burdened by filling such needs, though the recognition that one has filled such needs often creates a sense of virtue in the carer. I am reminded here of the ferocious demands for food that infants make on their parents with astonishing regularity. Filling psychological needs can often be more fulfilling. It is more likely to be done in a reciprocal relationship and in such a relationship filling psychological needs requires that both parties share the roles of carer and cared for. I needn't respond to every need. In choosing how and when to respond, I should consider the seriousness of the need, the benefit to the one needing care of filling this particular need, and the competing needs of others, including myself, that will be affected by my filling this particular need.

Objects of Care

I can care for persons, animals, values, institutions, and objects. My choice of objects of caring about should reflect my own need to be cared for and my capacity to care. But decisions about what to care for should not depend exclusively on my own needs and capacities. I should also be sensitive to the needs that summon the obligation to care for. If I understand my obligation to care for as following from the existence of need and helplessness, I should care for institutions, values, and practices that would diminish such needs. One might argue that we could virtually

eliminate the need to care for by creating such institutions, values, and practices and hence undermine our capacity to care. But even in a perfectly just world, children would need care and people and animals would get sick. Furthermore, human needs include more than needs for physical sustenance. Human needs for companionship and intimacy would exist even in a world free from the horrors of war, homelessness, sickness, and disease.

Defense of a General Obligation to Care

The obligation to respond as carer when appropriate can be defended on three grounds. The first is the need. Here I would appeal to Peter Singer's principle, "if it is in our power to prevent something very bad happening without thereby sacrificing anything of comparable moral significance, we ought to do it."[10]

The second is the recognition that human relationships require a continuous kind of caring. This caring involves three components: being receptive to the other, being accepting of the other, and being on-call for the other when s/he is in need.[11] Unless we want to do away with human relationships, we must be open to the demands of caring that such relationships require. But caring in human relationships is, as human relationships are, reciprocal.

The third defense is that I cannot develop and sustain my ability to care unless I do some active caring. This is an empirical claim and we must look both to social science and to our own experience in evaluating it, but there is an obvious way in which caring for enhances our ability to care. When I make the real attempt to care for, I must understand the needs of the one cared for. I must also see how that one wants the needs to be addressed. This ability to notice needs and wants, to empathize as well as sympathize is de-

10. Peter Singer, *Practical Ethics* (Cambridge: Cambridge University Press, 1979), 168.
11. This analysis is from Milton Mayeroff, *On Caring* (New York: Harper & Row, 1971).

veloped through caring. Of course, one might ask why one should want to develop this capacity to care. It seems to me that the right response is to point out that human lives devoid of caring impulses and responses would be nasty, brutish, short, and lonely.

Limitation on Obligations to Care

I don't think that we are obligated to be like Mother Teresa. Mother Teresa cares for continuously.[12] We can limit our obligation to care for by focusing on the defenses of this obligation. First, I have a prima facie obligation to care for when I come across a creature in need who is unable to meet that need without help, when my caring is called on as a part of a reciprocal relationship, or when indicated as part of my role responsibility. My actual obligation rests on the seriousness of the need, my assessment of the appropriateness of filling the need, and my ability to do something about filling it. But I must also recognize that I am a person who must be cared for and that I must recognize and respond to my own need to be cared for. The continuous caring for required to respond to needs for physical sustenance is, for most of us, incompatible with caring for ourselves. But not all caring for involves responding to physical needs. The caring for required to sustain relationships, which is usually reciprocal, can be a source of great strength to the person doing the caring for. Finally, allowing myself to suffer caring burnout also diminishes my ability to care for others in the future. I don't mean to argue that caring for requires no sacrifice. Indeed, where the need is great and my ability to meet it sufficient, I am required to sacrifice. But I am not required to adopt this as a form of life.

My obligation to care for is not an all-or-nothing thing. Being unable to care for now

does not eliminate the possibility that I may be obligated to meet this need later. This is a general point about obligations. I might owe someone money and be unable to pay it back now, through no fault of my own. If I later come into a windfall, I am obligated to pay the money back then. In addition, there is no one right way to care for. My assessment of the appropriateness of the need, my ability to meet the need, and my sense of the most successful way of doing so provide some guidance here. Perhaps immediate caring for is the best way to meet a need in one case, and cooperative political activity the most successful way of meeting other needs. I would want to leave these kinds of choices up to the agent.

Rules and Rights

In my model, rules and rights serve three purposes. They can be used to persuade, to sketch a moral minimum below which no one should fall and beyond which behavior is condemned, and they can be used to deliberate in some cases.

My attention to rules and rights here does not reflect my unwillingness to make appeals to virtues and practices. I think it is fair to describe caring as a virtue. I do include other virtues and practices as fulfilling each of the three functions that rules and rights play in my model. We certainly can and do persuade by reminding others of virtues: "Would an honest man do that?" We likewise persuade by pointing to practices: "Native Americans don't have that kind of an attitude about the earth." Virtues and practices can serve as minimums: "I can see that you won't be doing me any favors, but at least give me the courtesy of an honest reply."

We don't live in a caring world. By that I mean that not everyone recognizes his or her obligation to care. Our society does not encourage the flourishing of this capacity, but undermines it in various ways. In a world infamous for its lack of caring, we need tools of persuasion to protect the helpless. This is one of the roles that rules and rights fill. We can reason in the language of rules with those who lack a sufficient degree of

---

12. The inappropriateness of slavish caring has long been a theme in feminist thought. Betty Friedan called thinking that one's role in life requires such caring "the problem that has no name." See *The Feminine Mystique* (New York: Dell, 1963).

caring. If their natural sympathies are not engaged by the presence of suffering, we can attempt to appeal to reason: "How would you feel if you were in their place?" "What would be the consequences of such behavior on a large scale?" I am not convinced of the effect of such persuasion, and it is, I think, an empirical question whether such appeals would persuade where caring did not, but I suspect that such socially agreed on minimums could seve as persuasive appeals.

Rules and rights provide a minimum below which no one should fall and beyond which behavior is morally condemned. Rules provide a minimum standard for morality. Rights provide a measure of protection for the helpless. But on this level of moral discourse, morality is, like politics, the art of the possible. In the face of large-scale selfishness and inattention, perhaps the best we can hope for is a minimum below which no one should fall and beyond which behavior is roundly condemned. But we shouldn't fool ourselves into thinking that staying above this minimum is a sufficient condition for being a morally decent person. I don't want to deny the importance of these socially agreed on minimums; in a less than perfect world, they provide some real protection. They are not, in principle, incompatible with caring but can, I think, encourage caring. Much caring requires collective action and without a shared sense of moral minimums it will be difficult to organize such collective action.

Elizabeth Wolgast, in *The Grammar of Justice,* argues against the claim that treating patients in a moral fashion is entirely a matter of respecting their rights.[13] She points out that patients are often sick and in need of caring for. In this situation, she argues, we want doctors and other health-care workers to care for the patient. This involves far more than respecting rights. One could talk, I suppose, about a patient's right to be cared for, but as Wolgast points out, rights talk suggests a minimum below which the doctor should not fall, and in this case, we are less interested in the minimum than in the maximum. We want all our moral citizens to be open to the obligation to care for.

Rules and rights can also be used to deliberate under some conditions. Often we don't need to appeal to rules in deciding whom to care for and how to care for them. A creature's need and our ability to meet it identifies it as a candidate for caring for. We decide how to care for by appeal to the need, the strategies for meeting it, and the desires of the one in need about how best to meet the need. But when I am not in direct contact with the objects of care, my actions cannot be guided by the expressed and observed desires of those cared for, and hence I might want to appeal to rules. In these cases, I must make assumptions about their desires. I shall assume that they do not wish to fall below some minimum. Rules that provide a minimum standard for acceptable behavior ought to be sensitive to the general desires and aims of creatures, so I may take these into account. I am also free to appeal to my needs for care and on that basis decide that I do not wish to violate some socially approved minimum standard of behavior. I can also appeal to rules and rights when care must be allocated. For example, in a hospital emergency room we must make sure that the needs of the first accident victim of the night do not cause us to ignore the later victims. Finally, since rules and rights can express a consensus about morally acceptable behavior, I should be sensitive to the expectations generated in the one cared for by the public recognition of such roles and rights. For example, suppose I want to make sure that my family and friends are happy and involved in the wedding of my son. I might be tempted to ignore the rules of etiquette in making sure that my guests are uniquely provided for. But if the mother of the bride feels slighted because I didn't treat her the way she expected to be treated (i.e., as the etiquette rules say you should treat the mother of the bride), then I haven't really responded to her in a caring manner.

One might argue here that meeting some expressed needs might violate the moral minimums in our society. I am willing to grant that this can

13. See Elizabeth Wolgast, *The Grammar of Justice* (Ithaca, N.Y.: Cornell University Press, 1987), Chapter 3.

happen. If if does, we must remember that the rules do not have a life of their own, but are guides. They help us to formulate a caring response because they speak to us of what most of us would want as a caring response in a similar situation. If the one needing care does not want the response suggested by the appropriate rule, we should listen to them very carefully and be willing to ignore the rule. For example, suppose someone wanted us to help him/her commit suicide. I suspect that ideally we could and should settle this kind of a case without appealing to rules. Instead, we should appeal to the facts of the case. Is the person terminally ill or merely depressed? These conditions require different remedies. In the first case, one might be doing the right thing to aid in the suicide. Here, one must count the cost to oneself, as well as the needs and desires of the one cared for. In the second case, we appeal beyond the expressed needs to the unexpressed needs. This person probably needs some other care. Here, we make every attempt to listen to this person, to understand his or her pain, but we also remind ourselves that suicide is the final option for dealing with pain. We make this decision, not by appeal to a rule, but by reminding ourselves of the times when we or someone we know came close to suicide. We remember how it felt and how it was resolved.

In some cases, though, I cannot respond as one caring. As I approach caring burnout, I can then appeal to rules and rights. I do not want my behavior to fall below some minimum standard, nor do I want the one in need of care to fall below some moral minimum.

In the ideal caring society with sufficient resources to meet needs and to provide for some sort of flourishing, each of us would spend roughly the same amount of time being cared for. We would experience this as children and as adults. Hence, we would be surrounded by a nexus of caring. We would be persons who cared for and were supported by a history of being cared for. We would be free, to some extent, to choose whom to care for because there would be others to provide for needs and for flourishing. We would not be totally free, because social roles would commit us to some responsibilities to care. It's not clear that rules and rights would play a very big part in this world, but this is certainly not the world in which we live.

The people in our world differ in their ability and their willingness to care for others. Since I am both a creature who can care and a creature who needs care, I would, if I were committed to caring, be faced with enormous needs for care while sometimes suffering from a lack of caring for myself. This is true even if we grant that the kind of caring (in particular, psychological caring) involved in reciprocal relationships sustains all parties in the relationship. But since such relationships don't come easily and naturally, I would have to spend some time and energy establishing a nexus of care to support myself. In creating and maintaining this nexus of care, I would be developing bonds and responsibilities of care.

But spending much of one's time getting one's own needs for care satisfied leaves little time for caring for others. At the same time, everyone else is in much the same boat. And the gross inequality in the distribution of resources means that many slip between the caring cracks and into dire need. This puts the caring person in a bind. Real need presents itself to a person who is often running a caring deficit of his or her own. Caring burnout results. The only way to effectively reduce caring burnout is to change cultural and social institutions toward a model of caring. This it not the path that our culture has taken. Instead we careen from me-firstisms to paroxysms of guilt about the tremendous needs that have resulted. We make renewed commitments to care which are rejected as softheaded a generation later.

What are caring persons to do? Caring persons should try to respond to need by caring for, but they must pay attention to their own needs for care. They must navigate through an uncaring world without falling into total caring burnout. They should work for institutions, cultures, and practices that would reduce subsistence needs by redistributing resources and increasing the supply of caretakers, and they should encourage social change toward a culture of reciprocity in meeting psychological needs. But while struggling in our pre-caring world, caring persons are not obligated to care until they slip into caring burnout. This denies their own status as persons who deserve care and is counterproductive. It diminishes, in the long run, the amount of care they can provide. As they approach caring burnout, they should refill their care tanks by taking care of their own needs. During this period of renewal, they are still required to respect the moral minimums represented by rules and rights.

I haven't talked about what the rules and rights should be. In drafting a set of rules and rights, I should be sensitive to two considerations. The first is that rules and rights provide a moral minimum. The second is that rules and rights reflect a consensus about moral minimums. In this sense, morality is the art of the possible.

The morally preferred way to live is to appeal to caring. This suggests that rules and rights should reflect a sense of what counts as need, and a conception of flourishing, and a recognition of what would usually be accepted, by the ones cared for, as appropriate ways of responding to need and providing for flourishing. Notions of need and flourishing ought to be sensitive to empirical considerations about human nature, interaction, social organization, and so on, but they also have an irreducibly normative component. A defense of rules and rights would need to defend this normative component. We would also want rules and rights that would provide a climate for moral growth toward a caring society.

Rules and rights do play an important role in my ethics of caring, but we shouldn't forget that our primary responsibility is to care for. If this means that we are often unsure about just what to do, then we must live with this uncertainty. Discovering what to do requires that we listen carefully to the ones cared for. We should also recognize that it is often painful to be confronted by those in need, and even by those whom we could enrich. Appealing to rules provides a measure of security for ourselves, but we shouldn't allow it to distance us from the objects of care.

Suggestions for Further Reading

Since Gilligan's research has inspired some of the ethical theories developed by feminist philosophers, it is helpful to read Gilligan's *In a Different Voice* (Cambridge: Harvard University Press, 1982). See *An Ethics of Care: Feminist and Interdisciplinary Perspectives* edited by Mary Jeanne Larrabee (New York: Routledge, 1993) for an excellent collection of articles critiquing and extending Gilligan's work.

Nel Noddings, *Caring: A Feminine Approach to Ethics and Moral Education* (Berkeley: University of California Press, 1984) has had a major impact of the field. See Chapter 5 of Eve Browning Cole's *Philosophy and Feminist Criticism: An Introduction* (New York: Paragon House, 1993) for an overview of feminist ethics written for the beginning student. She also includes an excellent bibliography.

You may also wish to read the other essays in *Explorations in Feminist Ethics: Theory and Practice,* from which Manning's article is taken. Also see *Women and Values: Readings in Recent Feminist Philosophy,* edited by Marilyn Pearsall (Belmont, CA: Wadsworth Publishing Co., 1986). See Chapter 7 of Jean Crimshaw's *Philosophy and Feminist Thinking* (Minneapolis: University of Minnesota Press, 1986) for a critique of some of the ideas associated with feminist ethical theories.

Chapter 4

What Makes a Society Just?

HAVE YOU EVER WONDERED, "What is justice?" Have you ever been curious about why we have governments? What is the best form of government? Who should rule? Where does the authority to rule come from? Have you ever thought, "Why should there be laws and why should we obey them? Are all people naturally wicked and need to be restrained from doing bad or forced to do good? Is it morally justifiable to break the law?" Have you noticed that we talk a lot about liberty, equality, and justice, but have a hard time defining these concepts? Should liberty be sacrificed to promote equality? Or should liberty be protected at all costs, even if it means some people won't get an equal opportunity?

Have you ever wondered, "What should the government give the people—what they want or what is good for them? Who knows what is good for them? Should the state serve the interests of the individual or should the interests of the individual be subordinate to the interests of the state?"

If you have thought about these sorts of questions, you have been concerned with the kinds of issues and problems that are normally studied by social and political philosophers. **Social and political philosophy** deal with issues of moral value at the level of the group. Political philosophy is primarily concerned with the justification of governmental authority to rule and with the nature of government or the state. Social philosophy is primarily concerned with who gets what and how. Your pursuit of your own good occurs within a social context, that is, within a context in which others are also pursuing their own good. Inevitably, in such a social context, issues of fairness, social rights and responsibilities, the limits of political and economic power, and the welfare of your fellow human beings arise.

Like ethics, social-political philosophy is normative rather than simply descriptive. For example, one goal of political philosophy is not just to describe the kinds of governments there are and how they function, but also to figure out which are the best forms of government and by what standards such a judgment can be made.

There are many issues and problems relating to social-political philosophy, and we can do no more than investigate a few of them in this chapter. However, two concepts central to many of the debates in this field are authority and justice. A government is the exercise of power and coercive force by one person or group over the rest in a society. A fundamental political question has to do with what gives one group the authority to exercise such power. **Anarchism** is the position that governments are by nature immoral and should not be established. Those who argue in favor of anarchism maintain that each individual has the ultimate moral authority to live and act as he or she chooses. It is immoral for one group to rule another, and it is immoral of you, as an individual, to surrender your moral responsibility for the conduct of your own life to another. Of course many people believe that anarchism would lead to social chaos, and so government of some kind seems necessary. But the question remains, by whose authority does one person or group rule another? And even if we grant that some kind of government is needed, the issues of what kind and what are the limits of its power must be answered.

Some people have argued that one of the purposes of government is to ensure justice, to promote a just society. But what is justice? Philosophers often distinguish among **compensatory justice, retributive justice,** and **distributive justice.** Affirmative action programs which provide for preferential treatment constitute examples of compensatory (also called "corrective") justice because they involve providing corrective benefits to persons who have suffered undeserved hardships or who have been denied benefits they deserve. The imposition of legal penalties (e.g., putting someone in prison) is an example of retributive justice because it involves placing burdens on people who have enjoyed benefits they did not deserve or who are guilty of failing to fulfill their responsibilities. Distributive justice is the fair distribution of both burdens and benefits to persons in situations of conflict of interest and relative scarcity. For example, not everyone can get into medical school, so how can we decide who should be accepted in a manner fair to all?

These three notions indicate that the concepts of fairness and desert are central to the concept of justice. But what about the notion of equality? Isn't treating everyone equally the same as treating them justly? **Egalitarians** argue that all persons, simply because they are persons, should share equally in the distribution of all benefits and burdens. But treating everyone equally may not always be the just thing to do. Paying Harry $40,000 and paying Chong the same, even though Harry has worked only five years for the company and has a poor performance record whereas Chong is a fifteen-year veteran with an excellent record, doesn't seem just. Harry and Chong are both persons, but in the case of salary should this be the only consideration? However, allowing some people, because of good luck or birth, to become extremely wealthy and others, because of misfortune or birth, to become extremely poor doesn't seem fair either. Is there a fair way to distribute wealth?

4.1. The Theocratic State

Who ought to have the ultimate authority to rule in a community? Should it be one person, several, or all people? And which type of rule is best? What are the standards we can use to judge types of states?

Aristotle (see Section 2.4) divided governments into three types: rule of one, rule of some, and rule of all. He divided these types again into those that were good because they had the common good in view and those that were bad because they had only self-interest or special interests in mind.

Type	Good	Bad
one	monarchy	tyranny
some	aristocracy	oligarchy
all	polity	democracy

It might surprise you to find **democracy** (rule by the people) listed as the bad form of the rule of all, but Aristotle believed that democracies did not promote the common good. Rather, they promote the special interests of those who are able to exercise the most influence. For Aristotle, the moral entitlement to rule derives from whether those in power have their own interest in view or the interests of all segments of society. In other words, good governments promote the common good, and they do this by making human flourishing possible.

Aristotle did not list theocracy (the theory that God and only God has the right to rule) among his governmental types, but this has been a widespread and long-lasting theory of sovereignty. The Hebrew Bible endorses a theocratic state in which a king rules with God's proxy. The monarchs of the ancient world ruled as divine stand-ins, and the emperors of China had the mandate of Heaven as their charter. During the Middle Ages the divine right of kings was a widely held political theory which said, in effect, that the moral entitlement to exercise the power to rule is a divine right, but this right can be granted by God to those of his choice. Even today in the United States one hears talk of the "restoration" of a theocratic state, and the modern world is not without its theocracies.

Most of you have probably heard of the Ayatollah Khomeini and the Islamic revolution he led in Iran. Some of you may even know that Iran is a theocratic state. But how many of you know much about the theory that justifies such a state? How many of you have ever considered whether such a form of government might constitute a legitimate alternative to a secular democracy?

Muhammad (570–632) is considered by Muslims to be a prophet of **Allah** (God). A **Muslim** is one who submits to the will of Allah, and Islam is the name of a religious community that seeks to obey the commands of Allah. According to Islam, Allah revealed his will to the prophet Muhammad. Those revelations are recorded in the *Qur'an*, the holy book of Islam. Central to Islamic practice are the **five pillars of Islam:** witnessing that there is no God but Allah and that Muhammad is his Apostle; mandatory prayers or *salat;* mandatory alms (*zakat*); fasting during the month of Ramadan; and *hajj,* or pilgrimage to Mecca.

The selection that follows analyzes and supports one kind of Islamic political theory. It was presented as a lecture to the Inter-Collegiate Muslim Brotherhood at Punjab University in Lahore, Pakistan, in October, 1939 by Abu'l A'la Mawdudi, a prominent Muslim thinker and social reformer who was born in India in 1903. His life was dedicated to the cause of an Islamic renaissance, and he spent 14 years in jail because of his political activities. World War II was beginning when this lecture was given. Mawdudi was well aware of the Fascist states of Italy and Germany (**fascism,** the view that the interests of the state are always more important than the interests of the individual, is usually associated with right-wing movements that celebrate military might and use the power of the state to stop dissent), the Communist dictatorship of the Soviet Union, and the democracies of Britain and the United States. He underscores the distinctive features of Islamic political theory in this context.

It is important to draw a distinction between **Sunni** and **Shi'a** branches of Islam. Shi'is see political authority vested by Allah in religious leaders (Imams) while Sunni's believe it was given by Allah to the whole community, not just to the religious leaders. Mawdudi belongs to the Sunni branch of Islam (about 80% to 90% of Muslims are Sunni). The kind of theocracy found in Iran and advocated by the Ayatollah Khomeini represents the Shi'a viewpoint.

It must also be noted that there are and have been many kinds of government in the Islamic world ranging from democracies to dictatorships. It is clear from Mawdudi's address that he is arguing for one kind of political theory as the most authentically Islamic, but, of course, he would not need to make such an argument if there was widespread agreement among Muslims on political matters.

Reading Questions

1. According to Mawdudi, what motivates those who claim that Islamic political ideas are in harmony with modern political theories?

2. What are the main characteristics of an Islamic state?

3. Why does the author describe Islamic government as a "theo-democracy?" In what way is it like and unlike a theocracy and in what way is it like and unlike a democracy?

4. Why has Allah (God) restricted the authority to rule (sovereignty) to himself, according to Mawdudi?

5. What, according to the author, is wrong with Western secular democracy? How would you respond in defense of democracy?

6. What are "divine limits?" Give some examples. Do you agree that they do not deprive humans of any essential liberty and that they contribute to achieving a balanced and moderate life?

7. What is the purpose of the Islamic state, and why is it universal, all-embracing, and ideological?

8. What are the implications, according to Mawdudi, of the concepts of vicegerency (popular caliphate) for society?

9. How do you think Mawdudi would answer the question, "Should the state serve the interests of the individual, or should the individual serve the interests of the state?" How would you answer it? Present an argument in support of your position.

10. How do you think Mawdudi would answer the question, "What makes a society just?"

Political Theory of Islam

ABU'L A'LA MAWDUDI

WITH CERTAIN PEOPLE it has become a sort of fashion to somehow identify Islam with one or the other system of life in vogue at the time. So at this time also there are people who say that Islam is a democracy, and by this they mean to imply that there is no difference between Islam

From The Islamic Law and Constitution, *translated by Khurshid Ahmad. Copyright © 1955, 1960 by Abu'l A'la Mawdudi. Pages 131–132; 145–161. Reprinted by permission of Islamic Publications.*

and the democracy as in vogue in the West. Some others suggest that Communism is but the latest and revised version of Islam and it is in the fitness of things that Muslims imitate the Communist experiment of Soviet Russia. Still some others whisper that Islam has the elements of dictatorship in it and we should revive the cult of "obedience to the *Amīr*" (the leader). All these people, in this misinformed and misguided zeal to serve what they hold to be the cause of Islam, are always at great pains to prove that Islam contains within itself the elements of all types of contemporary social and political thought and action. Most of the people who indulge in this prattle have no clear idea of the Islamic way of life. They have never made nor try to make a systematic study of the Islamic political order—the place and nature of democracy, social justice, and equality in it. Instead they behave like the proverbial blind men who gave altogether contradictory descriptions of an elephant because one had been able to touch only its tail, the other its legs, the third its belly and the fourth its ears only. Or perhaps they look upon Islam as an orphan whose sole hope for survival lies in winning the patronage and the sheltering care of some dominant creed. That is why some people have begun to present apologies on Islam's behalf. As a matter of fact, this attitude emerges from an inferiority complex, from the belief that we as Muslims can earn no honor or respect unless we are able to show that our religion resembles the modern creeds and it is in agreement with most of the contemporary ideologies. These people have done a great disservice to Islam; they have reduced the political theory of Islam to a puzzle, a hotchpotch. They have turned Islam into a juggler's bag out of which can be produced anything that holds a demand! Such is the intellectual plight in which we are engulfed. Perhaps it is a result of this sorry state of affairs that some people have even begun to say that Islam has no political or economic system of its own and anything can fit into its scheme.

In these circumstances it has become essential that a careful study of the political theory of Islam should be made in a scientific way, with a view to grasp its real meaning, nature, purpose and significance. Such a systematic study alone can put an end to this confusion of thought and silence those who out of ignorance proclaim that there is nothing like Islamic political theory, Islamic social order and Islamic culture. I hope it will also bring to the world groping in darkness the light that it urgently needs, although it is not yet completely conscious of such a need. . . .

First Principle of Islamic Political Theory

The belief in the Unity and the sovereignty of Allah is the foundation of the social and moral system propounded by the Prophets. It is the very starting-point of the Islamic political philosophy. The basic principle of Islam is that human beings must, individually and collectively, surrender all rights of overlordship, legislation and exercising of authority over others. No one should be allowed to pass orders or make commands *in his own right* and no one ought to accept the obligation to carry out such commands and obey such orders. None is entitled to make laws on his own authority and none is obliged to abide by them. This right vests in Allah alone:

> The Authority rests with none but Allah. He commands you not to surrender to any one save Him. This is the right way (of life). (Qur'ān 12:40)
>
> They ask: "have we also got some authority?" Say: "all authority belongs to God alone." (3:154)
>
> Do not say wrongly with your tongues that this is lawful and that is unlawful. (16:116)
>
> Whoso does not establish and decide by that which Allah has revealed, such are disbelievers. (5:44)

According to this theory, sovereignty belongs to Allah. He alone is the law-giver. No man, even if he be a Prophet, has the right to order others *in his own right* to do or not to do certain things. The Prophet himself is subject to God's commands:

> I do not follow anything except what is revealed to me. (6:50)

Other people are required to obey the Prophet because he enunciates not his own but God's commands:

> We sent no messenger save that he should be obeyed by Allah's command. (4:64)
>
> They are the people to whom We gave the Scripture and Command and Prophethood. (6:90)
>
> It is not (possible) for any human being to whom Allah has given the Scripture and the Wisdom and the Prophethood that he should say to people: Obey me instead of Allah. Such a one (could only say): be solely devoted to the Lord. (3:79)

Thus the main characteristics of an Islamic state that can be deduced from these express statements of the Holy Qur'ān are as follows:—

1. No person, class or group, not even the entire population of the state as a whole, can lay claim to sovereignty. God alone is the real sovereign; all others are merely His subjects;

2. God is the real law-giver and the authority of absolute legislation vests in Him. The believers cannot resort to totally independent legislation nor can they modify any law which God has laid down, even if the desire to effect such legislation or change in Divine laws is unanimous; and

3. An Islamic state must, in all respects, be founded upon the law laid down by God through His Prophet. The government which runs such a state will be entitled to obedience in its capacity as a political agency set up to enforce the laws of God and only in so far as it acts in that capacity. If it disregards the law revealed by God, its commands will not be binding on the believers.

The Islamic State

ITS NATURE AND CHARACTERISTICS

The preceding discussion makes it quite clear that Islam, speaking from the view-point of political philosophy, is the very antithesis of secular Western democracy. The philosophical foundation of Western democracy is the sovereignty of the people. In it, this type of absolute powers of legislation—of the determination of values and of the norms of behavior—rest in the hands of the people. Law-making is their prerogative and legislation must correspond to the mood and temper of their opinion. If a particular piece of legislation is desired by the masses, howsoever ill-conceived it may be from a religious and moral viewpoint, steps have to be taken to place it on the statute book; if the people dislike any law and demand its abrogation, howsoever just and rightful it might be, it has to be expunged forthwith. This is not the case in Islam. On this count, Islam has no trace of Western democracy. Islam, as already explained, altogether repudiates the philosophy of popular sovereignty and rears its polity on the foundations of the sovereignty of God and the vicegerency (*Khilāfah*) of man.

A more apt name for the Islamic polity would be the "kingdom of God" which is described in English as a "theocracy." But Islamic theocracy is something altogether different from the theocracy of which Europe has had a bitter experience wherein a priestly class, sharply marked off from the rest of the population, exercises unchecked domination and enforces laws of its own making in the name of God, thus virtually imposing its own divinity and godhood upon the common people. Such a system of government is satanic rather than divine. Contrary to this, the theocracy built up by Islam is not ruled by any particular religious class but by the whole community of Muslims including the rank and file. The entire Muslim population runs the state in accordance with the Book of God and the practice of His Prophet. If I were permitted to coin a new term, I would describe this system of government as a "theo-democracy," that is to say a divine democratic government, because under it the Muslims have been given a limited popular sovereignty under the suzerainty of God. The executive under this system of government is constituted by the general will of the Muslims who have also the right to depose it. All administrative matters and all questions about which no explicit injunction is to be found in the *sharī'ah* are settled by the consensus of opinion among the Muslims.[1] Every Muslim who is capable and qualified to give a sound opinion on matters of Islamic law, is entitled to interpret the law of God when such interpretation becomes necessary. In this sense the Islamic polity is a democracy. But, as has been explained above, it is a theocracy in the sense that where an explicit command of God or His Prophet already exists, no Muslim leader or legislature, or any religious scholar can form an independent judgment, not even all the Muslims of the world put together have any right to make the least alteration in it.

Before proceeding further, I feel that I should put in a word of explanation as to why these limitations and restrictions have been placed upon popular sovereignty in Islam, and what is the nature of these limitations and restrictions. It may be said that God has, in this manner, taken away the liberty of the human mind and intellect instead of safeguarding it as I was trying to prove. My reply is that God has retained the right of legislation in His own hand not in order to deprive man of his natural freedom but to safeguard that very freedom. His purpose is to save man from going astray and inviting his own ruin.

One can easily understand this point by attempting a little analysis of the so-called Western secular democracy. It is claimed that this democracy is founded on popular sovereignty. But everybody knows that the people who constitute a state do not all of them take part either in legislation or in its administration. They have to delegate their sovereignty to their elected representatives so that the latter may make and enforce laws on their behalf. For this purpose, an electoral system is set up. But as a divorce has been effected between politics and religion, and as a result of this secularization, the society and particularly its politically active elements have ceased to attach much or any importance to morality and ethics. And this is also a fact that only those persons generally come to the top who can dupe the masses by their wealth, power, and deceptive propaganda. Although these representatives come into power by the votes of the common people, they soon set themselves up as an independent authority and assume the position of overlords (*ilāhs*). They often make laws not in the best interest of the people who raised them to power but to further their own sectional and class interests. They impose their will on the people by virtue of the authority delegated to them by those over whom they rule. This is the situation which besets people in England, America and in all those countries which claim to be the haven of secular democracy.

Even if we overlook this aspect of the matter and admit that in these countries laws are made according to the wishes of the common people, it has been established by experience that the great mass of the common people are incapable of perceiving their own true interests. It is the natural weakness of man that in most of the affairs concerning his life he takes into consideration only some one aspect of reality and loses sight of other aspects. His judgments are usually one-sided and he is swayed by emotions and desires to such an extent that rarely, if ever, can he judge important matters with the impartiality and objectivity of scientific reason. Quite often he rejects the plea of reason simply because it conflicts with his passions and desires. I can cite many instances in support of this contention but to avoid prolixity I shall content myself with giving only one example: the Prohibition Law of America. It had been rationally and logically established that drinking is injurious to health, produces deleterious effects on mental and intellectual faculties and leads to disorder in human society. The American public accepted these facts and agreed to the enactment of the Prohibition Law. Accordingly the law was passed by the majority vote. But when it was put into effect, the very same people by whose vote it had been passed, revolted against it. The worst kinds of wine were illicitly manufactured and consumed, and their use and consumption became more widespread than before. Crimes increased in

1. *Sharī'ah Qur'anic* commands, together with the *Sunnah* (whatever Muhammad said or did), constitute the *Shari'ah* (which means "basic laws"). The *Sunnis* accept the *Sunnah* as authoritative, but the *Shiites* do not.—Ed.]

number, and eventually drinking was legalized by the vote of the same people who had previously voted for its prohibition. This sudden change in public opinion was not the result of any fresh scientific discovery or the revelation of new facts providing evidence against the advantages of prohibition, but because the people had been completely enslaved by their habit and could not forgo the pleasures of self-indulgence. They delegated their own sovereignty to the evil spirit in them and set up their own desires and passions as their *ilāhs* (gods) at whose call they all went in for the repeal of the very law they had passed after having been convinced of its rationality and correctness. There are many other similar instances which go to prove that man is not competent to become an absolute legislator. Even if he secures deliverance from the service of other *ilāhs*, he becomes a slave to his own petty passions and exalts the devil in him to the position of a supreme Lord. Limitations on human freedom, provided they are appropriate and do not deprive him of all initiative are absolutely necessary in the interest of man himself.

That is why God has laid down those limits which, in Islamic phraseology, are termed "divine limits." These limits consist of certain principles, checks and balances and specific injunctions in different spheres of life and activity, and they have been prescribed in order that man may be trained to lead a balanced and moderate life. They are intended to lay down the broad framework within which man is free to legislate, decide his own affairs and frame subsidiary laws and regulations for his conduct. These limits he is not permitted to overstep and if he does so, the whole scheme of his life will go awry.

Take for example man's economic life. In this sphere God has placed certain restrictions on human freedom. The right to private property has been recognized, but it is qualified by the obligation to pay *Zakāh* (poor dues) and the prohibition of interest, gambling and speculation. A specific law of inheritance for the distribution of property among the largest number of surviving relations on the death of its owner has been laid down and certain forms of acquiring, accumulat-

ing and spending wealth have been declared unlawful. If people observe these just limits and regulate their affairs within these boundary walls, on the one hand their personal liberty is adequately safeguarded and, on the other, the possibility of class war and domination of one class over another, which begins with capitalist oppression and ends in working-class dictatorship, is safely and conveniently eliminated.

Similarly in the sphere of family life, God has prohibited the unrestricted intermingling of the sexes and has prescribed *Pardah*, recognized man's guardianship of woman, and clearly defined the rights and duties of husband, wife and children.[2] The laws of divorce and separation have been clearly set forth, conditional polygamy has been permitted and penalties for fornication and false accusations of adultery have been prescribed. He has thus laid down limits which, if observed by man, would stabilize his family life and make it a haven of peace and happiness. There would remain neither that tyranny of male over female which makes family life an inferno of cruelty and oppression, nor that satanic flood of female liberty and licence which threatens to destroy human civilization in the West.

In like manner, for the preservation of human culture and society God has, by formulating the law of *Qisyāsy* (Retaliation) commanding to cut off the hands for theft, prohibiting wine-drinking, placing limitations on uncovering of one's private parts and by laying down a few similar permanent rules and regulations, closed the door of social disorder forever. I have no time to present to you a complete list of all the divine limits and show in detail how essential each one of them is for maintaining equilibrium and poise in life. What I want to bring home to you here is that through these injunctions God has provided a permanent and immutable code of behavior for man, and that it does not deprive him of any essential liberty nor does it dull the edge of his mental faculties. On the contrary,

2. [*Pardah* refers to practices of secluding women, such as veiling.—Ed.]

it sets a straight and clear path before him, so that he may not, owing to his ignorance and weaknesses which he inherently possesses, lose himself in the maze of destruction and instead of wasting his faculties in the pursuit of wrong ends, he may follow the road that leads to success and progress in this world and the hereafter. If you have ever happened to visit a mountainous region, you must have noticed that in the winding mountain paths which are bounded by deep caves on the one side and lofty rocks on the other, the border of the road is barricaded and protected in such a way as to prevent travellers from straying towards the abyss by mistake. Are these barricades intended to deprive the wayfarer of his liberty? No, as a matter of fact, they are meant to protect him from destruction; to warn him at every bend of the dangers ahead and to show him the path leading to his destination. That precisely is the purpose of the restrictions which God has laid down in His revealed Code. These limits determine what direction man should take in life's journey and they guide him at every turn and pass and point out to him the path of safety which he should steadfastly follow.

As I have already stated, this code, enacted as it is by God, is unchangeable. You can, if you like, rebel against it, as some Muslim countries have done. But you cannot alter it. It will continue to be unalterable till the last day. It has its own avenues of growth and evolution, but no human being has any right to tamper with it. Whenever an Islamic State comes into existence, this code would form its fundamental law and will constitute the mainspring of all its legislation. Everyone who desires to remain a Muslim is under an obligation to follow the Qur'ān and the Sunnah which must constitute the basic law of an Islamic State.

THE PURPOSE OF THE ISLAMIC STATE

The purpose of the state that may be formed on the basis of the Qur'ān and the *Sunnah* has also been laid down by God. The Qur'ān says:

We verily sent Our messengers with clear proofs, and revealed with them the Scripture and the Balance, that mankind may observe right measure; and We revealed iron, wherein is mighty power and (many) uses for mankind. (57:25)

In this verse steel symbolizes political power and the verse also makes it clear that the mission of the Prophets is to create conditions in which the mass of people will be assured of social justice in accordance with the standards enunciated by God in His Book which gives explicit instructions for a well-disciplined mode of life. In another place God has said:

(Muslims are) those who, if We give them power in the land, establish the system of *Ṣalāh* (worship) and *Zakāh* (poor dues) and enjoin virtue and forbid evil and inequity. (22:41)

You are the best community sent forth to mankind; you enjoin the Right conduct and forbid the wrong; and you believe in Allah. (3:110)

It will readily become manifest to anyone who reflects upon these verses that the purpose of the state visualized by the Holy Qur'ān is not negative but positive. The object of the state is not merely to prevent people from exploiting each other, to safeguard their liberty and to protect its subjects from foreign invasion. It also aims at evolving and developing that well-balanced system of social justice which has been set forth by God in His Holy Book. Its object is to eradicate all forms of evil and to encourage all types of virtue and excellence expressly mentioned by God in the Holy Qur'ān. For this purpose political power will be made use of as and when the occasion demands; all means of propaganda and peaceful persuasion will be employed; the moral education of the people will also be undertaken; and social influence as well as the force of public opinion will be harnessed to the task.

ISLAMIC STATE IS UNIVERSAL AND ALL-EMBRACING

A state of this sort cannot evidently restrict the scope of its activities. Its approach is universal and all-embracing. Its sphere of activity is coextensive with the whole of human life. It seeks to mould every aspect of life and activity in consonance with its moral norms and program of social reform. In such a state no one can regard any field of his affairs as personal and private. Considered from this aspect the Islamic state bears a kind of resemblance to the Fascist and Communist states. But you will find later on that, despite its all-inclusiveness, it is something vastly and basically different from the modern totalitarian and authoritarian states. Individual liberty is not suppressed under it nor is there any trace of dictatorship in it. It presents the middle course and embodies the best that the human society has ever evolved. The excellent balance and moderation that characterize the Islamic system of government and the precise distinctions made in it between right and wrong—elicit from all men of honesty and intelligence the admiration and the admission that such a balanced system could not have been framed by anyone but the Omniscient and All-Wise God.

ISLAMIC STATE IS AN IDEOLOGICAL STATE

Another characteristic of the Islamic State is that it is an ideological state. It is clear from a careful consideration of the Qur'ān and the *Sunnah* that the state in Islam is based on an ideology and its objective is to establish that ideology. The state is an instrument of reform and must act likewise. It is a dictate of this very nature of the Islamic State that such a state should be run only by those who believe in the ideology on which it is based and in the Divine Law which it is assigned to administer. The administrators of the Islamic state must be those whose whole life is devoted to the observance and enforcement of this Law, who not only agree with its reformatory program and fully believe in it but thoroughly comprehend its spirit and are acquainted with its details. Islam does not recognize any geographical, linguistic or colour bars in this respect. It puts forward its code of guidance and the scheme of its reform before all men. Whoever accepts this pro-

gram, no matter to what race, nation or country he may belong, can join the community that runs the Islamic state. But those who do not accept it are not entitled to have any hand in shaping the fundamental policy of the State. They can live within the confines of the State as non-Muslim citizens (*Dhimmīs*). Specific rights and privileges have been accorded to them in the Islamic Law. A *Dhimmī*'s life, property and honor will be fully protected, and if he is capable of any service, his services will also be made use of. He will not, however, be allowed to influence the basic policy of this ideological state. The Islamic state is based on a particular ideology and it is the community which believes in the Islamic ideology which pilots it. Here again, we notice some sort of resemblance between the Islamic and the Communist states. But the treatment meted out by the Communist states to persons holding creeds and ideologies other than its own bears no comparison with the attitude of the Islamic state. Unlike the Communist state, Islam does not impose its social principles on others by force, nor does it confiscate their properties or unleash a reign of terror by mass executions of the people and their transportation to the slave camps of Siberia. Islam does not want to eliminate its minorities, it wants to protect them and give them the freedom to live according to their own culture. The generous and just treatment which Islam has accorded to non-Muslims in an Islamic state and the fine distinction drawn by it between justice and injustice and good and evil will convince all those who are not prejudiced against it, that the prophets sent by God accomplish their task in an altogether different manner—something radically different and diametrically opposed to the way of the false reformers who strut about here and there on the stage of history.

The Theory of the Caliphate and the Nature of Democracy in Islam

I will now try to give a brief exposition of the composition and structure of the Islamic state. I have already stated that in Islam, God alone is the real sovereign. Keeping this cardinal principle in mind, if we consider the position of those persons who set out to enforce God's law on earth, it is but natural to say that they should be regarded as representatives of the Supreme Ruler. Islam has assigned precisely this very position to them. Accordingly the Holy Qur'ān says:

Allah has promised to those among you who believe and do righteous deeds that He will assuredly make them to succeed (the present rulers) and grant them vicegerency in the land just as He made those before them to succeed (others).

The verse illustrates very clearly the Islamic theory of state. Two fundamental points emerge from it.

1. The first point is that Islam uses the term "vicegerency" (*Khilāfah*) instead of sovereignty. Since, according to Islam, sovereignty belongs to God alone, anyone who holds power and rules in accordance with the laws of God would undoubtedly be the vicegerent of the Supreme Ruler and would not be authorized to exercise any powers other than those delegated to him.

2. The second point stated in the verse is that the power to rule over the earth has been promised to *the whole community of believers;* it has not been stated that any particular person or class among them will be raised to that position. From this it follows that all believers are repositories of the Caliphate. The Caliphate granted by God to the faithful is the popular vicegerency and not a limited one. There is no reservation in favor of any family, class or race. Every believer is a Caliph of God in his individual capacity. By virtue of this position he is individually responsible to God. The Holy Prophet has said: "Everyone of you is a ruler and everyone is answerable for his subjects." Thus one Caliph is in no way inferior to another.

This is the real foundation of democracy in Islam. The following points emerge from an analysis of this conception of popular vicegerency:

(a) A society in which everyone is a Caliph of God and an equal participant in this Caliphate, cannot tolerate any class divisions based on distinctions of birth and social position. All men enjoy equal status and position in such a society. The only criterion of superiority in this social order is personal ability and character. This is what has been repeatedly and explicitly asserted by the Holy Prophet:

No one is superior to another except in point of faith and piety. All men are descended from Adam and Adam was made of clay.

An Arab has no superiority over a non-Arab nor a non-Arab over an Arab; neither does a white man possess any superiority over a black man nor a black man over a white one, except in point of piety.

After the conquest of Mekka, when the whole of Arabia came under the domination of the Islamic state, the Holy Prophet addressing the members of his own clan, who in the days before Islam enjoyed the same status in Arabia as the Brahmins did in ancient India, said:

O people of Quraysh! Allah has rooted out your haughtiness of the days of ignorance and the pride of ancestry. O men, all of you are descended from Adam and Adam was made of clay. There is no pride whatever in ancestry; there is no merit in an Arab as against a non-Arab nor in a non-Arab against an Arab. Verily the most meritorious among you in the eyes of God is he who is the most pious.

(b) In such a society no individual or group of individuals will suffer any disability on account of birth, social status, or profession that may in any way impede the growth of his faculties or hamper the development of his personality.

Every one would enjoy equal opportunities of progress. The way would be left open for him to make as much progress as possible according to his inborn capacity and personal merits without prejudice to similar rights of other people. Thus, unrestricted scope for personal achievement has always been the hallmark of Islamic society. Slaves and their descendants were appointed as military officers and governors of provinces, and noblemen belonging to the highest families did not feel ashamed to serve under them. Those who used to stitch and mend shoes rose in the social scale and became leaders of highest order (*imāms*); weavers and cloth-sellers became judges (*muftīs*) and jurists and to this day they are reckoned as the heroes of Islam. The Holy Prophet has said:

> Listen and obey even if a negro is appointed as a ruler over you.

(c) There is no room in such a society for the dictatorship of any person or group of persons since everyone is a Caliph of God herein. No person or group of persons is entitled to become an absolute ruler by depriving the rank and file of their inherent right of Caliphate. The position of a man who is selected to conduct the affairs of the state is no more than this; that all Muslims (or, technically speaking, all Caliphs of God) delegate their Caliphate to him for administrative purposes. *He is answerable to God on the one hand and on the other to his fellow "Caliphs" who have delegated their authority to him.* Now, if he raises himself to the position of an irresponsible absolute ruler, that is to say a dictator, he assumes the character of a usurper rather than a Caliph, because dictatorship is the negation of popular vicegerency. No doubt the Islamic state is an all-embracing state and comprises within its sphere all departments of life, but this all-inclusiveness and universality are based upon the universality of Divine Law which an Islamic ruler has to observe and enforce. The guidance given by God about every aspect of life will certainly be enforced in its entirety. But an Islamic ruler cannot depart from these instructions and adopt a policy of regimentation on his own. He cannot force people to follow or not to follow a particular profession; to learn or not to learn a special art; to use or not to use a certain script; to wear or not to wear a certain dress and to educate or not to educate their children in a certain manner. The powers which the dictators of Russia, Germany and Italy have appropriated or which Ataturk has exercized in Turkey have not been granted by Islam to its *Amīr* (leader). Besides this, another important point is that in Islam *every individual is held personally answerable to God.* This personal responsibility cannot be shared by anyone else. Hence, an individual en-

joys full liberty to choose whichever path he likes and to develop his faculties in any direction that suits his natural gifts. If the leader obstructs him or obstructs the growth of his personality, he will himself be punished by God for this tyranny. That is precisely the reason why there is not the slightest trace of regimentation in the rule of the Holy Prophet and of his Rightly-Guided Caliphs; and

(d) In such a society every sane and adult Muslim, male or female, is entitled to express his or her opinion, for each one of them is the repository of the Caliphate. God has made this Caliphate conditional, not upon any particular standard of wealth or competence but only upon faith and good conduct. Therefore all Muslims have equal freedom to express their opinions.

EQUILIBRIUM BETWEEN INDIVIDUALISM AND COLLECTIVISM

Islam seeks to set up, on the one hand, this superlative democracy and on the other it has put an end to that individualism which militates against the health of the body politic. The relations between the individual and the society have been regulated in such a manner that neither the personality of the individual suffers any diminution, or corrosion as it does in the Communist and Fascist social system, nor is the individual allowed to exceed his bounds to such an extent as to become harmful to the community, as happens in the Western democracies. In Islam, the purpose of an individual's life is the same as that of the life of the community, namely, the execution and enforcement of Divine Law and the acquisition of God's pleasure. Moreover, Islam has, after safeguarding the rights of the individual, imposed upon him certain duties towards the community. In this way requirements of individualism and collectivism have been so well harmonized that the individual is afforded the fullest opportunity to develop his potentialities and is thus enabled to employ his developed faculties in the service of the community at large.

These are, briefly, the basic principles and essential features of the Islamic political theory.

Suggestions for Further Reading

A good beginning introduction to Islam is *Concept of Islam* by Mahmoud Abu-Saud (Indianapolis: American Trust Publications, 1983). Chapter 8 deals with Islamic social order. Chapter 3 of Fazlu Rahman's *Major Themes of the Qur'an* (Minneapolis: Bibliotheca Islamica, 1980) discusses Qur'anic views of society. Also see Chapter 8 "Questions of Modern Time" in Kenneth Craig and R. Marston Splight, *The House of Islam,* 3d ed. (Belmont, CA: Wadsworth, 1988).

See *Islam and Revolution: Writings and Declarations of Imam Khomeini,* translated by Hamid Algar (Berkeley: Mizam Press, 1981), for a collection of writings on Islamic politics by Khomeini himself. *Voices of Resurgent Islam,* edited by John L. Esposito (New York: Oxford University Press, 1983), and *Islam in Transition: Muslim Perspectives,* edited by John J. Donohue and John L. Esposito (New York: Oxford University Press, 1982), provide a good sampling of writings on Islamic political and social theory in the modern world.

Videos

Islam: There is No God But God (52 minutes, Insight Media) explores the appeal of Islam, one of the fastest growing religions today. Filmed in Egypt.

Islam Today (30 minutes) recounts the conflicts between traditional Islamic values and modern values and lifestyles. Produced by Films for Humanities, Inc. See also *Iran: A Revolution Betrayed* (30 minutes, Films Incorporated). See your Media Services Catalogue for more information.

4.2. The Individual and Society

Which should be given top priority, the individual or the state? Inevitably, their interests will conflict. Should the interests of the individual be sacrificed for the interests of society? How much of your freedom are you willing to give up for the sake of the common good? A **paternalistic** government believes it knows what is in the best interests of its citizens. But does it? And do we want a **totalitarian** government which believes that its entitlement to rule extends to all aspects of our life?

Classical liberalism, stemming from European political thinkers of the eighteenth century, supports the idea of individual sovereignty and advocates maximizing freedom from societal and governmental interference. The less government, the better. Indeed, the only legitimate purposes of government are to guarantee security and the individual freedoms of citizens.

John Stuart Mill (see Section 3.2) believed both paternalism and totalitarianism were unjustified. In his essay *On Liberty* (which he wrote in conjunction with his wife Harriet Taylor whose name, curiously, does not appear as an author even though Mill was a strong supporter of women's rights—see his *The Subjection of Women*) he explores the question, "What are the limits of societies' power over the individual?" He argues that society is not justified in interfering with a citizen's liberty unless there is harm or the threat of harm to others.

Mill begins with a description (not included here) of the fight of individuals against tyrannical government. He contends that liberty means the setting of limits to governmental power so that the rulers could not oppress the ruled through abuse of their power. This liberty was obtained by getting the rulers to recognize certain rights of the ruled which, if violated, justified resistance or rebellion and by establishing constitutional checks which allowed the rulers to govern only by consent of the governed. However, when governments became democratic, many thought that the elected officials would represent the will and interests of the people. Setting limits to governmental power seemed less important. Nevertheless, it became apparent that democratically elected representatives did not always represent the will of the people, but only the will of the most numerous or the most active part of the people. Hence arose the possibility of the "tyranny of the majority." At the same time it became possible for society itself, not just the State, to exercise a sort of "social tyranny" by imposing its opinions, values, and beliefs on all citizens. Social conformity emerges in democracies as a powerful force. The ideas and practices of the majority become the norm and independence of thought and nonconforming values and practices become suppressed. If protection from political despotism was required in the past, now, Mill argues, there is need for protection against social control and the pressures for conformity. Democracies have a natural tendency to try to minimize diversity and get us all to think alike.

It should be noted that Mill's ideas have inspired modern day libertarians who hold that government's primary role is the protection of its citizens, modern day liberals who believe in state regulations designed to insure the welfare of citizens, but who loath to curtail freedom of expression, and modern day conservatives who celebrate the claim "the less government the better," but do believe the government should play a role in legislating personal morality. Perhaps this is due to the fact that Mill adopts both a paternalistic attitude towards those more "backward" who have "less cultivated tastes" and a libertarian attitude towards those who are mature "rational" adults. But who gets to decide which camp you and I fall into?

Reading Questions

1. What, according to Mill, is the object of his essay?

2. Mill places some limits on his doctrine of individual sovereignty. What are those limits? Could any of those limits justify British colonialism?

3. What is the appropriate region of human liberty?

4. How does Mill defend his claim that freedom of thought and discussion should be allowed?

5. How does Mill answer the question, "How much of human life should be assigned to individuality, and how much to society?"

6. Mills denies society is founded on a social contract, yet argues that everyone who receives the protection of society owes a return to society for this benefit. In what does this "return" consist?

7. How does Mill answer the objection that his ideas amount to selfish indifference to the suffering of others?

8. How does Mill respond to the objection that his distinction between what has come to be called the private sphere and the public sphere is false because no person is an entirely isolated being and if people who practice vices are allowed to do so, they will, at the very least, provide a bad example for others?

9. What is the strongest argument against public interference in purely personal conduct?

10. Suppose somebody argues that Neo-Nazi propaganda should be censored on the grounds that it advocates violence and racism and that it may lead to Neo-Nazis gaining politi-

cal power. How do you think Mill would respond to such an argument? Would he agree or disagree? Why?

11. Mill has been criticized for assuming that greater knowledge necessarily benefits humans and for holding that only the absence of constraint is conducive to the development of the individual. Do you think these are valid criticisms? Why or why not?

12. How do you think Mill would respond to Mawdudi's claim that the Islamic state is justified in being both all-embracing and ideological?

13. How would Mill answer the question, "What makes a society just?"

On Liberty

JOHN STUART MILL

THE OBJECT OF THIS ESSAY is to assert one very simple principle, as entitled to govern absolutely the dealings of society with the individual in the way of compulsion and control, whether the means used be physical force in the form of legal penalties or the moral coercion of public opinion. That principle is, that the sole end for which mankind are warranted, individually or collectively, in interfering with the liberty of action of any of their number, is self-protection. That the only purpose for which power can be rightfully exercised over any member of a civilized community, against his will, is to prevent harm to others. His own good, either physical or moral, is not a sufficient warrant. He cannot rightfully be compelled to do or forbear because it will be better for him to do so, because it will make him happier, because, in the opinions of others, to do so would be wise or even right. These are good reasons for remonstrating with him, or reasoning with him, or persuading him, or entreating him, but not for compelling him or visiting him with any evil in case he do otherwise. To justify that, the conduct from which it is desired to deter him must be calculated to produce evil to someone else. The only part of the conduct of anyone, for which he is amenable to society, is that which concerns others. In the part which merely concerns himself, his independence is, of right, absolute. Over himself, over his own body and mind, the individual is sovereign.

It is, perhaps, hardly necessary to say that this doctrine is meant to apply only to human beings in the maturity of their faculties. We are not speaking of children, or of young persons below the age which the law may fix as that of manhood or womanhood. Those who are still in a state to require being taken care of by others, must be protected against their own actions as well as against external injury. For the same reason, we may leave out of consideration those backward states of society in which the race itself may be considered as in its nonage. The early difficulties in the way of spontaneous progress are so great, and there is seldom any choice of means for overcoming them; and a ruler full of the spirit of improvement is warranted in the use of any expedients that will attain an end, perhaps otherwise unattainable. Despotism is a legitimate mode of government in dealing with barbarians, provided the end be their improvement, and the means justified by actually effecting that end. Liberty, as a principle, has no application to any state of things anterior to the time when mankind have become capable of being improved by free and equal discussion. Until then, there is nothing for

Excerpts from On Liberty, *by John Stuart Mill (London, 1859)*

them but implicit obedience to an Akbar or a Charlemagne, if they are so fortunate as to find one. But as soon as mankind have attained the capacity of being guided to their own improvement by conviction or persuasion (a period long since reached in all nations with whom we need here concern ourselves), compulsion, either in the direct form or in that of pains and penalties for noncompliance, is no longer admissible as a means to their own good, and justifiable only for the security of others.

It is proper to state that I forego any advantage which could be derived to my argument from the idea of abstract right, as a thing independent of utility. I regard utility as the ultimate appeal on all ethical questions; but it must be utility in the largest sense, grounded on the permanent interests of a man as a progressive being. These interests, I contend, authorized the subjection of individual spontaneity to external control, only in respect to those actions of each which concern the interest of other people. If anyone does an act hurtful to others, there is a *prima facie* case for punishing him, by law, or, where legal penalties are not safely applicable, by general disapprobation. There are also many positive acts for the benefit of others, which he may rightfully be compelled to perform: such as to give evidence in a court of justice; to bear his fair share in the common defense, or in any other joint work necessary to the interest of the society of which he enjoys the protection; and to perform certain acts of individual beneficence, such as saving a fellow-creature's life, or interposing to protect the defenseless against ill-usage, things which whenever it is obviously a man's duty to do, he may rightfully be made responsible to society for not doing. A person may cause evil to others not only by his actions but by his inaction, and in either case he is justly accountable to them for the injury. The latter case, it is true, requires a much more cautious exercise of compulsion than the former. To make anyone answerable for doing evil to others is the rule; to make him answerable for not preventing evil is, comparatively speaking, the exception. Yet there are many cases clear enough and grave enough to justify that exception. . . .

But there is a sphere of action in which society, as distinguished from the individual, has, if any, only an indirect interest; comprehending all that portion of a person's life and conduct which affects only himself, or if it also affects others, only with their free, voluntary, and undeceived consent and participation. When I say only himself, I mean directly, and in the first instance; for whatever affects himself, may affect others through himself; and the objection which may be grounded on this contingency, will receive consideration in the sequel. This, then is the appropriate region of human liberty. It comprises, *first*, the inward domain of consciousness; demanding liberty of conscience in the most comprehensive sense; liberty of thought and feeling; absolute freedom of opinion and sentiment on all subjects, practical or speculative, scientific, moral or theological. The liberty of expressing and publishing opinions may seem to fall under a different principle, since it belongs to that part of the conduct of an individual which concerns other people; but, being almost of as much importance as the liberty of thought itself, and resting in great part on the same reasons, is practically inseparable from it. *Secondly,* the principle requires liberty of tastes and pursuits; of framing the plan of our life to suit our own character; of doing as we like, subject to such consequences as may follow: without impediment from our fellow-creatures, so long as what we do does not harm them, even though they should think our conduct foolish, perverse, or wrong. *Thirdly,* from this liberty of each individual, follows the liberty, within the same limits, of combinations among individuals; freedom to unite, for any purpose not involving harm to others: the persons combining being supposed to be of full age, and not forced or deceived.

No society in which these liberties are not, on the whole, respected, is free, whatever may be its form of government; and none is completely free in which they do not exist absolute and unqualified. The only freedom which deserves the name, is that of pursuing our own good in our own way, as long as we do not attempt to deprive others of theirs, or impede their efforts to obtain it. Each is the proper guardian of his own health, whether bodily, or mental and spiritual. Mankind are greater gainers by suffering each other to live as seems good to themselves, than by compelling each to live as seems good to the rest. . . .

Of the Liberty of Thought and Discussion

The time, it is to be hoped, is gone by, when any defense would be necessary of the "liberty of the press" as one of the securities against corrupt or tyrannical government. No argument, we may suppose, can now be needed against permitting a legislature or an executive, not identified in interest with the people, to prescribe opinions to them, and determine what doctrines or what arguments they shall be allowed to hear. . . . Let us suppose . . . that government is entirely at one with the people, and never thinks of exerting any power of coercion unless in agreement with what it conceives to be their voice. But I deny the right of the people to exercise such coercion, either by themselves or by their government. The power itself is illegitimate. The best government has no more title to it than the worst. It is as noxious, or more noxious, when exerted in accordance with public opinion than when in opposition to it. If all mankind minus one were of one opinion, mankind would be no more justified in silencing that one person than he, if he had the power, would be justified in silencing mankind. Were an opinion a personal possession of no value except to the owner, if to be obstructed in the enjoyment of it were simply a private injury, it would make some difference whether the injury was inflicted only on a few persons or on many. But the peculiar evil of silencing the expression of an opinion is that it is robbing the human race, posterity as well as the existing generation—those who dissent from the opinion, still more than those who hold it. If the opinion is right, they are deprived of the opportunity of exchanging error for truth; if wrong, they lose, what is almost as great a benefit, the clearer perception and livelier impression of truth produced by its collision with error.

It is necessary to consider separately these two hypotheses, each of which has a distinct branch of the argument corresponding to it. We can never be sure that the opinion we are endeavoring to stifle is a false opinion; and if we were sure, stifling it would be an evil still.

First, the opinion which it is attempted to suppress by authority may possibly be true. Those who desire to suppress it, of course, deny its truth; but they are not infallible. They have no authority to decide the question for all mankind and exclude every other person from the means of judging. To refuse a hearing to an opinion because they are sure that it is false to assume that *their* certainty is the same thing as *absolute* certainty. All silencing of discussion is an assumption of infallibility. Its condemnation may be allowed to rest on this common argument, not the worst for being common.

Unfortunately for the good sense of mankind, the fact of their fallibility is far from carrying the weight in their practical judgment which is always allowed to it in theory; for while everyone well knows himself to be fallible, few think it necessary to take any precautions against their own fallibility, or admit the supposition that any opinion of which they feel very certain may be one of the examples of the error to which they acknowledge themselves to be liable.

The objection likely to be made to this argument would probably take some such form as the following. There is no greater assumption of infallibility in forbidding the propagation of error than in any other thing which is done by public authority on its own judgment and responsibility. . . . It is the duty of governments, and of individuals, to form the truest opinions they can; to form them carefully, and never impose them upon others unless they are quite sure of being right. But when they are sure (such reasoners may say), it is not conscientiousness but cowardice to shrink from acting on their opinions and allow doctrines which they honestly think dangerous to the welfare of mankind, either in this life or in another, to be scattered abroad without restraint, because other people, in less enlightened times, have persecuted opinions now believed to be true. . . . There is no such thing as absolute certainty, but there is assurance sufficient for the purposes of human life. We may, and must, assume our opinion to be true for the guidance of our own conduct; and it is assuming no more when we forbid bad men to pervert society by the propagation of opinions which we regard as false and pernicious.

I answer, that it is assuming very much more. There is the greatest difference between presuming an opinion to be true because, with every opportunity for contesting it, it has not been refuted, and assuming its truth for the purpose of not permitting its refutation. Complete liberty of contradicting and disproving our opinion is the very condition which justifies us in assuming its truth for purposes of action; and on no other terms can a being with human faculties have any rational assurance of being right. . . .

Let us now pass to the second division of the argument, and dismissing the supposition that any of the received opinions may be false, let us assume them to be true and examine into the worth of the manner in which they are likely to be held when their truth is not freely and openly canvassed. However unwillingly a person who has a strong opinion may admit the possibility that his opinion may be false, he ought to be moved by the consideration that, however true it may be, if it is not fully, frequently, and fearlessly discussed, it will be held as a dead dogma, not a living truth. . . .

If the cultivation of the understanding consists in one thing more than in another, it is surely in learning the grounds of one's own opinions. Whatever people believe, on subjects on which it is of the first importance to believe rightly, they ought to be able to defend against at least the common objections. . . . On every subject on which difference of opinion is possible, the truth depends on a balance to be struck between two sets of conflicting reasons. Even in natural philosophy, there is always some other explanation possible of the same facts; some geocentric theory instead of heliocentric, some phlogiston instead of oxygen; and it has to be shown why that other theory cannot be the true one; and until this is shown, and until we know how it is shown, we do not understand the grounds of our opinion. But when we turn to subjects infinitely more complicated, to morals, religion, politics, social relations, and the business of life, three-fourths of the arguments for every disputed opinion consist in dispelling the appearances which favor some opinion different from it. The greatest orator, save one, of antiquity, has left it on record that he always studied his adversary's case with as great, if not still greater, intensity than even his own. What Cicero practiced as the means of forensic success requires to be imitated by all who study any subject in order to arrive at the truth. He who knows only his own side of the case knows little of that. His reasons may be good, and no one may have been able to refute them. But if he is equally unable to refute the reasons on the opposite side, if he does not so much as know what they are, he has no ground for preferring either opinion. The rational position for him would be suspension of judgment, and unless he contents himself with that, he is either led by authority or adopts, like the generality of the world, the side to which he feels most inclination. Nor is it enough that he should hear the arguments of adversaries from his own teachers, presented as they state them, and accompanied by what they offer as refutations. That is not the way to do justice to the arguments or bring them into real contact with his own mind. He must be able to hear them from persons who actually believe them, who defend them in earnest and do their very utmost for them. He must know them in their most plausible and persuasive form; he must feel the whole force of the difficulty which the true view of the subject has to encounter and dispose of, else he will never really possess himself of the portion of truth which meets and removes that difficulty. . . .

The fact . . . is that not only the grounds of the opinion are forgotten in the absence of discussion, but too often the meaning of the opinion itself. The words which convey it cease to suggest ideas, or suggest only a small portion of those they were originally employed to communicate. Instead of a vivid conception and a living belief, there remain only a few phrases retained by rote; or, if any part, the shell and husk only of the meanings is retained, the finer essence being lost. The great chapter in human history which this fact occupies and fills cannot be too earnestly studied and meditated on.

It is illustrated in the experience of almost all ethical doctrines and religious creeds. They are all full of meaning and vitality to those who originate them, and to the direct disciples of the originators. Their meaning continues to be felt in undiminished strength, and is perhaps brought out into even fuller consciousness, so long as the struggle lasts to give the doctrine or creed an ascendancy over other creeds. At last it either prevails and becomes the general opinion, or its progress stops; it keeps possession of the ground it has gained, but ceases to spread further. When either of these results has become apparent, controversy on the subject flags, and gradually dies away. The doctrine has taken its place, if not as a received opinion, as one of the admitted sects of divisions of opinion; those who hold it have generally inherited, not adopted it; and conversion from one of these doctrines to another, being now an exceptional fact, occupies little place in the thoughts of their professors. Instead of being, as at first, constantly on the alert either to defend themselves against the world or to bring the world over to them, they have subsided into acquiescence and neither listen, when they can help it, to arguments against their creed, nor trouble dissentients (if there be such) with arguments in its favor. From this time may usually be dated the decline in the living power of the doctrine. . . .

We have hitherto considered only two possibilities: that the received opinion may be false, and some other opinion, consequently, true; or that, the received opinion being true, a conflict with the opposite error is essential to a clear apprehension and deep feeling of its truth. But there is a commoner case than either of these: when the conflicting doctrines, instead of being one true and the other false, share the truth between them, and the non-conforming opinion is needed to supply the remainder of the truth of which the received doctrine embodies only a part. Popular opinions, on subjects not palpable

to sense, are often true, but seldom or never the whole truth. They are a part of the truth, sometimes a greater, sometimes a smaller part, but exaggerated, distorted, and disjointed from the truths by which they ought to be accompanied and limited. Heretical opinions, on the other hand, are generally some of these suppressed and neglected truths, bursting the bonds which kept them down, and either seeking reconciliation with the truth contained in the common opinion, or fronting it as enemies, and setting themselves up, with similar exclusiveness, as the whole truth. The latter case is hitherto the most frequent, as, in the human mind, one-sidedness has always been the rule, and many-sidedness the exception. Hence, even in revolutions of opinion, one part of the truth usually sets while another rises. Even progress, which ought to superadd, for the most part only substitutes one partial and incomplete truth for another; improvement consisting chiefly in this, that the new fragment of truth is more wanted, more adapted to the needs of the time than that which it displaces. Such being the partial character of prevailing opinions, even when resting on a true foundation, every opinion which embodies somewhat of the portion of truth which the common opinion omits ought to be considered precious, with whatever amount of error and confusion that truth may be blended. . . .

We have now recognized the necessity to the mental well-being of mankind (on which all their other well-being depends) of freedom of opinion, and freedom of the expression of opinion, on four distinct grounds, which we will now briefly recapitulate:

First, if any opinion is compelled to silence, that opinion may, for aught we can certainly know, be true. To deny this is to assume our own infallibility.

Secondly, although the silenced opinion be an error, it may, and very commonly does, contain a portion of truth; and since the general or prevailing opinion on any subject is rarely or never the whole truth, it is only by the collision of adverse opinions that the remainder of the truth has any chance of being supplied.

Thirdly, even if the received opinion be not only true, but the whole truth; unless it is suffered to be, and actually is, vigorously and earnestly contested, it will, by most of those who receive it, be held in the manner of a prejudice, with little comprehension or feeling of its rational grounds. And not only this, but fourthly, the meaning of the doctrine itself will be in danger of being lost or enfeebled, and deprived of its vital effect on the character and conduct: the dogma becoming a mere formal profession, inefficacious for good, but cumbering the ground and preventing the growth of any real and heartfelt conviction from reason or personal experience. . . .

[In the next section, entitled "Of Individuality, as One of the Elements of Well-Being," Mill argues that as long as no one is harmed, diversity of views and lifestyles need to flourish in society so that individual happiness can be achieved. Social control and conformity threatens to erase all individuality as pressure is increasingly placed on people to think and act alike. This will ultimately harm society by hindering progress through the disappearance of eccentricity, innovation, and experimentation.—Ed.]

Of the Limits to the Authority of Society Over the Individual

What, then, is the rightful limit to the sovereignty of the individual over himself? Where does the authority of society begin? How much of human life should be assigned to individuality, and how much to society?

Each will receive its proper share, if each has that which more particularly concerns it. To individuality should belong the part of life in which it is chiefly the individual that is interested; to society, the part which chiefly interests society.

Though society is not founded on a contract, and though no good purpose is answered by inventing a contract in order to deduce social obligations from it, everyone who receives the protection of society owes a return for the benefit, and the fact of living in society renders it indispensable that each should be bound to observe a certain line of conduct towards the rest. This conduct consists, *first,* in not injuring the interests of one another; or rather certain interests, which either by express legal provision or by tacit understanding, ought to be considered as rights; and *secondly,* in each person's bearing his share (to be fixed on some equitable principle) of the labors and sacrifices incurred for defending the society or its members from injury and molestation. These conditions society is justified in enforcing, at all costs to those who endeavor to withhold fulfillment. Nor is this all that society may do. The acts of an individual may be hurtful to others, or wanting in due consideration for their welfare, without going to the length of violating any of their constituted rights. The offender may then be justly punished by opinion, though not by law. As soon as any part of a person's conduct affects prejudicially the interests of others, society has jurisdiction over it, and the question whether the general welfare will or will not be promoted by interfering with it, becomes open to discussion. But there is no room for entertaining any such question when a person's conduct affects the interests of no persons besides himself, or need not affect them unless they like (all the persons concerned being of full age, and the ordinary amount of understanding). In all such cases, there should be perfect freedom, legal and social, to do the action and stand the consequences.

It would be a great misunderstanding of this doctrine to suppose that it is one of selfish indifference, which pretends that human beings have no business with each other's conduct in life, and that they should not concern themselves about the well-doing or well-being of one another, unless their own interest is involved. Instead of any diminution, there is need of a great increase of disinterested exertion to promote the good of others. But disinterested benevolence can find other instruments to persuade people to their good than whips and scourges, either of the literal or the metaphorical sort. I am the last person to undervalue the self-regarding virtues: they are only second in importance, if even second, to the social. It is equally the business of education to cultivate both. But even education works by conviction and persuasion as well as by compulsion, and it is by the former only that, when the period of education is passed, the self-regarding virtues should be inculcated. Human beings owe to each other help to distinguish the better from the worse, and encouragement to choose the former and avoid the latter. They should be forever stimulating each other to increased exercise of their higher faculties, and increased direction of their feelings and aims towards wise instead of foolish, elevating instead of degrading, objects and contemplations. But neither one person, nor any number of persons, is warranted in saying to another human creature of ripe years, that he shall not do with his life for his own benefit what he chooses to do with it. He is the person most interested in his own well-being: the interest which any other person, except in cases of strong personal attachment, can have in it, is trifling, compared with that which he himself has; the interest which society has in him individually (except as to conduct to others) is fractional, and altogether indirect; while with respect to his own feelings and circumstances, the most ordinary man or woman has means of knowledge immeasurably surpassing those that can be possessed by anyone else. The interference of society to overrule his judgment and purposes in what only regards himself must be grounded on general presumptions; which may be altogether wrong, and even if right, are as likely as not to be misapplied to individual cases, by persons no better acquainted with the circumstances of such cases than those are who look at them merely from without. In this department, therefore, of human affairs, individuality has its proper field of action. In the conduct of human beings towards one another it is necessary that general rules should for the most part be observed, in order that people may know what they have to expect; but in each person's own concerns his individual spontaneity is entitled to free exercise. Considerations to aid his judgment, exhortations to strengthen his

will, may be offered to him, even obtruded on him, by others: but he himself is the final judge. All errors which he is likely to commit against advice and warning are far outweighed by the evil of allowing others to constrain him to what they deem his good. . . .

The distinction here pointed out between the part of a person's life which concerns only himself, and that which concerns others, many persons will refuse to admit. How (it may be asked)—can any part of the conduct of a member of society be a matter of indifference to the other members? No person is an entirely isolated being; it is impossible for a person to do anything seriously or permanently hurtful to himself, without mischief reaching at least to his near connections, and often far beyond them. If he injures his property, he does harm to those who directly or indirectly derived support from it, and usually diminishes, by a greater or less amount, the general resources of the community. If he deteriorates his bodily or mental faculties, he not only brings evil upon all who depended on him for any portion of their happiness, but disqualifies himself for rendering the services which he owes to his fellow-creatures generally; perhaps becomes a burden on their affection or benevolence; and if such conduct were very frequent, hardly an offense that is committed would detract more from the general sum of good. Finally, if by his vices or follies a person does not direct harm to others, he is nevertheless (it may be said) injurious by his example; and ought to be compelled to control himself, for the sake of those whom the sight or knowledge of his conduct might corrupt or mislead.

And even (it will be added) if the consequences of misconduct could be confined to the vicious or thoughtless individual, ought society to abandon to their own guidance those who are manifestly unfit for it? If protection against themselves is confessedly due to children and persons under age, is not society equally bound to afford it to persons of mature years who are equally incapable of self-government? If gambling, or drunkenness, or incontinence, or idleness, or uncleanliness, are as injurious to happiness, and as great a hindrance to improvement, as many or most of the acts prohibited by law, why (it may be asked) should not law, so far as is consistent with practicability and social convenience, endeavor to repress these also? And as a supplement to the unavoidable imperfections of law, ought not opinion at least to organize a powerful police against these vices, and visit rigidly with social penalties those who are known to practice them? There is no question here (it may be said) about restricting individuality, or impeding the trial of new and original experiments in living. The only things it is sought to prevent are things which have been tried and condemned from the beginning of the world until now; things which experience has shown not to be useful or suitable to any person's individuality. There must be some length of time and amount of experience after which a moral or prudential truth may be regarded as established: and it is merely desired to prevent generation after generation from falling over the same precipice which has been fatal to their predecessors.

I fully admit that the mischief which a person does to himself may seriously affect, both through their sympathies and their interests, those nearly connected with him and, in a minor degree, society at large. When, by conduct of this sort, a person is led to violate a distinct and assignable obligation to any other person or persons, the case is taken out of the self-regarding class and becomes amenable to moral disapprobation in the proper sense of the term. If, for example, a man, through intemperance or extravagance, becomes unable to pay his debts, or, having undertaken the moral responsibility of a family, becomes from the same cause incapable of supporting or educating them, he is deservedly reprobated, and might be justly punished; but it is for the breach of duty to his family or creditors, not for the extravagance. If the resources which ought to have been devoted to them, had been diverted from them for the most prudent investment, the moral culpability would have been the same. George Barnwell murdered his uncle to get money for his mistress, but if he had done it to set himself up in business he would equally

have been hanged. Again, in the frequent case of a man who causes grief to his family by addiction to bad habits, he deserves reproach for his unkindness or ingratitude; but so he may for cultivating habits not in themselves vicious, if they are painful to those with whom he passes his life, or who from personal ties are dependent on him for their comfort. Whoever fails in the consideration generally due to the interests and feelings of others, not being compelled by some more imperative duty, or justified by allowable self-preference, is a subject of moral disapprobation for that failure, but not for the cause of it, nor for the errors, merely personal to himself, which may have remotely led to it. In like manner, when a person disables himself, by conduct purely self-regarding, from the performance of some definite duty incumbent on him to the public, he is guilty of a social offense. No person ought to be punished simply for being drunk; but a soldier or policeman should be punished for being drunk on duty. Whenever, in short, there is a definite damage, or a definite risk of damage, either to an individual or to the public, the case is taken out of the province of liberty and placed in that of morality or law.

But with regard to the merely contingent or, as it may be called, constructive injury which a person causes to society by conduct which neither violates any specific duty to the public, nor occasions perceptible hurt to any assignable individual except himself, the inconvenience is one which society can afford to bear, for the sake of the greater good of human freedom. If grown persons are to be punished for not taking proper care of themselves, I would rather it were for their own sake than under pretense of preventing them from impairing their capacity or rendering to society benefits which society does not pretend it has a right to exact. But I cannot consent to argue the point as if society had no means of bringing its weaker members up to its ordinary standard of rational conduct, except waiting till they do something irrational, and then punishing them, legally or morally, for it. Society has had absolute power over them during all the early portion of their existence; it has had the whole period of childhood and nonage in which to try whether it could make them capable of rational conduct in life. The existing generation is master both of the training and the entire circumstances of the generation to come; it cannot indeed make them perfectly wise and good, because it is itself so lamentably deficient in goodness and wisdom; and its best efforts are not always, in individual cases, its most successful ones; but it is perfectly well able to make the rising generation, as a whole, as good as, and a little better than, itself. If society lets any considerable number of its members grow up mere children, incapable of being acted on by rational consideration of distant motives, society has itself to blame for the consequences. Armed not only with all the powers of education, but with the ascendancy which the authority of a received opinion always exercises over the minds who are least fitted to judge for themselves, and aided by the *natural* penalties which cannot be prevented from falling on those who incur the distaste or the contempt of those who know them—let not society pretend that it needs, besides all this, the power to issue commands and enforce obedience in the personal concerns of individuals in which, on all principles of justice and policy, the decision ought to rest with those who are to abide the consequences. Nor is there anything which tends more to discredit and frustrate the better means of influencing conduct than a resort to the worse. If there be among those whom it is attempted to coerce into prudence or temperance any of the material of which vigorous and independent characters are made, they will infallibly rebel against the yoke. No such person will ever feel that others have a right to control him in his concerns, such as they have to prevent him from injuring them in theirs; and it easily comes to be considered a mark of spirit and courage to fly in the face of such usurped authority and do with ostentation the exact opposite of what it enjoins, as in the fashion of grossness which succeeded, in the time of Charles II, to the fanatical moral intolerance of the Puritans. With respect to what is said of the necessity of protecting society from the bad example set to others by the vicious or the self-indulgent, it is true that bad example may have a pernicious effect, especially the example of doing wrong to others with impunity to the wrong-doer. But we are now speaking of conduct which, while it does no wrong to others, is supposed to do great harm to the agent himself; and I do not see how those who believe this can think otherwise than that the example, on the whole, must be more salutary than hurtful, since, if it displays the misconduct, it displays also the painful or degrading consequences which, if the conduct is justly censured, must be supposed to be in all or most cases attendant on it.

But the strongest of all the arguments against the interference of the public with purely personal conduct is that, when it does interfere, the odds are that it interferes wrongly and in the wrong place. On questions of social morality, of duty to others, the opinion of the public, that is, of an overruling majority, though often wrong, is likely to be still oftener right, because on such questions they are only required to judge of their own interests, of the manner in which some mode of conduct, if allowed to be practiced, would affect themselves. But the opinion of a similar majority, imposed as a law on the minority, on questions of self-regarding conduct is quite as likely to be wrong as right, for in these cases public opinion means, at the best, some people's opinions of what is good or bad for other people, while very often it does not even mean that—the public, with the most perfect indifference, passing over the pleasure or convenience of those whose conduct they censure and considering only their own preference. There are many who consider as an injury to themselves any conduct which they have a distaste for, and resent it as an outrage to their feelings; as a religious bigot, when charged with disregarding the religious feelings of others, has been known to retort that they disregard his feelings by persisting in their abominable worship or creed. But there is no parity between the feeling of a person for his own opinion and the feeling of another who is offended at his holding it, no more than between the desire of a thief to take a purse and the desire of the right owner to keep it. And a person's taste is as much his own peculiar concern as his opinion or his purse. It is easy for anyone to imagine an ideal public which leaves the freedom and choice of individuals in all uncertain manners undisturbed and only requires them to abstain from modes of conduct which universal experience has condemned. But where has there been seen a public which set any such limit to its censorship? Or when does the public trouble itself about universal experience? In its interferences with personal conduct it is seldom thinking of anything but the enormity of acting or feeling differently from itself. . . .

Suggestions for Further Reading

See Volume 3 of *World Philosophy* for a summary and interpretation of *On Liberty*. Robert Paul Wolff in *The Poverty of Liberalism* (Boston: Beacon Press, 1968) gives a particularly insightful critique of Mill's argument. Also see Gertrude Himmelfarb, *On Liberty and Liberalism: The Case of John Stuart Mill* (New York: Alfred A. Knopf, 1974) for a balanced and thorough discussion. Both contain excellent bibliographies.

Douglas MacLean and Claudia Mills have edited a useful collection of studies evaluating various issues in liberalism. See their *Liberalism Reconsidered* (Totowa, NJ: Rowman & Allanheld, 1983).

4.3. Labor and Alienation

Should people be allowed to own their own property? That may be a startling question. We are so used to the notion of private property that it seems absurd to even ask such a question. Of course we should be able to own our own property and, furthermore, do with it as we see fit. But which society is better: One in which the wealthy are allowed to accumulate as much wealth as they can or one in which the state regulates the distribution of wealth for the sake of the common good? After all, we are not all born equal. Some of us are born into wealth and privilege. We can afford a good education, good medical care, excellent legal representation. But others of us are born into poverty. We cannot afford education, medical care, and legal counsel. Is that fair?

Adam Smith (1723–1790), in his influential book, *The Wealth of Nations*, published in 1776, argued for an economic philosophy called **laissez-faire capitalism.** He supported what has come to be called a free enterprise system. He believed that in the long run a free competitive market would work for the common good. Smith believed that even though we are all selfish by nature, the laws that guided self-interested competitors would work like an "invisible hand" to the benefit of all.

Smith argued that the value of a commodity equals the amount of labor it commands (the *labor theory of value*). Those who acquire capital or "stock" can hire labor to produce a product. If a division of labor is efficiently set up (in a famous example, Smith divided the process of making pins into eighteen different jobs, thereby increasing the number of pins per worker that could be produced), a *surplus value* over and above the expense of wages and materials will result. This profit is a repayment to the capitalists for their efforts and ingenuity.

Central to this theory is the concept of private property. John Locke (1632–1704), an English philosopher, articulated this concept long before Smith. He writes in his book *Concerning Civil Government,* that God has given nature to humans to use for their benefit. The use of nature involves human labor. Once labor is mixed with the material God has given to humans, private property results. He wrote, "Whatsoever then, he [a human being] removes out of a state that nature hath provided and left it in, he hath mixed his labor with, and joined to it something that is his own, and thereby makes it his property." Since this property is private (owned by the individual), the individual should be free to use it as he or she sees fit. Thus Locke argued for certain individual rights, among them, the right to life, liberty and the preservation of property. If those words sound at least partly familiar it is because Thomas Jefferson (1743–1826) in the *Declaration of Independence* borrowed them from Locke, but made one change, substituting the "pursuit of happiness" for "preservation of property."

The view that the freedom of the individual takes priority over the group is subject to some serious objections. For one thing, a community is more than an atomistic collection of individuals. It is an organic whole and the good of each is not necessarily the good of all. In addition, human rights go beyond leaving people alone to compete with one another. Human rights include an equal opportunity to participate in and contribute to society. The right to work under safe conditions, to have access to education, to obtain adequate medical care, to enjoy a decent standard of living and a secure retirement—there is no provision for such rights in *Laissez-faire* capitalism. And what about the intrinsic value of cooperation? Should not society promote cooperation? *Laissez-faire* capitalism promotes competition. Alienation, envy, corruption, greed—such can be the results when petty self-interest prevails.

Karl Marx (1818–1883) saw the results of Adam Smith's economic theory. He saw workers abused and degraded, children exploited, and society divided into two antagonistic classes: the *proletariat* (an urban population of wage-earning workers) and the *bourgeoisie* (the owners of production along with bankers and financiers). All this was the result of the activity of capitalists whose primary interest was to maximize profits.

Marx argued that the division of labor results in meaningless repetitive jobs that alienate workers from the product of their labors. The workers, even though they have "mixed" their labor with natural materials, do not own the result. The capitalist owns the product and can dispose of it as she or he wishes. Marx also argued that wage labor is necessarily exploitation because workers give more than they receive. If this were not the case, it would be crazy for a capitalist to hire a worker because the value produced by an hour's labor would not be worth more than the money paid for that hour's worth of work (plus materials and overhead). The so-called "surplus value" from which the capitalist makes a profit is, in fact, created by paying workers less than full value for their efforts.

Marx advocated **socialism** in place of capitalism. All citizens should own the means of production, and there should be rational planning of economic investment and growth. Production should exist for the sake of human need, not private profit. There should be a just distribution of goods and services. At first, a strong governmental role is needed in order to create such a system. But eventually, as full equality and universal prosperity are achieved, the classes will disappear and a society of naturally cooperative individuals will emerge. The need for a state will simply wither away. When this happens, **communism,** in its ideal form, will be achieved.

There are, of course, serious objections to Marx's position. For one thing, socialism, at least in centrally planned, one-party, totalitarian states, does not seem to work well.

People do not work very hard when they lack economic incentives. Voluntary cooperation is one thing, but forced cooperation is entirely different. The notion that eventually there will be a classless society and government will disappear seems to be wishful thinking. If anything, government may get stronger and more absolute. Abuse of power and costly errors may increase as control increases. The state may become more totalitarian and, while the human rights to education, employment, medical care, and shelter are insured, the human rights of free assembly, free speech, and freedom of religion are often denied.

Neither sacrificing the interests of the individual completely to the interests of the community nor sacrificing the interests of the community completely to the interests of the individual seems to be the best way to produce a just society. Perhaps this is why many economic systems have moved in a mixed direction, that is, creating a mixture of capitalism and socialism. We live today in the midst of this dynamic process.

The first selection below is from Marx's early writings, many of which were not published until this century. He is here concerned with a critique of capitalism. Socialism is a better economic system because it assures a just distribution of wealth. But before one can understand that, one has to see how capitalism not only fails to assure a just distribution of wealth, but also produces profound and damaging effects on the human psyche.

Marxist economic and political theory has had a profound impact on China. Mao Zedong (1893–1976) or Chairman Mao, as he came to be known, led the successful Communist revolution in China. In 1949 he became chairman of the central government council of the People's Republic of China. After the death of Stalin in 1953, Mao became the leading figure in the Communist world and one of its most prominent theoreticians.

In the first selection, Mao addresses the issue of freedom of thought and speech in Chinese society. Although modern communist states have gained a reputation for suppressing such freedoms, (and in 1989 the Tiananmen Square massacre lived up to that reputation), Mao argues for freedom of thought on grounds similar to Mill (see Section 4.2) at least with respect to those groups in society who are not trying to overthrow the government. In the second selection, Mao addresses the issue of democracy and how this relates to the rights people have. He invokes a vision of the Great Harmony when the need for state regulation and control will disappear.

Reading Questions

A. Questions on Reading from Karl Marx

1. What happens to the worker, what is the result of competition, and what happens to society under a capitalist system of political economy?

2. Do you think Marx is right when he claims that the wheel the political economy of capitalism sets in motion is greed?

3. What does Marx mean by alienation?

4. How does Marx answer the question, "Who owns the product of labor?"

5. What is the relationship between alienated labor and private property according to Marx?

6. Why won't paying higher wages be an equitable way to solve the problem of alienated labor?

7. What will solve the problem of alienated labor according to Marx?

8. Do you think private property is the cause of alienation as Marx claims? Why or why not?

B. Questions of the Readings from Mao Zedong

9. What conditions prompted the slogans, "Let a hundred flowers blossom," "Let a hundred schools of thought contend," and "Long-term coexistence and mutual supervision"?

10. What reasons does Mao give for the claim that it is necessary to "encourage free discussion and avoid hasty conclusions" in the arts and sciences?

11. Mao says that counter-revolutionaries and saboteurs should not have freedom of speech, but that Marxism can be criticized and wrong ideas among the people should not be suppressed. Do these two claims contradict one another? Why or why not?

12. What is the Great Harmony? Do you think a classless society without state power or political parties is ever possible? Why?

13. Who are "the people," and what does Mao mean by "democratic dictatorship?"

14. How does Mao justify the practice of a democratic dictatorship?

15. Do you think the concept of a democratic dictatorship is self-contradictory? Why?

16. Under what conditions, if any, is it justified to limit people's freedom? Is it ever justified to deny people such rights as freedom of speech, assembly, association, and religion? If so, under what circumstances?

17. How would Marx and Mao answer the question, "What makes a society just?"

Economic and Philosophical Manuscripts of 1844

KARL MARX

WE HAVE PROCEEDED from the premises of political economy. We have accepted its language and its laws. We presupposed private property, the separation of labor, capital and land, and of wages, profit of capital and rent of land—likewise division of labor, competition, the concept of exchange-value, etc. On the basis of political economy itself, in its own words, we have shown that the worker sinks to the level of a commodity and becomes indeed the most wretched of commodities; that the wretchedness of the worker is in inverse proportion to the power and magnitude of his production; that the necessary result of competition is the accumulation of capital in a few hands, and thus the restoration of monopoly in a more terrible form; and that finally the distinction between capitalist and land rentier, like that between the tiller of the soil and the factory worker, disappears and that the whole of society must fall apart into the two classes—the property *owners* and the propertyless *workers*.

Political economy starts with the fact of private property, but it does not explain it to us. It expresses in general, abstract formulas the *material* process through which private property actually passes, and these formulas it then takes for *laws*. It does not *comprehend* these laws, i.e., it does not demonstrate how they arise from the very nature of private property. Political economy does not disclose the source of the division between labor and capital, and between capital and land. When, for example, it defines the relationship of wages to profit, it takes the interest of the capitalists to be the ultimate cause, i.e., it takes for granted what it is supposed to explain. Similarly, competition comes in everywhere. It is explained from external circumstances. As to how far these external and apparently accidental circumstances are but the expression of a necessary course of development, political economy teaches us nothing. We have seen how exchange itself appears to it as an accidental fact. The only wheels which political economy sets in motion are *greed* and the war *amongst the greedy—competition.* . . .

We proceed from an economic fact *of the present.*

The worker becomes all the poorer the more wealth he produces, the more his production increases in power and size. The worker becomes an ever cheaper commodity the more commodities he creates. With the *increasing value* of the world of things proceeds in direct proportion the *devaluation* of the world of men.

Labor produces not only commodities, it produces itself and the worker as a *commodity*—and this in the same general proportion in which it produces commodities.

The fact expresses merely that the object which labor produces—labor's product—confronts it as *something alien,* as a *power independent* of the producer. The product of labor is labor which has been embodied in an object, which has become material: it is the *objectifications* of labor. Labor's realization is its objectification. In the sphere of political economy this realization of labor appears as *loss of realization* for the workers: objectification as *loss of the object* and *bondage to it;* appropriation as *estrangement,* as *alienation.* . . .

The *alienation* of the worker in his product means not only that this labor becomes an object, an *external existence,* but that it exists *outside him,* independently, as something alien to him, and that it becomes a power on its own confronting him. It means that the life which he has conferred on the object confronts him as something hostile and alien. . . .

Political economy conceals the estrangement inherent in the nature of labor by not considering the direct relationship between the worker (labor) *and production.* It is true that labor produces for the rich wonderful things—but for the worker it produces privation. It produces palaces—but for the worker, hovels. It produces beauty—but for the worker, deformity. It replaces labor by machines, but it throws a section of the workers back to a barbarous type of labor, and it turns the other workers into machines. It produces intelligence—but for the worker stupidity, cretinism. . . .

What, then, constitutes the alienation of labor?

First, the fact that labor is *external* to the worker, i.e., it does not belong to his essential being; that in his work, therefore, he does not affirm himself but denies himself, does not feel content but unhappy, does not develop freely his physical and mental energy but mortifies his body and ruins his mind. The worker therefore only feels himself outside his work, and in his work feels outside himself. He is at home when he is not working, and when he is working he is not at home. His labor is therefore not voluntary, but coerced, it is *forced labor.* It is therefore not the satisfaction of a need; it is merely a *means* to satisfy needs external to it. Its alien character emerges clearly in the fact that as soon as no physical or other compulsion exists, labor is shunned like the plague. External labor, labor in which man alienates himself, is a labor of self-sacrifice, of mortification. Lastly, the external character of labor for the worker appears in the fact that it is not his own, but someone else's, that it does not belong to him, that in it he belongs, not to himself, but to another. Just as in religion the spontaneous activity of the human imagination, of the human brain and the human heart, operates independently of the individual—that is, operates on him as an alien, divine or diabolical activity—so is the worker's activity not his spontaneous activity. It belongs to another; it is the loss of his self. . . .

We took our departure from a fact of political economy—the estrangement of the worker and his production. We have formulated this fact in conceptual terms as *estranged, alienated* labor. We have analyzed this concept—hence analyzing merely a fact of political economy.

Let us now see, further, how the concept of estranged, alienated labor must express and present itself in real life.

If the product of labor is alien to me, if it confronts me as an alien power, to whom, then, does it belong?

If my own activity does not belong to me, if it is an alien, a coerced activity, to whom, then, does it belong?

To a being *other* than myself.

Who is this being? . . .

If the product of labor does not belong to the worker, if it confronts him as an alien power, then this can only be because it belongs to some *other man than the worker.* If the worker's activity is a torment to him, to another it must be *delight* and his life's joy. Not the gods, not nature, but only man himself can be this alien power over man.

We must bear in mind the previous proposition that man's relation to himself only becomes for him *objective* and *actual* through his relation to the other man. Thus, if the product of his labor, his labor *objectified,* is for him an *alien,* hostile, powerful object independent of him, then his position towards it is such that someone else is master of this object, someone who is alien, hostile, powerful, and independent of him. If his own activity is to him related as an unfree activity, then he is related to it as an activity performed in the service, under the dominion, the coercion, and the yoke of another man. . . .

Through *estranged, alienated labor,* then, the worker produces the relationship to this labor of a man alien to labor and standing outside it. The relationship of the worker to labor creates the relation to it of the capitalist (or whatever one chooses to call the master of labor). *Private property* is thus the product, the result, the necessary consequence, of *alienated labor,* of the external relation of the worker to nature and to himself.

Private property thus results by analysis from the concept of *alienated labor,* i.e., of *alienated man,* of estranged labor, of estranged life, of *estranged* man.

True, it is as a result of the *movement of private property* that we have obtained the concept of *alienated labor* (*of alienated life*) from political economy. But on analysis of this concept it becomes clear that though private property appears to be the source, the cause of alienated labor, it is rather its consequence, just as the gods are *originally* not the cause but the effect of man's intellectual confusion. Later this relationship becomes reciprocal.

Only at the last culmination of the development of private property does this, its secret, appear again, namely, that on the one hand, it is the *product* of alienated labor, and that on the other it is the *means* by which labor alienates itself, the *realization of this alienation.*

This exposition immediately sheds light on various hitherto unsolved conflicts.

1. Political economy starts from labor as the real soul of production, yet to labor it gives nothing, and to private property everything. Confronting this contradiction, Proudhon has decided in favor of labor against private property. We understand, however, that this apparent contradiction is the contradiction of *estranged labor* with itself, and that political economy has merely formulated the laws of estranged labor.

We also understand, therefore, that *wages* and *private property* are identical: since the product, as the object of labor, pays for labor itself, therefore, the wage is but a necessary consequence of labor's estrangement. After all, in the wage of labor, labor does not appear as an end in itself, but as the servant of the wage. We shall develop this point later, and meanwhile will only derive some conclusions.

An enforced increase of wages (disregarding all other difficulties, including the fact that it would only be by force, too, that higher wages, being an anomaly, could be maintained) would therefore be nothing but *better payment for the slave,* and would not win either for the worker or for labor their human status and dignity.

Indeed, even the *equality of wages* demanded by Proudhon only transforms the relationship of the present-day worker to his labor into the relationship of all men to labor. Society is then conceived as an abstract capitalist.

Wages are a direct consequence of estranged labor, and estranged labor is the direct cause of private property. The downfall of the one must involve the downfall of the other.

2. From the relationship of estranged labor to private property it follows further that the emancipation of society from private property, etc., from servitude, is expressed in the *political* form of the *emancipation of the workers*, not that *their* emancipation alone is at stake, but because the emancipation of the workers contains universal human emancipation—and it contains this, because the whole of human servitude is involved in the relation of the worker to production, and every relation of servitude is but a modification and consequence of this relation. . . .

Let a Hundred Flowers Blossom

MAO ZEDONG

"LET A HUNDRED FLOWERS BLOSSOM, let a hundred schools of thought contend" and "long-term coexistence and mutual supervision"—how did these slogans come to be put forward? They were put forward in the light of China's specific conditions, on the basis of the recognition that various kinds of contradictions still exist in socialist society, and in response to the country's urgent need to speed up its economic and cultural development. Letting a hundred flowers blossom and a hundred schools of thought contend is the policy for promoting the progress of the arts and the sciences and a flourishing socialist culture in our land. Different forms and styles in art should develop freely and different schools in science should contend freely. We think that it is harmful to the growth of art and science if administrative measures are used to impose one particular style of art or school of thought and to ban another. Questions of right and wrong in the arts and sciences should be settled through free discussion in artistic and scientific circles and through practical work in these fields. They should not be settled in summary fashion. A period of trial is often needed to determine whether something is right or wrong. Throughout history, new and correct things have often failed at the outset to win recognition from the majority of people and have had to develop by twists and turns in struggle. Often correct and good things have first been regarded not as fragrant flowers but as poisonous weeds. Copernicus' theory of the solar system and Darwin's theory of evolution were once dismissed as erroneous and had to win through over bitter opposition. Chinese history offers many similar examples. In a socialist society, conditions for the growth of the new are radically different from and far superior to those in the old society. Nevertheless, it still often happens that new, rising forces are held back and rational proposals constricted. Moreover, the growth of new things may be hindered in the absence of deliberate suppression simply through lack of discernment. It is therefore necessary to be careful about questions of right and wrong in the arts and sciences, to encourage free discussion and avoid hasty conclusions. We believe that such an attitude can help to ensure a relatively smooth development of the arts and sciences.

People may ask, since Marxism is accepted as the guiding ideology by the majority of the people in our country, can it be criticized? Certainly it can. Marxism is scientific truth and fears no criticism. If it did, and if it could be overthrown by criticism, it would be worthless. In fact, aren't the idealists criticizing Marxism every day and in every way? Aren't those who harbor bourgeois and petty-bourgeois ideas and do not wish to change—aren't they also criticizing Marxism in every way? Marxists should not be afraid of criticism from any quarter. Quite the contrary, they need to temper and develop themselves and win new positions in the teeth of criticism and in the storm and stress of struggle. Fighting against wrong ideas is like being vaccinated—a man develops greater immunity from disease as a result of vaccination. Plants raised in hot-houses are unlikely to be sturdy. Carrying out the policy of letting a hundred flowers blossom and a hundred schools of thought contend will not weaken but strengthen the leading position of Marxism in the ideological field.

What should our policy be towards non-Marxist ideas? As far as unmistakable counter-revolutionaries and saboteurs of the socialist cause are concerned, the matter is easy: we sim-

ply deprive them of their freedom of speech. But incorrect ideas among the people are quite a different matter. Will it do to ban such ideas and deny them any opportunity for expression? Certainly not. It is not only futile but very harmful to use summary methods in dealing with ideological questions among the people, with questions concerned with man's mental world. You may ban the expression of wrong ideas, but the ideas will still be there. On the other hand, if correct ideas are pampered in hot-houses without being exposed to the elements or immunized from disease, they will not win out against erroneous ones. Therefore, it is only by employing the method of discussion, criticism and reasoning that we can really foster correct ideas and overcome wrong ones, and that we can really settle issues.

On the People's Democratic Dictatorship

MAO ZEDONG

THE FIRST OF JULY 1949 marks the fact that the Communist Party of China has already lived through 28 years. Like a man, a political party has its childhood, youth, manhood and old age. The Communist Party of China is no longer a child or a lad in his teens but has become an adult. When a man reaches old age, he will die; the same is true of a party. When classes disappear, all instruments of class struggle—parties and the state machinery—will lose their function, cease to be necessary, therefore gradually wither away and end their historical mission; and human society will move to a higher stage. We are the opposite of the political parties of the bourgeoisie. They are afraid to speak of the ex-

tinction of classes, state power and parties. We, on the contrary, declare openly that we are striving hard to create the very conditions which will bring about their extinction. The leadership of the Communist Party and the state power of the people's dictatorship are such conditions. Anyone who does not recognize this truth is no communist. Young comrades who have not studied Marxism-Leninism and have only recently joined the Party may not yet understand this truth. They must understand it—only then can they have a correct world outlook. They must understand that the road to the abolition of classes, to the abolition of state power and to the abolition of parties is the road all mankind must take; it is

These excerpts are from an address given June 30, 1949 in commemoration of the Twenty-eighth Anniversary of the Communist Party of China. Selected Works, *Volume IV. pp. 411–412; 417–419. Reprinted by permission of Foreign Languages Press. Footnotes deleted.*

only a question of time and conditions. Communists the world over are wiser than the bourgeoisie, they understand the laws governing the existence and development of things, they understand dialectics and they can see farther. The bourgeoisie does not welcome this truth because it does not want to be overthrown. To be overthrown is painful and is unbearable to contemplate for those overthrown, for example, for the Kuomintang reactionaries whom we are now overthrowing and for Japanese imperialism which we together with other peoples overthrew some time ago. But for the working class, the laboring people and the Communist Party the question is not one of being overthrown, but of working hard to create the conditions in which classes, state power and political parties will die out very naturally and mankind will enter the realm of Great Harmony. We have mentioned in passing the long-range perspective of human progress in order to explain clearly the problems we are about to discuss. . . .

"You are dictatorial." My dear sirs, you are right, that is just what we are. All the experience the Chinese people have accumulated through several decades teaches us to enforce the people's democratic dictatorship, that is, to deprive the reactionaries of the right to speak and let the people alone have that right.

Who are the people? At the present stage in China, they are the working class, the peasantry, the urban petty bourgeoisie and the national bourgeoisie. These classes, led by the working class and the Communist Party, unite to form their own state and elect their own government; they enforce their dictatorship over the running dogs of imperialism—the landlord class and bureaucrat-bourgeoisie, as well as the representatives of those classes, the Kuomintang reactionaries and their accomplices—suppress them, allow them only to behave themselves and not to be unruly in word or deed.[1] If they speak or act in an unruly way, they will be promptly stopped and punished. Democracy is practiced within the ranks of the people, who enjoy the rights of freedom of speech, assembly, association and so on. The right to vote belongs only to the people, not to the reactionaries. The combination of these two aspects, democracy for the people and dictatorship over the reactionaries, is the people's democratic dictatorship.

Why must things be done this way? The reason is quite clear to everybody. If things were not done this way, the revolution would fail, the people would suffer, the country would be conquered.

"Don't you want to abolish state power?" Yes, we do, but not right now; we cannot do it yet. Why? Because imperialism still exists, because domestic reaction still exists, because classes still exist in our country. Our present task is to strengthen the people's state apparatus—mainly the people's army, the people's police and the people's courts—in order to consolidate national defense and protect the people's interests. Given this condition, China can develop steadily, under the leadership of the working class and the Communist Party, from an agricultural into an industrial country and from a new-democratic into a socialist and communist society, can abolish classes and realize the Great Harmony. The state apparatus, including the army, the police and the courts, is the instrument by which one class oppresses another. It is an instrument for the oppression of antagonistic classes; it is violence and not "benevolence." "You are not benevolent!" Quite so. We definitely do not apply a policy of benevolence to the reactionaries and towards the reactionary activities of the reactionary classes. Our policy of benevolence is applied only within the ranks of the people, not beyond them to the reactionaries or to the reactionary activities of reactionary classes.

The people's state protects the people. Only when the people have such a state can they educate and remould themselves by democratic methods on a country-wide scale, with everyone taking part, and shake off the influence of domestic and foreign reactionaries (which is still very strong, will survive for a long time, and cannot be quickly destroyed), rid themselves of the bad habits and ideas acquired in the old society, not allow themselves to be led astray by the

---

1. The Kuomintang were once allied with Mao and the Communists, but split in 1927.

reactionaries, and continue to advance—to advance towards a socialist and communist society.

Here, the method we employ is democratic, the method of persuasion, not of compulsion. When anyone among the people breaks the law, he too should be punished, imprisoned or even sentenced to death; but this is a matter of a few individual cases, and it differs in principle from the dictatorship exercised over the reactionaries as a class.

As for the members of the reactionary classes and individual reactionaries, so long as they do not rebel, sabotage or create trouble after their political power has been overthrown, land and work will be given to them as well in order to allow them to live and remould themselves through labor into new people. If they are not willing to work, the people's state will compel them to work. Propaganda and educational work will be done among them too and will be done, moreover, with as much care and thoroughness as among the captured army officers in the past. This, too, may be called a "policy of benevolence" if you like, but it is imposed by us on the members of the enemy classes and cannot be mentioned in the same breath with the work of self-education which we carry on within the ranks of the revolutionary people.

Such remoulding of members of the reaction-ary classes can be accomplished only by a state of the people's democratic dictatorship under the leadership of the Communist Party. When it is well done, China's major exploiting classes, the landlord class and the bureaucrat-bourgeoisie (the monopoly capitalist class), will be eliminated for good. There remain the national bourgeoisie; at the present stage, we can already do a good deal of suitable educational work with many of them. When the time comes to realize socialism, that is, to nationalize private enterprise, we shall carry the work of educating and remoulding them a step further. The people have a powerful state apparatus in their hands—there is no need to fear rebellion by the national bourgeoisie.

The serious problem is the education of the peasantry. The peasant economy is scattered, and the socialization of agriculture, judging by the Soviet Union's experience, will require a long time and painstaking work. Without socialization of agriculture, there can be no complete, consolidated socialism. The steps to socialize agriculture must be co-ordinated with the development of a powerful industry having state enterprise as its backbone. The state of the people's democratic dictatorship must systematically solve the problems of industrialization. Since it is not proposed to discuss economic problems in detail in this article, I shall not go into them further.

Suggestions for Further Reading

See Jean Baechler's *The Origins of Capitalism,* translated by Barry Cooper (New York: St. Martin's Press, 1976), for a discussion of the nature and history of capitalism.

Marx and Marxisms, edited by G.H.R. Parkinson (New York: Cambridge University Press, 1982), provides a collection of evaluations of issues involved in Marxism. See *World Philosophy,* Volume 3, for summary and critical discussion of Marx's early writings as well as a good beginning bibliography. H. P. Adams discusses Marx's early views in *Karl Marx: In His Earlier Writings* (New York: Russell & Russell, 1965) as Dirk J. Struik in the "Introduction" to the volume from which the selection on Marx has been taken. See Tom Bottomore's edited collection of essays on Marx in *Karl Marx* (Englewood Cliffs, N.J.: Prentice-Hall, 1973). Anne Fremantle has edited *Mao Tse-Tung: An Anthology of His Writings* (New York: New American Library, 1962), which provides an overview of Mao's political, strategic, and philosophical works.

Videos

Mao by Mao (20 minutes, Films for the Humanities, P.O. Box 2053, Princeton, N.J. 08543-2053) shows scenes from Mao's life with a voiceover of his views and sayings.

4.4. Our Obligation to the State

In Chapter 2 we left Socrates condemned to death by the Athenian court. His execution is delayed because of a religious festival, and his friends make plans for his escape from prison. Crito goes to Socrates and tries to persuade him to leave. Socrates argues that the right thing for him to do is to obey the law. This is a surprising argument because in the *Apology* he made it quite clear that his mission to search for the truth was of more value than conforming to the laws of Athens. Even if the Athenians should order him to stop his activities, he would continue because, as he so dramatically puts it, "the unexamined life is not worth living."

So why does Socrates argue now that he should obey the laws of Athens and drink the hemlock? Should all laws be obeyed just because they are legally established? Where do governments get the authority to pass laws? Where do they get the authority to take human life? If the laws are bad laws, isn't it right to break them? If someone is unjustly condemned, isn't it right for them to try to escape punishment? Or is it morally right to suffer the consequences of your actions, even if what you did was right?

At one point in his argument, Socrates makes an allusion to an implied agreement that he has with the state. According to this agreement, the city-state of Athens had provided him and his family with certain benefits in return for his promise to keep the laws. By living in Athens he has tacitly entered into a contract and to break that contract now would be dishonest. Here we find the seeds for what has emerged as one of the dominant modern Western theories of political authority, the theory of the **social contract.**

Social contract theory states that the authority of government derives from a voluntary agreement among all the people to form a political community and to obey the laws passed by a government they collectively select. Thomas Hobbes (1588–1679), in his book *Leviathan,* imagined a state of nature that was presocial. This condition he characterized as a "war of all against all" in which people pursued their own self-interest and the only right was the right to self-preservation. Rationality and the desire for self-preservation eventually made it clear that peace was a desirable goal and that the only way to secure this was to give the "sword of sovereignty" to someone who could guarantee order.

Jean-Jacques Rousseau (1712–1778), in his book *Social Contract,* rejected Hobbes's view that humans are by nature selfish and warlike. Human nature is basically good, he argued; evil arises with society. Civilization corrupts us. But even though we are born free and good, we are bound together in a social contract and obliged to obey the decisions of the group to which our agreement has bound us. Individually we have unique desires and interests that express our individual will. But as voting citizens of a community, we manifest the "general will" of the group, and it is this general will that forms the foundation of political authority.

Social contract theory makes clear how closely political theories are tied to theories of human nature. If we think humans are by nature evil, governments will be seen as necessary goods that restrain evil and prevent chaos. Governments provide law and order. The stronger the government, the better. If we think humans are by nature good, governments will be seen as necessary evils that hamper free and spontaneous expression. Governments restrict our freedom, and the less government, the better. (See Section 10.1 for a further discussion of this issue in the context of Confucian philosophy.)

Reading Questions

1. What are Crito's main arguments in favor of Socrates' escape?
2. Socrates first responds by stating certain principles with which he gets Crito to agree. What are these principles?
3. Socrates imagines the laws of Athens speaking to him. What are the most important points made in support of not escaping in this speech?
4. Socrates asserts that "the really important thing is not to live, but to live well." Do you agree or not? Why?
5. Assume you are Crito. Offer to Socrates your best argument for escaping which does not cause him to violate his principles.
6. Do you think the government is, as Socrates asserts, like your parents? Why?
7. Does living in a country amount to a tacit promise on your part to obey *all* its laws? Why or why not?
8. What do you think Socrates should do and why?
9. Create an analytical question about this selection and answer it.

Crito

PLATO

Socrates: WHY HAVE YOU COME at this hour, Crito? It must be quite early?

Crito: Yes, it certainly is.

Soc: What time is it?

Cr: The dawn is breaking.

Soc: I am surprised the keeper of the prison let you in.

Cr: He knows me because I come often, Socrates, and he owes me a favor.

Soc: Did you just get here?

Cr: No, I came some time ago.

Soc: Why did you sit and say nothing instead of waking me at once?

Cr: Why, indeed, Socrates, I myself would rather not have all this sleeplessness and sorrow. I have been wondering at your peaceful slumber and that was the reason why I did not (wake) you. I wanted you to be out of pain. I always thought you fortunate in your calm temperament but I never saw anything like the easy, cheerful way you bear this calamity.

Soc: Crito, when a man reaches my age he should not fear approaching death.

Cr: Other men of your age in similar situations fear death.

Soc: That may be. But you have not told me why you come at this early hour.

Cr: I bring you a sad and painful message; not sad, as I believe, for you, but to all of us who are your friends and saddest of all to me.

Soc: Has the ship come from Delos, on the arrival of which I am to die?

Cr: No, the ship has not actually arrived, but it will probably be here today because people who came from Sunium tell me they left it there. Therefore tomorrow, Socrates, will be the last day of your life.

Soc: Very well, Crito. If it is the will of the

The original translation is by Benjamin Jowett and has been revised and updated by Christopher Biffle, A Guided Tour of Five Works by Plato *(Mountain View, CA: Mayfield, 1988), pp. 57–67. Reprinted by permission of Mayfield Publishing Company.*

gods, I am willing but I believe there will be a delay of a day.

Cr: Why do you say that?

Soc: I will tell you. I am to die on the day after the arrival of the ship?

Cr: Yes, that is what the authorities say.

Soc: I do not think the ship will be here until tomorrow. I had a dream last night, or rather only just now, when you fortunately allowed me to sleep.

Cr: What was your dream?

Soc: I saw the image of a wondrously beautiful woman, clothed in white robes, who called to me and said: "O Socrates, the third day hence to fertile Phthia shalt thou go."

Cr: What a strange dream, Socrates!

Soc: I think there can be no doubt about the meaning, Crito.

Cr: Perhaps the meaning is clear to you. But, oh my beloved Socrates, let me beg you once more to take my advice and escape! If you die I shall not only lose a friend who can never be replaced, but there is another evil: People who do not know you and me will believe I might have saved you if I had been willing to spend money, but I did not care to do so. Now, can there be a worse disgrace than this—that I should be thought to value money more than the life of a friend? The many will not be persuaded I wanted you to escape and you refused.

Soc: But why, my dear Crito, should we care about the opinion of the many? Good men, and they are the only persons worth considering, will think of these things as they happened.

Cr: But do you see, Socrates, the opinion of the many must be regarded, as is clear in your own case, because they can do the very greatest evil to anyone who has lost their good opinion.

Soc: I only wish, Crito, they could. Then they could also do the greatest good and that would be excellent. The truth is, they can do neither good nor evil. They cannot make a man wise or make him foolish and whatever they do is the result of chance.

Cr: Well, I will not argue about that. But please tell me, Socrates, if you are acting out of concern for me and your other friends. Are you afraid if you escape we may get into trouble with the informers for having stolen you away and lose either the whole or a great part of our property, or even a worse evil may happen to us? Now, if this is your fear, be at ease. In order to save you we should surely run this, or even a greater, risk. Be persuaded, then, and do as I say.

Soc: Yes, Crito, that is one fear which you mention, but by no means the only one.

Cr: Do not be afraid. There are persons who at no great cost are willing to save you and bring you out of prison. As for the informers, they are reasonable in their demands, a little money will satisfy them. My resources, which are ample, are at your service and if you are troubled about spending all mine, there are strangers who will give you theirs. One of them, Simmias the Theban, brought a sum of money for this very purpose. Cebes and many others are willing to spend their money, too. I say therefore, do not hesitate about making your escape and do not say, as you did in the court, you will have difficulty in knowing what to do with yourself if you escape. Men will love you in other places you may go and not only in Athens. There are friends of mine in Thessaly, if you wish to go to them, who will value and protect you and no Thessalian will give you any trouble. Nor can I think you are justified, Socrates, in betraying your own life when you might be saved. This is playing into the hands of your enemies and destroyers. Besides, I say you are betraying your children. You should bring them up and educate them; instead you go away and leave them, and they will have to grow up on their own. If they do not meet with the usual fate of orphans, there will be small thanks to you. No man should bring children into the world who is unwilling to continue their nurture and education. You are choosing the easier part, as I think, not the better and manlier, which you should as one who professes virtue in all his actions. Indeed, I am ashamed not only of you, but of us, your friends, when I think this entire business of yours will be attributed to our lack of courage. The trial need never have started or might have been brought to another conclusion. The end of it all, which is the crowning absurdity, will seem to have been permitted by us, through cowardice and baseness, who might have saved you. You might have saved yourself, if we had been good for anything, for there was no difficulty in escaping, and we did not see how disgraceful, Socrates, and also miserable all this will be to us as well as to you. Make up your mind then. Or rather, have your mind already made up, for the time of deliberation is over. There is only one thing to be done, which must be done if at all this very night, and which any delay will render all but impossible. I plead with you therefore, Socrates, to be persuaded by me, and do as I say.

Soc: Dear Crito, your zeal is invaluable if right. If wrong, the greater the zeal the greater the evil. Therefore we must consider whether these things should be done or not. I am, and always have been, someone who must be guided by reason, whatever the reason may be which, upon reflection, appears to me to be the best. Now that this misfortune has come upon me, I cannot put away my old beliefs. The principles I honored and revered I still honor and unless we can find other and better principles, I will not agree with you. I would not even if the power of the multitude could inflict many more imprisonments, confiscations and deaths, frightening us like children with foolish terrors.

What will be the best way of considering the question? Shall I return to your old argument about the opinions of men, some of which should be considered, and others, as we were saying, are not to be considered. Now were we right in maintaining this before I was condemned? And has the argument which was once good, now proved to be talk for the sake of talking—in fact an amusement only and altogether foolish? That is what I want to consider with your help, Crito: whether, under my present circumstances, the argument appears to be in any way different or not and is to be followed by me or abandoned. That argument, I believe, is held by many who claim to be authorities, was to the effect, that the opinions of some men are to be considered and of other men not to be considered. Now you, Crito, are not going to die tomorrow—at least,

there is no probability of this. You are therefore not likely to be deceived by the circumstances in which you are placed. Tell me, then, whether I am right in saying that some opinions are to be valued and other opinions are not to be valued. I ask you whether I was right in believing this?

Cr: Certainly.

Soc: The good opinions are to be believed and not the bad?

Cr: Yes.

Soc: And the opinions of the wise are good and the opinions of the foolish are evil?

Cr: Certainly.

Soc: And what was said about another matter? Is the gymnastics student supposed to attend to the praise and blame and opinion of every man, or of one man only—his physician or trainer, whoever that is?

Cr: Of one man only.

Soc: And he should fear the blame and welcome praise of that one only, and not of the many?

Cr: That is clear.

Soc: He should live and train, eat and drink in the way which seems good to his single teacher who has understanding, rather than according to the opinion of all other men put together?

Cr: True.

Soc: And if he disobeys and rejects the opinion and approval of the one, and accepts the opinion of the many who have no understanding, will he not suffer evil?

Cr: Certainly he will.

Soc: And how will the evil affect the disobedient student?

Cr: Clearly, it will affect his body; that is what is destroyed by the evil.

Soc: Very good. Is this not true, Crito, of other things which we need not separately consider? In the matter of the just and unjust, the fair and foul, the good and evil, which are the subjects of our present discussion, should we follow the opinion of the many and fear them, or the opinion of the one man who has understanding? Is he the one we ought to fear and honor more than all the rest of the world? If we leave him, we shall destroy and injure that principle in us which may be assumed to be improved by justice and deteriorated by injustice? Is there not such a principle?

Cr: Certainly there is, Socrates.

Soc: Take a similar case. If, acting under the advice of men who have no understanding, we ruined what is improved by health and destroyed by disease—when the body has been destroyed, I say, would life be worth having?

Cr: Yes.

Soc: Could we live having an evil and corrupted body?

Cr: Certainly not.

Soc: And will life be worth having, if the soul is crippled, which is improved by justice and harmed by injustice? Do we suppose the soul to be inferior to the body?

Cr: Certainly not.

Soc: More important, then?

Cr: Far more important.

Soc: Then, my friend, we must not consider what the many say of us, but what he, the one man who has understanding of the just and unjust will say, and what the truth will say. Therefore you begin in error when you suggest we should consider the opinion of the many about the just and unjust, the good and evil, the honorable and dishonorable, but what if someone says, "But the many can kill us."

Cr: Yes, Socrates, that will clearly be the answer.

Soc: Still I believe our old argument is unshaken. I would like to know whether I may say the same of another proposition—that not life, but a good life, is to be chiefly valued?

Cr: Yes, that is also true.

Soc: And a good life is equivalent to a just and honorable one—that is also true?

Cr: Yes, that is true.

Soc: From these beliefs I am ready to consider whether I should or should not try to escape without the consent of the Athenians. If I am clearly right in escaping, then I will make the attempt, but if not, I will remain here. The other considerations which you mention, of money and loss of reputation and the duty of educating children, are, I fear, only the beliefs of the many,

who would be as ready to bring people to life, if they were able, as they are to put them to death. The only question remaining to be considered is whether we shall do right escaping or allowing others to aid our escape and paying them money and thanks or whether we shall not do right. If the latter, then death or any other calamity which may result from my remaining here must not be allowed to influence us.

Cr: I think you are right, Socrates. But, how shall we proceed?

Soc: Let us consider the matter together and either refute me if you can and I will be convinced; or else cease, my dear friend, from repeating to me that I ought to escape against the wishes of the Athenians. I am extremely eager to be persuaded by you, but not against my own better judgment. And now please consider my first position and do your best to answer me.

Cr: I will do my best.

Soc: Are we to say we are never intentionally to do wrong, or that in one way we should and in another way we should not do wrong? Or is doing wrong always evil and dishonorable, as I was just now saying? Are all our former admissions to be thrown away because of these last few days? Have we, at our age, been earnestly discoursing with one another all our life long only to discover we are no better than children? Or, are we convinced in spite of the opinion of the many and in spite of consequences of the truth of what we said, that injustice is always an evil and dishonor to him who acts unjustly? Shall we agree to that?

Cr: Yes.

Soc: Then we must do no wrong?

Cr: Certainly not.

Soc: Nor when injured should we injure in return, as the many imagine. We must injure no one at all?

Cr: Clearly not.

Soc: Again, Crito, can we do evil?

Cr: Surely not, Socrates.

Soc: And what of doing evil in return for evil, which is the morality of the many—is that just or not?

Cr: Not just.

Soc: For doing evil to another is the same as injuring him.

Cr: Very true.

Soc: Then we ought not to retaliate or render evil for evil to any one, whatever evil we may have suffered from him. But I would have you consider, Crito, whether you really mean what you are saying. For this opinion has never been held, and never will be held, by many people. Those who are agreed and those who are not agreed upon this point have no common ground, and can only despise one another when they see how widely they differ. Tell me, then, whether you agree with my first principle, that neither injury nor retaliation nor returning evil for evil is ever right. Shall that be the premise of our argument? Or do you disagree? For this has been and still is my opinion; but, if you are of another opinion, let me hear what you have to say. If, however, you remain of the same mind as formerly, I will go to the next step.

Cr: You may proceed, for I have not changed my mind.

Soc: The next step may be put in the form of a question: Ought a man to do what he admits to be right, or ought he to betray the right?

Cr: He ought to do what he thinks right.

Soc: But if this is true, what is the application? In leaving the prison against the will of the Athenians, do I wrong anyone? Or do I wrong those whom I ought least to wrong? Do I abandon the principles which were acknowledged by us to be just. What do you say?

Cr: I cannot tell, Socrates, because I do not know.

Soc: Then consider the matter in this way— imagine I am about to escape, and the Laws and the State come and interrogate me: "Tell us, Socrates," they say, "what are you doing? Are you going to overturn us—the Laws and the State, as far as you are able? Do you imagine that a State can continue and not be overthrown, in which the decisions of Law have no power, but are set aside and overthrown by individuals?"

What will be our answer, Crito, to these and similar words? Anyone, and especially a clever orator, will have a good deal to say about the evil of setting aside the Law which requires a sentence to be carried out. We might reply, "Yes, but the State has injured us and given an unjust sentence." Suppose I say that?

Cr: Very good, Socrates.

Soc: "And was that our agreement with you?" the Law would say, "Or were you to abide by the sentence of the State?" And if I was surprised at their saying this, the Law would probably add: "Answer, Socrates, instead of opening your eyes: you are in the habit of asking and answering questions. Tell us what complaint you have against us which justifies you in attempting to destroy us and the State? In the first place did we not bring you into existence? Your father married your mother by our aid and conceived you. Say whether you have any objection against those of us who regulate marriage?" None, I should reply. "Or against those of us who regulate the system of care and education of children in which you were trained? Were not the Laws, who have the charge of this, right in commanding your father to train you in the arts and exercise?" Yes, I should reply.

"Well then, since you were brought into the world, nurtured and educated by us, can you deny in the first place that you are our child and slave, as your fathers were before you? And if this is true you are not on equal terms with us. Nor can you think you have a right to do to us what we are doing to you. Would you have any right to strike or do any other evil to a father or to your master, if you had one, when you have been struck or received some other evil at his hands? And because we think it is right to destroy you, do you think that you have any right to destroy us in return, and your country so far as you are able? And will you, O expounder of virtue, say you are justified in this? Has a philosopher like you failed to discover your country is more to be valued and higher and holier by far than mother and father or any ancestor, and more regarded in the eyes of the gods and of men of understanding? It should be soothed and gently and reverently entreated when angry, even more than a father, and if not persuaded, it should be obeyed. And when we are punished by the State, whether with imprisonment or whipping, the punishment is to be endured in silence. If the State leads us to wounds or death in battle, we follow as is right; no one can yield or leave his rank, but whether in battle or in a court of law, or in any other place, he must do what his city and his country order him. Or, he must change their view of what is just. If he may do no violence to his father or mother, much less may he do violence to his country." What answer shall we make to this, Crito? Do the Laws speak truly, or do they not?

Cr: I think that they do.

Soc: Then the Laws will say: "Consider, Socrates, if this is true, that in your present attempt you are going to do us wrong. For, after having brought you into the world, nurtured and educated you, and given you and every other citizen a share in every good we had to give, we further give the right to every Athenian, if he does not like us when he has come of age and has seen the ways of the city, he may go wherever else he pleases and take his goods with him. None of us Laws will forbid or interfere with him. Any of you who does not like us and the city, and who wants to go to a colony or to any other city, may go where he likes, and take his possessions with him. But he who has experience of the way we order justice and administer the State, and still remains, has entered into an implied contract to do as we command him. He who disobeys us is, as we maintain, triply wrong; first, because in disobeying us he is disobeying his parents; second, because we are the authors of his education; third, because he has made an agreement with us that he will duly obey our commands. He neither obeys them nor convinces us our commands are wrong. We do not rudely impose our commands but give each person the alternative of obeying or convincing us. That is what we offer and he does neither. These are the sort of accusations to which, as we were saying Socrates, you will be exposed if you do as you were intending; you, above all other Athenians."

Suppose I ask, why is this? They will justly answer that I above all other men have acknowledged the agreement.

"There is clear proof," they will say, "Socrates, that we and the city were not displeasing to you. Of all Athenians you have been the most constant resident in the city, which, as you never leave, you appear to love. You never went out of the city either to see the games, except once when you went to the Isthmus, or to any other place unless you were on military service; nor did you travel as other men do. Nor had you any curiosity to know other States or their Laws: Your affections did not go beyond us and our State; we were your special favorites and you agreed in our government of you. This is the State in which you conceived your children, which is a proof of your satisfaction. Moreover, you might, if you wished, have fixed the penalty at banishment in the course of the trial—the State which refuses to let you go now would have let you go then. You pretended you preferred death to exile and that you were not grieved at death. And now you have forgotten these fine sentiments and pay no respect to us, the Laws, who you destroy. You are doing what only a miserable slave would do, running away and turning your back upon the agreements which you made as a citizen. First of all, answer this very question: Are we right in saying you agreed to be governed according to us in deed, and not in word only? Is that true or not?"

How shall we answer that, Crito? Must we not agree?

Cr: We must, Socrates.

Soc: Then will the Laws say: "You, Socrates, are breaking the agreements which you made with us at your leisure, not in any haste or under any compulsion or deception, but having had 70 years to think of them, during which time you were at liberty to leave the city, if we were not to your liking, or if our covenants appeared to you to be unfair. You might have gone either to Lacedaemon or Crete, which you often praise for their good government, or to some other Hellenic or foreign state. You, above all other Athenians, seemed to be so fond of the State and of us, her Laws, that you never left her. The lame, the blind, the maimed were not more stationary in the State than you were. Now you run away and forsake your agreements. Now, Socrates, if you will take our advice; do not make yourself ridiculous by escaping out of the city.

"Just consider, if you do evil in this way, what good will you do either yourself or your friends? That your friends will be driven into exile and lose their citizenship, or will lose their property, is reasonably certain. You yourself, if you fly to one of the neighboring cities, like Thebes or Megara, both of which are well-governed cities, will come to them as an enemy, Socrates. Their government will be against you and all patriotic citizens will cast suspicious eye upon you as a destroyer of the laws. You will confirm in the minds of the judges the justice of their own condemnation of you. For he who is a corruptor of the laws is more than likely to be corruptor of the young. Will you then flee from well-ordered cities and virtuous men? Is existence worth having on these terms? Or will you go to these cities without shame and talk to them, Socrates? And what will you say to them? Will you say what you say here about virtue, justice, institutions and laws being the best things among men? Would that be decent of you? Surely not.

"If you go away from well-governed states to Crito's friends in Thessaly, where there is a great disorder and immorality, they will be charmed to have the tale of your escape from prison, set off with ludicrous particulars of the manner in which you were wrapped in a goatskin or some other disguise and metamorphosed as the fashion of runaways is—that is very likely. But will there be no one to remind you in your old age you violated the most sacred laws from a miserable desire of a little more life. Perhaps not, if you keep them in a good temper. But if they are angry you will hear many degrading things; you will live, but how? As the flatterer of all men, and the servant of all men. And doing what? Eating and drinking in Thessaly, having gone abroad in order that you may get a dinner. Where will your

fine sentiments about justice and virtue be then? Say that you wish to live for the sake of your children, that you may bring them up and educate them—will you take them into Thessaly and deprive them of Athenian citizenship? Is that the benefit which you would confer upon them? Or are you under the impression that they will be better cared for and educated here if you are still alive, although absent from them because your friends will take care of them? Do you think if you are an inhabitant of Thessaly they will take care of them, and if you are an inhabitant of the other world they will not take care of them? No, if they who call themselves friends are truly friends, they surely will.

"Listen, then, Socrates, to us who have brought you up. Think not of life and children first, and of justice afterwards, but of justice first, that you may be justified before the rulers of the other world. For neither will you nor your children be happier or holier in this life, or happier in another, if you do as Crito bids. Now you depart in innocence, a sufferer and not a doer of evil; a victim, not of the Laws, but of men. But if you escape, returning evil for evil and injury for injury, breaking the agreements which you have made with us, and wronging those whom you ought least to wrong, that is to say, yourself, your friends, your country, and us, we shall be angry with you while you live. Our brethren, the Laws in the other world, will receive you as an enemy because they will know you have done your best to destroy us. Listen, then, to us and not to Crito."

This is the voice which I seem to hear murmuring in my ears, like the sound of a divine flute in the ears of the mystic. That voice, I say, is humming in my ears and prevents me from hearing any other. I know anything more which you may say will be useless. Yet speak, if you have anything to say.

Cr: I have nothing to say, Socrates.

Soc: Then let me follow what seems to be the will of the god.

Suggestions for Further Reading

See John Locke's *Two Treatises on Government* (originally published in 1689 and available in a critical edition, edited by Peter Laslett, Cambridge: Cambridge University Press, 1963) for a classic treatment of the issues of political authority, the justification of property and punishment, the social contract theory, and the idea of tacit consent.

See Robert Nozick's *Anarchy, State, and Utopia* (New York: Basic Books, 1974) for an argument in support of individual sovereignty and John Rawls's *A Theory of Justice* (Cambridge: Harvard University Press, 1971) for a modern use of a modified social contract theory in the development of a theory of justice.

Society and the Individual: Readings in Political and Social Philosophy, edited by Richard T. Garner and Andrew Oldenquist (Belmont, CA: Wadsworth, 1990), provides a good selection of texts on issues of liberty, equality, and authority.

Videos

The Trial of Socrates (29 minutes, Insight Media) covers both the trial and death of Socrates including material from the Crito.

4.5. Civil Disobedience

Are there times when disobeying the law is morally justified? What are the responsibilities of a citizen? The dialogue *Crito* raised these issues, but in one way or another we have been asking these questions whenever the issue of governmental authority has arisen. The issue of civil disobedience also raises fundamental questions about the rule of law. In Chapter 2, we read about the Confucian recommendation for rule by moral example. If that would work, why should we need laws?

A case against the rule of law might go something like this. Laws limit human freedom and hinder spontaneity. Laws are sometimes unfair, and repressive. Common sense, social custom, and religion already provide enough guidance so that laws are unnecessary. Besides, virtue comes from within, hence morality can never be legislated.

Many, of course, believe that the rule of law is both good and necessary. Laws protect people, create social stability, and provide opportunities to create rights that people might not otherwise enjoy. The rights to life, liberty, and the pursuit of happiness (property?) need to be protected and defined by laws. In pluralistic societies, we cannot depend on customs and traditions to unite people. Nor can we depend on the virtue and goodwill of our leaders. Only the rule of law can prevent abuse of power.

But how can we tell the difference between good laws and bad laws? Are there minimal conditions for good laws? We might argue that good laws guarantee access to the resources necessary to live, provide for enforcement of contracts, and give security from violence. Such laws should be fairly enforced, adjudicated in courts free from prejudice, provide for due process, and be free from vagueness and ambiguity. Should we also add that the right of civil disobedience be granted, or would such a right undermine entirely the rule of law?

Civil disobedience has played and continues to play a major role in effecting political and legal change. In the 19th century, Henry David Thoreau went to jail for refusing to pay his taxes to a government that supported slavery. He argued that conscience constitutes a higher law than the law of any land. We all have a moral duty to obey our consciences. However, he allowed that the person who commits civil disobedience must pay the legal penalty.

Civil disobedience has become a political strategy in many nations in the 20th century. Gandhi used it to liberate India from British colonial rule. He carried a copy of Thoreau's *On Civil Disobedience* with him and used it as a blueprint for nonviolent resistance. Nelson Mandela symbolizes the use of civil disobedience to change the apartheid system of South Africa. Unlike Gandhi, however, Mandela and the National African Congress, which he represents, will not renounce the use of force. When does civil disobedience become political revolution? When violence is used? Must one be willing to suffer the consequences of breaking the law in order to engage in a morally justifiable act of civil disobedience?

Martin Luther King, Jr. (1929–1968), a Baptist minister and winner of the Nobel Peace Prize, devoted his life to the struggle for racial justice in the United States. Like Thoreau and Gandhi, he argued for nonviolent methods. As a result, he found himself opposing those African-Americans who did advocate the use of violence. He died from an assassin's bullet in Memphis, Tennessee. A year before he won the Nobel Peace Prize and five years before his death, he served a sentence in the Birmingham, Alabama jail for participating in a civil rights demonstration. Eight prominent Alabama clergy wrote an open letter critical of Dr. King's methods. In his famous "Letter from Birmingham Jail," Dr. King responds to their criticisms and, in the process, writes a moving justification of civil disobedience.

Reading Questions

1. Do you agree with Dr. King's claim that "Injustice anywhere is a threat to justice everywhere?" Why?

2. Do you think groups are more immoral than individuals? Why?

3. What are the differences, according to King, between unjust laws and just laws? Are all the differences compatible? For example, could not a law code passed and obeyed by the majority that respects the rights of the minority be unjust in the sense that it is not in harmony with God's law? Can you think of an example?

4. Under what conditions is it permissible, according to King, to break the law? Do you agree? Why?

5. According to King, what is the purpose of law and order? Do you agree?

6. According to King, what is the proper role of the Christian church with respect to issues of social justice? Do you think he is right?

7. Write a brief letter in response to King from the point of view of the clergy who originally criticized him.

8. Create and answer any analytical or critical question you wish about this piece.

Letter from Birmingham Jail

MARTIN LUTHER KING, JR.

MY DEAR FELLOW CLERGYMEN,

While confined here in the Birmingham city jail, I came across your recent statement calling our present activities "unwise and untimely." Seldom, if ever, do I pause to answer criticism of my work and ideas. If I sought to answer all of the criticisms that cross my desk, my secretaries would be engaged in little else in the course of the day, and I would have no time for constructive work. But since I feel that you are men of genuine good will and your criticisms are sincerely set forth, I would like to answer your statement in what I hope will be patient and reasonable terms.

I think I should give the reason for my being in Birmingham, since you have been influenced by the argument of "outsiders coming in." I have the honor of serving as president of the Southern Christian Leadership Conference, an organization operating in every southern state, with headquarters in Atlanta, Georgia. We have some 85 affiliate organizations all across the South—one being the Alabama Christian Movement for Human Rights. Whenever necessary and possible we share staff, educational and financial resources with our affiliates. Several months ago our local affiliate here in Birmingham invited us to be on call to engage in a nonviolent direct-action program if such were deemed necessary. We readily consented and when the hour came we lived up to our promises. So I am here, along with several members of my staff, because we were invited here. I am here because I have basic organizational ties here.

Beyond this, I am in Birmingham because injustice is here. Just as the eighth century prophets left their little villages and carried their "thus saith the Lord" far beyond the boundaries of their hometowns; and just as the Apostle Paul left his little village of Tarsus and carried the gospel of Jesus Christ to practically every hamlet and city of the Graeco-Roman world, I too am compelled to carry the gospel of freedom beyond my particular hometown. Like Paul, I must constantly respond to the Macedonian call for aid.

Moreover, I am cognizant of the interrelatedness of all communities and states. I cannot sit idly by in Atlanta and not be concerned about what happens in Birmingham. Injustice anywhere is a threat to justice everywhere. We are caught in an inescapable network of mutuality, tied in a single garment of destiny. Whatever affects one directly affects all indirectly. Never again can we afford to live with the narrow, provincial "outside agitator" idea. Anyone who lives in the United States can never be considered an outsider anywhere in this country.

You deplore the demonstrations that are presently taking place in Birmingham. But I am sorry that your statement did not express a similar concern for the conditions that brought the demonstrations into being. I am sure that each of you would want to go beyond the superficial social analyst who looks merely at effects, and does not grapple with underlying causes. I would not hesitate to say that it is unfortunate that so-called demonstrations are taking place in Birmingham at this time, but I would say in more emphatic terms that it is even more unfortunate that the white power structure of this city left the Negro community with no other alternative.

In any nonviolent campaign there are four basic steps: (1) collection of the facts to determine whether injustices are alive, (2) negotiation, (3) self-purification, and (4) direct action. We have gone through all of these steps in Birmingham. There can be no gainsaying of the fact that racial injustice engulfs this community.

Birmingham is probably the most thoroughly segregated city in the United States. Its ugly record of police brutality is known in every section of this country. Its unjust treatment of Negroes in the courts is a notorious reality. There have been more unsolved bombings of Negro homes and churches in Birmingham than any city in this nation. These are the hard, brutal and unbelievable facts. On the basis of these conditions Negro leaders sought to negotiate with the city fathers. But the political leaders consistently refused to engage in good faith negotiation.

Then came the opportunity last September to talk with some of the leaders of the economic community. In these negotiating sessions certain promises were made by the merchants—such as the promise to remove the humiliating racial signs from the stores. On the basis of these promises Rev. Shuttlesworth and the leaders of the Alabama Christian Movement for Human Rights agreed to call a moratorium on any type of demonstrations. As the weeks and months unfolded we realized that we were the victims of a broken promise. The signs remained. Like so many experiences of the past we were confronted with blasted hopes, and the dark shadow of a deep disappointment settled upon us. So we had no alternative except that of preparing for direct action, whereby we would present our very bodies as a means of laying our case before the conscience of the local and national community. We were not unmindful of the difficulties involved. So we decided to go through a process of self-purification. We started having workshops on nonviolence and repeatedly asked ourselves the questions, "Are you able to accept blows without retaliating?" "Are you able to endure the ordeals of jail?" We decided to set our direct-action program around the Easter season, realizing that with the exception of Christmas, this was the largest shopping period of the year. Knowing that a strong economic withdrawal program would be the by-product of direct action, we felt that this was the best time to bring pressure on the merchants for the needed changes. Then it occurred

to us that the March election was ahead and so we speedily decided to postpone action until after election day. When we discovered that Mr. Connor was in the run-off, we decided again to postpone action so that the demonstrations could not be used to cloud the issues. At this time we agreed to begin our nonviolent witness the day after the run-off.

This reveals that we did not move irresponsibly into direct action. We, too, wanted to see Mr. Connor defeated; so we went through postponement after postponement to aid in this community need. After this we felt that direct action could be delayed no longer.

You may well ask, "Why direct action? Why sit-ins, marches, etc.? Isn't negotiation a better path?" You are exactly right in your call for negotiation. Indeed, this is the purpose of direct action. Nonviolent direct action seeks to create such a crisis and establish such creative tension that a community that has constantly refused to negotiate is forced to confront the issue. It seeks so to dramatize the issue that it can no longer be ignored. I just referred to the creation of tension as a part of the work of the nonviolent resister. This may sound rather shocking. But I must confess that I am not afraid of the word tension. I have earnestly worked and preached against violent tension, but there is a type of constructive nonviolent tension that is necessary for growth. Just as Socrates felt that it was necessary to create a tension in the mind so that individuals could rise from the bondage of myths and half-truths to the unfettered realm of creative analysis and objective appraisal, we must see the need of having nonviolent gadflies to create the kind of tension in society that will help men to rise from the dark depths of prejudice and racism to the majestic heights of understanding and brotherhood. So the purpose of the direct action is to create a situation so crisis-packed that it will inevitably open the door to negotiation. We, therefore, concur with you in your call for negotiation. Too long has our beloved Southland been bogged down in the tragic attempt to live in monologue rather than dialogue.

One of the basic points in your statement is

that our acts are untimely. Some have asked, "Why didn't you give the new administration time to act?" The only answer that I can give to this inquiry is that the new administration must be prodded about as much as the outgoing one before it acts. We will be sadly mistaken if we feel that the election of Mr. Boutwell will bring the millennium to Birmingham. While Mr. Boutwell is much more articulate and gentle than Mr. Connor, they are both segregationists, dedicated to the task of maintaining the status quo. The hope I see in Mr. Boutwell is that he will be reasonable enough to see the futility of massive resistance to desegregation. But he will not see this without pressure from the devotees of civil rights. My friends, I must say to you that we have not made a single gain in civil rights without determined legal and nonviolent pressure. History is the long and tragic story of the fact that privileged groups seldom give up their privileges voluntarily. Individuals may see the moral light and voluntarily give up their unjust posture; but as Reinhold Niebuhr has reminded us, groups are more immoral than individuals.

We know through painful experience that freedom is never voluntarily given by the oppressor; it must be demanded by the oppressed. Frankly, I have never yet engaged in a direct action movement that was "well-timed," according to the timetable of those who have not suffered unduly from the disease of segregation. For years now I have heard the words "Wait!" It rings in the ear of every Negro with a piercing familiarity. This "Wait" has almost always meant "Never." It has been a tranquilizing thalidomide, relieving the emotional stress for a moment, only to give birth to an ill-formed infant of frustration. We must come to see with the distinguished jurist of yesterday that "justice too long delayed is justice denied." We have waited for more than 340 years for our constitutional and God-given rights. The nations of Asia and Africa are moving with jetlike speed toward the goal of political independence, and we still creep at horse and buggy pace toward the gaining of a cup of coffee at a lunch counter. I guess it is easy for those who have never felt the stinging darts of segregation to say,

"Wait." But when you have seen vicious mobs lynch your mothers and fathers at will and drown your sisters and brothers at whim; when you have seen hate-filled policemen curse, kick, brutalize and even kill your black brothers and sisters with impunity; when you see the vast majority of your twenty million Negro brothers smothering in an airtight cage of poverty in the midst of an affluent society; when you suddenly find your tongue twisted and your speech stammering as you seek to explain to your six-year-old daughter why she can't go to the public amusement park that has just been advertised on television, and see tears welling up in her little eyes when she is told that Funtown is closed to colored children, and see the depressing clouds of inferiority begin to form in her little mental sky, and see her begin to distort her little personality by unconsciously developing a bitterness toward white people; when you have to concoct an answer for a five-year-old son asking in agonizing pathos: "Daddy, why do white people treat colored people so mean?"; when you take a cross-country drive and find it necessary to sleep night after night in the uncomfortable corners of your automobile because no motel will accept you; when you are humiliated day in and day out by nagging signs reading "white" and "colored"; when your first name becomes "nigger" and your middle name becomes "boy" (however old you are) and your last name becomes "John," and when your wife and mother are never given the respected title "Mrs."; when you are harried by day and haunted by night by the fact that you are a Negro, living constantly at tiptoe stance never quite knowing what to expect next, and plagued with inner fears and outer resentments; when you are forever fighting a degenerating sense of "nobodiness"; then you will understand why we find it difficult to wait. There comes a time when the cup of endurance runs over, and men are no longer willing to be plunged into an abyss of injustice where they experience the blackness of corroding despair. I hope, sirs, you can understand our legitimate and unavoidable impatience.

You express a great deal of anxiety over our willingness to break laws. This is certainly a legitimate concern. Since we so diligently urge people to obey the Supreme Court's decision of 1954 outlawing segregation in the public schools, it is rather strange and paradoxical to find us consciously breaking laws. One may well ask, "How can you advocate breaking some laws and obeying others?" The answer is found in the fact that there are two types of laws: there are *just* and there are *unjust* laws. I would agree with Saint Augustine that "An unjust law is no law at all."

Now what is the difference between the two? How does one determine when a law is just or unjust? A just law is a man-made code that squares with the moral law or the law of God. An unjust law is a code that is out of harmony with the moral law. To put it in the terms of Saint Thomas Aquinas, an unjust law is a human law that is not rooted in eternal and natural law. Any law that uplifts human personality is just. Any law that degrades human personality is unjust. All segregation statutes are unjust because segregation distorts the soul and damages the personality. It gives the segregator a false sense of superiority, and the segregated a false sense of inferiority. To use the words of Martin Buber, the great Jewish philosopher, segregation substitutes an "I-it" relationship for the "I-thou" relationship, and ends up relegating persons to the status of things. So segregation is not only politically, economically and sociologically unsound, but it is morally wrong and sinful. Paul Tillich has said that sin is separation. Isn't segregation an existential expression of man's tragic separation, an expression of his awful estrangement, his terrible sinfulness? So I can urge men to disobey segregation ordinances because they are morally wrong.

Let us turn to a more concrete example of just and unjust laws. An unjust law is a code that a majority inflicts on a minority that is not binding on itself. This is difference made legal. On the other hand a just law is a code that a majority compels a minority to follow that it is willing to follow itself. This is sameness made legal.

Let me give another explanation. An unjust law is a code inflicted upon a minority which that minority had no part in enacting or creating be-

cause they did not have the unhampered right to vote. Who can say that the legislature of Alabama which set up the segregation laws was democratically elected? Throughout the state of Alabama all types of conniving methods are used to prevent Negroes from becoming registered voters and there are some counties without a single Negro registered to vote despite the fact that the Negro constitutes a majority of the population. Can any law set up in such a state be considered democratically structured?

These are just a few examples of unjust and just laws. There are some instances when a law is just on its face and unjust in its application. For instance, I was arrested Friday on a charge of parading without a permit. Now there is nothing wrong with an ordinance which requires a permit for a parade, but when the ordinance is used to preserve segregation and to deny citizens the First Amendment privilege of peaceful assembly and peaceful protest, then it becomes unjust.

I hope you can see the distinction I am trying to point out. In no sense do I advocate evading or defying the law as the rabid segregationist would do. This would lead to anarchy. One who breaks an unjust law must do it *openly, lovingly* (not hatefully as the white mothers did in New Orleans when they were seen on television screaming, "nigger, nigger, nigger"), and with a willingness to accept the penalty. I submit that an individual who breaks a law that conscience tells him is unjust, and willingly accepts the penalty by staying in jail to arouse the conscience of the community over its injustice, is in reality expressing the very highest respect for law.

Of course, there is nothing new about this kind of civil disobedience. It was seen sublimely in the refusal of Shadrach, Meshach and Abednego to obey the laws of Nebuchadnezzar because a higher moral law was involved. It was practiced superbly by the early Christians who were willing to face hungry lions and the excruciating pain of chopping blocks, before submitting to certain unjust laws of the Roman Empire. To a degree academic freedom is a reality today because Socrates practiced civil disobedience.

We can never forget that everything Hitler

did in Germany was "legal" and everything the Hungarian freedom fighters did in Hungary was "illegal." It was "illegal" to aid and comfort a Jew in Hitler's Germany. But I am sure that if I had lived in Germany during that time I would have aided and comforted my Jewish brothers even though it was illegal. If I lived in a Communist country today where certain principles dear to the Christian faith are suppressed, I believe I would openly advocate disobeying these antireligious laws. I must make two honest confessions to you, my Christian and Jewish brothers. First, I must confess that over the last few years I have been gravely disappointed with the white moderate. I have almost reached the regrettable conclusion that the Negro's great stumbling block in the stride toward freedom is not the White Citizen's Counciler or the Ku Klux Klanner, but the white moderate who is more devoted to "order" than to justice; who prefers a negative peace which is the absence of tension to a positive peace which is the presence of justice; who constantly says, "I agree with you in the goal you seek, but I can't agree with your methods of direct action"; who paternalistically feels that he can set the timetable for another man's freedom; who lives by the myth of time and who constantly advised the Negro to wait until a "more convenient season." Shallow understanding from people of good will is more frustrating than absolute misunderstanding from people of ill will. Lukewarm acceptance is much more bewildering than outright rejection.

I had hoped that the white moderate would understand that law and order exist for the purpose of establishing justice, and that when they fail to do this they become dangerously structured dams that block the flow of social progress. I had hoped that the white moderate would understand that the present tension of the South is merely a necessary phase of the transition from an obnoxious negative peace, where the Negro passively accepted his unjust plight, to a substance-filled positive peace, where all men will respect the dignity and worth of human personality. Actually, we who engage in nonviolent direct action are not the creators of tension. We merely bring to the surface the hidden tension that is already alive. We bring it out in the open where it can be seen and dealt with. Like a boil that can never be cured as long as it is covered up but must be opened with all its pus-flowing ugliness to the natural medicines of air and light, injustice must likewise be exposed, with all of the tension its exposing creates, to the light of human conscience and the air of national opinion before it can be cured.

In your statement you asserted that our actions, even though peaceful, must be condemned because they precipitate violence. But can this assertion be logically made? Isn't this like condemning the robbed man because his possession of money precipitated the evil act of robbery? Isn't this like condemning Socrates because his unswerving commitment to truth and his philosophical delvings precipitated the misguided popular mind to make him drink the hemlock? Isn't this like condemning Jesus because His unique God-consciousness and never-ceasing devotion to His will precipitated the evil act of crucifixion? We must come to see, as federal courts have consistently affirmed, that it is immoral to urge an individual to withdraw his efforts to gain his basic constitutional rights because the quest precipitates violence. Society must protect the robbed and punish the robber.

I had also hoped that the white moderate would reject the myth of time. I received a letter this morning from a white brother in Texas which said: "All Christians know that the colored people will receive equal rights eventually, but it is possible that you are in too great of a religious hurry. It has taken Christianity almost two thousand years to accomplish what it has. The teachings of Christ take time to come to earth." All that is said here grows out of a tragic misconception of time. It is the strangely irrational notion that there is something in the very flow of time that will inevitably cure all ills. Actually time is neutral. It can be used either destructively or constructively. I am coming to feel that the people of ill will have used time much more effectively than the people of good will. We will have to repent in this generation not merely for the vitriolic words and actions of the bad people, but for the appalling silence of the good people. We must come to see that human progress never rolls in on wheels of inevitability. It comes through the tireless efforts and persistent work of men willing to be co-workers with God, and without this hard work time itself becomes an ally of the forces of social stagnation. We must use time creatively, and forever realize that the time is always ripe to do right. Now is the time to make real the promise of democracy, and transform our pending national elegy into a creative psalm of brotherhood. Now is the time to lift our national policy from the quicksand of racial injustice to the solid rock of human dignity.

You spoke of our activity in Birmingham as extreme. At first I was rather disappointed that fellow clergymen would see my nonviolent efforts as those of the extremist. I started thinking about the fact that I stand in the middle of two opposing forces in the Negro community. One is a force of complacency made up of Negroes who, as a result of long years of oppression, have been so completely drained of self-respect and a sense of "somebodiness" that they have adjusted to segregation, and, of a few Negroes in the middle class who, because of a degree of academic and economic security, and because at points they profit by segregation, have unconsciously become insensitive to the problems of the masses. The other force is one of bitterness and hatred, and comes perilously close to advocating violence. It is expressed in the various black nationalist groups that are springing up over the nation, the largest and best known being Elijah Muhammad's Muslim movement. This movement is nourished by the contemporary frustration over the continued existence of racial discrimination. It is made up of people who have lost faith in America, who have absolutely repudiated Christianity, and who have concluded that the white man is an incurable "devil." I have tried to stand between these two forces, saying that we need not follow the "do-nothingism" of the complacent or the hatred and despair of the black nationalist. There is the more excellent way of love and nonviolent protest. I'm grateful to God that,

through the Negro church, the dimension of nonviolence entered our struggle. If this philosophy had not emerged, I am convinced that by now many streets of the South would be flowing with floods of blood. And I am further convinced that if our white brothers dismiss us as "rabble-rousers" and "outside agitators" those of us who are working through the channels of nonviolent direct action and refuse to support our nonviolent efforts, millions of Negroes, out of frustration and despair, will seek solace and security in black nationalist ideologies, a development that will lead inevitably to a frightening racial nightmare.

Oppressed people cannot remain oppressed forever. The urge for freedom will eventually come. This is what happened to the American Negro. Something within has reminded him of his birthright of freedom; something without has reminded him that he can gain it. Consciously and unconsciously, he has been swept in by what the Germans call the *Zeitgeist,* and with his black brothers of Africa, and his brown and yellow brothers of Asia, South America and the Caribbean, he is moving with a sense of cosmic urgency toward the promised land of racial justice. Recognizing this vital urge that has engulfed the Negro community, one should readily understand public demonstrations. The Negro has many pent-up resentments and latent frustrations. He has to get them out. So let him march sometime; let him have his prayer pilgrimages to the city hall; understand why he must have sit-ins and freedom rides. If his repressed emotions do not come out in these nonviolent ways, they will come out in ominous expressions of violence. This is not a threat; it is a fact of history. So I have not said to my people "get rid of your discontent." But I have tried to say that this normal and healthy discontent can be channelized through the creative outlet of nonviolent direct action. Now this approach is being dismissed as extremist. I must admit that I was initially disappointed in being so categorized.

But as I continued to think about the matter, I gradually gained a bit of satisfaction from being considered an extremist. Was not Jesus an extremist in love—"Love your enemies, bless them that curse you, pray for them that despitefully use you." Was not Amos an extremist for justice—"Let justice roll down like waters and righteousness like a mighty stream." Was not Paul an extremist for the gospel of Jesus Christ—"I bear in my body the marks of the Lord Jesus." Was not Martin Luther an extremist—"Here I stand; I can do none other so help me God." Was not John Bunyan an extremist—"I will stay in jail to the end of my days before I make a butchery of my conscience." Was not Abraham Lincoln an extremist—"This nation cannot survive half slave and half free." Was not Thomas Jefferson an extremist—"We hold these truths to be self-evident, that all men are created equal." So the question is not whether we will be extremist but what kind of extremist will we be. Will we be extremists for hate or will we be extremists for love? Will we be extremists for the preservation of injustice—or will we be extremists for the cause of justice? In that dramatic scene on Calvary's hill, three men were crucified. We must not forget that all three were crucified for the same crime—the crime of extremism. Two were extremists for immorality, and thusly fell below their environment. The other, Jesus Christ, was an extremist for love, truth and goodness, and thereby rose above his environment. So, after all, maybe the South, the nation and the world are in dire need of creative extremists.

I had hoped that the white moderate would see this. Maybe I was too optimistic. Maybe I expected too much. I guess I should have realized that few members of a race that has oppressed another race can understand or appreciate the deep groans and passionate yearnings of those that have been oppressed and still fewer have the vision to see that injustice must be rooted out by strong, persistent and determined action. I am thankful, however, that some of our white brothers have grasped the meaning of this social revolution and committed themselves to it. They are still all too small in quantity, but they are big in quality. Some like Ralph McGill, Lillian Smith, Harry Golden and James Dabbs have written about our struggle in eloquent, prophetic and

understanding terms. Others have marched with us down nameless streets of the South. They have languished in filthy roach-infested jails, suffering the abuse and brutality of angry policemen who see them as "dirty nigger-lovers." They, unlike so many of their moderate brothers and sisters, have recognized the urgency of the moment and sensed the need for powerful "action" antidotes to combat the disease of segregation.

Let me rush on to mention my other disappointment. I have been so greatly disappointed with the white church and its leadership. Of course, there are some notable exceptions. I am not unmindful of the fact that each of you has taken some significant stands on this issue. I commend you, Rev. Stallings, for your Christian stance on this past Sunday, in welcoming Negroes to your worship service on a non-segregated basis. I commend the Catholic leaders of this state for integrating Springhill College several years ago.

But despite these notable exceptions I must honestly reiterate that I have been disappointed with the church. I do not say that as one of the negative critics who can always find something wrong with the church. I say it as a minister of the gospel, who loves the church; who was nurtured in its bosom; who has been sustained by its spiritual blessings and who will remain true to it as long as the cord of life shall lengthen.

I had the strange feeling when I was suddenly catapulted into the leadership of the bus protest in Montgomery several years ago that we would have the support of the white church. I felt that the white ministers, priests and rabbis of the South would be some of our strongest allies. Instead, some have been outright opponents, refusing to understand the freedom movement and misrepresenting its leaders; all too many others have been more cautious than courageous and have remained silent behind the anesthetizing security of the stained-glass windows.

In spite of my shattered dreams of the past, I came to Birmingham with the hope that the white religious leadership of this community would see the justice of our cause, and with deep moral concern, serve as the channel through which our just grievances would get to the power structure. I had hoped that each of you would understand. But again I have been disappointed. I have heard numerous religious leaders of the South call upon their worshippers to comply with a desegregation decision because it is the *law,* but I have longed to hear white ministers say, "Follow this decree because integration is morally *right* and the Negro is your brother." In the midst of blatant injustices inflicted upon the Negro, I have watched white churches stand on the sideline and merely mouth pious irrelevancies and sanctimonious trivialities. In the midst of a mighty struggle to rid our nation of racial and economic injustice, I have heard so many ministers say, "Those are social issues with which the gospel has no real concern," and I have watched so many churches commit themselves to a completely otherworldly religion which made a strange distinction between body and soul, the sacred and the secular.

So here we are moving toward the exit of the twentieth century with a religious community largely adjusted to the status quo, standing as a taillight behind other community agencies rather than a headlight leading men to higher levels of justice.

I have traveled the length and breadth of Alabama, Mississippi and all the other southern states. On sweltering summer days and crisp autumn mornings I have looked at her beautiful churches with their lofty spires pointing heavenward. I have beheld the impressive outlay of her massive religious education buildings. Over and over again I have found myself asking: "What kind of people worship here? Who is their God? Where were their voices when the lips of Governor Barnett dripped with words of interposition and nullification? Where were they when Governor Wallace gave the clarion call for defiance and hatred? Where were their voices of support when tired, bruised and weary Negro men and women decided to rise from the dark dungeons of complacency to the bright hills of creative protest?"

Yes, these questions are still in my mind. In deep disappointment, I have wept over the laxity of the church. But be assured that my tears have been tears of love. There can be no deep disappointment where there is not deep love. Yes, I love the church; I love her sacred walls. How could I do otherwise? I am in the rather unique position of being the son, the grandson and the great-grandson of preachers. Yes, I see the church as the body of Christ. But, oh! How we have blemished and scarred that body through social neglect and fear of being nonconformists.

There was a time when the church was very powerful. It was during that period when the early Christians rejoiced when they were deemed worthy to suffer for what they believed. In those days the church was not merely a thermometer that recorded the ideas and principles of popular opinion; it was a thermostat that transformed the mores of society. Wherever the early Christians entered a town the power structure got disturbed and immediately sought to convict them for being "disturbers of the peace" and "outside agitators." But they went on with the conviction that they were "a colony of heaven," and had to obey God rather than man. They were small in number but big in commitment. They were too God-intoxicated to be "astronomically intimidated." They brought an end to such ancient evils as infanticide and gladiatorial contest.

Things are different now. The contemporary church is often a weak, ineffectual voice with an uncertain sound. It is so often the archsupporter of the status quo. Far from being disturbed by the presence of the church, the power structure of the average community is consoled by the church's silent and often vocal sanction of things as they are.

But the judgment of God is upon the church as never before. If the church of today does not recapture the sacrificial spirit of the early church, it will lose its authentic ring, forfeit the loyalty of millions, and be dismissed as an irrelevant social club with no meaning for the twentieth century. I am meeting young people every day whose disappointment with the church has risen to outright disgust.

Maybe again, I have been too optimistic. Is organized religion too inextricably bound to the status quo to save our nation and the world?

Maybe I must turn my faith to the inner spiritual church, the church within the church, as the true *ecclesia* and the hope of the world. But again I am thankful to God that some noble souls from the ranks of organized religion have broken loose from the paralyzing chains of conformity and joined us as active partners in the struggle for freedom. They have left their secure congregations and walked the streets of Albany, Georgia, with us. They have gone through the highways of the South on tortuous rides for freedom. Yes, they have gone to jail with us. Some have been kicked out of their churches, and lost support of their bishops and fellow ministers. But they have gone with the faith that right defeated is stronger than evil triumphant. These men have been the leaven in the lump of the race. Their witness has been the spiritual salt that has preserved the true meaning of the gospel in these troubled times. They have carved a tunnel of hope through the dark mountain of disappointment.

I hope the church as a whole will meet the challenge of this decisive hour. But even if the church does not come to the aid of justice, I have no despair about the future. I have no fear about the outcome of our struggle in Birmingham, even if our motives are presently misunderstood. We will reach the goal of freedom in Birmingham and all over the nation, because the goal of America is freedom. Abused and scorned though we may be, our destiny is tied up with the destiny of America. Before the Pilgrims landed at Plymouth we were here. Before the pen of Jefferson etched across the pages of history the majestic words of the Declaration of Independence, we were here. For more than two centuries our foreparents labored in this country without wages; they made cotton king; and they built the homes of their masters in the midst of brutal injustice and shameful humiliation—and yet out of a bottomless vitality they continued to thrive and develop. If the inexpressible cruelties of slavery could not stop us, the opposition we now face will surely fail. We will win our freedom because the sacred heritage of our nation and the eternal will of God are embodied in our echoing demands.

I must close now. But before closing I am impelled to mention one other point in your statement that troubled me profoundly. You warmly commended the Birmingham police force for keeping "order" and "preventing violence." I don't believe you would have so warmly commended the police force if you had seen its angry violent dogs literally biting six unarmed, nonviolent Negroes. I don't believe you would so quickly commend the policemen if you would observe their ugly and inhuman treatment of Negroes here in the city jail; if you would watch them push and curse old Negro women and young Negro girls; if you would see them slap and kick old Negro men and young boys; if you will observe them, as they did on two occasions, refuse to give us food because we wanted to sing our grace together. I'm sorry that I can't join you in your praise for the police department.

It is true that they have been rather disciplined in their public handling of the demonstrators. In this sense they have been rather publicly "nonviolent." But for what purpose? To preserve the evil system of segregation. Over the last few years I have consistently preached that nonviolence demands that the means we use must be as pure as the ends we seek. So I have tried to make it clear that it is wrong to use immoral means to attain moral ends. But now I must affirm that it is just as wrong, or even more so, to use moral means to preserve immoral ends. Maybe Mr. Connor and his policemen have been rather publicly nonviolent, as Chief Pritchett was in Albany, Georgia, but they have used the moral means of nonviolence to maintain the immoral end of flagrant racial injustice. T. S. Eliot has said that there is no greater treason than to do the right deed for the wrong reason.

I wish you had commended the Negro sit-inners and demonstrators of Birmingham for their sublime courage, their willingness to suffer and their amazing discipline in the midst of the most inhuman provocation. One day the South will recognize its real heroes. They will be the James Merediths, courageously and with a majestic sense of purpose facing jeering and hostile mobs and the agonizing loneliness that characterizes the life of the pioneer. They will be old, oppressed, battered Negro women, symbolized in a seventy-two-year-old woman of Montgomery, Alabama, who rose up with a sense of dignity and with her people decided not to ride the segregated buses, and responded to one who inquired about her tiredness with ungrammatical profundity: "My feet is tired, but my soul is rested." They will be the young high school and college students, young ministers of the gospel and a host of their elders courageously and nonviolently sitting-in at lunch counters and willingly going to jail for conscience's sake. One day the South will know that when these disinherited children of God sat down at lunch counters they were in reality standing up for the best in the American dream and the most sacred values in our Judeo-Christian heritage, and thusly, carrying our whole nation back to those great wells of democracy which were dug deep by the Founding Fathers in the formulation of the Constitution and the Declaration of Independence.

Never before have I written a letter this long (or should I say a book?). I'm afraid that it is much too long to take your precious time. I can assure you that it would have been much shorter if I had been writing from a comfortable desk, but what else is there to do when you are alone for days in the dull monotony of a narrow jail cell other than write long letters, think strange thoughts, and pray long prayers?

If I have said anything in this letter that is an overstatement of the truth and is indicative of an unreasonable impatience, I beg you to forgive me. If I have said anything in this letter that is an understatement of the truth and is indicative of my having a patience that makes me patient with anything less than brotherhood, I beg God to forgive me.

I hope this letter finds you strong in the faith. I also hope that circumstances will soon make it possible for me to meet each of you, not as an integrationist or a civil rights leader, but as a fellow clergyman and a Christian brother. Let us all hope that the dark clouds of racial prejudice will soon pass away and the deep fog of misunderstanding will be lifted from our fear-drenched communities and in some not too distant tomorrow the radiant stars of love and brotherhood will shine over our great nation with all of their scintillating beauty.

Yours for the cause of Peace and Brotherhood,
Martin Luther King, Jr.

Suggestions for Further Reading

Henry David Thoreau's *On Civil Disobedience* is a classic. See *Civil Disobedience,* edited by Hugo Bedau (New York: Pegasus, 1969), for a collection of essays on the topic.

Hannah Arendt's *Crises of the Republic* (New York: Harcourt Brace Jovanovich, 1969) deals with a number of issues ranging from civil disobedience and violence to political revolution. Ronald Dworkin in *Taking Rights Seriously* (Cambridge: Harvard University Press, 1970) argues that any society that recognizes rights must abandon "the notion of a general duty to obey the law that holds in all cases."

Martin Luther King, Jr. was using civil disobedience to gain African-American liberation and a racially integrated society. There is an immense literature on the topic of racism and black liberation. See Franz Fanon, *The Wretched of the Earth* (New York: Grove Press, 1965); *Philosophy and Opinions of Marcus Garvey* (Volume I of *The American Negro: His History and Literature* published by Arno Press, Salem, NH, 1968); Eldridge Cleaver's famous *Soul on Ice* (New York: Dell Publishing, 1968); *The Autobiography of Malcolm X* (New York: Grove Press, 1965); and S. Carmichael's and C. Hamilton's *Black Power* (New York: Vintage Press, 1967), for starters. William R. Jones, "Liberation Strategies in Black Theology: Mao, Martin, or Malcolm?" in *Philosophy Born of Struggle: Anthology of Afro-American Philosophy from 1917,* edited by Leonard Harris (Dubuque, IA.: Kendell/Hunt Publishing company, 1983), pp. 229–241, argues that for nonviolent civil disobedience to work, the oppressor must accept the co-humanity of the oppressed. But in a racist society, this presupposition is absent and so self-sacrificing love will not have its intended effect.

For the perspective of an African-American woman, see Angela Davis, *Women, Race, and Class* (New York: Random House, 1982).

Videos

Martin Luther King, Jr.: A Personal Portrait (53 minutes, produced by Michaelis Tapes). *Martin Luther King, Jr.: I Have a Dream* (28 minutes, produced by API) shows King's "I Have a Dream" speech on the steps of the Lincoln memorial. *Eyes on the Prize: No Easy Walk 1961–63* (PBS Video, 1986). A video of King's speeches. *Promised Land* (50 minutes, Filmakers Library) is a recollection of the promise and legacy of the civil rights movement. Also, from the same source, *Are we Different?* (27 minutes), shows African-American students talking about race, racism, and race relations. *The Meeting* (60 minutes, PBS Video) is a dramatization of a fictional secret meeting between Dr. King and Malcom X in which they debate the use of violence versus nonviolence in attaining just social ends. *Ethnic Notions* (57 minutes, California Newsreel) traces the development of black stereotypes. See *Racism on Campus* (210 miutes, Governor's State University) for an examination of racism on college campuses from both an historical and contemporary perspective. For more information see your Media Services Catalogue.

4.6. Liberation of the Oppressed

Have you ever wondered why oppression exists in societies? Have you ever wondered how oppression might be eliminated? Surely one of the features of societies that makes them unjust is the existence of oppression. Oppression can take many forms: economic, racial, sexual. The rich dominate the poor and get richer at their expense. In the United States and elsewhere, the whites discriminate against the blacks. Men limit the opportunities for women. Gays and lesbians are denied the rights and opportunities others enjoy. Native Americans, north and south, have suffered near extinction and cultural destruction at the hands of the European invaders and their descendants. Mexican Americans have been brutally exploited as farm laborers, and prevented, until recently, from gaining any significant political power. Unfortunately I could go on and on recounting example after example.

Oppressors need to justify their position and so they convince themselves that those whom they oppress are inferior, immoral, heathen, lazy, stupid, dirty, or somehow deserving of their lot in life. In effect, they dehumanize the oppressed while keeping for themselves the image of full humanity. For example, during the period of slavery in the United States, many slaveholders viewed African-Americans as less then human. And today how many of you have heard the claim, "Well, the poor are just lazy and don't want to work?" One of the most damaging things about oppression is that the oppressed come to adopt the views about themselves held by the oppressor. Their sense of pride, dignity, self-worth, and self-respect is slowly but surely eroded by a social situation that reminds them at every turn just how inferior they are. So women come to believe they have no more value than their physical appearance and almost starve themselves to death (some, unfortunately, succeeding) so they will have some value in a world dominated by males who treat women as sex objects. They adopt a false consciousness, false because these negative and dehumanizing images are the product of oppression and serve to justify the power one group holds over another. But the oppressor suffers from a false consciousness as well, believing that they are indeed somehow truly superior to others. Liberation from oppression cannot occur until a true consciousness replaces a false one, and the oppressed and oppressor come to recognize their common humanity.

The negative image of the oppressed created by the oppressors is conveyed and reinforced in thousands of ways. Television and movies are two obvious examples. Less obvious is education. Not only does the content of what is taught reflect various kinds of prejudices, the very method of teaching can as well. Yet education can also be the means of liberation from oppression. The education of the oppressed can be a powerful liberating tool because it can make them aware of their oppression and inspire them to take the action necessary to eliminate injustice.

Recent Latin American philosophy has been very concerned with liberation. The gap between the rich and poor is so great in so many Latin American countries, the poverty so severe and crippling, the oppression so stifling and all-pervasive that liberation from oppression and the relationship between the oppressor and the oppressed has become a primary concern for philosophical **praxis** (reflection on the human social condition and action undertaken to transform it).

Paulo Friere (1921–   ), the author of the following selection, was born in Recife, Brazil and became a professor of the Philosophy of Education at the University of Recife. He developed a theory for the education of adult illiterates based on the notion that every human being is capable of looking critically upon his or her situation. In 1964 he was "asked" to leave the country because of his political views and activities. He moved first to Chile, eventually emigrating to the United States. Central to his philosophy is the concept of "*conscientização*"—"learning to perceive social, political, and economic contradictions, and to take action against the oppressive elements of reality." This, he argues, is the ultimate goal of education.

Reading Questions

1. What characterizes the "banking" concept of education?

2. Why does the "banking" concept of education turn the teacher into an oppressor and the students into the oppressed?

3. What constitutes reconciling the teacher-student contradiction?

4. How does the "banking" concept of education avoid the threat of student *conscientizacao*?

5. On what assumption about human beings and the world does the "banking" concept of education depend?

6. Why must those committed to liberation reject the "banking" concept and adopt instead "problem-posing" education?

7. Make a list of the differences between "banking" education and problem-posing education.

8. Do questions 1–7 above reflect a "banking" concept of education or a "problem-posing" concept? Why or why not?

9. Which type of education ("banking" or "problem-posing") has been more prevalent in your experience? Which type of education do you prefer? Why?

10. What is wrong with Friere's analysis of educational philosophy? Why do you think it is wrong? If you cannot think of anything wrong with it, why can't you?

11. How do you think Friere would answer the question, "What makes a society just?"

Pedagogy of the Oppressed

PAULO FREIRE

A CAREFUL ANALYSIS of the teacher-student relationship at any level, inside or outside the school, reveals its fundamentally *narrative* character. This relationship involves a narrating Subject (the teacher) and patient, listening objects (the students). The contents, whether values or empirical dimensions of reality, tend in the process of being narrated to become lifeless and petrified. Education is suffering from narration sickness.

The teacher talks about reality as if it were motionless, static, compartmentalized, and predictable. Or else he expounds on a topic completely alien to the existential experience of the students. His task is to "fill" the students with the contents of his narration—contents which are detached from reality, disconnected from the totality that engendered them and could give them significance. Words are emptied of their concreteness and become a hollow, alienated, and alienating verbosity.

The outstanding characteristic of this narrative education, then, is the sonority of words, not their transforming power. "Four times four is sixteen; the capital of Pará is Belém." The student records, memorizes, and repeats these phrases without perceiving what four times four really means, or realizing the true significance of "capital" in the affirmation "the capital of Pará is Belém," that is, what Belém means for Pará and what Pará means for Brazil.

Narration (with the teacher as narrator) leads the students to memorize mechanically the narrated content. Worse yet, it turns them into "containers," into "receptacles" to be "filled" by the teacher. The more completely he fills the receptacles, the better a teacher he is. The more meekly the receptacles permit themselves to be filled, the better students they are.

Education thus becomes an act of depositing, in which the students are the depositories and the teacher is the depositor. Instead of communicating, the teacher issues communiqués and makes deposits which the students patiently receive, memorize, and repeat. This is the "banking" concept of education, in which the scope of action allowed to the students extends only as far as receiving, filing, and storing the deposits. They do, it is true, have the opportunity to become collectors or cagaloguers of the things they store. But in the last analysis, it is men themselves who are filed away through the lack of creativity, transformation, and knowledge in this (at best) misguided system. For apart from inquiry, apart from the praxis, men cannot be truly human. Knowledge emerges only through invention and re-invention, through the restless, impatient, continuing, hopeful inquiry men pursue in the world, with the world, and with each other.

In the banking concept of education, knowledge is a gift bestowed by those who consider themselves knowledgeable upon those whom they consider to know nothing. Projecting an absolute ignorance onto others, a characteristic of the ideology of oppression, negates education and knowledge as processes of inquiry. The teacher presents himself to his students as their necessary opposite; by considering their ignorance absolute, he justifies his own existence. The students, alienated like the slave in the Hegelian dialectic, accept their ignorance as justifying the teacher's existence—but, unlike the slave, they never discover that they educate the teacher.

The *raison d'être* of libertarian education, on the other hand, lies in its drive towards reconciliation. Education must begin with the solution of the teacher-student contradiction, by reconciling the poles of the contradiction so that both are simultaneously teachers *and* students.

This solution is not (nor can it be) found in the banking concept. On the contrary, banking education maintains and even stimulates the contradiction through the following attitudes and practices, which mirror oppressive society as a whole:

1. the teacher teaches and the students are taught;

2. the teacher knows everything and the students know nothing;

3. the teacher thinks and the students are thought about;

4. the teacher talks and the students listen—meekly;

5. the teacher disciplines and the students are disciplined;

6. the teacher chooses and enforces his choice, and the students comply;

7. the teacher acts and the students have the illusion of acting through the action of the teacher;

8. the teacher chooses the program content and the students (who were not consulted) adapt to it;

9. the teacher confuses the authority of knowledge with his own professional authority, which he sets in opposition to the freedom of the students;

10. the teacher is the Subject of the learning process, while the pupils are mere objects.

It is not surprising that the banking concept of education regards men as adaptable, manageable beings. The more students work at storing the deposits entrusted to them, the less they develop the critical consciousness which would result from their intervention in the world as transformers of that world. The more completely they accept the passive role imposed on them, the more they tend simply to adapt to the world as it is and to the fragmented view of reality deposited in them.

The capability of banking education to minimize or annul the students' creative power and to stimulate their credulity serves the interests of the oppressors, who care neither to have the world revealed nor to see it transformed. The oppressors use their "humanitarianism" to preserve a profitable situation. Thus they react almost instinctively against any experiment in education which stimulates the critical faculties and is not content with a partial view of reality but always seeks out the ties which link one point to another and one problem to another.

Indeed, the interests of the oppressors lie in "changing the consciousness of the oppressed, not the situation which oppresses them"; for the more the oppressed can be led to adapt to that situation, the more easily they can be dominated. To achieve this end, the oppressors use the banking concept of education in conjunction with a paternalistic social action apparatus, within which the oppressed receive the euphemistic title of "welfare recipients." They are treated as individual cases, as marginal men who deviate from the general configuration of a "good, organized, and just" society. The oppressed are regarded as the pathology of the healthy society, which must therefore adjust these "incompetent and lazy" folk to its own patterns by changing their mentality. These marginals need to be "integrated," "incorporated" into the healthy society that they have "forsaken."

The truth is, however, that the oppressed are not "marginals," are not men living "outside" society. They have always been "inside"—inside the structure which made them "beings for others." The solution is not to "integrate" them into the structure of oppression, but to transform that structure so that they can become "beings for themselves." Such transformation, of course, would undermine the oppressors' purposes; hence their utilization of the banking concept of education to avoid the threat of student *conscientização*.

The banking approach to adult education, for example, will never propose to students that they critically consider reality. It will deal instead with such vital questions as whether Roger gave green grass to the goat, and insist upon the importance of learning that, on the contrary, *Roger* gave green grass to the *r*abbit. The "humanism" of the banking approach masks the effort to turn men into automatons—the very negation of their ontological vocation to be more fully human.

Those who use the banking approach, knowingly or unknowingly (for there are innumerable well-intentioned bank-clerk teachers who do not realize that they are serving only to dehumanize), fail to perceive that the deposits themselves contain contradictions about reality. But, sooner or later, these contradictions may lead formerly passive students to turn against their domestication and the attempt to domesticate reality. They may discover through existential experience that their present way of life is irreconcilable with their vocation to become fully human. They may perceive through their relations with reality that reality is really a *process,* undergoing constant transformation. If men are searchers and their ontological vocation is humanization, sooner or later they may perceive the contradiction in which banking education seeks to maintain them, and then engage themselves in the struggle for their liberation.

But the humanist, revolutionary educator cannot wait for this possibility to materialize. From the outset, his efforts must coincide with those of the students to engage in critical thinking and the quest for mutual humanization. His efforts must be imbued with a profound trust in men and their creative power. To achieve this, he must be a partner of the students in his relations with them.

The banking concept does not admit to such partnership—and necessarily so. To resolve the teacher-student contradiction, to exchange the role of depositor, prescriber, domesticator, for the role of student among students would be to undermine the power of oppression and serve the cause of liberation.

Implicit in the banking concept is the assumption of a dichotomy between man and the world: man is merely *in* the world, not *with* the world or with others; man is spectator, not re-creator. In this view, man is not a conscious being (*corpo consciente*); he is rather the possessor of *a* consciousness: an empty "mind" passively open to the reception of deposits of reality from the world outside. For example, my desk, my books, my coffee cup, all the objects before me—as bits

of the world which surrounds me—would be "inside" me, exactly as I am inside my study right now. This view makes no distinction between being accessible to consciousness and entering consciousness. The distinction, however, is essential: the objects which surround me are simply accessible to my consciousness, not located within it. I am aware of them, but they are not inside me.

It follows logically from the banking notion of consciousness that the educator's role is to regulate the way the world "enters into" the students. His task is to organize a process which already occurs spontaneously, to "fill" the students by making deposits of information which he considers to constitute true knowledge. And since men "receive" the world as passive entities, education should make them more passive still, and adapt them to the world. The educated man is the adapted man, because he is better "fit" for the world. Translated into practice, this concept is well suited to the purposes of the oppressors, whose tranquility rests on how well men fit the world the oppressors have created, and how little they question it.

The more completely the majority adapt to the purposes which the dominant minority prescribe for them (thereby depriving them of the right to their own purposes), the more easily the minority can continue to prescribe. The theory and practice of banking education serve this end quite efficiently. Verbalistic lessons, reading requirements, the methods for evaluating "knowledge," the distance between the teacher and the taught, the criteria for promotion: everything in this ready-to-wear approach serves to obviate thinking.

The bank-clerk educator does not realize that there is no true security in his hypertrophied role, that one must seek to live *with* others in solidarity. One cannot impose oneself, nor even merely co-exist with one's students. Solidarity requires true communication, and the concept by which such an educator is guided fears and proscribes communication.

Yet only through communication can human life hold meaning. The teacher's thinking is authenticated only by the authenticity of the students' thinking. The teacher cannot think for his students, nor can he impose his thought on them. Authentic thinking, thinking that is concerned about *reality*, does not take place in ivory tower isolation, but only in communication. If it is true that thought has meaning only when generated by action upon the world, the subordination of students to teachers becomes impossible. . . .

Education as the exercise of domination stimulates the credulity of students, with the ideological intent (often not perceived by educators) of indoctrinating them to adapt to the world of oppression. This accusation is not made in the naïve hope that the dominant elites will thereby simply abandon the practice. Its objective is to call the attention of true humanists to the fact that they cannot use banking educational methods in the pursuit of liberation, for they would only negate that very pursuit. Nor may a revolutionary society inherit these methods from an oppressor society. The revolutionary society which practices banking education is either misguided or mistrusting of men. In either event, it is threatened by the specter of reaction.

Unfortunately, those who espouse the cause of liberation are themselves surrounded and influenced by the climate which generates the banking concept, and often do not perceive its true significance or its dehumanizing power. Paradoxically, then, they utilize this same instrument of alienation in what they consider an effort to liberate. Indeed, some "revolutionaries" brand as "innocents," "dreamers," or even "reactionaries" those who would challenge this educational practice. But one does not liberate men by alienating them. Authentic liberation—the process of humanization—is not another deposit to be made in men. Liberation is a praxis: the action and reflection of men upon their world in order to transform it. Those truly committed to the cause of liberation can accept neither the mechanistic concept of consciousness as an empty vessel to be filled, nor the use of banking methods of domination (propaganda, slogans—deposits) in the name of liberation. . . .

Liberating education consists in acts of cognition, not transferrals of information. It is a learning situation in which the cognizable object (far from being the end of the cognitive act) intermediates the cognitive actors—teacher on the one hand and students on the other. Accordingly, the practice of problem-posing education entails at the outset that the teacher-student contradiction be resolved. Dialogical relations—indispensable to the capacity of cognitive actors to cooperate in perceiving the same cognizable object—are otherwise impossible.

Indeed, problem-posing education, which breaks with the vertical patterns characteristic of banking education, can fulfill its function as the practice of freedom only if it can overcome the above contradiction. Through dialogue, the teacher-of-the-students and the students-of-the-teacher cease to exist and a new term emerges: teacher-student with students-teachers. The teacher is no longer merely the-one-who-teaches, but one who is himself taught in dialogue with the students, who in turn while being taught also teach. They become jointly responsible for a process in which all grow. In this process, arguments based on "authority" are no longer valid; in order to function, authority must be *on the side of* freedom, not *against* it. Here, no one teaches another, nor is anyone self-taught. Men teach each other, mediated by the world, by the cognizable objects which in banking education are "owned" by the teacher. . . .

The problem-posing method does not dichotomize the activity of the teacher-student: he is not "cognitive" at one point and "narrative" at another. He is always "cognitive," whether preparing a project or engaging in dialogue with the students. He does not regard cognizable objects as his private property, but as the object of reflection by himself and the students. In this way, the problem-posing educator constantly re-forms his reflections in the reflection of the students. The students—no longer docile listeners—are now critical co-investigators in dialogue with the teacher. The teacher presents the material to the students for their consideration, and re-considers his earlier considerations as the students express their own. The role of the problem-posing educator is to create, together with the students, the conditions under which knowledge at the level of the *doxa* is superseded by true knowledge, at the level of the *logos*.

Whereas banking education anesthetizes and inhibits creative power, problem-posing education involves a constant unveiling of reality. The former attempts to maintain the *submersion* of consciousness; the latter strives for the *emergence* of consciousness and *critical intervention* in reality.

Students, as they are increasingly posed with problems relating to themselves in the world and with the world, will feel increasingly challenged and obliged to respond to that challenge. Because they apprehend the challenge as interrelated to other problems within a total context, not as a theoretical question, the resulting comprehension tends to be increasingly critical and thus constantly less alienated. Their response to the challenge evokes new challenges, followed by new understandings; and gradually the students come to regard themselves as committed.

Education as the practice of freedom—as opposed to education as the practice of domination—denies that man is abstract, isolated, independent, and unattached to the world; it also denies that the world exists as a reality apart from men. Authentic reflection considers neither abstract man nor the world without men, but men in their relations with the world. In these relations consciousness and world are simultaneous: consciousness neither precedes the world nor follows it.

In one of our culture circles in Chile, the group was discussing . . . the anthropological concept of culture. In the midst of the discussion, a peasant who by banking standards was completely ignorant said: "Now I see that without man there is no world." When the educator responded: "Let's say, for the sake of argument, that all the men on earth were to die, but that the earth itself remained, together with trees, birds, animals, rivers, seas, the stars . . . wouldn't all this be a world?" "Oh no," the peasant replied emphatically. "There would be no one to say: 'This is a world'."

The peasant wished to express the idea that there would be lacking the consciousness of the world which necessarily implies the world of consciousness. *I* cannot exist without a *not-I*. In turn, the *not-I* depends on that existence. The world which brings consciousness into existence becomes the world *of* that consciousness . . . .

Banking education (for obvious reasons) attempts, by mythicizing reality, to conceal certain facts which explain the way men exist in the world; problem-posing education sets itself the task of demythologizing. Banking education resists dialogue; problem-posing education regards dialogue as indispensable to the act of cognition which unveils reality. Banking education treats students as objects of assistance; problem-posing education makes them critical thinkers. Banking education inhibits creativity and domesticates (although it cannot completely destroy) the *intentionality* of consciousness by isolating consciousness from the world, thereby denying men their ontological and historical vocation of becoming more fully human. Problem-posing education bases itself on creativity and stimulates true reflection and action upon reality, thereby responding to the vocation of men as beings who are authentic only when engaged in inquiry and creative transformation. In sum: banking theory and practice, as immobilizing and fixating forces, fail to acknowledge men as historical beings; problem-posing theory and practice take man's historicity as their starting point . . . .

Problem-posing education, as a humanist and liberating praxis, posits as fundamental that men subjected to domination must fight for their emancipation. To that end, it enables teachers and students to become Subjects of the educational process by overcoming authoritarianism and an alienating intellectualism; it also enables men to overcome their false perception of reality. The world—no longer something to be described with deceptive words—becomes the object of that transforming action by man which results in their humanization. Problem-posing education does not and cannot serve the interests of the oppressor. No oppressive order could permit the oppressed to begin to question: Why? While only a revolutionary society can carry out this education in systematic terms, the revolutionary leaders need not take full power before they can employ the method. In the revolutionary process, the leaders cannot utilize the banking method as an interim measure, justified on grounds of expediency, with the intention of *later* behaving in a genuinely revolutionary fashion. They must be revolutionary—that is to say, dialogical—from the outset.

Suggestions for Further Readings

Enrique Dussel's *Philosophy of Liberation,* translated by Aquilina Martinez and Christine Morkovsky (Mary Knoll, NY: Orbis Books, 1985) presents the basic concepts of liberation philosophy. Ofelia Schutie, "Origins and Tendencies of the Philosophy of Liberation in Latin American Thought: A Critique of Dussel's Ethics" in *The Philosophical Forum,* Vol. XXII (Spring, 1991), pp. 270–295 will take you deeper into the issues. Also see *The Philosophical Forum,* Vol. XX (Fall–Winter, 1988–89) for a complete issue devoted to "Latin American Philosophy Today." Sheldon B. Liss and Peggy K. Liss have edited a useful volume on *Man, State, and Society in Latin American History,* (New York: Praeger Publishers, 1972) which collects essays on the historical, social, and political developments. Roberto E. Villarreal and Norma G. Hernandez edited a volume, *Latinos and Political Coalitions: Political Empowerment for the 1990s* (New York: Praeger, 1991) that shifts the focus to North America and the struggle for liberation in that context. In the same vein, see Kate Lindemann, "Philosophy of Liberation in the North American Context," *Contemporary Philosophy,* Vol. XIV, No. 4, pp. 5–9 which draws heavily on Freire's ideas. *Latin American Philosophy In the Twentieth Century,* ed. by Jorge J. E. Gracia (Buffalo, NY: Prometheus Books, 1986) provides brief excerpts from the writings of influential Latin American philosophers. There has been a massive amount of scholarship on the issue of liberation from a theological viewpoint. See Micheal R. Candelaria's *Popular Religion and Liberation: The Dilemma of Liberation Theology,* (Albany, N.Y.: State University of New York Press, 1990) for starters.

If you wish to pursue the philosophy of education, see *Selected Readings in the Philosophy of Education,* 4th ed., edited by Joe Park, (New York: Macmillan, 1974) and Neil Postman and Charles Weingartner, *Teaching as a Subversive Activity* (New York: Delta, 1969). Also the work of Ivan Ilich will prove rewarding.

Chapter 5

Is Justice for All Possible?

WHEN I ASK MY STUDENTS to write a brief essay on whether they think a just society is possible, the responses I get are overwhelmingly negative. They do not think a just society is possible because, as one student put it, "Someone will always be unhappy with the way things are."

The United States, and other countries as well, face a number of complex issues requiring some sort of legislation. Yet every time a law is passed or a judicial decision is made someone is going to feel cheated. Even so, decisions must be made, and one can only hope that the decisions make good moral sense even if someone may be "unhappy."

Should people be put to death because they have taken another person's life? It only seems fair. But what gives a group of people (society) the moral right to do what they claim is not a moral right for the individual to do? Then there is abortion. Once it was illegal. Now it is legal. But the forces against its legality are very vocal. Do the rights of a woman outweigh the rights of a potential person? What about sex roles and equal opportunity? Is sex-stereotyping compatible with equal opportunity? If women are viewed, in general, as weaker and less capable than males at certain tasks, is this compatible with equal opportunity, a goal which is compatible with justice? Should someone's sexual orientation be grounds for restricting their rights? We hear the chant, "No gays or lesbians in the military." But why? Does the chant, "No heterosexuals in the military" make any more sense?

Philosophers distinguish between the **material principle of justice** and the **formal principle of justice.** The material principle is some particular trait which is used as a basis for distributing benefits and burdens. If someone claimed that race, ethnic background, sex, or sexual orientation is the basis upon which he or she decided to deny (or give) someone a job, what would you say? Is this fair? If someone claimed that seniority, skill, and a record of good performance is the basis upon which she or he decided to deny (or give) someone a job, what would you say? Is this fair? The formal principle of justice requires that benefits and burdens be distributed fairly according to relevant differences and similarities. So if I decide to award an A to all my students who wear something red on the first Tuesday of each month, is that fair?

"But," you might properly retort, "that is not relevant."

"Why isn't it?"

168

"Because," you say, "it has nothing to do with how well they perform on the exams."

That is a reasonable response. But why is performance on exams relevant? *How do we decide what is fair?*

One way that philosophers have recommended deciding what is fair, is to listen carefully to both sides of an argument and see which makes most sense. In this chapter arguments on both sides of some contemporary controversial issues will be given and you can decide which position provides "justice for all." But I must warn you: if you wish to consider the issues fairly and objectively, you will need to set aside, as you read, your preconceived ideas so that the voice of those who differ can be heard by you and fairly evaluated.

5.1. The Death Penalty

One of the major topics of public debate today is the death penalty. Those who favor it (usually called *retentionists*) argue that murderers deserve to die because the horribleness of their crimes renders them unfit to live. Those who oppose it (usually called *abolitionists*) argue that the death penalty is a cruel practice worthy of barbarians bloodthirsty for revenge rather than civilized people guided by sober rationality and a respect for life.

Retentionists' arguments are generally of two kinds: (1) those relying on considerations of justice, and (2) those relying on considerations of social utility. Immanuel Kant (see Section 3.1) argued that punishment must be inflicted in a measure that equalizes the offense. When the moral order is upset by some offense, it is only right that this order be rectified by a punishment equal in intensity. Justice demands retribution. Death is the just dessert for those who take life. Utilitarians (see Section 3.2) normally argue that capital punishment is socially useful in *protecting* society from those who have killed (and are likely to kill again) and in *deterring* those who have not murdered others, but might.

Abolitionists generally begin with the assumption that the lives of persons are valuable and every person has the right to life. If this is so, then any deliberate taking of a person's life must be carefully and fully justified. Some abolitionists hold to the absolute sanctity of personal life and argue that there can be no justification for killing of any sort under any circumstances. Some abolitionists are willing to concede that taking human life is justified under some circumstances, but, they argue, the death penalty is inhumane and cruel. The retentionists, they say, have the burden of proof, and their arguments are simply not convincing. Against the just retribution argument, abolitionists respond by claiming that the demand for justice is really a mask for indulging the emotion of vengeance. Against the social utility viewpoint, they point out that there are other, more humane punishments that will serve equally well.

Capital punishment is not just a moral issue, it is an issue of public policy. The Eighth Amendment to the Constitution of the United States prohibits "cruel and unusual" punishment. In *Furman* v. *Georgia* (1972) the Supreme Court held that the death penalty *as then administered* was unconstitutional. Justices Marshall and Brennan argued that the death penalty is cruel and unusual punishment by its very nature, but the majority held that because it was administered in an arbitrary and capricious manner it was cruel and unusual, although it was not cruel and unusual by its very nature.

The majority opinion cleared the way for the states to pass new laws that set standards for the fair administration of capital punishment. Some states (e.g., Georgia) established standards that provided guidance for juries in deciding between life and death, and in *Gregg* v. *Georgia* (1976) those standards came under review. The majority found that the death penalty is constitutional when imposed at the discretion of a jury (or judge) for the crime of murder provided there are appropriate safeguards against arbitrary imposition. Mr. Justice Stewart, with Justices Powell and Stevens concurring, wrote the majority opinion.

Mr. Justice Potter Stewart (1915–1985) was appointed to the court by President Eisenhower in 1958. Prior to that appointment, he served as a judge of the Sixth Circuit Court of Appeals. He was a graduate of Yale Law School. Mr. Justice Thurgood Marshall, who served as a United States circuit judge (1961–1965) and solicitor general (1965–1967), was the first African-American to serve on the Supreme Court. He wrote the dissenting opinion in *Gregg* v. *Georgia*. Mr. Justice Brennan agreed with Mr. Justice Marshall. What follows is an excerpt from that opinion in which Mr. Justice Stewart and Mr. Justice Marshall present their case.

Reading Questions

1. How would you define punishment? How does punishment differ from harm in general?

2. Why, according to Mr. Justice Stewart, is not capital punishment "excessive?"

3. According to Mr. Justice Stewart, what two social purposes must the death penalty serve? Can you think of a third?

4. Why does Mr. Justice Stewart continue to use the deterrence argument when he admits that there is no empirical evidence that supports it?

5. Create your own set of questions, both analytical and critical, about Mr. Justice Marshall's opinion and answer them.

6. How does Mr. Justice Marshall refute the argument that the death penalty is morally justified because the wrongdoer deserves it? Do you agree or not? Why?

Majority Opinion in Gregg v. Georgia

POTTER STEWART

MR. JUSTICE STEWART, *with Justices Powell and Stevens Concurring:* . . . We address initially the basic contention that the punishment of death for the crime of murder is, under all circumstances, "cruel and unusual" in violation of the Eighth and Fourteenth Amendments of the Constitution. [Later in] this opinion, we will consider the sentence of death imposed under the Georgia statutes at issue in this case. . . .

The substantive limits imposed by the Eighth

Justices Potter and Stewart, United States Supreme Court. 428 U.S. 153 (1976).

Amendment on what can be made criminal and punished were discussed in *Robinson* v. *California*, 370 U.S. 660 (1962). The Court found unconstitutional a state statute that made the status of being addicted to a narcotic drug a criminal offense. It held, in effect, that it is "cruel and unusual" to impose any punishment at all for the mere status of addiction. The cruelty in the abstract of the actual sentence imposed was irrelevant: "Even one day in prison would be a cruel and unusual punishment for the 'crime' of having a common cold." *Id.,* at 667. Most recently, in *Furman* v. *Georgia, supra,* three Justices in separate concurring opinions found the Eighth Amendment applicable to procedures employed to select convicted defendants for the sentence of death.

It is clear from the foregoing precedents that the Eighth Amendment has not been regarded as a static concept. As Mr. Chief Justice Warren said, in an oft-quoted phrase, "[t]he Amendment must draw its meaning from the evolving standards of decency that mark the progress of a maturing society." . . . Thus, an assessment of contemporary values concerning the infliction of a challenged sanction is relevant to the application of the Eighth Amendment. As we develop below more fully, . . . this assessment does not call for a subjective judgment. It requires, rather, that we look to objective indicia that reflect the public attitude toward a given sanction.

But our cases also make clear that public perceptions of standards of decency with respect to criminal sanctions are not conclusive. A penalty also must accord with "the dignity of man," which is the "basic concept underlying the Eighth Amendment." *Trop* v. *Dulles* . . . This means, at least, that the punishment not be "excessive." When a form of punishment in the abstract (in this case, whether capital punishment may ever be imposed as a sanction for murder) rather than in the particular (the propriety of death as a penalty to be applied to a specific defendant for a specific crime) is under consideration, the inquiry into "excessiveness" has two aspects. First, the punishment must not involve the unnecessary and wanton infliction of pain. . . .

Second, the punishment must not be grossly out of proportion to the severity of the crime. . . .

The imposition of the death penalty for the crime of murder has a long history of acceptance both in the United States and in England. The common-law rule imposed as mandatory death sentence on all convicted murderers. . . .

It is apparent from the text of the Constitution itself that the existence of capital punishment was accepted by the Framers. At the time the Eighth Amendment was ratified, capital punishment was a common sanction in every State. Indeed, the First Congress of the United States enacted legislation providing death as the penalty for specified crimes. . . .

Four years ago, the petitioners in *Furman* and its companion cases predicted their argument primarily upon the asserted proposition that standards of decency had evolved to the point where capital punishment no longer could be tolerated. The petitioners in those cases said, in effect, that the evolutionary process had come to an end, and that standards of decency required that the Eighth Amendment be construed finally as prohibiting capital punishment for any crime regardless of its depravity and impact on society. This view was accepted by two Justices. Three other Justices were unwilling to go so far; focusing on the procedure by which convicted defendants were selected for the death penalty rather than on the actual punishment inflicted, they joined in the conclusion that the statutes before the Court were constitutionally invalid.

The petitioners in the capital cases before the Court today renew the "standards of decency" argument, but developments during the four years since *Furman* have undercut substantially the assumptions upon which their argument rested. Despite the continuing debate, dating back to the 19th century, over the morality and utility of capital punishment, it is now evident that a large proportion of American society continues to regard it as an appropriate and necessary criminal sanction.

The most marked indication of society's endorsement of the death penalty for murder is the legislative response to *Furman*. The legislatures of at least 35 States have enacted new statutes that provide for the death penalty for at least some crimes that result in the death of another person. And the Congress of the United States, in 1974, enacted a statute providing the death penalty for aircraft piracy that results in death. These recently adopted statutes have attempted to address the concerns expressed by the Court in *Furman* primarily (i) by specifying the factors to be weighed and the procedures to be followed in deciding when to impose a capital sentence, or (ii) by making the death penalty mandatory for specified crimes. . . .

[H]owever, the Eighth Amendment demands more than that a challenged punishment be acceptable to contemporary society. The Court also must ask whether it comports with the basic concept of human dignity at the core of the Amendment. . . .

The death penalty is said to serve two principal social purposes: retribution and deterrence of capital crimes by prospective offenders.

In part, capital punishment is an expression of society's moral outrage at particularly offensive conduct. This function may be unappealing to many, but it is essential in an ordered society that asks its citizens to rely on legal processes rather than self-help to vindicate their wrongs.

> The instinct for retribution is part of the nature of man, and channeling that instinct in the administration of criminal justice serves an important purpose in promoting the stability of a society governed by law. When people begin to believe that organized society is unwilling or unable to impose upon criminal offenders the punishment they 'deserve,' then there are sown the seeds of anarchy—of self-help, vigilante justice, and lynch law. *Forman* v. *Georgia, supra,* at 308 (Stewart, J., concurring).

"Retribution is no longer the dominant objective of the criminal law," *Williams* v. *New York,* 337 U.S. 241, 248 (1949), but neither is it a forbidden objective nor one inconsistent with our respect for the dignity of men. . . . Indeed, the decision that capital punishment may be the appropriate sanction in extreme cases is an expression of the community's belief that certain crimes are themselves so grievous an affront to humanity that the only adequate response may be the penalty of death.

Statistical attempts to evaluate the worth of the death penalty as a deterrent to crimes by potential offenders have occasioned a great deal of debate. The results simply have been inconclusive. . . .

Although some of the studies suggest that the death penalty may not function as a significantly greater deterrent than lesser penalties, there is no convincing empirical evidence either supporting or refuting this view. We may nevertheless assume safely that there are murderers, such as those who act in passion, for whom the threat of death has little or no deterrent effect. But for many others, the death penalty undoubtedly is a significant deterrent. There are carefully contemplated murders, such as murders for hire, where the possible penalty of death may well enter into the cold calculus that precedes the decision to act. And there are some categories of murder, such as murder by a life prisoner, where other sanctions may not be adequate. . . .

Finally, we must consider whether the punishment of death is disproportionate in relation to the crime for which it is imposed. There is no question that death as a punishment is unique in its severity and irrevocability. . . . When a defendant's life is at stake, the Court has been particularly sensitive to insure that every safeguard is observed. . . . But we are concerned here only with the imposition of capital punishment for the crime of murder, and when a life has been taken deliberately by the offender, we cannot say that the punishment is invariably disproportionate to the crime. It is an extreme sanction, suitable to the most extreme of crimes.

We hold that the death penalty is not a form of punishment that may never be imposed, regardless of the circumstances of the offense, regardless of the character of the offender, and regardless of the procedure followed in reaching the decision to impose it.

In summary, the concerns expressed in *Furman* that the penalty of death not be imposed in an arbitrary or capricious manner can be met by a carefully drafted statute that ensures that the sentencing authority is given adequate information and guidance. As a general proposition these concerns are best met by a system that provides for a bifurcated proceeding at which the sentencing authority is apprised of the information relevant to the imposition of sentence and provided with standards to guide its use of the information. . . .

Dissenting Opinion in Gregg v. Georgia

THURGOOD MARSHALL

In Furman v. Georgia (1972) (concurring opinion), I set forth at some length my views on the basic issue presented to the Court in [this case]. The death penalty, I concluded, is a cruel and unusual punishment prohibited by the Eighth and Fourteenth Amendments. That continues to be my view.

I have no intention of retracing the "long and tedious journey" that led to my conclusion in *Furman*. My sole purposes here are to consider the suggestion that my conclusion in *Furman* has been undercut by developments since then, and briefly to evaluate the basis for my Brethren's holding that the extinction of life is a permissible form of punishment under the Cruel and Unusual Punishments Clause.

In *Furman* I concluded that the death penalty is constitutionally invalid for two reasons. First, the death penalty is excessive. And second, the American people, fully informed as to the purposes of the death penalty and its liabilities, would in my view reject it as morally unacceptable.

Since the decision in *Furman*, the legislatures of 35 States have enacted new statutes authorizing the imposition of the death sentence for certain crimes, and Congress has enacted a law providing the death penalty for air piracy resulting in death. I would be less than candid if I did not acknowledge that these developments have a significant bearing on a realistic assessment of the moral acceptability of the death penalty to the American people. But if the constitutionality of the death penalty turns, as I have urged, on the opinion of an *informed* citizenry, then even the enactment of new death statutes cannot be viewed as conclusive. In *Furman*, I observed that the American people are largely unaware of the information critical to a judgment on the morality of the death penalty, and concluded that if they were better informed they would consider it shocking, unjust, and unacceptable. A recent study, conducted after the enactment of the post-*Furman* statutes, has confirmed that the American people know little about the death penalty, and that the opinions of an informed public would differ significantly from those of a public unaware of the consequences and effects of the death penalty.

Even assuming, however, that the post-*Furman* enactment of statutes authorizing the death penalty renders the prediction of the views of an informed citizenry an uncertain basis for a constitutional decision, the enactment of those statutes has no bearing whatsoever on the conclusion that the death penalty is unconstitutional because it is excessive. An excessive penalty is invalid under the Cruel and Unusual Punishments Clause "even though popular sentiment may favor" it. The inquiry here, then, is simply whether the death penalty is necessary to accomplish the

Justice Thurgood Marshall, United States Supreme Court. 428 U.S. 153 (1976).

legitimate legislative purposes in punishment, or whether a less severe penalty—life imprisonment—would do as well.

The two purposes that sustain the death penalty as nonexcessive in the Court's view are general deterrence and retribution. In *Furman,* I canvassed the relevant data on the deterrent effect of capital punishment. The state of knowledge at that point, after literally centuries of debate, was summarized as follows by a United Nations Committee:

> It is generally agreed between the retentionists and abolitionists, whatever their opinions about the validity of comparative studies of deterrence, that the data which now exist show no correlation between the existence of capital punishment and lower rates of capital crime.

The available evidence, I concluded in *Furman,* was convincing that "capital punishment is not necessary as a deterrent to crime in our society." . . .

The evidence I reviewed in *Furman* remains convincing, in my view, that "capital punishment is not necessary as a deterrent to crime in our society." The justification for the death penalty must be found elsewhere.

The other principal purpose said to be served by the death penalty is retribution. The notion that retribution can serve as a moral justification for the sanction of death finds credence in the opinion of my Brothers STEWART, POWELL, and STEVENS. . . . It is this notion that I find to be the most disturbing aspect of today's unfortunate [decision].

The concept of retribution is a multifaceted one, and any discussion of its role in the criminal law must be undertaken with caution. On one level, it can be said that the notion of retribution or reprobation is the basis of our insistence that only those who have broken the law be punished, and in this sense the notion is quite obviously central to a just system of criminal sanctions. But our recognition that retribution plays a crucial role in determining who may be punished by no means requires approval of retribution as a general justification for punishment. It

is the question whether retribution can provide a moral justification for punishment—in particular, capital punishment—that we must consider.

My Brothers STEWART, POWELL, and STEVENS offer the following explanation of the retributive justification for capital punishment:

> The instinct for retribution is part of the nature of man, and channeling that instinct in the administration of criminal justice serves an important purpose in promoting the stability of a society governed by law. When people begin to believe that organized society is unwilling or unable to impose upon criminal offenders the punishment they "deserve," then there are sown the seeds of anarchy—of self-help, vigilante justice, and lynch law.

This statement is wholly inadequate to justify the death penalty. As my Brother BRENNAN stated in *Furman,* "[t]here is no evidence whatever that utilization of imprisonment rather than death encourages private blood feuds and other disorders." It simply defies belief to suggest that the death penalty is necessary to prevent the American people from taking the law into their own hands.

In a related vein, it may be suggested that the expression of moral outrage through the imposition of the death penalty serves to reinforce basic moral values—that it marks some crimes as particularly offensive and therefore to be avoided. The argument is akin to a deterrence argument, but differs in that it contemplates the individual's shrinking from antisocial conduct, not because he fears punishment, but because he has been told in the strongest possible way that the conduct is wrong. This contention, like the previous one, provides no support for the death penalty. It is inconceivable that any individual concerned about conforming his conduct to what society says is "right" would fail to realize that murder is "wrong" if the penalty were simply life imprisonment.

The foregoing contentions—that society's expression of moral outrage through the imposition of the death penalty pre-empts the citizenry from taking the law into its own hands and reinforces moral values—are not retributive in the purest sense. They are essentially utilitarian in that they portray the death penalty as valuable because of its beneficial results. These justifications for the death penalty are inadequate because the penalty is, quite clearly I think, not necessary to the accomplishment of those results.

There remains for consideration, however, what might be termed the purely retributive justification for the death penalty—that the death penalty is appropriate, not because of its beneficial effect on society, but because the taking of the murderer's life is itself morally good. Some of the language of the opinion of my Brothers STEWART, POWELL, and STEVENS . . . appears positively to embrace this notion of retribution for its own sake as a justification for capital punishment. They state:

> [T]he decision that capital punishment may be the appropriate sanction in extreme cases is an expression of the community's belief that certain crimes are themselves so grievous an affront to humanity that the only adequate response may be the penalty of death.

They then quote with approval from Lord Justice Denning's remarks before the British Royal Commission on Capital Punishment:

> The truth is that some crimes are so outrageous that society insists on adequate punishment, because the wrong-doer deserves it, irrespective of whether it is a deterrent or not.

Of course, it may be that these statements are intended as no more than observations as to the popular demands that it is thought must be responded to in order to prevent anarchy. But the implication of the statements appears to me to be quite different—namely, that society's judgment that the murderer "deserves" death must be respected not simply because the preservation of order requires it, but because it is appropriate that society make the judgment and carry it out. It is this latter notion, in particular, that I consider to be fundamentally at odds with the Eighth Amendment. The mere fact that the community demands the murderer's life in return for the evil he has done cannot sustain the death penalty, for as JUSTICES STEWART, POWELL, and STEVENS remind us, "the Eighth Amendment demands more than that a challenged punishment be acceptable to contemporary society." To be sustained under the Eighth Amendment, the death penalty must "compor[t] with the basic concept of human dignity at the core of the Amendment;" the objective in imposing it must be "[consistent] with our respect for the dignity of [other] men." Under these standards, the taking of life "because the wrongdoer deserves it" surely must fail, for such a punishment has as its very basis the total denial of the wrongdoer's dignity and worth.

The death penalty, unnecessary to promote the goal of deterrence or to further any legitimate notion of retribution, is an excessive penalty forbidden by the Eighth and Fourteenth Amendments. I respectfully dissent from the Court's judgment upholding the [sentence] of death imposed upon the [petitioner in this case].

Suggestions for Further Reading

Gertrude Ezorsky has edited a useful volume on the morality of punishment in general with a section devoted explicitly to the issue of capital punishment: *Philosophical Perspectives on Punishment* (Albany: State University of New York Press, 1972). Along the same lines is Jeffrie G. Murphy's *Punishment and Rehabilitation,* 2d ed. (Belmont, CA: Wadsworth, 1985).

Hugo Adam Bedau's *The Death Penalty in America,* 3d ed. (New York: Oxford University Press, 1982) provides a rich selection of material relevant to the death penalty controversy, as does Ernest Van Den Haag and John P. Conrad's *The Death Penalty: A Debate* (New York: Plenum, 1983).

Videos

Crime and Punishment (60 minutes, produced by Annenberg) examines the issues surrounding the death penalty. See also *Crime I: Death Penalty* (28 minutes, National Institute of Justice). See your Media Services Catalogue for more information.

5.2. Abortion

In addition to capital punishment, another hotly debated issue in the United States is abortion. With the landmark decision of the Supreme Court in *Roe v. Wade* (1973), restrictive abortion laws were ruled unconstitutional. Since that decision, various subsequent rulings have opened the door to the states to restrict abortions in various ways. Whatever the legal status of abortion may be, it is still a widely contested ethical issue.

For many people, the moral status of the fetus has been a pivotal issue because if the fetus has a moral status, then we might believe that it has rights. But what sort of rights? The same as the woman or as a baby or a child? Does it have the right to life even if that right conflicts with the woman's right to control her own biological processes? Some claim that the fetus has full moral status and hence its right to life is nearly absolute (those who support this view usually argue for the *Right-to-life*). Others claim that the fetus has no moral status and hence no more rights than a piece of tissue such as an appendix. Still others claim that the fetus, because it is a potential person, has some moral status, but its right to life is by no means absolute, and the woman's rights may outweigh whatever rights the fetus may have in many instances (this is often called the *Pro-choice* position).

As a matter of social policy, the debate has to take into account what compelling interests, if any, the state might have in the regulation of abortion. The right-to-life forces support a Human Life Amendment, which is worded in such a fashion that the fetus is accorded personhood. Such an amendment is calculated to achieve the legal prohibition of abortion except in cases where the woman's life is at stake. Because the fetus is an innocent human life, the State has a compelling moral interest in protecting it, or so the right-to-life forces contend. The pro-choice forces insist that a woman has the right to choose whether she wants to deliver the fetus or not. The Human Life Amendment represents nothing more than an illicit attempt to impose the moral and religious views of one group on those who have different views, or so the pro-choice forces contend. The power of the State should not be used, they argue, to enforce the moral or religious views of one segment of society.

This is a complex debate, and one has to be careful to distinguish the issues. One set of issues is religious. Should the religious views, whatever they may be, determine the law of the land? Another set of issues has to do with whether or not the fetus is a human being in a morally relevant sense. Still another set of issues has to do with the rights of the woman when they conflict with the rights (?) of the fetus. And yet another set of issues has to do with the compelling interest of the State to intervene in what appears to be a private decision.

I present two views. One, by Dr. Judith Jarvis Thomson, a philosopher at MIT who has most recently published a volume on *The Realm of Rights* (Cambridge, MA.: Harvard University Press, 1990) and the other by Dr. Baruch Brody (1943–   ), Professor of Ethics at Rice University, who takes issue with Thomson's views.

Reading Questions

1. According to Thomson, those who are pro-life often rely on a "slippery slope argument." What is the argument and what is wrong with it?

2. What is the point of Thomson's analogy with the violinist?

3. What is the "extreme view" and how does Thomson respond?

4. Does the right to life mean that everyone, under all circumstances, has the moral obligation to preserve the life of another?

5. What is the difference between killing and killing unjustly? Why is this distinction important for Thomson's argument?

6. How does Thomson respond to the point that pregnancy often results from a case of voluntary sex, so the violinist analogy does not hold?

7. Although Thomson intends her argument to support a pro-choice position, does it not in fact justify abortion only in a narrow range of cases? For example, many unwanted pregnancies occur because contraception was not used at all. In such cases one might argue the woman is (partly) to blame and so the resulting fetus should be given the right to use her body? How do you think Thomson would respond?

8. What is Brody's basic criticism of Thomson's position? How do you think Thomson might respond?

9. What is Brody's "essentialist" argument for when a fetus is a human being?. How do you think Thomson might respond to this "essentialist" argument?

10. Create an analytical and a critical question about these two selections and respond.

A Defense of Abortion

JUDITH JARVIS THOMSON

MOST OPPOSITION TO ABORTION relies on the premise that the fetus is a human being, a person, from the moment of conception. The premise is argued for, but, as I think, not well. Take, for example, the most common argument. We are asked to notice that the development of a human being from conception through birth into childhood is continuous; then it is said that to draw a line, to choose a point in this development and say "before this point the thing is not a person, after this point it is a person" is to make an arbitrary choice, a choice for which in the nature of things no good reason can be given. It is concluded that the fetus is, or anyway that we had better say it is, a person from the moment of conception. But this conclusion does not follow. Similar things might be said about the development of an acorn into an oak tree, and it does not follow that acorns are oak trees, or that we had better say they are. Arguments of this form are sometimes called "slippery slope arguments"—the phrase is perhaps self-explanatory—and it is dismaying

Excerpts from Judith Jarvis Thomson's "A Defense of Abortion," Philosophy and Public Affairs, *Vol. 1 (1971), pp. 47–66. Copyright © 1971 by Princeton University Press. Reprinted by permission of Princeton University Press. Section titles added.*

that opponents of abortion rely on them so heavily and uncritically.

I am inclined to agree, however, that the prospects for "drawing a line" in the development of the fetus look dim. I am inclined to think also that we shall probably have to agree that the fetus has already become a human person well before birth. Indeed, it comes as a surprise when one first learns how early in its life it begins to acquire human characteristics. By the tenth week, for example, it already has a face, arms and legs, fingers and toes; it has internal organs, and brain activity is detectable. On the other hand, I think that the premise is false, that the fetus is not a person from the moment of conception. A newly fertilized ovum, a newly implanted clump of cells, is no more a person than an acorn is an oak tree. But I shall not discuss any of this. For it seems to me to be of great interest to ask what happens if, for the sake of argument, we allow the premise. How, precisely, are we supposed to get from there to the conclusion that abortion is morally impermissible? Opponents of abortion commonly spend most of their time establishing that the fetus is a person, and hardly any time explaining the step from there to the impermissibility of abortion. Perhaps they think the step too simple and obvious to require much comment. Or perhaps instead they are simply being economical in argument. Many of those who defend abortion rely on the premise that the fetus is not a person, but only a bit of tissue that will become a person at birth; and why pay out more arguments than you have to? Whatever the explanation, I suggest that the step they take is neither easy nor obvious, that it calls for closer examination than it is commonly given, and that when we do give it this closer examination we shall feel inclined to reject it.

I propose, then, that we grant that the fetus is a person from the moment of conception. How does the argument go from here? Something like this, I take it. Every person has a right to life. So the fetus has a right to life. No doubt the mother has a right to decide what shall happen in and to her body; everyone would grant that. But surely a person's right to life is stronger and more stringent than the mother's right to decide what happens in and to her body, and so outweighs it. So the fetus may not be killed; an abortion may not be performed.

It sounds plausible. But now let me ask you to imagine this. You wake up in the morning and find yourself back to back in bed with an unconscious violinist. A famous unconscious violinist. He has been found to have a fatal kidney ailment, and the Society of Music Lovers has canvassed all the available medical records and found that you alone have the right blood type to help. They have therefore kidnapped you, and last night the violinist's circulatory system was plugged into yours, so that your kidneys can be used to extract poisons from his blood as well as your own. The director of the hospital now tells you, "Look, we're sorry the Society of Music Lovers did this to you—we would never have permitted it if we had known. But still, they did, it, and the violinist now is plugged into you. To unplug you would be to kill him. But never mind, it's only for nine months. By then he will have recovered from his ailment, and can safely be unplugged from you." Is it morally incumbent on you to accede to this situation? No doubt it would be very nice of you if you did, a great kindness. But do you *have* to accede to it? What if it were not nine months, but nine years? Or longer still? What if the director of the hospital says, "Tough luck, I agree, but you've now got to stay in bed, with the violinist plugged into you, for the rest of your life. Because remember this. All persons have a right to life, and violinists are persons. Granted you have a right to decide what happens in and to your body, but a person's right to life outweighs your right to decide what happens in and to your body. So you cannot ever be unplugged from him." I imagine you would regard this as outrageous, which suggests that something really is wrong with that plausible-sounding argument I mentioned a moment ago.

In this case, of course, you were kidnapped; you didn't volunteer for the operation that plugged the violinist into your kidneys. Can those who oppose abortion on the ground I mentioned make an exception for a pregnancy due to rape? Certainly. They can say that persons have a right to life only if they didn't come into existence because of rape; or they can say that all persons have a right to life, but that some have less of a right to life than others, in particular, that those who come into existence because of rape have less. But these statements have a rather unpleasant sound. Surely the question of whether you have a right to life at all, or how much of it you have, shouldn't turn on the question of whether or not you are the product of a rape. And in fact the people who oppose abortion on the ground I mentioned do not make this distinction, and hence do not make an exception in case of rape.

Nor do they make an exception for a case in which the mother has to spend the nine months of her pregnancy in bed. They would agree that would be a great pity, and hard on the mother; but all the same, all persons have a right to life, the fetus is a person, and so on. I suspect, in fact, that they would not make an exception for a case in which, miraculously enough, the pregnancy went on for nine years, or even the rest of the mother's life.

Some won't even make an exception for a case in which continuation of the pregnancy is likely to shorten the mother's life; they regard abortion as impermissible even to save the mother's life. Such cases are nowadays very rare, and many opponents of abortion do not accept this extreme view. All the same, it is a good place to begin: a number of points of interest come out in respect to it.

The Extreme View

Let us call the view that abortion is impermissible even to save the mother's life "the extreme view." I want to suggest first that it does not issue from the argument I mentioned earlier without the addition of some fairly powerful premises. Suppose a woman has become pregnant, and now learns that she has a cardiac condition such that she will die if she carries the baby to term. What

may be done for her? The fetus, being a person, has a right to life, but as the mother is a person too, so has she a right to life. Presumably they have an equal right to life. How is it supposed to come out that an abortion may not be performed? If mother and child have an equal right to life, shouldn't we perhaps flip a coin? Or should we add to the mother's right to life her right to decide what happens in and to her body, which everybody seems to be ready to grant—the sum of her rights now outweighing the fetus' right to life?

The most familiar argument here is the following. We are told that performing the abortion would be directly killing the child, whereas doing nothing would not be killing the mother, but only letting her die. Moreover, in killing the child, one would be killing an innocent person, for the child has committed no crime, and is not aiming at his mother's death. . . . If directly killing an innocent person is murder, and thus is impermissible, then the mother's directly killing the innocent person inside her is murder, and thus is impermissible. But it cannot seriously be thought to be murder if the mother performs an abortion on herself to save her life. It cannot seriously be said that she *must* refrain, that she *must* sit passively by and wait for her death. Let us look again at the case of you and the violinist. There you are, in bed with the violinist, and the director of the hospital says to you, "It's all most distressing, and I deeply sympathize, but you see this is putting an additional strain on your kidneys, and you'll be dead within the month. But you *have* to stay where you are all the same. Because unplugging you would be directly killing an innocent violinist, and that's murder, and that's impermissible." If anything in the world is true, it is that you do not commit murder, you do not do what is impermissible, if you reach around to your back and unplug yourself from that violinist to save your life. . . .

In sum, a woman surely can defend her life against the threat to it posed by the unborn child, even if doing so involves its death. And this shows . . . that the extreme view of abortion is false, and so we need not canvass any other possible ways of arriving at it from the argument I mentioned at the outset.

The Right to Life

Where the mother's life is not at stake, the argument I mentioned at the outset seems to have a much stronger pull. "Everyone has a right to life, so the unborn person has a right to life." And isn't the child's right to life weightier than anything other than the mother's own right to life, which she might put forward as ground for an abortion?

This argument treats the right to life as if it were unproblematic. It is not, and this seems to me to be precisely the source of the mistake.

For we should now, at long last, ask what it comes to, to have a right to life. In some views having a right to life includes having a right to be given at least the bare minimum one needs for continued life. But suppose that what in fact *is* the bare minimum a man needs for continued life is something he has no right at all to be given? If I am sick unto death, and the only thing that will save my life is the touch of Henry Fonda's cool hand on my fevered brow, then all the same, I have no right to be given the touch of Henry Fonda's cool hand on my fevered brow. It would be frightfully nice of him to fly in from the West Coast to provide it. It would be less nice, though no doubt well meaning, if my friends flew out to the West Coast and carried Henry Fonda back with them. But I have no right at all against anybody that he should do this for me. Or again, to return to the story I told earlier, the fact that for continued life that violinist needs the continued use of your kidneys does not establish that he has a right to be given the continued use of your kidneys. He certainly has no right against you that *you* should give him continued use of your kidneys. For nobody has any right to use your kidneys unless you give him such a right; and nobody has the right against you that you shall give him this right—if you do allow him to go on using your kidneys, this is a kindness on your part, and not something he can claim from

you as his due. Nor has he any right against anybody else that *they* should give him continued use of your kidneys. Certainly he had no right against the Society of Music Lovers that they should plug him into you in the first place. And if you now start to unplug yourself, having learned that you will otherwise have to spend nine years in bed with him, there is nobody in the world who must try to prevent you, in order to see to it that he is given something he has a right to be given.

Some people are rather stricter about the right to life. In their view, it does not include the right to be given anything, but amounts to, and only to, the right not to be killed by anybody. But here a related difficulty arises. If everybody is to refrain from killing that violinist, then everybody must refrain from doing a great many different sorts of things. Everybody must refrain from slitting his throat, everybody must refrain from shooting him—and everybody must refrain from unplugging you from him. But does he have a right against everybody that they shall refrain from unplugging you from him? To refrain from doing this is to allow him to continue to use your kidneys. It could be argued that he has a right against us that *we* should allow him to continue to use your kidneys. That is, while he had no right against us that we should give him the use of your kidneys, it might be argued that he anyway has a right against us that we shall not now intervene and deprive him of the use of your kidneys. I shall come back to third-party interventions later. But certainly the violinist has no right against you that *you* shall allow him to continue to use your kidneys. As I said, if you do allow him to use them, it is a kindness on your part, and not something you owe him. . . .

The Right to Use the Mother's Body

There is another way to bring out the difficulty. In the most ordinary sort of case, to deprive someone of what he has a right to is to treat him unjustly. Suppose a boy and his small brother are jointly given a box of chocolates for Christmas. If the older boy takes the box and refuses to give his brother any of the chocolates, he is unjust to him, for the brother has been given a right to half of them. But suppose that, having learned that otherwise it means nine years in bed with that violinist, you unplug yourself from him. You surely are not being unjust to him for you gave him no right to use your kidneys, and no one else can have given him any such right. But we have to notice that in unplugging yourself, you are killing him; and violinists, like everybody else, have a right to life, and thus in the view we were considering just now, the right not to be killed. So here you do what he supposedly has a right you shall not do, but you do not act unjustly to him in doing it.

The emendation which may be made at this point is this: the right to life consists not in the right not to be killed, but rather in the right not to be killed unjustly. This runs a risk of circularity, but never mind; it would enable us to square the fact that the violinist has a right to life with the fact that you do not act unjustly toward him in unplugging yourself, thereby killing him. For if you do not kill him unjustly, you do not violate his right to life, and so it is no wonder you do him no injustice.

But if this emendation is accepted, the gap in the argument against abortion stares us plainly in the face: it is by no means enough to show that the fetus is a person, and to remind us that all persons have a right to life—we need to be shown also that killing the fetus violates its right to life, i.e., that abortion is unjust killing. And is it?

I suppose we may take it as a datum that in a case of pregnancy due to rape the mother has not given the unborn person a right to the use of her body for food and shelter. Indeed, in what pregnancy could it be supposed that the mother has given the unborn person such a right? It is not as if there were unborn persons drifting about the world, to whom a woman who wants a child says, "I invite you in."

But it might be argued that there are other ways one can have acquired a right to the use of another person's body than by having been invited to use it by that person. Suppose a woman voluntarily indulges in intercourse, knowing of the chance it will issue in pregnancy, and then she does become pregnant; is she not in part responsible for the presence, in fact the very existence, of the unborn person inside her? No doubt she did not invite it in. But doesn't her partial responsibility for its being there itself give it a right to the use of her body? If so, then her aborting it would be more like the boy's taking away the chocolates, and less like your unplugging yourself from the violinist—doing so would be depriving it of what it does have a right to, and thus would be doing it an injustice.

And then, too, it might be asked whether or not she can kill it even to save her own life: If she voluntarily called it into existence, how can she now kill it, even in self-defense?

The first thing to be said about this is that it is something new. Opponents of abortion have been so concerned to make out the independence of the fetus, in order to establish that it has a right to life, just as its mother does, that they have tended to overlook the possible support they might gain from making out that the fetus is *dependent* on the mother, in order to establish that she has a special kind of responsibility for it, a responsibility that gives it rights against her which are not possessed by any independent person—such as an ailing violinist who is a stranger to her.

On the other hand, this argument would give the unborn person a right to its mother's body only if her pregnancy resulted from a voluntary act, undertaken in full knowledge of the chance a pregnancy might result from it. It would leave out entirely the unborn person whose existence is due to rape. Pending the availability of some further argument, then, we would be left with the conclusion that unborn persons whose existence is due to rape have no right to the use of their mothers' bodies, and thus that aborting them is not depriving them of anything they have a right to and hence is not unjust killing.

And we should also notice that it is not at all plain that this argument really does go even as far as it purports to. For there are cases and cases, and the details make a difference. If the room is stuffy, and I therefore open a window to air it, and a burglar climbs in, it would be absurd to say,

"Ah, now he can stay, she's given him a right to the use of her house—for she is partially responsible for his presence there, having voluntarily done what enabled him to get in, in full knowledge that there are such things as burglars, and that burglars burgle." It would be still more absurd to say this if I had had bars installed outside my windows, precisely to prevent burglars from getting in, and a burglar got in only because of a defect in the bars. It remains equally absurd if we imagine it is not a burglar who climbs in, but an innocent person who blunders or falls in. Again, suppose it were like this: people-seeds drift about in the air like pollen, and if you open your windows, one may drift in and take root in your carpets or upholstery. You don't want children, so you fix up your windows with fine mesh screens, the very best you can buy. As can happen, however, and on very, very rare occasions does happen, one of the screens is defective; and a seed drifts in and takes root. Does the person-plant who now develops have a right to the use of your house? Surely not—despite the fact that you voluntarily opened your windows, you knowingly kept carpets and upholstered furniture, and you knew that screens were sometimes defective. Someone may argue that you are responsible for its rooting, that it does have a right to your house, because after all you *could* have lived out your life with bare floors and furniture, or with sealed windows and doors. But this won't do—for by the same token anyone can avoid a pregnancy due to rape by having a hysterectomy, or anyway by never leaving home without a (reliable!) army. . . .

There is room for yet another argument here, however. We surely must all grant that there may be cases in which it would be morally indecent to detach a person from your body at the cost of his life. Suppose you learn that what the violinist needs is not nine years of your life, but only one hour: all you need do to save his life is to spend one hour in that bed with him. Suppose also that letting him use your kidneys for that one hour would not affect your health in the slightest. Admittedly you were kidnapped. Admittedly you did not give anyone permission to plug him into you. Nevertheless it seems to me plain you *ought* to allow him to use your kidneys for that hour—it would be indecent to refuse.

Again, suppose pregnancy lasted only an hour, and constituted no threat to life or health. And suppose that a woman becomes pregnant as a result of rape. Admittedly she did not voluntarily do anything to bring about the existence of a child. Admittedly she did nothing at all which would give the unborn person a right to the use of her body. All the same it might well be said, as in the newly emended violinist story, that she *ought* to allow it to remain for that hour—that it would be indecent in her to refuse. . . .

So my own view is that even though you ought to let the violinist use your kidneys for the one hour he needs, we should not conclude that he has a right to do so—we would say that if you refuse, you are, like the boy who owns all the chocolates and will give none away, self-centered and callous, indecent in fact, but not unjust. And similarly, that even supposing a case in which a woman pregnant due to rape ought to allow the unborn person to use her body for the hour he needs, we should not conclude that he has a right to do so; we should conclude that she is self-centered, callous, indecent, but not unjust, if she refuses. The complaints are no less grave; they are just different. . . .

What we should ask is not whether anybody should be compelled by law to be a Good Samaritan, but whether we must accede to a situation in which somebody is being compelled—by nature, perhaps—to be a Good Samaritan. . . . There you are, you were kidnapped, and nine years in bed with that violinist lie ahead of you. You have your own life to lead. You are sorry, but you simply cannot see giving up so much of your life to the sustaining of his. You cannot extricate yourself, and ask us to do so. I should have thought that—in light of his having no right to the use of your body—it was obvious that we do not have to accede to your being forced to give up so much. We can do what you ask. There is no injustice to the violinist in our doing so. . . .

Abortion and the Sanctity of Human Life: A Philosophical View

BARUCH BRODY

The Woman's Right to Her Body

It is a common claim that a woman ought to be in control of what happens to her body to the greatest extent possible, that she ought to be able to use her body in ways that she wants to and refrain from using it in ways that she does not want to. This right is particularly pressed where certain uses of her body have deep and lasting effects upon the character of her life, personal, social, and economic. Therefore, it is argued, a woman should be free either to carry her fetus to term, thereby using her body to support it, or to abort the fetus, thereby not using her body for that purpose.

In some contexts in which this argument is advanced, it is clear that it is not addressed to the issue of the morality of abortion at all. Rather, it is made in opposition to laws against abortion on the ground that the choice to abort or not is a moral decision that should belong only to the mother. But that specific direction of the argument is irrelevant to our present purposes; I will consider it [later] when I deal with the issues raised by laws prohibiting abortions. For the moment, I am concerned solely with the use of this principle as a putative ground tending to show the permissibility of abortion, with the claim that because it is the woman's body that carries the fetus and upon which the fetus depends, she has certain rights to abort the fetus that no one else may have.

We may begin by remarking that it is obviously correct that, as carrier of the fetus, the mother has it within her power to choose whether or not to abort the fetus. And, as an autonomous and responsible agent, she must make this choice. But let us notice that this in no way entails either that whatever choice she makes is morally right or that no one else has the right to evaluate the decision that she makes.

At first glance, it would seem that this argument cannot be used by anyone who supposes, as we do for the moment, that there is a point in fetal development from which time on the fetus is a human being. After all, people do not have the right to do anything whatsoever that may be necessary for them to retain control over the uses of their bodies. In particular, it would seem wrong for them to kill another human being in order to do so.

In a recent article, Professor Judith Thomson has, in effect, argued that this simple view is mistaken. How does Professor Thomson defend her claim that the mother has a right to abort the fetus, even if it is a human being, whether or not her life is threatened and whether or not she has consented to the act of intercourse in which the fetus is conceived? At one point, discussing just the case in which the mother's life is threatened, she makes the following suggestion:

> In [abortion], there are only two people involved, one whose life is threatened and one who threatens it. Both are innocent: the one who is threatened is not threatened because of any fault, the one who threatens does not threaten because of any fault. For this reason, we may feel that we bystanders cannot intervene. But the person threatened can.

But surely this description is equally applicable to the following case: *A* and *B* are adrift on a lifeboat, *B* has a disease that he can survive, but *A,* if he contracts it, will die, and the only way that *A* can avoid that is by killing *B* and pushing him overboard. Surely, *A* has no right to do this. So there must be some special reason why the mother has, if she does, the right to abort the fetus.

There is, to be sure, an important difference between our lifeboat case and abortion, one that leads us to the heart of Professor Thomson's argument. In the case that we envisaged, both *A* and *B* have equal rights to be in the lifeboat, but the mother's body is hers and not the fetus's and she has first rights to its use. The primacy of these rights allow an abortion whether or not her life is threatened. Professor Thomson summarizes this argument in the following way:

> I am arguing only that having a right to life does not guarantee having either a right to be given the use of, or a right to be allowed continued use of, another person's body—even if one needs it for life itself.

One part of this claim is clearly correct. I have no duty to *X* to save *X's* life by giving him the use of my body (or my life savings, or the only home I have, and so on), and *X* has no right, even to save his life, to any of those things. Thus, the fetus conceived in the laboratory that will perish unless it is implanted into a woman's body has in fact no right to any woman's body. But this portion of the claim is irrelevant to the abortion issue, for in abortion of the fetus that is a human being the mother must kill *X* to get back the sole use of her body, and that is an entirely different matter.

This point can also be put as follows: . . . we must distinguish the taking of *X's* life from the saving of *X's* life, even if we assume that one has a duty not to do the former and to do the latter. Now that latter duty, if it exists at all, is much weaker than the first duty; many circumstances may relieve us from the latter duty that will not relieve us from the former one. Thus, I am certainly relieved from my duty to save *X's* life by the fact that fulfilling it means the loss of my life savings. It may be noble for me to save *X's* life at the cost of everything I have, but I certainly have no duty to do that. And the same observation may be made about cases in which I can save *X's* life by giving him the use of my body for an extended period of time. However, I am not relieved of my duty not to take *X's* life by the fact that fulfilling it means the loss of everything I have and not even by the fact that fulfilling it means the loss of my life. . . .

At one point in her paper, Professor Thomson does consider this objection. She has previously imagined the following case: a famous violinist, who is dying from a kidney ailment, has been, without your consent, plugged into you for a period of time so that his body can use your kidneys:

> Some people are rather stricter about the right to life. In their view, it does not include the right to be given anything, but amounts to, and only to, the right not to be killed by anybody. But here a related difficulty arises. If everybody is to refrain from killing that violinist, then everybody must refrain from doing a great many different sorts of things . . . everybody must refrain from unplugging you from him. But does he have a right against everybody that they shall refrain from unplugging you from him? To refrain from doing this is to allow him to continue to use your kidneys . . . certainly the violinist has no right against you that you shall allow him to continue to use your kidneys.

Applying this argument to the case of abortion, we can see that Professor Thomson's argument would run as follows:

1. Assume that the fetus's right to life includes the right not to be killed by the woman carrying him.

2. But to refrain from killing the fetus is to allow him the continued use of the woman's body.

3. So our first assumption entails that the fetus's right to life includes the right to the continued use of the woman's body.

4. But we all grant that the fetus does not have the right to the continued use of the woman's body.

5. Therefore, the fetus's right to life cannot include the right not to be killed by the woman in question.

And it is also now clear what is wrong with this argument. When we granted that the fetus has no right to the continued use of the woman's body, all that we meant was that he does not have this right merely because the continued use saves his life. But, of course, there may be other reasons why he has this right. One would be that the only way to take the use of the woman's body away from the fetus is by killing him, and that is something that neither she nor we have the right to do. So, I submit, the way in which Assumption 4 is true is irrelevant, and cannot be used by Professor Thomson, for Assumption 4 is true only in cases where the saving of the life of the fetus is at stake and not in cases where the taking of his life is at stake.

I conclude therefore that Professor Thomson has not established the truth of her claims about abortion, primarily because she has not sufficiently attended to the distinction between our duty to save *X's* life and our duty not to take it. Once one attends to that distinction, it would seem that the mother, in order to regain control over her body, has no right to abort the fetus from the point at which it becomes a human being.

It may also be useful to say a few words about the larger and less rigorous context of the argument that the woman has a right to her own body. It is surely true that one way in which women have been oppressed is by their being denied authority over their own bodies. But it seems to me that, as the struggle is carried on for meaningful amelioration of such oppression, it ought not to be carried so far that it violates the steady responsibilities all people have to one another. Parents may not desert their children, one class may not oppress another, one race or nation may not exploit another. For parents, powerful groups in society, races or nations in ascendancy, there are penalties for refraining from these wrong actions, but those penalties can in no way be taken as the justification for such

wrong actions. Similarly, if the fetus is a human being, the penalty of carrying it cannot, I believe, be used as the justification for destroying it. . . .

Abortion to Save the Mother

Let us begin by considering the case in which the continued existence of the fetus threatens the life of the mother. This would seem to be the case in which she has the strongest claim for the right to abort the fetus even if it is a human being with a right to life. . . .

Why would it not be permissible for the mother to have an abortion in order to save her life even after that point at which the fetus becomes a human being? After all, the fetus's continued existence poses a threat to the life of the mother, and why can't she void that threat by taking the life of the fetus, as an ultimate act of defense?

To be sure, it may be the physician, or other agent, who will cause the abortion, and not the mother herself, but that difference seems to be irrelevant. Our intuition is that the person whose life is threatened (call that person A) may either take the life of the person (B) who threatens his life or call upon someone else (C) to do so. And more important, it seems permissible (and perhaps even obligatory in some cases) for C to take B's life in order to save A's life. Put in traditional terms, we were really speaking of the mother's right as the pursued, or anyone else's right as an onlooker, to take the life of the fetus who is the pursuer.

Pope Pius XI observed, in objecting to this argument from self-defense, that in the paradigm case of killing the pursuer B is unjustly attempting to take A's life and is responsible for this attempt. It is the resulting guilt, based in part on B's intention (found in the attempt to kill A), together with the fact that A will die unless B is stopped, which permits the taking of B's life. The reader will notice that the abortion situation is quite different. Leaving aside for now—we shall return to it later on—the question as to whether the fetus can properly be described as attempting to take the mother's life, we can certainly agree that the fetus is not responsible for such an attempt (if it is occurring), that the fetus is therefore innocent, not guilty, and that the taking of fetal life cannot be compared to the paradigm case of killing the pursuer.

There is another way of putting Pope Pius' point. Consider the following case: there is, let us imagine, a medicine that A needs to stay alive, C owns some, and C will give it to A only if A kills B. Moreover, A has no other way of getting the medicine. In this case, the continued existence of B certainly poses a threat to the life of A; A can survive only if B does not survive. Still, it is not permissible for A to kill B in order to save A's life. Why not? How does this case differ from the paradigm case of killing the pursuer? The simplest answer is that in this case, while B's continued existence poses a threat to the life of A, B is not guilty of attempting to take A's life because there is no attempt to be guilty about it in the first place. Now if we consider the case of a fetus whose continued existence poses a threat to the life of the mother, we see that it is like the medicine case and not like the paradigm case of killing the pursuer. The fetus does pose (in our imagined situation) a threat to the life of its mother, but it is not guilty of attempting to take its mother's life. Consequently, in an analogue to the medicine case, the mother (or her agent) could not justify destroying the fetus on the ground that it would be a permissible act of killing the pursuer.

The persuasiveness of both of the preceding arguments indicates that we have to analyze the whole issue of pursuit far more carefully before we can definitely decide whether an abortion to save the life of the mother could be viewed as a permissible act of killing the pursuer. If we look again at a paradigm case of pursuit, we see that there are three factors involved:

1. The continued existence of B poses a threat to the life of A, a threat that can be met only by the taking of B's life (we shall refer to this as the condition of *danger*).

2. B is unjustly attempting to take A's life (we shall refer to this as the condition of *attempt*).

3. B is responsible for his attempt to take A's life (we shall refer to this as the condition of *guilt*).

In the medicine case, only the danger condition was satisfied. Our intuition that it would be wrong for A to take B's life in that case reflects our belief that the mere fact that B is a danger to A is not sufficient to establish that killing B will be a justifiable act of killing a pursuer. But it would be rash to conclude, as Pope Pius did, that all three conditions must be satisfied before the killing of B will be a justifiable act of killing a pursuer. What would happen, for example, if the first two conditions, but not the guilt condition, were satisfied?

There are good reasons for supposing that the satisfaction of the first two conditions is sufficient justification for taking B's life as an act of killing the pursuer. Consider, for example, a variation of the pursuit paradigm—one in which B is about to shoot. A, and the only way by which A can stop him is by killing him first—but one in which B is a minor who is not responsible for his attempt to take A's life. In this case, the only condition not satisfied is the condition of guilt. Still, despite that fact, it seems that A may justifiably take B's life as a permissible act of killing a pursuer. The guilt of the pursuer, then, is not a requirement for legitimacy in killing the pursuer. . . .

To summarize, then, our general discussion of killing the pursuer, we can say the following: the mere satisfaction of the danger condition is not sufficient to justify the killing of the pursuer. If, in addition . . . the attempt condition . . . is satisfied, then one would be justified in killing the pursuer to save the life of the pursued. In any case, the condition of guilt, arising from full knowledge and intent, need not be satisfied. . . .

Is, then, the aborting of the fetus, when necessary to save the life of the mother, a permissible act of killing a pursuer? It is true that in such cases the fetus is a danger to his mother. But it is also clear that the condition of attempt is not satisfied. The fetus has neither the beliefs nor the intentions to which we have referred. Furthermore, there is on the part of the fetus no action that threatens the life of the mother. . . . It seems to follow, therefore, that aborting the fetus could not be a permissible act of killing a pursuer. . . .

Two Additional Cases

All of the arguments that we have looked at so far are attempts to show that there is something special about abortion that justifies its being treated differently from other cases of the taking of human life. We shall now consider claims that are confined to certain special cases of abortion: the case in which the mother has been raped . . . and the case in which having the child may cause a problem for the rest of her family (the latter case is a particular case of the societal argument). In addressing these issues, we shall see whether there is any point to the permissibility of abortions in some of the cases covered by the Model Penal Code proposals.

When the expectant mother has conceived after being raped, there are two different sorts of considerations that might support the claim that she has the right to take the life of the fetus. They are the following: (A) the woman in question has already suffered immensely from the act of rape and the physical and/or psychological after-effects of that act. It would be particularly unjust, the argument runs, for her to have to live through an unwanted pregnancy owing to that act of rape. Therefore, even if we are at a stage at which the fetus is a human being, the mother has the right to abort it; (B) the fetus in question has no right to be in that woman. It was put there as a result of an act of aggression upon her by the rapist, and its continued presence is an act of aggression against the mother. She has a right to repel that aggression by aborting the fetus.

The first argument is very compelling. We can all agree that a terrible injustice has been committed on the woman who is raped. The question that we have to consider, however, is whether it follows that it is morally permissible for her to abort the fetus. We must make that consideration reflecting that, however unjust the act of rape, it was not the fetus who committed or commissioned it. The injustice of the act, then, should in no way impinge upon the rights of the fetus, for it is innocent. What remains is the initial misfor-

tune of the mother (and the injustice of her having to pass through the pregnancy, and, further, to assume responsibility of at least giving the child over for adoption or assuming the burden of its care.) However unfortunate that circumstance, however unjust, the misfortune and the injustice are not sufficient cause to justify the taking of the life of an innocent human being as a means of mitigation.

It is at this point that Argument B comes in, for its whole point is that the fetus, by its mere presence in the mother, is committing an act of aggression against her, one over and above the one committed by the rapist, and one that the mother has a right to repel by abortion. But . . . (1) the fetus is certainly innocent (in the sense of not responsible) for any act of aggression against the mother and that (2) the mere presence of the fetus in the mother, no matter how unfortunate for her, does not constitute an act of aggression by the fetus against the mother. Argument B fails then at just that point at which Argument A needs its support, and we can therefore conclude that the fact that pregnancy is the result of rape does not give the mother the right to abort the fetus. . . .

We come finally to those cases in which the continuation of the pregnancy would cause serious problems for the rest of the family. There are a variety of cases that we have to consider here together. Perhaps the health of the mother will be affected in such a way that she cannot function effectively as a wife and mother during, or even after, the pregnancy. Or perhaps the expenses incurred as a result of the pregnancy would be utterly beyond the financial resources of the family. The important point is that the continuation of the pregnancy raises a serious problem for other innocent people involved besides the mother and the fetus, and it may be argued that the mother has the right to abort the fetus to avoid that problem.

By now, the difficulties with this argument should be apparent. We have seen earlier that the mere fact that the continued existence of the fetus threatens to harm the mother does not, by itself, justify the aborting of the fetus. Why should anything be changed by the fact that the threatened harm will accrue to the other members of the family and not to the mother? Of course, it would be different if the fetus were committing an act of aggression against the other members of the family. But, once more, this is certainly not the case.

We conclude, therefore, that none of these special circumstances justifies an abortion from that point at which the fetus is a human being. . . .

Fetal Humanity and Brain Function

The question which we must now consider is the question of fetal humanity. Some have argued that the fetus is a human being with a right to life (or, for convenience, just a human being) from the moment of conception. Others have argued that the fetus only becomes a human being at the moment of birth. Many positions in between these two extremes have also been suggested. How are we to decide which is correct?

The analysis which we will propose here rests upon certain metaphysical assumptions which I have defended elsewhere. These assumptions are: (a) the question is when has the fetus acquired all the properties essential (necessary) for being a human being, for when it has, it is a human being; (b) these properties are such that the loss of any one of them means that the human being in question has gone out of existence and not merely stopped being a human being; (c) human beings go out of existence when they die. It follows from these assumptions that the fetus becomes a human being when it acquires all those characteristics which are such that the loss of any one of them would result in the fetus's being dead. We must, therefore, turn to the analysis of death. . . .

We will first consider the question of what properties are essential to being human if we suppose that death and the passing out of existence occur only if there has been an irreparable cessation of brain function (keeping in mind that the condition itself, as we have noted, is a matter of medical judgment). We shall then consider the same question on the supposition that [Paul] Ramsey's more complicated theory of death (the modified traditional view) is correct.

According to what is called the brain-death theory, as long as there has not been an irreparable cessation of brain function the person in question continues to exist, no matter what else has happened to him. If so, it seems to follow that there is only one property—leaving aside those entailed by this one property—that is essential to humanity, namely, the possession of a brain that has not suffered an irreparable cessation of function.

Several consequences follow immediately from this conclusion. We can see that a variety of often advanced claims about the essence of humanity are false. For example, the claim that movement, or perhaps just the ability to move, is essential for being human is false. A human being who has stopped moving, and even one who has lost the ability to move, has not therefore stopped existing. Being able to move, and a fortiori moving, are not essential properties of human beings and therefore are not essential to being human. Similarly, the claim that being perceivable by other human beings is essential for being human is also false. A human being who has stopped being perceivable by other humans (for example, someone isolated on the other side of the moon, out of reach even of radio communication) has not stopped existing. Being perceivable by other human beings is not an essential property of human beings and is not essential to being human. And the same point can be made about the claims that viability is essential for being human, that independent existence is essential for being human, and that actual interaction with other human beings is essential for being human. The loss of any of these properties would not mean that the human being in question had gone out of existence, so none of them can be essential to that human being and none of them can be essential for being human.

Let us now look at the following argument: (1) A functioning brain (or at least, a brain that, if not functioning, is susceptible of function) is a property that every human being must have because it is essential for being human. (2) By the time an entity acquires that property, it has all the other properties that are essential for being human. Therefore, when the fetus acquires that property it becomes a human being. It is clear that the property in question is, according to the brain-death theory, one that is had essentially by all human beings. The question that we have to consider is whether the second premise is true. It might appear that its truth does follow from the brain-death theory. After all, we did see that the theory entails that only one property (together with those entailed by it) is essential for being human. Nevertheless, rather than relying solely on my earlier argument, I shall adopt an alternative approach to strengthen the conviction that this second premise is true: I shall note that the important ways in which the fetus resembles and differs from an ordinary human being by the time it definitely has a functioning brain (about the end of the sixth week of development). It shall then be evident, in light of our theory of essentialism, that none of these differences involves the lack of some property in the fetus that is essential for its being human.

Structurally, there are few features of the human being that are not fully present by the end of the sixth week. Not only are the familiar external features and all the internal organs present, but the contours of the body are nicely rounded. More important, the body is functioning. Not only is the brain functioning, but the heart is beating sturdily (the fetus by this time has its own completely developed vascular system), the stomach is producing digestive juices, the liver is manufacturing blood cells, the kidney is extracting uric acid from the blood, and the nerves and muscles are operating in concert, so that reflex reactions can begin.

What are the properties that a fetus acquires after the sixth week of its development? Certain structures do appear later. These include the fingernails (which appear in the third month), the completed vocal chords (which also appear then), taste buds and salivary glands (again, in the third month), and hair and eyelashes (in the fifth month). In addition, certain functions begin later than the sixth week. The fetus begins to urinate (in the third month), to move spontaneously (in the third month), to respond to external stimuli (at least in the fifth month), and to breathe (in the sixth month). Moreover, there is a constant

growth in size. And finally, at the time of birth the fetus ceases to receive its oxygen and food through the placenta and starts receiving them through the mouth and nose.

I will not examine each of these properties (structures and functions) to show that they are not essential for being human. The procedure would be essentially the one used previously to show that various essentialist claims are in error. We might, therefore, conclude, on the supposition that the brain-death theory is correct, that the fetus becomes a human being about the end of the sixth week after its development.

There is, however, one complication that should be noted here. There are, after all, progressive stages in the physical development and in the functioning of the brain. For example, the fetal brain (and nervous system) does not develop sufficiently to support spontaneous motion until some time in the third month after conception. There is, of course, no doubt that that stage of development is sufficient for the fetus to be human. No one would be likely to maintain that a spontaneously moving human being has died; and similarly, a spontaneously moving fetus would seem to have become human. One might, however, want to claim that the fetus does not become a human being until the point of spontaneous movement. So then, on the supposition that the brain-death theory is correct, one ought to conclude that the fetus becomes a human being at some time between the sixth and twelfth week after its conception.

But what if we reject the brain-death theory, and replace it with its equally plausible contender, Ramsey's theory of death? According to that theory—which we can call the brain, heart, and lung theory of death—the human being does not die, does not go out of existence, until such time as the brain, heart and lungs have irreparably ceased functioning naturally. What are the essential features of being human according to this theory?

Actually, the adoption of Ramsey's theory requires no major modifications. According to that theory, what is essential to being human, what each human being must retain if he is to continue to exist, is the possession of a functioning (actually or potentially) heart, lung, or brain. It is only when a human being possesses none of these that he dies and goes out of existence; and the fetus comes into humanity, so to speak, when he acquires one of these.

On Ramsey's theory, the argument would now run as follows: (1) The property of having a functioning brain, heart, or lungs (or at least organs of the kind that, if not functioning, are susceptible of function) is one that every human being must have because it is essential for being human. (2) By the time that an entity acquires that property it has all the other properties that are essential for being human. Therefore, when the fetus acquires that property it becomes a human being. There remains, once more, the problem of the second premise. Since the fetal heart starts operating rather early, it is not clear that the second premise is correct. Many systems are not yet operating, and many structures are not yet present. Still, following our theory of essentialism, we should conclude that the fetus becomes a human being when it acquires a functioning heart (the first of the organs to function in the fetus).

There is, however, a further complication here, and it is analogous to the one encountered if we adopt the brain-death theory: When may we properly say that the fetal heart begins to function? At two weeks, when occasional contrac-tions of the primitive fetal heart are present? In the fourth to fifth week, when the heart, although incomplete, is beating regularly and pumping blood cells through a closed vascular system, and when the tracings obtained by an ECG exhibit the classical elements of an adult tracing? Or after the end of the seventh week, when the fetal heart is functioning complete and "normal"?

We have not reached a precise conclusion in our study of the question of when the fetus becomes a human being. We do know that it does so some time between the end of the second week and the end of the third month. But it surely is not a human being at the moment of conception and it surely is one by the end of the third month. Though we have not come to a final answer to our question, we have narrowed the range of acceptable answers considerably.

[In summary] we have argued that the fetus becomes a human being with a right to life some time between the second and twelfth week after conception. We have also argued that abortions are morally impermissible after that point except in rather unusual circumstances. What is crucial to note is that neither of these arguments appeal to any theological considerations. We conclude, therefore, that there is a human-rights basis for moral opposition to abortions. . . .

Suggestions for Further Reading

Joel Feinberg has edited an excellent collection of essays entitled *The Problem of Abortion* (Belmont, CA: Wadsworth, 1984).

James M. Humber's "Abortion: The Avoidable Moral Dilemma," in *Journal of Value Inquiry,* Vol. 9 (Winter, 1975), pp. 282–302, defends a conservative view, contending that pro-choice arguments are little more than "after-the-fact rationalizations."

In the now classic "On the Moral and Legal Status of Abortion," in *The Monist,* Vol. 57 (January, 1973), pp. 43–61, Mary Ann Warren argues that abortion is morally justified if the woman who is pregnant wants it because the fetus is not a person. For a nearly complete survey of all the relevant arguments see Bonnie Steinbock, *Life Before Birth: The Moral and Legal Status of Embryos and Fetuses,* (New York: Oxford University Press. 1992).

Audio-Video

Abortion: Listen to the Woman (Planned Parenthood Producers, audiotape only). The problems of parenthood are discussed by women. *Roe vs. Wade* (92 minutes, Paramount) dramatizes the circumstances surrounding this landmark decision on abortion. See your Media Services Catalogue for more information.

5.3. Sex-Stereotyping and Equal Opportunity

Are sex roles morally justifiable? Should we, can we, abolish sex roles? According to the formal principle of justice (see the introduction to this chapter), equals should be treated as equals and unequals should be treated as unequals in proportion to their relevant differences. Are sex roles consistent with this principle, or do they violate it? Are men and women equal or unequal? Is sex a relevant difference?

It is clear that we live in a society in which the division of labor is based, in part, on sex roles. There is "women's work" and "men's work." Female workers earn less than male workers for doing the same job. Women are clustered in the lowest-paid occupations. We hear comments like, "Women are too emotional for that job." Or "Women can't be engineers because they are poor at math." Or "Women aren't assertive enough to be good managers."

The concept of "sex roles" involves two basic ideas:

1. People are expected to develop different behavioral and psychological characteristics because of their sex.
2. Society reinforces what it considers "sex-appropriate" behavior through various systems of reward and punishment.

Women are expected to be nurturing and men aggressive. If a woman acts aggressively or a man nurturingly, they will be encouraged by others to change their behavior. The woman might be called a "bitch" and the man a "wimp." Sex roles are dependent on sex-stereotyping, that is, lumping all men and women into separate categories based on alleged differences in abilities and aptitude.

It is important to keep in mind a distinction between sex and gender. Sex refers to a biological concept that involves chromosomal and anatomical differences. Gender refers to the psychological/behavioral concepts of masculinity and femininity. A person who is sexually a male might have some characteristics traditionally associated with femininity (e.g., gentleness), while a person who is sexually a female might have so-called "masculine" traits (e.g., assertiveness).

Is the sex of an individual relevant to the performance of certain tasks? Some argue that sex is relevant because it is correlated with cognitive, psychological, and physical differences. There are differences between the sexes that are relevant to job performance and, so the argument goes, these differences are natural. Therefore, some unequal treatment is justified because women *by their very nature* are unequal to men in relevant ways.

Some argue that even if it were not the case that men and women are naturally different and hence deserving of unequal treatment, it is pointless to dream about the abolition of sex roles. What alternatives should we adopt if the old gender stereotypes are abandoned? Should we deliberately begin to train all men to be in touch with their feelings and to openly express affection while we train all women to be assertive and less openly expressive? Sometimes people talk of an "androgynous" society. An androgynous personality has all the positive traits traditionally associated with both masculinity and femininity. Should society seek to mold such personality types (assuming it has the power and skill), or should society simply encourage people to develop the personalities, interests, and abilities with which they are most comfortable?

There can be little doubt that widespread discrimination based on not only sex, but race, ethnicity, religion, and sexual preference has occurred in the United States and elsewhere. There is also widespread agreement today that hiring, promotion, housing, and educational practices that routinely work to the disadvantage of African-Americans, women, Hispanics, Native Americans, Asians, and others because of their race, sex, or ethnicity are morally wrong. They are morally wrong because they violate the formal principle of justice, which requires that we make decisions based on relevant criteria. It is simply not fair to refuse to hire someone who can do a job perfectly well just because he or she is black or brown or a he or a she.

In recognition of past wrongs and in the hope of producing a more just society, *affirmative action* programs have been started. There are a wide variety of such programs, but the most controversial are often called "preferential treatment" programs. Such programs may involve quotas or they may just require that "all things being equal," preferential treatment should be given to minority and female applicants.

Such preferential treatment programs are often justified by appeal to the principle of compensatory justice, which states that whenever an injustice has happened, a just compensation must be made to those who have been injured. If Hispanics, for example, have been "disadvantaged" in the past because of their ethnicity, it is only right to "advantage" them now. Sometimes such programs are justified by appeal to the principle of utility, which states that when the interests of everyone affected are given equal weight, that action is morally correct that will, on balance, produce better consequences than any alternative. Preferential treatment programs may temporarily disadvantage white male "majority" applicants, but there is no better alternative for producing good consequences for society as a whole in the long run.

The fact that preferential treatment programs can disadvantage one group because of their race, sex, or ethnicity and advantage another because of these same factors has led some to charge that such programs amount to *reverse discrimination*. If past discrimination based on sex, ethnicity, or race was wrong because it violated the formal principle of justice, then present discrimination based on those factors is also wrong, or so it would seem.

Michael Levin (1943–   ), Professor of Philosophy at the City College of New York, in the first selection that follows argues that feminism is antidemocratic because it advocates equality of outcome (an equal number of females in all professions) and that entails inequality of opportunity (males are disadvantaged). He also argues that sex-stereotyping is inevitable, legitimate, and compatible with both sexes acting freely and having equal opportunity. Susan Leigh Anderson (Professor of Philosophy at the University of Connecticut) counters that sex-stereotyping is not compatible with equal opportunity and freedom.

Reading Questions

1. What is Levin's thesis?
2. Levin believes that sex roles cannot be overcome because they are biologically inevitable. But if they are inevitable, why does society need to impose and reinforce sex roles?

3. In order for standards "that men are more likely to meet" to be discriminatory against women, what has to be shown according to Levin?

4. Why does Levin argue that sex-stereotypes should not be interfered with?

5. What does Anderson intend to argue?

6. What is the difference between the formal interpretation of equal opportunity and the substantive interpretation?

7. Anderson argues that the formal interpretation of equal opportunity is at best a necessary, but not sufficient condition of equal opportunity. Why?

8. Anderson argues that a "non-sexist" individual would never support giving a job to someone who is less qualified because of their sex. But what about a situation in which both a male and a female are equally qualified? Should preferential treatment based on sex be given in such a case?

9. According to Anderson, what is wrong with Levin's argument that "people will never freely act in ways which produce a world devoid of sexism?"

10. What is Anderson's argument for fighting sex-stereotyping?

11. How does Anderson counter Levin's argument that while sex-stereotyping will hurt a few, it will benefit most?

12. Who do you think is right, Levin or Anderson? Why?

Feminism and Freedom

MICHAEL LEVIN

WHEN THE 88 WOMEN who took the New York City Fire Department's entrance examination in 1977 failed its physical strength component, they filed a class-action sex discrimination lawsuit in federal court. The court found for the plaintiffs, agreeing in *Berkman v. NYFD* that the strength test was not job-related and therefore in violation of Title VII of the Civil Rights Act. The court thereupon ordered the city to hire forty-five female firefighters and to construct a special, less demanding physical examination for female candidates, with males still to be held to the extant, more difficult—and ostensibly inappropriate—standard. In addition, the court ordered the city to provide special training to the eighty-eight female plaintiffs—but none for the 54 percent of the males who also failed the test—on the grounds that certain "tricks of the trade" available to all male candidates were not available to them.

New York declined to appeal *Berkman* and instructed its regular firemen to maintain public silence. Since *Berkman,* 38 of the original group of 145 women given special training by the NYFD have entered service as firefighters, and almost all personnel actions taken by the NYFD have required the approval of the presiding judge, Charles Sifton. Continuing litigation has resulted in further easing of the physical standards applied to female firefighting applicants.

The use of statistics in *Berkman* is particularly instructive. According to the guidelines of the Equal Employment Opportunity Commission, which are controlling in cases like *Berkman,* a test for a job is presumed to be discriminatory if the passing rate for women is less than 80 percent of that rate for men. The wider the gap, the less defeasible is the presumption. The court accordingly asked how likely it would be, in the absence of discrimination, that none of the eighty-eight women passed while 46 percent of the men did. As the court correctly noted, "the pass rates were separated by more than eight standard deviations" (1982 at 205), and the probability that this could happen is so small—less than one in 10 trillion—as to amount to virtual impossibility. The court's conclusion that discrimination must have occurred is entirely cogent, *if strength is assumed to be uncorrelated with sex*. A difference in failure rates on a strength test is consistent with the absence of bias if it is allowed that men are on average stronger than women. The court found an outcome of fewer than 37 passes unacceptably improbable because it adopted the hypothesis that gender and strength are independent variables. Rejecting the hypothesis that gender and strength are in any way connected, the court construed an observed correlation between gender and strength as an artifact to be eliminated by special treatment for one sex. Since women are the same as men, the EEOC and the court reasoned, special steps must be taken to compensate for their manifest differences.

Public reaction to *Berkman* varied. The local tabloids treated it as a joke ("Firebelles!" headlined one), while the more serious press took it, in the words of one slick magazine, as a matter of "opening the doors for women." Other commentators drew attention to the decision's conflict with common sense, public safety, the judgement of the public officials closest to the matter at hand, and the undoubted preferences of the majority. It remained for the Special Counsel for the New York City Commission on the Status of Women to draw the most appropriate connection: The NYFD's latest employees "would never have had the chance to show what [they] could do . . . were it not for the efforts of the feminists and 'women's libbers.'" That is so: Were it not for the ascendancy of feminist ideas, the hypothe-

sis that strength varies randomly with sex would have been unthinkable as the basis for a finding of fact and a guide for policy.

Berkman illustrates as well the extent to which feminism has achieved its effects through the state, particularly unelected officials of the courts and the regulatory agencies, and those elected officials most remote from their constituencies. Gender quotas, limitations on free speech to combat "psychological damage to women" (to cite EEOC guidelines once again), among many other feminist innovations, are all state actions. What is more, the vagueness of such feminist-inspired initiatives as have been passed by elected officials—chiefly civil rights legislation governing gender, and the Equal Rights Amendments of various states—require that they be constantly interpreted, usually by unelected officials.

This, in short, is the thesis of the present book: It is not by accident that feminism has had its major impact through the necessarily co-ercive machinery of the state rather than through the private decisions of individuals. Although feminism speaks the language of liberation, self-fulfillment, options, and the removal of barriers, these phrases invariably mean their opposites and disguise an agenda at variance with the ideals of a free society. Feminism has been presented and widely received as a liberating force, a new view of the relations between the sexes emphasizing openness and freedom from oppressive stereotypes. The burden of the present book is to show in broad theoretical perspective and factual detail that this conventional wisdom is mistaken. Feminism is an antidemocratic, if not totalitarian, ideology.

Feminism is a program for making different beings—men and women—turn out alike, and like that other egalitarian, Procrustes, it must do a good deal of chopping to fit the real world into its ideal. More precisely, feminism is the thesis that males and females are already innately alike, with the current order of things—in which males and females appear to differ and occupy quite different social roles—being a harmful distortion of this fundamental similarity. Recognizing no innate gender differences that might explain observed gender differences and the broad structure of society, feminists are compelled to interpret these manifest differences as artifacts, judged by feminists to benefit men unfairly. Believing that overtly uncoerced behavior is the product of oppression, feminists must devise ever subtler theories about the social pressures "keeping women in their place"—pressures to be detected and cancelled.

The reader may feel an impulse to object that I am talking about radical feminism while ignoring moderate feminism, a more responsible position which concedes innate sex differences and wishes only to correct wrongs undeniably done to women. For now I refer the reader to the review of feminist literature in the following chapter, which shows, I believe definitively, that complete environmentalism—the denial that innate sex differences have anything to do with the broad structure of society—is central to feminism, and that moderate feminism is a chimera. But even the reader wishing to distinguish moderate from radical feminism must concede that *Berkman* is radical by any standards, and that if radical feminism is sufficiently influential to sway the federal judiciary, its credentials and implications deserve close scrutiny.

The second major contention of this book complements the first. If . . . those broad features of society attributed by feminism to discriminatory socialization are in fact produced by innate gender differences, efforts to eradicate those features must be futile and never-ending. Reforms designed to end when sexism disappears will have to be retained indefinitely, imposing increasingly heavy costs on their nonmalleable subjects. Since innate gender differences express themselves as differences in the typical preferences of men and women, so that people will never freely act in ways which produce a world devoid of sexism, the equalization of the sexes in personal behavior and in the work world demands implacable surveillance and interference. In the end it is impossible to overcome the biological inevitability of sex roles, but it is possible to try—and to violate

liberal values in the process. A good summary of my main thesis might run: equality of outcome entails inequality of opportunity.

Akin to the idea that radical feminism exaggerates a more tenable moderate position is the idea that, whatever its exaggerations, the radical feminism that emerged in the 1960s was a response to genuine injustices. This claim collapses under the demand for a specification of these injustices. The denial of the vote to women and long-void laws against the possession of property by women are patently irrelevant, since the issue raised here is the character of *contemporary* society. Indeed, it is a serious distortion of history to view the suffragettes of a century ago as forerunners of today's feminists. In addition to being concerned with well-defined legal reforms, nineteenth-century feminists were if anything more convinced than anyone is today not only of innate sex differences, but of the innate superiority of women. The old feminists hoped that greater female participation in public life would raise the moral tone of society, and, in particular, by reducing drunkenness and allowing a woman to be more confident of a sober husband's income, make it easier for her to stay home and raise her children. (The suffragettes were a major force behind the prohibition movement.) Contemporary feminism, by contrast, is best viewed as an extension of the racial civil rights movement, which emphasizes the similarity of populations.

Feminists themselves are strikingly ready to dismiss as superficial the reforms won by their nineteenth-century predecessors. Kate Millet admits that "the male's *de jure* property has recently been modified through the granting of divorce, protection, citizenship, and property to women. [However,] their chattel status continues." She goes on to chide early feminist "concentration on suffrage" for "its failure to challenge patriarchal ideology at a sufficiently deep and radical level." Despite the propensity of feminists and their commentators to frame issues in terms of the "politics" of women's status, legal reform is of interest to most feminists mainly as an instrument for working wholesale changes on society. Indifference to legal reform is in any case forced on feminists by the absence of anything to reform. Private discrimination against women has been illegal since 1964, and public discrimination at the state and municipal levels has been illegal since 1972. When at the behest of President Ronald Reagan the State of Georgia reviewed its statutes for possible discrimination, it reported that the most serious inequity in the state code was the occurrence of 10,000 "he's" as against 150 "she's." Popular discourse continues to allude to "much outright sex discrimination," but the examples of discrimination cited invariably concern the use of criteria in various activities that men are more likely to meet. Without some showing that these criteria are deployed *for the purpose* of excluding women, or that the discrepant effects of these criteria are *caused by* arbitrary socialization, these effects are not "discriminatory." The actual state of affairs is well illustrated by *Berkman:* extensive institutionalized preference favoring women over men. Feminists who explain their grievances in terms of laws against women driving buses may have a legitimate case, but it is one against Edwardian England, not a society in which female bus drivers are promoted over males with greater seniority.

To be sure, the claim that women do not yet enjoy equal opportunity is most frequently made not in connection with legal barriers but in terms of the tendency of people to think sex-stereotypically and to communicate sex-typed norms to the young. This claim will be considered in due course, but it suffices for now to reflect that, if the formation of stereotypic beliefs is a spontaneous response to perceptions of the world, altering these possibly oppressive beliefs will require manipulation of both the average person's spontaneous tendency to form beliefs and the social environment which prompts them. If the social environment is itself a spontaneous expression of innate sex differences, attempting (and inevitably failing) to alter this environment will require yet further intrusion. . . .

Because feminism is regularly called the "women's movement," any criticism of feminism is apt to be viewed as an attack on women. It is a measure of the ability of slogans to paralyze thought that any writer should have to explicitly disavow the patent absurdity that men are better than women, but I shall enter one such disavowal here. Men are not better than women and women are not better than men; men and women differ. Feminists may describe their opponents as those who think that "men are better than women," but it is not clear who in Western society holds such a view or what it might mean. "Better" is ill-defined in isolation—one thing being better than another only in some specific respect. To say, as the evidence suggests, that men are better than women at mathematics while women are better than men at caring for children is not to say that mathematics is more important than caring for children or vice versa. Anyone who insists that merely asserting these facts amounts to insulting women must himself believe that male talents are self-evidently more important than female talents. It is this sort of advocate of the cause of women who believes women to be inferior. . . .

It is impossible to say at this point how many responses to new situations are learned projections from the lessons of old situations, but no doubt much of our behavior toward men and women *is* learned. This does not mean, however, that these acquired responses can be unlearned. People are bound to base their behavior and expectations on past experience, and if someone has always observed men and women to act differently, his subsequent attitudes are bound to reflect the belief that these regularities will continue. Probability assessments coalesce too unconsciously and impressionistically to be altered by formula—by just how much should one reduce one's estimate of the chances that the next woman he meets will want children?—and anyway belief is not subject to the will. The reader might try as an exercise to will himself to believe that Jews make terrible lawyers. Conversely, there is little point to urging people to change their stereotypes, because stereotypes change unprompted when the world does. After 1948 people stopped believing that Jews could not fight.

If women cease being more interested in children than men, that stereotype too will vanish.

Many thoughtful persons continue to apply the liberal ideal of women out of concern that the persistence of stereotypes unfairly penalizes unusual women. To the extent that this concern denies the influence of biology and experience on attitudes, it is not a *moral* qualm, but it might be mentioned in passing that the right of unusual people to be treated as such is almost certainly imaginary. On what could such a right be based? Kantian considerations of reciprocity impose an omnilateral obligation to refrain from inflicting harm, but not an obligation to appreciate. Moreover, while a woman with atypical abilities may, thanks to stereotyping, face difficulties that a man with those same but more typically male abilities will escape, these difficulties must be balanced against the benefits conferred by stereotyping on the majority of typical men and women, who are told via stereotypes that their preferences are normal and desirable. While the one woman in fifty who does not want children may be made uncomfortable by the message that there is something wrong with her, the same message is reinforcing the other forty-nine women.

Whether the discomfort of the atypical few is too high a price for the comfort of the many is not a question that concerns me here, and I trust it will not deflect attention from my main point: The formation of stereotypes, like the formation of other generalizations, is a direct expression of individual spontaneity, and any attempt to interfere with it requires interference with processes whose variations between persons are important marks of individuality. Liberal open-mindedness risks running athwart individual liberty just as surely as does "radical" egalitarianism.

It is not hard to see why there *seems* to be a middle ground between feminism and the platitude of open-mindedness. One may begin with the platitude, edge toward the social oppression theory under pressure to be specific, and hasten back to the platitude as the oppression theory becomes implausible. Shuttle back and forth quickly enough, and the resultant blur can be taken for a position. That some such self-deception is at work is suggested by the difficulty experienced by self-described moderate feminists in detailing what they are *for*. Benjamin Barber writes:

> Once feminism is liberated from the narrow perspectives that put it at odds with the femininity its name ennobles, it can begin its true struggle to rescue the polity in which our humanity resides from its myriad enemies, and thereby to rescue women from the precarious perch somewhere between animality and divinity where their search for liberation has left them.

Who, then, are "the real foes of liberation" that enlightened feminism will oppose? They are "the materialists and bureaucrats and interest-mongers and technocrats and behaviorists and ideologues and hedonists and bigots who together conspire to annihilate our human identity." This miscellany cannot be called a helpful guide to what positive views moderate feminism might advocate.

Against the pious hope that one keep an open mind about women there stands a coherent theory about the nature of women issuing in an extensive program of action. I will *give* the word *feminism* to anyone who wishes to use it out of pious hope, and return to examining the coherent theory under any name anyone prefers for it.

Equal Opportunity, Freedom and Sex-Stereotyping[1]

SUSAN LEIGH ANDERSON

ABSTRACT: Michael Levin, in *Feminism and Freedom*[2], argues that sex-stereotyping is inevitable and legitimate since there are innate non-anatomical differences between the sexes. He, further, believes that sex-stereotyping is compatible with members of both sexes acting *freely* and having *equal opportunity* in the job market and other areas of life. I will attack both claims, but I will particularly concentrate on the second one. I believe that Levin is only able to make his view sound plausible because of his minimal definitions of "freedom" and "equal opportunity" which I shall argue are not acceptable. The results of his mistake is that he presents us with a false dilemma: We must choose between either a Libertarian ideal—which includes freedom, equal opportunity, the inevitable sex-stereotyping and resulting patriarchal society (since it cannot be eliminated voluntarily)—and Feminism—which denies the legitimacy of sex-stereotyping, insists that unequal outcome means inequality of opportunity and so supports a quota system, and *attempts* to accomplish its aims, at great cost, by depriving people of freedom.

BEFORE TURNING TO MY criticisms of Levin's theses, two preliminary comments are in order:

First, I will not question Levin's controversial assumption that there are innate non-anatomical differences between the sexes. I do not feel qualified to evaluate this factual claim; and I am much more interested in what, if anything, is supposed to follow from the assumption that these differences exist. It is very important that we understand exactly what Levin and others claim. Those who believe in innate non-anatomical sex differences do *not* believe that there are *any* non-anatomical properties which *all* and *only* members of one sex possess. Even Levin admits that "innate sex differences are statistical. . . . Neither sex monopolizes any nonanatomical trait." The most that can be said is that there are some non-anatomical characteristics where the *mean* of one sex is higher than the *mean* of the other. It has been claimed, for instance, that as far as mathematical ability is concerned, the male mean is higher than the female mean.

Second, I will not question Levin's definition of "Feminism" which I also believe to be controversial if it is supposed to capture the way the word is commonly used. Levin assumes that it is central to Feminism that "anatomical differences apart, men and women are the same . . . if raised identically [they] would develop identically." He is right, I think, to maintain that given his definition of "Feminism," a moderate form of Feminism is not possible.[3] Since a Feminist, on Levin's understanding of the term, is a "complete environmentalist," he or she will believe that unequal outcome means inequality of opportunity and so a quota system seems inevitable. "Gender differences should not be allowed to have consequences."

I propose that we simply give Levin the term "Feminism." Is it possible to defend a view which would oppose favoring members of one sex over the other in competitive situations where a person's sex is irrelevant to success, and have us fight

---

1. This was an invited symposium paper presented at the Pacific Division APA meeting held in Portland, Oregon, March 1988. I am indebted to my colleagues Diana Meyers and Ruth Millikan for their helpful comments on an earlier version of this paper.

2. Transaction Books, New Brunswick, New Jersey, 1987.

3. "I believe definitively, that complete environmentalism—the denial that innate sex differences have anything to do with the broad structure of society—is central to feminism, and that moderate feminism is a chimera."

From Susan Leigh Anderson, "Equal Opportunity, Freedom and Sex-Stereotyping," Journal of Philosophical Research, *Vol. XVI, 1990–91, pp. 1–10. Used with permission of the Philosophy Documentation Center, publisher of the* Journal of Philosophical Research.

against sex stereotyping in an attempt to insure equality of opportunity between the sexes, yet would not assume that unequal outcome shows inequality of opportunity and so would be opposed to a quota system? Furthermore, could we maintain that putting this view into practice would give people the maximum amount of freedom? I believe that we can answer both questions affirmatively. If Levin would not let us call this view Feminism, let us call it Non-Sexism. Levin, presumably, believes that Non-Sexism is incoherent. I shall attempt to argue—by analyzing the concepts "equal opportunity" and "freedom" and discussing whether they are compatible with sex-stereotyping—that Non-Sexism is not only coherent but defensible.

Equal Opportunity

According to Levin, people have equal opportunity to do X as long as none of them is barred from doing X. Since "private discrimination against women has been illegal since 1964, and public discrimination at the state and municipal levels has been illegal since 1972," Levin cannot see how women can complain that they are unable to compete equally with men.

Levin clearly is assuming what Onora O'Neill calls the "Formal Interpretation" of "equal opportunity" which

> sees two persons, A and B, as having equal opportunities in some respect if neither faces a legal or quasi-legal obstacle in doing something which the other does not face. . . . If women are not barred from engineering school on account of their sex, then they have equal opportunity to become engineers, and the fact that very few do so cannot be attributed to any inequality of opportunity.[4]

Like O'Neill, I believe that the minimal "Formal Interpretation" of "equal opportunity" is not defensible, but neither is her "Substantive Interpretation" which insists that equal opportunity and equal rewards must go hand in hand, at least as far as "major social groups" are concerned:

> An equal opportunity society on the substantive view is one in which the success rates of all major social groups are the same. On the substantive interpretation of equal opportunity, preferential and quota admissions and hirings and promotions are justifiable . . . because they confer equal . . . rewards.[5]

O'Neill here is confusing equality of opportunity with equality of worth. There is, I think, a more defensible interpretation of "equal opportunity" than either of these extreme views.

Let us imagine a planet inhabited by pink and blue beings who are commonly referred to as Pinks and Blues respectively. Let us, further, suppose that it is believed by *both* types of beings that Blues are more naturally suited to doing job X than are Pinks. Until recently no Pink even considered applying for openings to do job X, but a law recently passed forbids an employer from using color as a criterion for hiring workers. Now, along comes a Pink, P, who discovers through a career aptitude test that he should be good at job X. All P's life, however, he has been given the message that it is unpinklike to do X; he has never heard of a pink doing X. As a result, he has never attempted to acquire the skills necessary to do X. B, a Blue, on the other hand, has been groomed all his life to do X, like his parents and grandparents before him. He has received the appropriate education necessary to do job X and he received positive feedback as he developed the potential he had to do X. Assume that there is only one opening for job X, and an unconfident P decides to compete with B for it. Can we say, even if the employer attempts to have an open mind, that P and B have equal opportunity as far as getting this job is concerned? I don't think so, even though neither one is barred from getting the position.

The point of this example is to show that someone may be handicapped in his ability to

4. Onora O'Neill, "How Do We Know When Opportunities Are Equal?," in *Sex Equality*, edited by Jane English, Prentice-Hall, Inc., Englewood Cliffs, N.J., 1977, p. 145.

5. *Ibid.*, p. 148.

compete with another for a certain job if that job requires a skill which takes years to acquire and years before he/she was discouraged from acquiring that skill, while the other was encouraged to acquire it, even though their native abilities were similar. The situation is unjust, rather than simply unfortunate, if the one was discouraged just because of his/her sex, race or religion.

Thus, we see that the "Formal Interpretation" of "equal opportunity" does not guarantee that people have genuinely equal opportunities. It provides us with a necessary, but not sufficient condition for equal opportunity to obtain. We need to add as a further requirement something like: individuals with similar native abilities are encouraged[6] to the same extent to develop those abilities. A society can claim that its members have true equality of opportunity when desired educational and occupational positions are awarded only on the basis of relevant native abilities and effort expended to develop those abilities.

What should we do about the fact that P will be at a competitive disadvantage compared to B with respect to getting this particular job X? I don't think we can justify doing anything. Assuming that B is more qualified—that is, B has acquired skills and/or experience P has not which will enable him to do job X better—B should get the position. And the sad fact is that P may *never* recover from his deficient background sufficiently to enable him to compete equally with others with similar native abilities for future jobs of this type.

Let us apply what we have just said to the case of a male and female competing for a single job, a position as a mechanic for instance. Joe and Sally both enjoyed tinkering with various machines when they were young and they equally impressed their parents with their ability to diagnose and solve mechanical problems; but Joe was encouraged to develop his talent while Sally was not. Joe received the appropriate schooling and has had, at twenty-five, five years of experience working as a mechanic. Sally, on the other hand, was told that she must have a more "ladylike" occupation. She was sent to secretarial school and she has worked for many years as a secretary, hating every minute of it. Meanwhile, Sally has kept her interest in mechanics as a hobby, working on cars and other machines only on weekends. Now, at twenty-five, she would like a job as a mechanic and is applying for the same position as Joe. Since, as a result of his schooling and job experience, Joe is more qualified than Sally, he should be given the job. I don't see how you can favor a less qualified woman just because she is a woman, even if you believe that her being a woman has unjustly handicapped her, and call yourself a non-sexist. A non-sexist would never favor a member of one sex in a competitive situation where the reproductive organs one has are irrelevant to being successful.

What we can, and *should,* do as non-sexists is to prevent young girls from becoming handicapped women. I think that proper education, particularly in the early grades, is the key to insuring equal opportunity between the sexes. I would like to see educators in the early grades being more concerned with individual students' strengths—with spotting and encouraging the development of natural talent. And I would particularly like to see encouragement given to the development of an atypical child's natural abilities because this child is likely to become discouraged more easily otherwise. So for instance if a girl seems to have unusual mathematical ability, I would like to see her praised for this and encouraged to develop this talent as far as she can. Similarly, atypical boys should be encouraged to develop their unusual talents.[7]

In emphasizing education, I am not naively

---

6. Of course "encouragement" must be thought of as including not only offering incentives and rewards for developing those abilities ("carrots") but also eliminating the currently existing *dis*incentives ("sticks") which might disincline individuals to develop those abilities. For example, girls with aptitude in mathematics would not only receive praise for developing that ability, but also care should be taken to see that they are not made to feel in any way unfeminine for doing so.

7. I realize that there may be many practical problems involved in implementing the theoretical reforms in early educational practices I am proposing, but the working out of the details lie beyond the scope of a philosophy paper.

supposing that there are no other factors which affect whether or not a girl becomes a handicapped woman. Certainly family and society also play an important role in determining what sort of opportunities females will see themselves as having; but I don't know how we can change family members' and society's views other than through education. I would hope that attitudes of parents, grandparents and others in society would gradually begin to change as those children who were taught in school that girls and boys have equal opportunities in life reached adulthood.

Freedom

Levin basically thinks of freedom in the compatibilist sense as the ability to do what you want to do without external interference. But, in at least one place in *Feminism and Freedom,* he construes "external interference" so broadly that he suggests that to the extent to which others have influenced your desires at all you are less free, even if you are doing just what you want to do!

> Man is never freer than when he is acting on his biologically determined preferences.

Surely this is an overly narrow conception of freedom since no human being is capable of developing to adulthood without the aid of others, and very few wish to do without the company of others even after reaching that state. Thus we are bound to be influenced by others, and so our actions will never be completely free on this understanding of freedom.

Fortunately, Levin seems to rely on the customary interpretation of "without external interference" in giving the following argument to show that, not only is the Feminist movement not needed to insure that women act freely, it will actually have the *opposite* effect!

1. "noninterference . . . is the idea of freedom behind everyday ascriptions of responsibility. . . . More pertinently, it is also the idea of freedom implicit in the feminist demand that women be given power and control over their lives."

2. "One may wonder how women can be said to be unfree in this sense when so much characteristically female behavior is, as it seems to be, quite voluntary."

3. Perhaps it will be said that "while women under patriarchy may be doing what they want, the conditions under which their wants were formed were constrained. Women have had no chance to acquire different wants."

4. "Now that women have not chosen their wants is insufficient reason to deny that women are free, since no one, male or female, chooses his wants."

5. Still "the idea that voluntary sex-typed behavior is inauthentic explains the readiness to call for state action that is prominent in the feminist political agenda." Feminism has achieved its "major impact through the necessarily coercive machinery of the state rather than through the private decisions of individuals."

6. Therefore, "Since innate gender differences express themselves as differences in the typical preferences of men and women, . . . people will never freely act in ways which produce a world devoid of sexism. . . ."

The main thing that is wrong with this argument, in my opinion, is Levin's insistence that it is enough to point out that an action was done voluntarily to be assured that it was done freely.

Let us return to my planet inhabited by Pinks and Blues. Recall that the Blue B has been groomed all his life to do job X and, as a result, he naturally chooses that occupation when the time comes for him to apply for a job. Should we say that his decision to apply for the job X opening is a free one? Of course he acted voluntarily, but did he ever seriously consider that he had any other options? If he didn't, then I wouldn't say that his "decision" to apply for job X was free in the fullest sense of the word.

I will not insist that a person in *fact* be able to do more than one action, without altering the antecedent conditions, in order to say that he or she acted freely. This would require that freedom presuppose Indeterminism which is certainly controversial. I am, rather, only suggesting that for us to say that a person did X freely, he / she must have believed him/herself to have at least one other option. In other words, he/she must have been able to imagine him/herself doing at least one other thing besides X.[8]

I also believe that the more options a person realistically feels him/herself to have, the more free he/she is. Of course, Sartre has shown us that there is a price to pay for such freedom: the realization that one has many options can have a paralyzing effect on the individual. Few, however, would suggest that we eliminate the person's options in order to lessen the anxiety.

Again, I believe that encouraging young people to develop whatever talents they have will lead to them seeing themselves as realistically having a number of options as to what they can do with their lives. It is necessary that people develop their talents to *in fact* have more options; and to see *themselves* as realistically having these options, they need to acquire a certain amount of confidence in their own abilities. For the latter, approval from others is usually essential.

Sex-Stereotyping

Michael Levin believes that sex-stereotyping is inevitable:

> it is pointless to expect society to ignore inescapably obvious inductive generalizations which are, on the evidence, rooted in biology.

We don't have to worry about incorrect stereotypes, he thinks, because if at any point they no longer represent the way the world is, they would be altered. ["stereotypes change unprompted when the world does."]

Levin not only sees nothing wrong with sex-stereotyping, but he believes that if we attempt to eliminate it we would deprive people of freedom:

> The formation of stereotypes, like the formation of other generalizations, is a direct expression of

individual spontaneity, and any attempt to interfere with it . . . risks running athwart individual liberty. . . .

Why do I believe that we should fight against sex-stereotyping? Because even if stereotypers are careful to claim only that *most* women or men are X, their believing this will mean that they will not be as open to the possibility of a woman or man who is *not* X as they would have been had they not had the belief. Since such women/men exist, their stereotyping is unfair to these individuals and may cause them difficulties. This has particularly been a problem for exceptional women in the workplace since stereotypically it has been assumed that a working woman is either just passing time until she finds a husband and starts a family or else is just supplementing a husband's income.

Levin anticipates this objection. His response is that while "unusual women" may suffer as the result of sex-stereotyping, the benefits which the more numerous "typical women" receive greatly outweigh this small negative consequence:

> while a woman with atypical abilities may, thanks to stereotyping, face difficulties that a man with those same but more typically male abilities will escape, these difficulties must be balanced against the benefits conferred by stereotyping on the majority of typical men and women, who are told via stereotypes that their preferences are normal and desirable. While the one woman in fifty who does not want children may be made uncomfortable by the message that there is something wrong with her, the same message is reinforcing the other 49 women.

What has happened to Levin's concern with individual freedom? Isn't his willingness to sacrifice the unusual individual, out of concern for the majority's wishes, in conflict with his Libertarian ideal?[9] Levin is assuming here that *either* the unusual woman *or* the typical woman must

8. I have developed this view of freedom more fully in my article "A Picture of the Self Which Supports Moral Responsibility" which appears in *The Monist,* January 1991.

9. As Joyce Trebilcot has noted: "Indeed, if individual freedom is valued, those who vary from the statistical norm should not be required to conform to it." ("Sex Roles: The Argument from Nature," in *Sex Equality, Op Cit.,* p. 126).

suffer, but perhaps it's possible to discourage sex-stereotyping (which would benefit the unusual woman) while still allowing typical women to feel "normal."

Levin envisions, and has seen, the fight against sex-stereotyping in early education as taking the form of *lying* to children. Feminists, he says, want classroom material "to pretend that the world is as it should be in order to make the way it should be into the way it will be."

I can imagine another approach to fighting against sex-stereotyping. I would like to see educators encouraging students not to have any expectations as to what someone will be able to do based solely on that person's sex because neither sex happens to have a monopoly on any non-anatomical characteristics. Teachers should themselves use, and ask their students to use, sex-neutral language whenever possible. But, as Douglas Hofstadter has pointed out,[10] this will probably not be enough to counteract the pervasive, unconscious sex-stereotyping which exists in our society. Even if the teacher is careful, when speaking of a commercial airline pilot, for example, to say that "he or she needs lots of training to learn to fly a large airplane," the students will probably have unconsciously made the default sexist assumption immediately upon hearing the word "pilot" that the pilot is a man. But if, as Hofstadter says, "the passive approach of merely avoiding sexist usages isn't enough," he also points out that "the active approach of throwing in jolting stereotype violations can be too much." Referring to a typical commercial airline pilot as "she" not only seems strange because almost all commercial airline pilots *are* men (we can see why Levin accuses the teacher who does this of "lying" to children), it also "st[icks] out like a sore thumb." It "ma[kes] one think so much about sexism that the main point of the passage often [goes] unnoticed."

What I think teachers need to do (in addition to using sex-neutral language whenever pos-

sible), to correct default sexist assumptions, is to point out examples of non-sex-stereotypical behavior in real life and, even more importantly, look for and encourage non-sex-stereotypical talents and desires in their students.

I cannot foresee any adverse effects following from this practice. The "average" girl or boy will not receive *extra* praise and encouragement, but this should not make her/him feel abnormal. Students have never been singled out for being average.

I can envision several good consequences resulting from this practice: (1) Talent will be developed which might not have been otherwise. (2) We can feel assured that males and females will have equal opportunity to compete for the desirable positions in life because we will be preventing competitive disadvantages from arising; and (3) employers raised in this way will be less likely to be influenced by sex-stereotypes in their hiring practices. (4) We might even find that there turn out to be fewer differences between the sexes than we thought after years of discouraging sex-stereotyping in favor of adopting a non-sexist policy. (But, then again, differences between the sexes—that is between the *average* male and the *average* female—may persist.) Finally, (5) I believe that people raised in a non-sexist society will be freer because they will consider themselves as having more options than the stereotypes of their sexes will allow.

Levin may object that we have deprived people of the freedom to generalize from experience, but we certainly can't *force* people not to think certain thoughts. I have only proposed that we attempt to discourage sex-stereotyping in the formative years by pointing out that generalizations about the sexes, when they take the form "All males/females are X," are not correct, and even those of the form "Most males/females are X" can cause harmful consequences.

In conclusion, I believe, contrary to Michael Levin, that sex-stereotyping is incompatible with both equal opportunity and freedom. Adopting the position of Non-Sexism—which maintains that it is wrong to favor members of one sex over the other in competitive situations where

---

10. Douglas R. Hofstadter, "Changes in Default Words and Images, Engendered by Rising Consciousness," in *Metamagical Themas,* Basic Books, New York, 1985, pp. 136–138.

having certain reproductive organs is not essential to success, and discourages the practice of sex-stereotyping—will lead to members of both sexes enjoying more freedom and ensure equal opportunity between the sexes in competitive situations.

Suggestions for Further Reading

Simone de Beauvoir's *The Second Sex,* translated by H. M. Parshley (New York: Knopf, 1952), is a classic and should be read along with Kate Millett's *Sexual Politics* (New York: Doubleday, 1969). See Joyce Trebilcot's "Sex Roles: The Argument from Nature," *Ethics,* Vol. 85 (April, 1975), pp. 249–255, for a concise and cogent refutation of the traditional arguments supporting sex roles.

Mary Briody Mahowald has edited an excellent book of readings, *Philosophy of Woman: An Anthology of Classic and Current Concepts,* 2d ed. (Indianapolis: Hackett, 1983). Also see *Women, Knowledge, and Reality: Explorations in Feminist Philosophy,* edited by Ann Garry and Marilyn Pearsall (Boston: Unwin Hyman, 1989), for a wider treatment of topics from a feminist perspective. For a useful collection of essays and discussion of issues on this and other topics in applied ethics that I have found particularly helpful see Thomas A. Mappes' and Jane S. Zembaty's *Social Ethics: Morality and Social Policy* (New York: McGraw-Hill, 1987). For a good collection of articles on the issue of reverse discrimination see *Equality and Preferential Treatment,* edited by Marshall Cohen, Thomas Nagel, and Thomas Scanlon (Princeton: Princeton University Press, 1977).

Videos

Affirmative Action Versus Reverse Discrimination (60 minutes, produced by Annenberg) examines charges that affirmative action policies amount to reverse discrimination. See your Media Services Catalogue for more information.

5.4. Discrimination

Is it fair to discriminate against a person because he or she possesses qualities some may find objectionable? To discriminate is to deny rights to some people which most people are given. At one time, it was legal to discriminate on the basis of sex, race, skin color, ethnicity, and religious belief. It is no longer, at least in the United States, legal to do so, and it is widely thought to be unjust as well. This is because most people have come to see that there are characteristics some possess (e.g., skin color) that they cannot help and that there are beliefs (e.g., religious orientations) which, while they can be helped, people are free to choose. It seems unfair to deny rights to some which are afforded others just because they are different.

However, you might argue that if the differences are relevant, that is, if they constitute inability to perform a certain task adequately, then discrimination is justified. But what about sexual orientation? Should gays and lesbians be allowed to serve in the military? Should they be allowed to marry? Is there something about a person's sexual orientation which makes him or her unfit and hence not qualified to do certain jobs?

As I write these words, President Clinton appears to be losing his battle with the Congress of the United States on allowing gays and lesbians to serve openly in the military. But if they can do the job, if they are as good or better than "straights," why should there be a law preventing them from such service? If a woman can perform as well as a man in combat, why deny her that opportunity? Would we think of denying that opportunity to a Christian, or a male, or an Asian, or an African-American, or a Native American, or a Mexican American? What makes gays and lesbians different?

In the following selection, Richard D. Mohr considers many issues surrounding homosexuality, reviewing the pro and con arguments. He argues that prejudice against homosexuals is largely due to unfair stereotyping.

Reading Questions

1. What important consequences follow from the fact that homosexuals are found throughout society in all walks of life?
2. What are the two main types of anti-gay stereotypes, and why are they contradictory?
3. What forms stereotypes, and why are they socially useful?
4. Why has society been profoundly immoral when it comes to gay stereotyping?
5. Why does it matter that gays are discriminated against?
6. If something is immoral descriptively, why is not that enough to make it immoral normatively?
7. What is wrong with arguing that homosexuality is immoral because the Bible says so?
8. If I argued that homosexuality is immoral because it is unnatural, what would be wrong with my argument according to Mohr?
9. If sexual orientation is not a matter of choice (and the author thinks it is not) why does that make discrimination against gays and lesbians especially deplorable?
10. How would society benefit if gays and lesbians were given the same rights as heterosexuals?
11. Do you believe the arguments presented by Mohr are adequate to support the claim that homosexuals are unfairly discriminated against? Why or why not? If you think not, what must be done to make the arguments stronger?
12. Create your own question (analytical or critical) about this essay and answer it.

Gay Basics: Some Questions, Facts, and Values

RICHARD E. MOHR

Who Are Gays Anyway?

A recent Gallup poll found that only one in five Americans reports having a gay or lesbian acquaintance.[1] This finding is extraordinary given

1. "Public Fears—and Sympathies," *Newsweek* (August 12, 1985), p. 23.

the number of practicing homosexuals in America. Alfred Kinsey's 1948 study of the sex lives of 5,000 white males shocked the nation: 37 percent had at least one homosexual experience to orgasm in their adult lives; an additional 13 percent had homosexual fantasies to orgasm; 4 percent were exclusively homosexual in their practices; another 5 percent had virtually no heterosexual experience; and nearly one-fifth had at least as many homosexual as heterosexual experiences.[2]

Two out of five men one passes on the street have had orgasmic sex with men. Every second family in the country has a member who is essentially homosexual, and many more people regularly have homosexual experiences. Who are homosexuals? They are your friends, your minister, your teacher, your bank teller, your doctor, your mail carrier, your secretary, your congressional representative, your sibling, parent, and spouse. They are everywhere, virtually all ordinary, virtually all unknown.

Several important consequences follow. First, the country is profoundly ignorant of the actual experience of gay people. Second, social attitudes and practices that are harmful to gays have a much greater overall harmful impact on society than is usually realized. Third, most gay people live in hiding—in the closet—making the "coming out" experience the central fixture of gay consciousness and invisibility the chief characteristic of the gay community.

Ignorance, Stereotype, and Morality

Ignorance about gays, however, has not stopped people from having strong opinions about them. The void which ignorance leaves has been filled with stereotypes. Society holds chiefly two groups of antigay stereotypes; the two are an oddly contradictory lot. One set of stereotypes revolves around alleged mistakes in an individual's gender identity: Lesbians are women that want to be, or at least look and act like, men—bulldykes, diesel dykes; while gay men are those who want to be, or at least look and act like, women— queens, fairies, limp-wrists, nellies. These stereotypes of mismatched genders provide the materials through which gays and lesbians become the butts of ethnic-like jokes. These stereotypes and jokes, though derisive, basically view gays and lesbians as ridiculous.

Another set of stereotypes revolves around gays as a pervasive sinister conspiratorial threat. The core stereotype here is the gay person as child molester and, more generally, as sex-crazed maniac. These stereotypes carry with them fears of the very destruction of family and civilization itself. Now, that which is essentially ridiculous can hardly have such a staggering effect. Something must be afoot in this incoherent amalgam.

Sense can be made of this incoherence if the nature of stereotypes is clarified. Stereotypes are not *simply* false generalizations from a skewed sample of cases examined. Admittedly, false generalizing plays some part in the stereotypes a society holds. If, for instance, one takes as one's sample homosexuals who are in psychiatric hospitals or prisons, as was done in nearly all early investigations, not surprisingly one will probably find homosexuals to be of a crazed and criminal cast. Such false generalizations, though, simply confirm beliefs already held on independent grounds, ones that likely led the investigator to the prison and psychiatric ward to begin with. Evelyn Hooker, who in the late '50s carried out the first rigorous studies to use nonclinical gays, found that psychiatrists, when presented with case files including all the standard diagnostic psychological profiles—but omitting indications of sexual orientation—were unable to distinguish gay files from straight ones, even though they believed gays to be crazy and supposed themselves to be experts in detecting craziness.[3] These studies proved a profound embarrassment to the psychiatric establishment, the financial well-being of which has been substantially enhanced by "curing" allegedly insane gays. The studies led the way to the American Psychiatric Association finally dropping homosexuality from its registry of mental illnesses in 1973.[4] Nevertheless, the stereotype of gays as sick continues apace in the mind of America.

2. Alfred C. Kinsey, *Sexual Behavior in the Human Male* (Philadelphia: Saunders, 1948), pp. 650–51. On the somewhat lower incidences of lesbianism, see Alfred C. Kinsey, *Sexual Behavior in the Human Female* (Philadelphia: Saunders, 1953), pp. 472–75.

3. Evelyn Hooker, "The Adjustment of the Male Overt Homosexual," *Journal of Projective Techniques* 21 (1957), pp. 18–31, reprinted in Hendrik M. Ruitenbeek, ed., *The Problem of Homosexuality* (New York: Dutton, 1963), pp. 141–61.

4. See Ronald Bayer, *Homosexuality and American Psychiatry* (New York: Basic Books, 1981).

False generalizations *help maintain* stereo-types, they do not *form* them. As the history of Hooker's discoveries shows, stereotypes have a life beyond facts; their origin lies in a culture's ideology—the general system of beliefs by which it lives—and they are sustained across genera-tions by diverse cultural transmissions, hardly any of which, including slang and jokes, even pur-port to have a scientific basis. Stereotypes, then, are not the products of bad science but are social constructions that perform central functions in maintaining society's conception of itself.

On this understanding, it is easy to see that the antigay stereotypes surrounding gender iden-tification are chiefly means of reinforcing still powerful gender roles in society. If, as this ste-reotype presumes and condemns, one is free to choose one's social roles independently of gen-der, many guiding social divisions, both domestic and commercial, might be threatened. The so-cially gender-linked distinctions between bread-winner and homemaker, boss and secretary, doc-tor and nurse, protector and protected would blur. The accusations "fag" and "dyke" exist in significant part to keep women in their place and to prevent men from breaking ranks and ceding away theirs.

The stereotypes of gays as child molesters, sex-crazed maniacs, and civilization destroyers function to displace (socially irresolvable) prob-lems from their actual source to a foreign (and so, it is thought, manageable) one. Thus the stereotype of child molester functions to give the family unit a false sheen of absolute innocence. It keeps the unit from being examined too closely for incest, child abuse, wife battering, and the ter-rorism of constant threats. The stereotype teaches that the problems of the family are not internal to it, but external.[5]

One can see these cultural forces at work in society's and the media's treatment of current re-ports of violence, especially domestic violence. When a mother kills her child or a father rapes his daughter—regular Section B fare even in ma-jor urban papers—this is never taken by report-ers, columnists, or pundits as evidence that there is something wrong with heterosexuality or with traditional families. These issues are not even raised. But when a homosexual child molestation is reported, it is taken as confirming evidence of the way homosexuals are. One never hears of heterosexual murders, but one regularly hears of "homosexual" ones. Compare the social treat-ment of Richard Speck's sexually motivated mass murder of Chicago nurses with that of John Wayne Gacy's murders of Chicago youths. Gacy was in the culture's mind taken as symbolic of gay men in general. To prevent the possibility that "The Family" was viewed as anything but an innocent victim in this affair, the mainstream press knowingly failed to mention that most of Gacy's adolescent victims were homeless hus-tlers. That knowledge would be too much for the six o'clock news and for cherished beliefs.

Because "the facts" largely don't matter when it comes to the generation and maintenance of stereotypes, the effects of scientific and academic research and of enlightenment generally will be, at best, slight and gradual in the changing for-tunes of lesbians and gay men. If this account of stereotypes holds, society has been profoundly immoral. For its treatment of gays is a grand scale rationalization, a moral sleight-of-hand. The problem is not that society's usual standards of evidence and procedure in coming to judg-ments of social policy have been misapplied to gays; rather, when it comes to gays, the standards themselves have simply been ruled out of court and disregarded in favor of mechanisms that en-courage unexamined fear and hatred.

5. For studies showing that gay men are no more likely—indeed, are less likely—than heterosexuals to be child moles-ters and that the largest classes and most persistent sexual abusers of children are the children's fathers, stepfathers, or mother's boyfriends, see Vincent DeFrancis, *Protecting the Child Victim of Sex Crimes Committed by Adults* (Denver: The American Humane Association, 1969), pp. *vii*, 38, 69–

70; A. Nicholas Groth, "Adult Sexual Orientation and At-traction to Underage Persons," *Archives of Sexual Behavior* 7 (1978), pp. 175–81; Mary J. Spencer, "Sexual Abuse of Boys," *Pediatrics* 78:1 (July 1986), pp. 133–38.

Are Gays Discriminated Against? Does It Matter?

Partly because lots of people suppose they don't know any gay people and partly through willful ignorance of its own workings, society at large is unaware of the many ways in which gays are subject to discrimination in consequence of widespread fear and hatred. Contributing to this social ignorance of discrimination is the difficulty for gay people, as an invisible minority, even to complain of discrimination. For if one is gay, to register a complaint would suddenly target one as a stigmatized person, and so in the absence of any protections against discrimination, would simply invite additional discrimination. Further, many people, especially those who are persistently downtrodden and so lack a firm sense of self to begin with, tend either to blame themselves for their troubles or to view injustice as a matter of bad luck rather than as indicating something wrong with society. The latter recognition would require doing something to rectify wrong, and most people, especially the already beleaguered, simply aren't up to that. So for a number of reasons discrimination against gays, like rape, goes seriously underreported.

First, gays are subject to violence and harassment based simply on their perceived status rather than because of any actions they have performed. A recent extensive study by the National Gay Task Force found that over 90 percent of gays and lesbians had been victimized in some form on the basis of their sexual orientation.[6] Greater than one in five gay men and nearly one in ten lesbians had been punched, hit, or kicked, a quarter of all gays had had objects thrown at them, a third had been chased, a third had been sexually harassed, and 14 percent had been spit on—all just for being perceived as gay.

The most extreme form of antigay violence is queerbashing—where groups of young men target a person who they suppose is a gay man and beat and kick him unconscious and sometimes to death amid a torrent of taunts and slurs. Such seemingly random but in reality socially encouraged violence has the same social origin and function as lynchings of blacks—to keep a whole stigmatized group in line. As with lynchings of the recent past, the police and courts have routinely averted their eyes, giving their implicit approval to the practice.

Few such cases with gay victims reach the courts. Those that do are marked by inequitable procedures and results. Frequently judges will describe queerbashers as "just all-American boys." Recently a District of Columbia judge handed suspended sentences to queerbashers whose victim had been stalked, beaten, stripped at knifepoint, slashed, kicked, threatened with castration, and pissed on, because the judge thought the bashers were good boys at heart—after all, they went to a religious prep school.[7]

Police and juries will simply discount testimony from gays; they typically construe assaults on and murders of gays as "justified" self-defense—the killer need only claim his act was a panicked response to a sexual overture. Alternatively, when guilt seems patent, juries will accept highly implausible "diminished capacity" defenses, as in the case of Dan White's 1978 assassination of openly gay San Francisco city [supervisor] Harvey Milk—Hostess Twinkies made him do it.[8]

These inequitable procedures and results collectively show that the life and liberty of gays, like those of blacks, simply count for less than the life and liberty of members of the dominant culture.

The equitable rule of law is the heart of an orderly society. The collapse of the rule of law for gays shows that society is willing to perpetrate the worst possible injustices against them. Conceptually there is only a difference in degree between the collapse of the rule of law and systematic extermination of members of a population simply for having some group status indepen-

6. See National Gay Task Force, *Antigay/Lesbian Victimization* (New York: NGTF, 1984).

7. "2 St. John's Students Given Probation in Assault on Gay," *The Washington Post* (May 15, 1984), p. 1.

8. See Randy Shilts, *The Mayor of Castro Street: The Life and Times of Harvey Milk* (New York: St. Martin's, 1982), pp. 308–25.

dently of any act an individual has performed. In the Nazi concentration camps, gays were forced to wear pink triangles as identifying badges, just as Jews were forced to wear yellow stars. In remembrance of that collapse of the rule of law, the pink triangle has become the chief symbol of the gay rights movement.[9]

Gays are subject to widespread discrimination in employment—the very means by which one puts bread on one's table and one of the chief means by which individuals identify themselves to themselves and achieve personal dignity. Governments are leading offenders here. They do a lot of discriminating themselves, require that others do it ([such as] government contractors), and set precedents favoring discrimination in the private sector. The federal government explicitly discriminates against gays in the armed forces, the CIA, FBI, National Security Agency, and the State Department. The federal government refuses to give security clearances to gays and so forces the country's considerable private-sector military and aerospace contractors to fire known gay employees. State and local governments regularly fire gay teachers, policemen, firemen, social workers, and anyone who has contact with the public. Further, states through licensing laws officially bar gays from a vast array of occupations and professions—everything from doctors, lawyers, accountants, and nurses to hairdressers, morticians, and used car dealers. The American Civil Liberties Union's handbook *The Rights of Gay People* lists 307 such prohibited occupations.[10]

Gays are subject to discrimination in a wide variety of other ways, including private-sector employment, public accommodations, housing, immigration and naturalization, insurance of all types, custody and adoption, and zoning regulations that bar "singles" or "nonrelated" couples. All of these discriminations affect central components of a meaningful life; some even reach to the

9. See Richard Plant, *The Pink Triangle: The Nazi War Against Homosexuals* (New York: Holt, 1986).
10. E. Carrington Boggan, *The Rights of Gay People: The Basic ACLU Guide to a Gay Person's Rights,* 1st ed. (New York: Avon, 1975), pp. 211–35.

means by which life itself is sustained. In half the states, where gay sex is illegal, the central role of sex to meaningful life is officially denied to gays.

All these sorts of discriminations also affect the ability of people to have significant intimate relations. It is difficult for people to live together as couples without having their sexual orientation perceived in the public realm and so becoming targets for discrimination. Illegality, discrimination, and the absorption by gays of society's hatred of them all interact to impede or block altogether the ability of gays and lesbians to create and maintain significant personal relations with loved ones. So every facet of life is affected by discrimination. Only the most compelling reasons could justify it.

But Aren't They Immoral?

Many people think society's treatment of gays is justified because they think gays are extremely immoral. To evaluate this claim, different senses of *moral* must be distinguished. Sometimes by *morality* is meant the overall beliefs affecting behavior in a society—its mores, norms, and customs. On this understanding, gays certainly are not moral: Lots of people hate them and social customs are designed to register widespread disapproval of gays. The problem here is that this sense of morality is merely a *descriptive* one. On this understanding *every* society has a morality—even Nazi society, which had racism and mob rule as central features of its "morality" understood in this sense. What is needed in order to use the notion of morality to praise or condemn behavior is a sense of morality that is *prescriptive* or *normative*—a sense of morality whereby, for instance, the descriptive morality of the Nazi is found wanting.

As the Nazi example makes clear, that something is descriptively moral is nowhere near enough to make it normatively moral. [The fact that] a lot of people in a society say something is good, even over eons, does not make it so. Our rejection of the long history of socially approved and state-enforced slavery is another good example of this principle at work. Slavery would be wrong even if nearly everyone liked it. So consistency and fairness require that we abandon the belief that gays are immoral simply because most people dislike or disapprove of gays or gay acts, or even because gay sex acts are illegal.

Furthermore, recent historical and anthropological research has shown that opinion about gays has been by no means universally negative. Historically, it has varied widely even within the larger part of the Christian era and even within the church itself.[11] There are even societies—current ones—where homosexuality is not only tolerated but a universal compulsory part of social maturation.[12] Within the last thirty years, American society has undergone a grand turnabout from deeply ingrained, near total condemnation to near total acceptance on two emotionally charged "moral" or "family" issues: contraception and divorce. Society holds its current descriptive morality of gays not because it has to, but because it chooses to.

If popular opinion and custom are not enough to ground moral condemnation of homosexuality, perhaps religion can. Such argument[s] proceed along two lines. One claims that the condemnation is a direct revelation of God, usually through the Bible; the other claims to be able to detect condemnation in God's plan as manifested in nature.

One of the more remarkable discoveries of recent gay research is that the Bible may not be as univocal in its condemnation of homosexuality as has been usually believed.[13] Christ never mention[ed] homosexuality. Recent interpreters of the Old Testament have pointed out that the story of Lot at Sodom is probably intended to condemn inhospitality rather than homosexuality. Further, some of the Old Testament condemnations of homosexuality seem simply to be ways of tarring those of the Israelites' opponents who happen to accept homosexual practices when the Israelites themselves did not. If so, the condemnation is merely a quirk of history and rhetoric rather than a moral precept.

What does seem clear is that those who regularly cite the Bible to condemn an activity like homosexuality do so by reading it selectively. Do ministers who cite what they take to be condemnations of homosexuality in Leviticus maintain in their lives all the hygienic and dietary laws of Leviticus? If they cite the story of Lot at Sodom to condemn homosexuality, do they also cite the story of Lot in the cave to praise incestuous rape? It seems then not that the Bible is being used to ground condemnations of homosexuality as much as society's dislike of homosexuality is being used to interpret the Bible.[14]

Even if a consistent portrait of condemnation could be gleaned from the Bible, what social significance should it be given? One of the guiding principles of society, enshrined in the [U.S.] Constitution as a check against the government, is that decisions affecting social policy are not made on religious grounds. If the real ground of the alleged immorality invoked by governments to discriminate against gays is religious (as it has explicitly been even in some recent court cases involving teachers and guardians), then one of the major commitments of our nation is violated.

But Aren't They Unnatural?

The most noteworthy feature of the accusation of something being unnatural (where a moral rather than an advertising point is being made) is that the plaint is so infrequently made. One used

11. John Boswell, *Christianity, Social Tolerance, and Homosexuality: Gay People in Western Europe from the Beginning of the Christian Era to the Fourteenth Century* (Chicago: The University of Chicago Press, 1980).

12. See Gilbert Herdt, *Guardians of the Flute: Idioms of Masculinity* (New York: McGraw-Hill, 1981), pp. 232–39, 284–88, and see generally Gilbert Herdt, ed., *Ritualized Homosexuality in Melanesia* (Berkeley: University of California Press, 1984). For another eye-opener, see Walter J. Williams, *The Spirit and the Flesh: Sexual Diversity in American Indian Culture* (Boston: Beacon, 1986).

13. See especially Boswell, *op. cit.,* Chapter 4.

14. For Old Testament condemnations of homosexual acts, see Leviticus 18:22, 21:3. For hygienic and dietary codes, see, for example, Leviticus 15:19–27 (on the uncleanliness of women) and Leviticus 11:1–47 (on not eating rabbits, pigs, bats, finless water creatures, legless creeping creatures, and so on). For Lot at Sodom, see Genesis 19:1–25. For Lot in the cave, see Genesis 19:30–38.

to hear the charge leveled against abortion, but that has pretty much faded as antiabortionists have come to lay all their chips on the hope that people will come to view abortion as murder. Incest used to be considered unnatural but discourse now usually assimilates it to the moral machinery of rape and violated trust. The charge comes up now in ordinary discourse only against homosexuality. This suggests that the charge is highly idiosyncratic and has little, if any explanatory force. It fails to put homosexuality in a class with anything else so that one can learn by comparison with clear cases of the class just exactly what it is that is allegedly wrong with it.

Though the accusation of unnaturalness looks whimsical, in actual ordinary discourse when applied to homosexuality, it is usually delivered with venom of forethought. It carries a high emotional charge, usually expressing disgust and evincing queasiness. Probably it is nothing but an emotional charge. For people get equally disgusted and queasy at all sorts of things that are perfectly natural—to be expected in nature apart from artifice—and that could hardly be fit subjects for moral condemnation. Two typical examples in current American culture are some people's responses to mothers' suckling in public and to women who do not shave body hair. When people have strong emotional reactions, as they do in these cases, without being able to give good reasons for them, we think of them not as operating morally, but rather as being obsessed and manic. So the feelings of disgust that some people have toward gays will hardly ground a charge of immorality. People fling the term *unnatural* against gays in the same breath and with the same force as when they call gays "sick" and "gross." When they do this, they give every appearance of being neurotically fearful and incapable of reasoned discourse.

When *nature* is taken in *technical* rather than ordinary usage, it looks like the notion also will not ground a charge of homosexual immorality. When *unnatural* means "by artifice" or "made by humans," it need only be pointed out that virtually everything that is good about life is unnatural in this sense, that the chief feature that

distinguishes people from other animals is their very ability to make over the world to meet their needs and desires, and that their well-being depends upon these departures from nature. On this understanding of human nature and the natural, homosexuality is perfectly unobjectionable.

Another technical sense of *natural* is that something is natural, and so, good, if it fulfills some function in nature. Homosexuality on this view is unnatural because it allegedly violates the function of genitals, which is to produce babies. One problem with this view is that lots of bodily parts have lots of functions and just because some one activity can be fulfilled by only one organ (say, the mouth for eating) this activity does not condemn other functions of the organ to immorality (say, the mouth for talking, licking stamps, blowing bubbles, or having sex). So the possible use of the genitals to produce children does not, without more, condemn the use of the genitals for other purposes, say, achieving ecstasy and intimacy.

The functional view of nature will only provide a morally condemnatory sense to the unnatural if a thing which might have many uses has but one proper function to the exclusion of other possible functions. But whether this is so cannot be established simply by looking at the thing. For what is seen is all its possible functions. The notion of function seemed like it might ground moral authority, but instead it turns out that moral authority is needed to define proper function. Some people try to fill in this moral authority by appeal to the "design" or "order" of an organ, saying, for instance, that the genitals are designed for the purpose of procreation. But these people cheat intellectually if they do not make explicit *who* the designer and orderer is. If it is God, we are back to square one—holding others accountable for religious beliefs.

Further, ordinary moral attitudes about child-rearing will not provide the needed supplement, which, in conjunction with the natural function view of bodily parts, would produce a positive obligation to use the genitals for procreation. Society's attitude toward a childless couple is that of pity not censure—even if the couple could have children. The pity may be an unsympathetic one, that is, not registering a course one would choose *for oneself,* but this does not make it a course one would *require* of others. The couple who discovers it cannot have children is viewed not as having thereby had a debt canceled, but rather as having to forgo some of the richness of life, just as a quadriplegic is not viewed as absolved from some moral obligation to hop, skip, and jump, but is viewed as missing some of the richness of life. Consistency requires then that, at most, gays who do not or cannot have children are to be pitied rather than condemned. What *is* immoral is the willful preventing of people from achieving the richness of life. Immorality in this regard lies with those social customs, regulations, and statutes that prevent lesbians and gay men from establishing blood or adoptive families, not with gays themselves.

Sometimes people attempt to establish authority for a moral obligation to use bodily parts in a certain fashion simply by claiming that moral laws are natural laws and vice versa. On this account, inanimate objects and plants are good in that they follow natural laws by necessity, animals by instinct, and persons by a rational will. People are special in that they must first discover the laws that govern them. Now, even if one believes the view—dubious in the post-Newtonian, post-Darwinian world—that natural laws in the usual sense (e = mc², for instance) have some moral content, it is not at all clear how one is to discover the laws in nature that apply to people.

If, on the one hand, one looks to people themselves for a model—and looks hard enough—one finds amazing variety, including homosexuality as a social ideal (upper-class 5th-century Athenians) and even as socially mandatory (Melanesia today). When one looks to people, one is simply unable to strip away the layers of social custom, history, and taboo in order to see what's really there to any degree more specific than that people are the creatures that make over their world and are capable of abstract thought. That this is so should raise doubts that neutral principles are to be found in human nature that will condemn homosexuality.

On the other hand, if one looks to nature apart from people for models, the possibilities are staggering. There are fish that change gender over their lifetimes: Should we "follow nature" and be operative transsexuals? Orangutans, genetically our next of kin, live completely solitary lives without social organization of any kind: Ought we to "follow nature" and be hermits? There are many species where only two members per generation reproduce: Shall we be bees? The search in nature for people's purpose—far from finding sure models for action—is likely to leave one morally rudderless.

But Aren't Gays Willfully the Way They Are?

It is generally conceded that if sexual orientation is something over which an individual—for whatever reason—has virtually no control, then discrimination against gays is especially deplorable, as it is against racial and ethnic classes, because it holds people accountable without regard for anything they themselves have done. And to hold a person accountable for that over which the person has no control is a central form of prejudice.

Attempts to answer the question whether or not sexual orientation is something that is reasonably thought to be within one's own control usually appeal simply to various claims of the biological or "mental" sciences. But the ensuing debate over genes, hormones, twins, early childhood development, and the like is as unnecessary as it is currently inconclusive.[15] All that is needed to answer the question is to look at the actual experience of gays in current society, and it becomes fairly clear that sexual orientation is not likely a matter of choice. For coming to have a

15. The preponderance of the scientific evidence supports the view that homosexuality is either genetically determined or a permanent result of early childhood development. See the Kinsey Institute's study by Alan Bell, Martin Weinberg, and Sue Hammersmith, *Sexual Preference: Its Development in Men and Women* (Bloomington: Indiana University Press, 1981); Frederick Whitam and Robin Mathy, *Male Homosexuality in Four Societies* (New York: Praeger, 1986), Chapter 7.

homosexual identity simply does not have the same sort of structure that decision-making has.

On the one hand, the "choice" of the gender of a sexual partner does not seem to express a trivial desire which might be as easily well fulfilled by a simple substitution of the desired object. Picking the gender of a sex partner is decidedly dissimilar, that is, to such activities as picking a flavor of ice cream. If an ice-cream parlor is out of one's flavor, one simply picks another. And if people were persecuted, threatened with jail terms, shattered careers, loss of family and housing and the like for eating, say, rocky road ice cream, no one would ever eat it; everyone would pick another easily available flavor. That gay people abide in being gay even in the face of persecution shows that being gay is not a matter of easy choice.

On the other hand, even if establishing a sexual orientation is not like making a relatively trivial choice, perhaps it is nevertheless relevantly like making the central and serious life choices by which individuals try to establish themselves as being of some type. Again, if one examines gay experience, this seems not to be the case. For one never sees anyone setting out to become a homosexual, in the way one does see people setting out to become doctors, lawyers, and bricklayers. One does not find gays-to-be picking some end— "At some point in the future, I want to become a homosexual"—and then set[ting] about planning and acquiring the ways and means to that end, in the way one does see people deciding that they want to become lawyers, and then sees them plan[ning] what courses to take and what sort of temperaments, habits, and skills to develop in order to become lawyers. Typically gays-to-be simply find themselves having homosexual encounters and yet at least initially resisting quite strongly the identification of being homosexual. Such a person even very likely resists having such encounters but ends up having them anyway. Only with time, luck, and great personal effort, but sometimes never, does the person gradually come to accept her or his orientation, to view it as a given material condition of life, coming as materials do with certain capacities and limita-

tions. The person begins to act in accordance with his or her orientation and its capacities, seeing its actualization as a requisite for an integrated personality and as a central component of personal well-being. As a result, the experience of coming out to oneself has for gays the basic structure of a discovery, not the structure of a choice. And far from signaling immorality, coming out to others affords one of the few remaining opportunities in ever more bureaucratic, mechanistic, and socialistic societies to manifest courage.

How Would Society at Large Be Changed if Gays Were Socially Accepted?

Suggestions to change social policy with regard to gays are invariably met with claims that to do so would invite the destruction of civilization itself: After all, isn't that what did Rome in? Actually Rome's decay paralleled not the flourishing of homosexuality, but its repression under the later Christianized emperors.[16] Predictions of American civilization's imminent demise have been as premature as they have been frequent. Civilization has shown itself rather resilient here, in large part because of the country's traditional commitments to a respect for privacy, to individual liberties, and especially to people minding their own business. These all give society an open texture and the flexibility to try out things to see what works. And because of this, one now need not speculate about what changes reforms in gay social policy might bring to society at large. For many reforms have already been tried.

Half the states have decriminalized homosexual acts. Can you guess which of the following states still have sodomy laws? Wisconsin, Minnesota; New Mexico, Arizona; Vermont, New Hampshire; Nebraska, Kansas. One from each pair does and one does not have sodomy laws. And yet one would be hard pressed to point out any substantial difference between the members of each pair. (If you're interested: It is the second

16. See Boswell, *op. cit.*, Chapter 3.

of each pair with them.) Empirical studies have shown that there is no increase in other crimes in states that have decriminalized [homosexual acts].[17] Further, sodomy laws are virtually never enforced. They remain on the books not to "protect society" but to insult gays and, for that reason, need to be removed.

Neither has the passage of legislation barring discrimination against gays ushered in the end of civilization. Some 50 counties and municipalities, including some of the country's largest cities (like Los Angeles and Boston) have passed such statutes and among the states and [counties] Wisconsin and the District of Columbia have model protective codes. Again, no more brimstone has fallen in these places than elsewhere. Staunchly antigay cities, like Miami and Houston, have not been spared the AIDS crisis.

Berkeley, California, has even passed domestic partner legislation giving gay couples the same rights to city benefits as married couples, and yet Berkeley has not become more weird than it already was.

Seemingly hysterical predictions that the American family would collapse if such reforms would pass proved false, just as the same dire predictions that the availability of divorce would lessen the ideal and desirability of marriage proved completely unfounded. Indeed, if current discriminations, which drive gays into hiding and into anonymous relations, were lifted, far from seeing gays raze American families, one would see gays forming them.

Virtually all gays express a desire to have a permanent lover. Many would like to raise or foster children—perhaps [from among the] alarming number of gay kids who have been beaten up and thrown out of their "families" for being gay. But currently society makes gay coupling very difficult. A life of hiding is a pressure-cooker existence not easily shared with another. Members of nongay couples are here asked to imagine what it would take to erase every trace of their own sexual orientation for even just a week.

Even against oppressive odds, gays have shown an amazing tendency to nest. And those gay couples who have survived the odds show that the structure of more usual couplings is not a matter of destiny but of personal responsibility. The so-called basic unit of society turns out not to be a unique immutable atom but can adopt different parts, be adapted to different needs, and even be improved. Gays might even have a thing or two to teach others about divisions of labor, the relation of sensuality and intimacy, and stages of development in such relations.

If discrimination ceased, gay men and lesbians would enter the mainstream of the human community openly and with self-respect. The energies that the typical gay person wastes in the anxiety of systematic disguise would be released for use in personal flourishing. From this release would be generated the many spin-off benefits that accrue to a society when its individual members thrive.

Society would be richer for acknowledging another aspect of human richness and diversity. Families with gay members would develop relations based on truth and trust rather than lies and fear. And the heterosexual majority would be better off for knowing that they are no longer trampling their gay friends and neighbors.

Finally and perhaps paradoxically, in extending to gays the rights and benefits it has reserved for its dominant culture, America would confirm its deeply held vision of itself as a morally progressing nation, a nation itself advancing and serving as a beacon for others—especially with regard to human rights. The words with which our national pledge ends—"with liberty and justice for all"—are not a description of the present but a call for the future. Ours is a nation given to a prophetic political rhetoric which acknowledges that morality is not arbitrary and that justice is

17. See Gilbert Geis, "Reported Consequences of Decriminalization of Consensual Adult Homosexuality in Seven American States," *Journal of Homosexuality* 1:4 (1976), pp. 419–26; Ken Sinclair and Michael Ross, "Consequences of Decriminalization of Homosexuality: A Study of Two Australian States," *Journal of Homosexuality* 12:1 (1985), pp. 119–27.

not merely the expression of the current collective will. It is this vision that led the black civil rights movement to its successes. Those congressmen who opposed that movement and its centerpiece, the 1964 Civil Rights Act, on obscurantist grounds, but who lived long enough and were noble enough came in time to express their heartfelt regret and shame at what they had done. It is to be hoped and someday to be expected that those who now grasp at anything to oppose the extension of that which is best about America to gays will one day feel the same.

Suggestions for Further Reading

The footnotes of Mohr's article will lead you into some of the literature. Also see *Gays/Justice: A Study of Ethics, Society, and Law* (New York: Columbia University Press, 1988) as well as Gerre Goodman, *No Turning Back: Lesbian and Gay Liberation for the '80s* (Philadelphia, New Society Publishers, 1983).

5.5. Animal Rights

Do other-than-human animals have moral rights? That is, do we as humans have a moral obligation or duty to animals that are not human?

At first you might be inclined to answer, "Yes." After all, if someone has a pet cat or dog and they neglect or mistreat that animal do we not hold them both morally and legally responsible for their actions? What if my neighbor kicks or injures my dog Arthur? Isn't that wrong and can I not call on the police to prosecute my neighbor for animal abuse?

But why do we hold people responsible for pet abuse? "Well," you might say, "because to harm a pet harms the owner of the pet or at least harms the interests that other humans have in that pet and its safety." But doesn't it harm the animal too? If we only argue that it is wrong to harm animals because it is in the interests of human animals not to do so, we would be assuming that animals have no intrinsic rights, and we have only indirect duties to them. But do we not have direct obligations? Isn't it wrong to harm pets not only because it harms human interests in having healthy and happy other-than-human companions, but also because it inflicts suffering on our pets directly, and they have a right to be free from suffering?

Some of you, however, might view pets as a special case. While it is true our society punishes and forbids pet abuse, our society also permits painful medical, cosmetic, and chemical research to be done on dogs, cats, rabbits, monkeys and other animals (although we forbid such research on human animals). We allow farmers to raise calves in confined quarters in order to produce better quality veal, and we allow slaughter houses to kill and butcher animals so people can eat them, not to mention permitting hunters to hunt them, trappers to trap them, furriers to skin them and sell their hides for fur coats. Clearly our society allows quite a bit of animal suffering to legally occur, so maybe we don't have any moral obligations to animals in general, only to our pets and the pets of others.

But why single out one group? If we have a direct moral obligation to prevent suffering in animals, why not all animals, human and other-than-human alike?

In the first selection that follows, Peter Singer (1946–   ), Professor of Philosophy at Monash University in Melbourne, argues that most of us are speciesist, that is, we put the interest of our own species over the interests of other species. This is not different from racism and sexism and should be rejected for the same reasons that we reject racism and sexism. The book from which this selection is taken is often called "the bible of the Animal Liberation Movement" and, to continue the analogy, just like the rejection of racism and sexism has led to Black and feminist liberation movements, so the rejection of speciesism has led to the animal liberation movements. Singer relies on utilitarian moral theory (see Section 3.2) to build his case that the interest of other-than-human animals deserves consideration equal to the interests of human animals.

R. G. Frey, Professor of Philosophy at the University of Liverpool, takes issue with the whole idea that animals have interests and hence rights. What gives something a moral right? According to one theory, if something has interests it has rights. It seems to follow, assuming this theory is correct, that animals (all animals) have rights if they have interests. But what is it to have an interest? Frey explores this question carefully and concludes that other-than-human animals do not have interests in the relevant sense. Frey's argument leaves open the possibility that animals still might have rights, but to prove that you would need a theory of rights that was not based on the notion of interests (assuming, of course, that Frey has made his case that animals do not have interests in the relevant sense).

Who is right, Singer or Frey? Read what they have to say and decide. Perhaps when you first thought about the question, "Is justice for all possible?" you thought only about "all human beings" when you read that word "all." Perhaps it is time to be more inclusive and to think about the possibility of justice for other-than-human animals too.

Reading Questions

1. What is Singer's central thesis or main point?
2. Summarize the argument Singer offers on behalf of animal rights.
3. What sorts of counter-arguments have philosophers offered to Singer's line of reasoning? Why does he think they are unconvincing?
4. What practical consequences, according to Singer, follow from the conclusion that animals feel pain and that the principle of equal consideration applies to them?
5. Defend one of the counter-arguments to his own position that Singer discusses by answering Singer's objections to that counter-argument.
6. What is Frey's thesis or central point?
7. Summarize the argument Frey presents in support of his position.
8. How does Frey respond to the counter-argument that animals (say cats) do have a language? What do you think about the response? Is it a good one? Why or why not?
9. How does Frey respond to the counter-argument that animals have simple desires which do not require linguistic ability? Do you think this refutation is persuasive? Why or why not?
10. How do you think Singer would respond to Frey's argument?
11. In your opinion, who presents the better case on the issue of animal rights, Singer or Frey? Why?

All Animals Are Equal . . .

or Why Supporters of Liberation for Blacks and Women Should Support Animal Liberation too

PETER SINGER

"Animal Liberation" may sound more like a parody of other liberation movements than a serious objective. The idea of "The Rights of Animals" actually was once used to parody the case for women's rights. When Mary Wollstonecraft, a forerunner of today's feminists, published her *Vindication of the Rights of Women* in 1792, her views were widely regarded as absurd, and before long an anonymous publication appeared entitled *A Vindication of the Rights of Brutes.* The author of this satirical work (now known to have been Thomas Taylor, a distinguished Cambridge philosopher) tried to refute Mary Wollstonecraft's arguments by showing that they could be carried one stage further. If the argument for equality was sound when applied to women, why should it not be applied to dogs, cats, and horses? The reasoning seemed to hold for these "brutes" too; yet to hold that brutes had rights was manifestly absurd; therefore the reasoning by which this conclusion had been reached must be unsound, and if unsound when applied to brutes, it must also be unsound when applied to women, since the very same arguments had been used in each case.

In order to explain the basis of the case for the equality of animals, it will be helpful to start with an examination of the case for the equality of women. Let us assume that we wish to defend the case for women's rights against the attack by Thomas Taylor. How should we reply?

One way in which we might reply is by saying that the case for equality between men and women cannot validly be extended to nonhuman animals. Women have a right to vote, for instance, because they are just as capable of making rational decisions about the future as men are; dogs, on the other hand, are incapable of understanding the significance of voting, so they cannot have the right to vote. There are many other obvious ways in which men and women resemble each other closely, while humans and animals differ greatly. So, it might be said, men and women are similar beings and should have similar rights, while humans and nonhumans are different and should not have equal rights.

The reasoning behind this reply to Taylor's analogy is correct up to a point, but it does not go far enough. There *are* important differences between humans and other animals, and these differences must give rise to *some* differences in the rights that each have. Recognizing this obvious fact, however, is no barrier to the case for extending the basic principle of equality to nonhuman animals. The differences that exist between men and women are equally undeniable, and the supporters of Women's Liberation are aware that these differences may give rise to different rights. Many feminists hold that women have the right to an abortion on request. It does not follow that since these same feminists are campaigning for equality between men and women they must support the right of men to have abortions too. Since a man cannot have an abortion, it is meaningless to talk of his right to have one. Since a dog can't vote, it is meaningless to talk of its right to vote. There is no reason why either Women's Liberation or Animal Liberation should get involved in such nonsense. The extension of the basic principle of equality from one group to another does not imply that we must treat both groups in exactly the same way, or grant exactly the same rights to both groups. Whether we should do so will depend on the nature of the members of the two groups. The basic principle of equality does not require equal or identical *treatment;* it requires equal *consideration.* Equal consideration for different beings may lead to different treatment and different rights.

So there is a different way of replying to Taylor's attempt to parody the case for women's rights, a way that does not deny the obvious differences between humans and nonhumans but goes more deeply into the question of equality and concludes by finding nothing absurd in the idea that the basic principle of equality applies to so-called "brutes." At this point such a conclusion may appear odd; but if we examine more deeply the basis on which our opposition to discrimination on grounds of race or sex ultimately rests, we will see that we would be on shaky ground if we were to demand equality for blacks, women, and other groups of oppressed humans while denying equal consideration to nonhumans. To make this clear we need to see, first, exactly why racism and sexism are wrong.

When we say that all human beings, whatever their race, creed, or sex, are equal, what is it that we are asserting? Those who wish to defend hierarchical, inegalitarian societies have often pointed out that by whatever test we choose it simply is not true that all humans are equal. Like it or not we must face the fact that humans come in different shapes and sizes; they come with different moral capacities, different intellectual abilities, different amounts of benevolent feeling and sensitivity to the needs of others, different abilities to communicate effectively, and different capacities to experience pleasure and pain. In short, if the demand for equality were based on the actual equality of all human beings, we would have to stop demanding equality.

Still, one might cling to the view that the demand for equality among human beings is based on the actual equality of the different races and sexes. Although, it may be said, humans differ as individuals there are no differences between the races and sexes *as such.* From the mere fact that a person is black or a woman we cannot infer anything about that person's intellectual or moral capacities. This, it may be said, it why racism and sexism are wrong. The white racist claims that whites are superior to Blacks, but this is false—although there are differences among individuals, some Blacks are superior to some whites in all of the capacities and abilities that could conceivably be relevant. The opponent of sexism would say the same: a person's sex is no guide of his or her abilities, and this is why it is unjustifiable to discriminate on the basis of sex.

The existence of individual variations that cut across the lines of race or sex, however, provides us with no defense at all against a more sophisticated opponent of equality, one who proposes that, say, the interests of all those with IQ scores below 100 be given less consideration than the interests of those with ratings over 100. Perhaps those scoring below the mark would, in this society, be made the slaves of those scoring higher. Would a hierarchical society of this sort really be so much better than one based on race or sex? I think not. But if we tie the moral principle of equality to the factual equality of the different races or sexes, taken as a whole, our opposition to racism and sexism does not provide us with any basis for objecting to this kind of inegalitarianism.

There is a second important reason why we ought not to base our opposition to racism and sexism on any kind of actual equality, even the limited kind that asserts that variations in capacities and abilities are spread evenly between the different races and sexes: we can have no absolute guarantee that these capacities and abilities really are distributed evenly, without regard to race or sex, among human beings. So far as actual abilities are concerned there do seem to be certain measurable differences between both races and sexes. These differences do not, of course, appear in each case, but only when averages are taken. More important still, we do not yet know how much of these differences is really due to the different genetic endowments of the different races and sexes, and how much is due to poor schools, poor housing, and other factors that are the result of past and continuing discrimination. Perhaps all of the important differences will eventually prove to be environmental rather than genetic. Anyone opposed to racism and sexism will certainly hope that this will be so, for it will make the task of ending discrimination a lot easier; nevertheless it would be dangerous to rest the case against racism and sexism on the belief that all significant differences are environmental in origin. The opponent of, say, racism who takes this line will be unable to avoid conceding that *if* differences in ability do after all prove to have some genetic connection with race, racism would in some way be defensible.

Fortunately there is no need to pin the case for equality to one particular outcome of a scientific investigation. The appropriate response to those who claim to have found evidence of genetically based differences in ability between the races or sexes is not to stick to the belief that the genetic explanation must be wrong, whatever evidence to the contrary may turn up: instead we should make it quite clear that the claim to equality does not depend on intelligence, moral capacity, physical strength, or similar matters of fact. Equality is a moral idea, not an assertion of fact. There is no logically compelling reason for assuming that a factual difference in ability between two people justifies any difference in the amount of consideration we give to their needs and interests. *The principle of the equality of human beings is not a description of an alleged actual equality among humans: it is a prescription of how we should treat humans.*

Jeremy Bentham, the founder of the reforming utilitarian school of moral philosophy, incorporated the essential basis of moral equality into his system of ethics by means of the formula: "Each to count for one and none for more than one." In other words, the interests of every being affected by an action are to be taken into account and given the same weight as the like interests of any other being. A later utilitarian, Henry Sidgwick, put the point in this way: "The good of any one individual is of no more importance, from

the point of view (if I may say so) of the Universe, than the good of any other." More recently the leading figures in contemporary moral philosophy have shown a great deal of agreement in specifying as a fundamental presupposition of their moral theories some similar requirement which operates so as to give everyone's interests equal consideration—although these writers generally cannot agree on how this requirement is best formulated.[1]

It is an implication of this principle of equality that our concern for others and our readiness to consider their interests ought not to depend on what they are like or on what abilities they may possess. Precisely what this concern or consideration requires us to do may vary according to the characteristics of those affected by what we do: concern for the well-being of a child growing up in America would require that we teach him to read; concern for the well-being of a pig may require no more than that we leave him alone with other pigs in a place where there is adequate food and room to run freely. But the basic element— the taking into account of the interests of the being, whatever those interests may be—must, according to the principle of equality, be extended to all beings, black or white, masculine or feminine, human or nonhuman.

Thomas Jefferson, who was responsible for writing the principle of the equality of men into the American Declaration of Independence, saw this point. It led him to oppose slavery even though he was unable to free himself fully from his slaveholding background. He wrote in a letter to the author of a book that emphasized the notable intellectual achievements of Negroes in

1. For Bentham's moral philosophy, see his *Introduction to the Principles of Morals and Legislation,* and for Sidgwick's see *The Methods of Ethics* (the passage quoted is from the seventh edition, p. 382). As examples of leading contemporary moral philosophers who incorporate a requirement of equal consideration of interests, see R. M. Hare, *Freedom and Reason* (New York: Oxford University Press, 1963) and John Rawls, *A Theory of Justice* (Cambridge: Harvard University Press, Belknap Press, 1972). For a brief account of the essential agreement on this issue between these and other positions, see R. M. Hare, "Rules of War and Moral Reasoning," *Philosophy and Public Affairs,* Vol. 1, no. 2 (1972).

order to refute the then common view that they had limited intellectual capacities:

> Be assured that no person living wishes more sincerely than I do, to see a complete refutation of the doubts I have myself entertained and expressed on the grade of understanding allotted to them by nature, and to find that they are on a par with ourselves . . . but whatever be their degree of talent it is no measure of their rights. Because Sir Isaac Newton was superior to others in understanding, he was not therefore lord of the property or person of others.[2]

Similarly when in the 1850s the call for women's rights was raised in the United States a remarkable black feminist named Sojourner Truth made the same point in more robust terms at a feminist convention:

> . . . they talk about this thing in the head; what do they call it? ["Intellect," whispered someone near by."] That's it. What's that got to do with women's rights or Negroes' rights? If my cup won't hold but a pint and yours holds a quart, wouldn't you be mean not to let me have my little half-measure full?[3]

It is on this basis that the case against racism and the case against sexism must both ultimately rest; and it is in accordance with this principle that the attitude that we may call "speciesism," by analogy with racism, must also be condemned. Speciesism—the word is not an attractive one, but I can think of no better term—is a prejudice or attitude of bias toward the interests of members of one's own species and against those of members of other species. It should be obvious that the fundamental objections to racism and sexism made by Thomas Jefferson and Sojourner Truth apply equally to speciesism. If possessing a higher degree of intelligence does not entitle one human to use another for his own ends, how can it entitle humans to exploit nonhumans for the same purpose?[4]

Many philosophers and other writers have proposed the principle of equal consideration of interests, in some form or other as a basic moral principle; but not many of them have recognized that this principle applies to members of other species as well as to our own. Jeremy Bentham was one of the few who did realize this. In a forward-looking passage written at a time when black slaves had been freed by the French but in the British dominions were still being treated in the way we now treat animals, Bentham wrote:

> The day *may* come when the rest of the animal creation may acquire those rights which never could have been witholden from them but by the hand of tyranny. The French have already discovered that the blackness of the skin is no reason why a human being should be abandoned without redress to the caprice of a tormentor. It may one day come to be recognized that the number of the legs, the villosity of the skin, or the termination of the *os sacrum* are reasons equally insufficient for abandoning a sensitive being to the same fate. What else is it that should trace the insuperable line? Is it the faculty of reason, or perhaps the faculty of discourse? But a full-grown horse or dog is beyond comparison a more rational, as well as a more conversable animal, than an infant of a day or a week or even a month, old. But suppose they were otherwise, what would it avail? The question is not, Can they *reason?* nor Can they *talk?* but, *Can they suffer?*[5]

In this passage Bentham points to the capacity for suffering as the vital characteristic that gives a being the right to equal consideration. The capacity for suffering—or more strictly, for suffering and/or enjoyment or happiness—is not just another characteristic like the capacity for language or higher mathematics. Bentham is not saying that those who try to mark "the insuperable line" that determines whether the interests of a being should be considered happen to have chosen the wrong characteristic. By saying that we must consider the interests of all beings with the capacity for suffering or enjoyment Bentham

2. Letter to Henri Gregoire, February 25, 1809.
3. Reminiscences by Francis D. Gage, from Susan B. Anthony, *The History of Woman Suffrage*, Vol. 1; the passage is to be found in the extract in Leslie Tanner, ed., *Voices from Women's Liberation* (New York: Signet, 1970).
4. I owe the term "speciesism" to Richard Ryder.

5. *Introduction to the Principles of Morals and Legislation*, chapter 17.

does not arbitrarily exclude from consideration any interests at all—as those who draw the line with reference to the possession of reason or language do. The capacity for suffering and enjoyment is *a prerequisite for having interests at all,* a condition that must be satisfied before we can speak of interests in a meaningful way. It would be nonsense to say that it was not in the interests of a stone to be kicked along the road by a schoolboy. A stone does not have interests because it cannot suffer. Nothing that we can do to it could possibly make any difference to its welfare. A mouse, on the other hand, does have an interest in not being kicked along the road, because it will suffer if it is.

If a being suffers there can be no moral justification for refusing to take that suffering into consideration. No matter what the nature of the being, the principle of equality requires that its suffering be counted equally with the like suffering—in so far as rough comparisons can be made—of any other being. If a being is not capable of suffering, or of experiencing enjoyment or happiness, there is nothing to be taken into account. So the limit of sentience (using the term as a convenient if not strictly accurate shorthand for the capacity to suffer and/or experience enjoyment) is the only defensible boundary of concern for the interests of others. To mark this boundary by some other characteristic like intelligence or rationality would be to mark it in an arbitrary manner. Why not choose some other characteristic, like skin color?

The racist violates the principle of equality by giving greater weight to the interests of members of his own race when there is a clash between their interests and the interests of those of another race. The sexist violates the principle of equality by favoring the interests of his own sex. Similarly the speciesist allows the interests of his own species to override the greater interests of members of other species. The pattern is identical in each case.

Most human beings are speciesists. The following chapters show that ordinary human beings—not a few exceptionally cruel or heartless humans, but the overwhelming majority of humans—take an active part in, acquiesce in, and allow their taxes to pay for practices that require the sacrifice of the most important interests of members of other species in order to promote the most trivial interests of our own species.

There is, however, one general defense of the practices to be described in the next two chapters that needs to be disposed of before we discuss the practices themselves. It is a defense which, if true, would allow us to do anything at all to nonhumans for the slightest reason, or for no reason at all, without incurring any justifiable reproach. This defense claims that we are never guilty of neglecting the interests of other animals for one breathtakingly simple reason: they have no interests. Nonhuman animals have no interests, according to this view, because they are not capable of suffering. By this is not meant merely that they are not capable of suffering in all the ways that humans are—for instance, that a calf is not capable of suffering from the knowledge that it will be killed in six months time. That modest claim is, no doubt, true; but it does not clear humans of the charge of speciesism, since it allows that animals may suffer in other ways—for instance, by being given electric shocks, or being kept in small, cramped cages. The defense I am about to discuss is the much more sweeping, although correspondingly less plausible, claim that animals are incapable of suffering in any way at all; that they are, in fact, unconscious automata, possessing neither thoughts nor feelings nor a mental life of any kind.

Although, as we shall see in a later chapter, the view that animals are automata was proposed by the seventeenth-century French philosopher René Descartes, to most people, then and now, it is obvious that if, for example, we stick a sharp knife into the stomach of an unanesthetized dog, the dog will feel pain. That this is so is assumed by the laws in most civilized countries which prohibit wanton cruelty to animals. Readers whose common sense tells them that animals do suffer may prefer to skip the remainder of this section, since the pages do nothing but refute a position which they do not hold. Implausible as it is, though, for the sake of completeness this skeptical position must be discussed.

Do animals other than humans feel pain? How do we know? Well, how do we know if anyone, human or nonhuman, feels pain? We know that we ourselves can feel pain. We know this from the direct experiences of pain that we have when, for instance, somebody presses a lighted cigarette against the back of our hand. But how do we know that anyone else feels pain? We cannot directly experience anyone else's pain, whether that "anyone" is our best friend or a stray dog. Pain is a state of consciousness, a "mental event," and as such it can never be observed. Behavior like writhing, screaming, or drawing one's hand away from the lighted cigarette is not pain itself; nor are the recordings a neurologist might make of activity within the brain observations of pain itself. Pain is something that we feel, and we can only infer that others are feeling it from various external indications.

In theory, we *could* always be mistaken when we assume that other human beings feel pain. It is conceivable that our best friend is really a very cleverly constructed robot, controlled by a brilliant scientist so as to give all the signs of feeling pain, but really no more sensitive than any other machine. We can never know, with absolute certainty, that this is not the case. But while this might present a puzzle for philosophers, none of us has the slightest real doubt that our best friends feel pain just as we do. This is an inference, but a perfectly reasonable one, based on observations of their behavior in situations in which we would feel pain, and on the fact that we have every reason to assume that our friends are beings like us, with nervous systems like ours that can be assumed to function as ours do, and to produce similar feelings in similar circumstances.

If it is justifiable to assume that other humans feel pain as we do, is there any reason why a similar inference should be unjustifiable in the case of other animals?

Nearly all the external signs which lead us to infer pain in other humans can be seen in other species, especially the species most closely related to us—other species of mammals, and birds. Behavioral signs—writhing, facial contortions, moaning, yelping or other forms of calling, attempts to avoid the source of pain, appearance of fear at the prospect of its repetition, and so on—are present. In addition, we know that these animals have nervous systems very like ours, which respond physiologically as ours do when the animal is in circumstances in which we would feel pain: an initial rise of blood pressure, dilated pupils, perspiration, an increased pulse rate, and, if the stimulus continues, a fall in blood pressure. Although humans have a more developed cerebral cortex than other animals, this part of the brain is concerned with thinking functions rather than with basic impulses, emotions, and feelings. These impulses, emotions, and feelings are located in the diencephalon, which is well developed in many other species of animals, especially mammals and birds.[6]

We also know that the nervous systems of other animals were not artificially constructed to mimic the pain behavior of humans, as a robot might be artificially constructed. The nervous systems of animals evolved as our own did, and in fact the evolutionary history of humans and other animals, especially mammals, did not diverge until the central features of our nervous systems were already in existence. A capacity to feel pain obviously enhances a species' prospects of survival, since it causes members of the species to avoid sources of injury. It is surely unreasonable to suppose that nervous systems which are virtually identical physiologically, have a common origin and a common evolutionary function, and result in similar forms of behavior in similar circumstances should actually operate in an entirely different manner on the level of subjective feelings.

It has long been accepted as sound policy in science to search for the simplest possible explanation of whatever it is we are trying to explain. Occasionally, it has been claimed that it is for this reason "unscientific" to explain the behavior of animals by theories that refer to the animal's conscious feelings, desires, and so on—the idea

6. Lord Brain, "Presidential Address" in C. A. Keele and R. Smith, eds., *The Assessment of Pain in Men and Animals* (London: Universities Federation for Animal Welfare, 1962).

being that if the behavior in question can be explained without invoking consciousness or feelings, that will be the simpler theory. Yet we can now see that such explanations, when placed in the over-all context of the behavior of both human and nonhuman animals, are actually far more complex than their rivals. For we know from our own experience that explanations of our own behavior that did not refer to consciousness and the feeling of pain would be incomplete; and it is simpler to assume that the similar behavior of animals with similar nervous systems is to be explained in the same way than to try to invent some other explanation for the behavior of nonhuman animals as well as an explanation for the divergence between humans and nonhumans in this respect.

The overwhelming majority of scientists who have addressed themselves to this question agree. Lord Brain, one of the most eminent neurologists of our time, has said:

> I personally can see no reason for conceding mind to my fellow men and denying it to animals. . . . I at least cannot doubt that the interests and activities of animals are correlated with awareness and feeling in the same way as my own, and which may be, for aught I know, just as vivid.[7]

While the author of a recent book on pain writes:

> Every particle of factual evidence supports the contention that the higher mammalian vertebrates experience pain sensations at least as acute as our own. To say that they feel less because they are lower animals is an absurdity; it can easily be shown that many of their senses are far more acute than ours—visual acuity in certain birds, hearing in most wild animals, and touch in others; these animals depend more than we do today on the sharpest possible awareness of a hostile environment. Apart from the complexity of the cerebral cortex (which does not directly perceive pain) their nervous systems are almost identical to ours and their reactions to pain remarkably similar, though lacking (so far as we

know) the philosophical and moral overtones. The emotional element is all too evident, mainly in the form of fear and anger.[8]

In Britain, three separate expert government committees on matters relating to animals have accepted the conclusion that animals feel pain. After noting the obvious behavioral evidence for this view, the Committee on Cruelty to Wild Animals said:

> . . . we believe that the physiological, and more particularly the anatomical, evidence fully justifies and reinforces the commonsense belief that animals feel pain.

And after discussing the evolutionary value of pain they concluded that pain is "of clear-cut biological usefulness" and this is "a third type of evidence that animals feel pain." They then went on to consider forms of suffering other than mere physical pain, and added that they were "satisfied that animals do suffer from acute fear and terror." In 1965, reports by British government committees on experiments on animals, and on the welfare of animals under intensive farming methods, agreed with this view, concluding that animals are capable of suffering both from straightforward physical injuries and from fear, anxiety, stress, and so on.[9]

That might well be thought enough to settle the matter; but there is one more objection that needs to be considered. There is, after all, one behavioral sign that humans have when in pain which nonhumans do not have. This is a developed language. Other animals may communicate with each other, but not, it seems, in the complicated way we do. Some philosophers, including Descartes, have thought it important that while

---

7. *Ibid.*, p. 11.

8. Richard Serjeant, *The Spectrum of Pain* (London: Hart-Davis, 1969), p. 72.

9. See the reports of the Committee on Cruelty to Wild Animals (Command Paper 8266, 1951), paragraphs 36–42; the Departmental Committee on Experiments on Animals (Command Paper 2641, 1965), paragraphs 179–182; and the Technical Committee to Enquire into the Welfare of Animals Kept under Intensive Livestock Husbandry Systems (Command Paper 2836, 1965), paragraphs 26–28 (London: Her Majesty's Stationery Office).

humans can tell each other about their experience of pain in great detail, other animals cannot. (Interestingly, this once neat dividing line between humans and other species has now been threatened by the discovery that chimpanzees can be taught a language.)[10] But as Bentham pointed out long ago, the ability to use language is not relevant to the question of how a being ought to be treated—unless that ability can be linked to the capacity to suffer, so that the absence of a language casts doubt on the existence of this capacity.

This link may be attempted in two ways. First, there is a hazy line of philosophical thought, stemming perhaps from some doctrines associated with the influential philosopher Ludwig Wittgenstein, which maintains that we cannot meaningfully attribute states of consciousness to beings without language. This position seems to me very implausible. Language may be necessary for abstract thought, at some level anyway; but states like pain are more primitive, and have nothing to do with language.

The second and more easily understood way of linking language and the existence of pain is to say that the best evidence that we can have that another creature is in pain is when he tells us that he is. This is a distinct line of argument, for it is not being denied that a non-language-user conceivably *could* suffer, but only that we could ever have sufficient reason to *believe* that he is suffering. Still, this line of argument fails too. As Jane Goodall has pointed out in her study of chimpanzees, *In the Shadow of Man,* when it comes to the expressions of feelings and emotions language is less important than in other areas. We tend to fall back on nonlinguistic modes of communication such as a cheering pat on the back, an exuberant embrace, a clasp of the hands, and so on. The basic signals we use to convey pain, fear, anger, love, joy, surprise, sexual arousal, and many other emotional states are not specific to our own species.[11]

Charles Darwin made an extensive study of this subject, and the book he wrote about it, *The Expression of the Emotions in Man and Animals,* notes countless nonlinguistic modes of expression. The statement "I am in pain" may be one piece of evidence for the conclusion that the speaker is in pain, but it is not the only possible evidence, and since people sometimes tell lies, not even the best possible evidence.

Even if there were stronger grounds for refusing to attribute pain to those who do not have a language, the consequences of this refusal might lead us to reject the conclusion. Human infants and young children are unable to use language. Are we to deny that a year-old child can suffer? If not, language cannot be crucial. Of course, most parents understand the responses of their children better than they understand the responses of other animals; but this is just a fact about the relatively greater knowledge that we have of our own species, and the greater contact we have with infants, as compared to animals. Those who have studied the behavior of other animals, and those who have pet animals, soon learn to understand their responses as well as we understand those of an infant, and sometimes better. Jane Goodall's account of the chimpanzees she watched is one instance of this, but the same can be said of those who have observed species less closely related to our own. Two among many possible examples are Konrad Lorenz's observations of geese and jackdaws, and N. Tinbergen's extensive studies of herring gulls.[12] Just as we can understand infant human behavior in the light of adult human behavior, so we can understand the behavior of other species in light of our own behavior—and

10. One chimpanzee, Washoe, has been taught the sign language used by deaf people, and acquired a vocabulary of 350 signs. Another, Lana, communicates in structured sentences by pushing buttons on a special machine. For a brief account of Washoe's abilities, see Jane van Lawick-Goodall, *In the Shadow of Man* (Boston: Houghton Mifflin, 1971), pp. 252–254; and for Lana, see *Newsweek,* 7 January 1974, and *New York Times,* 4 December 1974.

11. *In the Shadow of Man,* p. 225; Michael Peters makes a similar point in "Nature and Culture," in Stanley and Roslind Godlovitch and John Harris, eds., *Animals, Men and Morals* (New York: Taplinger Publishing Co., 1972).
12. Konrad Lorenz, *King Solomon's Ring* (New York: T. Y. Crowell, 1952); N. Tinbergen, *The Herring Gull's World,* rev. ed. (New York: Basic Books, 1974).

sometimes we can understand our own behavior better in the light of the behavior of other species.

So to conclude: there are no good reasons, scientific or philosophical, for denying that animals feel pain. If we do not doubt that other humans feel pain we should not doubt that other animals do so too.

Animals can feel pain. As we saw earlier, there can be no moral justification for regarding the pain (or pleasure) that animals feel as less important than the same amount of pain (or pleasure) felt by humans. But what exactly does this mean, in practical terms? To prevent misunderstanding I shall spell out what I mean a little more fully.

If I give a horse a hard slap across its rump with my open hand, the horse may start, but it presumably feels little pain. Its skin is thick enough to protect it against a mere slap. If I slap a baby in the same way, however, the baby will cry and presumably does feel pain, for its skin is more sensitive. So it is worse to slap a baby than a horse, if both slaps are administered with equal force. But there must be some kind of blow—I don't know exactly what it would be, but perhaps a blow with a heavy stick—that would cause the horse as much pain as we cause a baby by slapping it with our hand. That is what I mean by "the same amount of pain" and if we consider it wrong to inflict that much pain on a baby for no good reason then we must, unless we are speciesists, consider it equally wrong to inflict the same amount of pain on a horse for no good reason.

There are other differences between humans and animals that cause other complications. Normal adult human beings have mental capacities which will, in certain circumstances, lead them to suffer more than animals would in the same circumstances. If, for instance, we decided to perform extremely painful or lethal scientific experiments on normal adult humans, kidnapped at random from public parks for this purpose, every adult who entered a park would become fearful that he would be kidnapped. The resultant terror would be a form of suffering additional to the pain of the experiment. The same experiments performed on nonhuman animals would cause less suffering since the animals would not have the anticipatory dread of being kidnapped and experimented upon. This does not mean, of course, that it would be right to perform the experiment on animals, but only that there is a reason, which is *not* speciesist, for preferring to use animals rather than normal adult humans, if the experiment is to be done at all. It should be noted, however, that this same argument gives us a reason for preferring to use human infants—orphans perhaps—or retarded humans for experiments, rather than adults, since infants and retarded humans would also have no idea of what was going to happen to them. So far as this argument is concerned nonhuman animals and infants and retarded humans are in the same category; and if we use this argument to justify experiments on nonhuman animals we have to ask ourselves whether we are also prepared to allow experiments on human infants and retarded adults; and if we make a distinction between animals and these humans, on what basis can we do it, other than a barefaced—and morally indefensible—preference for members of our own species?

There are many areas in which the superior mental powers of normal adult humans make a difference: anticipation, more detailed memory, greater knowledge of what is happening, and so on. Yet these differences do not all point to greater suffering on the part of the normal human being. Sometimes an animal may suffer more because of his more limited understanding. If, for instance, we are taking prisoners in wartime we can explain to them that while they must submit to capture, search, and confinement they will not otherwise be harmed and will be set free at the conclusion of hostilities. If we capture a wild animal, however, we cannot explain that we are not threatening its life. A wild animal cannot distinguish an attempt to overpower and confine from an attempt to kill; the one causes as much terror as the other.

It may be objected that comparisons of the sufferings of different species are impossible to make, and that for this reason when the interests of animals and humans clash the principle of equality gives no guidance. It is probably true that comparisons of suffering between members of different species cannot be made precisely, but precision is not essential. Even if we were to prevent the infliction of suffering on animals only when it is quite certain that the interests of humans will not be affected to anything like the extent that animals are affected, we would be forced to make radical changes in our treatment of animals that would involve our diet, the farming methods we use, experimental procedures in many fields of science, our approach to wildlife and to hunting, trapping and the wearing of furs, and areas of entertainment like circuses, rodeos, and zoos. As a result, a vast amount of suffering would be avoided.

Rights, Interests, Desires, and Beliefs

R. G. FREY

I

The question of whether non-human animals possess moral rights is once again being widely argued. Doubtless the rise of ethology is partly responsible for this: as we learn more about the behavior of animals, it seems inevitable that we shall be led to focus upon the similarities between them and us, with the result that the extension of moral rights from human beings to non-human animals can appear, as the result of these similarities, to have a firm basis in nature. (Of course, this way of putting the matter assumes that human beings have moral rights, and on another occasion I should perhaps wish to challenge this assumption.) But the major impetus to renewed interest in the subject of animal rights almost certainly stems from a heightened and more critical awareness, among philosophers and non-philosophers alike, of the arguments for and against eating animals and using them in scientific research. For if animals *do* have moral rights, such as a right to live and to live free from unnecessary suffering, and if our present practices systematically tread upon these rights, then the case for eating and experimenting upon animals, especially when other alternatives are for the most part readily available, is going to have to be a powerful one indeed.

It is important, however, not to misconstrue the question: the question is not about *which* rights animals may or may not be thought to possess or about *whether* their alleged rights in a particular regard are on a par with the alleged rights of humans in this same regard but rather about the more fundamental issue of whether animals—or, in any event, the "higher" animals—are a kind of being which can be the logical subject of rights. It is this issue, and a particular position with respect to it, that I want critically to address here.

II

The position I have in mind is the widely influential one which links the possession of rights to the possession of interests. In his *System of Ethics,* Leonard Nelson is among the first, if not the first, to propound the view that all and only beings which have interests can have rights,[1] a

1. Leonard Nelson, *System of Ethics,* tr. by Norbert Guterman (New Haven, 1956), Part I, Section 2, Chapter 7, pp. 136–144.

From "Rights, Interests, Desires and Beliefs," by R. G. Frey. American Philosophical Quarterly, Vol. 16 (July 1979), pp. 233–239. Reprinted by permission. Sections renumbered.

view which has attracted an increasingly wide following ever since. For example, in his paper "Rights," H. J. McCloskey embraces the view but goes on to deny that animals have interests;[2] whereas Joel Feinberg, in his seminal paper "The Rights of Animals and Unborn Generations," likewise embraces the view but goes on to affirm that animals do have interests.[3] Nelson himself is emphatic that animals as well as human beings are, as he puts it, "carriers of interests,"[4] and he concludes, accordingly, that animals possess rights, rights which both deserve and warrant our respect. For Nelson, then, it is because animals have interests that they can be the logical subject of rights, and his claim that animals *do have* interests forms the minor premise, therefore, in an argument for the moral rights of animals:

> All and only beings which (can) have interests (can) have moral rights: Animals as well as humans (can) have interests: Therefore, animals (can) have moral rights.

Both McCloskey and Feinberg accept the major premise of this argument, which I shall dub the interest thesis, but disagree over the truth of the minor premise; and it is apparent that the minor premise is indeed the key to the whole matter. For given the truth of the major premise, given, that is, that the possession of interests *is* a criterion for the possession of rights, it is nevertheless only the truth of the minor premise that would result in the inclusion of creatures other than human beings within the class of right-holders. This premise is doubtful, however, and the case against it a powerful one, or so I want to suggest. . . .

III

To say that "Good health is in John's interests" is not at all the same thing as to say that "John has an interest in good health." The former is

intimately bound up with having a good or well-being to which good health is conducive, so that we could just as easily have said "Good health is conducive to John's good or well-being," whereas the latter—"John has an interest in good health"—is intimately bound up with wanting, with John's wanting good health. That these two notions of "interest" are logically distinct is readily apparent: good health may well be in John's interests, in the sense of being conducive to his good or well-being, even if John does not want good health, indeed, even if he wants to continue taking hard drugs, with the result that his health is irreparably damaged; and John may have an interest in taking drugs, in the sense of wanting to take them, even if it is apparent to him that it is not conducive to his good or well-being to continue to do so. In other words, something can be *in* John's interests without John's *having* an interest in it, and John can *have* an interest in something without its being *in* his interests.

If this is right, and there are these two logically distinct senses of "interest," we can go on to ask whether animals can have interests in either of these senses; and if they do, then perhaps the minor premise of Nelson's argument for the moral rights of animals can be sustained.

IV

Do animals, therefore, have interests in the first sense, in the sense of having a good or well-being which can be harmed or benefited? The answer, I think, is that they certainly do have interests in this sense; after all, it is plainly not good for a dog to be fed certain types of food or to be deprived of a certain amount of exercise. This answer, however, is of little use to the Nelsonian cause; for it yields the counter-intuitive result that manmade/manufactured objects and even things have interests, and, therefore, on the interest thesis, have or at least are candidates for having moral rights. For example, just as it is not good for a dog to be deprived of a certain amount of exercise, so it is not good for prehistoric cave drawings to be exposed to excessive amounts of carbon dioxide or for Rembrandt

2. H. J. McCloskey, "Rights," *Philosophical Quarterly,* Vol. 15 (1965), pp. 115–127.
3. Joel Feinberg, "The Rights of Animals and Unborn Generations," in W. T. Blackstone, (ed.), *Philosophy and Environmental Crisis* (Athens, Georgia, 1974), pp. 43–68.
4. Nelson, *op. cit.,* p. 138.

paintings to be exposed to excessive amounts of sunlight.

If, nevertheless, one is inclined to doubt that the notion of "not being good for" in the above examples shows that the object or thing in question "has a good," consider the case of tractors: anything, including tractors, can have a good, a well-being, I submit, if it is the sort of thing that can be good of its kind; and there are obviously good and bad tractors. A tractor which cannot perform certain tasks is not a good tractor, is not good of its kind; it falls short of those standards tractors must meet in order to be good ones. Thus, to say that it is in a tractor's interests to be well-oiled means only that it is conducive to the tractor's being a good one, good of its kind, if it is well-oiled. Just as John is good of his kind (i.e., human being) only if he is in health, so tractors are good of their kind only if they are well-oiled. Of course, farmers *have an interest* in their tractors being well-oiled; but this does not show that being well-oiled is not in a tractor's interest, in the sense of contributing to its being good of its kind. It *may* show that what makes good tractors good depends upon the purposes for which *we* make them; but the fact that we make them for certain purposes in no way shows that, once they are made, they cannot have a good of their own. Their good is being good of their kind, and being well-oiled is conducive to their being good of their kind and so, in this sense, in their interests. If this is right, if tractors do have interests, then on the interest thesis they have or can have moral rights, and this is a counter-intuitive result.

It is tempting to object, I suppose, that tractors cannot be harmed and benefited and, therefore, cannot have interests. My earlier examples, however, suffice to meet this objection. Prehistoric cave drawings are (not benefited but) positively harmed by excessive amounts of carbon dioxide, and Rembrandt paintings are likewise certainly harmed through the exposure to excessive amounts of sunlight. It must be emphasized that it is these objects themselves that are harmed, and that their owners are harmed only in so far as and to the extent that the objects themselves undergo harm. Accordingly, on the present objection, interests are present, and the interest thesis once again gives the result that objects or things have or can have moral rights. To accommodate those, should there be any, who just might feel that objects or things can have moral rights, when these objects or things are, e.g., significant works of art, the examples can be suitably altered, so that what is harmed is, e.g., a quite ordinary rug. But if drawings, paintings and rugs can be harmed, why not tractors? Surely a tractor is harmed by prolonged exposure to rain? And surely the harm the tractor's owner suffers comes through and is a function of the harm to the tractor itself?

In short, it cannot be in this first sense of "interest" that the case for animals and for the truth of Nelson's minor premise is to be made; for though animals do have interests in this sense, so, too, do tractors, with awkward results.

V

Do animals, therefore, have interests in the second sense, in the sense of having wants which can be satisfied or left unsatisfied? In this sense, of course, it appears that tractors do not have interests; for though being well-oiled may be conducive to tractors being good of their kind, tractors do not *have an interest* in being well-oiled, since they cannot *want* to be well-oiled, cannot, in fact, have any wants whatever. But farmers can have wants, and they certainly have an interest in their tractors being well-oiled.

What, then, about animals? Can they have wants? By "wants," I understand a term that encompasses both needs and desires, and it is these that I shall consider.[5]

If to ask whether animals can have wants is to ask whether they can have needs, then certainly animals have wants. A dog can need water. But *this* cannot be the sense of "want" on which having interests will depend, since it does not exclude things from the class of want-holders. Just as dogs need water in order to function normally, so tractors need oil in order to function nor-

---

5. See also my paper "Russell and The Essence of Desire," *Philosophy,* forthcoming.

mally; and just as dogs will die unless their need for water is satisfied, so trees and grass and a wide variety of plants and shrubs will die unless their need for water is satisfied. Though we should not give the fact undue weight, someone who in ordinary discourse says "The tractor wants oiling" certainly means the tractor needs oiling, if it is not to fall away from those standards which make tractors good of their kind. Dogs, too, need water, if they are not to fall away from the standards which make them good of their kind. It is perhaps worth emphasizing, moreover, as the cases of the tractor, trees, grass, etc., show, that needs do not require the presence either of consciousness or of knowledge of the lack which makes up the need. If, in sum, we are to agree that tractors, trees, grass, etc., do not have wants, and, therefore, interests, it cannot be the case that wants are to be construed as needs.

This, then, leaves desires, and the question of whether animals can have wants as desires. I may as well say at once that I do not think animals can have desires. My reasons for thinking this turn largely upon my doubts that animals can have beliefs, and my doubts in this regard turn partially,[6] though in large part, upon the view that having beliefs is not compatible with the absence of language and linguistic ability. I realize that the claim that animals cannot have desires is a controversial one; but I think the case to be made in support of it, complex though it is, is persuasive. This case, I should stress, consists in an analysis of desire and belief and of what it is to have and to entertain beliefs, and *not* in the adoption of anything like Chomsky's account of language as something radically unlike and completely discontinuous with animal behavior.

VI

Suppose I am a collector of rare books and desire to own a Gutenberg Bible: my desire to own this volume is *to be traced* to my belief that I do not now own such a work and that my rare book collection is deficient in this regard. By "to be

traced" here, what I mean is this: if someone were to ask *how* my belief that my book collection lacks a Gutenberg Bible is connected with my desire to own such a Bible, what better or more direct reply could be given than that, without this belief, I would not have this desire? For if I believed that my rare book collection *did* contain a Gutenberg Bible and so was complete in this sense, then I would not desire a Gutenberg Bible in order to make up what I now believe to be a notable deficiency in my collection. (Of course, I might desire to own more than one such Bible, but this contingency is not what is at issue here.)

Now what is it that I believe? I believe that my collection lacks a Gutenberg Bible; that is, I believe that the sentence "My collection lacks a Gutenberg Bible" is true. In constructions of the form "I believe that . . . ," what follows upon the "that" is a declarative sentence; and *what* I believe is that that sentence is true. The same is the case with constructions of the form. "He believes that . . .": what follows upon the "that" is a declarative sentence, and what the "he" in question believes is that that sentence is true. The difficulty in the case of animals should be apparent: if someone were to say, e.g., "The cat believes that the door is locked," then that person is holding, as I see it, that the cat holds the declarative sentence "The door is locked" to be true; and I can see no reason whatever for crediting the cat or any other creature which lacks language, including human infants, with entertaining declarative sentences and holding certain declarative sentences to be true.

Importantly, nothing whatever in this account is affected by changing the example, in order to rid it of sophisticated concepts like "door" and "locked," which in any event may be thought beyond cats, and to put in their place more rudimentary concepts. For the essence of this account is not about the relative sophistication of this or that concept but rather about the relationship between believing something and entertaining and regarding as true certain declarative sentences. If what is believed is that a certain declarative sentence is true, then no creature which lacks language can have beliefs; and without be-

6. I express doubts of a different kind elsewhere; see note 5.

liefs, a creature cannot have desires. And this is the case with animals, or so I suggest; and if I am right, not even in the sense, then, of wants as desires do animals have interests, which, to recall, is the minor premise in the Nelsonian argument for the moral rights of animals.

But is what is believed that a certain declarative sentence is true? I think there are three arguments of sorts that shore up the claim that this *is* what is believed.

First, I do not see how a creature could have the concept of belief without being able to distinguish between true and false beliefs. When I believe that my collection of rare books lacks a Gutenberg Bible, I believe that it is true that my collection lacks a Gutenberg Bible; put another way, I believe that it is false that my collection contains a Gutenberg Bible. I can distinguish, and do distinguish, between the sentences "My collection lacks a Gutenberg Bible" and "My collection contains a Gutenberg Bible," and it is only the former I hold to be true. According to my view, what I believe in this case is that this sentence is true; and sentences are the sorts of things we regard as or hold to be true. As for the cat, and leaving aside now all questions about the relative sophistication of concepts, I do not see how it could have the belief that the door is locked unless it could distinguish this true belief from the false belief that the door is unlocked. But what is true or false are not states of affairs which correspond to or reflect or pertain to these beliefs; states of affairs are not true or false but either are or are not the case, either do or do not obtain. If, then, one is going to credit cats with beliefs, and cats must be able to distinguish true from false beliefs, and states of affairs are not true or false, then what exactly is it that cats are being credited with distinguishing as true or false? Reflection on this question, I think, forces one to credit cats with language, in order for there to be something that can be true or false in belief; and it is precisely because they lack language that we cannot make this move.

Second, if in order to have the concept of belief a creature must be possessed of the difference between true and false belief, then in order for a creature to be able to distinguish true from false

beliefs that creature must—simply must, as I see it—have some awareness of, to put the matter in the most general terms, how language connects with, links up with the world; and I see no reason to credit cats with such an awareness. My belief that my collection lacks a Gutenberg Bible is true if and only if my collection lacks a Gutenberg Bible; that is, the *truth* of this belief cannot be entertained by me without it being the case that I am aware that the truth of the sentence "My collection lacks a Gutenberg Bible" is *at the very least* partially a function of how the world is. However difficult to capture, it is this relationship between language and the world a grasp of which is necessary if a creature is to grasp the difference between true and false belief, a distinction which it must grasp, if it is to possess the concept of belief at all.

Third, I do not see how a creature could have an awareness or grasp of how language connects with, links up with the world, to leave the matter at its most general, unless that creature was itself possessed of language; and cats are not possessed of language. If it were to be suggested, for example, that the sounds that cats make do amount to a language, I should deny it. This matter is far too large and complex to be tackled here; but the general line of argument I should use to support my denial can be sketched in a very few words. Can cats lie? If they cannot, then they cannot assert anything; and if they lack assertion, I do not see how they could possess a language. And I should be strict: I do not suggest that, lacking assertion, cats possess a language in some attenuated or secondary sense; rather, I suggest that, lacking assertion, they do not possess a language *at all.*

VII

It may be suggested, of course, that there might possibly be a class of desires—let us call them simple desires—which do not involve the intervention of belief, in order to have them, and which do not require that we credit animals with language. Such simple desires, for example, might be for some object or other, and we as language-users might try to capture these simple desires in the case of a dog by describing its behavior in such terms as "The dog simply desires the bone." (This position may have to be complicated, as the result of questions about whether the dog possesses the concept "bone" or even more general concepts such as "material object," "thing" and "thing in my visual field"; but these questions I shall leave aside here.) If all the dog's desires are simple desires, and this is the point, then my arguments to show that dogs lack beliefs may well be beside the point.

A subsidiary argument is required, therefore, in order to cover this possibility. Suppose, then, the dog simply desires the bone: is the dog aware that it has this simple desire or not? If it is alleged to have this desire but to be unaware that it has it, to want but to be unaware that it wants, then a problem arises. In the case of human beings, unconscious desire can be made sense of, but only because we first make sense of conscious desire; but where no desires are conscious ones, where the creature in question is alleged to have only unconscious desires, what cash value can the use of the term "desire" have in such a case? This question must be appreciated against the backdrop of what appears to ensue as a result of the present claim. On the strength of the dog's behavior, it is claimed that the dog simply desires the bone; the desire we claim for it is one which, if we concede that it has it, it is unaware that it has; and no distinction between conscious and unconscious desire is to be drawn in the dog's case. Consider then, a rubber plant which shuns the dark and through a series of movements, seeks the light: by parity of reasoning with the dog's case, we can endow the plant with an unconscious desire for the light, and claim as we do so that it, too, is a type of creature for whom no distinction between conscious and unconscious desire is possible. In other words, without an awareness-condition of some sort, it would seem that the world can be populated with an enormous number of unconscious desires in this way, and it no longer remains clear what, if anything, the cash value of the term "desire" is in such cases. If, however, the dog is alleged to have a simple desire for the bone and to be aware that it has this desire, then the dog is aware that it

simply desires the bone; it is, in other words, self-conscious. Now my objection to regarding the dog as self-conscious is not merely founded upon the view that self-consciousness presupposes the possession of language, which is too large a subject to go into here; it is also founded upon the fact that there is nothing the dog can do which can express the difference between desiring the bone and being aware of desiring the bone. Yet, the dog would have to be capable of expressing this difference in its behavior, if one is going to hold, *on the basis of that behavior,* that the dog is aware that it has a simple desire for the bone, aware that it simply desires the bone.

Even, then, if we concede for the sake of argument that there are simple desires, desires which do not involve the intervention of belief in order to have them, the suggestion that we can credit animals with these desires, without also having to credit them with language, is at best problematic. . . .

VIII

I conclude, then, that the Nelsonian position on the moral rights of animals is not a sound one: the truth of the minor premise in his argument— that animals have interests—is doubtful at best, and animals must have interests if, in accordance with the interest thesis, they are to be a logical subject of such rights. For animals either have interests in a sense which allows objects and things to have interests, and so, on the interest thesis, to have or to be candidates for having moral rights or they do not have interests at all, and so, on the interest thesis, do not have and are not candidates for having moral rights. I have reached this conclusion, moreover, without querying the correctness of the interest thesis itself, without querying, that is, whether the possession of interests *really is* a criterion for the possession of moral rights.[7]

---

7. An earlier version of this paper was read to a discussion group in Oxford and to a conference on the philosophy of Leonard Nelson in the University of Göttingen. I am indebted to the participants in each for helpful comments and suggestions.

Suggestions for Further Reading

The footnotes in Singer and Frey will take you deeper into the literature. Of special interest is Tom Regan's, *The Case for Animal Rights* (New York: Routledge, 1984) which has become a classic in the field. Also see Stephen Clark, *The Moral Status of Animals* (New York: Oxford University Press, 1977). Recently Peter Carruthers has published a book attacking both Singer's and Regan's position. See his *The Animals Issue: Moral Theory in Practice* (New York: Cambridge, 1992). Also see the sections on animal rights in *The Environmental Ethics and Policy Book: Philosophy, Ecology, Economics* (Belmont, CA: Wadsworth, 1994) and *People, Penguins, and Plastic Trees: Basic Issues in Environmental Ethics* (Belmont, CA: Wadsworth, 1986), both edited by Donald VanDeVeer and Christine Pierce. These books will also offer you good selections on other issues in environmental ethics.

Videos

Their Future in Your Hands (13 minutes, produced by Animal Aid) is an introduction to the issue of animal rights and the ethical treatment of animals. Also the film *Animal Film* (2hr and 15 minutes by Cinema Guild) lays out the issues and argues for animal rights. Your Media Services Catalogue will provide more information.

Chapter 6

Are We Free or Determined?

DETERMINISM (SOMETIMES CALLED simple determinism in order to distinguish it from other types) is the belief that all events are caused. For every event there is a set of conditions such that if the conditions were repeated, the event would reoccur. Simple determinism implies that the universe and what happens in it is lawful, that is, that the law of causality (or law of cause and effect) governs events. Hence we can assume that any given event is determined (caused) by some set of antecedent events even if we are not fully aware of what those antecedent events are.

Simple determinism should not be confused with **fatalism** nor with **predestination.** Fatalism is the belief that some or all events (including human actions) are predetermined by some impersonal cosmic force or power; predestination is the belief that some or all events are predetermined by some personal power. While fatalism and predestination differ about what predetermines events, they both agree that if an event or action is fated or predestined, it will happen *no matter what.*

Simple determinism does not claim that events or actions are predetermined by personal or impersonal cosmic powers, nor does it claim that events will happen no matter what. Rather, it holds that events happen *only if* particular causes of those events occur. If the causes of a possible event or action do not occur, that event will not occur.

Whatever the differences among simple determinism, fatalism, and predestination, it is clear that all three positions raise important questions about human freedom. If all events are caused (whether their cause be fate, a god, or some set of antecedent events), how can any human actions (assuming human actions are events), like your act of reading these words, be free? This is one way of formulating what philosophers call the **problem of freedom and determinism** (sometimes called the problem of free will).

This problem is important for a number of reasons. One of the most important has to do with moral responsibility. If the choices we make and the actions we perform are not free, it seems to make no sense to praise or blame people for what they do. Indeed, why bother to search for how one should live, or how to make correct moral choices, or how to create a just society if, in fact, all our choices are determined by antecedent factors over which we have no control?

The issue of moral responsibility allows us to probe more deeply the problem of freedom and determinism by formulating that problem as a dilemma.

1. Human choice is either free or it is not.
2. If it is free, then the law of causality is false.
3. If it is not free, then people are not responsible for their actions.
4. Therefore, either the law of causality is false or people are not responsible for their actions.

Neither of the choices given us in the conclusion is very attractive. On the one hand, we want to believe in the law of causality. All of science and technology depends on it. Surely, if there are uncaused events, then there are events that can never be explained, or predicted. So why search for a cure for cancer, or why try to eliminate crime, or why try to invent a pollution-free form of rapid transportation? There may be no causes for these things and hence no means of prediction or control. If the law of causality is false, the universe appears chaotic, disordered, unreliable, and events seem unexplainable.

On the other hand, we want to hold people morally responsible for what they do. What sense would praise or blame make if we aren't responsible? If you are not free and hence not responsible for what you do, then what sense does it make to say you *earned* a good grade in philosophy, or you *merited* a promotion, or you *ought* to be punished for behaving badly? Indeed, what sense would morality make if people cannot freely choose what they do?

In this chapter we will explore some of the solutions people have proposed to the problem of freedom and determinism. As we explore these solutions, our understanding of the problem will grow and alternatives that may not have occurred to us will present themselves.

6.1. We Are Determined

One proposed solution to the problem of freedom and determinism is a position known as **hard determinism.** Hard determinism holds that every event has a cause and that this fact is *incompatible* with free will. Nothing happens for which there is no sufficient reason, hence free will is an illusion. People should not be held morally responsible for their actions since a given act is unavoidable if the appropriate antecedent conditions obtain. If we want to change people's behavior, we need to develop a science of behavior that will show us how to manipulate the causes of human behavior.

Notice that hard determinism is a form of simple determinism insofar as it holds that every event has a cause. But *unlike* simple determinism, hard determinism claims, in addition, that determinism and free will are incompatible, that free will is an illusion, and that humans are not in fact responsible for what they do in the sense that they could have made choices other than they did.

Supporters of this position usually appeal to the natural sciences and concepts like "natural law" to back their views. Science seeks to give a description of objective facts. But more than this, it seeks to discover uniformity in nature. That is, it seeks to explain facts by discovering the networks of cause and effect according to which events are ordered.

Robert Blatchford (1851–1943) believed in hard determinism and crusaded in England for that position. He argued that heredity and environment determine human behavior. It is, he thought, still appropriate to reward and punish people for what they do, but rewards and punishments are only appropriate as means to change behavior. They should not be linked to the notion of responsibility. His arguments are aimed against a particular conception of free will, namely, that humans are free to do other than what their heredity and environment cause them to do. He did not deny that humans make choices and that they even make choices in accord with their wishes, desires, likes, and dislikes. Nor did he deny that many of the choices humans make are voluntary in the sense that no other person forced them to make a particular choice. All he denied is that humans are free to somehow rise above heredity and environment.

Reading Questions

1. According to Blatchford, what is the "point" on which the free will discussion turns?
2. What is Blatchford's main point?
3. What arguments does Blatchford present to support his main point?
4. Why, according to Blatchford, should we not blame someone for their conduct?
5. Present the best counter-argument you can to Blatchford's position.
6. If what you believe about the existence of free will is determined (as Blatchford claims) by heredity and environment, why would Blatchford even try to convince you that hard determinism is true?
7. Formulate any question you wish (analytic or critical) about what Blatchford has to say and answer it.

Not Guilty

ROBERT BLATCHFORD

THE FREE WILL DELUSION has been a stumbling block in the way of human thought for thousands of years. Let us try whether common sense and common knowledge cannot remove it.

Free will is a subject of great importance to us in this case; and it is one we must come to with our eyes wide open and our wits wide awake; not because it is very difficult, but because it has been tied and twisted into a tangle of Gordian knots by twenty centuries full of wordy but unsuccessful philosophers.

The free will party claim that man is responsible for his acts, because his will is free to choose between right and wrong.

From Not Guilty *by Robert Blatchford. Copyright © 1913, New York: Albert and Charles Boni, Inc. Pages 108–120; 130–131.*

We reply that the will is not free, and that if it were free man could not know right from wrong until he was taught.

As to the knowledge of good and evil the free will party will claim that conscience is an unerring guide. But I have already proved that conscience does not and cannot tell us what is right and what is wrong: it only reminds us of the lessons we have learnt as to right and wrong.

The "still small voice" is not the voice of God: it is the voice of heredity and environment.

And now to the freedom of the will.

When a man says his will is free, he means that it is free of all control or interference: that it can overrule heredity and environment.

We reply that the will is ruled by heredity and environment.

The cause of all the confusion on this subject may be shown in a few words.

When the free will party say that man has a free will, they mean that he is free to act as he chooses to act.

There is no need to deny that. *But what causes him to choose?*

That is the pivot upon which the whole discussion turns.

The free will party seem to think of the will as something independent of the man, as something outside him. They seem to think that the will decides without the control of the man's reason.

If that were so, it would not prove the man responsible. "The will" would be responsible, and not the man. It would be as foolish to blame a man for the act of a "free" will, as to blame a horse for the action of its rider.

But I am going to prove to my readers, by appeals to their common sense and common knowledge, that the will is not free; and that it is ruled by heredity and environment.

To begin with, the average man will be against me. He knows that he chooses between two courses every hour, and often every minute, and he thinks his choice is free. But that is a delusion: his choice is not free. He can choose, and does choose. But he can only choose as his heredity

and his environment cause him to choose. He never did choose and never will choose except as his heredity and his environment—his temperament and his training—cause him to choose. And his heredity and his environment have fixed his choice before he makes it.

The average man says "I know that I can act as I wish to act." But what causes him to wish?

The free will party say, "We know that a man can and does choose between two acts." But what settles the choice?

There is a cause for every wish, a cause for every choice; and every cause of every wish and choice arises from heredity, or from environment.

For a man acts always from temperament, which is heredity, or from training, which is environment.

And in cases where a man hesitates in his choice between two acts, the hesitation is due to a conflict between his temperament and his training, or as some would express it, "between his desire and his conscience."

A man is practising at a target with a gun, when a rabbit crosses his line of fire. The man has his eye and his sights on the rabbit, and his finger on the trigger. The man's will is free. If he press the trigger the rabbit will be killed.

Now, how does the man decide whether or not he shall fire? He decides by feeling, and by reason.

He would like to fire, just to make sure that he could hit the mark. He would like to fire, because he would like to have the rabbit for supper. He would like to fire, because there is in him the old, old hunting instinct, to kill.

But the rabbit does not belong to him. He is not sure that he will not get into trouble if he kills it. Perhaps—if he is a very uncommon kind of man—he feels that it would be cruel and cowardly to shoot a helpless rabbit.

Well. The man's will is free. He can fire if he likes: he can let the rabbit go if he likes. How will he decide? On what does his decision depend?

His decision depends upon the relative strength of his desire to kill the rabbit, and of his scruples about cruelty, and the law.

Not only that, but, if we knew the man fairly well, we could guess how his free will would act before it acted. The average sporting Briton would kill the rabbit. But we know that there are men who on no account shoot any harmless wild creature.

Broadly put, we may say that the sportsman would will to fire, and that the humanitarian would not will to fire.

Now, as both their wills are free, it must be something outside the wills that makes the difference.

Well. The sportsman will kill, because he is a sportsman: the humanitarian will not kill, because he is a humanitarian.

And what makes one man a sportsman and another a humanitarian? Heredity and environment: temperament and training.

One man is merciful, another cruel, by nature; or one is thoughtful and the other thoughtless, by nature. That is a difference of heredity.

One may have been taught all his life that to kill wild things is "sport"; the other may have been taught that it is inhuman and wrong: that is a difference of environment.

Now, the man by nature cruel or thoughtless, who has been trained to think of killing animals as sport, becomes what we call a sportsman, because heredity and environment have made him a sportsman.

The other man's heredity and environment have made him a humanitarian.

The sportsman kills the rabbit, because he is a sportsman, and he is a sportsman because heredity and environment have made him one.

That is to say the "free will" is really controlled by heredity and environment.

Allow me to give a case in point. A man who had never done any fishing was taken out by a fisherman. He liked the sport, and for some months followed it eagerly. But one day an accident brought home to his mind the cruelty of catching fish with a hook, and he instantly laid down his rod, and never fished again.

Before the change he was always eager to go fishing if invited: after the change he could not

be persuaded to touch a line. His will was free all the while. How was it that his will to fish changed to his will not to fish? It was the result of environment. He had learnt that fishing was cruel. This knowledge controlled his will.

But, it may be asked, how do you account for a man doing the thing he does not wish to do?

No man ever did a thing he did not wish to do. When there are two wishes the stronger rules.

Let us suppose a case. A young woman gets two letters by the same post; one is an invitation to go with her lover to a concert, the other is a request that she will visit a sick child in the slums. The girl is very fond of music, and is rather afraid of the slums. She wishes to go to the concert, and to be with her lover; she dreads the foul street and the dirty home, and shrinks from the risk of measles or fever. But she goes to the sick child, and she foregoes the concert. Why?

Because her sense of duty is stronger than her self-love.

Now, her sense of duty is partly due to her nature—that is, to her heredity—but it is chiefly due to environment. Like all of us, this girl was born without any kind of knowledge, and with only the rudiments of a conscience. But she has been well taught, and the teaching is part of her environment.

We may say that the girl is free to act as she chooses, but she *does* act as she has been *taught* that she *ought* to act. This teaching, which is part of her environment, controls her will.

We may say that a man is free to act as he chooses. He is free to act as *he* chooses, but *he* will choose as heredity and environment cause *him* to choose. For heredity and environment have made him that which he is. . . .

As we want to get this subject as clear as we can, let us take one or two familiar examples of the action of the will.

Jones and Robinson meet and have a glass of whisky. Jones asks Robinson to have another. Robinson says, "no thank you, one is enough." Jones says, "all right: have another cigarette." Robinson takes the cigarette. Now, here we have a case where a man refuses a second drink, but takes a second smoke. Is it because he would like another cigarette, but would not like another glass of whisky? No. It is because he knows that it is *safer* not to take another glass of whisky.

How does he know that whisky is dangerous? He has learnt it—from his environment.

"But he *could* have taken another glass if he wished."

But he could not wish to take another, because there was something he wished more strongly—to be safe.

And why did he want to be safe? Because he had learnt—from his environment—that it was unhealthy, unprofitable, and shameful to get drunk. Because he had learned—from his environment—that it is easier to avoid forming a bad habit than to break a bad habit when formed. Because he valued the good opinion of his neighbors, and also his position and prospects.

These feelings and this knowledge ruled his will, and caused him to refuse the second glass.

But there was no sense of danger, no well-learned lesson of risk to check his will to smoke another cigarette. Heredity and environment did not warn him against that. So, to please his friend, and himself, he accepted.

Now suppose Smith asks Williams to have another glass. Williams takes it, takes several, finally goes home—as he often goes home. Why?

Largely because drinking is a habit with him. And not only does the mind instinctively repeat an action, but, in the case of drink, a physical craving is set up, and the brain is weakened. It is easier to refuse the first glass than the second; easier to refuse the second than the third; and it is very much harder for a man to keep sober who has frequently got drunk.

So, when poor Williams has to make his choice, he has habit against him, he has a physical craving against him, and he has a weakened brain to think with.

"But Williams could have refused the first glass."

No. Because in this case the desire to drink, or to please a friend, was stronger than his fear of the danger. Or he may not have been so con-

scious of the danger as Robinson was. He may not have been so well taught, or he may not have been so sensible, or he may not have been so cautious. So that his heredity and environment, his temperament and training, led him to take the drink, as surely as Robinson's heredity and environment led him to refuse it.

And now, it is my turn to ask a question. If the will is "free," if conscience is a sure guide, how is it that the free will and the conscience of Robinson caused him to keep sober, while the free will and the conscience of Williams caused him to get drunk?

Robinson's will was curbed by certain feelings which failed to curb the will of Williams. Because in the case of Williams the feelings were stronger on the other side.

It was the nature and the training of Robinson which made him refuse the second glass, and it was the nature of the training of Williams which made him drink the second glass.

What had free will to do with it?

We are told that *every* man has a free will, and a conscience.

Now, if Williams had been Robinson, that is to say if his heredity and his environment had been exactly like Robinson's, he would have done exactly as Robinson did.

It was because his heredity and environment were not the same that his act was not the same.

Both men had free wills. What made one do what the other refused to do?

Heredity and environment. To reverse their conduct we should have to reverse their heredity and environment. . . .

And, again, as to that matter of belief. Some moralists hold that it is wicked not to believe certain things, and that men who do not believe those things will be punished.

But a man cannot believe a thing he is told to believe: he can only believe a thing which he *can* believe; and he can only believe that which his own reason tells him is true.

It would be no use asking Sir Roger Ball to believe that the earth is flat. He *could not* believe it.

It is no use asking an agnostic to believe the

story of Jonah and the whale. He *could not* believe it. He might pretend to believe it. He might try to believe it. But his reason would not allow him to believe it.

Therefore it is a mistake to say that a man "knows better," when the fact is that he has been told "better" and cannot believe what he has been told.

That is a simple matter, and looks quite trivial; but how much ill-will, how much intolerance, how much violence, persecution, and murder have been caused by the strange idea that a man is wicked because *his* reason *cannot* believe that which to another man's reason seems quite true.

Free will has no power over a man's belief. A man cannot believe by will, but only by conviction. A man cannot be forced to believe. You may threaten him, wound him, beat him, burn him; and he may be frightened, or angered, or pained; but he cannot *believe,* nor can he be made to believe. Until he is convinced.

Now, truism as it may seem, I think it necessary to say here that a man cannot be convinced by abuse, nor by punishment. He can only be convinced by *reason.*

Yes. If we wish a man to believe a thing, we shall find a few words of reason more powerful than a million curses, or a million bayonets. To burn a man alive for failing to believe that the sun goes round the world is not to convince him. The fire is searching, but it does not seem to him to be relevant to the issue. He never doubted that fire would burn; but perchance his dying eyes may see the sun sinking down into the west, as the world rolls on its axis. He dies in his belief. And knows no "better." . . .

We are to ask whether it is true that everything a man does is the only thing he could do, at the instant of his doing it.

This is a very important question, because if the answer is yes, all praise and all blame are undeserved.

All praise and *all* blame.

Let us take some revolting action as a test.

A tramp has murdered a child on the highway, has robbed her of a few coppers, and has thrown her body into a ditch.

"Do you mean to say that tramp could not help doing that? Do you mean to say he is not to blame? Do you mean to say he is not to be punished?"

Yes. I say all those things; and if all those things are not true this book is not worth the paper it is printed on.

Prove it? I have proved it. But I have only instanced venial acts, and now we are confronted with murder. And the horror of murder drives men almost to frenzy, so that they cease to think: they can only feel.

Murder. Yes, a brutal murder. It comes upon us with a sickening shock. But I said in my first chapter that I proposed to defend those whom God and man condemn, and to demand justice for those whom God and man have wronged. I have to plead for the *bottom* dog: the lowest, the most detested, the worst.

The tramp has committed a murder. Man would loathe him, revile him, hang him: God would cast him into outer darkness.

"Not," cries the pious Christian, "if he repent."

I make a note of the repentance and pass on.

The tramp has committed a murder. It was a cowardly and cruel murder, and the motive was robbery.

But I have proved that all motives and all powers; all knowledge and capacity, all acts and all words, are caused by heredity and environment.

I have proved that a man can only be good or bad as heredity and environment cause him to be good or bad; and I have proved these things because I have to claim that all punishments and rewards, all praise and blame, are undeserved. . . .

Punishment has never been just, has never been effectual. Punishment has always failed of its purpose: the greater its severity, the more abject its failure.

Men cannot be made good and gentle by means of violence and wrong. The real tamers and purifiers of human hearts are love and charity and reason. . . .

Suggestions for Further Reading

The articles entitled "Determinism," "Behaviorism," and "Determinism in History" in *The Encyclopedia of Philosophy* will provide general background information and a bibliography.

For arguments in favor of hard determinism and its application to the judicial system see Clarence Darrow, *Crime and Criminals* (New York: Charles H. Kerr, 1902).

B. F. Skinner, an influential psychologist, has touched on the issues of determinism, freedom, and control in a number of different writings. See his *Walden Two* (New York: Macmillan, 1948, 1976) and *Beyond Freedom and Dignity* (New York: Knopf, 1972) for popular and controversial treatments. The critical literature attacking Skinner's position is no less extensive than the literature defending it. For starters see Michael Scriven, "A Study of Radical Behaviorism," in *Minnesota Studies in the Philosophy of Science,* Vol. 1, edited by Herbert Feigl and Michael Scriven (Minneapolis: University of Minnesota Press, 1956).

More recent versions of hard determinism are associated with sociobiology. Sociobiology works on the hypothesis that all forms of social behavior can be biologically explained. The literature is extensive, but see E. O. Wilson's *Sociobiology: The New Synthesis* (Cambridge: Belknap, 1975). For a philosophical discussion, a critique, and a good bibliography see Michael Ruse's *Sociobiology: Sense or Nonsense?* 2d ed. (Dordrecht: Reidel, 1985).

Video

A Clockwork Orange (137 minutes, produced by Warner Home Video) illustrates, in a futuristic setting, how behavioral techniques can be used to modify destructive behavior. See your Media Services Catalogue for more information.

6.2. We Are Free

Some of you may find hard determinism unconvincing. Some of you might still be wondering whether we are free in the sense that our choices are not caused or determined by heredity or environment, but by our own free will.

Libertarianism is the position that some human choices, in particular moral choices for which we are responsible, are not determined by antecedent events. (Please note that this kind of libertarianism should not be confused with the political movement and theory of the same name.) One version of this theory holds that the self (sometimes called "soul") is an agent with free will, that is, with a power to choose, which transcends heredity and environment in the sense that the self can choose contrary to these factors. Another version of this view holds that humans are radically free in the sense that they are free to create their own self. The self is not a fixed essence determined by heredity, environment, or any other factor except our capacity for choice. We create who we are (our selves) by the choices we make. It follows that humans, when freely deciding to act in a particular way, not only can be but ought to be held responsible for what they do.

Jean-Paul Sartre (1905–1980) was a French novelist, playwright, and philosopher. In 1939 he was called up by the French army to fight the German invasion. He was captured by the Germans in 1940, but returned to France after the armistice and became active in the resistance movement. After the war he emerged as a leading French intellectual, a major figure in the philosophical movement called **existentialism,** and he became involved in a number of radical causes. His major philosophical work is *Being and Nothingness* (1943).

In 1945 Sartre gave a lecture which was published the following year as *L'Existentialisme est un humanisme*. The selection that follows is from that lecture. Sartre is not only concerned with defining existentialism and defending it against its critics, he is also concerned with free choice. Sartre realizes that if human nature is not something determined beforehand, but is something we create as we make the decisions that come to constitute our lives, then we are radically free. This is central to the existentialist view of human beings and, as Sartre also clearly realizes, has important implications for ethics. If you are free to do whatever you wish, if for you everything is permissible, then what will you do?

Reading Questions

1. What does "existence precedes essence" mean?
2. What is the first principle of existentialism?
3. Why does Sartre claim that "In choosing myself, I choose man?"
4. What is meant by anguish?
5. What does forlornness mean?
6. Do you agree with the contention that "everything is permissible if God does not exist?" Why or why not?
7. Why does Sartre say we are *condemned* to be free?
8. What is meant by despair?
9. If we create moral value and there is no guarantee that our values are correct or will produce good results, why bother to become socially and politically involved at all? How does Sartre answer this question? Do you agree or not with his answer? Why?
10. Create your own *critical* question about anything Sartre says and answer it.

Existentialism

JEAN-PAUL SARTRE

WHAT IS MEANT BY THE TERM EXISTENTIALISM? Most people who use the word would be rather embarrassed if they had to explain it, since, now that the word is all the rage, even the work of a musician or painter is being called existentialist. A gossip columnist in *Clartés* signs himself *The Existentialist,* so that by this time the word has been so stretched and has taken on so broad a meaning that it no longer means anything at all. It seems that for want of an advance-guard doctrine analogous to surrealism, the kind of people who are eager for scandal and flurry turn to this philosophy which in other respects does not at all serve their purposes in this sphere.

Jean-Paul Sartre, Existentialism, *translated by Bernard Frechtman (New York: The Philosophical Library, 1947), pp. 14–38. Reprinted by permission of The Philosophical Library, Inc.*

Actually, it is the least scandalous, the most austere of doctrines. It is intended strictly for specialists and philosophers. Yet it can be defined easily. What complicates matters is that there are two kinds of existentialist; first, those who are Christian, among whom I would include Jaspers and Gabriel Marcel, both Catholic; and on the other hand the atheistic existentialists, among whom I class Heidegger, and then the French existentialists and myself. What they have in common is that they think that existence precedes essence, or, if you prefer, that subjectivity must be the starting point.

Just what does that mean? Let us consider some object that is manufactured, for example, a book or a paper-cutter: here is an object which has been made by an artisan whose inspiration came from a concept. He referred to the concept of what a paper-cutter is and likewise to a known method of production, which is part of the concept, something which is, by and large, a routine. Thus, the paper-cutter is at once an object produced in a certain way and, on the other hand, one having a specific use; and one can not postulate a man who produces a paper-cutter but does not know what it is used for. Therefore, let us say that, for the paper-cutter, essence—that is, the ensemble of both the production routines and the properties which enable it to be both produced and defined—precedes existence. Thus, the presence of the paper-cutter or book in front of me is determined. Therefore, we have here a technical view of the world whereby it can be said that production precedes existence.

When we conceive God as the Creator, He is generally thought of as a superior sort of artisan. Whatever doctrine we may be considering, whether one like that of Descartes or that of Leibnitz, we always grant that will more or less follows understanding or, at the very least, accompanies it, and that when God creates He knows exactly what He is creating. Thus, the concept of man in the mind of God is comparable to the concept of paper-cutter in the mind of the manufacturer, and, following certain techniques and a conception, God produces man, just as the artisan, following a definition and a technique, makes a paper-cutter. Thus, the individual man is the realization of a certain concept in the divine intelligence.

In the eighteenth century, the atheism of the *philosophes* discarded the idea of God, but not so much for the notion that essence precedes existence. To a certain extent, this idea is found everywhere; we find it in Diderot, in Voltaire, and even in Kant. Man has a human nature; this human nature, which is the concept of the human, is found in all men, which means that each man is a particular example of a universal concept, man. In Kant, the result of this universality is that the wild-man, the natural man, as well as the bourgeois, are circumscribed by the same definition and have the same basic qualities. Thus, here too the essence of man precedes the historical existence that we find in nature.

Atheistic existentialism, which I represent, is more coherent. It states that if God does not exist, there is at least one being in whom existence precedes essence, a being who exists before he can be defined by any concept, and that this being is man, or, as Heidegger says, human reality. What is meant here by saying that existence precedes essence? It means that, first of all, man exists, turns up, appears on the scene, and, only afterwards, defines himself. If man, as the existentialist conceives him, is indefinable, it is because at first he is nothing. Only afterward will he be something, and he himself will have made what he will be. Thus, there is no human nature, since there is no God to conceive it. Not only is man what he conceives himself to be, but he is also only what he wills himself to be after this thrust toward existence.

Man is nothing else but what he makes of himself. Such is the first principle of existentialism. It is also what is called subjectivity, the name we are labeled with when charges are brought against us. But what do we mean by this, if not that man has a greater dignity than a stone or table? For we mean that man first exists, that is, that man first of all is the being who hurls himself toward a future and who is conscious of imagining himself as being in the future. Man is at the start a plan which is aware of itself, rather than a patch of moss, a piece of garbage, or a cauli-flower; nothing exists prior to this plan; there is nothing in heaven; man will be what he will have planned to be. Not what he will want to be. Because by the word "will" we generally mean a conscious decision, which is subsequent to what we have already made of ourselves. I may want to belong to a political party, write a book, get married; but all that is only a manifestation of an earlier, more spontaneous choice that is called "will." But if existence really does precede essence, man is responsible for what he is. Thus, existentialism's first move is to make every man aware of what he is and to make the full responsibility of his existence rest on him. And when we say that a man is responsible for himself, we do not only mean that he is responsible for his own individuality, but that he is responsible for all men.

The word subjectivism has two meanings, and our opponents play on the two. Subjectivism means, on the one hand, that an individual chooses and makes himself; and, on the other, that it is impossible for man to transcend human subjectivity. The second of these is the essential meaning of existentialism. When we say that man chooses his own self, we mean that every one of us does likewise; but we also mean by that that in making this choice he also chooses all men. In fact, in creating the man that we want to be, there is not a single one of our acts which does not at the same time create an image of man as we think he ought to be. To choose to be this or that is to affirm at the same time the value of what we choose, because we can never choose evil. We always choose the good, and nothing can be good for us without being good for all.

If, on the other hand, existence precedes essence, and if we grant that we exist and fashion our image at one and the same time, the image is valid for everybody and for our whole age. Thus, our responsibility is much greater than we might have supposed, because it involves all mankind. If I am a working man and choose to join a Christian trade-union rather than be a communist, and if by being a member I want to show that the best thing for man is resignation, that the

kingdom of man is not of this world, I am not only involving my own case—I want to be resigned for everyone. As a result, my action has involved all humanity. To take a more individual matter, if I want to marry, to have children; even if this marriage depends solely on my own circumstances or passion or wish, I am involving all humanity in monogamy and not merely myself. Therefore, I am responsible for myself and for everyone else. I am creating a certain image of man of my own choosing. In choosing myself, I choose man.

This helps us understand what the actual content is of such rather grandiloquent words as anguish, forlornness, despair. As you will see, it's all quite simple.

First, what is meant by anguish? The existentialists say at once that man is anguish. What that means is this: the man who involves himself and who realizes that he is not only the person he chooses to be, but also a law-maker who is, at the same time, choosing all mankind as well as himself, can not help escape the feeling of his total and deep responsibility. Of course, there are many people who are not anxious; but we claim that they are hiding their anxiety, that they are fleeing from it. Certainly, many people believe that when they do something, they themselves are the only ones involved, and when someone says to them, "What if everyone acted that way?" they shrug their shoulders and answer, "Everyone doesn't act that way." But really, one should always ask himself, "What would happen if everybody looked at things that way?" There is no escaping this disturbing thought except by a kind of double-dealing. A man who lies and makes excuses for himself by saying "not everybody does that," is someone with an uneasy conscience, because the act of lying implies that a universal value is conferred upon the lie.

Anguish is evident even when it conceals itself. This is the anguish that Kierkegaard called the anguish of Abraham. You know the story: an angel has ordered Abraham to sacrifice his son; if it really were an angel who has come and said, "You are Abraham, you shall sacrifice your son," everything would be all right. But everyone might first wonder, "Is it really an angel, and am I really Abraham? What proof do I have?"

There was a madwoman who had hallucinations; someone used to speak to her on the telephone and give her orders. Her doctor asked her, "Who is it who talks to you?" She answered, "He says it's God." What proof did she really have that it was God? If an angel comes to me, what proof is there that it's an angel? And if I hear voices, what proof is there that they come from heaven and not from hell, or from the subconscious, or a pathological condition? What proves that they are addressed to me? What proof is there that I have been appointed to impose my choice and my conception of man on humanity? I'll never find any proof or sign to convince me of that. If a voice addresses me, it is always for me to decide that this is the angel's voice; if I consider that such an act is a good one, it is I who will choose to say that it is good rather than bad.

Now, I'm not being singled out as an Abraham, and yet at every moment I'm obliged to perform exemplary acts. For every man, everything happens as if all mankind had its eyes fixed on him and were guiding itself by what he does. And every man ought to say to himself, "Am I really the kind of man who has the right to act in such a way that humanity might guide itself by my actions?" And if he does not say that to himself, he is masking his anguish.

There is no question here of the kind of anguish which would lead to quietism, to inaction. It is a matter of a simple sort of anguish that anybody who has had responsibilities is familiar with. For example, when a military officer takes the responsibility for an attack and sends a certain number of men to death, he chooses to do so, and in the main he alone makes the choice. Doubtless, orders come from above, but they are too broad; he interprets them, and on this interpretation depend the lives of ten or fourteen or twenty men. In making a decision he can not help having a certain anguish. All leaders know this anguish. That doesn't keep them from acting; on the contrary, it is the very condition of their action. For it implies that they envisage a number of possibilities, and when they choose one, they realize that it has value only because it is chosen. We shall see that this kind of anguish, which is the kind that existentialism describes, is explained, in addition, by a direct responsibility to the other men whom it involves. It is not a curtain separating us from action, but is part of action itself.

When we speak of forlornness, a term Heidegger was fond of, we mean only that God does not exist and that we have to face all the consequences of this. The existentialist is strongly opposed to a certain kind of secular ethics which would like to abolish God with the least possible expense. About 1880, some French teachers tried to set up a secular ethics which went something like this: God is a useless and costly hypothesis; we are discarding it; but, meanwhile, in order for there to be an ethics, a society, a civilization, it is essential that certain values be taken seriously and that they be considered as having an *a priori* existence. It must be obligatory, *a priori*, to be honest, not to lie, not to beat your wife, to have children, etc. So we're going to try a little device which will make it possible to show that values exist all the same, inscribed in a heaven of ideas, though otherwise God does not exist. In other words—and this, I believe, is the tendency of everything called reformism in France—nothing will be changed if God does not exist. We shall find ourselves with the same norms of honesty, progress, and humanism, and we shall have made of God an outdated hypothesis which will peacefully die off by itself.

The existentialist, on the contrary, thinks it very distressing that God does not exist, because all possibility of finding values in a heaven of ideas disappears along with Him; there can no longer be an *a priori* Good, since there is no infinite and perfect consciousness to think it. Nowhere is it written that the Good exists, that we must be honest, that we must not lie; because the fact is we are on a plane where there are only men. Dostoievsky said, "If God didn't exist, everything would be possible." That is the very starting point of existentialism. Indeed, everything is permissible if God does not exist, and as a result man is forlorn, because neither within him or without does he find anything to cling to. He can't start making excuses for himself.

If existence really does precede essence, there is no explaining things away by reference to a fixed and given human nature. In other words, there is no determinism, man is free, man is freedom. On the other hand, if God does not exist, we find no values or commands to turn to which legitimize our conduct. So, in the bright realm of values, we have no excuse behind us, nor justification before us. We are alone, with no excuses.

That is the idea I shall try to convey when I say that man is condemned to be free. Condemned, because he did not create himself, yet, in other respects is free; because, once thrown into the world, he is responsible for everything he does. The existentialist does not believe in the power of passion. He will never agree that a sweeping passion is a ravaging torrent which fatally leads a man to certain acts and is therefore an excuse. He thinks that man is responsible for his passion.

The existentialist does not think that man is going to help himself by finding in the world some omen by which to orient himself. Because he thinks that man will interpret the omen to suit himself. Therefore, he thinks that man, with no support and no aid, is condemned every moment to invent man. Ponge, in a very fine article, has said, "Man is the future of man." That's exactly it. But if it is taken to mean that this future is recorded in heaven, that God sees it, then it is false, because it would really no longer be a future. If it is taken to mean that, whatever a man may be, there is a future to be forged, a virgin future before him, then this remark is sound. But then we are forlorn.

To give you an example which will enable you to understand forlornness better, I shall cite the case of one of my students who came to see me under the following circumstances: His father was on bad terms with his mother, and, moreover, was inclined to be a collaborationist; his older brother had been killed in the German offensive of 1940, and the young man, with somewhat immature but generous feelings, wanted to avenge him. His mother lived alone with him,

very much upset by the half-treason of her husband and the death of her older son; the boy was her only consolation.

The boy was faced with the choice of leaving for England and joining the Free French Forces— that is, leaving his mother behind—or remaining with his mother and helping her to carry on. He was fully aware that the woman lived only for him and that his going-off—and perhaps his death—would plunge her into despair. He was also aware that every act that he did for his mother's sake was a sure thing, in the sense that it was helping her to carry on, whereas every effort he made toward going off and fighting was an uncertain move which might run aground and prove completely useless; for example, on his way to England he might, while passing through Spain, be detained indefinitely in a Spanish camp; he might reach England or Algiers and be stuck in an office at a desk job. As a result, he was faced with two very different kinds of action: one, concrete, immediate, but concerning only one individual; the other concerned an incomparably vaster group, a national collectivity, but for that very reason was dubious, and might be interrupted en route. And, at the same time, he was wavering between two kinds of ethics. On the one hand, an ethics of sympathy, of personal devotion; on the other, a broader ethics, but one whose efficacy was more dubious. He had to choose between the two.

Who could help him choose? Christian doctrine? No. Christian doctrine says, "Be charitable, love your neighbor, take the more rugged path, etc." But which is the more rugged path? Whom should he love as a brother? The fighting man or his mother? Which does the greater good, the vague act of fighting in a group, or the concrete one of helping a particular human being to go on living? Who can decide *a priori*? Nobody. No book of ethics can tell him. The Kantian ethics says, "Never treat any person as a means, but as an end." Very well, if I stay with my mother, I'll treat her as an end and not as a means; but by virtue of this very fact, I'm running the risk of treating the people around me who are fighting, as means; and, conversely, if I go to join those who are fighting, I'll be treating them as an end, and, by doing that, I run the risk of treating my mother as a means.

If values are vague, and if they are always too broad for the concrete and specific case that we are considering, the only thing left for us is to trust our instincts. That's what this young man tried to do; and when I saw him, he said, "In the end, feeling is what counts. I ought to choose whichever pushes me in one direction. If I feel that I love my mother enough to sacrifice everything else for her—my desire for vengeance, for action, for adventure—then I'll stay with her. If, on the contrary, I feel that my love for my mother isn't enough, I'll leave."

But how is the value of a feeling determined? What gives his feeling for his mother value? Precisely the fact that he remained with her. I may say that I like so-and-so well enough to sacrifice a certain amount of money for him, but I may say so only if I've done it. I may say "I love my mother well enough to remain with her" if I have remained with her. The only way to determine the value of this affection is, precisely, to perform an act which confirms and defines it. But, since I require this affection to justify my act, I find myself caught in a vicious circle.

On the other hand, Gide has well said that a mock feeling and a true feeling are almost indistinguishable; to decide that I love my mother and will remain with her, or to remain with her by putting on an act, amount something to the same thing. In other words, the feeling is formed by the acts one performs; so, I can not refer to it in order to act upon it. Which means that I can neither seek within myself the true condition which will impel me to act, nor apply to a system of ethics for concepts which will permit me to act. You will say, "At least, he did go to a teacher for advice." But if you seek advice from a priest, for example, you have chosen this priest; you already knew, more or less, just about what advice he was going to give you. In other words, choosing your adviser is involving yourself. The proof of this is that if you are a Christian, you will say, "Consult a priest." But some priests are collaborating, some are just marking time, some are

resisting. Which to choose? If the young man chooses a priest who is resisting or collaborating, he has already decided on the kind of advice he's going to get. Therefore, in coming to see me he knew the answer I was going to give him, and I had only one answer to give: "You're free; choose, that is, invent." No general ethics can show you what is to be done; there are no omens in the world. The Catholics will reply, "But there are." Granted—but, in any case, I myself choose the meaning they have.

When I was a prisoner, I knew a rather remarkable young man who was a Jesuit. He had entered the Jesuit order in the following way: he had had a number of very bad breaks; in childhood, his father died, leaving him in poverty, and he was a scholarship student at a religious institution where he was constantly made to feel that he was being kept out of charity; then, he failed to get any of the honors and distinctions that children like; later on, at about eighteen, he bungled a love affair; finally, at twenty-two, he failed in military training, a childish enough matter, but it was the last straw.

This young fellow might well have felt that he had botched everything. It was a sign of something, but of what? He might have taken refuge in bitterness or despair. But he very wisely looked upon all this as a sign that he was not made for secular triumphs, and that only the triumphs of religion, holiness, and faith were open to him. He saw the hand of God in all this, and so he entered the order. Who can help seeing that he alone decided what the sign meant?

Some other interpretation might have been drawn from this series of setbacks; for example, that he might have done better to turn carpenter or revolutionist. Therefore, he is fully responsible for the interpretation. Forlornness implies that we ourselves choose our being. Forlornness and anguish go together.

As for despair, the term has a very simple meaning. It means that we shall confine ourselves to reckoning only with what depends upon our will, or on the ensemble of probabilities which make our action possible. When we want something, we always have to reckon with probabilities. I may be counting on the arrival of a friend. The friend is coming by rail or street-car; this supposes that the train will arrive on schedule, or that the street-car will not jump the track. I am left in the realm of possibility; but possibilities are to be reckoned with only to the point where my action comports with the ensemble of these possibilities, and no further. The moment the possibilities I am considering are not rigorously involved by my action, I ought to disengage myself from them, because no God, no scheme, can adapt the world and its possibilities to my will. When Descartes said, "Conquer yourself rather than the world," he meant essentially the same thing.

The Marxists to whom I have spoken reply, "You can rely on the support of others in your action, which obviously has certain limits because you're not going to live forever. That means: rely on both what others are doing elsewhere to help you, in China, in Russia, and what they will do later on, after your death, to carry on the action and lead it to its fulfillment, which will be the revolution. You even *have* to rely upon that, otherwise you're immoral." I reply at once that I will always rely on fellow-fighters insofar as these comrades are involved with me in a common struggle, in the unity of a party or a group in which I can more or less make my weight felt; that is, one whose ranks I am in as a fighter and whose movements I am aware of at every moment. In such a situation, relying on the unity and will of the party is exactly like counting on the fact that the train will arrive on time or that the car won't jump the track. But, given that man is free and that there is no human nature for me to depend on, I can not count on men whom I do not know by relying on human goodness or

man's concern for the good of society. I don't know what will become of the Russian revolution; I may make an example of it to the extent that at the present time it is apparent that the proletariat plays a part in Russia that it plays in no other nation. But I can't swear that this will inevitably lead to a triumph of the proletariat. I've got to limit myself to what I see.

Given that men are free and that tomorrow they will freely decide what man will be, I can not be sure that, after my death, fellow-fighters will carry on my work to bring it to its maximum perfection. Tomorrow, after my death, some men may decide to set up Fascism, and the others may be cowardly and muddled enough to let them do it. Fascism will then be the human reality, so much the worse for us.

Actually, things will be as man will have decided they are to be. Does that mean that I should abandon myself to quietism? No. First, I should involve myself; then, act on the old saw, "Nothing ventured, nothing gained." Nor does it mean that I shouldn't belong to a party, but rather that I shall have no illusions and shall do what I can. For example, suppose I ask myself, "Will socialization, as such, ever come about?" I know nothing about it. All I know is that I'm going to do everything in my power to bring it about. Beyond that, I can't count on anything. Quietism is the attitude of people who say, "Let others do what I can't do." The doctrine I am presenting is the very opposite of quietism, since it declares, "There is no reality except in action." Moreover, it goes further, since it adds, "Man is nothing else than his plan; he exists only to the extent that he fulfills himself; he is therefore nothing else than the ensemble of his acts, nothing else than his life."

Suggestions for Further Reading

Start with Frederick A. Olafson's article "Sartre, Jean-Paul" in *The Encyclopedia of Philosophy* for an overview. The article on "Existentialism" by Alasdair MacIntyre in the same source will also provide more background information on this important philosophical movement.

The Philosophy of Jean-Paul Sartre, edited and introduced by Robert Denoon Cumming (New York: Random House, 1965), provides a good collection of primary sources and a helpful introduction to major themes in Sartre's philosophy.

Francis Jeanson's *Sartre and the Problem of Morality,* translated by Robert V. Stone (Bloomington: Indiana University Press, 1980), was first published in French in 1965. Sartre himself praised this study of his ethical views.

For a different sort of libertarian position, one which views human freedom as far more limited than Sartre, see Susan L. Anderson, "The Libertarian Conception of Freedom" *International Philosophical Quarterly* (Vol. 21, 1981; 391–404). Her bibliography will lead you into the standard philosophical literature on the topic.

6.3. Karma and Freedom

The contemporary Western discussion of the problem of freedom and determinism usually takes place in the context of the natural and social sciences. Many philosophers believe that determinism is one of the assumptions of the scientific point of view and therefore that there is a conflict between a scientific view and the moral or religious view of human freedom and responsibility. The law of causality, as understood by science, is an amoral law. That is, it operates regardless of moral considerations. The social or behavioral sciences (psychology, sociology, anthropology, economics, and history) have extended these views to human behavior. It is often assumed that human action, like physical action, is understandable only when the causal factors determining such action are described and explained by reference to some kind of "natural" law.

In the Eastern (primarily Indian) context, the discussion of the problem of freedom and determinism usually takes place in a moral and religious context. The law of causality that concerns much Indian and Buddhist philosophy is not amoral, but moral.

Very early in Indian philosophy (500 B.C.E.?) the idea of the *law of Karma* developed. (In Section 2.5 I discussed the idea of Karma [action], and you may wish to review that discussion before reading the following selection.) This law states that as each of us sows, so shall we reap. This is a moral causal law which holds that the actions of a living being have effects that determine the future spiritual, moral, and physical conditions of that being both in this life and in succeeding ones. Karma is thus linked to the Indian notion of reincarnation. Your past Karma (good or bad) has determined your present birth.

The teaching of Karma posits the existence of a perfect law of moral justice that operates automatically within the universe. Habitual liars in this life, for example, will pay for lying in the future. Perhaps they will be falsely accused at some future date or, when reborn, will have relatives who lie, cheat, and deceive them. In contrast, an honest person will be treated honestly by others.

The law of Karma provides a good deal of comfort. It assures us that the universe is a just place, that evil people and good people will eventually get their just desserts. But the notion of Karma also raises questions about human freedom. If what is happening to me now is the effect of my own actions in the past, how can I be free? Are not my life and the circumstances of my life determined? It seems to be the case, according to the law of Karma, that, for example, if you are poor, this condition is due to what you did in the past, and hence, it would seem, you are no more in control of your poverty than you are in control of the orbit of the earth.

Some Indian philosophers have drawn fatalistic conclusions from the doctrine of Karma and have denied human freedom. The majority of Indian philosophers, however, have affirmed human freedom and argued that freedom and Karma are compatible ideas. One such philosopher was Sir Sarvepalli Radhakrishnan (1888–1975), a scholar and statesman who held chairs of philosophy at several Indian universities and was president of India from 1962 until 1967. He was a leading exponent of neo-Hinduism, maintaining that all religions are but different expressions of one truth and that spiritual reality is more fundamental than material reality. The following selection comes from his book *An Idealist View of Life,* which contains his Hibbert lectures given in 1929 and 1930.

Radhakrishnan supports a type of libertarianism. While he believes that human action is determined to a large extent (and hence would not subscribe to Sartre's radical libertarianism), he also believes in "self-determination." If a choice is caused by the "whole self" rather than part of the self (such as character or environment) such choice is free. In other words, he subscribes to what is often called "agent causation." When your self (not a part of your self but your whole self) is the agent which causes you to chose and act, then you are free. But what is the "self?" That question leads to another whole set of issues (see Chapter 11).

Reading Questions

1. According to Radhakrishnan, what is the law of Karma?
2. What are the two aspects of Karma?
3. How does Radhakrishnan define freedom of the will?
4. What does he mean by self-determination?
5. How does he respond to the argument that self-determination is not really freedom?
6. How does he define choice?
7. Does the author's assertion that even though "the self is not free from the bonds of determination, it can subjugate the past to a certain extent and turn it into a new course" make sense?
8. Do you think Radhakrishnan's analogy with a game of bridge is a good one? Why?
9. Name one thing you learned from reading this selection that you did not know before.

Karma and Freedom

SARVEPALLI RADHAKRISHNAN

THE TWO PERVASIVE features of all nature, connection with the past and creation of the future, are present in the human level. The connection with the past at the human stage is denoted by the word "Karma" in the Hindu systems. The human individual is a self-conscious, efficient portion of universal nature with his own uniqueness. His history stretching back to an indefinite period of time binds him with the physical and vital conditions of the world. Human life is an organic

From S. Radhakrishnan's An Idealist View of Life *(London: George Allen & Unwin, 1932), pp. 218–223. Reproduced by kind permission of Unwin Hyman, an imprint of HarperCollins Publishers Limited. Footnotes deleted.*

whole where each successive phase grows out of what has gone before. We are what we are on account of our affinity with the past. Human growth is an ordered one and its orderedness is indicated by saying that it is governed by the law of Karma.

Karma literally means action, deed. All acts produce their effects which are recorded both in the organism and the environment. Their physical effects may be short-lived but their moral effects (samsskāra) are worked into the character of the self. Every single thought, word and deed enters into the living chain of causes which makes us what we are. Our life is not at the mercy of blind chance or capricious fate. The conception is not peculiar to the Oriental creeds. The Christian Scriptures refer to it. "Be not deceived; God is not mocked: for whatsoever a man soweth, that shall he also reap." Jesus is reported to have said on the Mount, "Judge not that ye be not judged, for with what judgment ye judge, ye shall be judged, and with what measure ye mete, it shall be measured to you again."

Karma is not so much a principle of retribution as one of continuity. Good produces good, evil, evil. Love increases our power of love, hatred our power of hatred. It emphasizes the great importance of right action. Man is continuously shaping his own self. The law of Karma is not to be confused with either a hedonistic or a juridical theory of rewards and punishments. The reward for virtue is not a life of pleasure nor is the punishment for sin pain. Pleasure and pain may govern the animal nature of man but not his human. Love which is a joy in itself suffers; hatred too often means a perverse kind of satisfaction. Good and evil are not to be confused with material well-being and physical suffering.

All things in the world are at once causes and effects. They embody the energy of the past and exert energy on the future. Karma or connection with the past is not inconsistent with creative freedom. On the other hand it is implied by it. The law that links us with the past also asserts that it can be subjugated by our free action. Though the past may present obstacles, they must all yield to the creative power in man in propor-

tion to its sincerity and insistence. The law of Karma says that each individual will get the return according to the energy he puts forth. The universe will respond to and implement the demands of the self. Nature will reply to the insistent call of spirit. "As is his desire, such is his purpose; as is his purpose, such is the action he performs; what action he performs, that he procures for himself." "Verily I say unto you that whoever shall say to this mountain, 'Be lifted up and cast into the sea,' and shall not doubt in his heart but believe fully that what he says shall be, it shall be done for him." When Jesus said, "Destroy this temple and I will raise it again in three days" he is asserting the truth that the spirit within us is mightier than the world of things. There is nothing we cannot achieve if we want it enough. Subjection to spirit is the law of universal nature. The principle of Karma has thus two aspects, a retrospective and a prospective, continuity with the past and creative freedom of the self.

The urge in nature which seeks not only to maintain itself at a particular level but advance to a higher becomes conscious in man who deliberately seeks after rules of life and principles of progress. "My father worketh hitherto, and I work." Human beings are the first among nature's children who can say "I" and consciously collaborate with the "father" the power that controls and directs nature, in the fashioning of the world. They can substitute rational direction for the slow, dark, blundering growth of the subhuman world. We cannot deny the free action of human beings however much their origin may be veiled in darkness. The self has conative tendencies, impulses to change by its efforts the given conditions, inner and outer, and shape them to its own purpose.

The problem of human freedom is confused somewhat by the distinction between the self and the will. The will is only the self in its active side and freedom of the will really means the freedom of the self. It is determination by the self.

It is argued that self-determination is not really freedom. It makes little difference whether the self is moved from without or from within. A spinning top moved from within by a spring is as mechanical as one whipped into motion from without. The self may well be an animated automaton. A drunkard who takes to his glass habitually does so in obedience to an element in his nature. The habit has become a part of his self. If we analyze the contents of the self, many of them are traceable to the influence of the environment and the inheritance from the past. If the individual's view and character are the product of a long evolution, his actions which are the outcome of these cannot be free. The feeling of freedom may be an illusion of the self which lives in each moment of the present, ignoring the determining past. In answer to these difficulties, it may be said that the self represents a form of relatedness or organization, closer and more intimate than that which is found in animal, plant or atom. Self-determination means not determination by any fragment of the self's nature but by the whole of it. Unless the individual employs his whole nature, searches the different possibilities and selects one which commends itself to his whole self, the act is not really free.

Sheer necessity is not to be found in any aspect of nature; complete freedom is divine and possible only when the self becomes co-extensive with the whole. Human freedom is a matter of degree. We are most free when our whole self is active and not merely a fragment of it. We generally act according to our conventional or habitual self and sometimes we sink to the level of our subnormal self.

Freedom is not caprice, nor is Karma necessity. Human choice is not unmotived or uncaused. If our acts were irrelevant to our past, then there would be no moral responsibility or scope for improvement. Undetermined beginnings, upstart events are impossible either in the physical or the human world. Free acts cannot negate continuity. They arise within the order of nature. Freedom is not caprice since we carry our past with us. The character, at any given point, is the condensation of our previous history. What we have been enters into the "me" which is now active and choosing. The range of one's natural freedom of action is limited. No man has the univer-

sal field of possibilities for himself. The varied possibilities of our nature do not all get a chance and the cosmic has its influence in permitting the development of certain possibilities and closing down others. Again, freedom is dogged by automatism. When we make up our mind to do a thing, our mind is different from what it was before. When a possibility becomes an actuality, it assumes the character of necessity. The past can never be cancelled, though it may be utilized. Mere defiance of the given may mean disaster, though we can make a new life spring up from the past. Only the possible is the sphere of freedom. We have a good deal of present constraint and previous necessity in human life. But necessity is not to be mistaken for destiny which we can neither defy nor delude. Though the self is not free from the bonds of determination, it can subjugate the past to a certain extent and turn it into a new course. Choice is the assertion of freedom over necessity by which it converts necessity to its own use and thus frees itself from it. "The human agent is free." He is not the plaything of fate or driftwood on the tide of uncontrolled events. He can actively mould the future instead of passively suffering the past. The past may become either an opportunity or an obstacle. Everything depends on what we make of it and not what it makes of us. Life is not bound to move in a specific direction. Life is a growth and a growth is undetermined in a measure. Though the future is the sequel of the past, we cannot say what it will be. If there is no indetermination, then human consciousness is an unnecessary luxury.

Our demand for freedom must reckon with a universe that is marked by order and regularity. Life is like a game of bridge. The cards in the game are given to us. We do not select them. They are traced to past Karma but we are free to make any call as we think fit and lead any suit. Only we are limited by the rules of the game. We are more free when we start the game than later on when the game has developed and our choices become restricted. But till the very end there is always a choice. A good player will see possibilities which a bad one does not. The more skilled a player the more alternatives does he perceive. A good hand may be cut to pieces by unskillful play and the bad play need not be attributed to the frowns of fortune. Even though we may not like the way in which the cards are shuffled, we like the game and we want to play. Sometimes wind and tide may prove too strong for us and even the most noble may come down. The great souls find profound peace in the consciousness that the stately order of the world, now lovely and luminous, now dark and terrible, in which man finds his duty and destiny, cannot be subdued to known aims. It seems to have a purpose of its own of which we are ignorant. Misfortune is not fate but providence.

The law of Karma does not support the doctrine of predestination. There are some who believe that only the predestination of certain souls to destruction is consistent with divine sovereignty. God has a perfect right to deal with his creatures even as a potter does with his clay. St. Paul speaks of "vessels of wrath fitted to destruction." Life eternal is a gracious gift of God. Such a view of divine sovereignty is unethical. God's love is manifested in and through law.

In our relations with human failures, belief in Karma inclines us to take a sympathetic attitude and develop reverence before the mystery of misfortune. The more understanding we are, the less do we pride ourselves on our superiority. Faith in Karma induces in us the mood of true justice or charity which is the essence of spirituality. We realize how infinitely helpless and frail human beings are. When we look at the warped lives of the poor, we see how much the law of Karma is true. If they are lazy and criminal, let us ask what chance they had of choosing to be different. They are more unfortunate than wicked. Again, failures are due not so much to "sin" as to errors which lead us to our doom. In Greek tragedy man is held individually less responsible and circumstances or the decisions of Moira more so. The tale of Oedipus Rex tells us how he could not avoid his fate to kill his father and marry his mother, in spite of his best efforts. The parting of Hector and Andromache in Homer is another illustration. In Shakespeare again, we see the artist leading on his characters to their destined ends by what seems a very natural development of their foibles, criminal folly in Lear or personal ambition in Macbeth. The artist shows us these souls in pain. Hamlet's reason is puzzled, his will confounded. He looks at life and at death and wonders which is worse. Goaded by personal ambition, Macbeth makes a mess of it all. Othello kills his wife and kills himself because a jealous villain shows him a handkerchief. When these noble souls crash battling with adverse forces we feel with them and for them; for it might happen to any of us. We are not free from the weaknesses that broke them, whatever we call them, stupidity, disorder, vacillation or, if you please, insane ambition and self-seeking. Today the evil stars of the Greek tragedians are replaced by the almighty laws of economics. Thousands of young men the world over are breaking their heads in vain against the iron walls of society like trapped birds in cages. We see in them the essence of all tragedy, something noble breaking down, something sublime falling with a crash. We can only bow our heads in the presence of those broken beneath the burden of their destiny. The capacity of the human soul for suffering and isolation is immense. Take the poor creatures whom the world passes by as the lowly and the lost. If only we had known what they passed through, we would have been glad of their company. It is utterly wrong to think that misfortune comes only to those who deserve it. The world is a whole and we are members one of another, and we must suffer one for another. In Christianity, it needed a divine soul to reveal how much grace there is in suffering. To bear pain, to endure suffering, is the quality of the strong in spirit. It adds to the spiritual resources of humanity.

Suggestions for Further Reading

Both the articles on "Karma" and "Radhakrishnan, Sarvepalli" by Ninian Smart in *The Encyclopedia of Philosophy* are good places to start for background information.

A. L. Herman's *An Introduction to Indian Thought* (Englewood Cliffs, NJ: Prentice-Hall, 1976, pp. 130ff.) provides a good discussion of the idea of Karma as found in the *Upanishads*. In *Religious Reason* (New York: Oxford University Press, 1978, pp. 203–222), Ronald M. Green tackles the issue of Karma and freedom, arguing that the idea of moral freedom is "an implicit assumption" of the law of Karma.

6.4. We Are Both Free and Determined

You might be thinking, "Hard determinism seems awfully hard. Human beings are not just pawns in the hands of heredity and environment. We are free. I am free. Indeed, right now, I can continue reading this book or I can stop, whichever is my pleasure. Yet Sartre's views seem unrealistic. Clearly heredity and environment play some role. However Radhakrishnan's ideas, while less radical than Sartre's with respect to the scope of human freedom, require me to believe in some kind of metaphysical notions about the self and reincarnation. I don't find that attractive. But I don't want to deny the law of causality. There must be some way to reconcile freedom and determinism."

If these are your thoughts, then you might like another answer that has been proposed to the problem of freedom and determinism, an answer called **soft determinism.** This position holds that every event has a cause, and that this fact is *compatible* with human freedom. Hence another name for soft determinism is **compatibilism.** According to the compatibilist, even if determinism is true, people ought to be held morally responsible for those actions they do voluntarily. Indeed many compatibilists argue that moral responsibility makes no sense unless determinism is true because it makes no sense to hold anyone responsible for uncaused (undetermined) actions.

Notice that soft determinism is, like hard determinism, a kind of determinism. Both the soft and hard determinists agree that every event has a cause. However, they disagree about whether this is compatible with human freedom and about the implications for moral responsibility.

As you might imagine, the harmony between freedom and determinism that the compatibilist wishes to defend is based on a particular understanding of human freedom. Compatibilists do *not* define a free event as an uncaused or undetermined event. The issue, according to many compatibilists, is not a question of events being caused or uncaused, rather it is a question of what kind of cause we are talking about. If my behavior is coerced or forced by circumstances over which I have no control, then I am not free and my behavior is involuntary. But if my behavior is caused by circumstances over which I do have control, it is free or voluntary.

Raymond M. Smullyan, author of the next selection, gives a slightly different twist to the compatibilist argument. In an imaginative dialogue between a "mortal" and "God" (here used to symbolize the **Dao** and express Smullyan's views), Smullyan applies his understanding of Daoism (see Prelude and Section 7.1 for more on Daoism) to the issue of free will and determinism. The Dao is the Way of Nature which harmonizes all opposites and so, for Smullyan, it makes sense to say that free choice is just built into the causal order of the universe. The so called "laws of nature" don't literally "determine" anything in the sense of forcing events. They simply describe the regularities we can observe in nature. Hence there can be no conflict between our wills and the way of nature because one of the ways nature operates is via the human will.

Is this a reasonable solution? Does it really answer the question, "Could we have done other that we did, all other conditions remaining the same?" Some philosophers argue that this is really the crucial question in the debate and that compatibilistic answers do not adequately address it. Read this fun dialogue and freely (?) decide for yourself.

Reading Questions

1. The dialogue opens with the mortal requesting that God take away its free will. But very soon the mortal is refusing to let God take its free will away. What happened to cause such a reversal?

2. What is the "double bind" the mortal finds itself in?

3. What is the "double bind" God finds itself in?

4. What argument does the mortal present supporting the conclusion that God should not have given free will to humans in the first place?

5. Why does the mortal finally wish that a replica of itself be created with free will?

6. What is wrong with the word "determined" as used in the controversy over free will?

7. How does God show determinism and free will compatible? What do you think of the argument? Is it convincing? Why or why not?

Is God a Taoist?

RAYMOND M. SMULLYAN

Mortal: And therefore, O God, I pray thee, if thou hast one ounce of mercy for this thy suffering creature, absolve me of *having* to have free will!

God: You reject the greatest gift I have given thee?

Mortal: How can you call that which was forced on me a gift? I have free will, but not of my own choice. I have never freely chosen to have free will. I have to have free will, whether I like it or not!

God: Why would you wish not to have free will?

Mortal: Because free will means moral responsibility, and moral responsibility is more than I can bear!

God: Why do you find moral responsibility so unbearable?

Mortal: Why? I honestly can't analyze why; all I know is that I do.

God: All right, in that case suppose I absolve you from all moral responsibility but leave you still with free will. Will this be satisfactory?

Mortal (after a pause): No, I am afraid not.

God: Ah, just as I thought! So moral responsibility is not the only aspect of free will to which you object. What else about free will is bothering you?

Mortal: With free will I am capable of sinning, and I don't want to sin!

God: If you don't want to sin, then why do you?

Mortal: Good God! I don't know why I sin, I just do! Evil temptations come along, and try as I can, I cannot resist them.

God: If it is really true that you cannot resist them, then you are not sinning of your own free will and hence (at least according to me) not sinning at all.

Mortal: No, no! I keep feeling that if only I tried harder I could avoid sinning. I understand that the will is infinite. If one wholeheartedly wills not to sin, then one won't.

God: Well now, you should know. Do you try as hard as you can to avoid sinning or don't you?

Mortal: I honestly don't know! At the time, I feel I am trying as hard as I can, but in retrospect, I am worried that maybe I didn't!

God: So in other words, you don't really know whether or not you have been sinning. So the possibility is open that you haven't been sinning at all!

Mortal: Of course this possibility is open, but maybe I have been sinning, and this thought is what so frightens me!

God: Why does the thought of your sinning frighten you?

Mortal: I don't know why! For one thing, you do have a reputation for meting out rather gruesome punishments in the afterlife!

God: Oh, that's what's bothering you! Why didn't you say so in the first place instead of all this peripheral talk about free will and responsibility? Why didn't you simply request me not to punish you for any of your sins?

Mortal: I think I am realistic enough to know that you would hardly grant such a request!

God: You don't say! *You* have a realistic knowledge of what requests I will grant, eh? Well, I'll tell you what I'm going to do! I will grant you a very, very special dispensation to sin as much as you like, and I give you my divine word of honor that I will never punish you for it in the least. Agreed?

Mortal (in great terror): No, no, don't do that!

God: Why not? Don't you trust my divine word?

Mortal: Of course I do! But don't you see, I don't want to sin! I have an utter abhorrence of sinning, quite apart from any punishments it may entail.

God: In that case, I'll go you one better. I'll remove your abhorrence of sinning. Here is a magic pill! Just swallow it, and you will lose all *abhorrence* of sinning. You will joyfully and merrily sin away, you will have no regrets, no abhorrence and I still promise you will never be punished by me, or yourself, or by any source whatever. You will be blissful for all eternity. So here is the pill!

Mortal: No, no!

God: Are you not being irrational? I am even removing your abhorrence of sin, which is your last obstacle.

Mortal: I still won't take it!

God: Why not?

Mortal: I believe that the pill will indeed remove my future abhorrence for sin, but my present abhorrence is enough to prevent me from being willing to take it.

God: I command you to take it!

Mortal: I refuse!

God: What, you refuse of your own free will?

Mortal: Yes!

God: So it seems that your free will comes in pretty handy, doesn't it?

Mortal: I don't understand!

God: Are you not glad now that you have the free will to refuse such a ghastly offer? How would you like it if I forced you to take this pill, whether you wanted it or not?

Mortal: No, no! Please don't!

God: Of course I won't; I'm just trying to illustrate a point. All right, let me put it this way. Instead of forcing you to take the pill, suppose I grant your original prayer of removing your free will—but with the understanding that the moment you are no longer free, then you *will* take the pill.

Mortal: Once my will is gone, how could I possibly choose to take the pill?

God: I did not say you would choose it; I merely said you would take it. You would act, let us say, according to purely deterministic laws which are such that you would as a matter of fact take it.

Mortal: I still refuse.

God: So you refuse my offer to remove your free will. This is rather different from your original prayer, isn't it?

Mortal: Now I see what you are up to. Your argument is ingenious, but I'm not sure it is really correct. There are some points we will have to go over again.

God: Certainly.

Mortal: There are two things you said which seem contradictory to me. First you said that one cannot sin unless one does so of one's own free will. But then you said you would give me a pill which would deprive me of my own free will, and then I could sin as much as I liked. But if I no longer had free will, then, according to your first statement, how could I be capable of sinning?

God: You are confusing two separate parts of our conversation. I never said the pill would deprive you of your free will, but only that it would remove your abhorrence of sinning.

Mortal: I'm afraid I'm a bit confused.

God: All right, then let us make a fresh start. Suppose I agree to remove your free will, but with the understanding that you will then commit an enormous number of acts which you now regard as sinful. Technically speaking, you will not then be sinning since you will not be doing these acts of your own free will. And these acts will carry no moral responsibility, nor moral culpability, nor any punishment whatsoever. Nevertheless, these acts will all be of the type which you presently regard as sinful; they will all have this quality which you presently feel as abhorrent, but your abhorrence will disappear; so you will not *then* feel abhorrence toward the acts.

Mortal: No, but I have present abhorrence toward the acts, and this present abhorrence is sufficient to prevent me from accepting your proposal.

God: Hm! So let me get this absolutely straight. I take it you no longer wish me to remove your free will.

Mortal (reluctantly): No, I guess not.

God: All right, I agree not to. But I am still not exactly clear as to why you now no longer wish to be rid of your free will. Please tell me again.

Mortal: Because, as you have told me, without free will I would sin even more than I do now.

God: But I have already told you that without free will you cannot sin.

Mortal: But if I choose now to be rid of free will, then all my subsequent evil actions will be sins, not of the future, but of the present moment in which I choose not to have free will.

God: Sounds like you are pretty badly trapped, doesn't it?

Mortal: Of course I am trapped! You have placed me in a hideous double bind! Now whatever I do is wrong. If I retain free will, I will continue to sin, and if I abandon free will (with your help, of course), I will now be sinning in so doing.

God: But by the same token, you place me in a double bind. I am willing to leave you free will or remove it as you choose, but neither alternative satisfies you. I wish to help you, but it seems I cannot.

Mortal: True!

God: But since it is not my fault, why are you still angry with me?

Mortal: For having placed me in such a horrible predicament in the first place!

God: But, according to you, there is nothing satisfactory I could have done.

Mortal: You mean there is nothing satisfactory you can now do, but that does not mean that there is nothing you could have done.

God: Why? What could I have done?

Mortal: Obviously you should never have given me free will in the first place. Now that you have given it to me, it is too late—anything I do will be bad. But you should never have given it to me in the first place.

God: Oh, that's it! Why would it have been better had I never given it to you?

Mortal: Because then I never would have been capable of sinning at all.

God: Well, I'm always glad to learn from my mistakes.

Mortal: What!

God: I know, that sounds sort of self-blasphemous, doesn't it? It almost involves a logical paradox! On the one hand, as you have been taught, it is morally wrong for any sentient being to claim that I am capable of making mistakes. On the other hand, I have the right to do anything. But I am also a sentient being. So the question is, Do I or do I not have the right to claim that I am capable of making mistakes?

Mortal: That is a bad joke! One of your premises is simply false. I have not been taught that it is wrong for any sentient being to doubt your omniscience, but only for a mortal to doubt it. But since you are not mortal, then you are obviously free from this injunction.

God: Good, so you realize this on a rational level. Nevertheless, you did appear shocked when I said, "I am always glad to learn from my mistakes."

Mortal: Of course I was shocked. I was shocked not by your self-blasphemy (as you jokingly called it), not by the fact that you had no right to say it, but just by the fact that you did say it, since I have been taught that as a matter of fact you don't make mistakes. So I was amazed that you claimed that it is possible for you to make mistakes.

God: I have not claimed that it is possible. All I am saying is that *if* I make mistakes, I will be happy to learn from them. But this says nothing about whether the *if* has or ever can be realized.

Mortal: Let's please stop quibbling about this point. Do you or do you not admit it was a mistake to have given me free will?

God: Well now, this is precisely what I propose we should investigate. Let me review your present predicament. You don't want to have free will because with free will you can sin, and you don't want to sin. (Though I still find this puzzling; in a way you must want to sin, or else you wouldn't. But let this pass for now.) On the other hand, if you agreed to give up free will, then you would now be responsible for the acts of the future. Ergo, I should never have given you free will in the first place.

Mortal: Exactly!

God: I understand exactly how you feel. Many mortals—even some theologians—have complained that I have been unfair in that it was I, not they, who decided that they should have free

will, and then I hold *them* responsible for their actions. In other words, they feel that they are expected to live up to a contract with me which they never agreed to in the first place.

Mortal: Exactly!

God: As I said, I understand the feeling perfectly. And I can appreciate the justice of the complaint. But the complaint arises only from an unrealistic understanding of the true issues involved. I am about to enlighten you as to what these are, and I think the results will surprise you! But instead of telling you outright, I shall continue to use the Socratic method.

To repeat, you regret that I ever gave you free will. I claim that when you see the true ramifications you will no longer have this regret. To prove my point, I'll tell you what I'm going to do. I am about to create a new universe—a new space-time continuum. In this new universe will be born a mortal just like you—for all practical purposes, we might say that you will be reborn. Now, I can give this new mortal—this new you—free will or not. What would you like me to do?

Mortal (in great relief): Oh, please! Spare him from having to have free will!

God: All right, I'll do as you say. But you do realize that this new *you* without free will, will commit all sorts of horrible acts.

Mortal: But they will not be sins since he will have no free will.

God: Whether you call them sins or not, the fact remains that they will be horrible acts in the sense that they will cause great pain to many sentient beings.

Mortal (after a pause): Good God, you have trapped me again! Always the same game! If I now give you the go-ahead to create this new creature with no free will who will nevertheless commit atrocious acts, then true enough he will not be sinning, but I again will be the sinner to sanction this.

God: In that case, I'll go you one better! Here, I have already decided whether to create this new *you* with free will or not. Now, I am writing my decision on this piece of paper and I won't show it to you until later. But my decision is now made and is absolutely irrevocable. There is nothing you can possibly do to alter it; you have no responsibility in the matter. Now, what I wish to know is this: Which way do you hope I have decided? Remember now, the responsibility for the decision falls entirely on my shoulders, not yours. So you can tell me perfectly honestly and without any fear, which way do you hope I have decided?

Mortal (after a very long pause): I hope you have decided to give him free will.

God: Most interesting! I have removed your last obstacle! If I do not give him free will, then no sin is to be imputed to anybody. So why do you hope I will give him free will?

Mortal: Because sin or no sin, the important point is that if you do not give him free will, then (at least according to what you have said) he will go around hurting people, and I don't want to see people hurt.

God (with an infinite sigh of relief): At last! At last you see the real point!

Mortal: What point is that?

God: That sinning is not the real issue! The important thing is that people as well as other sentient beings don't get hurt!

Mortal: You sound like a utilitarian!

God: I am a utilitarian!

Mortal: What!

God: Whats or no whats, I am a utilitarian. Not a unitarian, mind you, but a utilitarian.

Mortal: I just can't believe it!

God: Yes, I know, your religious training has taught you otherwise. You have probably thought of me more like a Kantian than a utilitarian, but your training was simply wrong.

Mortal: You leave me speechless!

God: I leave you speechless, do I! Well, that is perhaps not too bad a thing—you have a tendency to speak too much as it is. Seriously, though, why do you think I ever did give you free will in the first place?

Mortal: Why did you? I never have thought much about why you did; all I have been arguing for is that you shouldn't have! But why did you? I guess all I can think of is the standard religious explanation: Without free will, one is not capable of meriting either salvation or damnation. So

without free will, we could not earn the right to eternal life.

God: Most interesting! *I* have eternal life; do you think I have ever done anything to merit it?

Mortal: Of course not! With you it is different. You are already so good and perfect (at least allegedly) that it is not necessary for you to merit eternal life.

God: Really now? That puts me in a rather enviable position, doesn't it?

Mortal: I don't think I understand you.

God: Here I am eternally blissful without ever having to suffer or make sacrifices or struggle against evil temptations or anything like that. Without any of that type of "merit," I enjoy blissful eternal existence. By contrast, you poor mortals have to sweat and suffer and have all sorts of horrible conflicts about morality, and all for what? You don't even know whether I really exist or not, or if there really is any afterlife, or if there is, where you come into the picture. No matter how much you try to placate me by being "good," you never have any real assurance that your "best" is good enough for me, and hence you have no real security in obtaining salvation. Just think of it! I already *have* the equivalent of "salvation"—and have never had to go through this infinitely lugubrious process of earning it. Don't you ever envy me for this?

Mortal: But it is blasphemous to envy you!

God: Oh come off it! You're not now talking to your Sunday school teacher, you are talking to *me*. Blasphemous or not, the important question is not whether you have the right to be envious of me but whether you are. Are you?

Mortal: Of course I am!

God: Good! Under your present world view, you sure should be most envious of me. But I think with a more realistic world-view, you no longer will be. So you really have swallowed the idea which has been taught you that your life on earth is like an examination period and that the purpose of providing you with free will is to test you, to see if you merit blissful eternal life. But what puzzles me is this: If you really believe I am as good and benevolent as I am cracked up to be, why should I require people to merit things like happiness and eternal life? Why should I not grant such things to everyone regardless of whether or not he deserves them? . . .

God: [But] [w]e have gotten sidetracked as it is, and I would like to return to the question of what you believed my purpose to be in giving you free will. You're first idea of my giving you free will in order to test whether you merit salvation or not may appeal to many moralists, but the idea is quite hideous to me. You cannot think of any nicer reason—any more humane reason—why I gave you free will?

Mortal: Well now, I once asked this question to an Orthodox rabbi. He told me that the way we are constituted, it is simply not possible for us to enjoy salvation unless we feel we have earned it. And to earn it, we of course need free will.

God: That explanation is indeed much nicer than your former but still is far from correct. According to Orthodox Judaism, I created angels, and they have no free will. They are in actual sight of me and are so completely attracted by goodness that they never have even the slightest temptation towards evil. They really have no choice in the matter. Yet they are eternally happy even though they have never earned it. So if your rabbi's explanation were correct, why wouldn't I have simply created only angels rather than mortals?

Mortal: Beats me! Why didn't you?

God: Because the explanation is simply not correct. In the first place, I have never created any ready made angels. All sentient beings ultimately approach the state which might be called "angelhood." But just as the race of human beings is in a certain stage of biologic evolution, so angels are simply the end result of a process of Cosmic Evolution. The only difference between the so-called *saint* and the so-called *sinner* is that the former is vastly older than the latter. Unfortunately it takes countless life cycles to learn what is perhaps the most important fact of the universe—evil is simply painful. All the arguments of the moralists—all the alleged reasons why people *shouldn't* commit evil acts—simply pale into insignificance in light of the one basic truth that *evil is suffering*.

No, my dear friend, I am not a moralist. I am wholly a utilitarian. That I should have been conceived in the role of a moralist is one of the great tragedies of the human race. My role in the scheme of things (if one can use this misleading expression) is neither to punish nor reward, but to aid the process by which all sentient beings achieve ultimate perfection. . . .

Mortal: Anyway, putting all these pieces together, it occurs to me that the only reason you gave free will is because of your belief that with free will, people will tend to hurt each other—and themselves—less than without free will.

God: Bravo! That is by far the best reason you have yet given! I can assure you that had I *chosen* to give free will that would have been my very reason for so choosing.

Mortal: What! You mean to say you did not choose to give us free will?

God: My dear fellow, I could no more choose to give you free will than I could choose to make an equilateral triangle equiangular. I could choose to make or not to make an equilateral triangle in the first place, but having chosen to make one, I would then have no choice but to make it equiangular.

Mortal: I thought you could do anything!

God: Only things which are logically possible. As St. Thomas said, "It is a sin to regard the fact that God cannot do the impossible, as a limitation on His powers." I agree, except that in place of his using the word *sin* I would use the term *error.*

Mortal: Anyhow, I am still puzzled by your implication that you did not choose to give me free will.

God: Well, it is high time I inform you that the entire discussion—from the very beginning—has been based on one monstrous fallacy! We have been talking purely on a moral level—you originally complained that I gave you free will, and raised the whole question as to whether I should have. It never once occurred to you that I had absolutely no choice in the matter.

Mortal: I am still in the dark!

God: Absolutely! Because you are only able to look at it through the eyes of a moralist. The more fundamental *metaphysical* aspects of the question you never even considered.

Mortal: I still do not see what you are driving at.

God: Before you requested me to remove your free will, shouldn't your first question have been whether as a matter of fact you *do* have free will?

Mortal: That I simply took for granted.

God: But why should you?

Mortal: I don't know. Do I have free will?

God: Yes.

Mortal: Then why did you say I shouldn't have taken it for granted?

God: Because you shouldn't. Just because something happens to be true, it does not follow that it should be taken for granted.

Mortal: Anyway, it is reassuring to know that my natural intuition about having free will is correct. Sometimes I have been worried that determinists are correct.

God: They are correct.

Mortal: Wait a minute now, do I have free will or don't I?

God: I already told you you do. But that does not mean that determinism is incorrect.

Mortal: Well, are my acts determined by the laws of nature or aren't they?

God: The word *determined* here is subtly but powerfully misleading and has contributed so much to the confusions of the free will versus determinism controversies. Your acts are certainly in accordance with the laws of nature, but to say they are *determined* by the laws of nature creates a totally misleading psychological image which is that your will could somehow be in conflict with the laws of nature and that the latter is somehow more powerful than you, and could "determine" your acts whether you liked it or not. But it is simply impossible for your will to ever conflict with natural law. You and natural law are really one and the same.

Mortal: What do you mean that I cannot conflict with nature? Suppose I were to become very stubborn, and I *determined* not to obey the laws of nature. What could stop me? If I became sufficiently stubborn, even you could not stop me!

God: You are absolutely right! *I* certainly could not stop you. Nothing could stop you. But there is no need to stop you, because you could not even start! As Goethe very beautifully expressed it, "In trying to oppose Nature, we are in the very process of doing so, acting according to the laws of nature!" Don't you see, that the so-called "laws of nature" are nothing more than a description of how in fact you and other beings *do* act. They are merely a description of how you act, not a prescription of how you should act, nor a power or force which compels or determines your acts. To be valid a law of nature must take into account how in fact you do act, or, if you like, how you choose to act.

Mortal: So you really claim that I am incapable of determining to act against natural law?

God: It is interesting that you have twice now used the phrase "determined to act" instead of "chosen to act." This identification is quite common. Often one uses the statement "I am determined to do this" synonymously with "I have chosen to do this." This very psychological identification should reveal that determinism and choice are much closer than they might appear. Of course, you might well say that the doctrine of free will says that it is *you* who are doing the determining, whereas the doctrine of determinism appears to say that your acts are determined by something apparently outside you. But the confusion is largely caused by your bifurcation of reality into the "you" and the "not you." Really now, just where do you leave off and the rest of the universe begin? Or where does the rest of the universe leave off and you begin? Once you can see the so-called "you" and the so-called "nature" as a continuous whole, then you can never again be bothered by such questions as whether it is you who are controlling nature or nature who is controlling you. Thus the muddle of free will versus determinism will vanish. If I may use a crude analogy, imagine two bodies moving toward each other by virtue of gravitational attraction. Each body, if sentient, might wonder whether it is he or the other fellow who is exerting the "force." In a way it is both, in a way it is neither. It is best to say that it is the configuration of the two which is crucial.

Mortal: You said a short while ago that our whole discussion was based on a monstrous fallacy. You still have not told me what this fallacy is.

God: Why the idea that I could possibly have created you without free will! You acted as if this were a genuine possibility, and wondered why I did not choose it! It never occurred to you that a sentient being without free will is no more conceivable than a physical object which exerts no gravitational attraction. (There is, incidentally, more analogy than you realize between a physical object exerting gravitational attraction and a sentient being exerting free will!) Can you honestly even imagine a conscious being without free will? What on earth could it be like? I think that one thing in your life that has so misled you is your having been told that I gave man the *gift* of free will. As if I first created man, and then as an afterthought endowed him with the extra property of free will. Maybe you think I have some sort of "paint brush" with which I daub some creatures with free will, and not others. No, free will is not an "extra"; it is part and parcel of the very essence of consciousness. A conscious being without free will is simply a metaphysical absurdity. . . .

Suggestions for Further Reading

See "The Compatibility of Freedom and Determinism" in *Reason and Practice* by Kai Nielsen (New York: Harper & Row, 1971) for a sophisticated defense of soft determinism. Nielsen summarizes many of the contributions to the discussion by such modern philosophers as Hobbes, Hume, Mill, Schlick, and Ayer. Daniel Dennett's *Elbow Room: Varieties of Free Will Worth Wanting* (Cambridge: MIT Press, 1983) provides a well-reasoned defense of compatibilism. See *Determinism and Freedom in an Age of Modern Science,* edited by Sidney Hook (New York: New York University Press, 1958), for a collection of essays on a variety of topics relating to the problem of free will. Also see W. T. Stace *Religion and the Modern* (New York: HarperCollins Publishers, 1952), pp. 279–291, for a defense of compatibilism.

See Richard Taylor, *Metaphysics,* 3d ed. (Englewood Cliffs, NJ: Prentice-Hall, 1983), for a discussion of all three positions and an argument in favor of libertarianism.

Peter van Inwagen's *An Essay on Free Will* (Oxford: Oxford University Press, 1983) is one of the best critiques of compatibilism available. It is not easy going, however. See Gary Watson's *Free Will* (Oxford: Oxford University Press, 1982) for a good collection of recent articles on the subject.

Chapter 7

What Is Really Real?

HAVE YOU EVER WONDERED if what you think is real, actually is real? Someone has undoubtedly asked you, with a smile, "If a tree falls in a forest and no one is there, does it make a sound?" What do you think? Have you ever thought about the question, "Why is there something rather than nothing?" Have you ever thought, "Is the world we experience real or an illusion?" Have you ever been puzzled by the question, "What are time and space?" Do you think something can come from nothing? What are ideas made of? Is matter all there is, or is there some sort of supernatural reality?

If you have wondered about these sorts of questions, you have been concerned with what philosophers call metaphysics (see Section 1.1). Metaphysics has to do with the construction and criticism of theories about what is really real. Metaphysics deals with abstract issues, but its concerns arise out of everyday experiences. For example, you may have been traveling down a road and seen, ahead on the highway, what looked like an animal; but when you got closer, you discovered that it was really a bush. It appeared to be one thing and turned out to be another. The question of what is *really* real presupposes a distinction between appearance and reality. Metaphysics generalizes that distinction and asks, "Okay, if some things in the world appear to be real but turn out not to be, what about the world itself? Is the universe appearance or reality?"

Some philosophers maintain that the chief part of metaphysics is what they call **ontology** (literally "the study of being"). One ontological concern has to do with the *kinds of things* that exist. For example, try to categorize the items on the following list into two general groups, material and immaterial.

chairs	trees	cats	ideas
seeing	anger	stones	atoms
God	space	time	you

Did you have a hard time sorting these? One problem is that some things seem to be a mixture of the material and the immaterial. For example, you have a body, which is material, but you also have a mind, which some would claim to be immaterial. Another problem has to do with definitions. What do we mean by "material" and "immaterial?" How can we classify things until we know how to distinguish between them?

This last question leads us directly into a second concern of ontology, namely the *definition of different kinds of being*. For example, some philosophers have argued that material beings can be distinguished from immaterial beings according to the following characteristics:

Material	*Immaterial*
spatial	nonspatial
public	private
mechanical	teleological

According to this list, material things like chairs take up space (hence are spatial), but immaterial things like ideas don't take up space (hence are nonspatial). After all, it makes good sense to ask how wide a chair is, but does it make any sense to ask how wide my idea of a chair is? Material things are also public in the sense that they can be viewed by different people. I can see a chair or a tree and so can you. But I can't see your *idea* of a chair or a tree. Your idea is private; it is not open to public inspection. Finally, material objects are causally determined in a purely **mechanistic** way. They are nonintentional, that is, they behave not according to purposes, but according to the laws of physics. That chair is in the corner of the room not because it *wants* to be there, but because it was *placed* there by external forces. But what about you? Is your behavior purely mechanistic (machinelike)? Or is your behavior teleological, that is, governed by intentions and purposes? Are you in the corner of the room because of external forces, or are you there because you want to leave and the door is located there?

This last distinction between the mechanical and the teleological should remind you of the previous discussion of freedom and determinism. In one sense the problem of free will is ethical, since ethics depends on the notion of moral responsibility, and that notion seems to depend on the genuine possibility of free will. But in another sense that issue is metaphysical because if everything is material and if material objects behave according to mechanistic laws, then determinism appears to be the preferred theory. I'm free only if I can act according to my intentions. But if I am a purely material being, if there is nothing immaterial about me, then my teleological behavior (actions according to intentions and purposes) is just an illusion.

A third concern of ontology has to do with *what is ultimately real*. Once we have discovered all the kinds of beings that seem to exist and have adequately defined each of the kinds, which if any of these kinds are really real? Is matter the really real? If you answer "yes," you would be an advocate of **materialism.** Materialism is the metaphysical theory that matter is really real and immaterial things are not. Note that we should not confuse materialism with physical science. Physical science is clearly concerned with matter and the study of physical things. But the claim that *only* physical things are real is not a scientific claim, it is a metaphysical claim. It is a claim about the whole of reality.

Some of you might be inclined to argue that being, or reality, is fundamentally immaterial. One widespread philosophical version of this theory is called **idealism.** Idealism is a metaphysical theory that holds that ideas (in the broad sense of thoughts, concepts, minds) are ultimately real. Don't confuse idealism as a metaphysical doctrine with idealism as a moral theory about ideals. Idealism, as I am using that term here, has to do with ideas, not ideals.

One major problem with idealism, as you might expect, is to explain our experience of things that seem both material and real. The chair I am sitting on seems physical, solid, and real to me, and I certainly hope it is. But could it be that this chair is nothing more than a bundle of sensations? If materialism needs to explain the mental in terms of the physical, idealism must explain the physical in terms of the mental.

But maybe you want to suggest that both these sorts of things (the material and the immaterial) are really real. This seems the most reasonable way. It certainly escapes the problems of explaining away chairs, bodies, minds, and ideas. **Dualism** is the theory that reality is both material and immaterial. My body is real and the material chair it is sitting on is real (what a relief), but my mind and its ideas are also real (that's good to know, too). But if reality is both material and immaterial, how are the two related? How, for example, are our minds related to our brains? The major problem of dualism is to relate the material and the immaterial.

Those who argue that being, or reality, is fundamentally of one nature avoid this problem. They are called monists and their theory (in contrast to dualism) is called **monism.** Monism holds that not only is there a single reality, but also that the nature of reality is unified or undivided. Notice that a monist can be either a materialist or an idealist. The contrast here is between monism and dualism, not between materialism and idealism.

This takes us to the **problem of the one and the many.** Is there one reality whose nature is undivided, or are there many different real things that cannot be reduced to a single thing? **Pluralism** is the name for the position that there are many different real things. This question of one or many, along with the question about what is really real, constitute two fundamental metaphysical questions.

But enough of terminology and questions. It is time to look at some of the metaphysical views philosophers hold and at some of the arguments they use to try to convince others that they are right.

7.1. The *Dao*

The name "Daoism" was first coined by Han scholars to refer to the philosophy developed by Laozi and Zhuangzi. We have already encountered some of the thoughts of Zhuangzi in the Prelude to this book. We will focus here on the ideas of Laozi (Wade-Giles spelling, Lao Tzu) as found in a book entitled *Laozi,* but popularly known as the *Dao De Jing* (Wade-Giles spelling, *Tao Te Ching*).

We have legends about Laozi and when he lived, but we have very little firm historical information. According to tradition he was a contemporary of Confucius (551–479 B.C.E.), but some scholars have placed his book later, during the Warring States Period (403–221 B.C.E.).

The *Dao De Jing* is a classic of world literature. Each time you come back to it, you will find something new and profound. However, the first time you read it you are likely to find it obscure. This is why I have included the translator's comments along with the translation.

You may find it obscure for a variety of reasons. First of all, it is written in a poetic and cryptic style. Poetry employs symbols and metaphors, uses paradoxes and unexpected contrasts in order to stimulate thought. It thrives on ambiguity. Second, this is a translation from ancient Chinese, and our English words often do not convey the richness of the Chinese concepts. Third, although 80 percent of the book deals with ethics (how one should live) and politics (what is the best way to govern), the rest deals with difficult metaphysical issues about the basic principles of reality, and it is these metaphysical portions of the text that are included here.

According to Aristotelian logic, a good definition should be positive. But what if there are realities that transcend the definitional abilities of human language? In such cases (and the *Dao* is such a case) the best we might hope for are negative indications, analogies, metaphors, and symbols.

Daoism has been characterized as a **process ontology** in contrast to a **substance ontology.** Process ontologies emphasize change and becoming as fundamentally real. In addition, they often emphasize the interrelatedness of an everflowing reality in which nothing is totally independent. Substance ontologies emphasize permanence and unchanging being as fundamentally real. Reality, it is thought, is made up of one or more substances that can exist independently.

Before you plunge into this bewildering, fascinating, and thought-provoking book about the *Dao*, it may be helpful to say something about some of the key concepts of Daoism. Let us begin with the *Dao* itself.

The word *Dao* means "road" or "way" in Chinese. Before Laozi, the word had been used by the Confucians to refer to the Way of humans, that is, the proper way that human beings ought to live. Laozi extends the term and gives it a cosmic and metaphysical meaning. It now becomes the Way of the universe and the source of all reality. Reality consists of all the sorts of things we think exist (which we can classify as being) as well as what we take to be nonexistent (which we can classify as nonbeing). Already we encounter something odd from a traditional Western perspective. How can the nonexistent be real? Where we tend to identify the real with what exists (being) and the unreal with what does not (nonbeing), the Daoist distinguishes between reality and existence so that both the existent and nonexistent can be classified as real.

Since the *Dao* is the source of all reality, it is not a thing (a being or a substance). It is beyond distinctions and hence beyond the definitional powers of language. To define is to distinguish. But how do you define that which is the source of all distinctions? So the *Dao* is called "the nameless," i.e., the indefinable.

This negative designation suggests that the *Dao* is closer to nonbeing than to being, and indeed, Daoists say the *Dao* is nonbeing. But it is not nonbeing in the Western sense of total nothingness. It is nonbeing in the sense of "no-thingness." It is real, but not *a* thing. Hence it is compared to a *positive emptiness,* that is, an emptiness (like the hollow of a bowl) that makes being (the usefulness of the bowl) possible. This notion of nonbeing as positive and creative is a unique insight of the *Dao De Jing.* For the Greeks and much of the Western tradition since the Greeks, something cannot come from nothing. Nothing is absolute nothingness. It is a totally negative void. Laozi sees things differently. Something can come from nothing; indeed, this whole marvelous universe did come from the no-thing that is the Way of all things.

De can be translated as "virtue," "power," or "excellence." So the title of Laozi's mind-expanding poem has been translated as "The Book of the Way and Its Power." It is a book (*jing*) about the excellence of the *Dao. De* is sometimes thought of as the *Dao* itself viewed from the perspective of individual things. The excellence (perfection, power) of each thing is called its *de,* and this is the *Dao* manifesting itself on the individual level. To actualize the potential of one's nature and condition in an excellent way is to exhibit *de.* For humans (as for all natural things) this actualization occurs by living in accord with the *Dao.*

Wuwei literally means "no action" and refers to the manner in which the *Dao* acts. The Way that is no-thing acts by not acting! This rather mysterious claim can be elucidated somewhat by looking at the various levels of meaning of *wuwei*. Laozi provides advice to rulers in his book. He tells them to govern according to *wuwei*. In this political context, *wuwei* means that rulers should not interfere unnecessarily in the lives of the people. In other words, the less government the better. On a moral level, *wuwei* means acting unselfishly and spontaneously, free of all selfish attachment to the consequences of our actions. And on the cosmic level, *wuwei* refers to the way nature acts—spontaneously, freely, and naturally. There is nothing artificial in natural events. Nature does not calculate how to act, it just acts.

Finally, we need to speak of the Daoist use of the **yin/yang** concept. The Daoists adopted this concept in order to characterize the universe that stems from the *Dao*. *Yin* and *yang* stand for complementary opposites: *yin* for all things that manifest a passive or receptive force; *yang* for all things that manifest an active or aggressive force. The passive and the active are complementary opposites; you cannot have one without the other.

There is a little bit of *yang* in *yin* and a little bit of *yin* in *yang*. In time, opposites will change into each other. Hence the universe is essentially a vast, harmonious process. This can be illustrated by the seasonal cycle. Winter is the most *yin* season because it is cold and dark, and life processes are slow. However, winter contains an element of *yang*, which expands over time until we reach spring with its warmth, light, and flourishing life. *Yang* continues to expand and reaches its zenith in summer. Yet summer contains an element of *yin*, which expands into fall and eventually winter again. Such is the operation of *Dao* by means of *yin* and *yang*.

So the *Dao*, which is not a thing, acts naturally, freely, spontaneously, unselfishly, without force, thereby producing and sustaining a universe of harmonious processes in such a way that it is possible for each individual thing to manifest its own excellence. This is the Way of nature; the Way of reality. I hope this profound vision of reality whets your appetite for more. Read on, and as you do, see if you can answer the following questions.

Reading Questions

1. What does it mean to say that the *Dao* is nameless, and why do you think it is "named" that?

2. What is the main idea that Chapter 2 conveys about the nature of opposites?

3. How is it possible for the sage (wise person) to act without acting and teach without speaking?

4. What do you think the comparison between the *Dao* and a bowl implies about the relationship between the substance of a thing and its function?

5. Analogies are drawn between the *Dao* and a valley, a female, water, the hub of a wheel, a utensil, and a room. What do these analogies tell us about the *Dao*?

6. If the *Dao* is invisible, inaudible, and formless, how can it be known?

7. How does the *Dao* "run" the universe?

8. What does it mean to say that "reversion is the action of *Dao*?"

9. Is Daoist metaphysics a materialism, idealism, dualism, monism, or something that these categories fail to express adequately? Provide evidence to support your answer.

Dao De Jing

LAOZI

1

The Tao that can be told of is not the eternal Tao;
The name that can be named is not the eternal
name.
The Nameless is the origin of Heaven and Earth;
The Named is the mother of all things.

Therefore let there always be non-being, so we may
see their subtlety,
And let there always be being, so we may see their
outcome.
The two are the same,
But after they are produced, they have different
names.
They both may be called deep and profound.
Deeper and more profound,
The door of all subtleties!

COMMENT

This is the most important of all chapters, for in one stroke the basic characteristics of Tao as the eternal, the nameless, the source, and the substance of all things are explicitly or implicitly affirmed. It is no wonder the opening sentences are among the most often quoted or even chanted sayings in Chinese.

The key Taoist concepts of the named and the nameless are also introduced here. The concept of name is common to all ancient Chinese philosophical schools, but Taoism is unique in this respect. Most schools insist on the correspondence of names and actualities and accept names as necessary and good; Taoism, on the contrary, rejects names in favor of the nameless. This, among other things, shows its radical and unique character. To Lao Tzu, Tao is nameless and is the simplicity without names; when names arise, that is, when the simple oneness of Tao is split up into individual things with names, it is time to stop.

The cardinal ideas of being and non-being are also important here, for in Taoism the nameless (*wu-ming*) is equivalent to non-being and the named (*yu-ming*) is equivalent to being. For this reason, when he comments on the saying about the named and the nameless, Wang Pi says, "All being originated in non-being." As students of Chinese thought well know, the ideas of being and non-being have been dominant throughout the history of Chinese philosophy. They are central concepts in Neo-Taoism, Chinese Buddhism, and also Neo-Confucianism. It was the importance of these concepts, no doubt, that led the Neo-Confucianist Wang An-shih to deviate from tradition and punctuate the phrases "always be no desires" and "always be desires" to read "Let there always be non-being, so we may . . . ," and "Let there always be being, so we may. . . ."

Wang's punctuation not only underlines the importance of these ideas; it also shows the new metaphysical interest in Neo-Confucianism. Confucianism had been fundamentally ethical in tradition, but under the impact of Buddhist and Taoist metaphysics, the Neo-Confucianists developed Confucianism along metaphysical lines. In this case, in substituting the ideas of being and non-being for the ideas of having desires and having no desires, Wang shows a greater recognition of the philosophical content of the *Lao Tzu*, as it deserves.

2

When the people of the world all know beauty as
beauty,

There arises the recognition of ugliness.
When they all know the good as good,
There arises the recognition of evil.
Therefore:
  Being and non-being produce each other;
  Difficult and easy complete each other;
  Long and short contrast each other;
  High and low distinguish each other;
  Sound and voice harmonize each other;
  Front and behind accompany each other.

Therefore the sage manages affairs without action
And spreads doctrines without words.
All things arise, and he does not turn away from them.
He produces them but does not take possession of them.
He acts but does not rely on his own ability.
He accomplishes his task but does not claim credit for it.
It is precisely because he does not claim credit that his accomplishment remains with him.

COMMENT

That everything has its opposite, and that these opposites are the mutual causations of each other, form a basic part of Chuang Tzu's philosophy and later Chinese philosophy. It is important to note that opposites are here presented not as irreconcilable conflicts but as complements. The traditional Chinese ideal that opposites are to be synthesized and harmonized can be said to have originated with Lao Tzu.

The idea of teaching without words anticipated the Buddhist tradition of silent transmission of the mystic doctrine, especially in the Zen (Ch'an) school. This is diametrically opposed to the Confucian ideal, according to which a superior man acts and thus "becomes the model of the world," and speaks and thus "becomes the pattern for the world." It is true that Confucianists say that a superior man "is truthful without any words," but they would never regard silence itself as a virtue. . . .

4

Tao is empty (like a bowl).
  It may be used but its capacity is never exhausted.

It is bottomless, perhaps the ancestor of all things.
It blunts its sharpness,
It unties its tangles.
It softens its light.
It becomes one with the dusty world.
Deep and still, it appears to exist forever.
I do not know whose son it is.
It seems to have existed before the Lord.

COMMENT

This chapter, on the substance and function of Tao, shows clearly that in Taoism function is no less important than substance. Substance is further described in chapters 14 and 21, but here, as in chapters 11 and 45, function (*yung*, also meaning "use") is regarded with equal respect. There is no deprecation of phenomena, as is the case with certain Buddhist schools. To describe the world as dusty may suggest a lack of enthusiasm for it; indeed both Buddhism and later Taoism employ the word "dust" to symbolize the dirty world from which we should escape. It is significant to note, however, that Taoism in its true sense calls for identification with, not escape from, such a world. . . .

6

The spirit of the valley never dies.
  It is called the subtle and profound female.
The gate of the subtle and profound female
  Is the root of Heaven and Earth.
It is continuous, and seems to be always existing.
Use it and you will never wear it out.

COMMENT

The valley and the female, like the infant and water, are Lao Tzu's favorite symbols for Tao. The symbol of the valley is employed again and again. There is nothing mysterious about it or its spirit; it simply stands for vacuity, vastness, openness, all-inclusiveness, and lowliness or humility, all of which are outstanding characteristics of Tao. This is the interpretation of Wang Pi, and commentators, with only a few exceptions, have followed him. To understand the "continuous" operation as breathing, or the valley as the belly or the Void, and then to interpret the whole passage as one on the yoga technique of breathing, or to single out the characteristic of stillness of the valley and then to present it as an evidence of Taoist quietism, is to fail to interpret the passages in the context of the whole. These interpretations are not supported by the symbolic meaning of the valley elsewhere in the book.

The spirit of the chapter is far from quietism. Instead, it involves the idea of natural transformation and continuous creation. As Chu Hsi has said, "The valley is vacuous. As sound reaches it, it echoes. This is the spontaneity of spiritual transformation. To be subtle and profound means to be wonderful. The female is one who receives something and produces things. This is a most wonderful principle and it has the meaning of production and reproduction." . . .

8

The best (man)[1] *is like water.*
  Water is good; it benefits all things and does not
    compete with them.
It dwells in (lowly) places that all disdain.
This is why it is so near to Tao.

(The best man) in his dwelling loves the earth.
In his heart, he loves what is profound.
In his associations, he loves humanity.
In his words, he loves faithfulness.
In government, he loves order.
In handling affairs, he loves competence.
In his activities, he loves timeliness.
It is because he does not compete that he is without
  reproach.

1. Most commentators and translators have understood the Chinese phrase literally as the highest good, but some commentators and translators, including Lin Yutang, Cheng Lin (p. 15, Sec. 78), and Bynner, have followed Wang Pi and taken the phrase to mean the best man. Both interpretations are possible. The former interpretation has a parallel in Chapter 38, which talks about the highest virtue, while the latter has a parallel in Chapter 17, where both Wang Pi and Ho-shang Kung interpret "the best" to mean the best ruler. I have followed Wang Pi, not only because his commentary on the text is the oldest and most reliable, but also because the *Lao Tzu* deals with man's way of life more than abstract ideas.

COMMENT

Water is perhaps the most outstanding among Lao Tzu's symbols for Tao. The emphasis of the symbolism is ethical rather than metaphysical or religious. It is interesting to note that, while early Indian philosophers associated water with creation and the Greek philosophers looked upon it as a natural phenomenon, ancient Chinese philosophers, whether Lao Tzu or Confucius, preferred to learn moral lessons from it. Broadly speaking, Western thought, derived chiefly from the Greeks, has been largely interested in metaphysical and scientific problems, Indian thought largely interested in religious problems, and Chinese thought largely interested in moral problems. It is not too much to say that these different approaches to water characterize the Western, the Indian, and the Chinese systems of thought. . . .

11

Thirty spokes are united around the hub to make
  a wheel,
  But it is on its non-being that the utility of the
    carriage depends.
Clay is molded to form a utensil,
  But it is on its non-being that the utility of the
    utensil depends.
Doors and windows are cut out to make a room,
  But it is on its non-being that the utility of the
    room depends.
Therefore turn being into advantage, and turn
  non-being into utility.

COMMENT

Nowhere else in Chinese philosophy is the concept of non-being more strongly emphasized. This chapter alone should dispel any idea that Taoism is negativistic, for non-being—the hole in the hub, the hollowness of a utensil, the empty space in the room—is here conceived not as nothingness but as something useful and advantageous.

The Taoist interest in non-being has counteracted the positivistic tendency in certain Chinese philosophical schools, especially the Legalist and Confucian, which often overlook what seems to be nonexistent. It has prepared the Chinese mind for the acceptance of the Buddhist doctrine of Emptiness, although neither the Taoist concept of non-being nor that of vacuity is identical with that of the Buddhist Void. In addition, it was because of the Taoist insistence on the positive value of non-being that empty space has been utilized as a constructive factor in Chinese landscape painting. In this greatest art of China, space is used to combine the various elements into an organic whole and to provide a setting in which the onlooker's imagination may work. By the same token, much is left unsaid in Chinese poetry, for the reader must play a creative role to bring the poetic idea into full realization. The Zen Buddhists have developed to the fullest the themes that real existence is found in the nonexistent and that true words are spoken in silence, but the origin of these themes must be traced to early Taoism. . . .

14

We look at it and do not see it;
  Its name is The Invisible.
We listen to it and do not hear it;
  Its name is The Inaudible.
We touch it and do not find it;
  Its name is The Subtle (formless).

These three cannot be further inquired into,
And hence merge into one.
Going up high, it is not bright, and coming down
  low, it is not dark.
Infinite and boundless, it cannot be given any
  name;
It reverts to nothingness.
This is called shape without shape,
Form without objects.
It is The Vague and Elusive.
Meet it and you will not see its head.
Follow it and you will not see its back.
Hold on to the Tao of old in order to master the
  things of the present.
From this one may know the primeval beginning
  (of the universe).
This is called the bond[2] of Tao.

2. *Chi*, literally, "a thread," denotes tradition, discipline, principle, order, essence, etc. Generally it means the system, principle, or continuity that binds things together.

COMMENT

Subtlety is an important characteristic of Tao and is more important than its manifestations. The Confucianists, on the other hand, emphasize manifestation. There is nothing more manifest than the hidden (subtle), they say, and "a man who knows that the subtle will be manifested can enter into virtue." The Buddhists and Neo-Confucianists eventually achieved a synthesis, saying that "there is no distinction between the manifest and the hidden."

To describe reality in terms of the invisible, the inaudible, and the subtle is an attempt to describe it in terms of non-being. Because the three Chinese words are pronounced *i, hsi,* and *wei,* respectively, they have been likened to *Jod, Heh, Vav,* indicating the name Jehovah, and to the Hindu god Ishvara, but any similarity is purely accidental. The threefold description does not suggest any idea of trinity either. Basically, Taoist philosophy is naturalistic, if not atheistic, and any idea of a god is alien to it. . . .

16

Attain complete vacuity.
Maintain steadfast quietude.

All things come into being,
And I see thereby their return.
All things flourish,
But each one returns to its root.
This return to its root means tranquility.
It is called returning to its destiny.
To return to destiny is called the eternal (Tao).
To know the eternal is called enlightenment.
Not to know the eternal is to act blindly to result
  in disaster.
He who knows the eternal is all-embracing.
Being all-embracing, he is impartial.
Being impartial, he is kingly (universal).
Being kingly, he is one with Nature.
Being one with Nature, he is in accord with Tao.
Being in accord with Tao, he is everlasting
And is free from danger throughout his lifetime.

COMMENT

The central idea here is returning to the root, which is to be achieved through tranquility. Generally speaking, in Taoist philosophy Tao is revealed most fully through tranquility rather than activity. Under its influence, Wang Pi has commented on the hexagram *fu* (to return) in the *Book of Changes* in the same light. He says, "Although Heaven and Earth are vast, possessing the myriad things in abundance, where thunder moves and winds circulate, and while there is an infinite variety of changes and transformations, yet its original [substance] is absolutely quiet and perfect non-being. Therefore only with the cessation of activities within Earth can the mind of Heaven and Earth be revealed."

This Taoistic position is directly opposed by the Neo-Confucianists, who insist that the mind of Heaven and Earth is to be seen in a state of activity. As Ch'eng I says, "Former scholars all said that only in a state of tranquility can the mind of Heaven and Earth be seen. They did not realize that the mind of Heaven and Earth is found in the beginning of activity." . . .

22

To yield is to be preserved whole.
To be bent is to become straight.
To be empty is to be full.
To be worn out is to be renewed.
To have little is to possess.
To have plenty is to be perplexed.
Therefore the sage embraces the One
And becomes the model of the world.
He does not show himself; therefore he is luminous.
He does not justify himself; therefore he becomes
*   prominent.*
He does not boast of himself; therefore he is given
*   credit.*
He does not brag; therefore he can endure for long.

It is precisely because he does not compete that the
*   world cannot compete with him.*
Is the ancient saying, "To yield is to be preserved
*   whole," empty words?*
Truly he will be preserved and (prominence and
*   credit) will come to him.*

COMMENT

Taoism seems to be advocating a negative morality. In this respect, it is not much different from the Christian doctrine taught in the Sermon on the Mount, which extols meekness, poverty, and so forth. Whatever negativism there may seem to be, it pertains to method only; the objective is entirely positive. . . .

25

There was something undifferentiated and yet
*   complete,*
Which existed before heaven and earth.
Soundless and formless, it depends on nothing and
*   does not change.*
It operates everywhere and is free from danger.
It may be considered the mother of the universe.
I do not know its name; I call it Tao.
If forced to give it a name, I shall call it Great.
Now being great means functioning everywhere.
Functioning everywhere means far-reaching.
Being far-reaching means returning to the origi-
*   nal point.*

Therefore Tao is great.
Heaven is great.
Earth is great.
And the king[3] is also great.
There are four great things in the universe, and
*   the king is one of them.*
Man models himself after Earth.
Earth models itself after Heaven.
Heaven models itself after Tao.
And Tao models itself after Nature.

COMMENT

Taoist cosmology is outlined here simply but clearly. In the beginning there is something undifferentiated, which is forever operating; it produces heaven and earth and then all things. In essence this cosmology is strikingly similar to that of the *Book of Changes*. In the system of Change, the Great Ultimate produces the Two Modes (yin and yang), which in turn produce all

3. The Fu I and Fan Ying-yüan texts have "man" in place of "king." This substitution has been accepted by Hsi T'ung, Ma Hsü-lun, Ch'en Chu, Jen Chi-yü, and Ch'u Ta-kao. They have been influenced, undoubtedly, by the concept of the trinity of Heaven, Earth, and man, without realizing that the king is considered here as representative of men. Moreover, in Chapters 16 and 39, Heaven, Earth, and the king are spoken of together.

things. We don't know to what extent Taoist thought has influenced the *Book of Changes*, which the Confucianists have attributed to their ancient sages, chiefly Confucius. At any rate, this naturalistic philosophy has always been prominent in Chinese thought, and later contributed substantially to the naturalistic pattern of Neo-Confucian cosmology, especially through Chou Tun-i. As will be noted, he has added the concept of the Non-ultimate to the philosophy of the *Book of Changes* in order better to explain the originally undifferentiated. It is to be noted that the term "Non-ultimate" comes from the *Lao Tzu*. . . .

34

> *The Great Tao flows everywhere.*
> *It may go left or right.*
> *All things depend on it for life, and it does not turn away from them.*
> *It accomplishes its task, but does not claim credit for it.*
> *It clothes and feeds all things but does not claim to be master over them.*
> *Always without desires, it may be called The Small.*
> *All things come to it and it does not master them; it may be called The Great.*
> *Therefore (the sage) never strives himself for the great, and thereby the great is achieved.*

COMMENT

In commenting on this chapter, Yen Fu says that the left and the right, the small and the great, are relative terms, and that Tao in its original substance transcends all these relative qualities. Of greater significance, however, is the paradoxical character of Tao. This character is affirmed more than once in the *Lao Tzu*. In Neo-Confucianism, principle is both immanent and transcendent, as is the Christian God. Ultimate being or reality is by nature paradoxical. . . .

37

> *Tao invariably takes no action, and yet there is nothing left undone.*

> *If kings and barons can keep it, all things will transform spontaneously.*
> *If, after transformation, they should desire to be active,*
> *I would restrain them with simplicity, which has no name.*
> *Simplicity, which has no name, is free of desires.*
> *Being free of desires, it is tranquil.*
> *And the world will be at peace of its own accord.*

COMMENT

"Transform spontaneously" seems to be a passing remark here, but the idea became a key concept in the *Chuang Tzu* and later formed a key tenet in the Neo-Taoism of Kuo Hsiang. In the *Lao Tzu*, things transform themselves because Tao takes no action or leaves things alone. Chuang Tzu goes a step further, saying that everything is in incessant change and that is self-transformation. In his commentary on the *Chuang Tzu*, Kuo Hsiang goes even further, stressing that things transform themselves spontaneously because they are self-sufficient, and there is no Nature behind or outside of them. Nature, he says, is but a general name for things. . . .

40

> *Reversion is the action of Tao.*
> *Weakness is the function of Tao.*
> *All things in the world come from being.*
> *And being comes from non-being.*[4]

COMMENT

The doctrine of returning to the original is a prominent one in the *Lao Tzu*.[5] It has contrib-

---

4. Cf. Chapter 1. This seems to contradict the saying, "Being and non-being produce each other," in Chapter 2. But to produce means not to originate but to bring about.

5. The doctrine is also encountered in one sense or another in Chapters 14, 16, 25, 28, 30, and 52. To D. C. Lau, returning to the root is not a cyclical process. According to him, the main doctrine of the *Lao Tzu* is the preservation of life, which is to be achieved through "abiding by softness." Softness is real strength, because when strength is allowed to reach its limit, it falls, whereas softness preserves itself. Thus opposites are neither relative nor paradoxical, and their process is not

uted in no small degree to the common Chinese cyclical concept, according to which the Chinese believe that both history and reality operate in cycles. . . .

42

Tao produced the One.
The One produced the two.
The two produced the three.
And the three produced the ten thousand things.

The ten thousand things carry the yin and embrace the yang, and through the blending of the material force they achieve harmony.

People hate to be children without parents, lonely people without spouses, or men without food to eat,
And yet kings and lords call themselves by these names.
Therefore it is often the case that things gain by losing and lose by gaining.

What others have taught, I teach also:

"Violent and fierce people do not die a natural death."
I shall make this the father of my teaching.

COMMENT

It is often understood that the One is the original material force of the Great Ultimate, the two are yin and yang, the three are their blending with the original material force, and the ten thousand things are things carrying yin and embracing yang. The similarity of this process to that of the *Book of Changes,* in which the Great Ultimate produces the Two Forces (yin and yang) and then the myriad things, is amazing. The important point, however, is not the specific similarities, but the evolution from the simple to the complex. This theory is common to nearly all Chinese philosophical schools.

It should be noted that the evolution here, as in the *Book of Changes,* is natural. Production (*sheng*) is not personal creation or purposeful origination, but natural causation.

Suggestions for Further Reading

You should read the entire *Dao De Jing.* The selection I have made here is only a small portion of the text and focuses almost exclusively on its metaphysical parts. This selection is somewhat misleading since the book is as much a book about political philosophy and ethics as it is about metaphysics. Chan's translation reflects excellent scholarship and his introduction will provide you with more background. You may wish to compare his translation to the many others available (along with the Bible this is one of the world's most translated books). A popular "version" that is very readable but takes great liberties with the literal meaning of the text is Stephen Mitchell's *Tao Te Ching* (New York: Harper & Row, 1988). Also see Michael La-Fargue's *The Tao of the Tao Te Ching: A Translation and Commentary* (New York: State University of New York Press, 1992). LaFargue rejects a metaphysical reading of the text and argues for an ethical and political reading. He contends that the text embodies a "worldview" which stresses a philosophy of "organic harmony."

For more background information, check John Koller's chapter on Daoism in *Oriental Philosophies* (New York: Charles Scribner, 1985). His bibliography can guide you further. On Chinese philosophy in general, I recommend Thomé H. Fang's *Chinese Philosophy: Its Spirit and Its Development* (Taipei: Linking Publishing, 1981). Part II of this book discusses the impact of Daoism on the development of Chinese Buddhism and the first chapter sets forth the general characteristics of Chinese philosophy.

If you wish to explore the possible relationships between the Daoist vision of reality and

---

circular but a gradual development to the limit and then an inevitable and sudden decline. This idea may be implied in the *Lao Tzu* but there is no explicit passage to support Lau's theory. See his "The Treatment of Opposites in Lao Tzu," *Bulletin of the School of Oriental and African Studies,* XXI (1958), 349–50, 352–57.

modern physics, see Fritjof Capra's *The Tao of Physics: An Exploration of the Parallels Between Modern Physics and Eastern Mysticism* (Berkeley: Shambhala, 1975) and Gary Zukav's *The Dancing Wu Li Masters: An Overview of the New Physics* (New York: William Morrow, 1979).

Videos

Taoism (25 minutes, Insight Media) presents the story of Lao Tzu and his book. Also see *Flowing with the Tao* (20 minutes, Hartley Productions), narrated by Alan Watts, for an aesthetic approach.

7.2. Platonic Dualism

We have encountered Plato and Socrates before (see Section 2.3). Plato (428–347 B.C.E.) was Socrates' star pupil and one of the most creative and influential minds in the whole history of Western philosophy. He lived in Athens, founded the first "university" (called the Academy) in the West, and wrote a number of dialogues in which Socrates frequently appears.

Alfred North Whitehead, a twentieth-century British-American philosopher, remarked that "All Western philosophy is but a footnote to Plato." This might be overstating the case for Plato's importance, but there can be little doubt that his ideas have influenced and still influence the thoughts and values of people who do not even know his name.

Do you believe in the immortality of the soul? Do you think that there is a material reality and an immaterial or spiritual reality and that the latter is more important than the former? Do you regard logical and mathematical methods of reasoning ideal models for arriving at truth? Do you believe that things have an essential nature? Do you believe you ought to control your passions by the use of reason? Do you think politicians ought to have the good of the people in mind? Do you think virtue is its own reward? If you believe some of these things, you are reflecting ideas that Plato articulated almost twenty-five centuries ago.

Plato wrote on almost every aspect of philosophy. Here we are concerned primarily with his metaphysical ideas. Plato's metaphysics has been classified as dualistic because he argued that reality could be divided into two radically different sorts of things. There is the reality of matter characterized by change (becoming) and the reality of what he called the **Forms** or Ideas characterized by permanence (being). Being is immaterial and of greater value than the material. Along with this general ontological dualism between being and becoming, Plato taught a soul-body dualism. Human beings are composed of bodies and souls. One power that our souls have is the power of thought (the mind), and this is by far our most valuable thing. Our minds and souls are immaterial in contrast to our material bodies.

Plato's metaphysics is also classified as an idealism because it centers on the theory of Forms (Ideas) and because, although the reality of matter is not denied, matter is regarded as less real than the immaterial Forms. What is the theory of Forms? The English word "form" is often used to translate the Greek word for idea or concept. So, in the first instance, a form is the mental concept or idea we have of something. For example, how do you recognize a table as a table when you see one? After all, each table is different. How are you able to classify a whole group of different-looking objects into the class "table?" Well, you can do this, we might say, because you have the concept or idea of a table. If someone asked you what a table is, you could give a definition. This definition would constitute the expression of your concept.

Your definition (if it were the "correct" definition in Socrates' sense) would also express the essential nature of table. That is, it would not tell us what this or that *particular* table is, but it would tell us what *all* tables are insofar as they are tables. So, in the second place, a form is an essence.

Now most of us think that the concepts of things exist only in human minds and the essences of things (if there are such) either exist in our minds or somehow exist in the things themselves. If we might use the word "tableness" to designate the Form of tables, then most of us would be inclined to say that if there were no tables, there would be no tableness. Not so Plato. Or at least, not so Plato as interpreted by his star pupil, Aristotle. For Plato, according to Aristotle, essences (Forms) exist objectively apart from the minds that think them and the objects that instantiate them. They constitute ideals, perfect models if you will, that are even more real than the material things that reflect them.

Think of a square. Any particular material square you can draw will be imperfect. Its angles and lines will not be exact. But the square as such (squareness or the pure abstract geometric shape that we can define with mathematical precision) is another matter. It is perfect and its definition will never change. Is not that which is perfect and permanent more real than that which is imperfect and everchanging?

The selection that follows is from Plato's most famous dialogue, the *Republic*. This is one of the masterpieces of Western literature, and you should definitely read all of it. It is filled with stories, myths, striking analogies, and political ideas that are still hotly debated today. For now, we will have to be content with just a little bit. However, in order to appreciate this little bit, some idea of what the whole is about will help.

Socrates, along with others, has been invited to the home of Cephalus. The question, "What is justice?" arises and after examining and finding fault with several definitions, Thrasymachus (pronounced Thra-*sim*-a-kus) argues that justice is whatever is in the interest of the stronger party. Socrates attacks this "might makes right" position and argues that power and knowledge must be combined since the art of government, like other arts, requires skill and knowledge. In particular, it requires knowledge of what is good for people since government ought to serve the needs of those who are governed, not merely the interests of the strongest.

In Book II, Glaucon (Glau-kon) and Adeimantus (A-dei-man-tus) press Socrates to prove that the just life is worth living. Socrates argues that virtue is its own reward and begins an analysis of political justice. The ideal state needs guardians (rulers), auxiliaries (soldiers/police), and workers. When each class does its proper business without interfering with the others, political justice is achieved. By analogy with the state, Socrates argues that the just person is one in whom the three basic elements of human nature—the rational, the spirited, and the appetitive—are properly ordered. Proper order consists of the rule of rationality or reason over the spirited and appetitive parts of the soul.

Books III through V describe in some detail Socrates' vision of the ideal state. In the ideal republic, the classes are carefully controlled by breeding, education, and selection. Just as reason should rule in the individual if personal justice is to be realized, so the "lovers of wisdom" (philosophers) should rule the state. This means that the rulers (philosopher-kings) need to know what is good and so must be properly educated, which leads to a discussion of what the good is and what the proper education of the guardians should be. This discussion takes place in Books VI and VII, from which the following selection comes.

Socrates admits that the good itself is the proper object of the philosopher's quest, but he cannot say directly what the good is. He offers three analogies. The first compares the good to the sun. The second, called the simile of the divided line, compares *opinion* (which derives from sensations of material objects) with *knowledge* (which derives from knowing the Forms via reason and understanding). The third, called the allegory of the cave, compares the philosopher to a prisoner who has escaped from a cave and seen the light of the real world.

The last three books of the *Republic* deal with political change, the decline of the state, and various forms of government. It closes with an argument for the immortality of the soul. By loving justice (that is, by harmonizing reason, spirit, and appetite under the rule of rationality) we can keep our souls healthy and thereby prosper forever.

You should read what follows slowly and carefully, pausing to think about what Socrates is saying. Socrates is the main speaker. Please note that in this translation the words of the speaker who responds to Socrates are usually indicated only by a dash (—). The following questions should help you catch the main ideas.

Reading Questions

1. What is the difference between "the many things" and the Forms?
2. In what ways are the sun and the Good alike?
3. Give examples of what Socrates means by images and by objects of sense.
4. What is the difference between reasoning and understanding?
5. What do you think the allegory of the cave means?
6. What is the relationship between the image of the divided line and the story about the cave?
7. What conclusion about education does Socrates draw from the allegory of the cave?
8. Are you inclined to agree with Plato about the existence of some higher, immaterial, intelligible reality beyond this material world? Why?
9. Formulate a critical question about this text and answer it.
10. How would Plato answer the question, "What is really real?"

Republic

PLATO

. . . But you also, Socrates, must tell us whether you consider the good to be knowledge, or pleasure, or something else.

What a man! I said. It has been clear for some time that the opinion of others on this subject would not satisfy you.

From Plato's Republic, *translated by G. M. A. Grube, Hackett Publishing Co., Inc. Copyright © 1974, pp. 161–172. Reprinted with permission of Hackett Publishing Company, Inc., Indianapolis, IN, and Cambridge, MA. Translator's footnotes have been retained, but renumbered.*

Well, Socrates, he said, it does not seem right to me to be able to tell the opinions of others and not one's own, especially for a man who has spent so much time as you have occupying himself with this subject.

Why? said I. Do you think it right to talk about things one does not know as if one knew them?

Not as if one knew them, he said, but for a man who has an opinion to say what that opinion is.

And have you not noticed that opinions not based on knowledge are ugly things? The best of them are blind; or do you think that those who express a true opinion without knowledge are any different from blind people who yet follow the right road?—They are no different.

Do you want to contemplate ugly, blind, and crooked things when you can hear bright and beautiful things from others?

By Zeus, Socrates, said Glaucon, do not stand off as if you had come to the end. We shall be satisfied if you discuss the Good in the same fashion as you did justice, moderation, and the other things.

That, my friend, I said, would also quite satisfy me, but I fear I shall not be able to do so, and that in my eagerness I shall disgrace myself and make myself ridiculous. But, my excellent friends, let us for the moment abandon the quest for the nature of the Good itself, for that I think is a larger question than what we started on, which was to ascertain my present opinion about it. I am willing to tell you what appears to be the offspring of the Good and most like it, if that is agreeable to you. If not, we must let the question drop.

Well, he said, tell us. The story of the parent remains a debt which you will pay us some other time.

I wish, I said, that I could pay it in full now, and you could exact it in full and not, as now, only receive the interest.[1] However, accept then this offspring and child of the Good. Only be

careful that I do not somehow deceive you unwillingly by giving a counterfeit account of this offspring.—We shall be as careful as we can. Only tell us.

I will, I said, after coming to an agreement with you and reminding you of the things we said before, and also many times elsewhere—What are these things?

We speak of many beautiful things and many good things, and we say that they are so and so define them in speech—We do.

And Beauty itself and Goodness itself, and so with all the things which we then classed as many; we now class them again according to one Form of each, which is one and which we in each case call that which is—That is so.

And we say that the many things are the objects of sight but not of thought, while the Forms are the objects of thought but not of sight—Altogether true.

With what part of ourselves do we see the objects that are seen?—With our sight.

And so things heard are heard by our hearing, and all that is perceived is perceived by our other senses?—Quite so.

Have you considered how very lavishly the maker of our senses made the faculty of seeing and being seen?—I cannot say I have.

Look at it this way: Do hearing and sound need another kind of thing for the former to hear and the latter to be heard, and in the absence of this third element the one will not hear and the other not be heard—No, they need nothing else.

Neither do many other senses, if indeed any, need any such other thing, or can you mention one?—Not I.

But do you not realize that the sense of sight and that which is seen do have such a need?—How so?

Sight may be in the eyes, and the man who has it may try to use it, and colours may be present in the objects, but unless a third kind of thing is present, which is by nature designed for this very purpose, you know that sight will see nothing and the colours remain unseen—What is this third kind of thing?

What you call light, I said—Right.

So to no small extent the sense of sight and

---

1. Plato is punning on the Greek word *tokos* which means a child, and in the plural was used also of the interest on capital, a pleasant and common metaphor.

the power of being seen are yoked together by a more honorable yoke than other things which are yoked together, unless light is held in no honor—That is far from being the case.

Which of the gods in the heavens can you hold responsible for this, whose light causes our sight to see as beautifully as possible, and the objects of sight to be seen?—The same as you would, he said, and as others would; obviously the answer to your question is the sun.

And is not sight naturally related to the sun in this way?—Which way?

Sight is not the sun, neither itself nor that in which it occurs which we call the eye—No indeed.

But I think it is the most sunlike of the organs of sense—Very much so.

And it receives from the sun the capacity to see as a kind of outflow—Quite so.

The sun is not sight, but is it not the cause of it, and is also seen by it?—Yes.

Say then, I said, that it is the sun which I called the offspring of the Good, which the Good begot as analogous to itself. What the Good itself is in the world of thought in relation to the intelligence and things known, the sun is in the visible world, in relation to sight and things seen.—How? Explain further.

You know, I said, that when one turns one's eyes to those objects of which the colours are no longer in the light of day but in the dimness of the night, the eyes are dimmed and seem nearly blind, as if clear vision was no longer in them—Quite so.

Yet whenever one's eyes are turned upon objects brightened by sunshine, they see clearly, and clear vision appears in those very same eyes?—Yes indeed.

So too understand the eye of the soul: whenever it is fixed upon that upon which truth and reality shine, it understands and knows and seems to have intelligence, but whenever it is fixed upon what is mixed with darkness—that which is subject to birth and destruction—it opines and is dimmed, changes its opinions this way and that, and seems to have no intelligence—That is so.

Say that what gives truth to the objects of knowledge, and to the knowing mind the power

to know, is the Form of Good. As it is the cause of knowledge and truth, think of it also as being the object of knowledge. Both knowledge and truth are beautiful, but you will be right to think of the Good as other and more beautiful than they. As in the visible world light and sight are rightly considered sun-like, but it is wrong to think of them as the sun, so here it is right to think of knowledge and truth as Good-like, but wrong to think of either as the Good, for the Good must be honored even more than they.

This is an extraordinary beauty you mention, he said, if it provides knowledge and truth and is itself superior to them in beauty. You surely do not mean this to be pleasure!

Hush! said I, rather examine the image of it in this way.—How?

You will say, I think, that the sun not only gives to the objects of sight the capacity to be seen, but also that it provides for their generation, increase, and nurture, though it is not itself the process of generation—How could it be?

And say that as for the objects of knowledge, not only is their being known due to the Good, but also their reality being, though the Good is not being but superior to and beyond being in dignity and power.

Glaucon was quite amused and said: By Apollo, a miraculous superiority!

It is your own fault, I said, you forced me to say what I thought about it.

Don't you stop, he said, except for a moment, but continue to explain the similarity to the sun in case you are leaving something out.

I am certainly leaving out a good deal, I said—Don't omit the smallest point.

Much is omitted, I said. However, as far as the explanation can go at present, I will not omit anything—Don't you!

Understand then, I said, that, as we say, there are those two, one reigning over the intelligible kind and realm, the other over the visible (not to say heaven, that I may not appear to play the sophist about the name[2]). So you have two kinds, the visible and the intelligible—Right.

---

2. He means play on the similarity of sound between *ouranos,* the sky, and *horaton,* visible.

It is like a line divided[3] into two unequal parts, and then divide each section in the same ratio, that is, the section of the visible and that of the intelligible. You will then have sections related to each other in proportion to their clarity and obscurity. The first section of the visible consists of images—and by images I mean shadows in the first instance, then the reflections in water and all those on close-packed, smooth, and bright materials, and all that sort of thing, if you understand me—I understand.

In the other section of the visible, place the models of the images, the living creatures around us, all plants, and the whole class of manufactured things—I so place them.

Would you be willing to say that, as regards truth and untruth, the division is made in this proportion: as the opinable is to the knowable so the image is to the model it is made like?—Certainly.

Consider now how the section of the intelligible is to be divided—How?

In such a way that in one section the soul, using as images what before were models, is compelled to investigate from hypotheses, proceed-

ing from these not to a first principle but to a conclusion. In the second section which leads to a first principle that is not hypothetical, the soul proceeds from a hypothesis without using the images of the first section, by means of the Forms themselves and proceeding through these.—I do not, he said, quite understand what you mean.

Let us try again, I said, for you will understand more easily because of what has been said. I think you know that students of geometry, calculation, and the like assume the existence of the odd and the even, of figures, of three kinds of angles, and of kindred things in each of their studies, as if they were known to them. These they make their hypotheses and do not deem it necessary to give any account of them either to themselves or to others as if they were clear to all; these are their starting points, and going through the remaining steps they reach an agreed conclusion on what they started out to investigate—Quite so, I understand that.

You know also that they use visible figures and talk about them, but they are not thinking about them but about the models of which these are likenesses; they are making their points about the square itself, the diameter itself, not about the diameter which they draw, and similarly with the others. These figures which they fashion and draw, of which shadows and reflections in the water are images, they now in turn use as images, in seeking to understand those others in themselves, which one cannot see except in thought—That is true.

This is what I called the intelligible class, and said that the soul is forced to use hypotheses in its search for it, not travelling up to a first principle, since it cannot reach beyond its hypotheses, but it uses as images those very things which at a lower level were models and which, in comparison with their images, were thought to be clear and honored as such—I understand, he said, that you mean what happens in geometry and kindred sciences.

Understand also that by the other section of the intelligible I mean that which reason itself grasps by the power of dialectic. It does not consider its hypotheses as first principles, but as hypotheses in the true sense of stepping stones and

3. It is clear that Plato visualizes a vertical line . . . with *B* as the highest point in the scale of reality and *A* as the lowest form of existence. The main division is at *C*. *AC* is the visible, *CB* being the intelligible world, *AD* is the world of images (and perhaps, though Plato does not say so, works of art), mathematical realities are contained in *CE*, the Platonic Forms in *EB*, with the Good presumably at *B*.

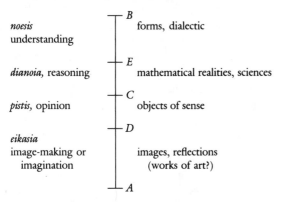

noesis understanding	B — forms, dialectic
dianoia, reasoning	E — mathematical realities, sciences
pistis, opinion	C — objects of sense
eikasia image-making or imagination	D — images, reflections (works of art?)
	A

The names of the four mental processes—*noesis, dianoia, pistis,* and *eikasia*—are more or less arbitrary, and Plato does not use them regularly in these precise senses in the rest of the *Republic*.

starting points, in order to reach that which is beyond hypothesis, the first principle of all that exists. Having reached this and keeping hold of what follows from it, it does come down to a conclusion without making use of anything visible at all, but proceeding by means of Forms and through Forms to its conclusions which are Forms.

I understand, he said, but not completely, for you seem to be speaking of a mighty task—that you wish to distinguish the intelligible reality contemplated by the science of dialectic as clearer than that viewed by the so-called sciences, for which their hypotheses are first principles. The students of these so-called sciences are, it is true, compelled to study them by thought and not by sense perception, yet because they do not go back to a first principle but proceed from hypotheses, you do not think that they have any clear understanding of their subjects, although these can be so understood if approached from a first principle. You seem to me to call the attitude of mind of geometers and such reasoning but not understanding, reasoning being midway between opinion and understanding.

You have grasped this very satisfactorily, I said. There are four such processes in the soul, corresponding to the four sections of our line: understanding for the highest, reasoning for the second; give the name of opinion to the third, and imagination to the last. Place these in the due terms of a proportion and consider that each has as much clarity as the content of its particular section shares in truth—I understand, and I agree and arrange them as you say.

Book VII

Next, I said, compare the effect of education and the lack of it upon our human nature to a situation like this: imagine men to be living in an underground cave-like dwelling place, which has a way up to the light along its whole width, but the entrance is a long way up. The men have been there from childhood, with their neck and legs in fetters, so that they remain in the same place and can only see ahead of them, as their bonds prevent them turning their heads. Light is provided by a fire burning some way behind and above them. Between the fire and the prisoners, some way behind them and on a higher ground, there is a path across the cave and along this a low wall has been built, like the screen at a puppet show in front of the performers who show their puppets above it—I see it.

See then also men carrying along that wall, so that they overtop it, all kinds of artifacts, statues of men, reproductions of other animals in stone or wood fashioned in all sorts of ways, and, as is likely, some of the carriers are talking while others are silent—This is a strange picture, and strange prisoners.

They are like us, I said. Do you think, in the first place, that such men could see anything of themselves and each other[4] except the shadows which the fire casts upon the wall of the cave in front of them?—How could they, if they have to keep their heads still throughout life?

And is not the same true of the objects carried along the wall?—Quite.

If they could converse with one another, do you not think that they would consider these shadows to be the real things?—Necessarily.

What if their prison had an echo which reached them from in front of them? Whenever one of the carriers passing behind the wall spoke, would they not think that it was the shadow passing in front of them which was talking? Do you agree?—By Zeus I do.

Altogether then, I said, such men would believe the truth to be nothing else than the shadows of the artifacts?—They must believe that.

Consider then what deliverance from their bonds and the curing of their ignorance would be if something like this naturally happened to them. Whenever one of them was freed, had to stand up suddenly, turn his head, walk, and look up toward the light, doing all that would give

---

4. These shadows of themselves and each other are never mentioned again. A Platonic myth or parable, like a Homeric simile, is often elaborated in considerable detail. These contribute to the vividness of the picture but often have no other function, and it is a mistake to look for any symbolic meaning in them. It is the general picture that matters.

him pain, the flash of the fire would make it impossible for him to see the objects of which he had earlier seen the shadows. What do you think he would say if he was told that what he saw then was foolishness, that he was now somewhat closer to reality and turned to things that existed more fully, that he saw more correctly? If one then pointed to each of the objects passing by, asked him what each was, and forced him to answer, do you not think he would be at a loss and believe that the things which he saw earlier were truer than the things now pointed out to him?—Much truer.

If one then compelled him to look at the fire itself, his eyes would hurt, he would turn round and flee toward those things which he could see, and think that they were in fact clearer than those now shown to him—Quite so.

And if one were to drag him thence by force up the rough and steep path, and did not let him go before he was dragged into the sunlight, would he not be in physical pain and angry as he was dragged along? When he came into the light, with the sunlight filling his eyes, he would not be able to see a single one of the things which are now said to be true—Not at once, certainly.

I think he would need time to get adjusted before he could see things in the world above; at first he would see shadows most easily, then reflections of men and other things in water, then the things themselves. After this he would see objects in the sky and the sky itself more easily at night, the light of the stars and the moon more easily than the sun and the light of the sun during the day—Of course.

Then, at last, he would be able to see the sun, not images of it in water or in some alien place, but the sun itself in its own place, and be able to contemplate it—That must be so.

After this he would reflect that it is the sun which provides the seasons and the years, which governs everything in the visible world, and is also in some way the cause of those other things which he used to see—Clearly that would be the next stage.

What then? As he reminds himself of his first dwelling place, of the wisdom there and of his fellow prisoners, would he not reckon himself happy for the change, and pity them?—Surely.

And if the men below had praise and honors from each other, and prizes for the man who saw most clearly the shadows that passed before them, and who could best remember which usually came earlier and which later, and which came together and thus could most ably prophesy the future, do you think our man would desire those rewards and envy those who were honored and held power among the prisoners, or would he feel, as Homer put it, that he certainly wished to be "serf to another man without possessions upon the earth"[5] and go through any suffering, rather than share their opinions and live as they do?—Quite so, he said, I think he would rather suffer anything.

Reflect on this too, I said. If this man went down into the cave again and sat down in the same seat, would his eyes not be filled with darkness, coming suddenly out of the sunlight?—They certainly would.

And if he had to contend again with those who had remained prisoners in recognizing those shadows while his sight was affected and his eyes had not settled down—and the time for this adjustment would not be short—would he not be ridiculed? Would it not be said that he had returned from his upward journey with his eyesight spoiled, and that it was not worthwhile even to attempt to travel upward? As for the man who tried to free them and lead them upward, if they could somehow lay their hands on him and kill him, they would do so—They certainly would.

This whole image, my dear Glaucon, I said, must be related to what we said before. The realm of the visible should be compared to the prison dwelling, and the fire inside it to the power of the sun. If you interpret the upward journey and the contemplation of things above as the upward journey of the soul to the intelligible realm, you will grasp what I surmise since you were keen to hear it. Whether it is true or not only the god

5. *Odyssey* 11, 489–90, where Achilles says to Odysseus, on the latter's visit to the underworld, that he would rather be a servant to a poor man on earth than king among the dead.

knows, but this is how I see it, namely that in the intelligible world the Form of the Good is the last to be seen, and with difficulty; when seen it must be reckoned to be for all the cause of all that is right and beautiful, to have produced in the visible world both light and the fount of light, while in the intelligible world it is itself that which produces and controls truth and intelligence, and he who is to act intelligently in public or in private must see it—I share your thought as far as I am able.

Come then, share with me this thought also: do not be surprised that those who have reached this point are unwilling to occupy themselves with human affairs, and that their souls are always pressing upward to spend their time there, for this is natural if things are as our parable indicates—That is very likely.

Further, I said, do you think it at all surprising that anyone coming to the evils of human life from the contemplation of the divine behaves awkwardly and appears very ridiculous while his eyes are still dazzled and before he is sufficiently adjusted to the darkness around him, if he is compelled to contend in court or some other place about the shadows of justice or the objects of which they are shadows, and to carry through the contest about these in the way these things are understood by those who have never seen Justice itself?—That is not surprising at all.

Anyone with intelligence, I said, would remember that the eyes may be confused in two ways and from two causes, coming from light into darkness as well as from darkness into light. Realizing that the same applies to the soul, whenever he sees a soul disturbed and unable to see something, he will not laugh mindlessly but will consider whether it has come from a brighter life and is dimmed because unadjusted, or has come from greater ignorance into greater light and is filled with a brighter dazzlement. The former he would declare happy in its life and experience, the latter he would pity, and if he should wish to laugh at it, his laughter would be less ridiculous than if he laughed at a soul that has come from the light above.—What you say is very reasonable.

We must then, I said, if these things are true,

think something like this about them, namely that education is not what some declare it to be; they say that knowledge is not present in the soul and that they put it in, like putting sight into blind eyes—They surely say that.

Our present argument shows, I said, that the capacity to learn and the organ with which to do so are present in every person's soul. It is as if it were not possible to turn the eye from darkness to light without turning the whole body; so one must turn one's whole soul from the world of becoming until it can endure to contemplate reality, and the brightest of realities, which we say is the Good—Yes.

Education then is the art of doing this very thing, this turning around, the knowledge of how the soul can most easily and most effectively be turned around; it is not the art of putting the capacity of sight into the soul; the soul possesses that already but it is not turned the right way or looking where it should. This is what education has to deal with—That seems likely.

Now the other so-called virtues of the soul seem to be very close to those of the body—they really do not exist before and are added later by habit and practice—but the virtue of intelligence belongs above all to something more divine, it seems, which never loses its capacity but, according to which way it is turned, becomes useful and beneficial or useless and harmful. Have you never noticed in men who are said to be wicked but clever, how sharply their little soul looks into things to which it turns its attention? Its capacity for sight is not inferior, but it is compelled to serve evil ends, so that the more sharply it looks the more evils it works—Quite so.

Yet if a soul of this kind had been hammered at from childhood and those excrescences had been knocked off it which belong to the world of becoming and have been fastened upon it by feasting, gluttony, and similar pleasures, and which like leaden weights draw the soul to look downward—if, being rid of these, it turned to look at things that are true, then the same soul of the same man would see these just as sharply as it now sees the things towards which it is directed— That seems likely.

Further, is it not likely, I said, indeed it follows inevitably from what was said before, that the uneducated who have no experience of truth would never govern a city satisfactorily, nor would those who are allowed to spend their whole life in the process of educating themselves; the former would fail because they do not have a single goal at which all their actions, public and private, must aim; the latter because they would refuse to act, thinking that they have settled, while still alive, in the faraway islands of the blessed—True.

It is then our task as founders, I said, to compel the best natures to reach the study which we have previously said to be the most important, to see the Good and to follow that upward journey. When they have accomplished their journey and seen it sufficiently, we must not allow them to do what they are allowed to do today—What is that?

To stay there, I said, and to refuse to go down again to the prisoners in the cave, there to share both their labors and their honors, whether these be of little or of greater worth.

Suggestions for Further Reading

There is so much written on Plato that this list could go on for pages. I will make just a few suggestions, each of which contains bibliographies that will take you as deep into the scholarship as you wish to go. Of course, there is no substitute for reading the primary sources, which are widely available in a number of different translations.

The article on the *Republic* (p. 233 of Volume 1) in *World Philosophy* will provide a more detailed summary of the leading ideas, and the article on Plato in the *Encyclopedia of Philosophy* will provide basic background information. Of the many works on Plato, G. M. A. Grube's *Plato's Thought* (Indianapolis: Hackett Publishing, 1980) is an old standby that provides an excellent introduction to the whole of Plato's philosophy.

Videos

The Cave (10 minutes, produced by McGraw-Hill Films) explores the meaning of Plato's parable. *The Minds of Men* (52 minutes, Films for the Humanities and Sciences) explores the life and ideas of Socrates and Plato and the cultural world of Herodotus and Thucydides. See your Media Services Catalogue for more information.

7.3. Nondualism

Shankara (c. 788–c. 820) is one of the most important figures in Indian philosophy. In his short life he traveled extensively, founded four monasteries, and made major contributions to the development of philosophical and religious ideas. He wrote extensive commentaries interpreting important Hindu scriptures and became the leading advocate for a school of philosophy known as **Advaita** (nondual) **Vedanta.** Shankara preferred to be thought of as a *nondualist* rather than a monist because he taught that ultimate reality is an undifferentiated unity beyond all positive predication. Hence it can only be defined by saying what it is not.

Brahman was the word used by Shankara for the ultimate divine essence of reality. The word **Atman** had been used for the true Self (the real identity behind our individual egos). Shankara thought of the *Atman* as pure consciousness (consciousness per se) and identified it with the *Brahman*. Hence, *Atman* is the word used for the

Brahman "within," and *Brahman* is the word used for the *Atman* "without." But, of course, since they are one and since there is no other absolute reality, ultimately there is no division between within and without. Philosophically Shankara struggled to articulate more precisely what these ideas mean and to understand how they are related. Religiously he sought to discover the way to experience the identity of *Atman* and *Brahman.*

Like Plato, Shankara believed that the more permanent something is, the more real it is. That which is absolutely permanent is absolutely real. Everything else is but an appearance of this eternal reality. The supposed "reality" of the impermanent is nothing but an illusion. We must learn how to discriminate between the permanent and the impermanent if we want to know what is really real.

In order to distinguish things, we need a principle of discrimination, which we can term **sublation.** Sublation is the act of correcting a previous judgment in light of a subsequent one. For example, when I think the shiny surface up ahead on the road is water but decide, as I get closer, that it is only the sun reflecting off the asphalt, I am engaging in an act of sublation and thereby discriminating appearance from reality. Sublatability is the quality a thing has that allows us to correct our judgment about it. If something is sublatable, it must be impermanent. If the "water" I saw up ahead were permanent, when I got closer I would still see water. It would not be a mirage.

Shankara defines *reality* as that which cannot be sublated, *appearance* as that which can be sublated, and *unreality* as neither sublatable nor unsublatable because it does not exist. Armed with these distinctions and the principle of sublation, our task is to examine all the sorts of things we think are real to see if they really are real or just the appearance of what is real.

In the selection from *The Crest-Jewel of Discrimination* which follows, Shankara, speaking as the master, leads a disciple through an examination of various "coverings" in search of the true Self (*Atman*). The master then claims that the *Atman,* which is unsublatable, is the same as the *Brahman,* the really real. It should be noted that some scholars do not believe Shankara is the author of this text. Nevertheless, tradition has attributed it to him and there can be little doubt that it expresses ideas associated with his philosophy, even if he did not write it.

Read the text slowly and carefully, keeping in mind that in order to qualify as really real, something must be permanent and unsublatable. I have added footnotes at key points to explain technical terms. Be sure to read them; they will help.

Reading Questions

1. What does discrimination mean?
2. Why do you think renunciation, tranquillity, self-control, faith, self-surrender, the longing for liberation, and devotion are necessary in order to gain knowledge of the *Atman*?
3. Shankara says all kinds of things about the *Atman* and yet claims that it cannot be defined. Isn't this a contradiction? Why?
4. What is ignorance, and how is it overcome?
5. Why is your body (physical covering) not your true Self?
6. What are the differences among the fool, the intelligent person, and the wise person?
7. Why are the vital covering, the mental covering, and the covering of the intellect not the *Atman*?

8. Do you agree that the "mind of the experiencer creates all the objects which he experiences" while in the waking *and* the dreaming state? Why?

9. How does the master answer the disciple's question, "How, then, can there be an existence which the wise man may realize as one with his Atman?" Do you find the answer convincing? Why?

10. How is the universe related to *Brahman?*

11. If you were in a debate with Shankara, what would be the major objection you would make to his ideas? How do you think he would defend himself?

The Crest-Jewel of Discrimination

SHANKARA

A MAN SHOULD BE intelligent and learned, with great powers of comprehension, and able to overcome doubts by the exercise of his reason. One who has these qualifications is fitted for knowledge of the Atman.

He alone may be considered qualified to seek Brahman who has discrimination, whose mind is turned away from all enjoyments, who possesses tranquillity and the kindred virtues, and who feels a longing for liberation.

In this connection, the sages have spoken of four qualifications for attainment. When these are present, devotion to the Reality will become complete. When they are absent, it will fail.

First is mentioned discrimination between the eternal and the non-eternal. Next comes renunciation of the enjoyment of the fruits of action, here and hereafter. Then come the six treasures of virtue, beginning with tranquillity. And last, certainly, is the longing for liberation.

Brahman is real; the universe is unreal. A firm conviction that this is so is called *discrimination* between the eternal and the noneternal.

Renunciation is the giving-up of all the pleasures of the eyes, the ears, and the other senses, the giving-up of the desire for a physical body as well as for the highest kind of spirit-body of a god.

To detach the mind from all objective things by continually seeing their imperfection, and to direct it steadfastly toward Brahman, its goal—this is called *tranquillity.*

To detach both kinds of sense-organs—those of perception and those of action—from objective things, and to withdraw them to rest in their respective centers—this is called *self-control.* True *mental poise* consists in not letting the mind react to external stimuli.

To endure all kinds of afflictions without rebellion, complaint or lament—this is called *forbearance.*

A firm conviction, based upon intellectual understanding that the teachings of the scriptures and of one's master are true—this is called by the sages the *faith* which leads to realization of the Reality.

To concentrate the intellect repeatedly upon the pure Brahman and to keep it fixed there always—this is called *self-surrender.* This does not mean soothing the mind, like a baby, with idle thoughts.

Longing for liberation is the will to be free

From Shankara's Crest-Jewel of Discrimination with a Garland of Questions and Answers, *translated by Swami Prabhavananda and Christopher Isherwood (New York: New American Library, 1970), pp. 37–39; 52–61; 65–69. Reprinted by permission of Vedanta Press, 1946 Vedanta Pl., Hollywood, CA 90068.*

from the fetters forged by ignorance—beginning with the ego-sense and so on, down to the physical body itself—through the realization of one's true nature.

Even though this longing for liberation may be present in a slight or moderate degree, it will grow intense through the grace of the teacher, and through the practice of renunciation and of virtues such as tranquillity, etc. And it will bear fruit.

When renunciation and the longing for liberation are present to an intense degree within a man, then the practice of tranquillity and the other virtues will bear fruit and lead to the goal.

Where renunciation and longing for liberation are weak, tranquillity and the other virtues are a mere appearance, like the mirage in the desert.

Among all means of liberation, devotion is supreme. To seek earnestly to know one's real nature—this is said to be devotion.

In other words, devotion can be defined as the search for the reality of one's own Atman. The seeker after the reality of the Atman, who possesses the above-mentioned qualifications, should approach an illumined teacher from whom he can learn the way to liberation from all bondage. . . .

Now I shall tell you the nature of the Atman. If you realize it, you will be freed from the bonds of ignorance, and attain liberation.

There is a self-existent Reality, which is the basis of our consciousness of ego. That Reality is the witness of the three states of our consciousness, and is distinct from the five bodily coverings.[1]

That Reality is the knower in all states of consciousness—waking, dreaming and dreamless sleep. It is aware of the presence or absence of the mind and its functions. It is the Atman.

That Reality sees everything by its own light. No one sees it. It gives intelligence to the mind and the intellect, but no one gives it light.

That Reality pervades the universe, but no one penetrates it. It alone shines. The universe shines with its reflected light.

Because of its presence, the body, senses, mind and intellect apply themselves to their respective functions, as though obeying its command.

Its nature is eternal consciousness. It knows all things, from the sense of ego to the body itself. It is the knower of pleasure and pain and of the sense-objects. It knows everything objectively—just as a man knows the objective existence of a jar.

This is the Atman, the Supreme being, the ancient. It never ceases to experience infinite joy. It is always the same. It is consciousness itself. The organs and vital energies function under its command.

Here, within this body, in the pure mind, in the secret chamber of intelligence, in the infinite universe within the heart, the Atman shines in its captivating splendor, like a noonday sun. By its light, the universe is revealed.

It is the knower of the activities of the mind and of the individual man. It is the witness of all the actions of the body, the sense-organs and the vital energy. It seems to be identified with all these, just as fire appears identified with an iron ball. But it neither acts nor is subject to the slightest change.

The Atman is birthless and deathless. It neither grows nor decays. It is unchangeable, eternal. It does not dissolve when the body dissolves. Does the ether cease to exist when the jar that enclosed it is broken?

The Atman is distinct from Maya,[2] the primal cause, and from her effect, the universe. The na-

1. [The five bodily coverings will be discussed later. They are the physical, the vital, the mental, the intellectual, and the covering of bliss. These are called "coverings" because Shankara pictures them as progressively thinner bodies or sheaves (like those dolls within dolls) that cover the *Atman*. This is based on the idea that matter extends from a gross level (the physical body as we think of it) to subtler or finer levels. Notice that things like mind and intellect, which in the West have usually been thought of as immaterial, are here thought of as material (but matter of a finer sort).—Ed.]

2. [*Maya* is sometimes translated as "illusion" and sometimes as "appearance." It refers to the illusions done by magicians and Shankara uses this analogy to indicate the process by which Brahman produces the universe. In general, *Maya* is the impermanent which appears to be real but is not. It stands in contrast to the permanence of *Atman-Brahman,* which is what is truly real.—Ed.]

ture of the Atman is pure consciousness. The Atman reveals this entire universe of mind and matter. It cannot be defined. In and through the various states of consciousness—the waking, the dreaming and the sleeping—it maintains our unbroken awareness of identity. It manifests itself as the witness of the intelligence.

The Mind

With a controlled mind and an intellect which is made pure and tranquil, you must realize the Atman directly, within yourself. Know the Atman as the real I. Thus you cross the shoreless ocean of worldliness, whose waves are birth and death. Live always in the knowledge of identity with Brahman, and be blessed.

Man is in bondage because he mistakes what is non-Atman for his real Self. This is caused by ignorance. Hence follows the misery of birth and death. Through ignorance, man identifies the Atman with the body, taking the perishable for the real. Therefore he nourishes this body, and anoints it, and guards it carefully. He becomes enmeshed in the things of the senses like a caterpillar in the threads of its cocoon.

Deluded by his ignorance, a man mistakes one thing for another. Lack of discernment will cause a man to think that a snake is a piece of rope. When he grasps it in this belief he runs a great risk. The acceptance of the unreal as real constitutes the state of bondage. Pay heed to this, my friend.

The Atman is indivisible, eternal, one without a second. It is eternally made manifest by the power of its own knowledge. Its glories are infinite. The veil of tamas[3] hides the true nature of the Atman, just as an eclipse hides the rays of the sun.

When the pure rays of the Atman are thus concealed, the deluded man identifies himself with his body, which is non-Atman. Then rajas, which has the power of projecting illusory forms, afflicts him sorely. It binds him with chains of lust, anger and the other passions.

His mind becomes perverted. His consciousness of the Atman is swallowed up by the shark of total ignorance. Yielding to the power of rajas, he identifies himself with the many motions and changes of the mind. Therefore he is swept hither and thither, now rising, now sinking, in the boundless ocean of birth and death, whose waters are full of the poison of sense-objects. This is indeed a miserable fate.

The sun's rays bring forth layers of cloud. By them, the sun is concealed; and so it appears that the clouds alone exist. In the same way, the ego, which is brought forth by the Atman, hides the true nature of the Atman; and so it appears that the ego alone exists.

On a stormy day the sun is swallowed up by thick clouds; and these clouds are attacked by sharp, chill blasts of wind. So, when the Atman is enveloped in the thick darkness of tamas, the terrible power of rajas attacks the deluded man with all kinds of sorrows.

Man's bondage is caused by the power of these two—tamas and rajas. Deluded by these, he mistakes the body for the Atman and strays on to the path that leads to death and rebirth.

Man's life in this relative world may be compared to a tree. Tamas is the seed. Identification of the Atman with the body is its sprouting forth. The cravings are its leaves. Work is its sap. The body is its trunk. The vital forces are its branches. The sense-organs are its twigs. The sense-objects are its flowers. Its fruits are the sufferings caused by various actions. The individual man is the bird who eats the fruit of the tree of life.

The Atman's bondage to the non-Atman springs from ignorance. It has no external cause. It is said to be beginningless. It will continue indefinitely until a man becomes enlightened. As long as a man remains in this bondage it subjects him to a long train of miseries—birth, death, sickness, decrepitude, and so forth.

This bondage cannot be broken by weapons, or by wind, or by fire, or by millions of acts. Nothing but the sharp sword of knowledge can

---

3. [*Tamas* are one of the three *gunas* that make up all material things. *Gunas* are qualities. In ancient Hindu cosmology it was thought that everything material is made up of some combination or mixture of the *gunas*. *Tamas* is the quality of stupor, laziness, stupidity, heaviness, and inaction in general. *Rajas,* another *guna,* is the active principle and hence the opposite of *tamas. Sattva,* the third *guna,* is associated with the pure, the fine, and the calm.—Ed.]

cut through this bondage. It is forged by discrimination and made keen by purity of heart, through divine grace.

A man must faithfully and devotedly fulfill the duties of life as the scriptures prescribe. This purifies his heart. A man whose heart is pure realizes the supreme Atman. Thereby he destroys his bondage to the world, root and all.

Wrapped in its five coverings, beginning with the physical, which are the products of its own Maya, the Atman remains hidden, as the water of a pond is hidden by a veil of scum.

When the scum is removed, the pure water is clearly seen. It takes away a man's thirst, cools him immediately and makes him happy.

When all the five coverings are removed, the pure Atman is revealed. It is revealed as God dwelling within; as unending, unalloyed bliss; as the supreme and self-luminous Being.

The wise man who seeks liberation from bondage must discriminate between Atman and non-Atman. In this way, he can realize the Atman, which is Infinite Being, Infinite Wisdom and Infinite Love. Thus he finds happiness.

The Atman dwells within, free from attachment and beyond all action. A man must separate this Atman from every object of experience, as a stalk of grass is separated from its enveloping sheath. Then he must dissolve into the Atman all those appearances which make up the world of name and form. He is indeed a free soul who can remain thus absorbed in the Atman alone.

The Body

This body is the "physical covering." Food made its birth possible; on food it lives; without food it must die. It consists of cuticle, skin, flesh, blood, bone and water. It cannot be the Atman, the ever-pure, the self-existent.

It did not exist before birth, it will not exist after death. It exists for a short while only, in the interim between them. Its very nature is transient, and subject to change. It is a compound, not an element. Its vitality is only a reflection. It is a sense-object, which can be perceived, like a jar. How can it be the Atman—the experiencer of all experiences?

The body consists of arms, legs and other limbs. It is not the Atman—for when some of these limbs have been cut off, a man may continue to live and function through his remaining organs. The body is controlled by another. It cannot be the Atman, the controller.

The Atman watches the body, with its various characteristics, actions and states of growth. That this Atman, which is the abiding reality, is of another nature than the body, must be self-evident.

The body is a bundle of bones held together by flesh. It is very dirty and full of filth. The body can never be the same as the self-existent Atman, the knower. The nature of the Atman is quite different from that of the body.

It is the ignorant man who identifies himself with the body, which is compounded of skin, flesh, fat, bone and filth. The man of spiritual discrimination knows the Atman, his true being, the one supreme reality, as distinct from the body.

The fool thinks, "I am the body." The intelligent man thinks, "I am an individual soul united with the body." But the wise man, in the greatness of his knowledge and spiritual discrimination, sees the Atman as reality and thinks, "I am Brahman."

O fool, stop identifying yourself with this lump of skin, flesh, fat, bones and filth. Identify yourself with Brahman, the Absolute, the Atman in all beings. That is how you can attain the supreme peace.

The intelligent man may be learned in Vedanta and the moral laws. But there is not the least hope of his liberation until he stops mistakenly identifying himself with the body and the sense-organs. This identification is caused by delusion.

You never identify yourself with the shadow cast by your body, or with its reflection, or with the body you see in a dream or in your imagination. Therefore you should not identify yourself with this living body, either.

Those who live in ignorance identify the body with the Atman. This ignorance is the root-cause of birth, death and rebirth. Therefore you must strive earnestly to destroy it. When your heart is free from this ignorance, there will no longer be any possibility of your rebirth. You will reach immortality.

That covering of the Atman which is called "the vital covering" is made up of the vital force and the five organs of action. The body is called "the physical covering." It comes to life when it is enveloped by the vital covering. It is thus that the body engages in action.

This vital covering is not the Atman—for it is merely composed of the vital airs. Air-like, it enters and leaves the body. It does not know what is good or bad for itself, or for others. It is always dependent upon the Atman.

Purification

The mind, together with the organs of perception, forms the "mental covering." It causes the sense of "I" and "mine." It also causes us to discern objects. It is endowed with the power and faculty of differentiating objects by giving them various names. It is manifest, enveloping the "vital covering."

The mental covering may be compared to the sacrificial fire. It is fed by the fuel of many desires. The five organs of perception serve as priests. Objects of desire are poured upon it like a continuous stream of oblations. Thus it is that this phenomenal universe is brought forth.

Ignorance is nowhere, except in the mind. The mind is filled with ignorance, and this causes the bondage of birth and death. When, in the enlightenment of the Atman, a man transcends the mind, the phenomenal universe disappears from him. When a man lives in the domain of mental ignorance, the phenomenal universe exists for him.

In dream, the mind is emptied of the objective universe, but it creates by its own power a complete universe of subject and object. The waking state is only a prolonged dream. The phenomenal universe exists in the mind.

In dreamless sleep, when the mind does not function, nothing exists. This is our universal experience. Man seems to be in bondage to birth and death. This is a fictitious creation of the mind, not a reality.

The wind collects the clouds, and the wind drives them away again. Mind creates bondage, and mind also removes bondage.

The mind creates attachment to the body and the things of this world. Thus it binds a man, as a beast is tied by a rope. But it is also the mind which creates in a man an utter distaste for sense-objects, as if for poison. Thus it frees him from his bondage.

The mind, therefore, is the cause of man's bondage and also of his liberation. It causes bondage when it is darkened by rajas. It causes liberation when it is freed from rajas and tamas, and made pure.

If discrimination and dispassion are practiced, to the exclusion of everything else, the mind will become pure and move toward liberation. Therefore the wise man who seeks liberation must develop both these qualities within himself.

That terrible tiger called an impure mind prowls in the forest of the sense-objects. The wise man who seeks liberation must not go there.

The mind of the experiencer creates all the objects which he experiences, while in the waking or the dreaming state. Ceaselessly, it creates the differences in men's bodies, color, social condition and race. It creates the variations of the gunas. It creates desires, actions and the fruits of actions.

Man is pure spirit, free from attachment. The mind deludes him. It binds him with the bonds of the body, the sense-organs and the life-breath. It creates in him the sense of "I" and "mine." It makes him wander endlessly among the fruits of the actions it has caused.

The error of identifying Atman with non-Atman is the cause of man's birth, death and rebirth. This false identification is created by the mind. Therefore, it is the mind that causes the misery of birth, death and rebirth for the man who has no discrimination and is tainted by rajas and tamas.

Therefore the wise, who know Reality, have declared that the mind is full of ignorance. Because of this ignorance, all the creatures of the universe are swept helplessly hither and thither, like masses of cloud before the wind.

Therefore, the seeker after liberation must work carefully to purify the mind. When the mind has been made pure, liberation is as easy to grasp as the fruit which lies in the palm of your hand.

Seek earnestly for liberation, and your lust for

sense-objects will be rooted out. Practice detachment toward all actions. Have faith in the Reality. Devote yourself to the practice of spiritual disciplines, such as hearing the word of Brahman, reasoning and meditating upon it. Thus the mind will be freed from the evil of rajas.

The "mental covering," therefore, cannot be the Atman. It has a beginning and an end, and is subject to change. It is the abode of pain. It is an object of experience. The seer cannot be the thing which is seen.

The Covering of Intellect

The discriminating faculty with its powers of intelligence, together with the organs of perception, is known as the "covering of intellect." To be the doer is its distinguishing characteristic. It is the cause of man's birth, death and rebirth.

The power of intelligence that is in the "covering of intellect" is a reflection of the Atman, the pure consciousness. The "covering of intellect" is an effect of Maya. It possesses the faculty of knowing and acting. It always identifies itself entirely with the body, sense-organs, etc.

It has no beginning. It is characterized by its sense of ego. It constitutes the individual man. It is the initiator of all actions and undertakings. Impelled by the tendencies and impressions formed in previous births, it performs virtuous or sinful actions and experiences their results.

It gathers experiences by wandering through many wombs of higher or lower degree. The states of waking and dreaming belong to this "covering of intellect." It experiences joy and sorrow.

Because of its sense of "I" and "mine," it constantly identifies itself with the body, and the physical states, and with the duties pertaining to the different stages and orders of life. This "covering of intellect" shines with a bright light because of its proximity to the shining Atman. It is a garment of the Atman, but man identifies himself with it and wanders around the circle of birth, death and rebirth because of his delusion.

The Atman, which is pure consciousness, is the light that shines in the shrine of the heart, the center of all vital force. It is immutable, but it becomes the "doer" and "experiencer" when it is mistakenly identified with the "covering of intellect."

The Atman assumes the limitations of the "covering of intellect" because it is mistakenly identified with that covering, which is totally different from itself. This man, who is the Atman, regards himself as being separate from it, and from Brahman, who is the one Atman in all creatures. An ignorant man, likewise, may regard a jar as being different from the clay of which it was made.

By its nature, the Atman is forever unchanging and perfect. But it assumes the character and nature of its coverings because it is mistakenly identified with them. Although fire is formless, it will assume the form of red-hot iron. . . .

Atman Is Brahman

The Disciple: Master, if we reject these five coverings as unreal, it seems to me that nothing remains but the void. How, then, can there be an existence which the wise man may realize as one with his Atman?

The Master: That is a good question, O prudent one. Your argument is clever. Nevertheless, there must be an existence, a reality, which perceives the ego-sense and the coverings and is also aware of the void which is their absence. This reality by itself remains unperceived. Sharpen your discrimination that you may know this Atman, which is the knower.

He who experiences is conscious of himself. Without an experiencer, there can be no self-consciousness.

The Atman is its own witness, since it is conscious of itself. The Atman is no other than Brahman.

The Atman is pure consciousness, clearly manifest as underlying the states of waking, dreaming and dreamless sleep. It is inwardly experienced as unbroken consciousness, the consciousness that I am I. It is the unchanging witness that experiences the ego, the intellect and the rest, with their various forms and changes. It is realized within one's own heart as existence, knowledge and bliss absolute. Realize this Atman within the shrine of your own heart.

The fool sees the reflection of the sun in the water of a jar, and thinks it is the sun. Man in the ignorance of his delusion sees the reflection of Pure Consciousness upon the coverings, and mistakes it for the real I.

In order to look at the sun, you must turn away from the jar, the water, and the sun's reflection in the water. The wise know that these three are only revealed by the reflection of the self-luminous sun. They are not the sun itself.

The body, the covering of intellect, the reflection of consciousness upon it—none of these is the Atman. The Atman is the witness, infinite consciousness, revealer of all things but distinct from all, no matter whether they be gross or subtle. It is the eternal reality, omnipresent, all-pervading, the subtlest of all subtleties. It has neither inside nor outside. It is the real I, hidden in the shrine of the heart. Realize fully the truth of the Atman. Be free from evil and impurity, and you shall pass beyond death.

Know the Atman, transcend all sorrows, and reach the fountain of joy. Be illumined by this knowledge, and you have nothing to fear. If you wish to find liberation, there is no other way of breaking the bonds of rebirth.

What can break the bondage and misery of this world? The knowledge that the Atman is Brahman. Then it is that you realize Him who is one without a second, and who is the absolute bliss.

Realize Brahman, and there will be no more returning to this world—the home of all sorrows. You must realize absolutely that the Atman is Brahman.

Then you will win Brahman for ever. He is the truth. He is existence and knowledge. He is absolute. He is pure and self-existent. He is eternal, unending joy. He is none other than the Atman.

The Atman is one with Brahman: this is the highest truth. Brahman alone is real. There is

none but He. When He is known as the supreme reality there is no other existence but Brahman.

The Universe

Brahman is the reality—the one existence, absolutely independent of human thought or idea. Because of the ignorance of our human minds, the universe seems to be composed of diverse forms. It is Brahman alone.

A jar made of clay is not other than clay. It is clay essentially. The form of the jar has no independent existence. What, then, is the jar? Merely an invented name!

The form of the jar can never be perceived apart from the clay. What, then, is the jar? An appearance! The reality is the clay itself.

This universe is an effect of Brahman. It can never be anything else but Brahman. Apart from Brahman, it does not exist. There is nothing beside Him. He who says that this universe has an independent existence is still suffering from delusion. He is like a man talking in his sleep.

"The universe is Brahman"—so says the great seer of the Atharva Veda. The universe, therefore, is nothing but Brahman. It is superimposed upon Him. It has no separate existence, apart from its ground.

If the universe, as we perceive it, were real, knowledge of the Atman would not put an end to our delusion. The scriptures would be untrue. The revelations of the Divine Incarnations would make no sense. These alternatives cannot be considered either desirable or beneficial by any thinking person.

Sri Krishna, the Incarnate Lord, who knows the secret of all truths, says in the Gita: "Although I am not within any creature, all creatures exist within me. I do not mean that they exist within me physically. That is my divine mystery. My Being sustains all creatures and brings them to birth, but has no physical contact with them."

If this universe were real, we should continue to perceive it in deep sleep. But we perceive nothing then. Therefore it is unreal, like our dreams.

The universe does not exist apart from the Atman. Our perception of it as having an independent existence is false, like our perception of blueness in the sky. How can a superimposed attribute have any existence, apart from its substratum? It is only our delusion which causes this misconception of the underlying reality.

No matter what a deluded man may think he is perceiving, he is really seeing Brahman and nothing else but Brahman. He sees mother-of-pearl and imagines that it is silver. He sees Brahman and imagines that it is the universe. But this universe, which is superimposed upon Brahman, is nothing but a name.

I Am Brahman

Brahman is supreme. He is the reality—the one without a second. He is pure consciousness, free from any taint. He is tranquillity itself. He has neither beginning nor end. He does not change. He is joy for ever.

He transcends the appearance of the manifold, created by Maya. He is eternal, for ever beyond reach of pain, not to be divided, not to be measured, without form, without name, undifferentiated, immutable. He shines with His own light. He is everything that can be experienced in this universe.

The illumined seers know Him as the uttermost reality, infinite, absolute, without parts—the pure consciousness. In Him they find that knower, knowledge and known have become one.

They know Him as the reality which can neither be cast aside (since He is ever-present within the human soul) nor grasped (since He is beyond the power of mind and speech). They know Him immeasurable, beginningless, endless, supreme in glory. They realize the truth: "I am Brahman."

Suggestions for Further Reading

Ninian Smart's article "Shankara" in Volume 7 of *The Encyclopedia of Philosophy* is a good starting place. Also, Volume 2 of *World Philosophy* (pp. 600ff.) will provide background information and a summary of the major ideas of the *Crest-Jewel*.

Chapter 7 of John M. Koller's *Oriental Philosophies* will take you deeper into the issues. For a more detailed account see Chapter 9 of R. Puligandla's *Fundamentals of Indian Philosophy* (New York: Abingdon Press, 1975). Eliot Deutsch's *Advaita Vedanta: A Philosophical Reconstruction* (Honolulu: East-West Center Press, 1966) is a real jewel, managing to make sense out of complicated arguments in a way the beginning student can grasp.

Video

Absorption in Brahman: The Story of Hinduism (30 minutes, produced by Video Outlines) summarizes the religious viewpoints of ancient India. See your Media Services Catalogue for more information.

7.4. Subjective Idealism

George Berkeley was born in 1685 in Kilkenny, Ireland. At age 15 he went to Trinity College, Dublin, where he studied classics, mathematics, and the then new and controversial physics of Newton. In 1704, after graduation, he became a Fellow of his college and was ordained to the ministry. By the age of 25 he had worked out the basic ideas of his philosophy in reaction to the philosophy of John Locke (1632–1704). He saw himself as a defender of common sense in a skeptical age and a defender of religion against a science that pictured the universe as a vast machine operating according to blind natural laws. Berkeley lived in the United States for awhile, married in 1728, and was appointed Bishop of Cloyne in south Ireland in 1734. He died at Oxford in 1753 while visiting his son.

Bishop Berkeley's metaphysics is called **subjective idealism.** His views constitute a variety of idealism because he argued that reality consists of finite or created minds, an infinite mind (God), and the ideas (thoughts, feelings, and sensations) these minds have. All of these things are immaterial. This idealism is termed "subjective" because physical objects (which are nothing more than complexes of ideas) do not exist apart from some subject (mind) who perceives them. This kind of idealism stands in contrast to **objective idealism,** which holds that although reality is mental, it does exist independently of the human knower because it is a manifestation of an absolute mind. Objective idealism is usually monistic (or at least nondualistic), maintaining that there is one absolute mind and the universe is a manifestation of it. Berkeley's subjective idealism, while nondualistic in the sense of asserting that all reality is mental or immaterial, is pluralistic in the sense that there are many finite minds independent of God's mind.

The denial of the objective existence of physical objects made out of matter seems so utterly fantastic that one wonders how Berkeley could view himself as a champion of common sense. Indeed, when he published his views in 1710 many thought him insane. However, Berkeley's rejection of matter seems more plausible if we understand the historical circumstances that led him to that conclusion. The hypothesis that physical objects do not exist independent of the mind seems more reasonable if it can be shown to be the only plausible alternative.

We must return, for a moment, to Plato. Plato was a dualist, arguing that reality is twofold: material and immaterial. This dualism was revived and given a modern formulation by the French philosopher René Descartes (sounds like "day kart") in the early seventeenth century (see Section 8.2). Descartes argued for a position known as **indirect or representational realism.** His position is called **realism** because he believed objects can exist apart from any knower or mind. It is called "indirect or representational" because he also argued that sensations indirectly represent objects that exist outside the mind. This sort of realism stands in contrast to **direct or naive realism** which holds that we are directly in touch with real objects via our senses.

John Locke, an English philosopher, combined Descartes's realism with **empiricism.** Empiricism is the view that knowledge derives from sense experience and that knowledge claims are tested by reference to sense experience. If empiricism is true, then all we can know *directly* or immediately are the ideas or sensations that occur in our minds. Although these ideas are themselves mental, they resemble and are caused by nonmental or physical objects existing outside the mind, or so the indirect realist claims. Hence, according to Locke, there are two substances: *immaterial substances* or minds, which have ideas caused by *material substances.*

This distinction between ideas and the objects they represent was accompanied by a distinction between **primary** and **secondary qualities.** Primary qualities are characteristics that constitute the properties of physical objects. Locke believed them to be extension, figure, motion, rest, solidity, and number. Secondary qualities are characteristics of our *sensation* of physical objects: color, flavor, odor, texture, sound, hot, cold, and the like. The theory of indirect realism combined with the distinction between secondary and primary qualities allowed Locke to explain, for example, how it is that an object looks a different color in different light, or feels cold to one person but hot to another. Direct realism was unable to explain such common experiences, because if we are *directly* in touch with real physical objects via our senses, an object would have to be both blue and green or hot and cold if it were so experienced. But if we are *indirectly* in touch with objects, and if color and heat sensation are secondary qualities, then we can say that the object *appears* both blue and green or feels both hot and cold, but in fact it is simply in a certain state of motion.

Berkeley pondered Locke's ideas as an undergraduate and found them nonsensical. He felt that since all we can really know are immaterial ideas, there is no way of knowing that they represent anything at all outside the mind. To know that this picture is a likeness of my friend, I can look at my friend and compare that image to the picture image. But I cannot do that with sensations because I can never get outside of sensations to compare them with the physical objects that supposedly caused them.

Locke, Berkeley thought, has created a duplex world. We have a world of physical objects duplicated by a world of mental images. It also turns out that there are problems involved in trying to explain how physical objects can cause nonphysical sensations. Why not just simplify things by getting rid of physical objects? Isn't it true that we only know for sure that ideas or sensations exist, but we have no way of knowing for sure that physical objects do? What we *do* know is that what we call a physical object is for us a bundle of sensations (colors, odors, flavors, etc.). Since sensations cannot exist without being sensed, why not say the obvious, that nothing can exist without being experienced. "*To be is to be perceived.*" We don't really need the materialistic hypothesis—or so Berkeley argued. But it is now time to turn to the details of that argument.

Reading Questions

1. Give an example of each of the three kinds of ideas that constitute, according to Berkeley, the objects of human knowledge.

2. What is the difference between ideas and the mind?

3. Why does Berkeley assert that the existence (*esse*) of the objects of knowledge consists in their being perceived (*percipi*)?

4. How would Berkeley answer that old question, "If a tree fell in the forest and no one was there to hear it, would it make a sound?"

5. How does Berkeley respond to the claim that there are things that exist apart from minds (unthinking or material substances), which our ideas copy or resemble? Do you find his response convincing? Why or why not?

6. Why does Berkeley reject the distinction between primary and secondary qualities, and why does he claim that the very notion of matter is contradictory?

7. In Sections 16–20, Berkeley advances a series of arguments against the idea that material objects exist outside our minds. Briefly summarize the main ideas of these arguments.

8. Do you find any of these arguments convincing? If so, which ones and why? If you find them all unconvincing, why?

9. If you got into a debate with Berkeley, what sort of objections would you raise against his claim that matter does not exist? How do you think he would respond to your objections?

10. Formulate and answer a question comparing Berkeley's views with any of the other metaphysical views you have studied in this chapter. How are they the same and how are they different?

The Principles of Human Knowledge

GEORGE BERKELEY

Part I

1. IT IS EVIDENT to anyone who takes a survey of the objects of human knowledge, that they are either *ideas* actually imprinted on the senses; or else such as are perceived by attending to the passions and operations of the mind; or lastly, *ideas* formed by help of memory and imagination— either compounding, dividing, or barely representing those originally perceived in the aforesaid ways.—By sight I have the ideas of light and colors, with their several degrees and variations. By touch I perceive hard and soft, heat and cold, motion and resistance, and of all these more and less either as to quantity or degree. Smelling furnishes me with odors; the palate with tastes; and hearing conveys sounds to the mind in all their variety of tone and composition.—And as several of these are observed to accompany each other, they come to be marked by one name, and so to be reputed as one THING. Thus, for example, a certain color, taste, smell, figure and consistence having been observed to go together, are accounted one distinct thing, signified by the name *apple;* other collections of ideas constitute a stone, a tree, a book, and the like sensible things— which as they are pleasing or disagreeable excite the passions of love, hatred, joy, grief, and so forth.

2. But, besides all that endless variety of ideas or objects of knowledge, there is likewise something which knows or perceives them; and exercises divers operations, as willing, imagining, remembering, about them. This perceiving, active being is what I call MIND, SPIRIT, SOUL, or MYSELF. By which words I do not denote any one of my ideas, but a thing entirely distinct from them, wherein they exist, or, which is the same

thing, whereby they are perceived—for the existence of an idea consists in being perceived.

3. That neither our thoughts, nor passions, nor ideas formed by the imagination, exist without the mind, is what everybody will allow.— And to me it is no less evident that the various SENSATIONS, or *ideas imprinted on the sense,* however blended or combined together (that is, whatever *objects* they compose), cannot exist otherwise than in a mind perceiving them—I think an intuitive knowledge may be obtained of this by anyone that shall attend to *what is meant by the term exist when applied to sensible things.* The table I write on I say exists, that is, I see and feel it; and if I were out of my study I should say it existed—meaning thereby that if I was in my study I might perceive it, or that some other spirit actually does perceive it. There was an odor, that is, it was smelt; there was a sound, that is, it was heard; a color or figure, and it was perceived by sight or touch. This is all that I can understand by these and the like expressions.—For as to what is said of the absolute existence of unthinking things without any relation to their being perceived, that is to me perfectly unintelligible. Their *esse* is *percipi,* nor is it possible they should have any existence out of the minds or thinking things which perceive them.

4. It is indeed an opinion strangely prevailing amongst men, that houses, mountains, rivers, and in a word all sensible objects, have an existence, natural or real, distinct from their being perceived by the understanding. But, with how great an assurance and acquiescence soever this principle may be entertained in the world, yet whoever shall find in his heart to call it in question may, if I mistake not, perceive it to involve a manifest contradiction. For, what are the

From George Berkeley, A Treatise Concerning the Principles of Human Knowledge *(Dublin, 1710), Sections 1–10; 14–20.*

forementioned objects but the things we perceive by sense? and what do we perceive besides our own ideas or sensations? and is it not plainly repugnant that any one of *these,* or any combination of them, should exist unperceived?

5. If we thoroughly examine this tenet it will, perhaps, be found at bottom to depend on the doctrine of *abstract ideas.* For can there be a nicer strain of abstraction than to distinguish the *existence* of sensible objects from their *being perceived,* so as to conceive them existing unperceived? Light and colors, heat and cold, extension and figures—in a word the things we see and feel—what are they but so many sensations, notions, ideas, or impressions on the sense? and is it possible to separate, even in thought, any of these from perception? For my part, I might as easily divide a thing from itself. I may, indeed, divide in my thoughts, or conceive apart from each other, those things which, perhaps, I never perceived by sense so divided. Thus, I imagine the trunk of a human body without the limbs, or conceive the smell of a rose without thinking on the rose itself. So far, I will not deny, I can abstract—if that may properly be called *abstraction* which extends only to the conceiving separately such objects as it is possible may really exist or be actually perceived asunder. But my conceiving or imagining power does not extend beyond the possibility of real existence or perception. Hence, as it is impossible for me to see or feel anything without an actual sensation of that thing, so is it impossible for me to conceive in my thoughts any sensible thing or object distinct from the sensation or perception of it.

6. Some truths there are so near and obvious to the mind that a man need only open his eyes to see them. Such I take this important one to be, viz. that all the choir of heaven and furniture of the earth, in a word all those bodies which compose the mighty frame of the world, have not any subsistence without a mind—that their *being* is *to be perceived or known;* that consequently so long as they are not actually perceived by me, or do not exist in my mind or that of any other created spirit, they must either have no existence at all, or else subsist in the mind of some

Eternal Spirit—it being perfectly unintelligible, and involving all the absurdity of abstraction, to attribute to any single part of them an existence independent of a spirit. To be convinced of which, the reader need only reflect, and try to separate in his own thoughts the *being* of a sensible thing from its *being perceived.*

7. From what has been said it is evident there is not any other Substance than SPIRIT, or *that which perceives.* But, for the fuller demonstration of this point, let it be considered the sensible qualities are color, figure, motion, smell, taste, etc., *i.e.,* the ideas perceived by sense. Now, for an idea to exist in an unperceiving thing is a manifest contradiction; for to have an idea is all one as to perceive; that therefore wherein color, figure, etc. exist must perceive them; hence it is clear there can be no unthinking substance or *substratum* of those ideas.

8. But, say you, though the ideas themselves do not exist without the mind, yet there may be things like them, whereof they are copies or resemblances, which things exist without the mind in an unthinking substance. I answer, an idea can be like nothing but an idea; a color or figure can be like nothing but another color or figure. If we look but never so little into our own thoughts, we shall find it impossible for us to conceive a likeness except only between our ideas. Again, I ask whether those supposed originals or external things, of which our ideas are the pictures or representations, be themselves perceivable or no? If they are, then they are ideas and we have gained our point; but if you say they are not, I appeal to anyone whether it be sense to assert a color is like something which is invisible; hard or soft, like something which is intangible; and so of the rest.

9. Some there are who make a distinction betwixt *primary* and *secondary* qualities. By the former they mean extension, figure, motion, rest, solidity or impenetrability, and number; by the latter they denote all other sensible qualities, as colors, sounds, tastes, and so forth. The ideas we have of these they acknowledge not to be the resemblances of anything existing without the mind, or unperceived, but they will have our

ideas of the primary qualities to be patterns or images of things which exist without the mind, in an unthinking substance which they call *matter.* By *matter,* therefore, we are to understand an inert, senseless substance, in which extension, figure, and motion do actually subsist. But it is evident, from what we have already shown, that extension, figure, and motion are only ideas existing in the mind, and that an idea can be like nothing but another idea, and that consequently neither they nor their archetypes can exist in an unperceiving substance. Hence, it is plain that the very notion of what is called *matter* or *corporeal substance,* involves a contradiction in it.

10. They who assert that figure, motion, and the rest of the primary or original qualities do exist without the mind in unthinking substances, do at the same time acknowledge that colors, sounds, heat, cold, and such like secondary qualities, do not—which they tell us are sensations existing in the mind alone, that depend on and are occasioned by the different size, texture, and motion of the minute particles of matter. This they take for an undoubted truth, which they can demonstrate beyond all exception. Now, if it be certain that those original qualities are inseparably united with the other sensible qualities, and not, even in thought, capable of being abstracted from them, it plainly follows that they exist only in the mind. But I desire any one to reflect and try whether he can, by any abstraction of thought, conceive the extension and motion of a body without all other sensible qualities. For my own part, I see evidently that it is not in my power to frame an idea of a body extended and moving, but I must withal give it some color or other sensible quality which is acknowledged to exist only in the mind. In short, extension, figure, and motion, abstracted from all other qualities, are inconceivable. Where therefore the other sensible qualities are, there must these be also, to wit, in the mind and nowhere else. . . .

14. I shall further add, that, after the same manner as modern philosophers prove certain sensible qualities to have no existence in matter, or without the mind, the same thing may be likewise proved of all other sensible qualities whatsoever. Thus, for instance, it is said that heat and cold are affections only of the mind, and not at all patterns of real beings, existing in the corporeal substances which excite them, for [the reason] that the same body which appears cold to one hand seems warm to another. Now, why may we not as well argue that figure and extension are not patterns or resemblances of qualities existing in matter, because to the same eye at different stations, or eyes of a different texture at the same station, they appear various, and cannot therefore be the images of anything settled and determinate without the mind? Again, it is proved that sweetness is not really in the sapid [tasty] thing, because the thing remaining unaltered the sweetness is changed into bitter, as in case of a fever or otherwise vitiated palate. Is it not as reasonable to say that motion is not without the mind, since if the succession of ideas in the mind become swifter, the motion, it is acknowledged, shall appear slower without any alteration in any external object?

15. In short, let any one consider those arguments which are thought manifestly to prove that colors and tastes exist only in the mind, and he shall find they may with equal force be brought to prove the same thing of extension, figure, and motion. Though it must be confessed this method of arguing does not so much prove that there is no extension or color in an outward object, as that we do not know by sense which is the true extension or color of the object. But the arguments foregoing plainly show it to be impossible that any color or extension at all, or other sensible quality whatsoever, should exist in an unthinking subject without the mind, or in truth, that there should be any such thing as an outward object.

16. But let us examine a little the received opinion.—It is said extension is a mode or accident of Matter, and that Matter is the *substratum* that supports it. Now I desire that you would explain to me what is meant by Matter's *supporting* extension. Say you, I have no idea of Matter and therefore cannot explain it. I answer, though you have no positive, yet, if you have any meaning at all, you must at least have a relative idea of Mat-

ter; though you know not what it is, yet you must be supposed to know what relation it bears to accidents, and what is meant by its supporting them. It is evident "support" cannot here be taken in its usual or literal sense—as when we say that pillars support a building; in what sense therefore must it be taken?

17. If we inquire into what the most accurate philosophers declare themselves to mean by *material substance,* we shall find them acknowledge they have no other meaning annexed to those sounds but the idea of *being in general,* together with the relative notion of its *supporting accidents.* The general idea of Being appeareth to me the most abstract and incomprehensible of all other; and as for its supporting accidents, this, as we have just now observed, cannot be understood in the common sense of those words; it must therefore be taken in some other sense, but what that is they do not explain. So that when I consider the two parts or branches which make the signification of the words *material substance,* I am convinced there is no distinct meaning annexed to them. But why should we trouble ourselves any further, in discussing this material *substratum* or "support" of figure, and motion, and other sensible qualities? Does it not suppose *they* have an existence without the mind? And is not this a direct repugnancy, and altogether inconceivable?

18. But, though it were possible that solid, figured, moveable *substances* may exist without the mind, corresponding to the ideas we have of bodies, yet how is it possible for us to know this? Either we must know it by Sense or by Reason.— As for our senses, by them we have the knowledge only of our sensations, ideas, or those things that are immediately perceived by sense, call them what you will: but they do not inform us that things exist without the mind, or unperceived, like to those which are perceived. This the Materialists themselves acknowledge.—It remains therefore that if we have any knowledge at all of external things, it must be by Reason inferring their existence from what is immediately perceived by sense. But what reason can induce us

to believe the existence of bodies without the mind, from what we perceive, since the very patrons of Matter themselves do not pretend there is any *necessary* connection betwixt them and our ideas? I say it is granted on all hands—and what happens in dreams, frenzies, and the like, puts it beyond dispute—that it is possible we might be affected with all the ideas we have now, though there were no bodies existing without resembling them. Hence, it is evident the supposition of external bodies is not necessary for producing our ideas; since it is granted they are produced sometimes, and might possibly be produced always in the same order we see them in at present, without their concurrence.

19. But, though we might possibly have all our sensations without them, yet perhaps it may be thought easier to conceive and explain the manner of their production, by supposing external bodies in their likeness rather than otherwise; and so it might be at least probable there are such things as bodies that excite their ideas in our minds. But neither can this be said; for, though we give the materialists their external bodies, they by their own confession are never the nearer knowing *how* our ideas are produced; since they own themselves unable to comprehend in what manner body can act upon spirit, or how it is possible it should imprint any idea in the mind. Hence it is evident the production of ideas or sensations in our minds can be no reason why we should suppose Matter or corporeal substances, since *that* is acknowledged to remain equally inexplicable with or without this supposition. If therefore it were possible for bodies to exist without the mind, yet to hold they do so must needs be a very precarious opinion; since it is to suppose, without any reason at all, that God has created innumerable beings that are entirely useless, and serve to no manner of purpose.

20. In short, if there were external bodies, it is impossible we should ever come to know it; and if there were not, we might have the very same reasons to think there were that we have now. Suppose—what no one can deny possible— an intelligence *without the help of external bodies,*

to be affected with the same train of sensations or ideas that you are, imprinted in the same order and with like vividness in his mind. I ask whether that intelligence hath not all the reason to believe the existence of corporeal substances, represented by his ideas, and exciting them in his mind, that you can possibly have for believing the same thing? Of this there can be no question—which one consideration were enough to make any reasonable person suspect the strength of whatever arguments he may think himself to have, for the existence of bodies without the mind.

Suggestions for Further Reading

The article "Berkeley, George" in volume 1 of *The Encyclopedia of Philosophy* will prove a good starting point for those who wish to pursue Berkeley's philosophy. Chapter 5 in William H. Brenner's *Elements of Modern Philosophy: Descartes Through Kant* (Englewood Cliffs, NJ: Prentice-Hall, 1989) also provides a good overview for the beginner.

G. J. Warnock's introduction of Berkeley's *The Principles of Human Knowledge* (Cleveland: World Publishing Company, 1963) provides excellent background information. See volume 2 of *World Philosophy* for a summary and interpretation of the main ideas of Berkeley's *Principles* as well as a guide to the secondary literature.

7.5. Materialism

Hugh Elliot (1881–1930) was an editor of the *Annual Register* in England and a champion of modern science. A student and biographer of Herbert Spencer, a famous philosopher of evolution, Elliot firmly believed that the genius of modern science was its ability to explain all of reality in materialistic terms. He argued that modern science holds the key to solving age old metaphysical questions.

Elliot invokes the authority of modern science to support his materialistic metaphysics. He asserts that the physical sciences imply a materialistic viewpoint. He agrees with Berkeley's subjective idealism up to a point. All knowledge, he concedes, is derived from sense experience. But unlike Berkeley, Elliot affirms the existence of matter and denies that the mind, understood as something immaterial, constitutes any sort of reality above and beyond the physical.

Part of Elliot's argument hinges on the principle known as **Occam's razor,** "Entities should not be multiplied beyond necessity" (*entia non sunt multiplicanda præter necessitatem*). In other words, you should not posit the existence of more things than you need in order to explain some event. Elliot argues that all events, even so-called mental events, can be explained materialistically. We do not need to posit some immaterial entity called "mind" in order to explain our experiences.

Reading Questions

1. What are the main points Elliot makes?
2. Are Elliot's arguments adequate to support his conclusions?
3. Formulate a critical question about Elliot's argument and answer it.
4. How would Elliot answer the question, "What is really real"?

Modern Science and Materialism

HUGH ELLIOT

WHEN WE THUS LOOK out on Nature with a philosophic eye, what is it that we behold? The Universe is made up of vast aggregates of matter, moving about in various directions, emitting light and heat, and displaying other physical manifestations. Nothing, we notice, appears to be still; while we look, there is no single particle of matter that has remained in the same position with regard to other particles, nor, out of the great aggregates of matter composing the various stars and nebulae, is there any which remains even for a moment just exactly what or where it was. In other words, we see that all things are in a state of change or flux; nothing remains unaltered for an instant. It is a moving and changing Universe with which we have to do.

In the next place, all that we behold may, as a first step, be classified into two or three categories of phenomena. Firstly (pending further analysis), there is what we call *matter*. This comprises all the *objects* which we discern. Then there are motion, heat, light, sound, electricity, etc., which are not matter, but which are all related to one another, and constitute one fundamental phenomenon; this we call *energy*. As we look further, we may think we see a third type of manifestation, which cannot be brought under the heading of either matter or energy. This third type we call life and mind. As regards life, indeed, we perceive it only on one insignificant portion of matter, namely, the Earth; and our eye is not yet sufficiently developed to inform us by direct vision whether it occurs elsewhere. As regards mind, we are still more circumscribed, for we know it directly only in our own person, and the perception of it elsewhere is no more than a matter of inference.

Leaving aside for the moment this third category of life and mind, we find, then, that the Universe consists of matter and energy in a state of permanent change. We perceive, moreover, that the whole course of that change is not haphazard, but that it follows certain fixed sequences—usually called laws—which are so definite that even in the present state of knowledge many future events can be prophesied with certainty; and that, if our knowledge was unlimited, *all* future events could be so prophesied.

All human knowledge is derived by observation and experiment. The facts thus made known are co-ordinated or systematized in the various sciences. They are the individual bricks out of which the edifice of a scientific theory is built. As isolated facts, they have little philosophic import; but in proportion as they can be co-ordinated into broad generalizations, they take on a deeper philosophic significance. Science, therefore, alone can furnish the data of philosophy. If there is any knowledge attainable that can truly be called philosophic, it is such knowledge only as is yielded by a study of the various sciences. Consequently, the first thing to be done in any search after philosophic principles is to travel over the special sciences with a view to extracting from them such information as is relevant to our purpose.

Stated differently, the problems usually comprised under the name of philosophy are those dealing with the great questions of profound human interest: what is man's place in the Universe? whether there is any transcendental purpose inherent in the eternal drifting of matter and energy? and so on. The answer—in so far as any answer is possible—to these ultimate questions must plainly be reached by marshalling together such information as we already possess concern-

From *Hugh Elliot*, Modern Science and Materialism *(New York: Longmans, Green and Co., 1919), pp. 9–11; 137–145.*

ing the Universe. The primitive mind has a small knowledge of real facts, and upon this narrow basis erects a vast fabric of mythology or ontology. The more developed mind has a larger knowledge of real facts; and upon this broader basis erects a far less ambitious superstructure of philosophy. Before we can discern the deeper relationships of existence and the Universe, we must know all that can be known about these ultimate facts. That is a task far transcending the powers of any single mind; nevertheless, if we limit our endeavour to the establishment of a few general principles, it does become possible to test them by application to the different branches of natural science. . . .

The main purpose of the present work is to defend the doctrine of materialism. It is, indeed, a materialism infinitely different from that of the ancients, for it makes vast concessions to Agnosticism, and it concedes the whole foundation of knowledge to idealism. Yet it remains materialism; for I shall endeavour to show that the whole of the positive knowledge available to mankind can be embraced within the limits of a single materialistic system. The outlines of this system are not new; the main features of it, indeed, have been admittedly associated with scientific progress for centuries past. An age of science is necessarily an age of materialism; ours is a scientific age, and it may be said with truth that we are all materialists now. The main principles which I shall endeavour to emphasize are three.

1. The uniformity of law. In early times events appeared to be entirely haphazard and unaccountable, and they still seem so, if we confine attention purely to the passing moment. But as science advances, there is disclosed a uniformity in the procedure of Nature. When the conditions at any one moment are precisely identical with those which prevailed at some previous moment, the results flowing from them will also be identical. It is found, for instance, that a body of given mass attracts some other body of given mass at a given distance with a force of a certain strength. It is found that when the masses, distances, and other conditions are precisely repeated, the attraction between the bodies is always exactly the

same. It is found, further, that when the distance between the bodies is increased the force of their attraction is diminished in a fixed proportion, and this again is found to hold true at all distances at which they may be placed. The force of their attraction again varies in a different but still constant proportion to their masses. And hence results the law of gravitation, by which the force of attraction can be precisely estimated from a knowledge of the masses and distances between any two bodies whatever. A uniformity is established which remains absolute within the experience of Man, and to an equivalent extent the haphazard appearance of events is found to be only an appearance. Innumerable other laws of a similar character are gradually discovered, establishing a sort of nexus between every kind of event. If oxygen and hydrogen in the proportion by weight of eight to one are mixed together, and an electric spark is passed through them, water is formed; and on every occasion where precisely the same conditions are realized precisely the same result ensues. This truth is the basis of the experimental method. If from similar conditions it were possible that dissimilar results should follow on various occasions, then experiments would be useless for advancing knowledge. . . .

2. The denial of teleology. Scientific materialism warmly denies that there exists any such thing as purpose in the Universe, or that events have any ulterior motive or goal to which they are striving. It asserts that all events are due to the interaction of matter and motion acting by blind necessity in accordance with those invariable sequences to which we have given the name of laws. This is an important bond of connection between the materialism of the ancient Greeks and that of modern science. Among all peoples not highly cultivated there reigns a passionate conviction, not only that the Universe as a whole is working out some pre-determined purpose, but that every individual part of it subserves some special need in the fulfillment of this purpose. Needless to say, the purpose has always been regarded as associated with human welfare. The Universe, down to its smallest parts, is regarded by primitive superstition as existing for the spe-

cial benefit of man. To such extreme lengths has this view been carried that even Bernardin de Saint-Pierre, who died only last century, argued that the reason why melons are ribbed is that they may be eaten more easily by families.

The reason for this early teleology is obvious. We all of us survey the Universe from the standpoint of our own centrality. Subjectively we all do stand actually at the centre of the Universe. Our entire experience of the Universe is an experience of it as it affects ourselves; for if it does not affect ourselves, we know of it only indirectly, and in primitive stages we do not know of it at all. As our education endows us with a wider outlook and a wider knowledge, we come to see that the objective Universe is very different from our own private subjective Universe. At first we discover that we as individuals are not the centre of the Universe, as appears to uncorrected experience, but that we are merely one individual among many others of equal status constituting a nation or society. We then perhaps regard our own society as the centre of the Universe, as many primitive peoples do, such, for instance, as the ancient Romans and the modern Chinese. Or we may regard our own sex as the purposed product of the Universe, as in many Mohammedan peoples, who hold that women have not souls like men, and that they exist purely for the benefit or use of men, in the same way that cattle exist in order to be eaten, or that melons are ribbed to indicate the proper amount of one portion.

With still further cultivation, the entire human species becomes regarded as the centre and object of all events in the Universe. This is the stage now reached by the masses in modern civilizations. Just as the existence of one particular individual has not the world-wide or cosmic importance that that individual is apt to suppose; just as the existence of a particular tribe or society is not of the profound historic import that that tribe or society very commonly imagines; so too the human species as a whole is far from being, as it too often believes, the sole object for which the Universe was created, with all things in it, great and small. The human species is, indeed, a mere incident in the universal redistribution of matter and motion; its existence has not the smallest cosmic significance. Our species is biologically very modern. Neither in numbers nor in antiquity can it compare with infinitely numerous species of other animals inhabiting the Earth. The Earth itself is one of the smaller planets, revolving round a minor star. The entire solar system, of which the Earth is so insignificant a portion, is itself a system of contemptible minuteness, set among other luminaries and other systems which surpass it many times in magnitude, in brightness, and in every other ascertainable quality that we are accustomed to admire.

When it is alleged that the Universe is purposive, it is assumed that humanity is intimately connected with the purpose. Without that assumption, none but the most transcendental of philosophers would have any interest in maintaining teleology. As the anthropocentric doctrine falls, therefore, the doctrine of teleology must fall with it. This, at all events, is the position taken up by scientific, as indeed by all materialism; it is the position that I hope I shall have little difficulty in defending in the following pages. Nevertheless, however obvious its truth, we must recognize that it involves a profound alteration in the existing mental point of view of the majority of mankind; for most men have as yet not shaken off the habit, which all men necessarily start from, that they themselves, or their family, nation or kind, are in fact, as in appearance, the very centre of the cosmos.

3. The denial of any form of existence other than those envisaged by physics and chemistry, that is to say, other than existences that have some kind of palpable material characteristics and qualities. It is here that modern materialism begins to part company with ancient materialism, and it is here that I expect the main criticisms of opponents to be directed. The modern doctrine stands in direct opposition to a belief in any of those existences that are vaguely classed as "spiritual." To this category belong not only ghosts, gods, souls, *et hoc genus omne*, for these have long been rejected from the beliefs of most advanced thinkers. The time has now come to include also in the condemned list that further imaginary entity which we call "mind," "con-

sciousness," etc., together with its various sub-species of intellect, will, feeling, etc., in so far as they are supposed to be independent or different from material existences or processes.

I beg that the reader will not hastily repudiate a suggestion which, until rightly understood, must appear almost as absurd as did Berkeley's original formulation of idealism. It seems to the ordinary observer that nothing can be more remotely and widely separated than some so-called "act of consciousness" and a material object. An act of consciousness or mental process is a thing of which we are immediately and indubitably aware: so much I admit. But that it differs in any sort of way from a material process, that is to say, from the ordinary transformations of matter and energy, is a belief which I very strenuously deny, and which I propose to discuss and elucidate at length in my final chapter. The proposition which I here desire to advance is that every event occurring in the Universe, including those events known as mental processes, and all kinds of human action or conduct, are expressible purely in terms of matter and motion. If we assume in the primeval nebula of the solar system no other elementary factors beyond those of matter and energy or motion, we can theoretically, as above remarked, deduce the existing Universe, including mind, consciousness, etc., without the introduction of any new factor whatsoever. The existing Universe and all things and events therein may be theoretically expressed in terms of matter and energy, undergoing continuous redistribution in accordance with the ordinary laws of physics and chemistry. If all manifestations within our experience can be thus expressed, as has for long been believed by men of science, what need is there for the introduction of any new entity of spiritual character, called mind? It has no part to play; it is impotent in causation. According to Huxley's theory it accompanies certain physical processes as a shadow, without any power, or any reason, or any use. The world, as Huxley and the great majority of physiologists affirm, would be just the same without it.

Now there is an ancient logical precept which retains a large validity: *entia non sunt multiplicanda præter necessitatem*. It is sometimes referred to as William of Occam's razor, which cuts off and rejects from our theories all factors or entities which are superfluous in guiding us to an explanation. "Mind" as a separate entity is just such a superfluity. I will not deny—indeed I cordially affirm—that it is a direct datum of experience; but there is no direct datum of experience to the effect that it is anything different from certain cerebral processes. If uneducated experience seems to deny the identity, the denial rests upon an inference or deduction which is just as faulty as was the denial of Berkeley's theory that what we call matter is no more than sense-impressions. In passing, I may point out the difference here disclosed between modern scientific materialism and the crude materialism of the ancients. They agree in declaring the uniformity of law; they agree in denying the doctrine of teleology; they agree that all existences are of a material character. But they disagree in their treatment of the alleged spiritual and unseen world. The ancient materialists believed to a certain extent in an unseen world; they believed even in the existence of souls. They asserted their materialism only by the theory that these entities were material in character. Democritus conceived the soul as consisting of smooth, round, material particles. The scientific materialist of today does not believe in any separate existence of this kind whatever. He regards what is called soul or mind as *identical* with certain physical processes passing in a material brain, processes of which the ancient Greeks knew nothing, and, indeed, which are still entirely unknown to all who have not acquired some smattering of physiology. . . .

Suggestions for Further Reading

See Edgar Wilson's *The Mental as Physical* (London: Routledge and Kegan Paul, 1979) for a detailed argument in support of physicalism and its implications for notions like free will. See John O'Connor's collection of readings in *Modern Materialism: Readings on Mind-Body Iden-*

tity (New York: Harcourt, Brace, and World, 1969) for a good sampling of views. James W. Cornman's *Materialism and Sensations* (New Haven: Yale University Press, 1971) discusses in detail both reductive and eliminative materialism. D. M. Armstrong's *A Materialistic Theory of the Mind* (New York: Humanities Press, 1968) tackles the hardest problem for materialism, the problem of developing a credible theory of the mind on strictly materialistic grounds. See also the essays edited by David M. Rosenthal, *Materialism and the Mind-Body Problem* (Englewood Cliffs, NJ: Prentice-Hall, 1971). J. J. C. Smart in "Sensations and Brain Processes," *Philosophical Review,* Vol. 68 (1959), pp. 141–156 has given a famous defense of the identity version of materialism.

Video

Heroic Materialism (52 minutes, Number 13 in Civilization Series) deals with the rise of modern materialism. See your Media Services Catalogue for more information.

7.6. So What Is Real?

I began this book with a tale from China which left Zhuangzi wondering whether he was a sage dreaming he was a butterfly or a butterfly dreaming he was a sage. Philosophers from around the world have wondered about whether there is some Archimedian point, some firm and solid foundation, some privileged perspective from which we can distinguish with confidence dreaming from waking, good from bad, reality from appearance. Some have claimed to have found such a foundation, others have claimed it does not exist. What do you think?

"Not that question again," I hear some of you say. Wondering can be frustrating business and being constantly challenged to think for ourselves can be intimidating. Yet thinking is what philosophy is about. Of course from time to time we all wonder what we have accomplished by all this thought. Sometimes it seems we just go in circles. But the circles get bigger and after awhile begin to form a spiral. New ideas arise. Fresh distinctions emerge. Questions are refined and plateaus of clarity reached. I do hope that this experience encourages you to continue to wonder because wondering has given birth to some of the greatest of human accomplishments. I also hope that you have come to value the ideas and insights from different countries and cultural groups. It is good to learn what the world looks like from a different perspective. Different viewpoints enrich our own and open up new paths for further exploration. As we move into the next century, it will become ever more necessary to understand the perspectives and values of others. Philosophy needs to become a global conversation which is stimulating, productive, and edifying. Each of you has something of value to contribute to this emerging global conversation, and I hope what you have learned has helped you to begin to find your voice in these matters.

I close this chapter with another tale of dreaming by Jorge Luis Borges (1899–1986), Argentina's greatest writer and a man with an active, ever probing mind and imagination who lived in constant wonder. He uses fiction to raise philosophical issues worth pondering. Can we ever be certain that our perspective is the right one? Can we ever be confident that our way of distinguishing appearance from reality is the one correct way? And if we cannot, then what? I have only one reading question, What does the tale mean? We can all wonder about that together.

The Circular Ruins

JORGE LUIS BORGES

And if he left off dreaming about you . . .
—*Through the Looking Glass,* VI

NO ONE SAW HIM DISEMBARK in the unanimous night. No one saw the bamboo canoe running aground on the sacred mud. But within a few days no one was unaware that the taciturn man had come from the South and that his home had been one of the infinity of hamlets which lie upstream, on the violent flank of the mountain, where the Zend language is uncontaminated by Greek, and where leprosy is infrequent. The certain fact is that the anonymous gray man kissed the mud, scaled the bank without pushing aside (probably without even feeling) the sharp-edged sedges lacerating his flesh, and dragged himself, bloody and sickened, up to the circular enclosure whose crown is a stone colt or tiger, formerly the color of fire and now the color of ash. This circular clearing is a temple, devoured by ancient conflagration, profaned by the malarial jungle, its god unhonored now of men. The stranger lay beneath a pedestal. He was awakened, much later, by the sun at its height. He was not astonished to find that his wounds had healed. He closed his pale eyes and slept, no longer from weakness of the flesh but from a determination of the will. He knew that this temple was the place required by his inflexible purpose; he knew that the incessant trees had not been able to choke the ruins of another such propitious temple down river, a temple whose gods also were burned and dead; he knew that his immediate obligation was to dream. The disconsolate shriek of a bird awoke him about midnight. The prints of bare feet, some figs, and a jug told him that the people of the region had reverently spied out his dreaming and solicited his protection or feared his magic. He felt the cold chill of fear, and sought in the dilapidated wall for a sepulchral niche where he concealed himself under some unfamiliar leaves.

The purpose which impelled him was not impossible though it was supernatural. He willed to dream a man. He wanted to dream him in minute totality and then impose him upon reality. He had spent the full resources of his soul on this magical project. If anyone had asked him his own name or about any feature of his former life, he would have been unable to answer. The shattered and deserted temple suited his ends, for it was a minimum part of the visible world, and the nearness of the peasants was also convenient, for they took it upon themselves to supply his frugal needs. The rice and fruits of the tribute were nourishment enough for his body, given over to the sole task of sleeping and dreaming.

At first his dreams were chaotic. A little later they were dialectical. The stranger dreamt he stood in the middle of a circular amphitheater which was in some measure the fired temple; clouds of taciturn students wearied the tiers; the faces of the last rows looked down from a distance of several centuries and from a stellar height, but their every feature was precise. The dreamer himself was delivering lectures on anatomy, cosmography, magic: the faces listened anxiously and strove to answer with understanding, as if they guessed the importance of that examination, which would redeem one of them from his insubstantial state and interpolate him into the real world. In dreams or in waking the man continually considered the replies of his phantoms; he did not let himself be deceived by the impostors; in certain paradoxes he sensed an expanding intelligence. He was seeking a soul worthy of participating in the universe.

At the end of nine or ten nights he realized,

with a certain bitterness, that he could expect nothing from those students who accepted his teaching passively, but that he could of those who sometimes risked a reasonable contradiction. The former, though deserving of love and affection, could never rise to being individuals; the latter already existed to a somewhat greater degree. One afternoon (now even the afternoons were tributaries of the dream; now he stayed awake for only a couple of hours at daybreak) he dismissed the entire vast illusory student body for good and retained only one pupil. This pupil was a silent, sallow, sometimes obstinate boy, whose sharp features repeated those of his dreamer. The sudden elimination of his fellow students did not disconcert him for very long; his progress, at the end of a few private lessons, made his master marvel. And nevertheless, catastrophe came. One day the man emerged from sleep as from a viscous desert, stared about at the vain light of evening, which at first he took to be dawn, and realized he had not dreamt. All that night and all the next day the intolerable lucidity of insomnia broke over him in waves. He was impelled to explore the jungle, to wear himself out; he barely managed some quick snatches of feeble sleep amid the hemlock, shot through with fugitive visions of a rudimentary type: altogether unserviceable. He strove to assemble the student body, but he had scarcely uttered a few words of exhortation before the college blurred, was erased. Tears of wrath scalded his old eyes in his almost perpetual vigil.

He realized that the effort to model the inchoate and vertiginous stuff of which dreams are made is the most arduous task a man can undertake, though he get to the bottom of all the enigmas of a superior or inferior order: much more arduous than to weave a rope of sand or mint coins of the faceless wind. He realized that an initial failure was inevitable. He vowed to forget the enormous hallucination by which he had been led astray at first, and he sought out another approach. Before essaying it, he dedicated a month to replenishing the forces he had squandered in delirium. He abandoned all premedita-

tion concerned with dreaming, and almost at once managed to sleep through a goodly part of the day. The few times he did dream during this period he took no notice of the dreams. He waited until the disk of the moon should be perfect before taking up his task again. Then, on the eve, he purified himself in the waters of the river, worshiped the planetary gods, pronounced the lawful syllables of a powerful name and went to sleep. Almost at once he dreamt of a beating heart.

He dreamt it active, warm, secret, the size of a closed fist, garnet-colored in the half-light of a human body that boasted as yet no sex or face. He dreamt this heart with meticulous love, for fourteen lucid nights. Each night he saw it more clearly. He never touched it, but limited himself to witnessing it, to observing it or perhaps rectifying it with a glance. He watched it, lived it, from far and from near and from many angles. On the fourteenth night he ran his index finger lightly along the pulmonary artery, and then over the entire heart, inside and out. The examination satisfied him. The next night, he deliberately did not dream. He then took up the heart again, invoked the name of a planet, and set about to envision another one of the principal organs. Before the year was up he had reached the skeleton, the eyelids. The most difficult task, perhaps, proved to be the numberless hairs. He dreamt a whole man, a fine lad, but one who could not stand nor talk nor open his eyes. Night after night he dreamt him asleep.

In the Gnostic cosmogonies, demiurges fashion a red Adam who never manages to get to his feet: as clumsy and equally as crude and elemental as this dust Adam was the dream Adam forged by the nights of the wizard. One afternoon, the man almost destroyed all his work, but then changed his mind. (It would have been better for him had he destroyed it.) Having expended all the votive offerings to the numina of the earth and the river, he threw himself at the feet of the effigy, which was perhaps a tiger or perhaps a colt, and implored its unknown help. That evening, at twilight, he dreamt of the statue. He dreamt it alive, tremulous: it was no atrocious bastard of a tiger and a colt, but both these vehement creatures at once and also a bull, a rose, a tempest. This multiple god revealed to him that its terrestrial name was Fire, that in this same circular temple (and in others like it) it once had been offered sacrifices and been the object of a cult, and that now it would magically animate the phantom dreamt by the wizard in such wise that all creatures—except Fire itself and the dreamer—would believe the phantom to be a man of flesh and blood. It directed that once the phantom was instructed in the rites, he be sent to the other broken temple, whose pyramids persisted down river, so that some voice might be raised in glorification in that deserted edifice. In the dream of the man who was dreaming, the dreamt man awoke.

The wizard carried out the directives given him. He dedicated a period of time (which amounted, in the end, to two years) to revealing the mysteries of the universe and the cult of Fire to his dream creature. In his intimate being, he suffered when he was apart from his creation. And so every day, under the pretext of pedagogical necessity, he protracted the hours devoted to dreaming. He also reworked the right shoulder, which was perhaps defective. At times, he had the uneasy impression that all this had happened before. . . . In general, though, his days were happy ones: as he closed his eyes he would think: *Now I shall be with my son.* Or, more infrequently: *The son I have engendered is waiting for me and will not exist if I do not go to him.*

Little by little he got his creature accustomed to reality. Once, he ordered him to plant a flag on a distant mountain top. The next day the flag was fluttering on the peak. He tried other analogous experiments, each one more audacious than the last. He came to realize, with a certain bitterness, that his son was ready—and perhaps impatient—to be born. That night he kissed his child for the first time, and sent him to the other temple, whose remains were whitening down river, many leagues across impassable jungle and swamp. But first, so that his son should never

know he was a phantom and should think himself a man like other men, he imbued him with total forgetfulness of his apprentice years.

His triumph and his respite were sapped by tedium. In the twilight hours of dusk or dawn he would prostrate himself before the stone figure, imagining his unreal child practicing identical rites in other circular ruins downstream. At night he did not dream, or dreamt as other men do. The sounds and forms of the universe reached him wanly, pallidly: his absent son was being sustained on the diminution of the wizard's soul. His life's purpose had been achieved; the man lived on in a kind of ecstasy. After a time—which some narrators of his story prefer to compute in years and others in lustra—he was awakened one midnight by two boatmen: he could not see their faces, but they told him of a magical man at a temple in the North, who walked on fire and was not burned. The wizard suddenly recalled the words of the god. He remembered that of all the creatures composing the world, only Fire knew his son was a phantom. This recollection, comforting at first, ended by tormenting him. He feared lest his son meditate on his abnormal privilege and somehow discover his condition of mere simulacrum. Not to be a man, to be the projection of another man's dream—what incomparable humiliation, what vertigo! Every father is concerned with the children he has procreated (which he has permitted) in mere confusion or felicity: it was only natural that the wizard should fear for the future of his son, thought out entrail by entrail and feature by feature on a thousand and one secret nights.

The end of his caviling was abrupt, but not without forewarnings. First (after a long drought) a remote cloud, light as a bird, appeared over a hill. Then, toward the South, the sky turned the rosy color of a leopard's gums. Smoke began to rust the metallic nights. And then came the panic flight of the animals. And the events of several centuries before were repeated. The ruins of the fire god's sanctuary were destroyed by fire. One birdless dawn the wizard watched the concentric conflagration close around the walls: for one instant he thought of taking refuge in the river, but then he understood that death was coming to crown his old age and to absolve him of further work. He walked against the florid banners of the fire. And the fire did not bite his flesh but caressed and engulfed him without heat or combustion. With relief, with humiliation, with terror, he understood that he, too, was all appearance, that someone else was dreaming him.

Chapter 8

Is Knowledge Possible?

HAVE YOU EVER THOUGHT that what you heard was just people's opinions, that they didn't really know what they were talking about? Have you ever wondered whether we can trust our intuition? Have you ever thought about the limits of human reason? Are there things that we cannot know? But how could we know that? Have you ever thought about history, about how we can know what happened before we were born? Does everything we know come from experience? Have you ever been puzzled by the question, "What is truth?" Have you ever wondered whether we can be certain about any of our beliefs?

If you have wondered about these kinds of questions, you have been thinking about what philosophers call epistemology. Epistemology means the study of knowledge, and the epistemologist is concerned with examining theories of knowledge. And just as the metaphysician is concerned with how we distinguish between appearance and reality, so the epistemologist wants to know how we can distinguish between opinion and knowledge.

We've all had the experience of listening to someone tell us something she thinks she knows. Perhaps we have dismissed what was said with the comment, "Oh, that's just your opinion." How do we know she doesn't really know? How do we know it is just her opinion? However we know it, the very fact that we call it opinion indicates that we assume that it is possible to distinguish between opinion and knowledge.

Let's start with a game. How do you know, if you know, the following:

that you exist	that this book exists
that it will snow tomorrow	that all fat cats are fat
that it rained yesterday	that two plus two equals four
that God exists	that every event has a cause

I imagine that you said you knew some of the things on this list because of sense experiences you've had. For example, you might have said that you know this book exists because you can see it and touch it. One important epistemological theory is called empiricism. According to this theory, we know things because we experience them with our senses. We see, touch, taste, smell, and hear things. That is how we gain knowledge about them. If someone tells me something is true, but what he says is based neither on experience nor verifiable by reference to experience, I would say, if I were an empiricist, "Oh, that's just a matter of opinion."

However, there are some things on this list that you might say you knew because of reason. For example, you might have said that you know two plus two equals four because that's the way it works out when you add. Addition is a rational activity, one that requires you to reason and you reason, in this case, by applying the rules of addition. If you apply the rules correctly, the answer has to be four.

If some of you identified reason as the source of knowledge, you would be reflecting the ideas of another important epistemological theory called *rationalism*. According to this theory, we know things by the use of reason. Reason tells us what is true. If someone says he knows there are some fat cats that are not fat because he has seen one, you might want to suggest that this is not merely a matter of opinion. Fat cats, by definition, are fat. Whatever he saw, he is mistaken.

Let us contrast these two basic theories of knowledge a bit more in order to be sure we grasp how they are different. Empiricism usually claims that the human mind, prior to sense experience, is like a blank slate (**tabula rasa**) or empty tablet. Sensations make impressions on this slate via our senses. It is from these impressions that we learn what is true and false and thereby, over the years, slowly build up a fund of knowledge. Hence our knowledge is **a posteriori** (after experience). We cannot know anything until after we have had experiences, and if we wish to test or verify what we believe, we do so by checking it against further experiences. Knowledge, according to the empiricist, is also largely inductive (see Appendix A) since we induce some future events from past or present experiences. Of course our inductions might be wrong. The conclusions we draw are only probable, but probability is the best we can hope for if we want to know something about the world in which we live.

Rationalists reject the idea that the human mind is blank. We have, they usually claim, *innate ideas* or ideas already built into our minds at birth, like the wiring built into a computer that allows it to compute. We use these innate ideas to make sense of our sensations. How do we know such innate ideas are true? By direct intellectual intuition (reason). Sensation does not tell us that every event has a cause since we cannot experience every event. Reason tells us that. We know it intuitively. Hence knowledge is **a priori** (prior to experience, in the sense of independent from). We do know things not learned from sensation, and we can prove things true without reference to sensation. Our proofs are deductive (see Appendix A), and we can deduce that a fat cat is fat from the definition of "fat cat." It follows necessarily. It is certain.

Ponder the contrast between:

Empiricism	*Rationalism*
tabula rasa	innate ideas
sensation	reason
a posteriori	*a priori*
inductive	deductive

"But wait," some of you might be saying, "what about those of us who are not sure that anything on that first list can be known at all? After all, you said, 'How do you know, *if you know*.' Well, I don't think some of these things can be known. For example, God. I think we just believe or we don't, but we can't know."

This response raises the issue of **skepticism.** The word "skepticism" comes from a

Greek word that means "to reflect on," "consider," or "examine." We often associate the word with doubt or the suspension of judgment. The skeptic is a doubter.

There are various kinds of skepticism. One kind, what we might call **commonsense skepticism,** refers to the activity of doubting or suspending judgment about some things at one time or another. In this sense we are all skeptics because we have all doubted. This sort of skepticism is healthy. It prevents an overly credulous attitude and is a good antidote to intellectual arrogance. If you are too gullible, you can be manipulated by others who claim to have knowledge when they don't.

Another kind of skepticism is **methodical skepticism.** This is the sort of skepticism that is used by some philosophers and scientists in their search for the truth. If, for example, I want to be as certain as I can be that water freezes at 32°F, I might doubt that hypothesis and conduct several experiments under differing circumstances to see if there is evidence supporting it. Such doubt can be enormously constructive, since it stimulates our intellectual curiosity and energizes our search for truth.

There is yet a third kind of skepticism, **absolute skepticism,** which, somewhat ironically, some philosophers have presented as a theory of knowledge. Unlike both rationalism and empiricism, this theory claims that knowledge of any kind is not possible. Pyrrho of Elis (about 300 B.C.E.) founded a school of philosophers who advocated absolute skepticism. He claimed to be following Socrates and just asking questions. But he also claimed that every argument cancels out its opposite. In other words, arguments on opposite sides of an issue balance out, thereby canceling any definitive conclusion. Try as we might, we cannot know what is true.

"Well," you might say, "that is certainly ridiculous. If we cannot know what is true, then how can Pyrrho or any other skeptic know that we cannot know?" That is a good question. You are suggesting that skepticism is self-refuting. If it is true that we cannot know anything, then how do we know that it is true that we cannot know anything? If absolute skepticism is true, then it must be false!

Pyrrho himself anticipated a similar criticism. He retorted that he was not certain that he was not certain of anything. Of course one wonders whether he was not certain that he was not certain that. . . . This conversation could go on forever! Yet self-refuting propositions are puzzling and provocative things. Consider:

The sentence in this box is false.

Think about that for a minute. If "the sentence in the box is false" is false, then it must be true. And if it is true, it must be false. Yet one claim central to two-valued logics is that sentences must be either true or false. They, presumably, cannot be both. Yet here we have a sentence that seems to be both. What are we to make of this? Is the claim of the absolute skeptic, "we cannot know anything," another example of a proposition of this sort? Perhaps certainty is simply not possible for humans, and, if we mean by "knowledge" certainty (knowing without the possibility of doubt that certain statements are true or false), then we may have to be more humble when we claim to know something. Perhaps our knowledge claims are fallible and truth or falsity a matter of degree.

8.1. Sufi Mysticism

Abu Hamid Muhammad al-Ghazali was born at Tus, Persia, in 450 A.H. (1058). He was appointed a professor of Islamic theology at the university in Baghdad at the early age of 33 (see Section 4.1 for general information on Islam). Four years later he had an emotional and spiritual crisis, which centered on the feeling that his way of life as an academic was too worldly. He left his post and became an ascetic, studying both the teachings and the practices of Islamic mystics. He later returned to teaching; he died in 505 A.H. *Deliverance from Error,* from which the following selection is taken, constitutes al-Ghazali's spiritual and intellectual autobiography.

Al-Ghazali is embarked on a quest for certainty. He studies theology, but is disappointed with its intellectual achievements. His quest prompts him to study philosophy, but once again he is disappointed, especially with its unfounded metaphysical claims and with the fact that philosophers hold beliefs contrary to Islamic revelation. He turns to the Batiniyah, who teach that truth is attained not by reason, but by accepting the pronouncements of the infallible Imam (religious leader). At the time, this teaching had important political implications since it was the official ideology of the Fatimid caliphate with its center in Cairo. However, al-Ghazali finds the teachings of the imams to be trivial. He characterizes their knowledge as "feeble" and "emaciated." Finally he investigates **Sufism,** an Islamic mystical movement teaching that direct and immediate experience of Allah is possible. It is among the Sufis that his restless soul finds peace.

Al-Ghazali is clearly not satisfied with empiricism, rationalism, or skepticism. Hence he seeks to discover a source or means to knowledge that escapes the skeptic's doubts, and provides a firmer foundation than either empiricism or rationalism. He believes he finds such a source in mystical experience, an intimate union with the Divine.

Of course al-Ghazali's motivation is not entirely philosophical or scientific. He does not merely want to know about the world sense experience can tell him about, nor about the abstract world of mathematics and metaphysics that reason can reveal. Nor is he content to be a doubter. His motivation is also spiritual, he wants to know about the Divine. His quest may reveal to us something about the limited nature of epistemological theories. Each theory may be appropriate in a limited domain. If you want to know about the world, empiricism is attractive. If you want to know about mathematics or abstract realities, rationalism commends itself. But what if you want to know about God? Is either empiricism or rationalism adequate?

Al-Ghazali's views are controversial, for many would be skeptical about the claim that adequate knowledge can be grounded in some sort of mystical experience. How do we know that mystical experience is not an illusion, just like some sense experiences? Within Islamic philosophy al-Ghazali was not without his critics. Another Islamic philosopher, Averroes (ibn-Roshid, 1126–1198) wrote a book called *The Incoherence of the Incoherence,* referring to a book al-Ghazali wrote entitled *The Incoherence of the Philosophers.* Averroes attacked al-Ghazali's views, arguing that the philosophic reliance on reason and sense experience as an adequate method for knowing is both proper and appropriate.

Reading Questions

1. How does al-Ghazali define knowledge?
2. What leads him to doubt beliefs based on sense-perception and on intellect?
3. What is distinctive about mysticism?
4. What creedal principles were firmly rooted in al-Ghazali after his study of theology and philosophy?
5. What is the mystic way, and what did al-Ghazali learn from following it?
6. How does the author distinguish among knowledge, immediate experience, and faith?
7. What does he mean by prophetic revelation? How is it related to other ways of obtaining knowledge? What is the proof of prophecy, and do you find the proof convincing? Why?
8. What method does he suggest we use to arrive at the knowledge that someone is a prophet? Why is this method better than relying on miracles as proof?
9. How does al-Ghazali answer the question, "Is knowledge possible?"

Deliverance from Error

AL-GHAZALI

TO THIRST AFTER A comprehesion of things as they really are was my habit and custom from a very early age. It was instinctive with me, a part of my God-given nature, a matter of temperament and not of my choice or contriving. Consequently as I drew near the age of adolescence the bonds of mere authority (*taqlīd*) ceased to hold me and inherited beliefs lost their grip upon me, for I saw that Christian youths always grew up to be Christians, Jewish youths to be Jews and Muslim youths to be Muslims. I heard, too, the Tradition related of the Prophet of God according to which he said: "Everyone who is born is born with a sound nature; it is his parents who make him a Jew or a Christian or a Magian." My inmost being was moved to discover what this original nature really was and what the beliefs derived from the authority of parents and teachers really were. The attempt to distinguish between these authority-based opinions and their principles developed the mind, for in distinguishing the true in them from the false differences appeared.

I therefore said within myself: "To begin with, what I am looking for is knowledge of what things really are, so I must undoubtedly try to find what knowledge really is." It was plain to me that sure and certain knowledge is that knowledge in which the object is disclosed in such a fashion that no doubt remains along with it, that no possibility of error or illusion accompanies it, and that the mind cannot even entertain such a supposition. Certain knowledge must also be infallible; and this infallibility or security from error is such that no attempt to show the falsity of the knowledge can occasion doubt or denial, even though the attempt is made by someone who turns stones into gold or a rod into a serpent. Thus, I know that ten is more than three. Let us suppose that someone says to me: "No, three is more than ten, and in proof of that I shall change this rod into a serpent"; and let us suppose that he actually changes the rod into a serpent and that I witness him doing so. No doubts about what I know are raised in me because of this. The only result is that I wonder precisely how he is able to produce this change. Of doubt about my knowledge there is no trace.

After these reflections I knew that whatever I do not know in this fashion and with this mode of certainty is not reliable and infallible knowledge; and knowledge that is not infallible is not certain knowledge.

Preliminaries: Skepticism and the Denial of All Knowledge

Thereupon I investigated the various kinds of knowledge I had, and found myself destitute of all knowledge with this characteristic of infallibility except in the case of sense-perception and necessary truths. So I said: "Now that despair has come over me, there is no point in studying any problems except on the basis of what is self-evident, namely, necessary truths and the affirmations of the senses. I must first bring these to be judged in order that I may be certain on this matter. Is my reliance on sense-perception and my trust in the soundness of necessary truths of the same kind as my previous trust in the beliefs I had merely taken over from others and as the trust most men have in the results of thinking? Or is it a justified trust that is in no danger of being betrayed or destroyed?"

I proceeded therefore with extreme earnestness to reflect on sense-perception and on necessary truths, to see whether I could make myself doubt them. The outcome of this protracted effort to induce doubt was that I could no longer trust sense-perception either. Doubt began to spread here and say: "From where does this reliance on sense-perception come? The most powerful sense is that of sight. Yet when it looks at the shadow (*sc.* of a stick or the gnomon of a sundial), it sees it standing still, and judges that there

is no motion. Then by experiment and observation after an hour it knows that the shadow is moving and, moreover, that it is moving not by fits and starts but gradually and steadily by infinitely small distances in such a way that it is never in a state of rest. Again, it looks at the heavenly body (*sc.* the sun) and sees it small, the size of a shilling; yet geometrical computations show that it is greater than the earth in size."

In this and similar cases of sense-perception the sense as judge forms his judgments, but another judge, the intellect, shows him repeatedly to be wrong; and the charge of falsity cannot be rebutted.

To this I said: "My reliance on sense-perception also has been destroyed. Perhaps only those intellectual truths which are first principles (or derived from first principles) are to be relied upon, such as the assertion that ten are more than three, that the same thing cannot be both affirmed and denied at one time, that one thing is not both generated in time and eternal, nor both existent and non-existent, nor both necessary and impossible."

Sense-perception replied: "Do you not expect that your reliance on intellectual truths will fare like your reliance on sense-perception? You used to trust in me; then along came the intellect-judge and proved me wrong; if it were not for the intellect-judge you would have continued to regard me as true. Perhaps behind intellectual apprehension there is another judge who, if he manifests himself, will show the falsity of intellect in its judging, just as, when intellect manifested itself, it showed the falsity of sense in its judging. The fact that such a supra-intellectual apprehension has not manifested itself is no proof that it is impossible."

My ego hesitated a little about the reply to that, and sense-perception heightened the difficulty by referring to dreams. "Do you not see," it said, "how, when you are asleep, you believe things and imagine circumstances, holding them to be stable and enduring, and, so long as you are in that dream-condition, have no doubts about them? And is it not the case that when you awake you know that all you have imagined and believed is unfounded and ineffectual? Why then are you confident that all your waking beliefs, whether from sense or intellect, are genuine? They are true in respect of your present state; but it is possible that a state will come upon you whose relation to your waking consciousness is analogous to the relation of the latter to dreaming. In comparison with this state your waking consciousness would be like dreaming! When you have entered into this state, you will be certain that all the suppositions of your intellect are empty imaginings. It may be that that state is what the Sufis claim as their special 'state' (*sc.* mystic union or ecstasy), for they consider that in their 'states' (or ecstasies), which occur when they have withdrawn into themselves and are absent from their senses, they witness states (or circumstances) which do not tally with these principles of the intellect. Perhaps that 'state' is death; for the Messenger of God (God bless and preserve him) says: 'The people are dreaming; when they die, they become awake.' So perhaps life in this world is a dream by comparison with the world to come; and when a man dies, things come to appear differently to him from what he now beholds, and at the same time the words are addressed to him: 'We have taken off thee thy covering, and thy sight today is sharp.'" (Q. 50, 21)

When these thoughts had occurred to me and penetrated my being, I tried to find some way of treating my unhealthy condition; but it was not easy. Such ideas can only be repelled by demonstration; but a demonstration requires a knowledge of first principles; since this is not admitted, however, it is impossible to make the demonstration. The disease was baffling, and lasted almost two months, during which I was a sceptic in fact though not in theory nor in outward expression. At length God cured me of the malady; my being was restored to health and an even balance; the necessary truths of the intellect became once more accepted, as I regained confidence in their certain and trustworthy character.

This did not come about by systematic demonstration or marshalled argument, but by a light which God most high cast into my breast. That light is the key to the greater part of knowledge.

Whoever thinks that the understanding of things Divine rests upon strict proofs has in his thought narrowed down the wideness of God's mercy. When the Messenger of God (peace be upon him) was asked about "enlarging" (*sharhy*) and its meaning in the verse, "Whenever God wills to guide a man, He enlarges his breast for *islām* (i.e., surrender to God)" (Q. 6, 125), he said, "It is a light which God most high casts into the heart." When asked, "What is the sign of it?" he said, "Withdrawal from the mansion of deception and return to the mansion of eternity." It was about this light that Muhammad (peace be upon him) said, "God created the creatures in darkness, and then sprinkled upon them some of His light." From that light must be sought an intuitive understanding of things Divine. That light at certain times gushes from the spring of Divine generosity, and for it one must watch and wait—as Muhammad (peace be upon him) said: "In the days of your age your Lord has gusts of favor; then place yourselves in the way of them."

The point of these accounts is that the task is perfectly fulfilled when the quest is prosecuted up to the stage of seeking what is not sought (but stops short of that). For first principles are not sought, since they are present and to hand; and if what is present is sought for, it becomes hidden and lost. When, however, a man seeks what is sought (and that only), he is not accused of falling short in the seeking of what is sought. . . .

The Ways of Mysticism

I knew that the complete mystic "way" includes both intellectual belief and practical activity; the latter consists in getting rid of the obstacles in the self and in stripping off its base characteristics and vicious morals, so that the heart may attain to freedom from what is not God and to constant recollection of Him.

The intellectual belief was easier to me than the practical activity. I began to acquaint myself with their belief by reading their books, such as *The Food of the Hearts* by Abū Ṭālib al-Makkī (God have mercy upon him), the works of al-Ḥārith al-Muḥāsibī, the various anecdotes about al-Junayd, ash-Shiblī and Abū Yazīd al-Bisṭāmī (may God sanctify their spirits), and other discourses of their leading men. I thus comprehended their fundamental teachings on the intellectual side, and progressed, as far as is possible by study and oral instruction, in the knowledge of mysticism. It became clear to me, however, that what is most distinctive of mysticism is something which cannot be apprehended by study, but only by immediate experience (*dhawq*—literally "tasting"), by ecstasy and by a moral change. What a difference there is between *knowing* the definition of health and satiety, together with their causes and presuppositions, and *being* healthy and satisfied! What a difference between being acquainted with the definition of drunkenness—namely, that it designates a state arising from the domination of the seat of the intellect by vapours arising from the stomach—and being drunk! Indeed, the drunken man while in that condition does not know the definition of drunkenness nor the scientific account of it; he has not the very least scientific knowledge of it. The sober man, on the other hand, knows the definition of drunkenness and its basis, yet he is not drunk in the very least. Again the doctor, when he is himself ill, knows the definition and causes of health and the remedies which restore it, and yet is lacking in health. Similarly there is a difference between knowing the true nature and causes and conditions of the ascetic life and actually leading such a life and forsaking the world.

I apprehended clearly that the mystics were men who had real experiences, not men of words, and that I had already progressed as far as was possible by way of intellectual apprehension. What remained for me was not to be attained by oral instruction and study but only by immediate experience and by walking in the mystic way.

Now from the sciences I had labored at and the paths I had traversed in my investigation of the revelational and rational sciences (that is, presumably, theology and philosophy), there had come to me a sure faith in God most high, in prophethood (or revelation), and in the Last Day. These three creedal principles were firmly rooted in my being, not through any carefully argued proofs, but by reason of various causes, coincidences and experiences which are not capable of being stated in detail.

It had already become clear to me that I had no hope of the bliss of the world to come save through a God-fearing life and the withdrawal of myself from vain desire. It was clear to me too that the key to all this was to sever the attachment of the heart to worldly things by leaving the mansion of deception and returning to that of eternity, and to advance towards God most high with all earnestness. It was also clear that this was only to be achieved by turning away from wealth and position and fleeing from all time-consuming entanglements.

Next I considered the circumstances of my life, and realized that I was caught in a veritable thicket of attachments. I also considered my activities, of which the best was my teaching and lecturing, and realized that in them I was dealing with sciences that were unimportant and contributed nothing to the attainment of eternal life.

After that I examined my motive in my work of teaching, and realized that it was not a pure desire for the things of God, but that the impulse moving me was the desire for an influential position and public recognition. I saw for certain that I was on the brink of a crumbling bank of sand and in imminent danger of hell-fire unless I set about to mend my ways.

I reflected on this continuously for a time, while the choice still remained open to me. One day I would form the resolution to quit Baghdad and get rid of these adverse circumstances; the next day I would abandon my resolution. I put one foot forward and drew the other back. If in the morning I had a genuine longing to seek eternal life, by the evening the attack of a whole host of desires had reduced it to impotence. Worldly desires were striving to keep me by their chains just where I was, while the voice of faith was calling, "To the road! to the road! What is left of life is but little and the journey before you is long. All that keeps you busy, both intellectually and practically, is but hypocrisy and delusion.

If you do not prepare *now* for eternal life, when will you prepare? If you do not now sever these attachments, when will you sever them?" On hearing that, the impulse would be stirred and the resolution made to take to flight. . . .

I left Baghdad, then. I distributed what wealth I had, retaining only as much as would suffice myself and provide sustenance for my children. This I could easily manage, as the wealth of 'Iraq was available for good works, since it constitutes a trust fund for the benefit of the Muslims. Nowhere in the world have I seen better financial arrangements to assist a scholar to provide for his children. . . .

In general, then, how is a mystic "way" (*tarīqah*) described? The purity which is the first condition of it (*sc.* as bodily purity is the prior condition of formal Worship for Muslims) is the purification of the heart completely from what is other than God most high; the key to it, which corresponds to the opening act of adoration in prayer, is the sinking of the heart completely in the recollection of God; and the end of it is complete absorption (*fanā'*) in God. At least this is its end relatively to those first steps which almost come within the sphere of choice and personal responsibility; but in reality in the actual mystic "way" it is the first step, what comes before it being, as it were, the ante-chamber for those who are journeying towards it.

With this first stage of the "way" there begin the revelations and visions. The mystics in their waking state now behold angels and the spirits of the prophets; they hear these speaking to them and are instructed by them. Later, a higher state is reached; instead of beholding forms and figures, they come to stages in the "way" which it is hard to describe in language; if a man attempts to express these, his words inevitably contain what is clearly erroneous.

In general what they manage to achieve is nearness to God; some, however, would conceive of this as "inherence" (*ḥulūl*), some as "union" (*ittiḥad*), and some as "connection" (*wuṣūl*). All that is erroneous. In my book, *The*

Noblest Aim, I have explained the nature of the error here. Yet he who has attained the mystic "state" need do no more than say:

Of the things I do not remember, what was, was;
Think it good; do not ask an account of it.
(Ibn al-Mu'tazz)

In general the man to whom He has granted no immediate experience at all, apprehends no more of what prophetic revelation really is than the name. The miraculous graces given to the saints are in truth the beginnings of the prophets; and that was the first "state" of the Messenger of God (peace be upon him) when he went out to Mount Ḥirā,' and was given up entirely to his Lord, and worshipped, so that the bedouin said, "Muhammad loves his Lord passionately."

Now this is a mystical "state" which is realized in immediate experience by those who walk in the way leading to it. Those to whom it is not granted to have immediate experience can become assured of it by trial (*sc.* contact with mystics or observation of them) and by hearsay, if they have sufficiently numerous opportunities of associating with mystics to understand that (*sc.* ecstasy) with certainty by means of what accompanies the "states." Whoever sits in their company derives from them this faith; and none who sits in their company is pained.

Those to whom it is not even granted to have contacts with mystics may know with certainty the possibility of ecstasy by the evidence of demonstration, as I have remarked in the section entitled *The Wonders of the Heart* of my *Revival of the Religious Sciences.*

Certainty reached by demonstration is *knowledge* (*'ilm*); actual acquaintance with that "state" is *immediate experience* (*dhawq*); the acceptance of it as probable from hearsay and trial (or observation) is *faith* (*īmān*). These are three degrees. "God will raise those of you who have faith and those who have been given knowledge in degrees (*sc.* of honor)" (Q. 58, 12).

Behind the mystics, however, there is a crowd of ignorant people. They deny this fundamentally, they are astonished at this line of thought, they listen and mock. "Amazing," they say. "What nonsense they talk!" About such people God most high has said: "Some of them listen to you, until, upon going out from you, they say to those to whom knowledge has been given, 'What did he say just now?' These are the people on whose hearts God sets a seal and they follow their passions." (Q. 47, 18) He makes them deaf, and blinds their sight.

Among the things that necessarily became clear to me from my practice of the mystic "way" was the true nature and special characteristics of prophetic revelation. The basis of that must undoubtedly be indicated in view of the urgent need for it.

The True Nature of Prophecy and the Compelling Need of All Creation for It

You must know that the substance of man in his original condition was created in bareness and simplicity without any information about the worlds of God most high. These worlds are many, not to be reckoned save by God most high Himself. As He said, "None knows the hosts of thy Lord save He" (Q. 74, 34). Man's information about the world is by means of perception; and every perception of perceptibles is created so that thereby man may have some acquaintance with a world (or sphere) from among existents. By "worlds (or spheres)" we simply mean "classes of existents."

The first thing created in man was the sense of *touch,* and by it he perceives certain classes of existents, such as heat and cold, moisture and dryness, smoothness and roughness. Touch is completely unable to apprehend colors and noises. These might be non-existent so far as concerns touch.

Next there is created in him the sense of *sight,* and by it he apprehends colors and shapes. This is the most extensive of the worlds of sensibles. Next *hearing* is implanted in him, so that he hears sounds of various kinds. After that *taste* is created in him; and so on until he has completed the world of sensibles.

Next, when he is about seven years old, there is created in him *discernment* (or the power of distinguishing—*tamyīz*). This is a fresh stage in his development. He now apprehends more than the world of sensibles; and none of these additional factors (*sc.* relations, etc.) exists in the world of sense.

From this he ascends to another stage, and *intellect* (or reason) (*'aql*) is created in him. He apprehends things necessary, possible, impossible, things which do not occur in the previous stages.

Beyond intellect there is yet another stage. In this another eye is opened, by which he beholds the unseen, what is to be in the future, and other things which are beyond the ken of intellect in the same way as the objects of intellect are beyond the ken of the faculty of discernment and the objects of discernment are beyond the ken of sense. Moreover, just as the man at the stage of discernment would reject and disregard the objects of intellect were these to be presented to him, so some intellectuals reject and disregard the objects of prophetic revelation. That is sheer ignorance. They have no ground for their view except that this is a stage which they have not reached and which for them does not exist; yet they suppose that it is non-existent in itself. When a man blind from birth, who has not learnt about colors and shapes by listening to people's talk, is told about these things for the first time, he does not understand them nor admit their existence.

God most high, however, has favored His creatures by giving them something analogous to the special faculty of prophecy, namely dreams. In the dream-state a man apprehends what is to be in the future, which is something of the unseen; he does so either explicitly or else clothed in a symbolic form whose interpretation is disclosed.

Suppose a man has not experienced this himself, and suppose that he is told how some people fall into a dead faint, in which hearing, sight and the other senses no longer function, and in this condition perceive the unseen. He would deny that this is so and demonstrate its impossibility. "The sensible powers," he would say, "are the causes of perception (or apprehension); if a man does not perceive things (*sc.* the unseen) when these powers are actively present, much less will he do so when the senses are not functioning." This is a form of analogy which is shown to be false by what actually occurs and is observed. Just as intellect is one of the stages of human development in which there is an "eye" which sees the various types of intelligible objects, which are beyond the ken of the senses, so prophecy also is the description of a stage in which there is an eye endowed with light such that in that light the unseen and other supra-intellectual objects become visible.

Doubt about prophetic revelation is either (a) doubt of its possibility in general, or (b) doubt of its actual occurrence, or (c) doubt of the attainment of it by a specific individual.

The proof of the possibility of there being prophecy and the proof that there has been prophecy is that there is knowledge in the world the attainment of which by reason is inconceivable; for example, in medical science and astronomy. Whoever researches in such matters knows of necessity that this knowledge is attained only by Divine inspiration and by assistance from God most high. It cannot be reached by observation. For instance there are some astronomical laws based on phenomena which occur only once in a thousand years; how can these be arrived at by personal observation? It is the same with the properties of drugs.

This argument shows that it is possible for there to be a way of apprehending these matters which are not apprehended by the intellect. This is the meaning of prophetic revelation. That is not to say that prophecy is merely an expression for such knowledge. Rather, the apprehending of this class of extra-intellectual objects is *one* of the properties of prophecy; but it has many other properties as well. The said property is but a drop in the ocean of prophecy. It has been singled out for mention because you have something analogous to it in what you apprehend in dreaming, and because you have medical and astronomical knowledge belonging to the same class, namely, the miracles of the prophets, for the intellectuals cannot arrive at these at all by any intellectual efforts.

The other properties of prophetic revelation are apprehended only by immediate experience (*dhawq*) from the practice of the mystic way, but this property of prophecy you can understand by an analogy granted you, namely, the dream-state. If it were not for the latter you would not believe in that. If the prophet possessed a faculty to which you had nothing analogous and which you did not understand, how could you believe in it? Believing presupposes understanding. Now that analogous experience comes to a man in the early stages of the mystic way. Thereby he attains to a kind of immediate experience, extending as far as that to which he has attained, and by analogy to a kind of belief (or assent) in respect of that to which he has not attained. Thus this single property is a sufficient basis for one's faith in the principle of prophecy.

If you come to doubt whether a specific person is a prophet or not, certainty can only be reached by acquaintance with his conduct, either by personal observation, or by hearsay as a matter of common knowledge. For example, if you are familiar with medicine and law, you can recognize lawyers and doctors by observing what they are, or, where observation is impossible, by hearing what they have to say. Thus you are not unable to recognize that al-Shāfi'ī (God have mercy upon him) is a lawyer and Galen a doctor; and your recognition is based on the facts and not on the judgment of someone else. Indeed, just because you have some knowledge of law and medicine, and examine their books and writings, you arrive at a necessary knowledge of what these men are.

Similarly, if you understand what it is to be a prophet, and have devoted much time to the study of the Qur'an and the Traditions, you will arrive at a necessary knowledge of the fact that Muhammad (God bless and preserve him) is in the highest grades of the prophetic calling. Convince yourself of that by trying out what he said about the influence of devotional practices on the purification of the heart—how truly he asserted that "whoever lives out what he knows will receive from God what he does not know"; how truly he asserted that "if anyone aids an evildoer, God will give that man power over him"; how truly he asserted that "if a man rises up in the morning with but a single care (*sc.* to please God), God most high will preserve him from all cares in this world and the next." When you have made trial of these in a thousand or several thousand instances, you will arrive at a necessary knowledge beyond all doubt.

By this method, then, seek certainty about the prophetic office, and not from the transformation of a rod into a serpent or the cleaving of the moon. For if you consider such an event by itself, without taking account of the numerous circumstances accompanying it—circumstances readily eluding the grasp of the intellect—then you might perhaps suppose that it was magic and deception and that it came from God to lead men astray; for "He leads astray whom He will, and guides whom He will." Thus the topic of miracles will be thrown back upon you; for if your faith is based on a reasoned argument involving

the probative force of the miracle, then your faith is destroyed by an ordered argument showing the difficulty and ambiguity of the miracle.

Admit, then, that wonders of this sort are one of the proofs and accompanying circumstances out of the totality of your thought on the matter; and that you attain necessary knowledge and yet are unable to say specifically on what it is based. The case is similar to that of a man who receives from a multitude of people a piece of information which is a matter of common belief. . . . He is unable to say that the certainty is derived from the remark of a single specific person; rather, its source is unknown to him; it is neither from outside the whole, nor is it from specific individuals. This is strong, intellectual faith. Immediate experience, on the other hand, is like actually witnessing a thing and taking it in one's hand. It is only found in the way of mysticism.

This is a sufficient discussion of the nature of prophetic revelation for my present purpose.

Suggestions for Further Reading

See Seyyed Hossein Nasr's *Ideals and Realities of Islam* (Boston: Beacon Press, 1972) for a general introduction to Islamic thought and practice. Chapter 4 of F. C. Copleston's *Medieval Philosophy* (New York: Harper & Row, 1961) will provide basic information on Islamic philosophy. *Philosophy in the Middle Ages,* edited by Arthur Hyman and James J. Walsh (Indianapolis: Hackett Publishing Company, 1973), provides original texts, background summaries, and a good bibliography.

Martin Ling's *What Is Sufism?* (Berkeley: University of California Press, 1977) will give you a good introduction to this fascinating type of mysticism. A. J. Arberry's *Revelation and Reason in Islam* (London: George Allen & Unwin, 1957) is a standard presentation of the diverse Islamic approaches to this problem.

See W. M. Watt's *Muslim Intellectual: A Study of al-Ghazali* (Edinburgh: University Press, 1963) for an excellent overview of al-Ghazali's thought. See Averroes, *Thafut al-Tahafat (The Incoherence of the Incoherence),* translated by Simon Van den Bergh (London: Luzac, 1969), for a critique of al-Ghazali's views by another Islamic philosopher (a secondary discussion and overview can be found in *World Philosophy.*)

Videos

The Five Pillars of Islam (30 minutes) presents a basic overview of the fundamental Islamic beliefs, and *Islamic Science and Technology* (30 minutes) recounts the significant contribution to the fields of astronomy, physics, medicine, and engineering made by Islamic thinkers. Both are available from Films for the Humanities and Sciences. See your Media Services Catalogue for further information.

8.2. Is Certainty Possible?

Have you ever been plagued by doubt? Would you like to be certain about something? Have you ever longed for an absolute truth that would never let you down? Have you ever gotten tired of questions, questions, questions?

You might be inclined to answer, "Yes, especially when studying philosophy." Uncertainty is not a pleasant state for anyone, even philosophers. It leaves us up in the air, juggling things that might fall and break at any moment. Uncertainty is unsettling. And yet if we really want to know what is true, if we really want absolutely certain knowledge, must we not question and doubt until we find it?

René Descartes was born in France in 1596 and died in Sweden in 1650. He was a brilliant philosopher and mathematician who has been called "the father" of modern philosophy. Like many of you, and like al-Ghazali (see Section 8.1), he sought something about which he could be absolutely certain. And he was willing to undergo the turmoil of doubt to find it because he believed that we should accept as true only that which is supported by sound arguments.

Descartes is a methodical skeptic because he employs the method of doubt in his quest for certainty. This method deals with *logical possibility*. He is not concerned with beliefs that people actually doubt or beliefs that are in fact false. Rather, he is concerned with those beliefs that it is logically possible to doubt. If it is possible for a belief to be false, then it is capable of being doubted, whether or not, as a matter of fact, anyone has ever doubted it and whether or not, as a matter of fact, it is false.

But Descartes could not be content with skepticism. Ultimately he sought knowledge firmly grounded in reason. Like Plato he was a rationalist, holding that beliefs based on sensations are little more than opinions, but beliefs based on reason constitute genuine knowledge. However, he refines Plato's distinction between opinion and knowledge. By "certainty" he meant that about which logical doubt is impossible. A belief is certain (or "clear and distinct" as Descartes liked to put it) if it is not logically possible to doubt its truth. Only such beliefs constitute knowledge. Since it is logically possible to doubt the truth of beliefs based on sensations, such beliefs must constitute opinion, not knowledge.

In order to grasp Descartes's philosophical project, we must take a brief look at the historical context. Descartes lived at the time when modern science was developing and was replacing medieval science, which had been based on the philosophies of Aristotle and Plato. Medieval science assumed as true a theory (ultimately derived from Aristotle) called "direct realism" (see Section 7.4). According to this theory, there is a reality that exists apart from human sensations, and our senses put us directly in touch with this reality.

This theory of direct realism had proved increasingly problematic because it seemed to lead to all sorts of contradictions. I see a house as small from a distance and as large when close up. Is the house both small and large? Hardly. But if our senses put us *directly* in touch with the *real* house, then what else can we conclude?

Galileo Galilei (1564–1642), who had reintroduced the atomistic theory of matter into physical science, also rejected direct realism because it was rather obvious that we do not directly sense atoms. If what is really out there are atoms and if we don't sense them, then we cannot be directly in touch with physical reality via our senses.

So what role do our senses play? Galileo proposed a theory called "indirect or representational realism" (see Section 7.4). According to this theory, our sensations represent physical reality. However, we are not directly in touch with that reality; we are only directly in touch with our sensations *of* that reality.

But how does Galileo know that? How does he know, or for that matter, how does anyone know that our sensations represent an external reality? We cannot get outside of sensations to see. We cannot compare our image of a fat cat with the real fat cat as we can compare a picture of a fat cat with our sensations of a fat cat. You may recall that this problem, among others, led Berkeley (Section 7.4) to deny the existence of matter.

Descartes, however, did not arrive at a conclusion as radical as Berkeley's. Descartes believed that science ought to provide us with certainty. Its great promise was to give us knowledge. Knowledge is certainty as far as Descartes is concerned, but how can science provide us with knowledge if the theory on which it is built, the theory of indirect or representational realism, cannot be proved true? Without a proof of representational realism, science is without a firm foundation, or so Descartes thought.

Descartes wrote his famous *Meditations on First Philosophy* in order to arrive at certainty and to prove representational realism correct. Here you will read only the first two *Meditations* because they deal directly with his epistemological theory. This is unfortunate because it is like stopping a play after you have seen only the first two acts. But you will have a chance to read more of the Meditations later, and I will provide you with the big picture surrounding the two Meditations you will read here.

In the first Meditation, Descartes employs the method of doubt to show that all our beliefs based on sensations can be doubted and that we cannot even be sure we have not made a mistake in calculation when we do mathematics. In the second Meditation, he shows that one thing cannot be doubted and this is that "I exist as a thinking thing when I think." This is the famous *"cogito, ergo sum"* ("I think, therefore I am") argument, and Descartes maintains this is an absolutely certain truth that cannot be doubted. In later Meditations Descartes attempts to rationally deduce the existence of God from his own existence as a thinking thing and to show that God is perfectly good and hence no deceiver.

"So what," you say? Well, if we can be certain that we exist and if we can be certain that God exists and if we can be certain that God is no deceiver, we can also be certain that our sensations must truly represent an external reality. If they did not, we would live in constant error and ignorance, like Plato's prisoners in the cave (see Section 7.2), and this, surely, a good and gracious God would not allow.

This may seem rather farfetched to you, but only after reading Descartes and struggling with the details of his argument will his real genius become clear, even if, in the end, you don't agree with him. So off we go, beginning on a sea of doubt with the first island of certainty looming ahead. Let's take along the following questions and answer them. They will help make the journey more understandable.

Reading Questions

1. What is Descartes's goal, and what is the method he is going to employ in order to get there?

2. Many of our beliefs are based on sensation. Descartes offers two arguments, the arguments from deception and dreaming, to show that beliefs based on sensations are not trustworthy. State these arguments in your own words.

3. List some examples of occasions when you have been deceived by your senses.

4. Have you ever had a dream that you were totally convinced was true? How do you know you are not now dreaming?

5. Some of our beliefs, for example, that two plus three equals five, are based on reasoning, not sensation. Descartes argues that even arithmetic calculations can be doubted. What is the argument?

6. Descartes ends the first Meditation with the famous evil demon argument. What is the point of this argument?

7. Play Descartes's game for a moment and imagine there is an all-powerful force that has nothing better to do than to deceive you. Give this force a name and imagine it, like some mad puppeteer pulling the strings behind the scenes, constantly arranging things so that your beliefs are false. Now ask yourself, "Is there anything about which this wicked force could not deceive me?" If there is anything you can think of, what is it?

8. Descartes concludes that the statement "I am, I exist" must be true whenever he thinks it. Why? What reasons support this conclusion?

9. The next step in Descartes's argument is to reach the conclusion that he is a thinking thing. How does he reach that conclusion? Why does he not conclude instead that he is a physical thing?

10. In the final paragraph of Meditation II, Descartes lists several things he has learned from his consideration of a piece of wax. What are they, and how does he arrive at these conclusions?

11. What similarities and differences do you notice between al-Ghazali's quest for knowledge (see Section 8.1) and Descartes's quest?

12. How does Descartes answer the question, "Is knowledge possible?"

Meditations I and II

RENÉ DESCARTES

Meditation I

ON WHAT CAN BE CALLED
INTO DOUBT

FOR SEVERAL YEARS NOW, I've been aware that I accepted many falsehoods as true in my youth, that what I built on the foundations of those falsehoods was dubious, and accordingly that once in my life I would need to tear down everything and begin anew from the foundations if I wanted to establish any stable and lasting knowledge. But the task seemed enormous, and

I waited until I was so old that no better time for undertaking it would be likely to follow. I have thus delayed so long that it would be wrong for me to waste in indecision the time left for action. Today, then, having rid myself of worries and having arranged for some peace and quiet, I withdraw alone, free at last earnestly and wholeheartedly to overthrow all my beliefs.

To do this, I don't need to show each of them to be false: I may never be able to do that. But, since reason now convinces me that I ought to withhold my assent just as carefully from what isn't obviously certain and indubitable as from

From René Descartes's Meditations on First Philosophy, *translated by Ronald Rubin (Claremont, CA: Areté Press, 1986), pp. 1–13. Reprinted by permission of Areté Press.*

what's obviously false, I can justify the rejection of all my beliefs if in each I can find some ground for doubt. And, to do this, I need not run through my beliefs one by one, which would be an endless task. Since a building collapses when its foundation is cut out from under it, I will go straight to the principles on which all my former beliefs rested.

Of course, whatever I have so far accepted as supremely true I have learned either from the senses or through the senses. But I have occasionally caught the senses deceiving me, and it's prudent never completely to trust those who have cheated us even once.

But, while my senses may deceive me about what is small or far away, there may still be other things which I take in by the senses but which I cannot possibly doubt—like that I am here, sitting before the fire, wearing a dressing gown, touching this paper. And on what grounds might I deny that my hands and the other parts of my body exist?—unless perhaps I liken myself to madmen whose brains are so rattled by the persistent vapors of melancholy that they are sure that they're kings when in fact they are paupers, or that they wear purple robes when in fact they're naked, or that their heads are clay, or that they are gourds, or made of glass. But these people are insane, and I would seem just as crazy if I were to apply what I say about them to myself.

This would be perfectly obvious—if I weren't a man accustomed to sleeping at night whose experiences while asleep are at least as far-fetched as those that madmen have while awake. How often, at night, I've been convinced that I was here, sitting before the fire, wearing my dressing gown, when in fact I was undressed and between the covers of my bed! But now I am looking at this piece of paper with my eyes wide open; the head that I am shaking has not been lulled to sleep; I put my hand out consciously and deliberately and feel. None of this would be as distinct if I were asleep. As if I can't remember having been tricked by similar thoughts while asleep! When I think very carefully about this, I see so plainly that there are no reliable signs by which I can distinguish sleeping from waking that I am

stupefied—and my stupor itself suggests that I am asleep!

Suppose, then, that I am dreaming. Suppose, in particular, that my eyes are not open, that my head is not moving, and that I have not put out my hand. Suppose that I do not have hands, or even a body. I must still admit that the things I see in sleep are like painted images which must have been patterned after real things and, hence, that things like eyes, heads, hands, and bodies are real rather than imaginary. For, even when painters try to give bizarre shapes to sirens and satyrs, they are unable to give them completely new natures; they only jumble together the parts of various animals. And, even if they were to come up with something so novel that no one had ever seen anything like it before, something entirely fictitious and unreal, at least there must be real colors from which they composed it. Similarly, while things like eyes, heads, and hands may be imaginary, it must be granted that some simpler and more universal things are real—the "real colors" from which the true and false images in our thoughts are formed.

Things of this sort seem to include general bodily nature and its extension, the shape of extended things, their quantity (that is, their size and number), the place in which they exist, the time through which they endure, and so on.

Perhaps we can correctly infer that, while physics, astronomy, medicine, and other disciplines that require the study of composites are dubious, disciplines like arithmetic and geometry, which deal only with completely simple and universal things without regard to whether they exist in the world, are somehow certain and indubitable. For, whether we are awake or asleep, two plus three is always five, and the square never has more than four sides. It seems impossible even to suspect such obvious truths of falsity.

Nevertheless, the traditional view is fixed in my mind that there is a God who can do anything and by whom I have been made to be as I am. How do I know that He hasn't brought it about that, while there is in fact no earth, no sky, no extended thing, no shape, no magnitude, and no place, all of these things seem to me to exist, just as they do now? I think that other people sometimes err in what they believe themselves to know perfectly well. Mightn't I be deceived when I add two and three, or count the sides of a square, or do even simpler things, if we can even suppose that there is anything simpler? Maybe it will be denied that God deceives me, since He is said to be supremely good. But, if God's being good is incompatible with His having created me so that I am deceived always, it seems just as out of line with His being good that He permits me to be deceived sometimes—as he undeniably does.

Maybe some would rather deny that there is an omnipotent God than believe that everything else is uncertain. Rather than arguing with them, I will grant everything I have said about God to be fiction. But, however these people think I came to be as I now am—whether they say it is by fate, or by accident, or by a continuous series of events, or in some other way—it seems that he who errs and is deceived is somehow imperfect. Hence, the less power that is attributed to my original creator, the more likely it is that I am always deceived. To these arguments, I have no reply. I'm forced to admit that nothing that I used to believe is beyond legitimate doubt—not because I have been careless or playful, but because I have valid and well-considered grounds for doubt. Hence, I must withhold my assent from my former beliefs as carefully as from obvious falsehoods if I want to arrive at something certain.

But it's not enough to have noticed this: I must also take care to bear it in mind. For my habitual views constantly return to my mind and take control of what I believe as if our long-standing, intimate relationship has given them the right to do so, even against my will. I'll never break the habit of trusting and giving in to these views while I see them for what they are—things somewhat dubious (as I have just shown) but nonetheless probable, things that I have much more reason to believe than to deny. That's why I think it will be good deliberately to turn my will around, to allow myself to be deceived, and to suppose that all my previous beliefs are false and

illusory. Eventually, when I have counterbalanced the weight of my prejudices, my bad habits will no longer distort my grasp of things. I know that there is no danger of error here and that I won't overindulge in skepticism, since I'm now concerned, not with action, but only with gaining knowledge.

I will suppose, then, not that there is a supremely good God who is the source of all truth, but that there is an evil demon, supremely powerful and cunning, who works as hard as he can to deceive me. I will say that sky, air, earth, color, shape, sound, and other external things are just dreamed illusions which the demon uses to ensnare my judgment. I will regard myself as not having hands, eyes, flesh, blood, and senses—but as having the false belief that I have all these things. I will obstinately concentrate on this meditation and will thus ensure by mental resolution that, if I do not really have the ability to know the truth, I will at least withhold assent from what is false and from what a deceiver may try to put over on me, however powerful and cunning he may be. But this plan requires effort, and laziness brings me back to my ordinary life. I am like a prisoner who happens to enjoy the illusion of freedom in his dreams, begins to suspect that he is asleep, fears being awakened, and deliberately lets the enticing illusions slip by unchallenged. Thus, I slide back into my old views, afraid to awaken and to find that after my peaceful rest I must toil, not in the light, but in the confusing darkness of the problems just raised.

Meditation II

ON THE NATURE OF THE HUMAN MIND, WHICH IS BETTER KNOWN THAN THE BODY

Yesterday's meditation has hurled me into doubts so great that I can neither ignore them nor think my way out of them. I am in turmoil, as if I have accidentally fallen into a whirlpool and can neither touch bottom nor swim to the safety of the surface. I will struggle, however, and try to follow the path that I started on yesterday. I will reject whatever is open to the slightest doubt just as though I have found it to be entirely false, and I will continue until I find something certain— or at least until I know for certain that nothing is certain. Archimedes required only one fixed and immovable point to move the whole earth from its place, and I too can hope for great things if I can find even one small thing that is certain and unshakable.

I will suppose, then, that everything I see is unreal. I will believe that my memory is unreliable and that none of what it presents to me ever happened. I have no senses. Body, shape, extension, motion, and place are fantasies. What then is true? Perhaps just that nothing is certain.

But how do I know that there isn't something different from the things just listed which I do not have the slightest reason to doubt? Isn't there a God, or something like one, who puts my thoughts into me? But why should I say so when I may be the author of those thoughts? Well, isn't it at least the case that I am something? But I now am denying that I have senses and a body. But I stop here. For what follows from these denials? Am I so bound to my body and to my senses that I cannot exist without them? I have convinced myself that there is nothing in the world—no sky, no earth, no minds, no bodies. Doesn't it follow that I don't exist? No, surely I must exist if it's I who is convinced of something. But there is a deceiver, supremely powerful and cunning, whose aim is to see that I am always deceived. But surely I exist, if I am deceived. Let him deceive me all he can, he will never make it the case that I am nothing while I think that I am something. Thus having fully weighed every consideration, I must finally conclude that the statement "I am, I exist" must be true whenever I state it or mentally consider it.

But I do not yet fully understand what this "I" is that must exist. I must guard against inadvertently taking myself to be something other than I am, thereby going wrong even in the knowledge that I put forward as supremely certain and evident. Hence, I will think once again about what I believed myself to be before beginning these meditations. From this concep-

tion, I will subtract everything challenged by the reasons for doubt which I produced earlier, until nothing remains except what is certain and indubitable.

What, then, did I formerly take myself to be? A man, of course. But what is a man? Should I say a rational animal? No, because then I would need to ask what an animal is and what it is to be rational. Thus, starting from a single question, I would sink into many which are more difficult, and I do not have the time to waste on such subtleties. Instead, I will look here at the thought which occurred to me spontaneously and naturally when I reflected on what I was. The first thought to occur to me was that I have a face, hands, arms, and all the other equipment (also found in corpses) which I call a body. The next thought to occur to me was that I take nourishment, move myself around, sense, and think— that I do things which I trace back to my soul. Either I didn't stop to think about what this soul was, or I imagined it to be a rarified air, or fire, or ether permeating the denser parts of my body. But, about physical objects, I didn't have any doubts whatever: I thought that I distinctly knew their nature. If I had tried to describe my conception of this nature, I might have said this: "When I call something a physical object, I mean that it is capable of being bounded by a shape and limited to a place; that it can fill a space so as to exclude other objects from it; that it can be perceived by touch, sight, hearing, taste, and smell; that it can be moved in various ways, not by itself, but by something else in contact with it." I judged that the powers of self-movement, of sensing, and of thinking did not belong to the nature of physical objects, and, in fact, I marveled that there were some physical objects in which these powers could be found.

But what should I think now, while supposing that a supremely powerful and "evil" deceiver completely devotes himself to deceiving me? Can I say that I have any of the things that I have attributed to the nature of physical objects? I concentrate, think, reconsider—but nothing comes to me; I grow tired of the pointless repetition. But what about the things that I have assigned to soul? Nutrition and self-movement? Since I have no body, these are merely illusions. Sensing? But I cannot sense without a body, and in sleep I've seemed to sense many things that I later realized I had not really sensed. Thinking? It comes down to this: Thought and thought alone cannot be taken away from me. I am, I exist. That much is certain. But for how long? As long as I think—for it may be that, if I completely stopped thinking, I would completely cease to exist. I am not now admitting anything unless it must be true, and I am therefore not admitting that I am anything at all other than a thinking thing—that is, a mind, soul, understanding, or reason (terms whose meaning I did not previously know). I know that I am a real, existing thing, but what kind of thing? As I have said, a thing that thinks.

What else? I will draw up mental images. I'm not the collection of organs called a human body. Nor am I some rarified gas permeating these organs, or air, or fire, or vapor, or breath—for I have supposed that none of these things exist. Still, I am something. But couldn't it be that these things, which I do not yet know about and which I am therefore supposing to be nonexistent, really aren't distinct from the "I" that I know to exist? I don't know, and I'm not going to argue about it now. I can only form judgments on what I do know. I know that I exist, and I ask what the "I" is that I know to exist. It's obvious that this conception of myself doesn't depend on anything that I do not yet know to exist and, therefore, that it does not depend on anything of which I can draw up a mental image. And the words "draw up" point to my mistake. I would truly be creative if I were to have a mental image of what I am, since to have a mental image is just to contemplate the shape or image of a physical object. I now know with certainty that I exist and at the same time that all images—and, more generally, all things associated with the nature of physical objects—may just be dreams. When I keep this in mind, it seems just as absurd to say "I use mental images to help me understand what I am" as it would to say "Now, while awake, I see something true—but, since I don't yet see it clearly enough, I'll go to sleep and let my dreams present it to me more clearly and truly." Thus I know that none of the things that I can comprehend with the aid of mental images bear on my knowledge of myself. And I must carefully draw my mind away from such things if it is to see its own nature distinctly.

But what then am I? A thinking thing. And what is that? Something that doubts, understands, affirms, denies, wills, refuses, and also senses and has mental images.

That's quite a lot, if I really do all of these things. But don't I? Isn't it me who now doubts nearly everything, understands one thing, affirms this thing, refuses to affirm other things, wants to know much more, refuses to be deceived, has mental images (sometimes involuntarily), and is aware of many things "through his senses?" Even if I am always dreaming, and even if my creator does what he can to deceive me, isn't it just as true that I do all these things as that I exist? Are any of these things distinct from my thought? Can any be said to be separate from me? That it's me who doubts, understands, and wills is so obvious that I don't see how it could be more evident. And it's also me who has mental images. While it may be, as I am supposing, that absolutely nothing of which I have a mental image really exists, the ability to have mental images really does exist and is a part of my thought. Finally, it's I who senses—or who seems to gain awareness of physical objects through the senses. For example, I am now seeing light, hearing a noise, and feeling heat. These things are unreal, since I am dreaming. But it is still certain that I seem to see, to hear, and to feel. This seeming cannot be unreal, and it is what is properly called sensing. Strictly speaking, sensing is just thinking.

From this, I begin to learn a little about what I am. But I still can't stop thinking that I apprehend physical objects, which I picture in mental images and examine with my senses, much more distinctly than I know this unfamiliar "I," of which I cannot form a mental image. I think this, even though it would be astounding if I comprehended things which I've found to be doubtful, unknown, and alien to me more distinctly than the one which I know to be real: my self. But I see what's happening. My mind enjoys wandering, and it won't confine itself to the truth. I will therefore loosen the reins on my mind for now so that later, when the time is right, I will be able to control it more easily.

Let's consider the things commonly taken to be the most distinctly comprehended: physical objects that we see and touch. Let's not consider physical objects in general, since general conceptions are very often confused. Rather, let's consider one, particular object. Take, for example, this piece of wax. It has just been taken from the honeycomb; it hasn't yet completely lost the taste of honey; it still smells of the flowers from which it was gathered; its color, shape, and size are obvious; it is hard, cold, and easy to touch; it makes a sound when rapped. In short, everything seems to be present in the wax that is required for me to know it as distinctly as possible. But, as I speak, I move the wax towards the fire; it loses what was left of its taste; it gives up its smell; it changes color; it loses its shape; it gets bigger; it melts; it heats up; it becomes difficult to touch; it no longer makes a sound when struck. Is it still the same piece of wax? We must say that it is: no one denies it or thinks otherwise. Then what was there in the wax that I comprehended so distinctly? Certainly nothing that I reached with my senses—for, while everything having to do with taste, smell, sight, touch, and hearing has changed, the same piece of wax remains.

Perhaps what I distinctly knew was neither the sweetness of honey, not the fragrance of flowers, nor a sound, but a physical object which once appeared to me one way and now appears differently. But what exactly is it of which I now have a mental image? Let's pay careful attention, remove everything that doesn't belong to the wax, and see what's left. Nothing is left except an extended, flexible, and changeable thing. But what is it for this thing to be flexible and changeable? Is it just that the wax can go from round to square and then to triangular, as I have mentally pictured? Of course not. Since I understand that the wax's shape can change in innumerable ways, and since I can't run through all the changes in my imagination, my comprehension of the wax's

flexibility and changeability cannot have been produced by my ability to have mental images. And what about the thing that is extended? Are we also ignorant of its extension? Since the extension of the wax increases when the wax melts, increases again when the wax boils, and increases still more when the wax gets hotter, I will be mistaken about what the wax is unless I believe that it can undergo more changes in extension than I can ever encompass with mental images. I must therefore admit that I do not have an image of what the wax is—that I grasp what it is with only my mind. (While I am saying this about a particular piece of wax, it is even more clearly true about wax in general.) What then is this piece of wax that I grasp only with my mind? It is something that I see, feel, and mentally picture—exactly what I believed it to be at the outset. But it must be noted that, despite the appearances, my grasp of the wax is not visual, tactile, or pictorial. Rather, my grasp of the wax is the result of a purely mental inspection, which can be imperfect and confused, as it was once, or clear and distinct, as it is now, depending on how much attention I pay to the things of which the wax consists.

I'm surprised by how prone my mind is to error. Even when I think to myself non-verbally, language stands in my way, and common usage comes close to deceiving me. For, when the wax is present, we say that we see the wax itself, not that we infer its presence from its color and shape. I'm inclined to leap from this fact about language to the conclusion that I learn about the wax by eyesight rather than by purely mental inspection. But, if I happen to look out my window and see men walking in the street, I naturally say that I see the men just as I say that I see the wax. What do I really see, however, but hats and coats that could be covering robots? I *judge* that there are men. Thus I comprehend with my judgment, which is in my mind, objects that I once believed myself to see with my eyes.

One who aspires to wisdom above that of the common man disgraces himself by deriving doubt from common ways of speaking. Let's go on, then, to ask when I most clearly and perfectly grasped what the wax is. Was it when I first looked at the wax and believed my knowledge of it to come from the external senses—or at any rate from the so-called "common sense," the power of having mental images? Or is it now, after I have carefully studied what the wax is and how I come to know it? Doubt would be silly here. For what was distinct in my original conception of the wax? How did that conception differ from that had by animals? When I distinguish the wax from its external forms—when I "undress" it and view it "naked"—there may still be errors in my judgments about it, but I couldn't possibly grasp the wax in this way without a human mind.

What should I say about this mind—or, in other words, about myself? (I am not now admitting that there is anything to me but a mind.) What is this "I" that seems to grasp the wax so distinctly? Don't I know myself much more truly and certainly, and also much more distinctly and plainly, than I know the wax? For, if I base my judgment that the wax exists on the fact that I see it, my seeing it much more obviously implies that I exist. It's possible that what I see is not really wax, and it's even possible that I don't have eyes with which to see—but it clearly is not possible that, when I see (or, what now amounts to the same thing, when I think I see), the "I" which thinks is not a real thing. Similarly, if I base

my judgement that the wax exists on the fact that I feel it, the same fact makes it obvious that I exist. If I base my judgment that the wax exists on the fact that I have a mental image of it or on some other fact of this sort, the same thing can obviously be said. And what I've said about the wax applies to everything else that is outside me. Moreover, if I seem to grasp the wax more distinctly when I detect it with several senses than when I detect it with just sight or touch, I must know myself even more distinctly—for every consideration that contributes to my grasp of the piece of wax or to my grasp of any other physical object serves better to reveal the nature of my mind. Besides, the mind has so much in it by which it can make its conception of itself distinct that what comes to it from physical objects hardly seems to matter.

And now I have brought myself back to where I wanted to be. I now know that physical objects are grasped, not by the senses or the power of having mental images, but by understanding alone. And, since I grasp physical objects in virtue of their being understandable rather than in virtue of their being tangible or visible, I know that I can't grasp anything more easily or plainly than my mind. But, since it takes time to break old habits of thought, I should pause here to allow the length of my contemplation to impress the new thoughts more deeply into my memory.

Suggestions for Further Reading

Start with Chapter 1 of William H. Brenner's little book *Elements of Modern Philosophy: Descartes Through Kant* (Englewood Cliffs, NJ: Prentice-Hall, 1989) for a lucid account and a good list of suggestions for further reading. The article on Descartes in the *Encyclopedia of Philosophy* will also prove helpful and provides a bibliography.

Volume 2 of *World Philosophy* (pp. 828ff) will give you a summary of the main ideas of the *Meditations*. You will find O. K. Bouwsma's "Descartes' Evil Genius" in *Philosophical Essays* (Lincoln: University of Nebraska Press, 1965) a real delight. Bouwsma tries to convince you that the evil demon of Descartes could not really deceive you without your being aware of it.

8.3. Empiricism and Limited Skepticism

David Hume (1711–1776) was a Scottish philosopher whom some regard as the greatest philosopher to write in the English language. There is little doubt about his brilliance. He graduated from the University of Edinburgh at the ripe old age of fifteen and headed for law school. Deciding he did not like law, he began writing a philosophical work called *A Treatise on Human Nature* (1739–40), which he hoped would bring him fame and fortune. It did not. Very few people understood what he was talking about. Disappointed, he wrote a more popular version called *An Enquiry Concerning Human Understanding* (1748) from which the following selection is taken. You can judge for yourself how popular this version might have been.

Hume presents an empiricist theory of knowledge: Everything we can know about the world is ultimately derived from our senses. He developed empiricism into a critical tool for checking ideas. If you want to know what an idea or concept means, says Hume, trace it back to the impressions from which it comes (see Section II). For example, in a famous section (VII, not included here) Hume seeks to find out what the concept of cause means. This is a basic idea because so much of science and, for that matter, common sense presupposes the law of cause and effect.

Usually people mean three things by "cause," namely, that event A is the cause of event B if A occurs *before B, A* is *contiguous* to B in some way, and A is *necessarily connected* with B. It is this last idea that has Hume puzzled. What is a necessary connection? From what impression does it arise? The only impression Hume can find is the impression of *constant conjunction.* We say A is the cause of B because in our experience A and B are constantly conjoined. Yet the concept of a necessary connection goes far beyond constant conjunction. If A and B are necessarily connected, then whenever A occurs, B will necessarily occur. But from the fact that A and B have been constantly conjoined in the past, can we conclude that they will be so connected in the future? It is likely that they will be connected, even highly probable, but high probability is not the same as necessity.

This conclusion shocked the intellectual community of Hume's day because, if Hume is right, a fundamental law of thought and of science is without foundation in experience. This issue of the foundation of knowledge was of central importance to Hume. The rationalists claimed there was a foundation found in reason; the empiricists claimed there was a foundation found in experience. Hume, while sympathetic to empiricism, questioned whether there are in fact any firm foundations on which knowledge rests other than customary and habitual associations of ideas.

Hume brought the assumption that knowledge had a foundation into question by discovering the **problem of induction** (see Section IV). Although Hume does not call it by this name, the problem of induction, simply stated, is the problem of discovering rational foundations for all the conclusions we draw based on experience. Let's examine this further.

Later philosophers, inspired by Hume, drew a distinction between **analytic** statements such as "All bachelors are unmarried men" and **synthetic** statements such as "My cat is fat." Hume used the terms "relations of ideas" and "matters of fact" for these because analytic statements are about how ideas are related and synthetic statements are about facts. You can test to see if any given statement is analytic by applying this rule: "If it is not logically possible for the negation of the statement to be true, the statement is analytic." The claim that "some bachelors are married" cannot be true because the word "bachelor" means "unmarried man." You can test to see if a statement is synthetic by applying this rule: "If it is logically possible for the negation of the statement to be true, the statement is synthetic." It is quite possible that in fact my cat is not fat.

See if you understand these rules by determining which of these statements are analytic and which synthetic.

1. The sun is round.
2. The lights are on.
3. $(2 + 2 = 4)$.
4. Philosophy is fun.
5. Blind bats cannot see.

Note that statements about the relation of ideas (analytic) are *necessarily true*. That is, they are true by virtue of the meaning of the terms. Statements about matters of fact (synthetic) are *contingently true* because their truth depends on a certain state of affairs actually obtaining. Philosophers have also maintained that the truth of analytic statements is justified *a priori* by deductive reasoning while the truth of synthetic statements is justified *a posteriori* by inductive reasoning.

Let us return to the problem of induction. Conclusions based on experience presuppose, according to Hume, that the future will resemble the past. Now how is this presupposition justified? There are two types of proof: deductive and inductive. We cannot justify the statement, "The future will resemble the past," deductively because it is not an analytic statement, but a synthetic statement. It is logically possible that the future will not resemble the past. So what about induction? Well, according to Hume, we cannot justify it inductively because that would be to beg the question (argue in a circle). It amounts to circular reasoning because the inductive method itself presupposes this rule, namely, that the future will resemble the past.

The question of whether there is a foundation of knowledge remains a major philosophical problem. In fact, philosophy today is deeply embroiled in this issue. For Hume, it was important because the then new physical sciences claimed to provide knowledge of the world based on conclusions drawn from experience. Can such scientific knowledge be philosophically justified?

In the last section (XII, "On the Academical or Skeptical Philosophy") of the *Enquiry* (not included here) Hume admits it is our natural instinct to believe that our senses provide us with information about an external world. But this is a philosophically naive attitude because serious objections can be raised that would lead us to doubt whether we do have access to an external world through our senses (remember Berkeley?). Our senses do not put us directly in touch with external objects. We never see a chair per se, only visual images which we infer to be *of* a chair.

There are two ways to overcome such objections. One way is to argue that assertions about matters of fact (synthetic statements) are justified by reference to sense experience or impressions (*a posteriori*). But all such proofs are bound to fail because all they can ever prove is that we have sensations. The other way is to try to prove deductively the existence of an external world (remember Descartes?). But this line of argument is also bound to fail because the most it can prove is that certain relations among ideas (analytic statements) are true *a priori*. Such arguments tell us what words mean, but do not tell us what the world is like.

If critical objections to the naive attitude cannot be overcome by either inductive or deductive reasoning, then skepticism about all claims to knowledge of the external world seems the only logical conclusion to draw. But absolute skepticism can be shown to lead to absurdities. If we really were totally skeptical about all our beliefs based on sensation, then we would never move because there is no proof that we can, nor would we ever eat because there is no proof that food exists or is good for us. Besides, absolute skepticism is self-refuting. So if inductive and deductive arguments fail and if absolute skepticism leads to absurdities, what are we to do?

Hume ends up advocating a limited or "mitigated" skepticism much like the commonsense skepticism I mentioned in the introduction. We should take claims to knowledge with a grain of salt. We should accept what seems reasonable and useful, but keep an open mind. We should avoid dogmatism and beware of a naive credulity. And we should limit our enquiries to subjects that are useful. These include mathematics, which provides us with useful analytic statements justified *a priori*, and the physical and social sciences, which provide us with synthetic statements justified *a posteriori*. All other subjects such as metaphysical speculations and theology are best left alone.

But enough of my telling you what Hume is about. Read him for yourself and see.

Reading Questions

1. Into what two categories can the "perceptions of the mind" be divided, and how are they distinguished from each other? Give an example of each.

2. Hume presents two arguments to prove "all our ideas . . . are copies of our impressions." State these arguments in your own words. What do you think of them? Are they convincing? Why or why not?

3. What is the difference between "matters of fact" and "relations of ideas?" Provide your own example of each.

4. According to Hume, all reasoning concerning matters of fact is founded on the relation of cause and effect. This relation, Hume argues, is not discoverable by reason, only by experience. Summarize the argument Hume uses to support this claim.

5. In answer to the question, "What is the foundation of all conclusions from experience?" Hume challenges the reader to supply the foundation for the inference from the fact that I have found objects (like bread) to produce certain effects (like nourishment) in the past to the conclusion that the same will occur in the future. Can you supply the basis for the connection or inference between these two statements? If so, what is it?

6. Why can we not prove the principle, "the future will resemble the past," deductively (Hume's term is "by demonstrative reasoning")?

7. Why can we not prove this principle inductively ("by moral reasoning")?

8. What don't you understand about what Hume is saying? Mark the passages in the text and bring them up in class.

9. How do you think Hume would answer the question, "Is knowledge possible?" How does his answer differ from the answers given by al-Ghazali and Descartes?

An Enquiry Concerning Human Understanding

DAVID HUME

Section II

OF THE ORIGIN OF IDEAS

EVERYONE WILL READILY allow that there is a considerable difference between the perceptions of the mind, when a man feels the pain of excessive heat, or the pleasure of moderate warmth, and when he afterwards recalls to his memory this sensation, or anticipates it by his imagination. These faculties may mimic or copy the perceptions of the senses; but they never can entirely reach the force and vivacity of the original sentiment. The utmost we say of them, even when they operate with greatest vigour, is, that they represent their object in so lively a manner, that we could *almost* say we feel or see it: But, except the mind be disordered by disease or madness, they never can arrive at such a pitch of vivacity, as to render these perceptions altogether indistinguishable. All the colors of poetry, however splendid, can never paint natural objects in such a manner as to make the description be taken for a real landscape. The most lively thought is still inferior to the dullest sensation.

We may observe a like distinction to run through all the other perceptions of the mind. A man in a fit of anger is actuated in a very different manner from one who only thinks of that emotion. If you tell me that any person is in love, I easily understand your meaning, and form a just conception of his situation; but never can mistake that conception for the real disorders and agitations of the passion. When we reflect on our past sentiments and affections, our thought is a faithful mirror, and copies its objects truly; but the colors which it employs are faint and dull, in comparison of those in which our original perceptions were clothed. It requires no nice discernment or metaphysical head to mark the distinction between them.

Here therefore we may divide all the perceptions of the mind into two classes or species, which are distinguished by their different degrees of force and vivacity. The less forcible and lively are commonly denominated *Thoughts* or *Ideas.* The other species want a name in our language, and in most others; I suppose, because it was not requisite for any, but philosophical purposes, to rank them under a general term or appellation. Let us, therefore, use a little freedom, and call them *Impressions;* employing that word in a sense somewhat different from the usual. By the term *impression,* then, I mean all our more lively perceptions, when we hear, or see, or feel, or love, or hate, or desire, or will. And impressions are distinguished from ideas, which are the less lively perceptions, of which we are conscious, when we reflect on any of those sensations or movements above mentioned.

Nothing, at first view, may seem more unbounded than the thought of man, which not only escapes all human power and authority, but is not even restrained within the limits of nature and reality. To form monsters, and join incongruous shapes and appearances, costs the imagination no more trouble than to conceive the most natural and familiar objects. And while the body is confined to one planet, along which it creeps with pain and difficulty; the thought can in an instant transport us into the most distant regions of the universe; or even beyond the universe, into the unbounded chaos, where nature is supposed to lie in total confusion. What never was seen, or heard of, may yet be conceived; nor is any thing beyond the power of thought, except what implies an absolute contradiction.

Excerpts from Sections II and IV of David Hume's An Enquiry Concerning Human Understanding *(Oxford: Clarendon Press, 1748).*

But though our thought seems to possess this unbounded liberty, we shall find, upon a nearer examination, that it is really confined within very narrow limits, and that all this creative power of the mind amounts to no more than the faculty of compounding, transposing, augmenting, or diminishing the materials afforded us by the senses and experience. When we think of a golden mountain, we only join two consistent ideas, *gold,* and *mountain,* with which we were formerly acquainted. A virtuous horse we can conceive; because, from our own feeling, we can conceive virtue; and this we may unite to the figure and shape of a horse, which is an animal familiar to us. In short, all the materials of thinking are derived either from our outward or inward sentiment: the mixture and composition of these belongs alone to the mind and will. Or, to express myself in philosophical language, all our ideas or more feeble perceptions are copies of our impressions or more lively ones.

To prove this, the two following arguments will, I hope, be sufficient. First, when we analyze our thoughts or ideas, however compounded or sublime, we always find that they resolve themselves into such simple ideas as were copied from a precedent feeling or sentiment. Even those ideas, which, at first view, seem the most wide of this origin, are found, upon a nearer scrutiny, to be derived from it. The idea of God, as meaning an infinitely intelligent, wise, and good Being, arises from reflecting on the operations of our own mind, and augmenting, without limit, those qualities of goodness and wisdom. We may prosecute this enquiry to what length we please; where we shall always find, that every idea which we examine is copied from a similar impression. Those who would assert that this position is not universally true nor without exception, have only one, and that an easy method of refuting it; by producing that idea, which, in their opinion, is not derived from this source. It will then be incumbent on us, if we would maintain our doctrine, to produce the impression, or lively perception, which corresponds to it.

Secondly. If it happens, from a defect of the organ, that a man is not susceptible of any species of sensation, we always find that he is as little susceptible of the correspondent ideas. A blind man can form no notion of colors; a deaf man of sounds. Restore either of them that sense in which he is deficient; by opening this new inlet for his sensations, you also open an inlet for the ideas; and he finds no difficulty in conceiving these objects. The case is the same, if the object, proper for exciting any sensation, has never been applied to the organ. A Laplander or Negro has no notion of the relish of wine. And though there are few or no instances of a like deficiency in the mind, where a person has never felt or is wholly incapable of a sentiment or passion that belongs to his species; yet we find the same observation to take place in a less degree. A man of mild manners can form no idea of inveterate revenge or cruelty; nor can a selfish heart easily conceive the heights of friendship and generosity. It is readily allowed that other beings may possess many senses of which we can have no conception; because the ideas of them have never been introduced to us in the only manner by which an idea can have access to the mind, to wit, by the actual feeling and sensation. . . .

Section IV

SKEPTICAL DOUBTS CONCERNING THE OPERATIONS OF THE UNDERSTANDING

PART I All the objects of human reason or enquiry may naturally be divided into two kinds, to wit, *Relations of Ideas,* and *Matters of Fact.* Of the first kind are the sciences of Geometry, Algebra, and Arithmetic; and in short, every affirmation which is either intuitively or demonstratively certain. *That the square of the hypotenuse is equal to the square of the two sides,* is a proposition which expresses a relation between these figures. *That three times five is equal to the half of thirty,* expresses a relation between these numbers. Propositions of this kind are discoverable by the mere operation of thought, without dependence on what is anywhere existent in the universe. Though there never were a circle or triangle in nature, the truths demonstrated by Euclid would for ever retain their certainty and evidence.

Matters of fact, which are the second objects of human reason, are not ascertained in the same manner; nor is our evidence of their truth, however great, of a like nature with the foregoing. The contrary of every matter of fact is still possible; because it can never imply a contradiction, and is conceived by the mind with the same facility and distinctness, as if ever so conformable to reality. *That the sun will not rise tomorrow* is no less intelligible a proposition, and implies no more contradiction than the affirmation, *that it will rise*. We should in vain, therefore, attempt to demonstrate its falsehood. Were it demonstratively false, it would imply a contradiction, and could never be distinctly conceived by the mind.

It may, therefore, be a subject worthy of curiosity, to enquire what is the nature of that evidence which assures us of any real existence and matter of fact, beyond the present testimony of our senses, or the records of our memory. This part of philosophy, it is observable, has been little cultivated, either by the ancients or moderns; and therefore our doubts and errors, in the prosecution of so important an enquiry, may be the more excusable; while we march through such difficult paths without any guide or direction. They may even prove useful, by exciting curiosity, and destroying that implicit faith and security, which is the bane of all reasoning and free enquiry. The discovery of defects in the common philosophy, if any such there be, will not, I presume, be a discouragement, but rather an incitement, as is usual, to attempt something more full and satisfactory than has yet been proposed to the public.

All reasonings concerning matter of fact seem to be founded on the relation of *Cause and Effect*. By means of that relation alone we can go beyond the evidence of our memory and senses. If you were to ask a man, why he believes any matter of fact, which is absent; for instance, that his friend is in the country, or in France; he would give you a reason; and this reason would be some other fact; as a letter received from him, or the knowledge of his former resolutions and promises. A man finding a watch or any other machine in a desert island, would conclude that there had once been men in that island. All our reasonings concerning fact are of the same nature. And here it is constantly supposed that there is a connection between the present fact and that which is inferred from it. Were there nothing to bind them together, the inference would be entirely precarious. The hearing of an articulate voice and rational discourse in the dark assures us of the presence of some person: Why? because these are the effects of the human make and fabric, and closely connected with it. If we anatomize all the other reasonings of this nature, we shall find that they are founded on the relation of cause and effect, and that this relation is either near or remote, direct or collateral. Heat and light are collateral effects of fire, and the one effect may justly be inferred from the other.

If we would satisfy ourselves, therefore, concerning the nature of that evidence, which assures us of matters of fact, we must enquire how we arrive at the knowledge of cause and effect.

I shall venture to affirm, as a general proposition, which admits of no exception, that the knowledge of this relation is not, in any instance, attained by reasonings *a priori;* but arises entirely from experience, when we find that any particular objects are constantly conjoined with each other. Let an object be presented to a man of ever so strong natural reason and abilities; if that object be entirely new to him, he will not be able, by the most accurate examination of its sensible qualities, to discover any of its causes or effects. Adam, though his rational faculties be supposed, at the very first, entirely perfect, could not have inferred from the fluidity and transparency of water that it would suffocate him, or from the light and warmth of fire that it would consume him. No object ever discovers, by the qualities which appear to the senses, either the causes which produced it, or the effects which will arise from it; nor can our reason, unassisted by experience, ever draw any inference concerning real existence and matter of fact. . . .

We fancy that were we brought on a sudden

into this world, we could at first have inferred that one Billiard-ball would communicate motion to another upon impulse; and that we needed not to have waited for the event, in order to pronounce with certainty concerning it. Such is the influence of custom, that, where it is strongest, it not only covers our natural ignorance, but even conceals itself, and seems not to take place, merely because it is found in the highest degree.

But to convince us that all the laws of nature, and all the operations of bodies without exception, are known only by experience, the following reflections may, perhaps, suffice. Were any object presented to us, and were we required to pronounce concerning the effect, which will result from it, without consulting past observation; after what manner, I beseech you, must the mind proceed in this operation? It must invent or imagine some event, which it ascribes to the object as its effect; and it is plain that this invention must be entirely arbitrary. The mind can never possibly find the effect in the supposed cause, by the most accurate scrutiny and examination. For the effect is totally different from the cause, and consequently can never be discovered in it. Motion in the second Billiard-ball is a quite distinct event from motion in the first; nor is there anything in the one to suggest the smallest hint of the other. A stone or piece of metal raised into the air, and left without any support, immediately falls: but to consider the matter *a priori*, is there anything we discover in this situation which can beget the idea of a downward, rather than an upward, or any other motion, in the stone or metal?

And as the first imagination or invention of a particular effect, in all natural operations, is arbitrary, where we consult not experience; so must we also esteem the supposed tie or connection between the cause and effect, which binds them together, and renders it impossible that any other effect could result from the operation of that cause. When I see, for instance, a Billiard-ball moving in a straight line towards another; even suppose motion in the second ball should by accident be suggested to me, as the result of their contact or impulse; may I not conceive that a hundred different events might as well follow from that cause? May not both these balls remain at absolute rest? May not the first ball return in a straight line, or leap off from the second in any line or direction? All these suppositions are consistent and conceivable. Why then should we give the preference to one, which is no more consistent or conceivable than the rest? All our reasonings *a priori* will never be able to show us any foundation for this preference. . . .

PART II But we have not yet attained any tolerable satisfaction with regard to the question first proposed. Each solution still gives rise to a new question as difficult as the foregoing, and leads us on to further inquiries. When it is asked, *What is the nature of all our reasonings concerning matter of fact?* the proper answer seems to be that they are founded on the relation of cause and effect. When again it is asked, *What is the foundation of all our reasonings and conclusions concerning that relation?* it may be replied in one word, Experience. But if we still carry on our sifting humor, and ask, *What is the foundation of all conclusions from experience?* this implies a new question, which may be of more difficult solution and explication. Philosophers that give themselves airs of superior wisdom and sufficiency have a hard task when they encounter persons of inquisitive dispositions, who push them from every corner to which they retreat, and who are sure at last to bring them to some dangerous dilemma. The best expedient to prevent this confusion is to be modest in our pretensions; and even to discover the difficulty ourselves before it is objected to us. By this means, we may make a kind of merit of our very ignorance.

I shall content myself, in this section, with an easy task, and shall pretend only to give a negative answer to the question here proposed. I say then, that, even after we have experience of the operations of cause and effect, our conclusions from that experience are *not* founded on reasoning, or any process of the understanding. This answer we must endeavour both to explain and to defend.

It must certainly be allowed that nature has kept us at a great distance from all her secrets, and has afforded us only the knowledge of a few superficial qualities of objects; while she conceals from us those powers and principles on which the influence of those objects entirely depends. Our senses inform us of the color, weight, and consistence of bread; but neither sense nor reason can ever inform us of those qualities which fit it for the nourishment and support of a human body. Sight or feeling conveys an idea of the actual motion of bodies; but as to that wonderful force or power, which would carry on a moving body for ever in a continued change of place, and which bodies never lose but by communicating it to others; of this we cannot form the most distant conception. But notwithstanding this ignorance of natural powers and principles, we always presume, when we see like sensible qualities, that they have like secret powers, and expect that effects, similar to those which we have experienced, will follow from them. If a body of like color and consistence with that bread, which we have formerly eaten, be presented to us, we make no scruple of repeating the experiment, and foresee, with certainty, like nourishment and support. Now this is a process of the mind or thought, of which I would willingly know the foundation. It is allowed on all hands that there is no known connection between the sensible qualities and the secret powers; and consequently, that the mind is not led to form such a conclusion concerning their constant and regular conjunction, by anything which it knows of their nature. As to past *Experience*, it can be allowed to give *direct* and *certain* information of those precise objects only, and that precise period of time, which fell under its cognizance: but why this experience should be extended to future times, and to other objects, which for aught we know, may be only in appearance similar; this is the main question on which I would insist. The bread, which I formerly ate, nourished me; that is, a body of such sensible qualities was, at that time, embued with such secret powers: but does it follow, that other bread must also nourish me at another time, and that like sensible qualities must always be attended with like secret powers? The consequence seems nowise necessary. At least, it

must be acknowledged that there is here a consequence drawn by the mind; that there is a certain step taken; a process of thought, and an inference, which wants to be explained. These two propositions are far from being the same, *I have found that such an object has always been attended with such an effect*, and *I foresee that other objects, which are, in appearance, similar, will be attended with similar effects*. I shall allow, if you please, that the one proposition may justly be inferred from the other: I know, in fact, that it always is inferred. But if you insist that the inference is made by a chain of reasoning, I desire you to produce that reasoning. The connection between these propositions is not intuitive. There is required a medium, which may enable the mind to draw such an inference, if indeed it be drawn by reasoning and argument. What that medium is, I must confess, passes my comprehension; and it is incumbent on those to produce it, who assert that it really exists; and is the origin of all our conclusions concerning matter of fact.

This negative argument must certainly, in process of time, become altogether convincing, if many penetrating and able philosophers shall turn their enquiries this way and no one be ever able to discover any connecting proposition or intermediate step, which supports the understanding in this conclusion. But as the question is yet new, every reader may not trust so far to his own penetration, as to conclude, because an argument escapes his enquiry, that therefore it does not really exist. For this reason it may be requisite to venture upon a more difficult task; and enumerating all the branches of human knowledge, endeavor to show that none of them can afford such an argument.

All reasonings may be divided into two kinds, namely, demonstrative reasoning, or that concerning relations of ideas, and moral reasoning, or that concerning matter of fact and existence. That there are no demonstrative arguments in the case seems evident; since it implies no contradiction that the course of nature may change, and that an object, seemingly like those which we have experienced, may be attended with different or contrary effects. May I not clearly and distinctly conceive that a body, falling from the clouds, and which, in all other respects, resembles snow, has yet the taste of salt or feeling of fire? Is there any more intelligible proposition than to affirm that all the trees will flourish in December and January, and decay in May and June? Now whatever is intelligible, and can be distinctly conceived, implies no contradiction, and can never be proved false by any demonstrative argument or abstract reasoning *a priori*.

If we be, therefore, engaged by arguments to put trust in past experience, and make it the standard of our future judgment, these arguments must be probable only, or such as regard matter of fact and real existence, according to the division above mentioned. But that there is no argument of this kind must appear, if our explication of that species of reasoning be admitted as solid and satisfactory. We have said that all arguments concerning existence are founded on the relation of cause and effect; that our knowledge of that relation is derived entirely from experience; and that all our experimental conclusions proceed upon the supposition that the future will be conformable to the past. To endeavor, therefore, the proof of this last supposition by probable arguments, or arguments regarding existence, must be evidently going in a circle, and taking that for granted, which is the very point in question.

In reality, all arguments from experience are founded on the similarity which we discover among natural objects, and by which we are in-duced to expect effects similar to those which we have found to follow from such objects. And though none but a fool or madman will ever pretend to dispute the authority of experience, or to reject that great guide of human life, it may surely be allowed a philosopher to have so much curiosity at least as to examine the principle of human nature, which gives this mighty authority to experience, and makes us draw advantage from that similarity which nature has placed among different objects. From causes which appear *similar* we expect similar effects. This is the sum of all our experimental conclusions. Now it seems evident that, if this conclusion were formed by reason, it would be as perfect at first, and upon one instance, as after ever so long a course of experience. But the case is far otherwise. Nothing so like as eggs; yet no one, on account of this appearing similarity, expects the same taste and relish in all of them. It is only after a long course of uniform experiments in any kind that we attain a firm reliance and security with regard to a particular event. Now where is that process of reasoning which, from one instance, draws a conclusion, so different from that which it infers from a hundred instances that are nowise different from that single one? This question I propose as much for the sake of information as with an intention of raising difficulties. I cannot find, I cannot imagine any such reasoning. But I keep my mind still open to instruction, if any one will vouchsafe to bestow it on me.

Suggestions for Further Reading

William Brenner's chapter on Hume in *Elements of Modern Philosophy: Descartes through Kant* will provide you with a section by section commentary on the *Enquiry* as well as introduce you to some of Hume's provocative writings on religion.

Norman Kemp Smith's *The Philosophy of David Hume* (London: Macmillan, 1941) is a classic interpretation, as is H. H. Price's *Hume's Theory of the External World* (Oxford: Oxford University Press, 1940).

For a contemporary discussion of the problem of induction and an attempt to resolve it by showing how it is a pseudoproblem, see Max Black's "The Justification of Induction" in *Philosophy of Science Today,* edited by Sidney Morgenbesser (New York: Basic Books, 1967).

8.4. Skepticism

Al-Ghazali (Section 8.1) is skeptical about (doubts) what sense experience, theologians, and philosophers can tell us about what we can know. Descartes (Section 8.2) employs methodical skepticism to arrive at certainty and Hume (Section 8.3) concludes that a limited skepticism is the best position to adopt. Contemporary Indian philosophy is concerned about the same issues and, in reflecting on its own tradition, discovers that traditional Indian philosophy is also concerned about what we can know.

Some often think of Indian philosophy as "spiritual" and unconcerned with technical issues relating to truth and knowledge. It is somehow "mystical" and beyond all that. But this is far from the case as the following selection from Binal Krishna Matilal (1935–1991), a contemporary Indian philosopher educated in both Eastern and Western philosophy and the former Spalding Professor of Eastern religions and Ethics at Oxford University, proves. He looks at the debate in the Indian tradition between those philosophers who argued there are reliable means of knowing and those who argued that all so-called means of knowledge were doubtful.

Udayana (ca. 1000), an Indian philosopher, combined two previous schools of Indian philosophy, the Vaisesika and the Nyaya ("nyah yah") schools, into what is usually called **Naiyayika**. This philosophic school advanced an epistemological theory (first developed in Nyaya philosophy) which influenced much of Indian philosophy. According to this theory, the correct means to knowledge (called *pramanas*) can be analyzed into four kinds: perception, inference, comparison (analogy), and reliable testimony. Perceptual knowledge arises from the contact of the senses (eye, ear, nose, etc.) with an object external to the senses, and such contact correctly represents the way the object is. Inferential knowledge arises from the inference from a bit of perceptual knowledge (I see smoke) to a correct conclusion concerning what is not immediately seen (There is a fire.) Analogical knowledge derives from drawing a correct conclusion about an unknown object from the similarities between it and a known object. Knowledge based on testimony occurs when the person telling you something is honest and reliable, knows what she or he is talking about, and you understand correctly what is said.

Naiyayika philosophers were very much concerned with epistemological and logical issues (among others). They viewed knowledge as a relation between self (subject) and nonself (object). Knowledge, they claimed, is like the light of a lamp that reveals objects. The light is not the object nor is it the subject, but it makes it possible for an object to be seen by a subject.

This view of knowledge did not go unquestioned. Nagarjuna ("nah-gar-joo-nah"), an Indian Buddhist philosopher who lived in the second century, mounted an astute critique of the traditional views of knowledge Indian Hindu philosophers had come to accept. He is the founder of the **Madhyamika** school of Buddhist philosophy. Madhyamika refers to the Middle Way (see Section 2.1) and the school took this name because it sought to avoid all extreme philosophical positions.

Nagarjuna found the Buddha's doctrine of **dependent origination** particularly profound. According to this doctrine, everything that exists owes its existence to something else. For example, I would not exist if my parents did not exist. If all existing things are conditioned by, related to, and dependent on other existing things, Nagarjuna reasoned, then all extreme positions (positions which maintained that only one view, independent of its opposite, is true) must be misleading. The claim of the Nyaya philosophers that only the *pramanas* constituted the correct standard of knowledge seemed, to Nagarjuna, an extreme view.

Nagarjuna was a master logician who used logic to deconstruct the positions held by other philosophers. The supporters of the *pramana* theory, he reasoned, have argued that their views provide a reliable rule which allows us to distinguish opinion from knowledge. They realize that not every perception, inference, analogy, or testimony is reliable. If it were, there would be no opinion, only knowledge. So they have tried to offer ways of distinguishing *correct* perception, inference, analogy, and testimony from incorrect. But how do they know that their rules for distinguishing correct from incorrect are right? Don't they need some further standard which assures them that these rules are indeed the right ones?

These sorts of questions move in the direction of skepticism, and Nagarjuna is a skeptic in the sense that he does not believe that absolutely true and certain *conceptual* knowledge of the way things really are is possible. The *pramana* standard relies on concepts, such as correct perception, inference, analogy, testimony. But, conceptual knowledge is limited. We cannot know, in the conventional sense of "forming true concepts about," what is really real. However, Nagarjuna is not an absolute skeptic. He does admit there is a "higher truth," and he maintains that wisdom (**prajna**) leads to it.

What is *prajna*? It is intuitive, direct, immediate insight. Such insight goes beyond conceptual knowledge because it is not dependent on concepts. It is immediate in the sense that it is not mediated by ideas or words. It is the sort of insight gained by the practice of meditation. The discipline of meditation can decondition the mind so that it is able to transcend the usual way of viewing things. Our language and culture condition us to see and understand things in specific ways. Meditation aids us in breaking out of the confines of this conditioning. But philosophy can also aid in the deconditioning process. Philosophy can reveal the limitations of conceptual thought. It can show us that every view is a partial view, just as every perception is necessarily conditioned by a particular perspective. Philosophy clears the ground, so to speak, and meditation takes us beyond concepts to a state of mind in which direct awareness of reality is possible. This state is "ineffable" in the sense that it cannot be completely and adequately expressed in language. The best language can do, to use a well-known Buddhist analogy, is point to the moon. *Prajna,* born of meditative insight, can give us the moon itself.

The debate in traditional Indian philosophy between those who believed there are valid means to knowledge and those that did not is highly technical and relies on subtle arguments. B. K. Matilal threads his way through these arguments believing that they are still relevant to the concerns of contemporary philosophers. He is not content to just describe the debate, but he enters the discussion and develops his own views. This is not an easy read. It will test your skill in following arguments and understanding subtle distinctions. You will have to read slowly, attend carefully to the arguments and counter-arguments, and think about the issues. But the effort is worth it. Matilal is clearly sympathetic to the skeptical case, but he also believes that the supporters of *pramana* have laid out a promising path for overcoming skepticism.

Reading Questions

1. Why does the charge that skepticism is impractical miss the mark according to Matilal?

2. According to the opponents (the Nyaya) of Nagarjuna, why is Nagarjuna's skepticism inconsistent and how does Nagarjuna respond?

3. Matilal thinks Nagarjuna's response is "satisfactory." Why?

4. What question does Nagarjuna raise about the means of knowing (*pramanas*) and why does he charge those who support the *pramana* doctrine with an infinite regress?

5. How might the *pramana* theorist respond to the charge of infinite regress?

6. Nagarjuna raises two objections to the defense against an infinite regress. What are they?

7. Matilal summarizes (part B of Section 2.2) the ways an alleged piece of knowledge can derive its authority from something other than itself. Summarize those three ways in your own words, indicate Nagarjuna's response to each, and how each might be defended in the face of Nagarjuna's critique.

8. In your opinion, in order for me to know that some proposition is true, say "My dog's name is Arthur," must I know that I know it is true? Why or why not?

9. How does Matilal answer the question, "Is radical skepticism feasible?" What is the difference between "propositional negation" and "illocutionary negation?"

10. Nagarjuna's ultimate goal was not to doubt for the sake of doubting, but to clear away unwarranted beliefs so that insight (*prajna*) into ultimate reality can dawn ("the sudden illumination theory"). How could you validate such a theory?

11. How do you think a Naiyashika philosopher, Nagarjuna, and Matilal would answer the question, "Is knowledge possible?"

Perception: An Essay on Classical Indian Theories of Knowledge

B. K. MATILAL

> The unexamined life is not worth living.
>
> Socrates

2.1. The Paradoxicality of Skepticism

UNCOMPROMISING EMPIRICISM LEADS to skepticism. One can stop short of the skeptical route by making some sort of a compromise. But compromises need not always be degrading or scandalous. The question arises, on the other hand, whether skepticism itself is a coherent position. Would not the skeptic himself run into some dilemma of his own? It may be claimed that even the "uncompromising" skeptic eventually makes a compromise of a sort. I shall pursue this question here, after presenting the arguments of the Indian skeptics, *viz.* those who reject altogether the *pramāṇa* doctrine along with its emphasis upon the empirical foundation of knowledge, while tentatively accepting the empiricist stance of their opponents.

A philosopher has to learn to live with the skeptic, for they are both in the same profession, so to speak. A skeptic is not an intruder in the "Temple of Truth," he shares the same concern for truth with the philosopher, and is reluctant to accept anything less. A skeptic is first and foremost an "inquirer," and in this regard, all philos-

From B. K. Matilal's Perception: An Essay on Classical Indian Theories of Knowledge. Copyright © 1986 by B. K. Matilal, pp. 46–57. Reprinted by permission of Oxford University Press. Footnotes deleted.

ophers participate in inquiries and play the role, at least provisionally, of a skeptic to varying degrees. Both persist in seeking and probing, but a skeptic is distinguished by his persistence or concern, which is (the philosopher rightly points out) out of proportion, and hence, "impractical." Thus Kumārila says about the hyperskeptic: "If somebody imagines (the existence of) even some unknown counter-argument, he, doubting his own self, would be destroyed in all practical behavior." But this rebuke which the skeptic receives from his opponent—the rebuke of being impractical, holding an impossible position and leading to an impossible situation—seldom matters to the skeptic, for I think (as will be shown below) he can argue his way out. Thus the frequent jokes and insults that are normally heaped upon the skeptic are wide of the mark. For instance, Udayana points out that if the skeptic does not *believe* what he does not *see,* then he should not believe that his wife is alive when he is out in the street and hence should mourn for her death. Against such attacks the skeptic can justifiably claim that his point has been seriously and severely misunderstood. Or if, as Russell has said, radical skepticism is untenable and impractical, for "from blank doubt, no argument can begin," the Indian skeptic might reply: (1) that he does not see a great virtue in practicality when one is seriously embarking upon a theoretical dispute; and (2) that he is again being misunderstood for he does not doubt simply for the sake of doubting, nor does he seek nothing beyond uncertainty ("blank doubt"); he simply refuses to prejudge the issue and to believe beforehand that there is "the rock or clay" (the indubitable ground for certainty) to be reached once we have "cast aside the loose earth."

The skeptic claims that his skeptical position is what is demanded by consistency for he sees that the *pro*-arguments and the *contra*-arguments for any thesis are equally balanced. If it is shown however that skepticism itself involves some inconsistency, or that it is an incoherent position to hold, then it would be a serious objection indeed and should be answered adequately. Nāgārjuna's skepticism about all existents (*bhāva*), or

about all philosophical positions was actually accused of paradoxicality and therefore inconsistency. This critique presented by the *pramāṇa* theorists such as Nyāya can be given in the form of a dilemma: if all things lack existence or all theses lack certainty (in Nāgārjuna's language, lack *svabhāva* or "essence" or "own-being"), then this particular thesis (and it is also a "thing") must not lack essence. For if it does, there is no reason for us to believe it and Nāgārjuna should refrain from asserting it. And if it does not, there is at least one counter-example to falsify Nāgārjuna's thesis. Objections of this sort were formulated in the *Nyāyasūtra* and in Vātsyāyana's commentary.

We can use the notion of utterance and meaning to formulate the same problem. If the skeptic's position is that all utterances are devoid of (i.e., empty (*śūnya*) of) meaning, then this itself cannot be an utterance. For if it is, it falsifies itself. We can think of "meaning" here as something that is not necessarily separable from thinking or intending. This is at least the non-technical sense of "meaning." For we cannot *mean* something by utterances unless we have thoughts that we intend our utterances to mean. Both Nāgārjuna and his opponents use such schematic terms as *bhāva* and *sva-bhāva* which are general enough to allow such interpretations. Their argument presupposes that a statement or an utterance is to be included in the domain of *bhāva*. For it is stated as follows: "If all *bhāvas* are empty of their *svabhāva*, then your utterance (*vacana* or saying) that all *bhāvas* are empty must also be empty of its *sva-bhāva* for it is also a *bhāva*."

Whether the above formulation expresses a genuine paradox or not, it did have the consequence of showing that pure skepticism (or the Mādhyamika skepticism) cannot be consistently maintained. (Nāgārjuna's reply is to be found in the *Vigrahavyāvartanī*.) He says: "I have no proposition, no thesis to defend (which may lack any essence). If I had any thesis, I would have been guilty of the faults you ascribe to me. But I do not, hence I have no fault."

This reply of Nāgārjuna is amazingly simple. But can he get away with this? The purport is that "no (philosophic) thesis has *svabhāva*, i.e., 'essence'" is itself not a thesis. It is not an assertion. It may be an utterance but only an *empty* utterance. To put it another way: "No statement is certain, or has *svabhāva*, or is meaningful" should not be regarded as a statement, so that we cannot raise such questions whether or not it is itself certain, has *svabhāva*, or is meaningful. I think this reply should be satisfactory, for at least it is not inconsistent on the face of it. For it is quite possible that every thesis lacks essence or *svabhāva*, and this will remain so even if there is nobody (not even a Nāgārjuna) who asserts it as a thesis. If anyone asserted it, he would falsify it; but if nobody did, there is no falsification. We can imagine a possible world where all assertions made are empty but there is nobody to make the crucial assertion that all assertions are empty. A. N. Prior once followed J. Buridan in resolving the paradox with "no statement is true" in more or less the same way: "But if God were to annihilate all negative propositions, there would in fact be no negative propositions, even if this were not then being asserted by any proposition at all." The air of paradoxicality in the sceptical position, then, can be resolved only at the expense of disallowing the skeptic to assert his own position. For it is possible for a skeptic to believe that all beliefs have dubious value, including the said belief in question! One can raise many questions here against Nāgārjuna. Is not his way of wriggling out of paradoxicality incomplete without a Buridan-like assumption that there is a higher power which decrees what is or is not in the world? I think Nāgārjuna would rephrase the point differently: "It just so *happens* that everything is empty (lacks *svabhāva*), but it must remain *unsaid*, for to assert (say) it is to falsify it."

Dismissing the air of paradoxicality in the above manner, Nāgārjuna proceeded to formulate some serious criticisms of his rivals, the *pramāṇa* theorists, the Naiyāyikas in particular. What he called in question was the very concept of *pramāṇa*, our standards of proof, our evidence for knowledge. He did not use what is generally called argument from illusion, nor did he appeal to the fallibility of our cognitive pro-

cess. He did not argue on the basis of the fact that we do misperceive on many occasions, or that we make false judgments more often than not. Instead he developed a very strong and devastating critique of the whole epistemological enterprise itself and therefore his arguments have a lasting philosophic value.

2.2 *Nāgārjuna's Critique of Knowledge and* Pramāṇas

If we claim that we have means of knowing (*pramāṇa*) the way the world is, or if we believe that we have such means available to us, it stands to reason to ask further: how do we *know* those means of knowing? For, obviously, we have to know or recognize that those are the means we have; otherwise, it would be like having in our pocket some money, the presence of which we are unaware and which therefore would be useless for all practical purposes. A means is not a means unless it does something and hence if we have the means, we have to make them effective. To make them effective, we have to *know* that they are there. Nāgārjuna therefore raises the legitimate question: how, or through what means, do we know that they are there? By raising such a question, Nāgārjuna is not simply urging a fault of circularity against his opponents. For there will be other serious logical difficulties in store for the Naiyāyika or the *pramāṇa* theorist.

In the above argument, the *pramāṇa* theorist seems to have conceded already that the means of knowing can also be, or can be turned into, the object of knowing. (A *pramāṇa* is also a *prameya*, i.e., is among the knowables. If this is so, then we need further *pramāṇa*s to "measure" them.) If our means is turned into an end, then to achieve that end we need further means. If our standards for determining others are themselves to be determined by another set of standards and then a further set is needed for the second set of standards, we may regress into infinity and our search for the final standard may never come to an end. In the words of Nāgārjuna: "If the proof of the *pramāṇa*s were by means of other *pra-*

māṇas, then there would be an 'infinite regress' (*anavasthā*). There would be no proof of the first, nor of the middle, nor of the last." In Sanskrit dialectics this fault is called *anavasthā,* literally "lack of a firm grounding." This situation as the skeptic envisions it would partly be comparable to the never-ending search for the rock-bottom certainty. In Cartesian epistemology for instance, a similar sort of skepticism is presupposed and the epistemologist tries to come forward with either the *cogito,* or the sense-impression, or the self-evident sense-data, as his final court of appeal.

There may be objections against my use of the term "skepticism" in connection with Nāgārjuna. One could say that Nāgārjuna was a Buddhist and not a skeptic. It may also be said that if a skeptic is simply one whom Descartes characterized as a person who doubts only "that he may doubt and seeks nothing beyond uncertainty itself," then he would try to cast doubt upon as many fundamental beliefs of the *pramāṇa* theorists as possible and certainly Nāgārjuna has not followed this method. In my defence I would point out that I do not have such a narrow definition of skepticism in my mind (as should be clear from the introductory comments). By calling Nāgārjuna a skeptic, or rather by using his arguments to delineate the position of my skeptical opponent of the *pramāṇa* theorists, I have only proposed a probable extension of the application of the term "skepticism." Here as well as elsewhere, I would urge my readers not to dispute too much over mere labels but to pay attention to the formulation of a position (in the Indian context) and the arguments adduced in favor of it. Sometimes descriptive labels are put on theories in order to familiarize them to readers and hence they need not always be too strictly interpreted.

It is worth noting that my extended use of the notion of skepticism can be discussed in the context of A. J. Ayer's characterization of "philosophical skepticism": ". . . his [the skeptic's] charge against our standards of proof is *not that they work badly;* he does not suggest that there are others which work better. The ground on which he attacks them is that they are *logically*

defective, or if not defective, at any rate logically questionable."

Such a general characterization would undoubtedly be applicable to Nāgārjuna, Jayarāśi, and Śrīharṣa, although I understand that even in Ayer's discussion the skeptic becomes more specific in raising some questions. He raises questions about such things as whether, or how, we are justified in making assertions about physical objects on the basis of our sense-experience, or in assuming and talking about other minds on the basis of their bodily behavior, or in regarding our memories as giving us knowledge of the past. Nāgārjuna, however, raises more fundamental questions about the consistency of the *pramāṇa* doctrine as a whole: he asks whether or not our so-called standards of proof form a coherent system, whether our fundamental assumptions are endowed with at least psychological certainty. It is his contention that in the long run the concept of the standard of proof would be found to be self-refuting or self-stultifying.

However, the charge of infinite regress against the *pramāṇa* theory is not a formidable objection for there are obviously several alternative ways of answering it. Nāgārjuna anticipated and countered most of them. Some of his counter-arguments will be examined here so that one may appreciate the position of the skeptic in so far as he offers formidable objections to the *pramāṇa* theory.

The purported answers of the *pramāṇa* theorists may fall into two general categories. First it may be claimed that there are some, if not all, means of knowing which do not require any further means for knowing them, for they are what may be called self-evident or self-supporting (*svataḥ prasiddhiḥ*). Second, the authoritativeness of the means of knowing may be derivative in a way that need not lead to any infinite regress. The *locus classicus* of this argument is *Vigrahavyāvartanī,* verse 51. I shall, however, rearrange the alternatives as follows:

A. Neither knowledge nor means of knowing derive their authority (or validity) from anything else. They have (intrinsic and natural) authority and validity.

A proof is used to prove something else but it itself does not require a further proof. A piece of evidence is evidence for something else but is itself self-evident. This can obviously have two ramifications:

1. Each piece of knowledge is self-validating, each means of knowing is self-supporting, each piece of evidence is self-evident.
2. A subset of knowledge-pieces or a subset of *pramāṇas* are self-supporting and self-evident and upon these we base others of their kind.

In either case the analogy would be fire or light which reveals itself besides revealing others. (Nāgārjuna confounds the argument based upon fire-analogy as we will see later.) The first view is upheld by the Mīmāṃsakas (including the Vedāntins) as well as the Buddhist *pramāṇa* theorists. The second view may be attributed to the epistemologists in the Cartesian or the Humean tradition who want to reach rock-bottom certainty, casting aside the loose earth and sand. Nāgārjuna's criticism is applicable to both of them with equal force. For in either case we have introduced a clear-cut dichotomy. The *pramāṇas* belong to a privileged class, the set of the self-evident, self-supporting items, while the other items, *viz. prameyas,* are not so. Nāgārjuna questions this dichotomy as well as the validity of the principle lying behind it.

The question is why certain items, the so-called self-evident or the self-supporting "means," should be sacrosanct, i.e., should enjoy the privilege of being independent of any requirement for further support. A dichotomy proposed by a philosopher should be based upon some dichotomizing principle and the philosopher concerned should be prepared to spell out the latter. In other words he should not only say what the difference is but also, and more importantly, account for the same. This is exactly what Nāgārjuna demands: " *Viśeṣa-hetuś ca vaktavyaḷi.*" And the reason for such differentiation should be stated.

What exactly is being asked here? The *pramāṇa* theorist has to account for the fact that why out of all items in the world certain items do not stand in need of being established or revealed

to us by a "means," while others necessarily do. What accounts for this difference in character? To say that it is the nature of one kind of things to reveal and that of the other to be revealed will not serve the purpose, for that will be hardly more helpful than saying, as we have already said, that one group comprises the "means" of knowledge (*pramāṇas*) while the other group comprises the "objects" of knowledge (*prameyas*). For in philosophy appeal to the nature of things is almost as good (or as bad) as an appeal to the caprices of Nature or Providence.

The second difficulty, Nāgārjuna points out, is that the *pramāṇa* theorist by introducing this dichotomy contradicts his original thesis—the very thesis that started the debate (*vihīyate vādaḥ*). The *pramāṇa* theorist started with the fundamental thesis that everything is established, or made known by, some *pramāṇa* or other. In fact the very well-known and much-debated Nyāya thesis is that to be an object of knowledge (*prameya*) is a feature shared by all things whatsoever. Now it is being suggested that there are certain things, self-supporting *pramāṇas* themselves or self-evident pieces of knowledge, which do not require a further *pramāṇa* or a further support. If to answer this difficulty it is urged that these self-supporting "means" of knowing are not absolutely independent but simply require nothing beyond themselves to be proven valid or sound, then Nāgārjuna could go back to his first criticism: how to account for the alleged difference or discrimination between *pramāṇas* and *prameyas*?

The question Nāgārjuna raises is fundamental to skepticism in the Indian tradition. The early Nyāya method is essentially a program that presupposes an initial doubt (*saṃśaya*), and through the employment of *pramāṇa,* moves on to reach a certitude (*nirṇaya*) at the end of the inquiry. (This is not exactly Descartes's project of pure inquiry which is carried on with the fictional *malin genie* who devotes all his efforts to deceive us.) According to Nyāya, if a state of dubiety is to be entertained with regard to the truth of any proposition (thesis) before certitude is reached through the application of *pramāṇas,* means of knowledge or evidence, then a similar state of doubt could *ipso facto* be entertained with regard to those very means of knowledge or evidence before certitude regarding their effectiveness or efficacy can be reached. This is presupposed by the Nyāya program for arriving at certitude. If the "means" or evidence for knowledge is not subjected to this procedure, then Nyāya is simply arguing for a preferential or privileged treatment for a set of items, the *pramāṇas,* which is unwarranted. By admitting the universal possibility of doubt Nyāya is committed by the same token, according to Nāgārjuna, to the possibility of universal doubt.

The Naiyāyika cannot say that he has chosen the means of knowing as requiring no further evidence and hence immune from doubt because of our subjective feeling about their certitude or indubitability. For one thing, this subjective feeling may not be universal. The Nyāya program is to establish objective evidence for all things whatsoever and hence the same requirement must be met for the means of knowing as well. It is true that the self-evidence or self-validity of knowledge, or its means, is not accepted by the Nyāya school. But in so far as the Nyāya method is partially accepted by philosophers who argue for the "self-evidence" thesis, Nāgārjuna's criticism would be relevant. In his skeptical refutation of the *pramāṇas,* a Nagarjunite obviously moves here from the universal possibility of doubt to the possibility of universal doubt, though this passage from one to the other may not be logically warranted. But more of this later.

I have already indicated that Nāgārjuna's critique of knowledge would be relevant even if we transpose it to the Cartesian program for the foundation of knowledge. Descartes himself paved the way for the super-critic by introducing the fiction of the *malin genie.* His own program was to reach a set of irresistible and indubitable propositions on which to lay the foundation of other kinds of knowledge. This was quite in line with the general task of any philosopher, whether of East or West: to cast doubt on everything in order to reach certainty, to destroy apparent platitudes in order to gain genuine certitudes. Or as Ryle once suggested, the task is comparable to "the destruction-tests by which engineers discover the strength of materials." "We all know

that the destructive side of the Cartesian program proved more convincing and successful than its positive side. To be sure, Descartes' search for truth was also a search for knowledge as well as a search for certainty. An obvious criticism was that he set his standards too high to make it attainable by his program. But this criticism does not apply to the Nyāya method, for there the standard for certainty is not set too high. Without doubt it is made to depend upon standard means of knowing and evidence. Once the standard means of knowing are recognized, very little remains to frustrate the program. If the initial doubt is removed through standard procedures, we have obtained a piece of knowledge. Hence Nāgārjuna's strategy was to find an internal inconsistency in the very presupposition of the program. If everything is to be considered certified (certain) when and only when the means of knowing certifies them, why should the means of knowing not be certified in a similar way?

Where Descartes would reach his set of irresistible and indubitable propositions, the *cogito* or the idea of a benevolent creator for the successful completion of his program, a Nagarjunite could very well say: "Why are the indubitables indubitable, while the others are not?" It is well known that Descartes involved himself into a circularity for he used the criterion of self-evidence in order to prove the existence of God and then used God to validate the criterion of self-evidence. A Nāgārjunite would have loved to expose this circularity for his skeptical claim is that either all propositions should be subjected to doubt to ensure their final and objective certitude, or none should be so subjected. If we select some, that would be unwarranted preferential treatment. The moment our program sets objective certitude of propositions as its goal we forfeit the claim to demand objective indubitability of our self-evident, subjectively irresistible propositions such as envisioned in the *cogito* or the benevolent creator.

The epistemologist may give up the claim of self-evidence or the non-derivative nature of the authority pertaining to the means of knowledge or knowledge itself. He may choose the second alternative and say:

B. A piece of knowledge or a means of knowing derives its authority and validity from something other than itself (*parataḥ*). This can lead to the following possible positions:

1. A piece of knowledge derives its authority from another piece of knowledge. One instance of perception is proven by another instance of perception or by an inference. One instance of inference is proven by an instance of perception or by another inference. A piece of verbal knowledge is proven by an instance of perception or an inference and so on. Nāgārjuna notes all these cases in his *Vṛtti* (verse 51).

2. A piece of knowledge is validated by its "object," which is part of the independently existent real. It assumes that there is a knowledge-independent world and that there are independently existing entities, the nature of which is known when we have knowledge. The "real" object validates knowledge as well as its means.

3. Our "means" of knowledge and our "objects" of knowledge are mutually dependent. They validate each other. (Notice that this answer tries to bypass the question of the existence of a knowledge-independent world.)

A third alternative C is also formulated by Nāgārjuna, which says that the validation of the means of knowledge is *a-kasmāt* "unaccountable," neither intrinsic nor derivative. This however could be included in alternative A (the non-derivativeness of the *pramāṇas*).

Alternative B(1) is summarily rejected on pain of the *regressus ad infinitum*. But this may not be as absurd as it is made to appear under the skeptic's scrutiny. This may be a very pragmatic solution of the age-old problem. To prove A we may need B and to prove B we may need C, but it is then possible that we do not need to prove C also. The reason for not requiring to prove C may not be the claim that C is self-evident, but that the question regarding C's validity has not arisen. Such contingency may stop the regress, but that is not the crux of the argument. The main point is: must we necessarily validate C before we use it as a means to prove B?

There is the dubiety principle which we must accept: If C proves B, and C is doubtful, then B

is also doubtful. There is also the invalidation principle. If C is the only way to prove B, and C is invalidated, then B is invalidated. But we may not require a validation principle along the same line: If C proves B, and C is validated, then and then only B is validated. For this would be too strong. We can simply say: If C proves B, then B is validated. The issue here is connected with two broader questions about the concept of knowledge. First, if I know that *p*, must I know that I know that *p*? Second, if I know that *p*, must I always feel certain or will there simply be an absence of doubt? As we shall see later, the Naiyāyika argued that from the fact that somebody knows that *p*, it does not necessarily follow that he knows that he knows that *p*. For example, on entering this room someone may know, on the basis of perception, that there are four chairs in this room without by the same token knowing that he knows that there are four chairs there. His knowledge-episode proves here that there are four chairs there, and hence the proposition that there are four chairs there is validated. But it would be too odd to claim that his knowledge-episode must also and always be validated by another knowledge-episode. (For he may not always know that he knows!) All these intricate problems will engage us later on. For the present we can only say (and I follow Vātsyāyana on this point) that the regress to infinity can be stopped, and is actually stopped, despite Nāgārjuna's insinuation.

Alternative B(2) can indeed be upheld. For a knowledge-independent world can indeed validate our knowledge and its means, provided they are *in accord* with that knowledge-independent world as it really is. But the skeptic is quick to point out that the existence of that very knowledge-independent world is what is in question here. An epistemologist can say of a cognitive situation that it yields knowledge only when it is in accord with his experience. For we cannot know about a cognitive situation that it is in accord with the world as it really is without encompassing that knowledge-independent world within the act of cognition. We thereby run into circularity. We posit the world (the *prameya*) to validate knowledge and then validate the world by the criteria of that knowledge itself. It is like Descartes' attempt to prove God through self-evidence and then use God to validate the criterion of self-evidence.

Alternative B(3) is rejected by Nāgārjuna because of the fault of mutual dependence, which is no doubt a kind of circularity. But why the position is asserted at all by explicitly courting the mutual dependence? Is there any sense in which it seems plausible? The answer is yes. I think the model of mutual dependence is not necessarily a faulty model. For when two sides are equally weak and uncertain, mutual dependence in the form of mutual reinforcement of certainty may be regarded as a virtue rather than a vice. If two propositions are mutually dependent upon each other, while both lack certitude, is there any comparative gain? It may be argued that both may be allowed to stand until either is proven wrong or right. There may be greater collective plausibility to both of them, although there is no strong argument in favor of either.

Besides, the mutuality of the means of knowing and the object of knowledge may point up another direction. If the object depends upon the means and the means upon the object, then both may be said to be knowledge-dependent. This position will then have a consequence that will be welcome to the Buddhist phenomenalists and other idealists. If we locate the object in what appears in experience, and identify knowledge with what makes it appear the way it does, we court some sort of mutuality between knowledge and its object, which may point up their essential non-difference. In any case, such a position cannot be treated lightly or rejected on frivolous grounds. . . .

2.4 Is Radical Skepticism Feasible?

The upshot is that a radical skepticism of this kind is not, or does not seem to be, a statable position. For if it is statable, it becomes incoherent or paradoxical. In other words such a position could be coherent only at the risk of being unstatable! It seems to me that both radical skepticism and Nāgārjunian Buddhism would welcome this situation, for here we may find the significance of the doctrine of silence in Mādhyamika. (The same point may also explain the ironical comment of Aristotle, though not the irony of it, regarding Cratylus who only wiggled his finger, instead of teaching anything.) Is it the only way to make radical skepticism a coherent position? If it is, then the teacher-philosopher is forced to remain mute and so lose any chance of success in communicating his doctrine. But there is another way. The skeptic may claim, as Śrīharṣa explicitly did, that he enters into a debate simply to refute others and it is not his responsibility to state his position, much less to defend it. Assuming the standards of argument and proof of his opponent as only provisionally correct or acceptable, he would be inclined to show that the opponent's position is wrong, and there ends his philosophic discourse. In other words, his philosophic activity consists in *refutation* only, not in *assertion*.

The obvious difficulty here would be that the skeptic would have to answer the following challenge: How can he logically not *assert* anything while he refutes something? Is refutation of a proposition possible without any (implicit) assertion? According to the standard notion of logic, refutation cannot be successful without negating something, i.e., some proposition, and negation of some proposition p is equivalent to assertion of *not-p*. If we follow this line of argument then it is difficult to see how the skeptic can simply refute without asserting or stating anything. In other words, it is impossible to maintain the position of "non-assertion" or "non-statement," even though the skeptic enters into debate only for the sake of refutation. I think the radical skeptic has an easy answer to this problem. He may say that his refutation should not, and need not, be equated with the negation as it is understood in standard logic (where to negate p means to assert *not-p*). His refutation is a strong refutation of a possibility (*cf.* Indian notion of *prasajya-pratiṣedha*) but without any implication for the contrary or contradictory possibilities. This notion of refutation is more or less prominent in our question-and-answer activity. It is a non-committal act of refutation or what I once called the commitment-less denial of the Mādhyamikas.

What emerges here is that the problem of negation or the ambiguity of negative statement is philosophically very central. Negation, as Richard Routley has commented (in private correspondence) "is a fundamental, but ill-understood, ill-explained, and much-disputed notion across a wide philosophical spectrum." The skeptic may or may not find his position paradoxical, but what we should not do is to attack or threaten the skeptic with the two very sharp horns of a dilemma, or a paradox which has been generated in the first place by our own standard classical logical definition of negation. The standard classical theory of negation in a two-valued system does capture, we must admit, a very pervasive sense of negation. But it is also a fact that some important uses of negation are left out in the account that we get from standard logic. The skeptic's use of negation, perhaps, can be better understood as an act of refutation, an illocutionary act where one negates some illocutionary force rather than a proposition.

I wish to refer here to J. R. Searle's distinction between a propositional negation and an illocutionary negation to explain the skeptic's point. This is, I think, quite suitable to explain the Sañjaya-type or the Nāgārjuna-type negation. Such negations were obviously formulated in the context of speech-acts. For example, Sañjaya said, "I do not say it is so. Nor do I say it is otherwise . . ." and so on. If we construe assertion as an illocutionary act and the proposition is represented by p, then we can write, "I assert that p." By illocutionary negation, we can then write for the skeptic's utterance, "I do not assert that p." Here the skeptic does not make another assertion such as "*not-p*," for illocutionary negation usually negates the act or the illocutionary force. A propositional negation would leave the illocutionary force unchanged, for the result would be another proposition, a negative one, similarly asserted as the affirmative one.

The skeptic's attitude of non-assertion is therefore a possible one, and this does not force him into a contradiction. He can very well say,

"I do not say that it is p. Nor do I say that it is *not-p*," just as I can say, "I do not promise to come, nor do I promise not to come." I think the Buddhist dilemma or tetralemma could be better explained in the context of such illocutionary acts. Consider also the following. Suppose p stands for the proposition that everything is empty or that all assertions are false. A Nāgārjunian skeptic has the perfect right to say, "I do not assert that p, nor do I assert that *not-p*." This does not seem to lead him to any position even when the skeptic participates in the debate only for the sake of refutation.

The skeptic in the Sañjaya–Nāgārjuna tradition is more in line with the Greek sophist or the Pyrrhonist (as described by Sextus Empiricus) than with the Cartesian skeptic. But, nevertheless, the critique of knowledge and evidence that the Indian skeptic has generated can hardly be ignored by an epistemologist in any tradition. In classical India, as I have already indicated, the generally accepted style of philosophizing was the formulation of a *pramāṇa* theory as the basis for the defense of some metaphysical system or other. The Nāgārjunian critique was that this style of philosophizing is at best a distortion and at worst an illusion. For it assumes more than what is warranted by pure experience. The force of such arguments was to persuade us to recognize our philosophic activity, our *pramāṇa* doctrine, for what it is, a fabrication, a convenient myth-making or make-believe, the inherent value of which lies only in making day-to-day life work smoothly and rendering inter-subjective communication successful. In short, the skeptic says that the *pramāṇa* theorist either begs the question (while talking about "evidence" or "ways" or "means" of knowing, such as perception and inference) by using a very questionable criterion to establish the standard for what should count as true, or he regresses to infinity to find out another criterion for this criterion and so on. I have already summed up how the *pramāṇa* theorists in general, and Nyāya in particular, would answer this challenge.

The skeptic's argumentation, through constant practice, is supposed to lead one to an *in-*

sight into the nature of what is ultimately real (*prajñā*). This transition from radical skepticism to some sort of mysticism (where the truth is supposed to dawn upon the person if he can rid himself of all false or unwarranted beliefs) is very pronounced in the Indian tradition, and it seems to be somewhat marginal in the Western tradition. Śrīharṣa claims that his Brahman does not need to be established through any means, for the eternal truth will illuminate and show itself as soon as the fabricated walls of misconceptions and false beliefs are destroyed, and dialectics only help to destroy them. Jayarāśi, however, does not say anything about how the truth will come to light. For him all philosophic questions remain open, and in practical life he recommends common sense and normal behavior. He says that those who understand the ultimate purpose recommend that we follow ordinary worldly behavior (*laukika mārga*), for "with regard to ordinary behavior the wise resembles the fool or the child." Sextus' own commendation is not very far from it: "We live in accordance with the normal rules of life, undogmatically, seeing that we cannot remain wholly inactive."

Even the "sudden illumination" theory of the Indian skeptic-mystic is matched by another comment of Sextus. He compares the skeptic with Apelles, court-painter of Alexander the Great. Once Apelles was painting a horse and wanted to paint the horse's foam. Being unsuccessful several times, in despair he flung a sponge at the picture and, lo and behold, the foam was automatically painted by the throwing of the sponge. Skeptics get their *ataraxia* in this way all of a sudden. A Buddhist Zen master would have loved this analogy.

Suggestions for Further Reading

A classic and influential discussion of Nyaya is S.C. Chatterjee's *The Nyaya Theory of Knowledge* (Calcutta: University of Calcutta Press, 1950). Ganganatha Jha's *The Nyaya Philosophy of Gautama* (Allahabad: Allahabad University Press, n.d.) provides an in-depth discussion. See John Koller's chapter on "Knowledge and Reality: Nyaya-Vaisheshika" in *Oriental Philosophies* (New York: Charles Scribner Sons, 1985) for an introductory account.

Nagarjuna is a fascinating and profound philosopher, but he is not easy to understand. Start with Ninian Smart's brief overview in Volume 5 of the *Encyclopedia of Philosophy* and branch out. See Frederick Streng's account in *Emptiness: A Study in Religious Meaning* (Nashville: Abingdon Press, 1967) and Kenneth K. Inada's *Nagarjuna: A Translation of His Mulamadhyamakakarika* (Tokyo: The Hokuseido Press, 1970) when you are ready for deeper waters.

An excellent translation of some of Nagarjuna's work with extensive notes can be found in *Master of Wisdom: Writings of the Buddhist Master Nagarjuna* (Oakland: Dharma Publishing, 1986), translated by C. Lindtner.

For a general account of Buddhist philosophy see David J. Kalupahana's *Buddhist Philosophy: A Historical Analysis* (Honolulu: University Press of Hawaii, 1976) and Edward Conze's *Buddhist Thought in India* (Ann Arbor: University of Michigan Press, 1970).

See Adi Parush, "Nietzsche on the Skeptic's Life" *Review of Metaphysics* (Vol. 29, 1976, 523–542) for a comparative study of skepticism in the Western tradition.

8.5. What Is Truth?

We have talked a lot about knowledge and how it might differ from opinion, but we have not said much directly about truth. Surely one difference between knowledge and opinion is that knowledge is true whereas opinion may be true or false. But what is truth? What does it mean to call something true?

William James (1842–1910) may well be the most famous and influential philosopher to be born in the United States. Along with Charles Peirce and John Dewey, he developed a philosophy called **pragmatism**, which some have claimed is the distinctive philosophy of U.S. culture.

James characterizes pragmatism (from the Greek word *pragma,* meaning "action") as a method for settling philosophical disputes. This method was based on a distinctive theory of truth, called the **pragmatic theory of truth.** According to this theory, some proposition *p* is true if and only if the belief that "*p* is true" works.

"And what does 'works' mean," you ask? James uses words like "useful," "adaptive," "serviceable," "satisfying," "verifiable," "agreeing with reality" to try to explain what it means. He also claims that for any proposition to "work" and hence to be taken as true, it must be consistent with what we already take to be true and it must be in agreement with our sense experience. Thus, my belief that "my fat, blind cat is on the rug by the fire" works as long as it is consistent with my other beliefs (he is not outside, he is not in the kitchen eating my dinner, he is not in the pool practicing his backstroke, etc.), and when I look at the rug I get "fat-blind-cat" type sensations.

We can grasp James's theory better by contrasting it with two other theories of truth, both of which derive from Plato. They have been the two dominant theories of truth in Western thought. The first is called the **correspondence theory**. According to this theory, *p* is true if and only if *p* corresponds to the facts. My believing *p* to be true or false has nothing to do with the matter of its truth, or so this theory would maintain. "My cat is on the rug" is true if, indeed, that is where the cat is and is false if the cat is not there. Even if I don't look and no matter how I feel or what I believe, it is true or false independent of my actions or beliefs.

The second theory of truth is called the **coherence theory**. According to this view, *p* is true if and only if *p* is logically implied by *q*, where *q* is a true statement, and *q*, in turn, is logically implied by *r*, and so on. Truth, on this account, is the coherence of a whole system of statements in which each statement is entailed by all the others. We have only fragments of this whole, but when and if we ever discover the entire system, we will have arrived at absolute truth. Thus, "My fat, blind cat is on the rug" is true if a whole host of other propositions are true such as "My cat is blind," "The rug exists," "Cats exist," and so on.

James ascribed both the correspondence and coherence theories to philosophers he called "intellectualists and rationalists." He objected to these theories on the grounds that they present truth as a static property existing prior to and independent of human experience and investigation. James sees truth as something dynamic, something that happens to ideas when they lead humans into ever more satisfactory experiences. The rationalists accused James, in turn, of denying objectivity, reducing truth to a matter of what we want to believe, and making it relative to the context in which we verify propositions.

Richard Rorty (1931–), a contemporary American philosopher and the Kenan Professor of Humanities at the University of Virginia, Charlottesville has, along with others, revived what he understands to be James's pragmatic viewpoint (although other philosophers have accused him of misunderstanding James). From the standpoint of neo-pragmatism (new pragmatism) he has criticized traditional theories of knowledge as dependent upon a misleading metaphor, a metaphor which construes the mind as if it were a mirror which when correctly reflecting its object, can be said to know that object. He has also criticized traditional views of rationality, views which construe rationality as the pursuit of objective knowledge about some reality external to the mind (see Section 1.2). Rorty's brand of neo-pragmatism has, in turn, been criticized for leading to relativism, i.e., the notion that truth is merely relative to a particular cultural or social community. In the essay that follows Rorty wishes to explain and defend his neo-pragmatism against the charge of relativism. He at first admits that if we mean a particular thing by relativism, then neo-pragmatism can be so characterized. But he does not like the term "relativism" and in the end wishes to disassociate neo-pragmatic views from the use of that term.

Rorty makes a number of references to other philosophers whose work you probably will not know. This will make him difficult to understand at times, but you will be able to grasp the general outline of his argument without extensive knowledge of those other philosophers with whom Rorty finds himself in conversation.

Reading Questions

1. What are the two principle ways reflective humans try to give sense to their lives according to Rorty?

2. According to those who wish to ground solidarity in objectivity, what constitutes truly rational procedures for justifying beliefs?

3. For pragmatists, what constitutes the desire for objectivity?

4. What are the three different views of relativism and which does the pragmatist hold?

5. The pragmatic view is not actually, according to Rorty, a relativistic view although there is a sense in which the term is used that appears to fit the pragmatist's case. Why isn't it?

6. What is the "incommensuability thesis," and why is it self-refuting (note Rorty does not say why it is, but claims that it is, so you will need to figure out what reasons he may have to support such a claim)?

7. What does Rorty mean by "ethnocentric?"

8. What is the root of scientism?

9. What is the pragmatist's justification of toleration, free inquiry, and the quest for undistorted communication?

10. What is the dilemma formed by ethnocentricism and relativism and which "horn" should the pragmatist grasp? Can you figure out a way out of this dilemma without supporting one side (horn) or the other?

11. What two sorts of metaphysical comfort does pragmatism take away?

12. What is the best argument partisans of solidarity have against realistic partisans of objectivity? Do you agree with this argument? Why or why not?

Solidarity or Objectivity?

RICHARD RORTY

THERE ARE TWO PRINCIPAL WAYS in which reflective human beings try, by placing their lives in a larger context, to give sense to those lives. The first is by telling the story of their contribu-

From Post-Analytic Philosophy, *edited by John Rajchman and Cornel West. Copyright © 1985 by Columbia University Press. Reprinted by permission of Columbia University Press.*

tion to a community. This community may be the actual historical one in which they live, or another actual one, distant in time or place, or a quite imaginary one, consisting perhaps of a dozen heroes and heroines selected from history or fiction or both. The second way is to describe themselves as standing in immediate relation to a nonhuman reality. This relation is immediate in the sense that it does not derive from a relation between such a reality and their tribe, or their nation, or their imagined band of comrades. I shall say that stories of the former kind exemplify the desire for solidarity, and that stories of the latter kind exemplify the desire for objectivity. Insofar as a person is seeking solidarity, he or she does not ask about the relation between the practices of the chosen community and something outside that community. Insofar as he seeks objectivity, he distances himself from the actual persons around him not by thinking of himself as a member of some other real or imaginary group, but rather by attaching himself to something which can be described without reference to any particular human beings.

The tradition in Western culture which centers around the notion of the search for Truth, a tradition which runs from the Greek philosophers through the Enlightenment, is the clearest example of the attempt to find a sense in one's existence by turning away from solidarity to objectivity. The idea of Truth as something to be pursued for its own sake, not because it will be good for oneself, or for one's real or imaginary community, is the central theme of this tradition. It was perhaps the growing awareness by the Greeks of the sheer diversity of human communities which stimulated the emergence of this ideal. A fear of parochialism, of being confined within the horizons of the group into which one happens to be born, a need to see it with the eyes of a stranger, helps produce the skeptical and ironic tone characteristic of Euripides and Socrates. Herodotus' willingness to take the barbarians seriously enough to describe their customs in detail may have been a necessary prelude to Plato's claim that the way to transcend skepticism is to envisage a common goal of humanity—a goal set by human nature rather than by Greek cul-

ture. The combination of Socratic alienation and Platonic hope gives rise to the idea of the intellectual as someone who is in touch with the nature of things, not by way of the opinions of his community, but in a more immediate way.

Plato developed the idea of such an intellectual by means of distinctions between knowledge and opinion, and between appearance and reality. Such distinctions conspire to produce the idea that rational inquiry should make visible a realm to which nonintellectuals have little access, and of whose very existence they may be doubtful. In the Enlightenment, this notion became concrete in the adoption of the Newtonian physical scientist as a model of the intellectual. To most thinkers of the eighteenth century, it seemed clear that the access to Nature which physical science had provided should now be followed by the establishment of social, political, and economic institutions which were in accordance with Nature. Ever since, liberal social thought has centered around social reform as made possible by objective knowledge of what human beings are like— not knowledge of what Greeks or Frenchmen or Chinese are like, but of humanity as such. We are the heirs of this objectivist tradition, which centers round the assumption that we must step outside our community long enough to examine it in the light of something which transcends it, namely, that which it has in common with every other actual and possible human community. This tradition dreams of an ultimate community which will have transcended the distinction between the natural and the social, which will exhibit a solidarity which is not parochial because it is the expression of an ahistorical human nature. Much of the rhetoric of contemporary intellectual life takes for granted that the goal of scientific inquiry into man is to understand "underlying structures," or, "culturally invariant factors," or "biologically determined patterns."

Those who wish to ground solidarity in objectivity—call them "realists"—have to construe truth as correspondence to reality. So they must construct a metaphysics which has room for a special relation between beliefs and objects which will differentiate true from false beliefs. They also must argue that there are procedures of justification of belief which are natural and not merely local. So they must construct an epistemology which has room for a kind of justification which is not merely social but natural, springing from human nature itself, and made possible by a link between that part of nature and the rest of nature. On their view, the various procedures which are thought of as providing rational justification by one or another culture may or may not really *be* rational. For to be truly rational, procedures of justification *must* lead to the truth, to correspondence to reality, to the intrinsic nature of things.

By contrast, those who wish to reduce objectivity to solidarity—call them "pragmatists"—do not require either a metaphysics or an epistemology. They view truth as, in William James' phrase, what it is good for *us* to believe. So they do not need an account of a relation between beliefs and objects called "correspondence," nor an account of human cognitive abilities which ensures that our species is capable of entering into that relation. They see the gap between truth and justification not as something to be bridged by isolating a natural and transcultural sort of rationality which can be used to criticize certain cultures and praise others, but simply as the gap between the actual good and the possible better. From a pragmatist point of view, to say that what is rational for us now to believe may not be *true,* is simply to say that somebody may come up with a better idea. It is to say that there is always room for improved belief, since new evidence, or new hypotheses, or a whole new vocabulary, may come along.[1] For pragmatists, the desire for ob-

jectivity is not the desire to escape the limitations of one's community, but simply the desire for as much intersubjective agreement as possible, the desire to extend the reference of "us" as far as we can. Insofar as pragmatists make a distinction between knowledge and opinion, it is simply the distinction between topics on which such agreement is relatively easy to get and topics on which agreement is relatively hard to get.

"Relativism" is the traditional epithet applied to pragmatism by realists. Three different views are commonly referred to by this name. The first is the view that every belief is as good as every other. The second is the view that "true" is an equivocal term, having as many meanings as there are procedures of justification. The third is the view that there is nothing to be said about either truth or rationality apart from descriptions of the familiar procedures of justification which a given society—*ours*—uses in one or another area of inquiry. The pragmatist holds the ethnocentric third view. But he does not hold the self-refuting first view, nor the eccentric second view. He thinks that his views are better than the realists, but he does not think that his views correspond to the nature of things. He thinks that the very flexibility of the word "true"—the fact that it is merely an expression of commendation—insures its univocity. The term "true," on his account, means the same in all cultures, just as equally flexible terms like "here," "there," "good," "bad," "you," and "me" mean the same in all cultures. But the identity of meaning is, of course, compatible with diversity of reference, and with diversity of procedures for assigning the terms. So he feels free to use the term "true" as a general term of commendation in the same way as his realist opponent does—and in particular to use it to commend his own view.

However, it is not clear why "relativist" should be thought an appropriate term for the ethnocentric third view, the one which the pragmatist *does* hold. For the pragmatist is not holding a

---

1. This attitude toward truth, in which the consensus of a community rather than a relation to a nonhuman reality is taken as central, is associated not only with the American pragmatic tradition but with the work of Popper and Habermas. Habermas' criticisms of lingering positivist elements in Popper parallel those made by Deweyan holists of the early logical empiricists. It is important to see, however, that the pragmatist notion of truth common to James and Dewey is not dependent upon either Peirce's notion of an "ideal end of inquiry" nor on Habermas' notion of an "ideally free community." For criticism of these notions, which in my view are insufficiently ethnocentric, see my "Pragmatism, Davidson, and Truth," forthcoming in a festschrift for Davidson edited

by Ernest LePore (University of Minnesota Press 1985), and "Habermas and Lyotard on Postmodernity" in *Praxis International*, 1984.

positive theory which says that something is relative to something else. He is, instead, making the purely *negative* point that we should drop the traditional distinction between knowledge and opinion, construed as the distinction between truth as correspondence to reality and truth as a commendatory term for well-justified beliefs. The reason that the realist calls this negative claim "relativistic" is that he cannot believe that anybody would seriously deny that truth has an intrinsic nature. So when the pragmatist says that there is nothing to be said about truth save that each of us will commend as true those beliefs which he or she finds good to believe, the realist is inclined to interpret this as one more positive theory about the nature of truth: a theory according to which truth is simply the contemporary opinion of a chosen individual or group. Such a theory would, of course, be self-refuting. But the pragmatist does not have a theory of truth, much less a relativistic one. As a partisan of solidarity, his account of the value of cooperative human inquiry has only an ethical base, not an epistemological or metaphysical one. Not having *any* epistemology, *a fortiori* he does not have a relativistic one.

The question of whether truth or rationality has an intrinsic nature, of whether we ought to have a positive theory about either topic, is just the question of whether our self-description ought to be constructed around a relation to human nature or around a relation to a particular collection of human beings, whether we should desire objectivity or solidarity. It is hard to see how one could choose between these alternatives by looking more deeply into the nature of knowledge, or of man, or of nature. Indeed, the proposal that this issue might be so settled begs the question in favour of the realist, for it presupposes that knowledge, man, and nature *have* real essences which are relevant to the problem at hand. For the pragmatist, by contrast, "knowledge" is, like "truth," simply a compliment paid to the beliefs which we think so well justified that, for the moment, further justification is not needed. An inquiry into the nature of knowledge can, on his view, only be a sociohistorical account of how various people have tried to reach agreement on what to believe.

This view which I am calling "pragmatism" is almost, but not quite, the same as what Hilary Putnam, in his recent *Reason, Truth and History,* calls "the internalist conception of philosophy." [2] Putnam defines such a conception as one which gives up the attempt at a God's eye view of things, the attempt at contact with the nonhuman which I have been calling "the desire for objectivity." Unfortunately, he accompanies his defense of the antirealist views I am recommending with a polemic against a lot of the other people who hold these views—e.g., Kuhn, Feyerabend, Foucault, and myself. We are criticized as "relativists." Putnam presents "internalism" as a happy *via media* between realism and relativism. He speaks of "the plethora of relativistic doctrines being marketed today" [3] and in particular of "the French philosophers" as holding "some fancy mixture of cultural relativism and 'structuralism.'" [4] But when it comes to criticizing these doctrines all that Putnam finds to attack is the so-called "incommensurability thesis": vis., "terms used in another culture cannot be equated in meaning or reference with any terms or expressions *we* possess." [5] He sensibly agrees with Donald Davidson in remarking that this thesis is self-refuting. Criticism of this thesis, however, is destructive of, at most, some incautious passages in some early writings by Feyerabend. Once this thesis is brushed aside, it is hard to see how Putnam himself differs from most of those he criticizes.

Putnam accepts the Davidsonian point that, as he puts it, "the whole justification of an interpretative scheme . . . is that it renders the behavior of others at least minimally reasonably by *our* lights." [6] It would seem natural to go on from

2. Hilary Putnam, *Reason, Truth, and History* (Cambridge: Cambridge University Press, 1981), pp. 49–50.
3. Ibid., p. 119.
4. Ibid., p. x.
5. Ibid., p. 114.
6. Ibid., p. 119. See Davidson's "On the very idea of a conceptual scheme," in his *Inquiries into Truth and Interpretation* (Oxford: Oxford University Press, 1984) for a more complete and systematic presentation of this point.

this to say that we cannot get outside the range of those lights, that we cannot stand on neutral ground illuminated only by the natural light of reason. But Putnam draws back from this conclusion. He does so because he construes the claim that we cannot do so as the claim that the range of our thought is restricted by what he calls "institutionalized norms," publicly available criteria for settling of arguments, including philosophical arguments. He rightly says that there are no such criteria, arguing that the suggestion that there are is as self-refuting as the "incommensurability thesis." He is, I think, entirely right in saying that the notion that philosophy is or should become such an application of explicit criteria contradicts the very idea of philosophy.[7] One can gloss Putnam's point by saying that "philosophy" is precisely what a culture becomes capable of when it ceases to define itself in terms of explicit rules, and becomes sufficiently leisured and civilized to rely on inarticulate knowhow, to substitute *phronesis* for codification, and conversation with foreigners for conquest of them.

But to say that we cannot refer every question to explicit criteria institutionalized by our society does not speak to the point which the people whom Putnam calls "relativists" are making. One reason these people are pragmatists is precisely that they share Putnam's distrust of the positivistic idea that rationality is a matter of applying criteria.

Such a distrust is common, for example, to Kuhn, Mary Hesse, Wittgenstein, Michael Polanyi and Michael Oakeshott. Only someone who did think of rationality in this way would dream of suggesting that "true" means something different in different societies. For only such a person could imagine that there was anything to pick out to which one might make "true" relative. Only if one shares the logical positivists' idea that we all carry around things called "rules of language" which regulate what we say when, will one suggest that there is no way to break out of one's culture.

In the most original and powerful section of

his book, Putnam argues that the notion that "rationality . . . is defined by the local cultural norms" is merely the demonic counterpart of positivism. It is, as he says, "a scientistic theory inspired by anthropology as positivism was a scientistic theory inspired by the exact sciences." By "scientism" Putnam means the notion that rationality consists in the application of criteria.[8] Suppose we drop this notion, and accept Putnam's own Quinean picture of inquiry as the continual reweaving of a web of beliefs rather than as the application of criteria to cases. Then the notion of "local cultural norms" will lose its offensively parochial overtones. For now to say that we must work by our own lights, that we must be ethnocentric, is merely to say that beliefs suggested by another culture must be tested by trying to weave them together with beliefs we already have. It is a consequence of this holistic view of knowledge, a view *shared* by Putnam and those he criticizes as "relativists," that alternative cultures are not to be thought of on the model of alternative geometries. Alternative geometries are irreconcilable because they have axiomatic structures, and contradictory axioms. They are *designed* to be irreconcilable. Cultures are not so designed, and do not have axiomatic structures. To say that they have "institutionalized norms" is only to say, with Foucault, that knowledge is never separable from power—that one is likely to suffer if one does not hold certain beliefs at certain times and places. But such institutional backups for beliefs take the form of bureaucrats and policemen, not of "rules of language" and "criteria of rationality." To think otherwise is the Cartesian fallacy of seeing axioms where there are only shared habits, of viewing statements which summarize such practices as if they reported constraints enforcing such practices. Part of the force of Quine's and Davidson's attack on the distinction between the conceptual and the empirical is that the distinction between different cultures does not differ in kind from the distinction between different theories held by members of a single culture. The Tasmanian aborigines

7. Putnam, p. 113.

8. Ibid., p. 126.

and the British colonists had trouble communicating, but this trouble was different only in extent from the difficulties in communication experienced by Gladstone and Disraeli. The trouble in all such cases is just the difficulty of explaining why other people disagree with us, of reweaving our beliefs so as to fit the fact of disagreement together with the other beliefs we hold. The same Quinean arguments which dispose of the positivists' distinction between analytic and synthetic truth dispose of the anthropologists' distinction between the intercultural and the intracultural.

On this holistic account of cultural norms, however, we do not need the notion of a universal transcultural rationality which Putnam invokes against those whom he calls "relativists." Just before the end of his book, Putnam says that once we drop the notion of a God's-eye point of view we realize that:

> we can only hope to produce a more rational *conception* of rationality or a better *conception* of morality if we operate from *within* our tradition (with its echoes of the Greek agora, of Newton, and so on, in the case of rationality, and with its echoes of scripture, of the philosophers, of the democratic revolutions, and so on . . . in the case of morality.) We are invited to engage in a truly human dialogue.[9]

With this I entirely agree, and so, I take it, would Kuhn, Hesse, and most of the other so-called "relativists"—perhaps even Foucault. But Putnam then goes on to pose a further question:

> Does this dialogue have an ideal terminus? Is there a *true* conception of rationality, an ideal morality, even if all we ever have are our *conceptions* of these?

I do not see the point of this question. Putnam suggests that a negative answer—the view that "there is only the dialogue"—is just another form of self-refuting relativism. But, once again, I do not see how a claim that something does not exist can be construed as a claim that something is relative to something else. In the

final sentence of his book, Putnam says that "The very fact that we speak of our different conceptions as different conceptions of *rationality* posits a *Grenzbegriff*, a limit-concept of ideal truth." But what is such a posit supposed to do, except to say that from God's point of view the human race is heading in the right direction? Surely Putnam's "internalism" should forbid him to say anything like that. To say that *we* think we're heading in the right direction is just to say, with Kuhn, that we can, by hindsight, tell the story of the past as a story of progress. To say that we still have a long way to go, that our present views should not be cast in bronze, is too platitudinous to require support by positing limit-concepts. So it is hard to see what difference is made by the difference between saying "there is only the dialogue" and saying "there is also that to which the dialogue converges."

I would suggest that Putnam here, at the end of the day, slides back into the scientism he rightly condemns in others. For the root of scientism, defined as the view that rationality is a matter of applying criteria, is the desire for objectivity, the hope that what Putnam calls "human flourishing" has a transhistorical nature. I think that Feyerabend is right in suggesting that until we discard the metaphor of inquiry, and human activity generally, as converging rather than proliferating, as becoming more unified rather than more diverse, we shall never be free of the motives which once led us to posit gods. Positing *Grenzbegriffe* seems merely a way of telling ourselves that a nonexistent God would, if he did exist, be pleased with us. If we could ever be moved solely by the desire for solidarity, setting aside the desire for objectivity altogether, then we should think of human progress as making it possible for human beings to do more interesting things and be more interesting people, not as heading towards a place which has somehow been prepared for humanity in advance. Our self-image would employ images of making rather than finding, the images used by the Romantics to praise poets rather than the images used by the Greeks to praise mathematicians. . . .

The ritual invocation of the "need to avoid

9. Ibid., p. 216.

relativism" is most comprehensible as an expression of the need to preserve certain habits of contemporary European life. These are the habits nurtured by the Enlightenment, and justified by it in terms of an appeal of Reason, conceived as a transcultural human ability to correspond to reality, a faculty whose possession and use is demonstrated by obedience to explicit criteria. So the real question about relativism is whether these same habits of intellectual, social, and political life can be justified by a conception of rationality as criterionless muddling through, and by a pragmatist conception of truth.

I think that the answer to this question is that the pragmatist cannot justify these habits without circularity, but then neither can the realist. The pragmatists' justification of toleration, free inquiry, and the quest for undistorted communication can only take the form of a comparison between societies which exemplify these habits and those which do not, leading up to the suggestion that nobody who has experienced both would prefer the latter. It is exemplified by Winston Churchill's defense of democracy as the worst form of government imaginable, except for all the others which have been tried so far. Such justification is not by reference to a criterion, but by reference to various detailed practical advantages. It is circular only in that the terms of praise used to describe liberal societies will be drawn from the vocabulary of the liberal societies themselves. Such praise has to be in *some* vocabulary, after all, and the terms of praise current in primitive or theocratic or totalitarian societies will not produce the desired result. So the pragmatist admits that he has no ahistorical standpoint from which to endorse the habits of modern democracies he wishes to praise. These consequences are just what partisans of solidarity expect. But among partisans of objectivity they give rise, once again, to fears of the dilemma formed by ethnocentrism on the one hand and relativism on the other. Either we attach a special privilege to our own community, or we pretend an impossible tolerance for every other group.

I have been arguing that we pragmatists should grasp the ethnocentric horn of this dilemma. We should say that we must, in practice, privilege our own group, even though there can be no noncircular justification for doing so. We must insist that the fact that nothing is immune from criticism does not mean that we have a duty to justify everything. We Western liberal intellectuals should accept the fact that we have to start from where we are, and that this means that there are lots of views which we simply cannot take seriously. To use Neurath's familiar analogy, we can *understand* the revolutionary's suggestion that a sailable boat can't be made out of the planks which make up ours, and that we must simply abandon ship. But we cannot take his suggestion seriously. We cannot take it as a rule for action, so it is not a live option. For some people, to be sure, the option *is* live. These are the people who have always hoped to become a New Being, who have hoped to be converted rather than persuaded. But we—the liberal Rawlsian searchers for consensus, the heirs of Socrates, the people who wish to link their days dialectically each to each—cannot do so. Our community—the community of the liberal intellectuals of the secular modern West—wants to be able to give a *post factum* account of any change of view. We want to be able, so to speak, to justify ourselves to our earlier selves. This preference is not built into us by human nature. It is just the way *we* live now.[10]

This lonely provincialism, this admission that we are just the historical moment that we are, not the representatives of something ahistorical,

10. This quest for consensus is opposed to the sort of quest for authenticity which wishes to free itself from the opinion of our community. See, for example, Vincent Descombes' account of Deleuze in *Modern French Philosophy* (Cambridge: Cambridge University Press, 1980), p. 153: "Even if philosophy is essentially demystificatory, philosophers often fail to produce authentic critiques; they defend order, authority, institutions, 'decency,' everything in which the ordinary person believes." On the pragmatist or ethnocentric view I am suggesting, all that critique can or should do is play off elements in "what the ordinary person believes" against other elements. To attempt to do more than this is to fantasize rather than to converse. Fantasy may, to be sure, be an incentive to more fruitful conversation, but when it no longer fulfills this function it does not deserve the name of "critique."

is what makes traditional Kantian liberals like Rawls draw back from pragmatism.[11] "Relativism," by contrast, is merely a red herring. The realist is, once again, projecting his own habits of thought upon the pragmatist when he charges him with relativism. For the realist thinks that the whole point of philosophical thought is to detach oneself from any particular community and look down at it from a more universal standpoint. When he hears the pragmatist repudiating the desire for such a standpoint, he cannot quite believe it. He thinks that everyone, deep down inside, *must* want such detachment. So he attributes to the pragmatist a perverse form of his own attempted detachment, and sees him as an ironic, sneering aesthete who refuses to take the choice between communities seriously, a mere "relativist." But the pragmatist, dominated by the desire

for solidarity, can only be criticized for taking his own community *too* seriously. He can only be criticized for ethnocentrism, not for relativism. To be ethnocentric is to divide the human race into the people to whom one must justify one's beliefs and the others. The first group—one's *ethnos*—comprises those who share enough of one's beliefs to make fruitful conversation possible. In this sense, everybody is ethnocentric when engaged in actual debate, no matter how much realist rhetoric about objectivity he produces in his study.[12]

What is disturbing about the pragmatist's picture is not that it is relativistic but that it takes

11. In *A Theory of Justice* Rawls seemed to be trying to retain the authority of Kantian "practical reason" by imagining a social contract devised by choosers "behind a veil of ignorance"—using the "rational self-interest" of such choosers as a touchstone for the ahistorical validity of certain social institutions. Much of the criticism to which that book was subjected, e.g., by Michael Sandel in his *Liberalism and the Limits of Justice* (Cambridge: Cambridge University Press, 1982), has centered on the claim that one cannot escape history in this way. In the meantime, however, Rawls has put forward a meta-ethical view which drops the claim to ahistorical validity. (See his "Kantian constructivism in moral theory," *Journal of Philosophy,* 1977, and his "Theory of Justice: Metaphysical or Political?" forthcoming in *Philosophy and Public Affairs.*) Concurrently, T. M. Scanlon has urged that the essence of a "contractualist" account of moral motivation is better understood as the desire to justify one's action to others than in terms of "rational self-interest." See Scanlon, "Contractualism and Utilitarianism," in A. Sen and B. Williams, eds., *Utilitarianism and Beyond,* (Cambridge, Cambridge University Press, 1982). Scanlon's emendation of Rawls leads in the same direction as Rawls' later work, since Scanlon's use of the notion of "justification to others on grounds they could not reasonably reject" chimes with the "constructivist" view that what counts for social philosophy is what can be justified to a particular historical community, not to "humanity in general." On my view, the frequent remark that Rawls' rational choosers look remarkably like twentieth-century American liberals is perfectly just, but not a criticism of Rawls. It is merely a frank recognition of the ethnocentrism which is essential to serious, nonfantastical, thought. I defend this view in "Postmodernist Bourgeois Liberalism," *Journal of Philosophy,* 1983.

12. In an important paper called "The Truth in Relativism," included in his *Moral Luck* (Cambridge: Cambridge University Press, 1981), Bernard Williams makes a similar point in terms of a distinction between "genuine confrontation" and "notional confrontation." The latter is the sort of confrontation which occurs, asymmetrically, between us and primitive tribespeople. The belief-systems of such people do not present, as Williams puts it, "real options" for us, for we cannot imagine going over to their view without "self-deception or paranoia." These are the people whose beliefs on certain topics overlap so little with ours that their inability to agree with us raises no doubt in our minds about the correctness of our own beliefs. Williams' use of "real option" and "notional confrontation" seems to me very enlightening, but I think he turns these notions to purposes they will not serve. Williams wants to defend ethical relativism, defined as the claim that when ethical confrontations are merely notional "questions of appraisal do not genuinely arise." He thinks they *do* arise in connection with notional confrontations between, e.g., Einsteinian and Amazonian cosmologies. (See Williams, p. 142). This distinction between ethics and physics seems to me an awkward result to which Williams is driven by his unfortunate attempt to find *something* true in relativism, an attempt which is a corollary of his attempt to be "realistic" about physics. On my (Davidsonian) view, there is no point in distinguishing between true sentences which are "made true by reality" and true sentences which are "made true by us," because the whole idea of "truth-makers" needs to be dropped. So I would hold that there is *no* truth in relativism, but this much truth in ethnocentrism: we cannot justify our beliefs (in physics, ethics, or any other area) to everybody, but only to those whose beliefs overlap ours to some appropriate extent. (This is not a theoretical problem about "untranslatability," but simply a practical problem about the limitations of argument; it is not that we live in different worlds than the Nazis or the Amazonians, but that conversion from or to their point of view, though possible, will not be a matter of inference from previously shared premises.)

away two sorts of metaphysical comfort to which our intellectual tradition has become accustomed. One is the thought that membership in our biological species carries with it certain "rights," a notion which does not seem to make sense unless the biological similarities entail the possession of something nonbiological, something which links our species to a nonhuman reality and thus gives the species moral dignity. This picture of rights as biologically transmitted is so basic to the political discourse of the Western democracies that we are troubled by any suggestion that "human nature" is not a useful moral concept. The second comfort is provided by the thought that our community cannot wholly die. The picture of a common human nature oriented towards correspondence to reality as it is in itself comforts us with the thought that even if our civilization is destroyed, even if all memory of our political or intellectual or artistic community is erased, the race is fated to recapture the virtues and the insights and the achievements which were the glory of that community. The notion of human nature as an inner structure which leads all members of the species to converge to the same point, to recognize the same theories, virtues, and works of art as worthy of honor, assures us that even if the Persians had won, the arts and sciences of the Greeks would sooner or later have appeared elsewhere. It assures us that even if the Orwellian bureaucrats of terror rule for a thousand years the achievements of the Western democracies will someday be duplicated by our remote descendants. It assures us that "man will prevail," that something reasonably like *our* world-view, *our* virtues, *our* art, will bob up again whenever human beings are left alone to cultivate their inner natures. The comfort of the realist picture is the comfort of saying not simply that there is a place prepared for our race in our advance, but also that we now know quite a bit about what that place looks like. The inevitable ethnocentrism to which we are all condemned is thus as much a part of the realist's comfortable view as of the pragmatist's uncomfortable one.

The pragmatist gives up the first sort of comfort because he thinks that to say that certain people have certain rights is merely to say that we should treat them in certain ways. It is not to give a *reason* for treating them in those ways. As to the second sort of comfort, he suspects that the hope that something resembling *us* will inherit the earth is impossible to eradicate, as impossible as eradicating the hope of surviving our individual deaths through some satisfying transfiguration. But he does not want to turn this hope into a theory of the nature of man. He wants solidarity to be our *only* comfort, and to be seen not to require metaphysical support.

My suggestion that the desire for objectivity is in part a disguised form of the fear of the death of our community echoes Nietzsche's charge that the philosophical tradition which stems from Plato is an attempt to avoid facing up to contingency, to escape from time and chance. Nietzsche thought that realism was to be condemned not only by arguments from its theoretical incoherence, the sort of argument we find in Putnam and Davidson, but also on practical, pragmatic, grounds. Nietzsche thought that the test of human character was the ability to live with the thought that there was no convergence. He wanted us to be able to think of truth as:

a mobile army of metaphors, metonyms, and anthromorphisms—in short a sum of human relations, which have been enhanced, transposed, and embellished poetically and rhetorically and which after long use seem firm, canonical, and obligatory to a people.[13]

Nietzsche hoped that eventually there might be human beings who could and did think of truth in this way, but who still liked themselves, who saw themselves as *good* people for whom solidarity was *enough*.[14]

I think that pragmatism's attack on the various structure-content distinctions which buttress

13. Nietzsche, "On Truth and Lie in an Extra-Moral Sense," in *The Viking Portable Nietzsche,* Walter Kaufmann, ed. and trans., pp. 46–47.

14. See Sabina Lovibond, *Realism and Imagination in Ethics* (Minneapolis: University of Minnesota Press, 1983), p. 158: "An adherent of Wittgenstein's view of language should equate that goal with the establishment of a language-game in which we could participate ingenuously, while retaining

the realist's notion of objectivity can best be seen as an attempt to let us think of truth in this Nietzschean way, as entirely a matter of solidarity. That is why I think we need to say, despite Putnam, that "there is only the dialogue," only *us,* and to throw out the last residues of the notion of "trans-cultural rationality." But this should not lead us to repudiate, as Nietzsche sometimes did, the elements in our movable host which embody the ideas of Socratic conversation, Christian fellowship, and Enlightenment science. Nietzsche ran together his diagnosis of philosophical realism as an expression of fear and resentment with his own resentful idiosyncratic idealizations of silence, solitude, and violence. Post-Nietzschean thinkers like Adorno and Heidegger and Foucault have run together Nietzsche's criticisms of the metaphysical tradition on the one hand with his criticisms of bourgeois civility, of Christian love, and of the nineteenth century's hope that science would make the world a better place to live, on the other. I do not think that there is any interesting connection between these two sets of criticisms. Pragmatism seems to me, as I have said, a philosophy of solidarity rather than of despair. From this point of view, Socrates' turn away from the gods, Christianity's turn from an Omnipotent Creator to the man who suffered on the Cross, and the Baconian turn from science as contemplation of eternal truth to science as instrument of social progress, can be seen as so many preparations for the act of social faith which is suggested by a Nietzschean view of truth.[15]

The best argument we partisans of solidarity have against the realistic partisans of objectivity is Nietzsche's argument that the traditional Western metaphysico-epistemological way of firming up our habits simply isn't working anymore. It isn't doing its job. It has become as transparent a device as the postulation of deities who turn out, by a happy coincidence, to have chosen *us* as their people. So the pragmatist suggestion that we substitute a "merely" ethical foundation for our sense of community—or, better, that we think of our sense of community as having no foundation except shared hope and the trust created by such sharing—is put forward on practical grounds. It is *not* put forward as a corollary of a metaphysical claim that the objects in the world contain no intrinsically action-guiding properties, nor of an epistemological claim that we lack a faculty of moral sense, nor of a semantical claim that truth is reducible to justification. It is a suggestion about how we might think of ourselves in order to avoid the kind of resentful belatedness—characteristic of the bad side of Nietzsche—which now characterizes much of high culture. This resentment arises from the realization, which I referred to at the beginning of this essay, that the Enlightenment's search for objectivity has often gone sour.

The rhetoric of scientific objectivity, pressed too hard and taken too seriously, has led us to people like B. F. Skinner on the one hand and people like Althusser on the other—two equally pointless fantasies, both produced by the attempt to be "scientific" about our moral and political lives. Reaction against scientism led to attacks on natural science as a sort of false god. But there is nothing wrong with science, there is only something wrong with the attempt to divinize it, the attempt characteristic of realistic philosophy. This reaction has also led to attacks on liberal social thought of the type common to Mill and Dewey and Rawls as a mere ideological superstructure, one which obscures the realities of our situation

---

our awareness of it as a specific historical formation. A community in which such a language-game was played would be one . . . whose members understood their own form of life and yet were not embarrassed by it."

15. See Hans Blumenberg, *The Legitimation of Modernity* (Cambridge: MIT Press, 1982), for a story about the history of European thought which, unlike the stories told by Nietzsche and Heidegger, sees the Enlightenment as a definitive step forward. For Blumberg, the attitude of "self-assertion," the kind of attitude which stems from a Baconian view of the nature and purpose of science, needs to be distinguished from "self-foundation," the Cartesian project of grounding such inquiry upon ahistorical criteria of rationality. Blumenberg remarks, pregnantly, that the "historicist" criticism of the op-

timism of the Enlightenment, criticism which began with the Romantics' turn back to the Middle Ages, undermines self-foundation but not self-assertion.

and represses attempts to change that situation. But there is nothing wrong with liberal democracy, nor with the philosophers who have tried to enlarge its scope. There is only something wrong with the attempt to see their efforts as failures to achieve something which they were not trying to achieve—a demonstration of the "objective" superiority of our way of life over all other alternatives. There is, in short, nothing wrong with the hopes of the Enlightenment, the hopes which created the Western democracies. The value of the ideals of the Enlightenment is, for us pragmatists, just the value of some of the institutions and practices which they have created. In this essay I have sought to distinguish these institutions and practices from the philosophical justifications for them provided by partisans of objectivity, and to suggest an alternative justification.

Suggestions for Further Reading

There is so much written about truth, James, and pragmatism it is hard to decide where to point you first for further study. Try the relevant articles in *The Encyclopedia of Philosophy*. See *World Philosophy* (Volume 4) for summaries of some of James's major writings and a good bibliography of primary and secondary sources.

See Rorty's *Philosophy and the Mirror of Nature* (Princeton, NJ: Princeton University Press, 1979) for a classic statement of Rorty's position. See the essays in *Relativism: Interpretation and Confrontation* edited by Michael Krausz (University of Notre Dame Press, 1989) for more on the issues Rorty is addressing. Also *Rationality and Relativism* edited by Marin Hollis and Steven Lukes (Oxford: Basil Blackwell, 1982) provides a collection of essays on the nature of rationality and issues surrounding the debate about relativism. Harold I. Brown's *Rationality* (London: Routledge, 1988) develops a new theory of rationality in response to relativism. Although it is quite difficult, Robert Nozick's *The Nature of Rationality* (Princeton, NJ: Princeton University Press, 1993) will provide some provocative ideas about instrumental rationality (rationality as a procedure for obtaining goals). For an article dealing with the issue of relativism from a feminist perspective, see Anne Seller's "Realism versus Relativism: Towards a Politically Adequate Epistemology" in *Feminist Perspectives in Philosophy* edited by Morwenna Griffiths and Margaret Whitford (Bloomington: Indiana University Press, 1988), pp. 169–186. Chapter 4 "Truth in Trouble" of Kenneth J. Gergen's *The Saturated Self: Dilemmas of Identity in Contemporary Life* (New York: Basic Books, 1991) presents a summary for the beginner of the kind of relativistic skepticism emerging in the postmodern world. Also see *Culture and Modernity: East-West Perspectives* edited by Eliot Deutsch (Honolulu: University of Hawaii Press, 1992) for a good collection of essays dealing with issues of rationality and relativism from both an Eastern and Western perspective.

Chapter 9

Is There a God?

HAVE YOU EVER WONDERED whether God exists? Of course; most people have. But have you wondered whether God's existence can be proved? Are there arguments that would convince any reasonable person? Is there evidence, I mean real hard-core scientific evidence, that God exists? When I ask my students how many of them believe God exists, almost all of them raise their hands. But when I ask them how many think God's existence can be *proved,* most are skeptical. "It is," they say, "a matter of faith."

The existence of God is a metaphysical question central to a branch of philosophy called **the philosophy of religion.** As the name implies, this area of philosophy applies philosophical methods to the study of a wide variety of religious issues including the existence of God. Philosophy of religion should be sharply distinguished from a type of **theology** called **revealed theology.** Theology literally means the study of God or issues relating to the divine. Revealed theology is a type of theology that claims our knowledge of God comes through special revelations such as the Bible, the Holy Spirit, or the Qur'an. St. Thomas Aquinas (Section 9.1) said that revealed theology provides "saving knowledge," that is, knowledge that will result in our salvation.

Another kind of theology, called **natural theology,** has to do with the knowledge of God that is possible based on the use of natural reason, that is, reason unaided by special revelations. St. Thomas says that this sort of theology can provide us with some knowledge of God's nature and can demonstrate that God exists, but it cannot provide saving knowledge because, after all, even the devils know that God exists.

Natural theology is sometimes called "rational theology" or "philosophical theology." As this last name indicates, this kind of theology is more closely related to the philosophy of religion than is revealed theology. Both natural theology and the philosophy of religion rely solely on the use of human reason in their attempts to discover something about the divine. They do not assume the truth of some special revelation; they allow only what reason can prove.

Although both philosophy of religion and natural theology rely on reason rather than on revelation, they differ in the range of topics considered. Philosophy of religion studies a wide range of religious issues and different notions of what constitutes ultimate reality. The concept of God is just one sort of religious notion of ultimate reality. The *Dao* or *Brahman-Atman,* for example (see Sections 7.1 and 7.3), both present conceptions of ultimate reality that appear quite different from theistic ideas. Needless to say, nontheistic philosophies have not been overly concerned with the issue of *God's* existence even though they have been concerned with the nature and existence of some kind of ultimate reality. However, theistic philosophies and the cultures—both Eastern and Western—influenced by theistic religions have regarded the topic of God's existence as an issue of immense significance.

Although the questions, "What is God like?" and "Does God exist?" are different, nevertheless they are closely related. The answer to the first question tells us something about God's nature; for example, that God or the divine, if there is such a being, is the creator of the universe, is all-powerful and all-knowing, is perfectly good and loving, and so on. The answer to the second question tells us whether a being of this sort exists. But these answers blend into each other because every argument for God's existence or nonexistence is an argument for the existence or nonexistence of a God of a certain sort. So, for example, those who argue that the existence of complex order and beauty in the universe is evidence that God created it and hence exists imply that God's nature is that of an intelligent being capable of producing beauty and order.

Arguments for God's existence fall into two broad types: *a posteriori* and *a priori*. *A posteriori* arguments attempt to demonstrate the existence of God by appealing to sense experience. Typically they argue from some feature of our experience of the world to the conclusion that God exists. We will be looking at two examples in what follows: the cosmological argument (Section 9.1) and the teleological argument (Section 9.4). *A priori* arguments attempt to show that God exists independently of any appeal to sense experience. Typically they argue from some definition of God's nature to the conclusion that God exists. We will look at one example, the argument from perfection (Section 9.3).

9.1. Cosmological Arguments

How many of you have thought, "There must be a God because the universe just couldn't happen by itself. Something must have caused it. Things don't just pop into existence out of nothing?" If you have had thoughts like this, you have been thinking along the lines of a **cosmological argument.** Cosmological arguments (there are several varieties) argue from the existence of the universe (world or cosmos) to the existence of God as its cause, its creator, or its explanation.

Cosmological arguments are very old, being found among the ancient Greek and Indian philosophers (for example Udayana [see Section 8.4] presents seven arguments for the existence of God). The Greek versions were most influential on Western thought. Since the Greeks believed the universe was eternal, they did not believe that God created it out of nothing. However, they did believe that there had to be a cause for an eternal universe and an explanation for it. Notice there is some ambiguity here. The cause of something is not necessarily the same as an explanation. "Maria got a haircut in order to appear well groomed for her job interview," explains why Maria got a haircut, but it does not state the cause of her haircut. The person who cut it and the tools used are the cause.

Aristotle (Section 2.4) argued from the existence of motion to the existence of an Unmoved Mover as the cause of motion. This Unmoved Mover he called God, in part because it was unmoved (that is, nothing caused it to move) but was responsible for the motion of other things (a prime mover). Aristotle's argument was based on three principles that operate as assumptions in practically all cosmological arguments, namely, that (1) something cannot be the cause of itself; (2) something cannot come from nothing; and (3) there cannot be an infinite series of causes and effects.

Christian and Islamic theologians inherited the Greek thinking on these matters, but most could not accept the notion that the universe was eternal. God, they believed, must be absolute and the existence of the world must be completely dependent on him. He alone is eternal. Therefore they interpreted the story of creation found in Genesis in a manner compatible with the doctrine of *creatio ex nihilo,* creation out of nothing. God, they argued, created the universe out of nothing and hence the universe is not eternal, but began to exist at some point.

Kalam, which means "speech" in Arabic, came to denote the statement of points in theological doctrine. Eventually it was used as a name for a movement in Islamic thought which, among other things, was much concerned with the problems involved in demonstrating God's existence. These Islamic theologians rejected the Greek idea of the eternity of the world and so reformulated the cosmological argument to explicitly recognize a temporal universe. A simple version of the *Kalam* cosmological argument runs:

1. Whatever begins to exist has a cause of its existence.
2. The universe began to exist.
3. Therefore, the universe has a cause of its existence, and this is Allah.

The first version of the cosmological argument that follows is from Moses ben Maimon, better known as Maimonides. He was born in Cordova, Spain in 4895 (1135 in the Christian calendar) and died in 4964 (1204) at the age of 69. Maimonides was a great Jewish theologian and philosopher who inherited both the Greek and Islamic thinking about cosmological proofs. "From Moses to Moses there is none like Moses" is a famous phrase showing how important Maimonides is in Jewish thought. The first Moses is the prophet through whom the Law was given. The second Moses is Maimonides who reconciled that Law with the science and philosophy of his day. In 1190 he transcribed a book called *Guide for the Perplexed* which shows Jews, who were perplexed by the relationship of Jewish tradition and law to science and philosophy, how to harmonize their religious tradition and scientific thinking.

Maimonides is critical of the Greek arguments because he thought the Greeks were unable to prove that the universe was eternal, and all their proofs depend on that assumption. But he was also critical of the *Kalam* arguments because he believed their assumption, namely that the universe was not eternal, also could not be proven. He therefore developed a version of the argument that attempts to prove that God exists no matter which assumption we make.

His argument makes reference to a "fifth essence" (better translated as "element") and to "heavenly spheres" because the science of his day taught that the earth was at the center of the universe (geocentrism, see diagram), surrounded by various layers of spheres where the stars were located. The material bodies within the terrestrial layer (everything below the sun and moon), it was thought, were made of various combinations of earth, air, fire, and water, and could move up and down. But the heavenly bodies were made out of a fifth element called "ether" because they moved in a circle and did not move up or down, i.e., fall toward the center (earth) or move away from it.

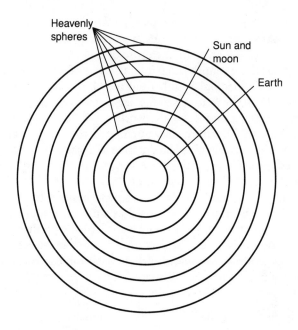

Heavenly spheres

Sun and moon

Earth

His argument begins with a list of "propositions" which he takes to be proven true. These propositions constitute what in his day were taken to be the fundamental ideas of physical science, a science adopted from the Greek physical theories of Aristotle. They provide an interesting contrast to modern physical science (see Section 9.2) and show how radically our conception of the universe has changed from the Middle Ages.

The second set of cosmological arguments comes from St. Thomas Aquinas (c. 1225–1274). St. Thomas was born in the family castle near Naples, Italy. His father, the Count of Aquino, hoped for a military career for his son. But Thomas became a monk instead and ended up teaching theology at the University of Paris. He was largely responsible for harmonizing Christian theology with the then recently discovered scientific and philosophical ideas of Aristotle. His major work is the *Summa Theologica,* which treats all the major theological issues of the day. Thomas was made a saint of the Catholic church in 1323 and in 1879 his ideas were proclaimed by Pope Leo XIII to be the official philosophy and theology of the Roman Catholic Church.

In the *Summa,* Thomas gives five separate arguments for God's existence, called the Five Ways. The selection included here presents two of these arguments, the second and third ways. It is evident that Thomas is heavily indebted to both Islamic and Jewish theology, not to mention the Greek philosophy of Aristotle. For example, following Maimonides, he constructs his arguments in such a way that they are compatible with either the assumption that the universe is eternal or the assumption that it is temporal. When he refers to an order of efficient causes, he is not thinking of a temporal order (although it could be temporal), but of a spatial order, i.e., a series of causes one on top of another like a ladder. This idea stems from the notion that the universe is made up of layers of spheres, each sphere acting as an efficient cause of a subsequent sphere. When he rejects the notion of an infinite regress, it is an infinite regress of spheres ("ladder rungs") that he is referring to, not an infinite temporal regression. However, the logic of the argument would be the same even if the regression were temporal.

The idea of an efficient cause is taken from Aristotle's idea of **four causes.** Things, Aristotle taught, had four causes: (1) efficient, (2) material, (3) formal, and (4) final. For example, the efficient cause of a statue is the agent (sculptor) and agency (sculpting) by which it is made. The material cause is the stuff (marble) out of which it is made. The formal cause is the idea or plan (essence) according to which the statue is made, and the final cause is the purpose for which the statue is made.

St. Thomas also borrows the ideas of necessity and contingency. Something is contingent if its existence is dependent on something else, and it is necessary if its existence does not depend on anything else. In one of the most influential versions of the cosmological argument, Thomas argues that the universe is contingent and hence dependent on something besides itself for existence.

Reading Questions

1. Of the 26 propositions listed by Maimonides, which do you not understand? Discuss them in class.

2. At the beginning of Chapter 1, Maimonides presents a long argument to show that the efficient motion of the sphere must be incorporeal and separate from the sphere. Summarize that argument in your own words using a premise and conclusion form (see Appendix A).

3. What is the conclusion of Maimonides' argument for God's existence presented in Chapter 2? Underline it.

4. Why must God be the creator of the spheres if the spheres are transient (that is, temporal), and why must God be the cause of the perpetual motion of the spheres if they are eternal?

5. According to St. Thomas, why is it not possible for the order of efficient causes to proceed to infinity?

6. Must a first efficient cause of the universe be God? Why or why not?

7. Why, according to St. Thomas, is it impossible for *all* things that exist to be capable of not existing?

8. If there was a time when nothing existed, why, according to St. Thomas, would it be impossible for anything to begin to exist?

9. How would St. Thomas answer the question, "Who caused God to exist?"

10. Do you think any of these arguments prove the existence of God? Why or why not? Can you formulate a better argument?

11. Just because everything in the universe has a cause and is contingent, does it follow that the universe itself, taken as whole, has a cause and is contingent?

Guide for the Perplexed

MAIMONIDES

Part II

INTRODUCTION

TWENTY-FIVE of the propositions which are employed in the proof for the existence of God, or in the arguments demonstrating that God is neither corporeal nor a force connected with a material being, or that He is One, have been fully established, and their correctness is beyond doubt. Aristotle and the Peripatetics who followed him

From Moses Maimonides, The Guide for the Perplexed, *translated by M. Friedlander (London: Routledge & Kegan Paul, Ltd., 1904), Part II, Chapters 1 & 2, pp.145–151, 154–155.*

have proved each of these propositions. There is, however, one proposition which we do not accept—namely, the proposition which affirms the Eternity of the Universe, but we will admit it for the present, because by doing so we shall be enabled clearly to demonstrate our own theory.

PROPOSITION I

The existence of an infinite magnitude is impossible.

PROPOSITION II

The coexistence of an infinite number of finite magnitudes is impossible.

PROPOSITION III

The existence of an infinite number of causes and effects is impossible, even if these were not magnitudes; if, e.g., one Intelligence were the cause of a second, the second the cause of a third, the third the cause of a fourth, and so on, the series could not be continued *ad infinitum*.

PROPOSITION IV

Four categories are subject to change:

1. *Substance*. Changes which affect the substance of a thing are called genesis and destruction.
2. *Quantity*. Changes in reference to quantity are increase and decrease.
3. *Quality*. Changes in the qualities of things are transformations.
4. *Place*. Change of place is called motion.

The term "motion" is properly applied to change of place, but is also used in a general sense of all kinds of changes.

PROPOSITION V

Motion implies change and transition from potentiality to actuality.

PROPOSITION VI

The motion of a thing is either essential or accidental; or it is due to an external force, or to the participation of the thing in the motion of another thing. This latter kind of motion is similar to the accidental one. An instance of essential motion may be found in the translation of a thing from one place to another. The accident of a thing, as, e.g., its black color, is said to move when the thing itself changes its place. The upward motion of a stone, owing to a force applied to it in that direction, is an instance of a motion due to an external force. The motion of a nail in a boat may serve to illustrate motion due to the participation of a thing in the motion of another thing; for when the boat moves, the nail is said to move likewise. The same is the case with everything composed of several parts: when the thing itself moves, every part of it is likewise said to move.

PROPOSITION VII

Things which are changeable are, at the same time, divisible. Hence everything that moves is divisible, and consequently corporeal; but that which is indivisible cannot move, and cannot therefore be corporeal.

PROPOSITION VIII

A thing that moves accidentally must come to rest, because it does not move of its own accord; hence accidental motion cannot continue forever.

PROPOSITION IX

A corporeal thing that sets another corporeal thing in motion can only effect this by setting itself in motion at the time it causes the other thing to move.

PROPOSITION X

A thing which is said to be contained in a corporeal object must satisfy either of the two following conditions: it either exists through that object, as is the case with accidents, or it is the cause of the existence of that object; such is, e.g., its essential property. In both cases it is a force existing in a corporeal object.

PROPOSITION XI

Among the things which exist through a material object, there are some which participate in the division of that object, and are therefore accidentally divisible, as, e.g., its color, and all other qualities that spread throughout its parts. On the other hand, among the things which form the essential elements of an object, there are some which cannot be divided in any way, as, e.g., the soul and the intellect.

PROPOSITION XII

A force which occupies all parts of a corporeal object is finite, that object itself being finite.

PROPOSITION XIII

None of the several kinds of change can be continuous, except motion from place to place, provided it be circular.

PROPOSITION XIV

Locomotion is in the natural order of the several kinds of motion the first and foremost. For genesis and corruption are preceded by transformation, which, in its turn, is preceded by the approach of the transforming agent to the object which is to be transformed. Also, increase and decrease are impossible without previous genesis and corruption.

PROPOSITION XV

Time is an accident that is related and joined to motion in such a manner that the one is never found without the other. Motion is only possible in time, and the idea of time cannot be conceived otherwise than in connection with motion; things which do not move have no relation to time.

PROPOSITION XVI

Incorporeal bodies can only be numbered when they are forces situated in a body; the several forces must then be counted together with substances or objects in which they exist. Hence purely spiritual beings, which are neither corporeal nor forces situated in corporeal objects, cannot be counted, except when considered as causes and effects.

PROPOSITION XVII

When an object moves, there must be some agent that moves it, from without, as, e.g., in the case of a stone set in motion by the hand; or from within, e.g., when the body of a living being moves. Living beings include in themselves, at the same time, the moving agent and the thing moved; when, therefore, a living being dies, and the moving agent, the soul, has left the body, i.e., the thing moved, the body remains for some time in the same condition as before, and yet cannot move in the manner it has moved previously. The moving agent, when included in the thing moved, is hidden from, and imperceptible to, the senses. This circumstance gave rise to the belief that the body of an animal moves without the aid of a moving agent. When we therefore affirm, concerning a thing in motion, that it is its own moving agent, or, as is generally said, that it moves of its own accord, we mean to say that the force which really sets the body in motion exists in that body itself.

PROPOSITION XVIII

Everything that passes over from a state of potentiality to that of actuality, is caused to do so by some external agent; because if that agent existed in the thing itself, and no obstacle prevented the transition, the thing would never be in a state of potentiality, but always in that of actuality. If, on the other hand, while the thing itself contained that agent, some obstacle existed, and at a certain time that obstacle was removed, the same cause which removed the obstacle would undoubtedly be described as the cause of the transition from potentiality to actuality, [and not the force situated within the body]. Note this.

PROPOSITION XIX

A thing which owes its existence to certain causes has in itself merely the possibility of existence; for only if these causes exist, the thing likewise exists. It does not exist if the causes do not exist at all, or if they have ceased to exist, or if there has been a change in the relation which implies the existence of that thing as a necessary consequence of those causes.

PROPOSITION XX

A thing which has in itself the necessity of existence cannot have for its existence any cause whatever.

PROPOSITION XXI

A thing composed of two elements has necessarily their composition as the cause of its present existence. Its existence is therefore not necessitated by its own essence; it depends on the existence of its two component parts and their combination.

PROPOSITION XXII

Material objects are always composed of two elements [at least], and are without exception subject to accidents. The two component elements of all bodies are substance and form. The accidents attributed to material objects are quantity, geometrical form, and position.

PROPOSITION XXIII

Everything that exists potentially, and whose essence includes a certain state of possibility, may at some time be without actual existence.

PROPOSITION XXIV

That which is potentially a certain thing is necessarily material, for the state of possibility is always connected with matter.

PROPOSITION XXV

Each compound substance consists of matter and form, and requires an agent for its existence, *viz.,* a force which sets the substance in motion, and thereby enables it to receive a certain form. The force which thus prepares the substance of a certain individual being, is called the immediate motor.

Here the necessity arises of investigating into the properties of motion, the moving agent and the thing moved. But this has already been explained sufficiently; and the opinion of Aristotle may be expressed in the following proposition: Matter does not move of its own accord—an important proposition that led to the investigation of the Prime Motor (the first moving agent).

Of these foregoing twenty-five propositions some may be verified by means of a little reflection and the application of a few propositions capable of proof, or of axioms or theorems of almost the same force, such as have been explained by me. Others require many arguments and propositions, all of which, however, have been established by conclusive proofs partly in the Physics and its commentaries, and partly in the Metaphysics and its commentary. I have already stated that in this work it is not my intention to copy the books of the philosophers or to explain difficult problems, but simply to mention those propositions which are closely connected with our subject, and which we want for our purpose.

To the above propositions one must be added which enunciates that the universe is eternal, and which is held by Aristotle to be true, and even more acceptable than any other theory. For the present we admit it, as a hypothesis, only for the purpose of demonstrating our theory. It is the following proposition:—

PROPOSITION XXVI

Time and motion are eternal, constant, and in actual existence.

In accordance with this proposition, Aristotle is compelled to assume that there exists actually a body with constant motion, *viz.*, the fifth element. He therefore says that the heavens are not subject to genesis or destruction, because motion cannot be generated nor destroyed. He also holds that every motion must necessarily be preceded by another motion, either of the same or of a different kind. The belief that the locomotion of an animal is not preceded by another motion, is not true; for the animal is caused to move, after it had been in rest, by the intention to obtain those very things which bring about that locomotion. A change in its state of health, or some image, or some new idea can produce a desire to seek that which is conducive to its welfare and to avoid that which is contrary. Each of these three causes sets the living being in motion, and each of them is produced by various kinds of motion. Aristotle likewise asserts that everything which is created must, before its actual creation, have existed *in potentiâ*. By inferences drawn from this assertion he seeks to establish his proposition, *viz.*, The thing that moves is finite, and its path finite; but it repeats the motion in its path an infinite number of times. This can only take place when the motion is circular, as has been stated in Proposition XIII. Hence follows also the existence of an infinite number of things which do not coexist but follow one after the other.

Aristotle frequently attempts to establish this proposition; but I believe that he did not consider his proofs to be conclusive. It appeared to him to be the most probable and acceptable proposition. His followers, however, and the commentators of his books, contend that it contains not only a probable but a demonstrative proof, and that it has, in fact, been fully established. On the other hand, the Mutakallemim try to prove that the proposition cannot be true, as, according to their opinion, it is impossible to conceive how an infinite number of things could even come into existence successively. They assume this impossibility as an axiom. I, however, think that this proposition is admissible, but neither demonstrative, as the commentators of Aristotle assert, nor, on the other hand, impossible, as the Mutakallemim say. We have no intention to explain here the proofs given by Aristotle, or to show our doubts concerning them, or to set forth our opinions on the creation of the universe. I here simply desire to mention those propositions which we shall require for the proof of the three principles stated above. Having thus quoted and admitted these propositions, I will now proceed to explain what may be inferred from them.

Chapter 1

According to Proposition XXV, a moving agent must exist which has moved the substance of all existing transient things and enabled it to receive Form. The cause of the motion of that agent is found in the existence of another motor of the same or of a different class, the term "motion," in a general sense, being common to four categories (Prop. IV). This series of motions is not infinite (Prop. III); we find that it can only be continued till the motion of the fifth element is arrived at, and then it ends. The motion of the fifth element is the source of every force that moves and prepares any substance on earth for its combination with a certain form, and is connected with that force by a chain of intermediate motions. The celestial sphere [or the fifth element] performs the act of locomotion which is the first of the several kinds of motion (Prop. XIV), and all locomotion is found to be the indirect effect of the motion of this sphere; e.g., a stone is set in motion by a stick, the stick by a man's hand, the hand by the sinews, the sinews by the muscles, the muscles by the nerves, the nerves by the natural heat of the body, and the heat of the body by its form. This is undoubtedly the immediate motive cause, but the action of this immediate cause is due to a certain design, e.g., to bring a stone into a hole by striking against it with a stick in order to prevent the draught from coming through the crevice. The motion of the air that causes the draught is the effect of the motion of the celestial sphere. Similarly it may be shown that the ultimate cause of all genesis and destruction can be traced to the motion of the sphere. But the motion of the sphere must likewise have been effected by an agent (Prop. XVII) residing either without the sphere or within it; a third case being impossible. In the first case, if the motor is without the sphere, it must either be corporeal or incorporeal; if incorporeal, it cannot be said that the agent is *without* the sphere; it can only be described as *separate* from it; because an incorporeal object can only be said metaphorically to reside without a certain corporeal object. In the second case, if the agent resides within the sphere, it must be either a force distributed throughout the whole sphere so that each part of the sphere includes a part of the force, as is the case with the heat of fire; or it is an indivisible force, e.g., the soul and the intellect (Props. X and XI). The agent which sets the sphere in motion must consequently be one of the following four things: a corporeal object without the sphere; an incorporeal object separate from it; a force spread throughout the whole of the sphere; or an indivisible force [within the sphere].

The first case, *viz.*, that the moving agent of the sphere is a corporeal object without the sphere is, impossible, as will be explained. Since the moving agent is corporeal, it must itself move while setting another object in motion (Prop. IX), and as the sixth element would likewise move when imparting motion to another body, it would be set in motion by a seventh element, which must also move. An infinite number of bodies would thus be required before the sphere could be set in motion. This is contrary to Proposition II.

The third case, *viz.*, that the moving object be a force distributed throughout the whole body, is likewise impossible. For the sphere is corporeal, and must therefore be finite (Prop. I); also the force it contains must be finite (Prop. XII), since each part of the sphere contains part of the force (Prop. XI): the latter can consequently not produce an infinite motion, such as we assumed according to Proposition XXVI, which we admitted for the present.

The fourth case is likewise impossible, *viz.*, that the sphere is set in motion by an indivisible force residing in the sphere in the same manner as the soul resides in the body of man. For this force, though indivisible, could not be the cause of infinite motion by itself alone; because if that were the case the prime motor would have an accidental motion (Prop. VI). But things that move accidentally must come to rest (Prop. VIII), and then the thing comes also to rest which is set in motion. [The following may serve as a further illustration of the nature of accidental motion. When man is moved by the soul, i.e., by his form, to go from the basement of the house to the upper storey, his body moves directly, while the soul, the really efficient cause of that motion, participates in it accidentally. For through the translation of the body from the basement to the upper storey, the soul has likewise changed its place, and when no fresh impulse for the motion of the body is given by the soul, the body which has been set in motion by such impulse comes to rest, and the accidental motion of the soul is discontinued]. Consequently the motion of that supposed first motor must be due to some cause which does not form part of things composed of two elements, *viz.*, a moving agent and an object moved; if such a cause is present the motor in that compound sets the other element in motion; in the absence of such a cause no motion takes place. Living beings do therefore not move continually, although each of them possesses an indivisible motive element; because this element is not constantly in motion, as it would be if it produced motion of its own accord. On the contrary, the things to which the action is due are separate from the motor. The action is caused either by desire for that which is agreeable, or by aversion from that which is disagreeable, or by some image, or by some ideal when the moving being has the capacity of conceiving it. When any of these causes are present then the motor acts; its motion is accidental, and must therefore come to an end (Prop. VIII). If the motor of the sphere were of this kind the sphere could not move *ad infinitum*. Our opponent, however, holds that the spheres move continually *ad infinitum;* if this were the case, and it is in fact possible (Prop. XIII), the efficient cause of the motion of the sphere must, according to the above division, be of the second kind, *viz.,* something incorporeal and separate from the sphere.

It may thus be considered as proved that the efficient cause of the motion of the sphere, if that motion be eternal, is neither itself corporeal nor does it reside in a corporeal object; it must move neither of its own accord nor accidentally; it must be indivisible and unchangeable (Prop. VII and Prop. V). This Prime Motor of the sphere is God, praised be His name! . . .

Chapter 2

The fifth essence, i.e., the heavenly spheres, must either be transient, and in this case motion would likewise be temporary, or, as our opponent assumes, it must be eternal. If the spheres are transient, then God is their Creator; for if anything comes into existence after a period of nonexistence, it is self-evident that an agent exists which has effected this result. It would be absurd to contend that the thing itself effected it. If, on the other hand, the heavenly spheres be eternal, with a regular perpetual motion, the cause of this perpetual motion, according to the Propositions enumerated in the Introduction, must be something that is neither a body, nor a force residing in a body, and that is God, praised be His name! We have thus shown that whether we believe in the *Creatio ex Nihilo,* or in the Eternity of the Universe, we can prove by demonstrative arguments the existence of God, i.e., an absolute Being, whose existence cannot be attributed to any cause, or admit in itself any potentiality.

Summa Theologica

ST. THOMAS AQUINAS

The Second Way: The Argument from Causation

THE SECOND WAY is taken from the idea of the Efficient cause. (1) For we find that there is among material things a regular order of efficient causes. (2) But we do not find, nor indeed is it possible, that anything is the efficient cause of itself, for in that case it would be prior to itself, which is impossible. (3) Now it is not possible to proceed to infinity in efficient causes. (4) For if we arrange in order all efficient causes, the first is the cause of the intermediate, and the intermediate the cause of the last, whether the intermediate be many or only one. (5) But if we remove a cause the effect is removed; therefore, if there is no *first* among efficient causes, neither will there be a last or an intermediate. (6) But if we proceed to infinity in efficient causes there will be no first efficient cause, and thus there will be no ultimate effect, nor any intermediate efficient causes, which is clearly false. Therefore it is necessary to suppose the existence of some first efficient cause, and this men call God.

From Thomas Aquinas, Summa Theologica, *translated by Lawrence Shapcotte (London: O. P. Benziger Brothers, 1911). Part 1, Article 3.*

The Third Way:
The Argument from Contingency

The Third Way rests on the idea of the "contingent" and the "necessary" and is as follows: (1) Now we find that there are certain things in the Universe which are capable of existing and of not existing, for we find that some things are brought into existence and then destroyed, and consequently are capable of being or not being. (2) But it is impossible for all things which exist to be of this kind, because anything which is capable of not existing, at some time or other does not exist. (3) If therefore *all* things are capable of not existing, there was a time when nothing existed in the Universe. (4) But if this is true there would also be nothing in existence now; because anything that does not exist cannot begin to exist except by the agency of something which has existence. If therefore there was once nothing which existed, it would have been impossible for anything to begin to exist, and so nothing would exist now. (5) This is clearly false. Therefore all things are not contingent, and there must be something which is necessary in the Universe. (6) But everything which is necessary either has or has not the cause of its necessity from an outside source. Now it is not possible to proceed to infinity in necessary things which have a cause of their necessity, as has been proved in the case of efficient causes. Therefore it is necessary to suppose the existence of something which is necessary in itself, not having the cause of its necessity from any outside source, but which is the cause of necessity in others. And this "something" we call God.

Suggestions for Further Reading

For a summary of the *Guide for the Perplexed* and the *Summa Theologica* plus a good starting bibliography on Maimonides and St. Thomas see Volume 2 of *World Philosophy*.

Donald R. Burrill has edited a useful collection of readings in *The Cosmological Arguments* (Garden City, NY: Anchor Books, 1967), and you can find a somewhat advanced discussion in William L. Rowe's *The Cosmological Argument* (Princeton: Princeton University Press, 1975). Richard Taylor has provided an introductory and sympathetic approach to the cosmological argument in the third edition of his *Metaphysics* (Englewood Cliffs, NJ: Prentice-Hall, 1983).

For a detailed discussion and defense of the *Kalam* version see William Lane Craig's *The Kalam Cosmological Argument* (London: Macmillan, 1979). The seven ways of Udayana can be found in his *Nyayakusumanjali*, translated by Jose Pereira, in *Hindu Theology: A Reader*, (New York: Doubleday, 1976).

9.2. The Origin of the Universe According to Modern Science

Victor Weisskopf, the author of the next essay, is the Institute Professor Emeritus at MIT. In 1988 he was awarded the Enrico Fermi Award from the U.S. Department of Energy for outstanding scientific achievement. He is one of the premier physicists of our age. The selection that follows is based on a talk he gave to the American Academy of Arts and Sciences.

You may be asking yourself, "What is an essay by a physicist on the origin of the universe doing in a chapter having to do with God's existence? What does religion have to do with science?" These are good questions. For many, religion is akin to poetry and myth. It speaks in metaphors and symbols. It expresses values and feelings. Science is fact. It speaks literally and realistically. It expresses what we know about the world, not how we feel about being in the world.

There is much to be said in favor of a sharp distinction between religion and science. They are very different. And yet, throughout history, especially modern history, they have repeatedly come into conflict. For example, Galileo (1564–1642) was prosecuted for heresy by the Roman Catholic Church for teaching heliocentrism (the view that the sun, not the earth, is the center of our solar system). And most of you are probably aware of the present-day conflict between fundamentalist Christians and biologists over evolution and "creationism."

The cosmological argument seems to beg for comparisons with scientific views. It is a theory about the origin of the universe and, insofar as science is interested in the origin of the universe, it seems inevitable that scientific theories and this argument should meet at some point. Indeed, the versions of the cosmological arguments presented in the last section all depended heavily on the science of their day. But science has changed. Geocentrism has been replaced by heliocentrism and the idea that matter is made up of earth, air, fire, and water has been replaced by the atomic theory of matter. No longer do we believe that the stars are made out of ether. We have also discovered that they are not attached to spheres that rotate in a perfect circle. In fact, the universe is expanding. Stars and planets are moving away from a "center."

Modern science is strongly influenced by **naturalism,** the theory that the universe is a self-existing, self-regulating, and homogeneous system (its parts differ in degree but not in kind). Pierre Laplace (1749–1827), the famous and influential French mathematician and astronomer, when asked why God played no role in scientific theories about the origin of the universe, remarked, "We have no need of that hypothesis." He believed that science can explain the universe quite well without recourse to anything outside the universe. This is a good example of a naturalistic attitude.

Of course, there have been attempts to develop ideas of God that are compatible with scientific theories. Many scientists have been attracted, for example, to a deistic theory of God. **Deism** is the view that God started the universe and established natural laws (the laws of physics) according to which it operates. It now runs on its own without God's interference or help. Such a view of God implies that there are no miracles, if what you mean by a miracle is God intervening in world affairs in violation of natural laws. Still others have been attracted to **pantheism,** the theory that nature is God. According to pantheism, God does not transcend the universe; God is the universe.

Both deistic and pantheistic views of God appear to conflict with theism. **Theism** is the view that God is an infinite, unitary, self-existent, all-powerful, all-knowing, perfectly good, and personal being who created the universe out of nothing and directs it according to teleological laws. Both Maimonides and St. Thomas had this theistic sort of God in mind when they presented their cosmological arguments. But do their arguments prove the existence of a theistic God, rather than the God of deists or of pantheists?

Of course, some people believe that some versions of the cosmological argument conflict with modern science. One of the laws of energy is called the law of the conservation of energy. According to this law, energy can be neither created nor destroyed (although it can be transformed). This would seem to directly contradict the view that God created the universe out of nothing. However, there appears to be less of a conflict with the notion that God is the cause of an eternally existing universe (the Greek view).

Many of you may have heard of the Big Bang. This is the notion that the universe began as a huge explosion. The Big Bang has been treated as a physical singularity, that is, as an occurrence whose physics is not understood. A physical singularity marks the limits of the conceptual resources of a theory. Singularities must be thought of as a kind of arbitrary initial condition or as a phenomenon awaiting explanation. Science is not content with singularities, and recently, new theories have been developed to explain the singularity of the Big Bang according to known physical laws. These theories are highly speculative and tentative, but they do show how scientists might explain the origin of the universe without recourse to the "God hypothesis." These theories raise the issue of what constitutes a sufficient explanation of the universe. In order to have a sufficient explanation do we need a concept like God as a stopping point in an otherwise infinite regress? Or will certain physical phenomena like "fluctuations" in a vacuum do just as well? Read this fascinating and lucid account of recent cosmogonic theory and decide.

Reading Questions

1. What is the quantum ladder?
2. How do we know that matter must have been very compressed at the time of the Big Bang?
3. What is the cosmic horizon?
4. How does Weisskopf define cosmology?
5. How does a false vacuum differ from a true vacuum, and what is the Big Bang?
6. How did the Big Bang start?
7. Why might we conclude that our universe is not the only universe?
8. Even though Weisskopf says that some aspects of the present scientific view complement religious views, he never mentions God as the creator of the universe. Does the scientific picture he paints support, contradict, or complement the cosmological argument? Why or why not?
9. Try to restate the cosmological argument in modern scientific terms. Can it be done?

The Origin of the Universe

VICTOR WEISSKOPF

1.

HOW DID THE UNIVERSE begin about 12 billion years ago? The question concerns the very large—space, galaxies, etc.—but also the very small, namely the innermost structure of matter. The reason is that the early universe was very hot, so that matter was then decomposed into its constituents. These two topics hang together, and this is what makes them so interesting.

One must start with a few words about the innermost structure of matter. The sketch in Figure 1 indicates, on the very left, a piece of metal. It is made of atoms. To the right of it you see one of the atoms symbolically designed with a nucleus in the middle and with electrons around it.

Victor Weisskopf, "The Origin of the Universe," The New York Review of Books XXXVI (February 16, 1989), pp. 10–14. Reprinted with permission from The New York Review of Books. Copyright © 1989 Nyrev Inc.

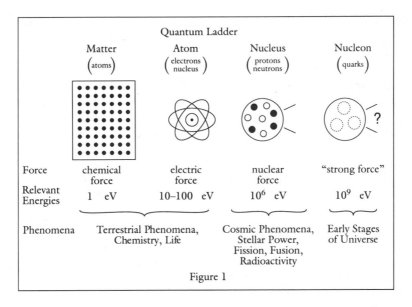

Figure 1

Here we proceed toward the innermost structure of matter in steps. That's why I call it the quantum ladder. Further to the right you see the nucleus, consisting of protons and neutrons, which I will call nucleons from now on. We have found out that the nucleons themselves are composite; they are made up of quarks, as seen in Figure 1.

Let us look at the forces that keep the constituents together in the four steps of the quantum ladder. The deeper you go, the stronger the forces become. In the piece of metal, the chemical force that keeps the atoms together has the strength of a few electron volts (this is a measure of force strength). In the atom, the electrons are bound to the nucleus by a few tens of electron volts. The protons and neutrons are bound within the nucleus by millions of electron volts, and the forces between the quarks in a nucleus are in the billions of electron volts. This leads us to the concept of conditional elementarity. When we apply small amounts of energy, we cannot overcome the forces that keep the constituents together. For example, if energies of less than a few electron volts are available, atoms cannot be decomposed into electrons and nuclei. They seem to be elementary, which means stable, or unchangeable. When energies above a few hundred but below a million electron volts are available, atoms may be decomposed, but nuclei and electrons seem elementary. For energies over a million electron volts, nuclei are decomposed, but the protons and neutrons are elementary. At a billion electron volts, the nucleons appear to be composed of quarks. Electrons, so far, have never been shown to be composite.

It will be important later on to understand the connection between energy and temperature. Heating a piece of material is equivalent to increasing the energy of motion of the constituents of that piece, be they atoms or electrons or other particles. In a hot material, the atoms or the electrons perform all kinds of motions, oscillations, straight flights, etc. The greater the temperature, the higher the energy of the motions. Thus, temperature is equivalent to energy. For example, one electron volt corresponds to about 12,000°C (about 22,000°F). The temperature at which atomic nuclei decompose is about 20 billion degrees. A billion electron volts would be about 20 trillion degrees Celsius.

On the last rung of the quantum ladder, when billions of electron volts are available—by means of accelerators or when the universe was very hot—new phenomena appear. Let us call it the subnuclear realm. Antimatter plays an important role at that stage. What is it? In the last 50 years it was discovered that there is an antiparticle to every particle; an antielectron called a positron, an antiproton and antineutron, an antiquark. They carry the opposite charge of the actual particle. Thus there ought to exist antiatoms, antimolecules, antimatter of all sorts, made of antielectrons and antinuclei. Why do we not find antimatter in our environment? Because of an important fact: when an antiparticle hits a particle, they "annihilate." A small explosion occurs, and the two entities disappear in a burst of light energy or other forms of energy. This is in agreement with the famous Einstein formula $E = mc^2$, which says that mass—in this case, the masses of the particle and the antiparticle—is a form of energy. The opposite process also occurs: a high concentration of energy can give rise to the birth of a particle and antiparticle. This is called pair creation.

To summarize the quantum ladder, let me quote a prophetic statement by Newton, who wrote three hundred years ago; it describes Figure 1 from the right to the left, as it were:

> Now the smallest particles of matter may cohere by the strongest attractions, and compose bigger particles of weaker virtue. And many of these may cohere, and compose bigger particles whose virtue is still weaker. And so on for diverse successions, until the progression ends in the biggest particles on which the operation in chemistry and the colors of natural bodies depend, which by cohering compose bodies of a sensible magnitude . . .

. . . like that piece of metal. He foresaw the ideas of the structure of matter that were developed centuries after his time.

2.

Let us now turn to our main subject: the universe. Let's first look at the universe as we see it today. There are six facts that are important to us. First, most of the stars we see in the universe consist of 93 percent hydrogen, 6 percent he-

lium, and only 1 percent all other elements. This has been determined by analyzing the light from the stars. Here on earth, things—including our bodies—consist mainly of other elements besides hydrogen. But this is a special case; the stars are made mostly of hydrogen. I have to mention something of which astronomers should be very much ashamed. It turned out that visible matter, the one that sends light to us, is only 10 percent of the total matter. Ninety percent of the matter of the universe is what is now called dark matter—dark because we don't see it; dark because we don't know what it is. How do we know that it is there? The dark matter, like any matter, attracts other matter by gravity. One has found motions of stars and galaxies that could not be explained by the gravitational attraction of the visible, luminous matter. For example, stars in the neighborhood of galaxies move much faster than they would if they were attracted only by the visible stars. So far the nature of that dark matter is unknown. We do not have the slightest idea of what 90 percent of the world is made of.

The second fact concerns the distribution of matter in space. We know that it is very uneven. We see stars, but nothing in between; we see galaxies and clusters of galaxies. However, if we average over a large part of space containing many stars and galaxies, we find that luminous matter is very thinly distributed, only about one hydrogen atom per cubic meter. To this we must add ten times as much dark matter.

The third fact is the expansion of the universe. The following astounding observation was made about 60 years ago, first by the American astronomer E. P. Hubble. It was Hubble who found that faraway objects like galaxies move away from us; the greater the distance, the faster they move away. For example, a galaxy that is as far as 1 million light years moves away from us with a speed of about 20 kilometers per second. Another galaxy, at a distance of two million light years, moves away at 40 kilometers per second; another, at three million light years, moves away at 60 kilometers per second; and so on. As a consequence, the distances between objects in space increase as time goes on. The universe gets more dilute with time. It is a kind of decompression of matter.

A most dramatic conclusion must be drawn from this: if we go backward in time, we conclude that galaxies were nearer to each other in the past. Therefore, at a certain time in the far distant past, the matter in the universe must have been extremely dense. Matter must have been highly compressed, far more than any compression achievable on earth by technical means. At that time there were no galaxies or stars: matter was so thoroughly compressed that everything merged. A little calculation shows that this happened about 12 billion years ago.

In this calculation, one has taken into account that the expansion was faster at an earlier time, since the gravitational attraction acts like a brake and slows down the expansion. Today's rate of expansion, the so-called Hubble constant, is not very well established. It could be 15 or 30, instead of 20, kilometers per second at a million light years. Therefore, the time of extreme compression—this is the time of the beginning of our universe, of the Big Bang—may not have been 12 billion years ago, but perhaps 10 or 15 billion years ago. Still, we can introduce a new chronology: the zero time is the time of extreme compression, the time of the Big Bang. Today is about 12 billion years since the beginning.

We now approach the fourth point regarding our present universe. How far can we see into space? Since the universe is about 12 billion years old, we cannot see farther than about 12 billion light years. We call this distance the cosmic horizon of today. As we will see later in more detail, the Big Bang was a tremendous explosion in which space expanded almost infinitely fast, creating matter over a region probably much larger than what is visible today. Light from those farther regions has not had enough time to reach us today but may do so in the future.

There is another interesting consequence: the farther we look within the cosmic horizons, the younger are the objects we see. After all, it took time for the light to reach us. The light we see of a galaxy, say, 100 million light years away, was emitted 100 million years ago. A picture of the

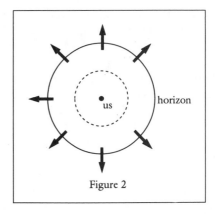

Figure 2

galaxy shows how it was 100 million years back. Figure 2 shows this schematically. The outer circle is the cosmic horizon. The broken circle is about 6 billion light years away, and objects there appear to us only 6 billion years old. What about objects at or very near the horizon? What we see there is matter in its first moments, matter just or almost just born. Thus, if we had very good telescopes, we could see the whole history of matter in the universe, starting far out and ending near us.

Beware of the following misunderstanding. One could wrongly argue that, say, the regions that are 6 billion light years away were much nearer to us when they did send out their light, and therefore we should see them earlier than 6 billion years after emission. This conclusion is false, because the light velocity must be understood as relative to the expanding space. Seen from a nonexpanding frame, a light beam running against the expansion—that is, toward us—moves slower than the usual light velocity. As it were, light is dragged along with the expansion.

Our fifth question has to do with the temperature in the universe. How hot is it out there? Let us consider a kiln, such as potters use, to understand the situation. Take a kiln and heat it up. First you can see no light, but the kiln radiates microwaves. When it gets hotter it radiates infrared radiation, which we do not see but can feel as heat radiation. At higher temperatures it becomes red, then yellow and white, then ultraviolet; at millions of degrees it will radiate X-rays.

Today, in the immediate surroundings within a few million light years, the temperature is very low in space. It was measured a few decades ago when two Princeton physicists, A. Penzias and R. Wilson, found a very cool microwave radiation in space corresponding to heat radiation of only 5 degrees above absolute zero—the lowest possible temperature, which is minus 460°F. An appropriate measure of very low temperatures is the Kelvin scale. Zero degree Kelvin is absolute zero. The Kelvin scale uses Celsius degrees above absolute zero. Thus, the space temperature in our neighborhood is 3°K. This is the temperature in space between the stars. The stars are much hotter inside, but there is so much space between them that their higher temperature does not count.

Was the temperature always 3°K.? No, it was much warmer at earlier times, a fact that is related to the expansion of the universe. Let us go back to the kiln again. Imagine a kiln made in such a way that we can expand or contract its volume at will. The laws of physics tell us that the temperature of a kiln drops when it expands and rises when it contracts. Thus, we must conclude that the expansion of the universe lowers the temperature. It must have been hotter at earlier times. For example, about 6 million years ago, the temperature was roughly twice as high— that is, near 6°K. At the very beginning, about 12 billion years ago, when space was extremely contracted, the temperature must have been extremely high. This has interesting consequences.

We know from the physics of radiation that matter is transparent for light when the temperature is below 1000°C. This is true only for very dilute matter, such as that found in the space between the stars. Matter of ordinary density, such as a piece of iron or wood, is not transparent, of course. But if the temperature is raised from 1000°C, even very dilute matter becomes opaque. Thus light from those outer regions near the cosmic horizon, which are so young that the temperature is over 1000°C, cannot penetrate space and will not reach us. We should emphasize that these regions are very near the cosmic horizon. A temperature of 1000°C was reached when the universe was about 300,000 years old, an age that is very young compared with 12 billion years. Hence, light reaches us not from the cosmic horizon but from a distance that is almost as far as the cosmic horizon. We see only matter older than 300,000 years, which is nevertheless pretty young. Even younger matter, younger than that, is hidden by the opaque space.

Figure 3 illustrates this schematically. The outermost circle is the cosmic horizon, where matter is just born at extreme density and extreme heat. But already a little nearer to us at the center, the temperature has fallen to and below 1000°C, and we can see it, since space inside that second circle is transparent.

But why do we not see that part of the universe glowing white-hot at 1000°C? The reason is the famous Doppler effect. That part of the universe moves away from us at a terrific speed according to the law of expansion, which states that the greater the distance of an object, the faster it moves away from us. The Doppler effect reduces the frequency of light if the emitting object moves away from us. Everybody has observed how the whistle of a fire engine lowers its pitch as the engine moves away. Reducing the frequency is equivalent to lowering the temperature. Red's frequency is lower than yellow's and much lower than violet's. Therefore, the heat radiation from that far away region of 1000°K is much cooled down because it moves away from us so fast. Indeed, it is cooled down from

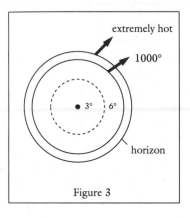

Figure 3

1000°K to 3°K. Thus, the cool radiation that Penzias and Wilson have observed is indeed the radiation from the hot universe 300,000 years after the Big Bang. The 3°K radiation can be considered the optical reverberation of the Big Bang. This is not quite correct, because it was emitted a little later. That is the explanation of the cool radiation of today.

3.

So far, we have discussed the present state of the universe and what one can deduce from it as to its past. Now we will recount the speculations and hypotheses as to the history of the universe from the Big Bang to today, and perhaps also what was before the Big Bang. Usually history does not enter physics. One studies the properties of matter as it is today. Other sciences, such as geology, anthropology, and biology, are historical sciences; the first one deals with the history of the earth, anthropology with the history of the human animal, and biology with the history of animal and plant species.

When physics becomes historical, it deals with the history of matter—that is, with the history of the universe. It is then called cosmology. It must be emphasized that most of the conclusions are much less reliable than those in other fields of physics. Facts are scarce and not known with any accuracy. The Russian physicist Lev Landau said that the cosmologists have very weak facts to work with but very strong convictions about what they think is going on. Whatever will be told here may turn out to be wrong in the near future. Nevertheless, it is so impressive that it is worth reporting.

As we have seen, our universe is expanding and cooling down. We are in principle able to see parts of the universe in earlier periods just by looking at distant objects. We have seen that this is possible to a point in time in the past 300,000 years after the Big Bang. Let us therefore call the time from 300,000 years after the Bang up to today the period of observable history. Of course, the history is observable only in principle. Actually, our instruments are not good

enough to get detailed information regarding very distant objects.

We will not say much about that period; the preobservable history is more interesting. At the beginning of observable history the temperature was around 1000°K, which was low enough so that atoms were not destroyed and robbed of their electrons. Therefore, space was filled mainly with hydrogen and helium atoms forming a hot gas. The density of things never was completely uniform. There were gas accumulations here and more dilute parts somewhere else. The accumulations grew because of gravity. They had more concentration of mass and therefore attracted the surrounding gas more strongly than the dilute parts. The further this accumulative process went, the more effective the gravitational pull became. Such accumulations finally formed "protostars" of much higher density than elsewhere. These protostars also became much hotter than the rest, since compression produces heat. When it became hot enough at the center of such protostars, nuclear reactions were ignited, producing even more energy. The protostar became a real star like the sun, whose radiation energy comes from the nuclear reactions at the center. Furthermore, the early deviations from complete uniformity caused the stars to be not uniformly distributed but to form agglomerations that we see today as galaxies.

The nuclear reactions inside a star produce helium out of hydrogen. When a star has used up its primary nuclear fuel—hydrogen—at its center, other nuclear processes form heavier elements, such as carbon, oxygen, up to iron. Finally the star explodes and becomes a supernova. In this process most other elements are formed and expelled into space. Then new accumulations and protostars are formed from the gases in space, which now contain traces of other heavier elements, such as oxygen, carbon, iron, gold, and uranium. The sun is an example of a "second-generation" star. Some of the stars are surrounded by planets like the sun. In some of the planets, such as the earth, heavier elements are present in higher concentration. This is because most hydrogen and helium atoms escape from smaller planets, since those atoms are light and planets exert only weak gravitational pull. The hydrogen found on earth is bound in molecules to heavier atoms. Life may develop under the mild warming of the nearby star. So much for the observable history.

Now let us turn to the period between the Big Bang and the onset of observable history at about 300,000 years. Let us call it preobservable history. Nothing about that period can be observed; space was opaque because the temperature was higher than 1000°C. But we are able to conclude from our knowledge of physics what happened during that period, at least for times that are not too near to the Big Bang. Pursuing the picture of an expanding and cooling universe, one comes to the conclusion that a microsecond after the Big Bang, the temperature must have reached about 10 trillion degrees, or a thermal energy of a billion electron volts. Our present knowledge is good enough that we can guess what has happened in the universe between a microsecond and 300,000 years. But conclusions about events at earlier times, when the energy concentrations were higher, are very uncertain.

Let us tell the story in reverse, going back in time from 300,000 years to a microsecond. In that inverse sense, the universe must be regarded as contracting and getting hotter. When the temperature was hotter than 10,000°K, the atoms were decomposed and formed a "plasma," a dense gas of nuclei and electrons. The plasma was bathed in shining light, visible light, during the time when the temperature was between a thousand and a few ten thousand degrees.

That light was more and more ultraviolet (that is, of a higher frequency) at earlier times, when the temperature was higher. This radiation should be considered the same as today's 3°K radiation but enormously compressed at the early seconds of the expansion. Compression makes light hotter and of higher frequency. Going back in time, we come to a moment at about one second after the Big Bang, when the temperature was about 10 billion degrees, corresponding to an energy concentration of about a few million electron volts. At that point the thermal energy

is high enough for creating pairs of electrons and antielectrons (positrons). This is the process of matter-antimatter formation mentioned before. Hence, at one second and earlier, when the temperature was even higher, space was filled by a plasma composed not only of hydrogen and helium nuclei and their electrons but also of a rather dense gas of electrons and positrons.

At a fraction of a second after the Bang, the temperature was high enough to split the helium and nuclei into neutrons and protons. Finally, when our backward history reaches the microsecond after the Bang, the heat and the corresponding energy concentration were high enough not only to decompose protons and neutrons into quarks but also to produce quark-antiquark pairs. At this point of our backward journey in time, the universe was filled with hot, dense gases of quarks and antiquarks, electrons and positrons, and a very intense, high-frequency thermal light radiation. There was also a hot, dense gas of neutrinos, which survived the whole evolution and should be present even today, though much less hot and dense, together with the cool three-degree light radiation. We stop at this point, which is a millionth of a second after the Big Bang. We are practically at it anyway.

The prehistory described here is based on a relatively firm knowledge of the properties of matter at energy concentrations up to several billion electron volts. This knowledge stems from experiments made with accelerators producing particle beams at these energies. The largest of these machines, the ones in Geneva, Switzerland, and in Batavia, Illinois, have reached energies of several hundred billion electron volts. It would be hard to guess what happened much earlier than a microsecond, since the energy concentrations were much higher than the ones reached with our accelerators, and we have no way to know how matter behaves at these enormous compressions and temperatures.

4.

We now have reached the point where we should ask the great questions: What was the Big Bang?

What caused it? And what existed before? When facing these exciting questions, it must be said that we have no reliable answers. There are speculation, guesswork led by intuition, and a great deal of imagination that may turn out to be wrong in a few years. However, the answers that are discussed in these days are so unusual and impressive that it is worthwhile to describe them in simple terms. The underlying ideas came mostly from four persons whom one might call the four apostles of the new story of Genesis: Alan Guth of MIT, Alexander Vilenkin of Tufts University, Andrei Linde in the USSR, and Stephen Hawking in England. Paul Steinhardt of the University of Pennsylvania also contributed to it.

In order to understand the basic ideas, we must introduce a concept that is suggested by some of the latest developments in particle physics. It is the so-called false vacuum. According to these ideas, there are two types of vacuum: the true vacuum and the false vacuum. The true one is very much what one would imagine: it is empty space, empty of matter and empty of energy. The false vacuum, however, is also empty of matter, but not of energy. The energy of the false vacuum is supposed to be none of the ordinary forms of energy, such as electric fields or gravity fields. It is imagined to be a new kind of field, of a type encountered in the current theories of radioactive processes. The most characteristic feature of the false vacuum follows directly from Einstein's general relativity theory. A region filled with energy but not with matter is bound to expand suddenly and explosively, filling more and more space with false vacuum. Alan Guth has called it, succinctly, an inflationary expansion, with a speed very much faster than the previously considered expansion of our universe at any time in its development. According to our four apostles, this sudden explosion is nothing else but the Big Bang.

How does this sudden inflationary expansion of a false vacuum start? Before the event, all space was in the state of a true vacuum. "The world was without form and void, and darkness was upon the face of the deep," as the Bible says. Now we must introduce a concept that is typical for quantum mechanics. According to the fundamental tenets of this well-established theory, there is nothing in nature that remains quiet. Everything, including the true vacuum, is subject to fluctuations—in particular to energy fluctuations. The field that provides the energy to the false vacuum is absent in the true vacuum, but not completely. There must be fluctuations of the field. Thus, at one moment a small region somewhere in space may have fluctuated into a false vacuum. It would happen very rarely but cannot be excluded. That region almost instantly expands tremendously and creates a large space filled with energy according to the properties of a false vacuum. That is supposed to be the Big Bang!

One might wonder where the energy comes from that fills the expanding false vacuum. There is no need to worry about conservation of energy. According to Einstein, energy is subject to gravity. The newly created energies interact via gravity, an effect that produces negative energy, so that the net energy remains essentially constant.

When a certain large size is reached, the inflationary explosion stops and a true vacuum emerges. But the vast amount of energy contained in the false vacuum must have shown up in some form. It filled the true vacuum with hot light, quark-antiquark pairs, electron-antielectron pairs, neutrinos, etc.—in other words, with all the stuff we have described as filling the space at a microsecond after the Big Bang. Our universe is born, the slow expansion takes over, the temperature falls, and the preobservable history develops and is followed by the observable history.

In short, the history of our universe started with a fluctuation of the empty true vacuum into a small region of false vacuum, which exploded, almost immediately, into a very much larger region of false vacuum. That was the primal Bang. Then it changed to a true vacuum, but the energy of the false vacuum created all light, all particles and antiparticles, which developed into what existed at about a microsecond after the explosion. Then the ordinary expansion of the universe took over; it cooled down; quarks and anti-quarks as well as electrons and antielectrons were annihilated, but a few supernumerary quarks and electrons remained. The quarks formed protons and neutrons. Then some of these nucleons formed helium nuclei. After 300,000 years it was cool enough that the protons and helium nuclei could grab and retain electrons and become atoms. A hot gas of hydrogen and helium appeared. The gas of atoms condensed to proto-stars, which became hot inside, allowing nuclear processes to start. Stars were born, grouping themselves in galaxies. The nuclear reactions in the center of the stars and in exploding super-novas produced heavier elements. The expelled gases of exploding stars condensed to protostars and then to stars containing traces of all elements, not only hydrogen and helium. The sun is one of these second-generation stars. It is surrounded by planets, some of which—such as the earth—are special concentrations of heavier elements, benignly supplied with energy from the nearby sun, so that life can start and develop the strange human animal that pretends to understand the whole process.

An interesting conclusion follows from this view of the birth of our universe, as the consequence of an energy fluctuation in the true vacuum. Such intense fluctuations creating a speck of false vacuum are very rare, but it may have happened at other places in infinite space at other times and may have developed into other universes. Thus, we may conclude that our universe is not the only one. It is not the center and the stage of everything in this world. There may be other universes much older or much younger or even not yet born somewhere else. Remember that our universe today is most probably con-siderably larger than our present cosmic horizon of about 12 billion light years, but there is room and time enough for many other universes. Maybe, in a few billion years, another universe will penetrate ours. Until then we cannot check this hypothesis. Our own universe, of which we see only a small part today, may not be unique. Its beginning is not the beginning of everything. Other universes may exist at an earlier or later stage.

It must be emphasized again that these are unproven hypotheses. They may turn out to be pure fantasies, but the ideas are impressively grandiose.

The origin of the universe is not only of scientific interest. It always was the subject of mythology, art, and religion. Such approaches are complementary to scientific ones. Most familiarly, the Old Testament describes the beginning of the world with the creation of light on the first day. It seemed contradictory that the sun, our terrestrial source of light, was only created on day four, but it turns out to be in line with current scientific thought, according to which the early universe was full of various kinds of radiation long before the sun appeared.

Those first days have been depicted in various forms, in pictures and poetry, but to me, Franz Josef Haydn's oratorio *The Creation* is the most remarkable rendition of the Big Bang. At the beginning we hear a choir of angels singing mysteriously and softly, "And God Said Let There Be Light." And at the words "And There Was Light" the entire choir and the orchestra explode into a blazing C major chord. There is no more beautiful and impressive presentation of the beginning of everything.

Suggestions for Further Reading

Try Ronald C. Pine's *Science and the Human Prospect* (Belmont: Wadsworth, 1989) for starters. You will learn a good deal about science and the philosophy of science. Stephen W. Hawking's *A Brief History of Time: From the Big Bang to Black Holes* (New York: Bantam Books, 1988) is a real gem by one of the greatest scientific minds of our time.

Milton K. Munitz has edited a useful but now somewhat dated collection: *Theories of the Universe: From Babylonian Myth to Modern Science* (New York: The Free Press, 1957). Munitz's

The Question of Reality (Princeton: Princeton University Press, 1990) presents an updated discussion of the philosophical and religious implications of modern cosmology.

Videos

Universe: Man's Changing Perceptions, (28 minutes, produced by Howard Preston Films, 1978, distributed by Kinetic Film Enterprise) traces the development of cosmological thought through five thousand years. *Universe* (28 minutes, produced by Benchmark films, 1970) describes the modern concept of the universe, its origin and development. See your Media Services Catalogue for more information.

9.3. An Ontological Argument for God's Existence

Cosmological arguments are *a posteriori*. They argue from our experience of the universe to the existence of God as the cause, creator, or explanation for the universe. **Ontological arguments** are *a priori*. They argue from a definition of God's being (ontological means the study of being) to God's existence.

St. Anselm (1033–1109) is credited with having invented the ontological argument. He reasoned that, by definition, God must be that than which nothing greater can be thought. In other words, God is the greatest possible being of which we can conceive. Now, if that is so, it follows necessarily that God must exist. Why? Well, let us assume, contrary to fact, that the greatest possible being of which we can conceive *does not* exist. If it does not, then we can image something still greater, namely, the greatest possible being of which we can conceive that *does* exist. But there can be, by definition, nothing greater than the greatest possible being because then the greatest possible being would not be the greatest possible being and that is a contradiction. So, if assuming "the greatest possible being of which we can conceive does not exist" leads to a contradiction, then the opposite must be true, namely, the greatest possible being of which we can conceive does exist.

You may have found that a little hard to follow because the reasoning employs the *reductio ad absurdum* form (see Appendix A) and hence is an indirect proof. It supports its conclusion by showing that the contradiction of its conclusion is logically absurd. Also, Anselm's proof assumes it is greater to exist than it is not to exist. This makes good sense if we accept Plato's idea that existence is a positive value. But it may not seem so obvious to many of us that something has greater value because it exists than it does if it does not exist.

The version of the ontological argument that follows will hopefully be easier to follow. It is called "the Argument from Perfection" and was developed by Descartes (see Section 8.2). Descartes defines God as a perfect being, that is, as a being that has all perfections. This is very close to St. Anselm's definition of God as "that than which nothing greater can be thought," and it coincides with the Jewish, Islamic, and Christian theological traditions. Descartes goes on to reason that if existence is one of the perfections (a perfection is any positive quality) and if God has all perfections, then it follows that God must exist.

Descartes's reasoning is a little more direct, although you may not find it too convincing. Normally an answer to the question, "What is *x*?" does not, in addition, constitute an answer to the question, "Is there any *x*?" So you, not knowing what a unicorn was, might ask me, and I might say, "It is a white horse with a single horn on its forehead." You now know what a unicorn is. But do you also know whether unicorns actually exist? No, it makes perfectly good sense to go on and ask, "Okay, I understand what it is; but now tell me, does any such animal exist?" In effect, Descartes is claiming that in the special case of God the answer to the question, "What is God?" also constitutes an answer to the question, "Is there any?" If you understood the answer to the first question, it would make no sense to ask the second. But why should the case of God be different?

Baruch Spinoza (1632–1677) was a Jewish philosopher who found Descartes's argument convincing. However, he interpreted God in a pantheistic way whereas Descartes thought of God theistically. Most other philosophers have not found Descartes's argument convincing, but there has been disagreement as to precisely what is wrong with it.

Immanuel Kant (see Section 3.1) said that the problem stems from the belief that "existence" is a real predicate (a property or perfection). Real predicates are those that add some descriptive information about the subject. For example, "Our dog Arthur loves to take walks" adds information to our *descriptive* understanding of Arthur the dog. We now know something about the dog named Arthur we did not know before. But we do not add to the *description* of a thing when we say it exists. To say something exists is to say that there is something in reality that corresponds to our description. It answers the question, "Is there any?" but it does not answer the question, "What is it?" In addition, Kant argued that existence is an all or nothing situation. Either the blind cat Peanut exists or he does not. But real predicates are not all or nothing. They are a matter of degree. Blindness, for example, is not necessarily the total loss of sight, but it falls within a range of a reduction in the power of vision.

We need to place Meditation V in its context. As you may recall (if you don't, review Section 8.2), we left Descartes with having established the existence of his own mind and its thoughts as absolutely certain—or at least that is what he believed he had established. But Descartes had to break out of the confines of his own mind or he would be trapped in a philosophical position known as **solipsism** (the view that you and your own mental life is the only thing that exists), and he would be unable to prove representational realism correct. In Meditation III Descartes takes a step away from solipsism by presenting an argument for God's existence, and in Meditation IV he argues that not only does God exist, but God is perfectly good and hence would not deceive us.

Somewhat unhappy about his first argument in Meditation III and being inspired by the notion of God's perfection, Descartes in Meditation V returns to the theme of God's existence and offers his own version of the ontological argument, the argument from perfection. If successful, this argument would establish with certainty that, in addition to his own mind and thoughts, there exists outside his mind a perfectly good God. He is now only one step short of the further deduction that there also exists a real world external to our senses, which our senses represent to us more or less correctly (see Section 11.1).

Descartes was trying to prove representational realism true in order to place science on a firm epistemological foundation. So we find once again a close connection between the desire to prove that God exists and scientific concerns.

Reading Questions

1. What is the main point Descartes is making about triangles and other geometric figures?
2. Can you state Descartes's argument for God's existence in clear, concise premise and conclusion form?
3. Why is God's relationship to his existence like the relationship between a mountain and a valley?
4. Descartes entertains an objection to his argument and refutes it. What is the objection, and how does he refute it?
5. What are the main points of the last two paragraphs of Meditation V?
6. Do you find Descartes's argument for God's existence convincing? Why or why not?
7. Formulate and answer both an analytical and critical question about anything Descartes says in this Meditation.

Meditation V

RENÉ DESCARTES

On the Essence of Material Objects and More on God's Existence

MANY QUESTIONS REMAIN about God's attributes and about the nature of my self or mind. I may return to these questions later. But now, having found what to do and what to avoid in order to attain truth, I regard nothing as more pressing than to work my way out of the doubts that I raised the other day and to see whether I can find anything certain about material objects.

But, before asking whether any such objects exist outside me, I ought to consider the ideas of these objects as they exist in my thoughts and see which are clear and which confused.

I have a distinct mental image of the quantity that philosophers commonly call continuous. That is, I have a distinct mental image of the extension of this quantity—or rather of the quantified thing—in length, breadth, and depth. I can distinguish various parts of this thing. I can ascribe various sizes, shapes, places, and motions to these parts and various durations to the motions.

In addition to having a thorough knowledge of extension in general, I grasp innumerable particulars about things like shape, number, and motion, when I pay careful attention. The truth of these particulars is so obvious and so consonant with my nature that, when I first think of one of these things, I seem not so much to be learning something novel as to be remembering something that I already knew—or noticing for the first time something that had long been in me without my having turned my mind's eye towards it.

What's important here, I think, is that I find in myself innumerable ideas of things which, though they may not exist outside me, can't be said to be nothing. While I have some control over my thoughts of these things, I do not make the things up: they have their own real and immutable natures. Suppose, for example, that I have a mental image of a triangle. While it may

From René Descartes's Meditations on First Philosophy, *trans. Ronald Rubin (Claremont, CA: Areté Press, 1986), Meditation V. Reprinted by permission of Areté Press.*

be that no figure of this sort does exist or ever has existed outside my thought, the figure has a fixed nature (essence or form), immutable and eternal, which hasn't been produced by me and isn't dependent on my mind. The proof is that I can demonstrate various propositions about the triangle, such as that its angles equal two right angles and that its greatest side subtends its greatest angle. Even though I didn't think of these propositions at all when I first imagined the triangle, I now clearly see their truth whether I want to or not, and it follows that I didn't make them up.

It isn't relevant that, having seen triangular physical objects, I may have gotten the idea of the triangle from external objects through my organs of sense. For I can think of innumerable other figures whose ideas I could not conceivably have gotten through my senses, and I can demonstrate facts about these other figures just as I can about the triangle. Since I know these facts clearly, they must be true, and they therefore must be something rather than nothing. For it's obvious that everything true is something, and, as I have shown, everything that I know clearly and distinctly is true. But, even if I hadn't shown this, the nature of my mind would have made it impossible for me to withhold my assent from these things, at least when I clearly and distinctly grasped them. As I recall, even when I clung most tightly to objects of sense, I regarded truths about shape and number—truths of arithmetic, geometry, and pure mathematics—as more certain than any others.

But, if anything whose idea I can draw from my thought must in fact have everything that I clearly and distinctly grasp it to have, can't I derive from this a proof of God's existence? Surely, I find the idea of God, a supremely perfect being, in me no less clearly than I find the ideas of figures and numbers. And I understand as clearly and distinctly that eternal existence belongs to His nature as that the things which I demonstrate of a figure or number belong to the nature of the figure or number. Accordingly, even if what I have thought up in the past few days

hasn't been entirely true, I ought to be at least as certain of God's existence as I used to be of the truths of pure mathematics.

At first, this reasoning may seem unclear and fallacious. Since I'm accustomed to distinguishing existence from essence in other cases, I find it easy to convince myself that I can separate God's existence from His essence and hence that I can think of God as nonexistent. But, when I pay more careful attention, it's clear that I can no more separate God's existence from his essence than a triangle's angles equaling two right angles from the essence of the triangle, or the idea of a valley from the idea of a mountain. It's no less impossible to think that God (the supremely perfect being) lacks existence (a perfection) than to think that a mountain lacks a valley.

Well, suppose that I can't think of God without existence, just as I can't think of a mountain without a valley. From the fact that I can think of a mountain with a valley, it doesn't follow that a mountain exists in the world. Similarly, from the fact that I can think of God as existing, it doesn't seem to follow that He exists. For my thought doesn't impose any necessity on things. It may be that, just as I can imagine a winged horse when no such horse exists, I can ascribe existence to God when no God exists.

No, there is a fallacy here. From the fact that I can't think of a mountain without a valley it follows, not that the mountain and valley exist, but only that whether they exist or not they can't be separated from one another. But, from the fact that I can't think of God without existence, it follows that existence is inseparable from Him and hence that He really exists. It's not that my thoughts make it so or impose a necessity on things. On the contrary, it's the fact that God does exist which necessitates my thinking of Him as I do. For I am not free to think of God without existence—of the supremely perfect being without supreme perfection—as I am free to think of a horse with or without wings.

Now someone might say this: "If I take God to have all perfections, and if I take existence to be a perfection, I must take God to exist, but I needn't accept the premise that God has all perfections. Similarly, if I accept the premise that every quadrilateral can be inscribed in a circle, I'm forced to the patently false view that every rhombus can be inscribed in a circle, but I need not accept the premise." But this should not be said. For, while it's not necessary that the idea of God occurs to me, it is necessary that, whenever I think of the primary and supreme entity and bring the idea of Him out of my mind's "treasury," I attribute all perfections to Him, even if I don't enumerate them or consider them individually. And this necessity ensures that, when I do notice that existence is a perfection, I can rightly conclude that the primary and supreme being exists. Similarly, while it's not necessary that I ever imagine a triangle, it is necessary that, when I do choose to consider a rectilinear figure having exactly three angles, I attribute to it properties from which I can rightly infer that its angles are no more than two right angles, perhaps without noticing that I am doing so. But, when I consider which shapes can be inscribed in the circle, there's absolutely no necessity for my thinking that all quadrilaterals are among them. Indeed, I can't even think that all quadrilaterals are among them, since I've resolved to accept only what I clearly and distinctly understand. Thus my false suppositions differ greatly from the true ideas implanted in me, the first and foremost of which is my idea of God. In many ways, I see that this idea is not a figment of my thought, but the image of a real and immutable nature. For one thing, God is the only thing that I can think of whose existence belongs to its essence. For another thing, I can't conceive of there being two or more such Gods, and, having supposed that one God now exists, I see that He has necessarily existed from all eternity and will continue to exist into eternity. And I also perceive many other things in God which I can't diminish or alter.

But, whatever proof I offer, it always comes back to the fact that I am only convinced of what I grasp clearly and distinctly. Of the things that I grasp in this way, some are obvious to everyone. Some are discovered only by those who examine things more closely and search more carefully, but, once these things have been discovered, they are regarded as no less certain than the others. That the square on the hypotenuse of a right triangle equals the sum of the squares on the other sides is not as readily apparent as that the hypotenuse subtends the greatest angle, but, once it has been seen, it is believed just as firmly. And, when I'm not overwhelmed by prejudices and my thoughts aren't besieged by images of sensible things, there surely is nothing that I know earlier or more easily than facts about God. For what is more self-evident than there is a supreme entity—that God, the only thing whose existence belongs to His essence, exists?

While I need to pay careful attention in order to grasp this, I'm now as certain of it as of anything that seems most certain. In addition, I now see that the certainty of everything else so depends on it that, if I weren't certain of it, I couldn't know anything perfectly.

Of course, my nature is such that, when I grasp something clearly and distinctly, I can't fail to believe it. But my nature is also such that I can't permanently fix my attention on a single thing so as always to grasp it clearly, and memories of previous judgments often come to me when I am no longer attending to the grounds on which I originally made them. Accordingly, if I were ignorant of God, arguments could be produced which would easily overthrow my opinions, and I therefore would have unstable and changing opinions rather than true and certain knowledge. For example, when I consider the nature of the triangle, it seems plain to me—steeped as I am in the principles of geometry—that its three angles equal two right angles: I can't fail to believe this as long as I pay attention to its demonstration. But, if I were ignorant of God, I might come to doubt its truth as soon as my mind's eye turned away from its demonstration, even if I recalled having once grasped it clearly. For I could convince myself that I've been so constructed by nature that I sometimes err about what I believe myself to grasp most plainly—especially if I remembered that, having taken many things to be true and certain, I had later found grounds on which to judge them false.

But now I grasp that God exists, and I understand both that everything else depends on Him and that He's not a deceiver. From this, I infer that everything I clearly and distinctly grasp must be true. Even if I no longer pay attention to the grounds on which I judged God to exist, my recollection that I once clearly and distinctly knew Him to exist ensures that no contrary ground can be produced to push me towards doubt. About God's existence, I have true and certain knowledge. And I have such knowledge, not just about this one thing, but about everything else that I remember having proven, like the theorems of geometry. For what can now be said against my believing these things? That I am so constructed that I always err? But I now know that I can't err about what I clearly understand. That much of what I took to be true and certain I later found

to be false? But I didn't grasp any of these things clearly and distinctly; ignorant of the true standard of truth, I based my belief on grounds that I later found to be unsound. Then what can be said? What about the objection (which I recently used against myself) that I may be dreaming and that the things I'm now experiencing may be as unreal as those that occur to me in sleep? No, even this is irrelevant. For, even if I am dreaming, everything that is evident to my understanding must be true.

Thus I plainly see that the certainty and truth of all my knowledge derives from one thing: my thought of the true God. Before I knew Him, I couldn't know anything else perfectly. But now I can plainly and certainly know innumerable things, not only about God and other mental beings, but also about the nature of physical objects, insofar as it is the subject-matter of pure mathematics.

Suggestions for Further Reading

There is a vast literature on the ontological argument, although most of it deals with St. Anselm's version. See the article "Ontological Argument for the Existence of God" in *The Encyclopedia of Philosophy* for starters. Part I (c) of Louis P. Pojman's (ed.) *Philosophy of Religion: An Anthology* (Belmont: Wadsworth Publishing, 1987) will provide a good selection of different viewpoints. Alvin Plantinga's (ed.) *The Ontological Argument: From St. Anselm to Contemporary Philosophers* (Garden City, NY: Anchor Books, 1965) will provide you with a useful compendium of materials. Also see Colin Grant's "Anslem's Argument Today" *Journal of the American Academy of Religion* (Winter, 1989) Vol. LVII (No. 4), pp. 791–806 for an excellent overview of the controversy surrounding St. Anselm's argument. It highlights how the basic assumptions of St. Anselm's "age of faith" differ from the assumptions of the "modern age of reason."

9.4. Teleological Arguments for God's Existence

Another type of *a posteriori* argument for God's existence, one that is extremely popular, is the **teleological argument** or the argument from design. This kind of argument begins with the premise that the universe exhibits purpose or order and draws the conclusion that a supreme, divine intelligence is responsible for the order of the universe.

Versions of the teleological argument are very old, but William Paley (1743–1805), a defender of the Christian evangelical cause in England, popularized it in his 1802 publication, *Natural Theology*. Paley was under the influence of Newtonian physics, which pictured the universe as a vast machine operating in accord with well-known laws. In addition, he was much taken by the naturalist's descriptions of the complex order of various plant and animal life. It seemed to Paley that the universe was one vast, harmonious, interconnected order designed for a purpose.

Although David Hume (see Section 8.3) lived before Paley and published posthumously in 1779 his *Dialogues Concerning Natural Religion,* in which he severely criticized the teleological argument, Paley seems to be unaware of his work. Among Hume's several objections to the argument, three stand out. First Hume argues, through a fictional character named Philo, a skeptic, that the universe is not sufficiently like the productions of human design to support the argument. The things between which the analogy is drawn (the world and designed objects) are the same in some respects and different in others. Although the universe may share some things in common with houses, ships, machines, and the like, it is also vastly different. For one thing it is bigger than anything any human has ever made. Second, Philo points out that we have no other universes with which to compare this one, and we would need to make comparisons in order to decide if it were the kind of thing that was designed or simply grew on its own. Would you know, if you had never seen a cut diamond and found one by accident on a beach, that this stone was designed (cut according to a pattern) and the other stones were not? Third, Philo argues that an effect must be proportionate to its cause. Since the universe is imperfect (evil and suffering occur), its cause must be imperfect. But no theologian wishes to admit that God is anything less than perfect.

You can judge for yourself how fatal these objections might be to Paley's version of the argument. Is Paley's argument a false analogy (see Appendix A)?

Reading Questions

1. According to Paley, how do you know a watch but not a rock is designed for a purpose? Do you agree with him or not? Why? What if you had never seen a watch or had no other watch with which to compare it? Would you still know that it was designed for a purpose?

2. Paley's teleological argument depends on an analogy. What is the analogy? Can you state the argument in premise and conclusion form?

3. How do you think Paley might respond to Hume's objection that we have only seen one universe and hence have no basis for comparison?

4. How do you think Paley would respond to Hume's objection that if the universe is designed, its designer must be imperfect since the universe contains evil and suffering?

5. Why, according to Paley, aren't other explanations of order such as a principle of order or the laws of nature as good as or better than the explanation of a divine intelligence?

6. What do you think of Paley's argument? Is it a good one? Why or why not?

The Watch : The Watchmaker :: The World : God

WILLIAM PALEY

Statement of the Argument

IN CROSSING A HEATH, suppose I pitched my foot against a *stone,* and were asked how the stone came to be there, I might possibly answer, that, for anything I knew to the contrary, it had lain there forever; nor would it, perhaps, be very easy to show the absurdity of this answer. But

From the first chapter of William Paley, Natural Theology, or Evidences of the Existence and Attributes of the Deity Collected from the Appearances of Nature, *1802.*

suppose I found a *watch* upon the ground, and it should be inquired how the watch happened to be in that place, I should hardly think of the answer which I had given—that, for anything I knew, the watch might have always been there. Yet why should not this answer serve for the watch as well as for the stone? why is it not as admissible in the second case as in the first? For this reason, and for no other; *viz.,* that, when we come to inspect the watch, we perceive (what we could not discover in the stone) that its several parts are framed and put together for a purpose, e.g., that they are so formed and adjusted as to produce motion, and that motion so regulated as to point out the hour of the day; that, if the different parts had been differently shaped from what they are, if a different size from what they are, or placed after any other manner, or in any other order than that in which they are placed, either no motion at all would have been carried on in the machine, or none which would have answered the use that is now served by it. To reckon up a few of the plainest of these parts, and of their offices, all tending to one result: We see a cylindrical box containing a coiled elastic spring, which, by its endeavor to relax itself, turns round the box. We next observe a flexible chain (artificially wrought for the sake of flexure) communicating the action of the spring from the box to the fusee. We then find a series of wheels, the teeth of which catch in, and apply to, each other, conducting the motion from the fusee to the balance, and from the balance to the pointer, and, at the same time, by the size and shape of those wheels, so regulating that motion as to terminate in causing an index, by an equable and measured progression, to pass over a given space in a given time. We take notice that the wheels are made of brass, in order to keep them from rust; the springs of steel, no other metal being so elastic; that over the face of the watch there is placed a glass, a material employed in no other part of the work, but in the room of which, if there had been any other than a transparent substance, the hour could not be seen without opening the case. This mechanism being observed (it requires indeed an examination of the instrument, and perhaps some previous knowledge of

the subject, to perceive and understand it; but being once, as we have said, observed and understood), the inference, we think, is inevitable, that the watch must have had a maker; that there must have existed, at some time, and at some place or other, an artificer or artificers who formed it for the purpose which we find it actually to answer; who comprehended its construction, and designed its use.

I. Nor would it, I apprehend, weaken the conclusion, that we had never seen a watch made; that we had never known an artist capable of making one; that we were altogether incapable of executing such a piece of workmanship ourselves, or of understanding in what manner it was performed; all this being no more than what is true of some exquisite remains of ancient art, of some lost arts, and, to the generality of mankind, of the more curious productions of modern manufacture. Does one man in a million know how oval frames are turned? Ignorance of this kind exalts our opinion of the unseen and unknown artist's skill, if he be unseen and unknown, but raises no doubt in our minds of the existence and agency of such an artist, at some former time, and in some place or other. Nor can I perceive that it varies at all the inference, whether the question arise concerning a human agent, or concerning an agent of a different species, or an agent possessing, in some respect, a different nature.

II. Neither, secondly, would it invalidate our conclusion, that the watch sometimes went wrong, or that it seldom went exactly right. The purpose of the machinery, the design, and the designer, might be evident, and, in the case supposed, would be evident, in whatever way we accounted for the irregularity of the movement, or whether we could account for it or not. It is not necessary that a machine be perfect, in order to show with what design it was made; still less necessary, where the only question is, whether it were made with any design at all.

III. Nor, thirdly, would it bring any uncertainty into the argument, if there were a few parts of the watch, concerning which we could not discover, or had not yet discovered, in what manner they conduced to the general effect; or even some parts, concerning which we could not ascertain whether they conduced to that effect in any manner whatever. For, as to the first branch of the case, if by the loss, or disorder, or decay of the parts in question, the movement of the watch were found in fact to be stopped, or disturbed, or retarded, no doubt would remain in our minds as to the utility or intention of these parts, although we should be unable to investigate the manner according to which, or the connection by which, the ultimate effect depended upon their action or assistance; and the more complex is the machine, the more likely is this obscurity to arise. Then, as to the second thing supposed, namely, that there were parts which might be spared without prejudice to the movement of the watch, and that he had proved this by experiment, these superfluous parts, even if we were completely assured that they were such, would not vacate the reasoning which we had instituted concerning other parts. The indication of contrivance remained, with respect to them, nearly as it was before.

IV. Nor, fourthly, would any man in his senses think the existence of the watch, with its various machinery, accounted for, by being told that it was one out of possible combinations of material forms; that whatever he had found in the place where he found the watch, must have contained some internal configuration or other; and that this configuration might be the structure now exhibited, *viz.*, of the works of a watch, as well as a different structure.

V. Nor, fifthly, would it yield his inquiry more satisfaction, to be answered, that there existed in things a principle of order, which had disposed the parts of the watch into their present form and situation. He never knew a watch made by the principle of order; nor can he even form to himself an idea of what is meant by a principle of order, distinct from the intelligence of the watchmaker.

VI. Sixthly, he would be surprised to hear that the mechanism of the watch was no proof of con-

trivance, only a motive to induce the mind to think so.

VII. And not less surprised to be informed, that the watch in his hand was nothing more than the result of the laws of *metallic* nature. It is a perversion of language to assign any law as the efficient, operative cause of anything. A law presupposes an agent; for it is only the mode according to which an agent proceeds; it implies a power; for it is the order according to which that power acts. Without this agent, without this power, which are both distinct from itself, the *law* does nothing, is nothing. The expression, "the law of metallic nature," may sound strange and harsh to a philosophic ear; but it seems quite as justifiable as some others which are more familiar to him such as "the law of vegetable nature," "the law of animal nature," or, indeed, as "the law of nature" in general, when assigned as the cause of phenomena in exclusion of agency and power, or when it is substituted into the place of these.

VIII. Neither, lastly, would our observer be driven out of his conclusion, or from his confidence in this truth, by being told that he knew nothing at all about the matter. He knows enough for his argument: he knows the utility of the end: he knows the subserviency and adaptation of the means to the end. These points being known, his ignorance of other points, his doubts concerning other points, affect not the certainty of his reasoning. The consciousness of knowing little need not beget a distrust of that which he does know. . . .

APPLICATION OF THE ARGUMENT

Every indication of contrivance, every manifestation of design which existed in the watch, exists in the works of nature; with the difference, on the side of nature, of being greater and more, and that in a degree which exceeds all computation. I mean that the contrivances of nature surpass the contrivances of art, in the complexity, subtlety, and curiosity of the mechanism; and still more, if possible, do they go beyond them in number and variety; yet in a multitude of cases, are not less evidently mechanical, not less evidently contrivances, not less evidently accommodated to their end, or suited to their office, than are the most perfect productions of human ingenuity. . . .

Suggestions for Further Reading

Read David Hume's *Dialogues Concerning Natural Religion* for the classic refutation and Richard Swineburne's *The Existence of God* (Oxford: Oxford University Press, 1979) for a recent defense. R. R. Tennant also provides a version of the argument that takes Hume's objections into account in his *Philosophical Theology* (Cambridge: Cambridge University Press, 1928). Thomas McPherson's *The Argument from Design* (London: Macmillan, 1972) provides an introduction to various forms of the argument.

9.5. The Watchmaker Is Blind

In 1859, some 58 years after Paley's *Natural Theology* was published, Charles Darwin published *On the Origin of the Species.* This book revolutionized the biological sciences by showing how the order exhibited in nature is the result of evolutionary processes. According to Aristotle (Section 2.4), species are fixed. This idea supported the sort of creationism Paley promoted: that God is the original creator and designer of species, which then proliferate by reproductive means. But by Darwin's time the fossil record and mounting biological evidence no longer supported the fixed species idea. Species change, develop, and evolve, Darwin claimed, and they do so by a mechanism he called "natural selection."

The theory of evolution has undergone considerable refinement since Darwin first formulated it. In one form or another it has emerged as the dominant theory of modern biology. Since Paley had argued that only a divine intelligence was a sufficient explanation for the order found in nature, evolutionary theory appears to offer a direct challenge to his views. It provides not only an alternative explanation, but also one far more sufficient from a scientific viewpoint.

The reaction to the theory of evolution on the part of those who believe in a divine creative intelligence has been both varied and intense. A theory of *instantaneous creation* has been advanced by those who reject the theory of evolution. According to this view, God is responsible for the immediate and direct creation of all distinct forms of life. Supporters of this outlook have been very persistent in attempting to get the public schools to teach what they call "creation science" in addition to evolution. *Guided evolution* is a theory advanced by those who wish to combine evolution and belief in a creator God. In this view God creates and designs the order in the world, but the means God uses is natural selection.

Evolutionary theory has had an impact on the way modern versions of the teleological argument are formulated. Recent versions of the argument tend to emphasize the idea of probability. In effect they claim that evolutionary explanations ultimately boil down to notions of chance. The next move is to point out the tremendous odds against the complex order of life which we experience evolving by chance. Someone has suggested, for example, that the odds against life evolving on this planet in its present form by chance alone is about as great as the chances of a tornado assembling the parts of a Boeing 747 scattered over a field into a functioning airplane. If your choice is between chance and intelligent design and if the odds are against chance and in favor of design, which constitutes the most plausible explanation?

The next selection is by Richard Dawkins, a zoologist who has taught at Berkeley and Oxford. He was born in Nairobi, Kenya in 1941 and moved to England in 1949. He is best known for his book *The Selfish Gene* (1976). Dawkins argues against Paley and in support of neo-Darwinian views of evolution. He maintains that the critics of evolution have misunderstood the mechanism by which life evolves. It does not evolve by chance (or at least the more complex forms do not), but by a nonrandom process he calls "cumulative selection" in contrast to "single-step selection." Single-step selection sorts or filters all items once and for all. It is like filtering sand through a sieve once and looking at the formation that results. Cumulative selection filters repeatedly, thus passing on some of the first results of the filtering to the next process of selection. In other words the first pile of sand resulting from the first filtering is filtered again, with a finer sieve. Hence the result will be different from the first result (smaller bits of sand will result). If this process is repeated over and over again, the result will be that the finest bits of sand survive each filtering, and the larger pieces do not. If natural selection operated as "single-step selection," then the odds *against* getting a heap of the finest sand the first time around would be very high. It would largely be a matter of chance. But if natural selection operates as "cumulative selection" (and it does according to evolutionary theory), the odds of eventually getting a heap of the finest sand would greatly increase. As the genetic traits of one generation are filtered by natural selection and passed on to the next, and again filtered and passed on to the next, and so on for many many generations, the chances of ending up with a complex, adaptive order increase greatly. Dawkins also argues that the major alternatives to neo-Darwinism are fatally flawed. Evolution remains the only viable scientific hypothesis for explaining the natural order.

You may have noted how discussions of both the cosmological and teleological arguments seem to return again and again to the issue of what constitutes a sufficient explanation. All parties agree that the existence of the universe and the order of life on earth require an explanation, but they disagree about what constitutes a sufficient one. Perhaps there can be no agreement on this matter, since what counts as sufficient depends on the conceptual scheme from which you approach the issue. Or does it?

Reading Questions

1. As you read, create your own set of analytical and critical questions for this selection and answer them.

2. What is the difference between single-step selection and cumulative selection, and why is that distinction so important to Dawkins's argument?

3. What are Dawkins's objections to theories like instantaneous creation and guided evolution? Do you agree with his views or not? Why?

4. Isn't the theory of evolution basically compatible with the design argument since it is always possible that God uses the mechanism of evolution to design life?

5. What do you think are the characteristics of a sufficient explanation? How would we know when we had one?

The Blind Watchmaker

RICHARD DAWKINS

THIS BOOK IS WRITTEN in the conviction that our own existence once presented the greatest of all mysteries, but that it is a mystery no longer because it is solved. Darwin and Wallace solved it, though we shall continue to add footnotes to their solution for a while yet. I wrote the book because I was surprised that so many people seemed not only unaware of the elegant and beautiful solution to this deepest of problems but, incredibly, in many cases actually unaware that there was a problem in the first place!

The problem is that of complex design. The computer on which I am writing these words has an information storage capacity of about 64 kilobytes (one byte is used to hold each character of text). The computer was consciously designed and deliberately manufactured. The brain with which you are understanding my words is an array of some ten million kiloneurones. Many of these billions of nerve cells have each more than a thousand "electric wires" connecting them to other neurones. Moreover, at the molecular genetic level, every single one of more than a trillion cells in the body contains about a thousand times as much precisely-coded digital information as my entire computer. The complexity of living organisms is matched by the elegant efficiency of their apparent design. If anyone doesn't agree that this amount of complex design cries out for an explanation, I give up. No, on second thought I don't give up, because one of my aims in the book is to convey something of the sheer wonder of biological complexity to those whose eyes have not been opened to it. But having built up the mystery, my other main aim is to remove it again by explaining the solution.

Explaining is a difficult art. You can explain something so that your reader understands the words, and you can explain something so that the reader feels it in the marrow of his bones. To do the latter, it sometimes isn't enough to lay the evidence before the reader in a dispassionate way. You have to become an advocate and use the tricks of the advocate's trade. This book is not a dispassionate scientific treatise. Other books on Darwinism are, and many of them are excellent and informative and should be read in conjunction with this one. Far from being dispassionate, it has to be confessed that in parts this book is written with a passion which, in a professional scientific journal, might excite comment. Certainly it seeks to inform, but it also seeks to persuade and even—one can specify *aims* without presumption—to inspire. I want to inspire the reader with a vision of our own existence as, on the face of it, a spine-chilling mystery; and simultaneously to convey the full excitement of the fact that it is a mystery with an elegant solution which is within our grasp. More, I want to persuade the reader, not just that the Darwinian world-view *happens* to be true, but that it is the only known theory that *could,* in principle, solve the mystery of our existence. This makes it a doubly satisfying theory. A good case can be made that Darwinism is true, not just on this planet but all over the universe wherever life may be found.

In one respect I plead to distance myself from professional advocates. A lawyer or a politician is paid to exercise his passion and his persuasion on behalf of a client or a cause in which he may not privately believe. I have never done this and I never shall. I may not always be right, but I care passionately about what is true and I never say anything that I do not believe to be right. I remember being shocked when visiting a university

From Richard Dawkins, The Blind Watchmaker, *1986, pp. ix–xii; 4–6; 43–49; 316–318. Reprinted by permission of W. W. Norton. Copyright © 1986 by Richard Dawkins.*

debating society to debate with creationists. At dinner after the debate, I was placed next to a young woman who had made a relatively powerful speech in favour of creationism. She clearly couldn't *be* a creationist, so I asked her to tell me honestly why she had done it. She freely admitted that she was simply practicing her debating skills, and found it more challenging to advocate a position in which she did not believe. Apparently it is common practice in university debating societies for speakers simply to be *told* on which side they are to speak. Their own beliefs don't come into it. I had come a long way to perform the disagreeable task of public speaking, because I believed in the truth of the motion that I had been asked to propose. When I discovered that members of the society were using the motion as a vehicle for playing arguing games, I resolved to decline future invitations from debating societies that encourage insincere advocacy on issues where scientific truth is at stake.

For reasons that are not entirely clear to me, Darwinism seems more in need of advocacy than similarly established truths in other branches of science. Many of us have no grasp of quantum theory, or Einstein's theories of special and general relativity, but this does not in itself lead us to *oppose* these theories! Darwinism, unlike "Einsteinism," seems to be regarded as fair game for critics with any degree of ignorance. I suppose one trouble with Darwinism is that, as Jacques Monod perceptively remarked, everybody *thinks* he understands it. It is, indeed, a remarkably simple theory; childishly so, one would have thought, in comparison with almost all of physics and mathematics. In essence, it amounts simply to the idea that nonrandom reproduction, where there is hereditary variation, has consequences that are farreaching if there is time for them to be cumulative. But we have good grounds for believing that this simplicity is deceptive. Never forget that, simple as the theory may seem, nobody thought of it until Darwin and Wallace in the mid-nineteenth century, nearly 300 years after Newton's *Principia,* and more than 2000 years after Eratosthenes measured the Earth. How could such a simple idea go so long undis-

covered by thinkers of the caliber of Newton, Galileo, Descartes, Leibniz, Hume and Aristotle? Why did it have to wait for two Victorian naturalists? What was *wrong* with philosophers and mathematicians that they overlooked it? And how can such a powerful idea go still largely unabsorbed into popular consciousness?

It is almost as if the human brain were specifically designed to misunderstand Darwinism, and to find it hard to believe. Take, for instance, the issue of "chance," often dramatized as *blind* chance. The great majority of people that attack Darwinism leap with almost unseemly eagerness to the mistaken idea that there is nothing other than random chance in it. Since living complexity embodies the very antithesis of chance, if you think that Darwinism is tantamount to chance you'll obviously find it easy to refute Darwinism! One of my tasks will be to destroy this eagerly believed myth that Darwinism is a theory of "chance." Another way in which we seem predisposed to disbelieve Darwinism is that our brains are built to deal with events on radically different *timescales* from those that characterize evolutionary change. We are equipped to appreciate processes that take seconds, minutes, years or, at most, decades to complete. Darwinism is a theory of cumulative processes so slow that they take between thousands and millions of decades to complete. All our intuitive judgments of what is probable turn out to be wrong by many orders of magnitude. Our well-tuned apparatus of skepticism and subjective probability theory misfires by huge margins, because it is tuned—ironically, by evolution itself—to work within a lifetime of a few decades. It requires effort of the imagination to escape from the prison of familiar timescale, an effort that I shall try to assist.

A third respect in which our brains seem predisposed to resist Darwinism stems from our great success as creative designers. Our world is dominated by feats of engineering and works of art. We are entirely accustomed to the idea that complex elegance is an indicator of premeditated, crafted design. This is probably the most powerful reason for the belief, held by the vast majority of people that have ever lived, in some kind of supernatural deity. It took a very large leap of the imagination for Darwin and Wallace to see that, contrary to all intuition, there is another way and, once you have understood it, a far more plausible way, for complex "design" to arise out of primeval simplicity. A leap of the imagination so large that, to this day, many people seem still unwilling to make it. It is the main purpose of this book to help the reader to make this leap. . . .

The watchmaker of my title is borrowed from a famous treatise by the eighteenth-century theologian William Paley. His *Natural Theology—or Evidences of the Existence and Attributes of the Deity Collected from the Appearances of Nature,* published in 1802, is the best-known exposition of the "Argument from Design," always the most influential of the arguments for the existence of a God. It is a book that I greatly admire, for in his own time its author succeeded in doing what I am struggling to do now. He had a point to make, he passionately believed in it, and he spared no effort to ram it home clearly. He had a proper reverence for the complexity of the living world, and he saw that it demands a very special kind of explanation. The only thing he got wrong—admittedly quite a big thing!—was the explanation itself. He gave the traditional religious answer to the riddle, but he articulated it more clearly and convincingly than anybody had before. The true explanation is utterly different, and it had to wait for one of the most revolutionary thinkers of all time, Charles Darwin.

Paley begins *Natural Theology* with a famous passage:

> In crossing a heath, suppose I pitched my foot against a *stone,* and were asked how the stone came to be there; I might possibly answer, that, for anything I knew to the contrary, it had lain there forever: nor would it perhaps be very easy to show the absurdity of this answer. But suppose I had found a *watch* upon the ground, and it should be inquired how the watch happened to be in that place; I should hardly think of the answer which I had before given, that for anything I knew, the watch might have always been there.

Paley here appreciates the differences between natural physical objects like stones, and designed and manufactured objects like watches. He goes on to expound the precision with which the cogs and springs of a watch are fashioned, and the intricacy with which they are put together. If we found an object such as a watch upon a heath, even if we didn't know how it had come into existence, its own precision and intricacy of design would force us to conclude

> that the watch must have had a maker: that there must have existed, at some time, and at some place or other, an artificer or artificers, who formed it for the purpose which we find it actually to answer; who comprehended its construction, and designed its use.

Nobody could reasonably dissent from this conclusion, Paley insists, yet that is just what the atheist, in effect, does when he contemplates the works of nature, for:

> every indication of contrivance, every manifestation of design, which existed in the watch, exists in the works of nature; with the difference, on the side of nature, of being greater or more, and that in a degree which exceeds all computation.

Paley drives his point home with beautiful and reverent descriptions of the dissected machinery of life, beginning with the human eye, a favorite example which Darwin was later to use and which will reappear throughout this book. Paley compares the eye with a designed instrument such as a telescope, and concludes that "there is precisely the same proof that the eye was made for vision, as there is that the telescope was made for assisting it." The eye must have had a designer, just as the telescope had.

Paley's argument is made with passionate sincerity and is informed by the best biological scholarship of his day, but it is wrong, gloriously and utterly wrong. The analogy between telescope and eye, between watch and living organism, is false. All appearances to the contrary, the only watchmaker in nature is the blind forces of physics, albeit deployed in a very special way. A true watchmaker has foresight: he designs his cogs and springs, and plans their interconnections, with a future purpose in his mind's eye. Natural selection, the blind, unconscious, automatic process which Darwin discovered, and which we now know is the explanation for the existence and apparently purposeful form of all life, has no purpose in mind. It has no mind and no mind's eye. It does not plan for the future. It has no vision, no foresight, no sight at all. If it can be said to play the role of watchmaker in nature, it is the *blind* watchmaker.

I shall explain all this, and much else besides. But one thing I shall not do is belittle the wonder of the living "watches" that so inspired Paley. On the contrary, I shall try to illustrate my feeling that here Paley could have gone even further. When it comes to feeling awe over living "watches" I yield to nobody. I feel more in common with the Reverend William Paley than I do with the distinguished modern philosopher, a well-known atheist, with whom I once discussed the matter at dinner. I said that I could not imagine being an atheist at any time before 1859, when Darwin's *Origin of Species* was published. "What about Hume?" replied the philosopher. "How did Hume explain the organized complexity of the living world?" I asked. "He didn't," said the philosopher. "Why does it need any special explanation?"

Paley knew that it needed a special explanation; Darwin knew it, and I suspect that in his heart of hearts my philosopher companion knew it too. In any case it will be my business to show it here. As for David Hume himself, it is sometimes said that that great Scottish philosopher disposed of the Argument from Design a century before Darwin. But what Hume did was criticize the logic of using apparent design in nature as *positive* evidence for the existence of a God. He did not offer any *alternative* explanation for apparent design, but left the question open. An atheist before Darwin could have said, following Hume: "I have no explanation for complex biological design. All I know is that God isn't a good explanation, so we must wait and hope that somebody comes up with a better one." I can't help feeling that such a position, though logically

sound, would have left one feeling pretty unsatisfied, and that although atheism might have been *logically* tenable before Darwin, Darwin made it possible to be an intellectually fulfilled atheist. I like to think that Hume would agree, but some of his writings suggest that he underestimated the complexity and beauty of biological design. The boy naturalist Charles Darwin could have shown him a thing or two about that, but Hume had been dead 40 years when Darwin enrolled in Hume's university of Edinburgh. . . .

We have seen that living things are too improbable and too beautifully "designed" to have come into existence by chance. How, then, did they come into existence? The answer, Darwin's answer, is by gradual, step-by-step transformations from simple beginnings, from primordial entities sufficiently simple to have come into existence by chance. Each successive change in the gradual evolutionary process was simple enough, *relative to its predecessor,* to have arisen by chance. But the whole sequence of cumulative steps constitutes anything but a chance process, when you consider the complexity of the final end-product relative to the original starting point. The cumulative process is directed by nonrandom survival. The purpose of this chapter is to demonstrate the power of this *cumulative selection* as a fundamentally nonrandom process.

If you walk up and down a pebbly beach, you will notice that the pebbles are not arranged at random. The smaller pebbles typically tend to be found in segregated zones running along the length of the beach, the larger ones in different zones or stripes. The pebbles have been sorted, arranged, selected. A tribe living near the shore might wonder at this evidence of sorting or arrangement in the world, and might develop a myth to account for it, perhaps attributing it to a Great Spirit in the sky with a tidy mind and a sense of order. We might give a superior smile at such a superstitious notion, and explain that the arranging was really done by the blind forces of physics, in this case the action of waves. The waves have no purposes and no intentions, no tidy mind, no mind at all. They just energetically throw the pebbles around, and big pebbles and small pebbles respond differently to this treatment so they end up at different levels of the beach. A small amount of order has come out of disorder, and no mind planned it.

The waves and the pebbles together constitute a simple example of a system that automatically generates nonrandomness. The world is full of such systems. The simplest example I can think of is a hole. Only objects smaller than the hole can pass through it. This means that if you start with a random collection of objects above the hole, and some force shakes and jostles them about at random, after a while the objects above and below the hole will come to be nonrandomly sorted. The space below the hole will tend to contain objects smaller than the hole, and the space above will tend to contain objects larger than the hole. Mankind has, of course, long exploited this simple principle for generating nonrandomness, in the useful device known as the sieve.

The solar system is a stable arrangement of planets, comets and debris orbiting the sun, and it is presumably one of many such orbiting systems in the universe. The nearer a satellite is to its sun, the faster it has to travel if it is to counter the sun's gravity and remain in stable orbit. For any given orbit, there is only one speed at which a satellite can travel and remain in that orbit. If it were traveling at any other velocity, it would either move out into deep space, or crash into the sun, or move into another orbit. And if we look at the planets of our solar system, lo and behold, every single one of them is traveling at exactly the right velocity to keep it in its stable orbit around the Sun. A blessed miracle of provident design? No, just another natural "sieve." Obviously all the planets that we see orbiting the sun must be traveling at exactly the right speed to keep them in their orbits, or we wouldn't see them there because they wouldn't be there! But equally obviously this is not evidence for conscious design. It is just another kind of sieve.

Sieving of this order of simplicity is not, on its own, enough to account for the massive amounts of nonrandom order that we see in living things. Nowhere near enough. Remember the analogy of the combination lock. The kind of nonrandomness that can be generated by simple sieving is roughly equivalent to opening a combination lock with one dial: it is easy to open it by sheer luck. The kind of nonrandomness that we see in living systems, on the other hand, is equivalent to a gigantic combination lock with an almost uncountable number of dials. To generate a biological molecule like hemoglobin, the red pigment in blood, by simple sieving would be equivalent to taking all the amino-acid building blocks of hemoglobin, jumbling them up at random, and hoping that the hemoglobin molecule would reconstitute itself by sheer luck. The amount of luck that would be required for this feat is unthinkable, and has been used as a telling mind-boggler by Isaac Asimov and others.

A hemoglobin molecule consists of four chains of amino acids twisted together. Let us think about just one of these four chains. It consists of 146 amino acids. There are 20 different kinds of amino acids commonly found in living things. The number of possible ways of arranging 20 kinds of thing in chains 146 links long is an inconceivably large number, which Asimov calls the "hemoglobin number." It is easy to calculate, but impossible to visualize the answer. The first link in the 146-link chain could be any one of the 20 possible amino acids. The second link could also be any one of the 20, so the number of possible two-link chains is 20×20, or 400. The number of possible three-link chains is $20 \times 20 \times 20$, or 8,000. The number of possible 146-link chains is 20 times itself 146 times. This is a staggeringly large number. A million is a 1 with 6 noughts after it. A billion (1000 million) is a 1 with 9 noughts after it. The number we seek, the "hemoglobin number," is (near enough) a 1 with 190 noughts after it! This is the chance against happening to hit upon hemoglobin by luck. And a hemoglobin molecule has only a minute fraction of the complexity of a living body. Simple sieving, on its own, is obviously nowhere near capable of generating the amount of order in a living thing. Sieving is an essential ingredient in the generation of living order, but it is very far from being the whole story. Something else is needed. To explain the point, I shall need to make a distinction between "single-step" selection and "cumulative" selection. The simple sieves we have been considering so far are all examples of single-step selection. Living organization is the product of cumulative selection.

The essential difference between single-step selection and cumulative selection is this. In single-step selection the entities selected or sorted, pebbles or whatever they are, are sorted once and for all. In cumulative selection, on the other hand, they "reproduce"; or in some other way the results of one sieving process are fed into a subsequent sieving, which is fed into . . ., and so on. The entities are subjected to selection of sorting over many "generations" in succession. The end-product of one generation of selection is the starting point for the next generation of selection, and so on for many generations. It is natural to borrow such words as "reproduce" and "generation," which have associations with living things, because living things are the main examples we know of things that participate in cumulative selection. They may in practice be the only things that do. But for the moment I don't want to beg that question by saying so outright.

Sometimes clouds, through the random kneading and carving of the winds, come to look like familiar objects. There is a much published photograph, taken by the pilot of a small aeroplane, of what looks a bit like the face of Jesus, staring out of the sky. We have all seen clouds that reminded us of something—a sea horse, say, or a smiling face. These resemblances come about by single-step selection, that is to say by a single coincidence. They are, consequently, not very impressive. The resemblance of the signs of the zodiac to the animals after which they are named, Scorpio, Leo, and so on, is as unimpressive as the predictions of astrologers. We don't feel overwhelmed by the resemblance, as we are by biological adaptations—the products of cumulative selection. We describe as weird, uncanny or spectacular, the resemblance of, say, a leaf insect to a leaf or a praying mantis to a cluster of pink flowers. The resemblance of a cloud to a weasel is only mildly diverting, barely worth calling to the attention of our companion. Moreover, we are quite likely to change our mind about exactly what the cloud most resembles.

Hamlet: Do you see yonder cloud that's almost in shape of a camel?

Polonius: By the mass, and 'tis like a camel, indeed.

Hamlet: Methinks it is like a weasel.

Polonius: It is backed like a weasel.

Hamlet: Or like a whale?

Polonius: Very like a whale.

I don't know who it was first pointed out that, given enough time, a monkey bashing away at random on a typewriter could produce all the works of Shakespeare. The operative phrase is, of course, given enough time. Let us limit the task facing our monkey somewhat. Suppose that he has to produce, not the complete works of Shakespeare but just the short sentence "Methinks it is like a weasel," and we shall make it relatively easy by giving him a typewriter with a restricted keyboard, one with just the 26 (capital) letters, and a space bar. How long will he take to write this one little sentence?

The sentence has 28 characters in it, so let us assume that the monkey has a series of discrete "tries," each consisting of 28 bashes at the keyboard. If he types the phrase correctly, that is the end of the experiment. If not, we allow him another "try" of 28 characters. I don't know any monkeys, but fortunately my 11-month-old daughter is an experienced randomizing device, and she proved only too eager to step into the role of monkey typist. Here is what she typed on the computer.

```
UMMK JK CDZZ F ZD DSDSKSM
S SS FMCV PU I DDRGLKDXRRDO
RDTE QDWFDVIOY UDSKZWDCCVYT
H CHVY NMGNBAYTDFCCVD D
RCDFYYYRM N DFSKD LD K WDWK
JJKAUIZMZI UXDKIDISFUMDKUDXI
```

She has other important calls on her time, so I was obliged to program the computer to simulate a randomly typing baby or monkey:

```
WDLDMNLT DTJBKWIRZREZLMQCO P
Y YVMQKZPGJXWVHGLAWFVCHQYOPY
```

MWR SWTNUXMLCDLEUBXTQHNZVJQF
FU OVAODVYKDGXDEKYVMOGGS VT
HZQZDSFZIHIVPHZPETPWVOVPMZGF
GEWRGZRPBCTPGQMCKHFDBGW ZCCF

And so on and on. It isn't difficult to calculate how long we should reasonably expect to wait for the random computer (or baby or monkey) to type METHINKS IT IS LIKE A WEASEL. Think about the total number of *possible* phrases of the right length that the monkey or baby or random computer *could* type. It is the same kind of calculation as we did for hemoglobin, and it produces a similarly large result. There are 27 possible letters (counting "space" as one letter) in the first position. The chance of the monkey happening to get the first letter—M—right is therefore 1 in 27. The chance of it getting the first two letters—ME—right is the chance of it getting the second letter—E—right (1 in 27) *given that* it has also got the first letter—M—right, therefore $1/27 \times 1/27$, which equals $1/729$. The chance of it getting the first word—METHINKS—right is $1/27$ for each of the 8 letters, therefore $(1/27) \times (1/27) \times (1/27) \times (1/27) \ldots$, 8 times, or $(1/27)$ to the power 8. The chance of it getting the entire phrase of 28 characters right is $(1/27)$ to the power 28, i.e., $(1/27)$ multiplied by itself 28 times. These are very small odds, about 1 in 10,000 million million million million million million. To put it mildly, the phrase we seek would be a long time coming, to say nothing of the complete works of Shakespeare.

So much for single-step selection of random variation. What about cumulative selection; how much more effective should this be? Very very much more effective, perhaps more so than we at first realize, although it is almost obvious when we reflect further. We again use our computer monkey, but with a crucial difference in its program. It again begins by choosing a random sequence of 28 letters, just as before:

WDLMNLT DTJBKWIRZREZLMQCO P

It now "breeds from" this random phrase. It duplicates it repeatedly, but with a certain chance of random error—"mutation"—in the copying.

The computer examines the mutant nonsense phrases, the "progeny" of the original phrase, and chooses the one which, *however slightly*, most resembles the target phrase, METHINKS IT IS LIKE A WEASEL. In this instance the winning phrase of the next "generation" happened to be:

WDLTMNLT DTJBSWIRZREZLMQCO P

Not an obvious improvement! But the procedure is repeated, again mutant "progeny" are "bred from" the phrase, and a new "winner" is chosen. This goes on, generation after generation. After 10 generations, the phrase chosen for "breeding" was:

MDLDMNLS ITJISWHRZREZ MECS P

After 20 generations it was:

MELDINLS IT ISWPRKE Z WECSEL

By now, the eye of faith fancies that it can see a resemblance to the target phrase. By 30 generations there can be no doubt:

METHINGS IT ISWLIKE B WECSEL

Generation 40 takes us to within one letter of the target:

METHINKS IT IS LIKE I WEASEL

And the target was finally reached in generation 43. A second run of the computer began with the phrase:

Y YVMQKZPFJXWVHGLAWFVCHQXYOPY,

passed through (again reporting only every tenth generation):

Y YVMQKSPFTXWSHLIKEFV HQYSPY
YETHINKSPITXISHLIKEFA WQYSEY
METHINKS IT ISSLIKE A WEFSEY
METHINKS IT ISBLIKE A WEASES
METHINKS IT ISJLIKE A WEASEO
METHINKS IT IS LIKE A WEASEP

and reached the target phrase in generation 64. In a third run the computer started with:

GEWRGZRPBCTPGQMCKHFDBGW ZCCF

and reached METHINKS IT IS LIKE A WEASEL in 41 generations of selective "breeding."

The exact time taken by the computer to reach the target doesn't matter. If you want to know, it completed the whole exercise for me, the first time, while I was out to lunch. It took about half an hour. (Computer enthusiasts may think this unduly slow. The reason is that the program was written in BASIC, a sort of computer baby-talk. When I rewrote it in Pascal, it took 11 seconds.) Computers are a bit faster at this kind of thing than monkeys, but the difference really isn't significant. What matters is the difference between the time taken by *cumulative* selection, and the time which the same computer, working flat out at the same rate, would take to reach the target phrase if it were forced to use the other procedure of *single-step selection:* about a million million million million million years. This is more than a million million million times as long as the universe has so far existed. Actually it would be fairer just to say that, in comparison with the time it would take either a monkey or a randomly programmed computer to type our target phrase, the total age of the universe so far is a negligibly small quantity, so small as to be well within the margin of error for this sort of back-of-an-envelope calculation. Whereas the time taken for a computer working randomly but with the constraint of *cumulative selection* to perform the same task is of the same order as humans ordinarily can understand, between 11 seconds and the time it takes to have lunch.

There is a big difference, then, between cumulative selection (in which each improvement, however slight, is used as a basis for future building), and single-step selection (in which each new "try" is a fresh one). If evolutionary progress had had to rely on single-step selection, it would never have got anywhere. If, however, there was any way in which the necessary conditions for *cumulative* selection could have been set up by the blind forces of nature, strange and wonderful might have been the consequences. As a matter of fact that is exactly what happened on this planet, and we ourselves are among the most recent, if not the strangest and most wonderful, of those consequences.

It is amazing that you can still read calculations like my hemoglobin calculation, used as though they constituted arguments *against* Darwin's theory. The people who do this, often expert in their own field, astronomy or whatever it may be, seem sincerely to believe that Darwinism explains living organization in terms of chance—"single-step selection"—alone. This belief, that Darwinian evolution is "random," is not merely false. It is the exact opposite of the truth. Chance is a minor ingredient in the Darwinian recipe, but the most important ingredient is cumulative selection which is quintessentially *non*random. . . .

We have dealt with all the alleged alternatives to the theory of natural selection except the oldest one. This is the theory that life was created, or its evolution master-minded, by a conscious designer. It would obviously be unfairly easy to demolish some particular version of this theory such as the one (or it may be two) spelled out in Genesis. Nearly all peoples have developed their own creation myth, and the Genesis story is just the one that happened to have been adopted by one particular tribe of Middle Eastern herders. It has no more special status than the belief of a particular West African tribe that the world was created from the excrement of ants. All these myths have in common that they depend upon the deliberate intentions of some kind of supernatural being.

At first sight there is an important distinction to be made between what might be called "instantaneous creation" and "guided evolution." Modern theologians of any sophistication have given up believing in instantaneous creation. The evidence for some sort of evolution has become too overwhelming. But many theologians who call themselves evolutionists, for instance the Bishop of Birmingham quoted in Chapter 2, smuggle God in by the back door: they allow Him some sort of supervisory role over the course that evolution has taken, either influencing key moments in evolutionary history (especially, of course, *human* evolutionary history), or even meddling more comprehensively in the day-to-day events that add up to evolutionary change.

We cannot disprove beliefs like these, especially if it is assumed that God took care that his interventions always closely mimicked what would be expected from evolution by natural selection. All that we can say about such beliefs is, firstly, that they are superfluous and, secondly, that they *assume* the existence of the main thing we want to *explain,* namely organized complexity. The one thing that makes evolution such a neat theory is that it explains how organized complexity can arise out of primeval simplicity.

If we want to postulate a deity capable of engineering all the organized complexity in the world, either instantaneously or by guiding evolution, that deity must already have been vastly complex in the first place. The creationist, whether a naive Bible-thumper or an educated bishop, simply *postulates* an already existing being of prodigious intelligence and complexity. If we are going to allow ourselves the luxury of postulating organized complexity without offering an explanation, we might as well make a job of it and simply postulate the existence of life as we know it! In short, divine creation, whether instantaneous or in the form of guided evolution, joins the list of other theories we have considered in this chapter. All give some superficial appearance of being alternatives to Darwinism, whose merits might be tested by an appeal to evidence. All turn out, on closer inspection, not to be rivals of Darwinism at all. The theory of evolution by cumulative natural selection is the only theory we know of that is in principle *capable* of explaining the existence of organized complexity. Even if the evidence did not favor it, it would *still* be the best theory available! In fact the evidence does favor it. But that is another story.

Let us hear the conclusion of the whole matter. The essence of life is statistical improbability on a colossal scale. Whatever is the explanation for life, therefore, it cannot be chance. The true explanation for the existence of life must embody the very antithesis of chance. The antithesis of chance is nonrandom survival, properly understood. Nonrandom survival, improperly understood, is not the antithesis of chance, it is chance itself. There is a continuum connecting these two extremes, and it is the continuum from single-step selection to cumulative selection. Single-step selection is just another way of saying pure

chance. This is what I mean by nonrandom survival improperly understood. *Cumulative selection,* by slow and gradual degrees, is the explanation, the only workable explanation that has ever been proposed, for the existence of life's complex design.

The whole book has been dominated by the idea of chance, by the astronomically long odds against the spontaneous arising of order, complexity and apparent design. We have sought a way of taming chance, of drawing its fangs. "Untamed chance," pure, naked chance, means ordered design springing into existence from nothing, in a single leap. It would be untamed chance if once there was no eye, and then, suddenly, in the twinkling of a generation, an eye appeared, fully fashioned, perfect and whole. This is possible, but the odds against it will keep us busy writing noughts till the end of time. The same applies to the odds against the spontaneous existence of any fully fashioned, perfect and whole beings, including—I see no way of avoiding the conclusion—deities.

To "tame" chance means to break down the very improbable into less improbable small components arranged in series. No matter how improbable it is that an X could have arisen from a Y in a single step, it is always possible to conceive of a series of infinitesimally graded intermediates between them. However improbable a large-scale change may be, smaller changes are less improbable. And provided we postulate a sufficiently large series of sufficiently finely graded intermediates, we shall be able to derive anything from anything else, without invoking astronomical improbabilities. We are allowed to do this only if there has been sufficient time to fit all the intermediates in. And also only if there is a mechanism for guiding each step in some particular direction, otherwise the sequence of steps will careen off in an endless random walk.

It is the contention of the Darwinian worldview that both these provisos are met, and that slow, gradual, cumulative natural selection is the ultimate explanation for our existence. If there are versions of the evolution theory that deny slow gradualism, and deny the central role of natural selection, they may be true in particular cases. But they cannot be the whole truth, for they deny the very heart of the evolution theory, which gives it the power to dissolve astronomical improbabilities and explain prodigies of apparent miracle.

Suggestions for Further Reading

See L. Stafford Betty's and Bruce Cordell's article "God and Modern Science: New Life for the Teleological Argument," *International Philosophical Quarterly,* Vol. 27 (December, 1987), 409–435, for a discussion of arguments for God's existence in light of recent scientific theories about the origin of the universe and of life. They argue in favor of a theistic explanation. For a critical review of Dawkins's book see *Dialogue and Alliance: A Journal of the International Religious Foundation,* Vol. 1 (Winter, 1987–88), 85–87.

The literature on the creation versus evolution debate is vast. See Niles Eldredge's *The Monkey Business: A Scientist Looks at Creationism* (New York: Washington Square Press, 1982) for a vigorous defense of evolution and Duane Gish's *Evolution? The Fossils Say No!* (San Diego: Institute for Creation Research, 1973) for an attack on evolutionary theory.

The issue of what constitutes an adequate scientific explanation is not an easy one to wade through. Both Ernest Nagel's *The Structure of Science* (New York: Harcourt, 1961) and Karl Popper's *The Logic of Scientific Discovery* (New York: Basic Books, 1959) provide penetrating, influential, and sophisticated discussions. T. S. Kuhn's *The Structure of Scientific Revolutions,* 2d ed. (Chicago: University of Chicago Press, 1970) is a classic. Also see *The Cosmos, God and Philosophy* by Ralph J. Moore and Brooke N. Moore (New York: Peter Lang, 1989) for a recent discussion of the arguments for God's existence in relationship to contemporary scientific views.

Videos

Evolution of Man (14 minutes, produced by Coronet Films, 1967) briefly presents Darwin's theory of evolution and the discovery of prehuman fossils. *God, Darwin, And Dinosaurs* (58 minutes, 1993) explores the debate about teaching evolution and creationism in the public schools and *The Creationist Argument* (26 minutes, 1993) lets Luther Sutherland have his say, while *The Evidence for Evolution* (26 minutes, 1993) presents the case for evolution. All three are available from Films for the Humanities and Sciences.

See your Media Services Catalogue for more information.

9.6. The Gender of God

There is an old story of the *Time* magazine reporter who was granted an interview with God. When the reporter returned, people eagerly asked, "Well, tell us, what is God like?"

"You will have to wait until I write my article," the reporter replied, "but I can tell you this much, she is Black."

The punch line makes us smile because it is unexpected. But why is it unexpected? Why shouldn't God be female and Black?

We have all been raised with certain images of God and the dominant one in Western culture has been the image of a white male (usually old and bearded!). Although the arguments for God's existence make no mention of God's sex, many who read the arguments undoubtedly imagine a male deity as the reference of these arguments.

How many of you, as you read the arguments and read the word "God" thought of a male deity? If you did, you can understand how these arguments reinforce, perhaps unconsciously and unintentionally, the idea that masculinity is powerful, necessary, perfect, and intelligent.

Mary Daly, Professor of Theology at Boston College, understands the goal of Christianity as the liberation of all humans. She thinks that traditional Christian images of God as Father do not promote the liberation of females. Therefore, she argues, we must get beyond the notion of God as Father. In the introduction to the book from which this selection is taken (a book which has become a classic statement in the field) she sets forth her presuppositions as follows:

1. Women exist in a sexual "caste" system subordinate to and dominated by men,
2. Sex role socialization perpetuates this system by convincing women to accept their "inferior" status and men to accept their "superior" status,
3. Women's lower status is disguised by sex role segregation ("women are 'equal' but different") and by providing them derivative status as a consequence of their relationships with men (Mr. and Mrs. *John* Gibbons),
4. Judaism, Christianity, and Islam (to mention only three of the major world religions) have helped to maintain women's subordination to men by their teachings about marriage, reproduction, and the roles women can assume in their respective religious organizations, and
5. People try to avoid acknowledging the issue of sexual caste by trivializing it ("After all there are more important issues, like war or racism") by particularizing it ("It's a problem for Muslims or Hindus or Jews, but not for Christians"), or by universalizing it ("The real problem is *human* liberation, so let's concentrate on that").

Her purpose is to show that the women's movement is a "spiritual revolution" that points us beyond the idolatries of a sexist society and religion. Her method, she writes, derives from the Biblical insight that "to exist humanly is to name the self, the world, and God. The method of evolving spiritual consciousness of women is nothing less than this beginning to speak humanly—reclaiming of the right to name. The liberation of language is rooted in the liberation of ourselves."

Reading Questions

1. How has the symbol of God as Father rendered service to male-dominated (patriarchical) societies?
2. How does Daly respond to the criticism that the liberation of women will not basically change the structures, ideologies, and values of society?
3. What are the differences between the masculine and the feminine stereotypes?
4. What do you think Daly means by "androgynous human persons?"
5. What is inadequate about popular preaching about God?
6. Why won't calling God "She" and stressing God's maternal qualities help the situation?
7. Why does the women's revolution even need to speak about God at all?
8. How does Daly interpret the "image of God?"
9. Who are the false deities (idols) and why are they false? Do you agree with Daly that there are false images of God? Why or why not?

Beyond God the Father

MARY DALY

> The first step in the elevation of women under all systems of religion is to convince them that the great Spirit of the Universe is in no way responsible for any of these absurdities.
> —Elizabeth Cady Stanton

THE BIBLICAL AND POPULAR image of God as a great patriarch in heaven, rewarding and punishing according to his mysterious and seemingly arbitrary will, has dominated the imagination of millions over thousands of years. The symbol of the Father God, spawned in the human imagination and sustained as plausible by patriarchy, has in turn rendered service to this type of society by making its mechanisms for the oppression of women appear right and fitting. If God in "his" heaven is a father ruling "his" people, then it is in the "nature" of things and according to divine plan and the order of the universe that society be male-dominated.

Within this context a mystification of roles takes place: the husband dominating his wife represents God "himself." The images and values of a given society have been projected into the realm of dogmas and "Articles of Faith," and these in turn justify the social structures which have given rise to them and which sustain their plausibility. The belief system becomes hardened and objectified, seeming to have an unchangeable independent existence and validity of its own. It resists social change that would rob it of its plausibility. Despite the vicious circle, however, change can occur in society, and ideologies can die, though they die hard.

As the women's movement begins to have its effect upon the fabric of society, transforming it from patriarchy into something that never existed before—into a diarchal situation that is radically new—it can become the greatest single challenge to the major religions of the world, Western and Eastern. Beliefs and values that have held sway for thousands of years will be questioned as never before. This revolution may well be also the greatest single hope for survival of spiritual consciousness on this planet.

The Challenge: Emergence of Whole Human Beings

There are some who persist in claiming that the liberation of women will only mean that new characters will assume the same old roles, and that nothing will change essentially in structures, ideologies, and values. This supposition is often based on the observation that the very few women in "masculine" occupations often behave much as men do. This kind of reasoning is not at all to the point, for it fails to take into account the fact that tokenism does not change stereotypes or social systems but works to preserve them, since it dulls the revolutionary impulse. The minute proportion of women in the United States who occupy such roles (such as senators, judges, business executives, doctors, etc.) have been trained by men in institutions defined and designed by men, and they have been pressured subtly to operate according to male rules. There are no alternate models. As sociologist Alice Rossi has suggested, this is not what the women's movement in its most revolutionary potential is all about.

What *is* to the point is an emergence of woman-consciousness such as has never before taken place. It is unimaginative and out of touch with what is happening in the women's movement to assume that the becoming of women will simply mean uncritical acceptance of structures, beliefs, symbols, norms, and patterns of behavior that have been given priority by society under male domination. Rather, this becoming will act as catalyst for radical change in our culture. It has been argued cogently by Piaget that structure is maintained by an interplay of transformation laws that never yield results beyond the system and never tend to employ elements external to the system. This is indicative of what *can* effect basic alteration in the system, that is, a potent influence *from without*. Women who reject patriarchy have this power and indeed *are* this power of transformation that is ultimately threatening to things as they are.

The roles and structures of patriarchy have been developed and sustained in accordance with an artificial polarization of human qualities into the traditional sexual stereotypes. The image of the person in authority and the accepted understanding of "his" role has corresponded to the eternal masculine stereotype, which implies hyperrationality (in reality, frequently reducible to pseudo-rationality), "objectivity," aggressivity, the possession of dominating and manipulative attitudes toward persons and the environment, and the tendency to construct boundaries between the self (and those identified with the self) and "the Other." The caricature of human being which is represented by this stereotype depends for its existence upon the opposite caricature— the eternal feminine. This implies hyperemotionalism, passivity, self-abnegation, etc. By becoming whole persons women can generate a counterforce to the stereotype of the leader, challenging the artificial polarization of human characteristics into sex-role identification. There is no reason to assume that women who have the support of each other to criticize not only the feminine stereotype but the masculine stereotype as well will simply adopt the latter as a model for ourselves. On the contrary, what is happening is that women are developing a wider range of qualities and skills. This is beginning to encourage and in fact demand a comparably liberating process in men—a phenomenon which has begun in men's liberation groups and which is taking place every day within the context of personal relationships. The becoming of androg-

ynous human persons implies a radical change in the fabric of human consciousness and in styles of human behavior.

This change is already threatening the credibility of the religious symbols of our culture. Since many of these have been used to justify oppression, such a challenge should be seen as redemptive. Religious symbols fade and die when the cultural situation that gave rise to them and supported them ceases to give them plausibility. Such an event generates anxiety, but it is part of the risk involved in a faith which accepts the relativity of all symbols and recognizes that clinging to these as fixed and ultimate is self-destructive and idolatrous.

The becoming of new symbols is not a matter that can be decided arbitrarily around a conference table. Rather, symbols grow out of a changing communal situation and experience. This does not mean that we are confined to the role of passive spectators. The experience of the becoming of women cannot be understood merely conceptually and abstractly but through active participation in the overcoming of servitude. Both activism and creative thought flow from and feed into the evolving woman-consciousness. The cumulative effect is a surge of awareness beyond the symbols and doctrines of patriarchal religion.

The Inadequate God of Popular Preaching

The image of the divine Father in heaven has not always been conducive to humane behavior, as any perceptive reader of history knows. The often cruel behavior of Christians toward unbelievers and toward dissenters among themselves suggests a great deal not only about the values of the society dominated by that image, but also about how that image itself functions in relation to behavior. There has been a basic ambivalence in the image of the heavenly patriarch—a split between the God of love and the jealous God who represents the collective power of "his" chosen people. As historian Arnold Toynbee has indicated, this has reflected and perpetuated a double standard of behavior. Without debating the details of his historical analysis, the insight is available on an experiential level. The character of Vito Corleone in *The Godfather* is a vivid illustration of the marriage of tenderness and violence so intricately blended in the patriarchal ideal. The worshippers of the loving Father may in a sense love their neighbors, but in fact the term applies only to those within a restricted and unstable circumference, and these worshippers can "justifiably" be intolerant and fanatic persecutors of those outside the sacred circle.

How this God operates is illustrated in contemporary American civil religion. In one of the White House sermons given during the first term of Richard Nixon, Rabbi Louis Finkelstein expressed the hope that a future historian may say "that in the period of great trials and great tribulations, the finger of God pointed to Richard Milhous Nixon, giving the vision and the wisdom to save the world and civilization; and also to open the way for our country to realize the good that the twentieth century offers mankind." Within this context, as Charles Henderson has shown, God is an American and Nixon is "his" annointed one. The preachers carefully selected for the White House sermons stress that this nation is "under God." The logical conclusion is that its politics are right. Under God, the President becomes a Christ figure. In 1969, the day the astronauts would set foot on the moon, and when the President was preparing to cross the Pacific "in search of peace," one of these preachers proclaimed:

> And my hope for mankind is strengthened in the knowledge that our intrepid President himself will soon go into orbit, reaching boldly for the moon of peace. God grant that he, too, may return in glory and that countless millions of prayers that follow him shall not have been in vain.

A fundamental dynamic of this "theology" was suggested by one of Nixon's speech writers, Ray Price, who wrote:

> Selection of a President has to be an act of faith. . . . This faith isn't achieved by reason: it's achieved by charisma, by a feeling of trust. . . .

Price also argued that the campaign would be effective only "if we can get people to make the *emotional* leap, or what theologians call 'leap of faith.'" This is, of course, precisely the inauthentic leap that Camus labeled as philosophical suicide. It is the suicide demanded by a civil religion in which "God," the Savior-President, and "our nation" more or less merge. When the "leap" is made, it is possible simply not to see what the great God-Father and his annointed one are actually doing. Among the chosen ones are scientists and professors who design perverse methods of torture and death such as flechette pellets that shred the internal organs of "the enemy" and other comparable inhumane "antipersonnel" weapons. Also among the elect are politicians and priests who justify and bestow their blessing upon the system that perpetrates such atrocities. "Under God" are included the powerful industrialists who are making the planet uninhabitable.

Sophisticated thinkers, of course, have never intellectually identified God with a Superfather in heaven. Nevertheless it is important to recognize that even when very abstract conceptualizations of God are formulated in the mind, images survive in the imagination in such a way that a person can function on two different and even apparently contradictory levels at the same time. Thus one can speak of God as spirit and at the same time imagine "him" as belonging to the male sex. Such primitive images can profoundly affect conceptualizations which appear to be very refined and abstract. So too the Yahweh of the future, so cherished by the theology of hope, comes through on an imaginative level as exclusively a He-God, and it is consistent with this that theologians of hope have attempted to develop a political theology which takes no explicit cognizance of the devastation wrought by sexual politics.

The widespread conception of the "Supreme Being" as an entity distinct from this world but controlling it according to plan and keeping human beings in a state of infantile subjection has been a not too subtle mask of the divine patriarch. The Supreme Being's plausibility and that of the static worldview which accompanies this projection has of course declined, at least among the more sophisticated, as Nietzsche prophesied. This was a projection grounded in specifically patriarchal societal structures and sustained as subjectively real by the usual processes of producing plausibility such as preaching, religious indoctrination, and cult. The sustaining power of the social structure has been eroded by a number of developments in recent history, including the general trend toward democratization of society and the emergence of technology. However, it is the women's movement which appears destined to play the key role in the overthrow of such oppressive elements in traditional theism, precisely because it strikes at the source of the societal dualism that is reflected in traditional beliefs. It presents a growing threat to the plausibility of the inadequate popular "God" not so much by attacking "him" as by leaving "him" behind. Few major feminists display great interest in institutional religion. Yet this disinterest can hardly be equated with lack of spiritual consciousness. Rather, in our present experience the woman-consciousness is being wrenched free to find its own religious expression.

It can legitimately be pointed out that the Judeo-Christian tradition is not entirely bereft of elements that can foster intimations of transcendence. Yet the liberating potential of these elements is choked off in the surrounding atmosphere of the images, ideas, values, and structures of patriarchy. The social change coming from radical feminism has the potential to bring about a more acute and widespread perception of qualitative differences between the conceptualizations of "God" and of the human relationship to God which have been oppressive in their connotations, and the kind of language that is spoken from and to the rising woman-consciousness.

Castrating "God"

I have already suggested that if God is male, then the male is God. The divine patriarch castrates women as long as he is allowed to live on in the human imagination. The process of cutting away the Supreme Phallus can hardly be a merely "rational" affair. The problem is one of transforming the collective imagination so that this distortion of the human aspiration to transcendence loses its credibility.

Some religious leaders, notably Mary Baker Eddy and Ann Lee, showed insight into the problem to some extent and tried to stress the "maternal" aspect of what they called "God." A number of feminists have referred to "God" as "she." While all of this has a point, the analysis has to reach a deeper level. The most basic change has to take place in women—in our being and self-image. Otherwise there is danger of settling for mere reform, reflected in the phenomenon of "crossing," that is, of attempting to use the oppressor's weapons against him. Black theology's image of the Black God illustrates this. It can legitimately be argued that a transsexual operation upon "God," changing "him" to "her," would be a far more profound alteration than a mere pigmentation change. However, to stop at this level of discourse would be a trivialization of the deep problem of human becoming in women. . . .

Why Speak About "God"?

It might seem that the women's revolution should just go about its business of generating a new consciousness, without worrying about God. I suggest that the fallacy involved in this would be an overlooking of a basic question that is implied in human existence and that the pitfall in such an oversight is cutting off the radical potential of the movement itself.

It is reasonable to take the position that sustained effort toward self-transcendence requires keeping alive in one's consciousness the question of ultimate transcendence, that is, of God. It implies recognition of the fact that we have no power *over* the ultimately real, and that whatever authentic power we have is derived from *participation in* ultimate reality. This awareness, always hard to sustain, makes it possible to be free of idolatry even in regard to one's own cause, since it tells us that all presently envisaged goals, lifestyles, symbols, and societal structures may be transitory. This is the meaning that the question of God should have for liberation, sustaining a concern that is really open to the future, in other words, that is really ultimate. Such a concern will not become fixated upon limited objectives. Feminists in the past have in a way been idolatrous about such objectives as the right to vote. Indeed, this right is due to women in justice and it is entirely understandable that feminists' energies were drained by the efforts needed to achieve even such a modicum of justice. But from the experience of such struggles we are in a position now to distrust token victories within a societal and structural framework that renders them almost meaningless. The new wave of feminism desperately needs to be not only many faceted but cosmic and ultimately religious in its vision. This means reaching outward and inward toward the God beyond and beneath the gods who have stolen our identity.

The idea that human beings are "to the image of God" is an intuition whose implications could hardly be worked through under patriarchal conditions. If it is true that human beings have projected "God" in their own image, it is also true that we can evolve beyond the projections of earlier stages of consciousness. It is the creative potential itself in human beings that is the image of God. As the essential victims of the archaic God-projections, women can bring this process of creativity into a new phase. This involves iconoclasm—the breaking of idols. Even—and perhaps especially—through the activity of its most militantly atheistic and a-religious members, the movement is smashing images that obstruct the becoming of the image of God. The basic idol-breaking will be done on the level of internalized images of male superiority, on the plane of exorcising them from consciousness and from the cultural institutions that breed them.

One aspect of this expurgation is dethronement of false Gods—ideas and symbols of God that religion has foisted upon the human spirit (granted that the human spirit has created the religions that do this). I have already discussed this to some extent, but it might be well to focus specifically upon three false deities who still haunt the prayers, hymns, sermons, and religious education of Christianity. The three usurpers I have

in mind have already been detected and made the targets of attack by liberal male theologians, but the point in mentioning them here is to indicate the specific relevance of feminism to their demise.

One of the false deities to be dethroned is the God of explanation, or "God as a stop-gap for the incompleteness of our knowledge," as Bonhoeffer called him. This serves sometimes as the legitimation of anomic occurrences such as the suffering of a child, a legitimation process which Peter Berger lucidly analyzes in discussing the problem of theodicy. Such phenomena are "explained" as being God's will. So also are socially prevailing inequalities of power and privilege, by a justifying process which easily encourages masochistic attitudes. Clearly, this deity does not encourage commitment to the task of analyzing and eradicating the social, economic, and psychological roots of suffering. As marginal beings who are coming into awareness, women are in a situation to see that "God's plan" is often a front for men's plans and a cover for inadequacy, ignorance, and evil. Our vantage point offers opportunities for dislodging this deity from its revered position on the scale of human delusions.

Another idol is the God of otherworldliness. The most obvious face of this deity in the past has been that of the Judge whose chief activity consists in rewarding and punishing after death. As de Beauvoir indicated, women have been the major consumers of this religious product. Since there has been so little self-realization possible by the female sex "in this life," it was natural to focus attention on the next. As mass consumers of this image, women have the power to remove it from the market, mainly by living full lives here and now. I do not mean to advocate a mere re-utterance of the "secularization" theology that was so popular in the sixties. This obvious shape of the God of otherworldliness has after all been the target of male theologians for some time, and the result has often been a kind of translation of religion into humanism to such an extent that there is a kind of "self-liquidation of theology." What I see beginning to happen with women coming into their own goes beyond this secularization. The rejection of the simplistic God of otherworldliness does not mean necessarily reduction to banal secularism. If women can sustain the courage essential to liberation this can give rise to a deeper "otherworldliness"—an awareness that the process of creating a counterworld to the counterfeit "this world" presented to consciousness by the societal structures that oppress us is participation in eternal life.

It should be noted that the God lurking behind some forms of Protestant piety has functioned similarly to the otherworldly God of popular Roman Catholic piety. In his analysis of the effects of Luther's doctrine of salvation by faith alone, Max Weber uncovers serious problems of ethical motivation, involving a complicated series of phenomena: "Every rational and planned procedure for achieving salvation, every reliance on good works, and above all every effort to surpass normal ethical behavior by ascetic achievement is regarded by religion based on faith as a wicked preoccupation with purely human powers." Transworldly asceticism and monasticism tend to be rejected when salvation by faith is stressed, and as a result there may be an increased emphasis upon vocational activity within the world. However, as Weber explains, emphasis upon personal religious relationship to God tends to be accompanied by an attitude of individualism in pursuit of such worldly vocational activity. One consequence is an attitude of patient resignation regarding institutional structures, both worldly and churchly. It is precisely this schizophrenic attitude that combines personal vocational ambition within the prevailing set of social arrangements and passive acceptance of the system that radical feminism recognizes as destructive.

A third idol, intimately related to those described above, is the God who is the Judge of "sin," who confirms the rightness of the rules and roles of the reigning system, maintaining false consciences and self-destructive guilt feelings. Women have suffered both mentally and physically from this deity, in whose name they have been informed that birth control and abortion are unequivocally wrong, that they should be subordinate to their husbands, that they must be present at rituals and services in which men have all the leadership roles and in which they are degraded not only by enforced passivity but also verbally and symbolically. Although this is most blatant in the arch-conservative religions, the God who imposes false guilt is hardly absent from liberal Protestantism and Judaism, where his presence is more subtle. Women's growth in self-respect will deal the death blow to this as well as to the other demons dressed as Gods.

Suggestions for Further Reading

Some have argued that before masculine symbolism was used for the divine, feminist symbolism was used. See Merlin Stone's *When God Was a Woman* (New York: Harcourt Brace Jovanovich, 1976) and Carol Ochs, *Behind the Sex of God* (Boston: Beacon Press, 1977) for starters. Also see Rosemary Radford Ruether's *New Women, New Earth: Sexist Ideologies and Human Liberation* (New York: Seabury, 1975). Also see Mary Daly's *Pure Lust: Elemental Feminist Philosophy* (Boston: Beacon Press, 1984) in which Daly develops a new feminist vocabulary.

For an exploration of a wide range of issues in feminist philosophy see *Philosophy of Woman: An Anthology of Classic and Current Concepts,* edited by Mary Briody Mahowald (Indianapolis: Hackett Publishing, 1983) and *Women and Values: Readings in Recent Feminist Philosophy,* edited by Marilyn Pearsall (Belmont, CA: Wadsworth Publishing, 1986). Also see the collection of essays from, *Womanspirit Rising: A Feminist Reader in Religion,* as well as the more pluralistic sequel, *Weaving the Visions: New Patterns in Feminist Spirituality,* both edited by Judith Plaskow and Carol P. Christ (San Francisco: Harper & Row, 1989). For an enlightening and depressing look at Buddhism with respect to the issue of women in religion, see *Women in Buddhism: Images of the Feminine in the Mahayana Tradition* by Diana Y. Paul (Berkeley, CA: University of California Press, 1985).

Chapter 10

Why Evil?

HAVE YOU EVER WONDERED why babies die? Have you ever seen an animal suffer in terrible pain and thought, "That shouldn't happen. It's not fair?" Have you ever read about or seen pictures of the Nazi concentration camps where millions of Jews and others were brutally murdered and wondered why? Why must innocent people suffer injury and death? Why do earthquakes kill thousands and floods destroy whole cities? Have you seen bad things happen to good people and good things happen to bad people? Have you or your loved ones suffered some terrible tragedy? Have you ever witnessed terrible and pointless suffering and wished we lived in a world where such pain did not occur?

If you have wondered about these things, you have been pondering the **problem of evil**. In its *broad sense,* the problem of evil refers to the problem of why evil exists and what it means. How can we make sense of the fact that innocent people suffer for no apparent good reason, that life is filled with death and destruction, and that people rape, maim, and kill their neighbors? In its *narrow* and more theological sense, the problem of evil refers to the difficulty of reconciling the existence of evil with the existence of a perfectly good, perfectly powerful, perfectly knowing creator God.

In this chapter we will be concerned with the problem of evil in both its broad and narrow (theological) sense. However, I wish to concentrate for a moment on the theological problem of evil. In the last chapter we considered some arguments for God's existence and some reasons to doubt whether those arguments actually proved that God exists. Of course, if such arguments do fail to convince, we cannot conclude God does not exist. After all, God may exist, and we may be unable to prove it. So perhaps we can settle the issue by trying to prove God does not exist. Are there any good reasons to think that God may not exist? Both philosophers and theologians think that there may be some reasons to think God does not, and one of them has to do with evil.

If we define God in a certain way, namely, as an all-powerful being who is perfect in knowledge and goodness and who created this universe, then the existence of that sort of God appears to be incompatible with the existence of evil. If God is all-powerful, God can do something to prevent evil, and if God is all-good, God must want to. If God's knowledge is perfect, then God must be aware of the existence of evil, and if God is the creator of this universe, God would appear to be responsible for evil's existence. But how can that be? I think the dilemma is clear, and it takes little ingenuity to formulate an argument for God's nonexistence based on it.

413

1. Either a Creator God perfect in goodness, power, and knowledge exists or evil exists.
2. Evil exists.
3. Therefore, a Creator God perfect in goodness, power, and knowledge does not exist.

Attempts to solve the problem of evil are called **theodicies**. In the broad sense, a theodicy is any answer to the question "why evil?" In the narrow sense, a theodicy is any answer that reconciles the existence of God with the existence of evil. So, for example, some have responded to the above argument by denying the existence of evil (in other words, they claim the second premise is false). Evil, they say, is a privation or lack of good. Everything is really good, but not all good things are perfect. Evil is just a name we give to the lack of perfection. This may not seem like a very successful theodicy to you because the argument can be rephrased so that the end of the first premise and the second premise read, "A lack of perfection exists." This wording may blunt the edge of the argument somewhat, but the problem still remains of reconciling the existence of a perfect God with the existence of an imperfect universe.

But what about attacking the first premise directly? How about denying that God is perfect or that God created the universe? We could do that, and it would solve the technical problem of evil. We could say, for example, that God doesn't care whether evil exists, or that God doesn't have enough power to prevent it, or that God doesn't know about it. This solution seems a bit extreme, and would not be very satisfying to traditional Jewish, Christian, and Muslim views of God's nature. So if we accept the second premise and the first half of the first premise as true, about the only move left is to deny that the "or" in the first premise is exclusive. It is not an either/or situation, but a both/and. We don't have to choose between the existence of a perfect God and the existence of evil. But why don't we? There's the rub.

10.1. Human Nature Is Evil

In traditional Chinese philosophy, the problem of evil in the theological sense does not occur because there is no doctrine of a perfect creator God. However, the problem of evil in the broad sense was discussed in a political and moral context. Indeed, an intense debate erupted among Confucian philosophers about whether human nature was good or bad or a mixture of both. This debate had important political implications. If we think humans are inherently good, we might be inclined to attribute evil to the corruption of society, culture, and the interference of government. If we believe human nature is evil, we are likely to think of society, culture, and government as necessary to correct and control human beings. Whether we advocate less or more governmental authority depends, in part, on where we stand on the issue of evil and human nature.

Xunzi (Hsun Tzu in Wade-Giles), the author of the following essay, lived sometime during the third century B.C.E. He was a Confucian philosopher (see Section 2.2 for background information on Confucian philosophy) who is sometimes identified with the naturalistic wing of Confucianism. The naturalistic wing is often contrasted with the idealistic wing represented by the philosopher Mengzi (Mencius is the Latinization) who lived about one hundred years before Xunzi. Since Xunzi repeatedly attacks

Mengzi's views in this essay, some background information on Mengzi's ideas is helpful.

Mengzi believed that human nature was generated by Heaven and, since Heaven was good, human nature was also good. By "Heaven" he meant a cosmic ruling force or power. By human nature he meant a tendency inherent in humans. This tendency, he argued, was basically good. Just as long life is a natural tendency that can flourish if proper food and care are given the body, so, argued Mengzi, moral goodness can flourish if given the proper care through education. However, unnatural interference on the part of government and society can prevent this goodness from flourishing.

Xunzi, as you shall soon see, repeatedly denounces Mengzi's views. He argues that humans are by nature bad, meaning by "nature" the qualities someone has to start with. If humans are evil by nature, then goodness must derive from culture. In this translation, goodness is characterized as the result of "activity." The word translated as "activity" is *wei*, which can mean both "doing" and "artifice." The translation "artifice" would probably be better since it would make clear the contrast between the original state of something (its nature) and the changes brought about by socialization (artifice). Xunzi is claiming that our original nature is evil and that our only hope for goodness is through education and the acquiring of culture. His ideas were used later by the Legalists to support a strong authoritarian view of the role of government.

Although Xunzi develops his views in opposition to Mengzi, the difference between them is not as great as it might first appear. Mengzi sees no opposition between nature and culture. Rather, he sees culture as helping to complete and nurture our original tendency to goodness. Hence both Xunzi and Mengzi are strong supporters of education.

A word of caution before you read. In Western philosophy and theology, the doctrines of egoism and original sin have been used to support the notion that humans, left to their own devices, will do evil. We will do this because we are naturally selfish (egoism) or because we are in rebellion against God's will (original sin). The conclusion that strong social and political control is needed is frequently justified by this line of reasoning. Xunzi agrees that strong social and political control is needed, but he does not mean by "evil" either selfishness or rebellion against God. Rather, he means that we are by nature "out of control" because of conflicting desires and hence we need to be taught control by the moderating forces of society. Although there are parallels to his ideas in the West, don't mistake his notion of evil for the Western concepts of selfishness and sin.

Xunzi answers the question "why evil" by attributing it to human nature. But, since human nature is given by Heaven, doesn't this amount to attributing evil to Heaven? We must be cautious here. Granted, human nature is given by Heaven. But Xunzi sees Heaven as morally neutral. The course of things goes neither for nor against humans. Although Heaven has endowed us with conflicting desires, this is just a neutral fact with which we have to deal, just as the seasons and the weather are neutral facts with which we have to deal. Heaven did not intend the seasons to produce evil or the weather to be bad even though it sometimes results in drought or storm. So Heaven did not intend conflicting desires to be bad, even though they sometimes lead to violence and strife. Of course, since Xunzi thinks of Heaven in nonpersonal terms, it is misleading to talk about Heaven "intending" anything.

Reading Questions

1. Do you agree with Xunzi's claim that "to follow man's nature and his feelings will inevitably result in strife and rapacity, combine with rebellion and disorder, and end in violence?" Why or why not?

2. Do you agree that "people who are influenced by teachers and laws, accumulate literature and knowledge, and follow propriety and righteousness are superior men" and that those "who give rein to their feelings, enjoy indulgence, violate propriety and righteousness are inferior men?" Why or why not?

3. What reasons does the author provide to support the contention that "people desire to be good because their nature is evil?" Do you find this a convincing argument? If people are evil by nature, then how can any goodness ever arise?

4. How does Xunzi define good and evil?

5. What is Xunzi's argument against anarchism? Do you agree with it?

Human Nature Is Evil

XUNZI

THE NATURE OF MAN is evil; his goodness is the result of his activity.[1] Now, man's inborn nature is to seek for gain. If this tendency is followed, strife and rapacity result and deference and compliance disappear. By inborn nature one is envious and hates others. If these tendencies are followed, injury and destruction result and loyalty and faithfulness disappear. By inborn nature one possesses the desires of ear and eye and likes sound and beauty. If these tendencies are followed, lewdness and licentiousness result, and the pattern and order of propriety and righteousness disappear. Therefore to follow man's nature and his feelings will inevitably result in strife and rapacity, combine with rebellion and disorder, and end in violence. Therefore there must be the civilizing influence of teachers and laws and

the guidance of propriety and righteousness, and then it will result in deference and compliance, combine with pattern and order, and end in discipline. From this point of view, it is clear that the nature of man is evil and that his goodness is the result of activity.

Crooked wood must be heated and bent before it becomes straight. Blunt metal must be ground and whetted before it becomes sharp. Now the nature of man is evil. It must depend on teachers and laws to become correct and achieve propriety and righteousness and then it becomes disciplined. Without teachers and laws, man is unbalanced, off the track, and incorrect. Without propriety and righteousness, there will be rebellion, disorder, and chaos. The sage-kings of antiquity, knowing that the nature of man is evil, and that it is unbalanced, off the track, incorrect, rebellious, disorderly, and undisciplined, created the rules of propriety and righteousness and instituted laws and systems in order to correct man's feelings, transform them, and direct them so that they all may become disciplined and con-

[1]. According to Yang Liang, *wei* (artificial) is "man's activity." It means what is created by man and not a result of natural conditions. This is accepted by most commentators, including Hao I-hsing, who has pointed out that in ancient times *wei* (ordinarily meaning false or artificial) and *wei* (activity) were interchangeable.

From Chan, W. editor, A Source Book in Chinese Philosophy. *Copyright © 1963, renewed 1991, by Princeton University Press. Reprinted by permission of Princeton University Press. Footnote edited. Pp. 128–132.*

form with the Way (Tao). Now people who are influenced by teachers and laws, accumulate literature and knowledge, and follow propriety and righteousness are superior men, whereas those who give rein to their feelings, enjoy indulgence, and violate propriety and righteousness are inferior men. From this point of view, it is clear that the nature of man is evil and that his goodness is the result of his activity.

> *Comment.* In the *Hsün Tzu,* rules of propriety and law are often spoken of together, giving the impression that, unlike Confucius and Mencius who advocated propriety (*li*) as inner control, Hsün Tzu advocated it for external control. Thus rules of propriety shifted from being a means of personal moral cultivation to one of social control.

Mencius said, "Man learns because his nature is good." This is not true. He did not know the nature of man and did not understand the distinction between man's nature and his effort. Man's nature is the product of Nature; it cannot be learned and cannot be worked for. Propriety and righteousness are produced by the sage. They can be learned by men and can be accomplished through work. What is in man but cannot be learned or worked for is his nature. What is in him and can be learned or accomplished through work is what can be achieved through activity. This is the difference between human nature and human activity. Now by nature man's eye can see and his ear can hear. But the clarity of vision is not outside his eye and the distinctness of hearing is not outside his ear. It is clear that clear vision and distinct hearing cannot be learned. Mencius said, "The nature of man is good; it [becomes evil] because man destroys his original nature." This is a mistake. By nature man departs from his primitive character and capacity as soon as he is born, and he is bound to destroy it. From this point of view, it is clear that man's nature is evil.

By the original goodness of human nature is meant that man does not depart from his primitive character but makes it beautiful, and does not depart from his original capacity but utilizes it, so that beauty being [inherent] in his primitive character and goodness being [inherent] in his will are like clear vision being inherent in the eye and distinct hearing being inherent in the ear. Hence we say that the eye is clear and the ear is sharp. Now by nature man desires repletion when hungry, desires warmth when cold, and desires rest when tired. This is man's natural feeling. But now when a man is hungry and sees some elders before him, he does not eat ahead of them but yields to them. When he is tired, he dares not seek rest because he wants to take over the work [of elders]. The son yielding to or taking over the work of his father, and the younger brother yielding to or taking over the work of his older brother—these two lines of action are contrary to original nature and violate natural feeling. Nevertheless, the way of filial piety is the pattern and order of propriety and righteousness. If one follows his natural feeling, he will have no deference or compliance. Deference and compliance are opposed to his natural feelings. From this point of view, it is clear that man's nature is evil and that his goodness is the result of his activity.

Someone may ask, "If man's nature is evil, whence come propriety and righteousness?" I answer that all propriety and righteousness are results of the activity of sages and not originally produced from man's nature. The potter pounds the clay and makes the vessel. This being the case, the vessel is the product of the artisan's activity and not the original product of man's nature. The artisan hews a piece of wood and makes a vessel. This being the case, the vessel is the product of the artisan's activity and not the original product of man's nature. The sages gathered together their ideas and thoughts and became familiar with activity, facts, and principles, and thus produced propriety and righteousness and instituted laws and systems. This being the case, propriety and righteousness, and laws and systems are the products of the activity of the sages and not the original products of man's nature.

As to the eye desiring color, the ear desiring sound, the mouth desiring flavor, the heart desiring gain, and the body desiring pleasure and ease—all these are products of man's original nature and feelings. They are natural reactions to stimuli and do not require any work to be produced. But if the reaction is not naturally produced by the stimulus but requires work before it can be produced, then it is the result of activity. Here lies the evidence of the difference between what is produced by man's nature and what is produced by his effort. Therefore the sages transformed man's nature and aroused him to activity. As activity was aroused, propriety and righteousness were produced, and as propriety and righteousness were produced, laws and systems were instituted. This being the case, propriety, righteousness, laws, and systems are all products of the sages. In his nature, the sage is common with and not different from ordinary people. It is in his effort that he is different from and superior to them.

It is the original nature and feelings of man to love profit and seek gain. Suppose some brothers are to divide their property. If they follow their natural feelings, they will love profit and seek gain, and thus will do violence to each other and grab the property. But if they are transformed by the civilizing influence of the pattern and order of propriety and righteousness, they will even yield to outsiders. Therefore, brothers will quarrel if they follow their original nature and feeling but, if they are transformed by righteousness and propriety, they will yield to outsiders.

People desire to be good because their nature is evil. If one has little, he wants abundance. If he is ugly, he wants good looks. If his circumstances are narrow, he wants them to be broad. If poor, he wants to be rich. And if he is in a low position, he wants a high position. If he does not have it himself, he will seek it outside. If he is rich, he does not desire more wealth, and if he is in a high position, he does not desire more power. If he has it himself, he will not seek it outside. From this point of view, [it is clear that] people desire to be good because their nature is evil.

Now by nature a man does not originally possess propriety and righteousness; hence he makes strong effort to learn and seeks to have them. By nature he does not know propriety and righteousness; hence he thinks and deliberates and seeks to know them. Therefore, by what is inborn alone, man will not have or know propriety

and righteousness. There will be disorder if man is without propriety and righteousness. There will be violence if he does not know propriety and righteousness. Consequently by what is inborn alone, disorder and violence are within man himself. From this point of view, it is clear that the nature of man is evil and that his goodness is the result of his activity.

Mencius said, "The nature of man is good." I say that this is not true. By goodness at any time in any place is meant true principles and peaceful order, and by evil is meant imbalance, violence, and disorder. This is the distinction between good and evil. Now do we honestly regard man's nature as characterized by true principles and peaceful order? If so, why are sages necessary and why are propriety and righteousness necessary? What possible improvement can sages make on true principles and peaceful order?

Now this is not the case. Man's nature is evil. Therefore the sages of antiquity, knowing that man's nature is evil, that it is unbalanced and incorrect, and that it is violent, disorderly, and undisciplined, established the authority of rulers to govern the people, set forth clearly propriety and righteousness to transform them, instituted laws and governmental measures to rule them, and made punishment severe to restrain them, so that all will result in good order and be in accord with goodness. Such is the government of sage-kings and the transforming influence of propriety and righteousness.

But suppose we try to remove the authority of the ruler, do away with the transforming influence of propriety and righteousness, discard the rule of laws and governmental measure, do away with the restraint of punishment, and stand and see how people of the world deal with one another. In this situation, the strong would injure the weak and rob them, and the many would do violence to the few and shout them down. The whole world would be in violence and disorder and all would perish in an instant. From this point of view, it is clear that man's nature is evil and that his goodness is the result of his activity.

The man versed in ancient matters will certainly support them with evidences from the present, and he who is versed in [the principles of] Nature will certainly support them with evidences from the world of men. In any discussion, the important things are discrimination and evidence. One can then sit down and talk about things, propagate them, and put them into practice. But now Mencius said that man's nature is good. He had neither discrimination nor evidence. He sat down and talked about the matter but rose and could neither propagate it nor put it into practice. Is this not going too far? Therefore if man's nature is good, sage-kings can be done away with and propriety and righteousness can be stopped. But if his nature is evil, sage-kings are to be followed and propriety and righteousness are to be greatly valued. For bending came into existence because there was crooked wood, the carpenter's square and ruler came into existence because things are not straight, and the authority of rule is instituted and propriety and righteousness are made clear because man's nature is evil. From this point of view, it is clear that man's nature is evil and that his goodness is the result of his activity. Straight wood does not depend on bending to become straight; it is straight by nature. But crooked wood must be bent and heated before it becomes straight because by nature it is not straight. Now, the nature of man is evil. It has to depend on the government of sage-kings and the transforming influence of propriety and righteousness, and then all will result in good order and be in accord with goodness. From this point of view, it is clear that man's nature is evil and that his goodness is the result of his activity. . . .

Suggestions for Further Reading

Chapters 6 and 12 in Fung Yu-Lan's *A History of Chinese Philosophy*, Volume 1, translated by Derk Bodde (Princeton, NJ: Princeton University Press, 1952) will provide you with more information on the philosophies of Mengzi and Xunzi with special attention to the debate over human nature. Especially helpful is A. C. Graham's discussion in *Disputers of the Tao: Philosophical Argument in Ancient China* (La Salle, IL: Open Court, 1989). See II. 1 and III. 2 in particular. For a contemporary Western treatment of this issue see John Kekes, *Facing Evil* (Princeton, NJ: Princeton University Press, 1990). Kekes argues that the main sources of evil are habitual actions produced by our character defects, and we can increase our control over the evil we cause by developing a more reflective temperament.

Video

The Lord of the Flies (100 minutes, produced by Diamond Video, 1963) documents the chilling descent into evil of a group of British school boys stranded on an island.

10.2. Evil and Karma

Buddhist philosophy, like other religious philosophies, has long been concerned with the apparent injustices of life. Dogen (1200–1253), a leading Japanese thinker and founder of Soto Zen Buddhism, begins a treatise on karmic retribution (see Section 2.5) by recounting the story of a monk who asked the nineteenth patriarch of Zen why his parents, who were good people and faithful Buddhists, suffered illness and economic misfortune while others, who lived a life directly contrary to Buddhist teachings, were healthy and prosperous. Why do bad things happen to good people? Is there no justice in the world?

Christmas Humphreys, the founder-president of the Buddhist Society of London (1924) and a prolific writer on Buddhist thought, presents his interpretation of the Buddhist response to the apparent injustices of life in the next selection. He is a European convert to a type of nontheistic Buddhism. Hence, the theological problem of evil is of little concern to him. One need not reconcile the existence of evil with the existence of a perfect God if one doesn't believe there is any such God. But still the broader problem of the "why" of evil remains. How can we make sense of the fact that some people are born healthy and talented and others are born brain damaged or severely retarded? How can we make sense of the fact that an innocent girl is kidnapped, raped, and horribly murdered while her killer, who is never caught, prospers?

Humphreys answers these questions by appealing to the doctrine of Karma (see Section 2.5). We reap what we sow. If something bad happens to you that you think you do not deserve, think again. Ultimately you are responsible. It is a just world after all. The innocent girl was not so innocent in a previous life and the prosperous killer will eventually get his just retribution, if not in this life, then in the next.

This hardly seems like a compassionate view. It appears to justify a "blame the victim" attitude. But does it follow that we should not help poor people because we believe those born in poverty are experiencing the karmic effects from a previous life? Yet if we fail to help the less fortunate will we not be storing up our own bad Karma for the future? It is comforting to think abstractly that every evil deed and every good deed will someday produce their just fruits, but when we apply the idea of karmic payback concretely to our own lives it may seem less comforting.

Reading Questions

1. How does Buddhism respond to the question, "Why is there inequality in the world?"
2. How many different Karmas do we have?
3. How does an understanding of Karma lead to self-reliance?
4. Do you agree with Humphreys's claim that the doctrine of rebirth is "immensely reasonable?" Why or why not?
5. Do you think the doctrine of Karma encourages a "blame the victim" mentality? For example, if a woman is raped, would not this doctrine say it is her own fault? Does that seem fair?
6. Formulate any sort of question you wish about this material and answer it.

What Karma Explains

CHRISTMAS HUMPHREYS

Karma or Cause-effect

KARMA (PALI: KAMMA) is literally "action," "doing," "deed." It is at once cause, effect and the law which equilibrates the two. It is Newton's third law of motion, that Action and Reaction are equal and opposite, applied to the moral and all other realms of sentient life. For

The first two sections are from C. Humphreys, Buddhism. *(London: Penguin Books, 1951). Copyright © C. Humphreys 1951, pp. 100–105, and the last two sections are from C. Humphreys,* Karma and Rebirth *(London: Curzon Press, 1983, 1987), pp. 54–57. Reproduced by permission of Penguin Books, Ltd. and Curzon Press. Footnotes deleted.*

two thousand years have Christians heard it proclaimed from their pulpits: "Be not deceived: God is not mocked, for whatsoever a man soweth, that shall he also reap," and Christ is reported to have said upon the Mount: "Judge not that ye be not judged, for with what judgment ye judge ye shall be judged, and with what measure ye mete, it shall be measured to you again."

From the Buddhist viewpoint, Karma stresses the converse of the Christian presentation of this law. Whatsoever a man reaps, say the Buddhists, that has he also sown. Believing in the operation of natural justice, Buddhism would say in reply to the Biblical enquiry: "Who did sin, this man or his parents, that he was born blind?" that it was this man who had "sinned," that is, had so behaved in a previous life as to cause in the life in question the effect of blindness. As Mrs. Rhys Davids says, "Afflictions are for Buddhists so many forms, not of prepayment, by which future compensation may be claimed, but of settlement of outstanding debts accruing from bad, that is to say from evil-bringing, unhappiness-promoting acts, done either in this life or in previous lives." In Karma is to be found, in conjunction with its common-sense corollary, Rebirth, a natural and therefore reasonable answer to the apparent injustice of the daily round. Why should this man be born a beggar, this a prince? Why this a cripple, this a genius, that a fool? Why this a high-born Indian woman, that a low-born Englishman? These are effects. Do the causes lie in the hands of an irresponsible and finite God or, as the Buddhists say, within the lap of law? As it is man who suffers the effects, so it is man who generates the cause, and having done so he cannot flee the consequences. Says the *Dhammapada* (v. 165): "By oneself evil is done; by oneself one suffers. By oneself evil is left undone; by oneself one is purified." And, again, "Not in the sky, not in the midst of the sea, nor anywhere else on earth is there a spot where a man may be freed from (the consequences of) an evil deed" (v. 127). Thus every man is the molder and the sole creator of his life to come, and master of his destiny. "Subsequents follow antecedents by a bond of inner consequence; no merely numerical sequence of arbitrary and isolated units, but a rational interconnection." So said the Emperor Marcus Aurelius, and speaking of the abstract laws of the universe, Emerson said that they "execute themselves. . . . In the soul of man there is a justice whose retributions are instant and entire. He who does a good deed is instantly ennobled. He who does a mean deed is by the action itself contracted." (*Miscellanies.*) And again: "Secret retributions are always restoring the level, when disturbed, of the divine justice. It is impossible to tilt the beam. Settles for evermore the ponderous equator to its line, and man and mote, and star and sun, must range to it, or be pulverized by the recoil."

It is the mind which molds man's destiny, action being but precipitated thought. It follows that one's lightest thought has vast effects, not only on the thinker, but on all that lives. Hence the tremendous power of hatred and love, which man, in childlike ignorance, is pouring out upon the world by night and day. Yet such dynamic qualities, controlled and cultivated, can make a man just what he wills to be. Karma is thus the very antithesis of fatalism. That which is done can by the doer be in time, as it were, neutralized. That which is yet to be depends on the deeds now being done. There is here no cruel Nemesis; only the slow and perfect action of an all-embracing law.

Omar Khayyam was a Buddhist when he wrote:

> The Moving Finger writes; and having writ,
> Moves on: nor all thy Piety nor Wit
> Shall lure it back to cancel half a line,
> Nor all thy Tears wash out a Word of it.

But though the record of a deed remains indelible, it is the sufferer whose finger wrote his destiny, and who had it in his power to choose whether the deed were good or bad. It is but just that he who disturbed should in the end restore the equilibrium.

An individual's karma, in the sense of the sum of unexpended causes generated by him in the past, the burden which he has to bear upon life's pilgrimage, is classified with great precision in the various Schools, but can be analyzed by any student for himself. Karma is an ever-generating force. It may be as a thundercloud, so fully charged that nothing can delay its equally complete discharge; it may be as a snowball on the mountainside, so small and slowly moving at first that a slight expenditure of effort will bring its growing power to rest. Other analogies may be found with ease, but it is more important to understand the nature of Karma than to analyze its complex functioning.

The Buddhist, then, replaces Nemesis and Providence, Kismet, Destiny and Fate, with a natural law, by his knowledge of which he molds his future hour by hour. In the words of an old jingle:

> Sow a thought, reap an act;
> Sow an act, reap a habit;
> Sow a habit, reap a character;
> Sow a character, reap a destiny.

But even as the causes generated by one man react upon that man, so the mass causation of a group, be it family, society or nation, reacts upon that group as such, and upon all whose karma placed them at the time therein. Each man has, therefore, several "karmas," racial, national, family, and personal, yet all quite properly *his,* else he would not have found himself subject to their sway.

An understanding of the law of Karma leads to self-reliance, for in proportion as we understand its operation we cease to complain of our circumstances, and cease from turning with the weakness of a child to a man-made God to save us from the natural consequences of our acts. Karma is no God, for the gods themselves are subject to its sway. Only the ignorant personify Karma, and attempt to bribe, petition or cajole it; wise men understand it and conform to it.

The universe itself is an effect; hence all the units in it, viewed as events, are at once both cause and effect within a vast effect. Each is at once the result of all that has preceded it and a contributing cause of all to come. Yet, as we saw when studying causation, Karma is not only cause and effect in time; rather is it the law which governs the interrelation and solidarity of the Universe in all its parts, and hence, in a way, the karma of one such unit is the karma of all. It is the interdependence of Humanity which is the cause of what is called *Distributive Karma,* and it is this law which affords the solution to the great question of collective suffering and relief. No man can rise superior to his individual failings without lifting, be it ever so little, the whole body of which he is an integral part. In the same way no one can sin, nor suffer the effects of sin, alone.

Rebirth

All action has its due result. A stone thrown into a pond causes wavelets to circle outwards to a distance proportionate to the initial disturbance; after which the initial state of equilibrium is restored. And since each disturbance must start from some particular point, it is clear that harmony can be restored only by the re-converging to that point of the forces set in motion. Thus the consequences of an act re-act, via all the universe, upon the doer with a force commensurate with his own.

Now Karma involves the element of time; and it is unreasonable to hold that all the causes generated in an average life will produce their full effect before the last day of that period. The oldest sage would admit that at the close of a life of study his wisdom was as a raindrop to the sea. Nor is the idea new. Almost every country of the East accepts the doctrine as too obvious to need proof, and anthropologists have traced its presence in the legends and indigenous ideas of nearly every country in the world. It is to be found in most of the greatest minds of Europe and America, from Plato to Origen, from Blake to Schopenhauer, from Goethe, Boehme, Kant, and Swedenborg to Browning, Emerson, Walt Whitman, and leading minds of the Western world today.

It is clearly present in such fragments of Christ's teachings as are still extant. Consider, for example, the widely current rumors that he was John the Baptist, Jeremiah, or Elijah come again. Even Herod seems to think that he was John the Baptist "risen from the dead."

The truth of the doctrine cannot of course be "proved," but it is at least immensely reasonable.

A life on earth is, to the Buddhist, as a wayside inn upon a road. At any moment there are many travellers therein, and even as we speak more enter through the doors of Birth, and others leave by one whose name is Death. Within the common meeting-rooms are men and women of every type whose relations to one another form that reaction to environment we call experience.

Such a belief affects all blood relationship. The child may be an older pilgrim than its parents, and is at least entitled to its point of view. In the West we say that the child of a musical father is musical (if it be so) because of heredity. In Buddhist lands it would be explained that the child was born into a musical family, because it (the child) had developed musical propensities in previous lives, and was attracted to an environment suitable for the expression of those "gifts," a reversal of the Western view. The age of the body is thus no criterion of the age of the entity using it. In the same way, "infant prodigies" are the outcome of a series of lives devoted to the development of a special faculty. The body alone is the product of its parents. So may a house be built by a landlord, but the tenant need not take it against his will. But even though the body be not the direct creation of that "Self" which uses it, yet was it chosen as the instrument most suited to the needs of the informing consciousness. Karma is therefore, with Rebirth, a double key to unexplained phenomena. Life does not die at the body's death, nor do the consequences of a deed. Forms are created and destroyed; they come into being, serve their purpose and then die; but the life within knows no such limitation.

> Nay, but as when one layeth
>   His worn-out robes away,
> And taking new ones, sayeth,
>   "These will I wear to-day!"
> So putteth by the spirit
>   Lightly its garb of flesh,
> And passeth to inherit
>   A residence afresh.

So wrote Sir Edwin Arnold in his verse translation of the *Bhagavad-Gita,* and subject to understanding what it is which passes from life to life, the Buddhist would agree.

What Karma Explains

Once the Law is reasonably understood it solves a large proportion of the problems which cloud our present mind, and certainly in the East, where Karma is as obvious as the law of gravity, these problems do not arise.

In the first place it explains the inequities and inequalities of daily life. Only Karma

> can explain the mysterious problem of Good and Evil, and reconcile man to the terrible *apparent* injustice of life. For when one unacquainted with the noble doctrine looks around him, and observes the inequalities of birth and fortune, of intellect and capacities; when one sees honor paid to fools and profligates, and their nearest neighbor, with all his intellect and noble virtues, perishing of want and for lack of sympathy; when one sees all this and has to turn away, helpless to relieve the undeserved suffering, that blessed knowledge of Karma alone prevents him from cursing life and men, as well as their supposed Creator.

On the other hand, nothing is more untrue than the cry that all men are born equal. They are not. Each is born with the burden, pleasant or unpleasant, of his own Karma, and no two men are equal, for no two are the same.

> All mankind is one family, but its members are of different ages. Therefore there is no equality of opportunity and no equality of responsibility. Although all are marching towards a common goal they cannot bear equal burdens, and would not be expected to if the Law of Karma were understood.

In the same way Karma explains the problem of Original Sin. There is no problem, for there is no original sin. First causes are necessarily unknowable, and as the Buddha insisted again and again, discussion of such matters is unprofitable, as leading in no way to the heart's enlightenment. But the teaching of the Wisdom is clear. Evil is man-made, and is of his choosing, and he who suffers suffers from his deliberate use of his own free will. Cripples, dwarfs and those born deaf or blind are the products of their own past actions, and one's pity should be used, not in bewailing the injustice of their condition, but in assisting the new-born brain to appreciate its own responsibility and to produce new causes whose result will be the undoing of the evil whose results are manifest. Infant prodigies, on the other hand, are clearly the result of specialization in some particular line, and even special aptitudes and preferences are the outcome of the Law.

Conscience is a Karmic memory. The Essence of Mind is deathless, and its ray, the consciousness (*vinnana*) which moves from life to life, is a store-house of immensely complex memory. Even though the brain, which is new in each life, has forgotten the lessons of past experience, the inner mind remembers, and when temptation murmurs again of the pleasures of a certain low desire, the voice of memory replies, "But what of the cost in suffering, the price that you paid?"

Heredity versus Environment

Karma explains. "Karma expresses, not that which a man inherits from his ancestors, but that which he inherits from himself in some previous state of existence." In the same way, environment is a product of one's own past actions, for each new birth accords with the Karma therein to be discharged. All that is inherited from parents is the body, the outermost garment of the many-robed, essential man. The mind, or returning unit of consciousness, so far from being the product of its body's parents, chose those parents, and the body which they would provide for the working out of a portion of past Karma. Heredity is therefore the servant of Karma and not its substitute. By the law of affinity, the magnetic law of attraction and repulsion, each new body attracts an appropriate "soul" or character, as each returning consciousness attracts or is attracted to a vehicle suitable for self-expression in the life to come. The staggering complexity of such elaborate choosing, allowing for period, race, sex, family and the compound circumstances of "environment," is a reason for the mind's humility before the Law, but no bar to its acceptance. If an automatic telephone exchange can be made to "choose" which of a dozen lines is the least "loaded" at the moment, how much more can the Namelessness in manifestation operate its own high purposes!

Suggestions for Further Reading

Arthur L. Herman's *The Problem of Evil and Indian Thought* (Delhi: Motilal Banarsidass, 1976) deals in a technical fashion with the issue of evil in the Indian context of Karma and rebirth. See p. 255 and following for a discussion and critique of Humphreys's views. Herman's bibliography will carry you into deeper waters. For Dogen's views see "Karmic Retribution in the Three Stages of Time" in *Zen Master Dogen: An Introduction with Selected Writings* by Yuho Yokoi (New York: Weatherhill, 1976).

For a general treatment of Karma in Indian philosophy see Surendranath Dasgupta's *A History of Indian Philosophy,* Volume I (London: Cambridge University Press, 1922) and Volume I of Sarvepalli Radhakrishnan's *Indian Philosophy* (London: George Allen & Unwin, 1929).

Gunapala Dharmasiri discusses the Buddhist concept of evil in *Fundamentals of Buddhist Ethics* (Antioch, CA: Golden Leaves Publishing, 1989). Ronald M. Green gives a perceptive analysis of the implications for social justice of the Karma teaching in Chapter 7 of *Religion and Moral Reason: A New Method for Comparative Study* (New York: Oxford University Press, 1988).

10.3. The Problem of Evil in African Thought

Traditional, preliterate societies have no written philosophical literature. The Anglo-European bias for written materials has led some philosophers to assume that the absence of written philosophical texts amounts to the absence of philosophical thinking. This inference is not warranted. When we turn to African culture we must carefully comb its proverbs, linguistic expressions, folktales, myths, customs, and religious beliefs to find its philosophical concepts. Kwame Gyekye (pronounced Qua-may Je-che), a professor of philosophy at the University of Ghana, has done just that.

Professor Gyekye is an Akan. The Akan are the largest ethnic group in Ghana, and Dr. Gyekye has studied the Akan oral traditions with philosophical sensitivity. In the selection that follows, we read the results of his research on Akan ideas about the problem of evil.

There is little doubt that the Akan recognize and respond to the problem of evil in its broad sense. Like most cultures, they are concerned with explaining evil. But, according to Professor Gyekye, one also finds awareness of the theological problem of evil, as well as attempts to solve it, among the Akan. These attempts have interesting parallels in Christian theology.

The first Akan response ascribes evil to deities other than the supreme God. Christian theology has ascribed evil to Satan and his demons and, while this is similar, remember that Satan and his helpers are not deities, but fallen angels. Apart from problems relating to the existence of deities, Satan, and demons, this sort of response does not solve the problem, but moves it one step back. Instead of having to explain why God allows evil in the world one now has to explain why God allows deities, Satan, and/or demons, to do evil. Doesn't the supreme God have the power to stop them?

The second Akan response is to ascribe evil to the free exercise of human will. Humans in their freedom do evil. This response is similar to the so-called *free will defense* which is popular in Christian theology. According to this theodicy, evil is not due to God, but to human beings who misuse the free will God has given them. Apart from the issue of whether or not our wills are really free (see Chapter 6), one might ask why God permits humans to misuse their freedom?

Reading Questions

1. According to Akan thought, what are the sources of evil?
2. Does making deities responsible for evil eliminate the theological problem of evil? Why or why not?
3. What is wrong with the claim that "evil stems from our inability to exercise the moral sense?"
4. What sort of objections does the author raise with respect to the free will defense, and how does he counter them? Do you find his answers satisfactory? Why or why not?
5. What do you think might be wrong with the free will defense?
6. Formulate a critical question about this material and answer it.

The Problem of Evil

KWAME GYEKYE

BECAUSE AKAN THINKERS hold that moral evil stems from the exercise of man's free will, it is appropriately treated here. The problem of evil appears to be more complex in Akan

Kwame Gyekye, An Essay on African Philosophical Thought. The Akan Conceptual Scheme, *1987, pp. 123–128. Reprinted by permission of Cambridge University Press. Footnotes deleted.*

thought than Western thought. The reason is that whereas in Western thought the problem centers round God, in Akan thought the problem centers round both the Supreme Being (God: Onyame) and the deities (that is, lesser spirits). In Western thought the problem arises out of seeming conflicts between the attributes of God and the existence of evil. In Akan thought the problem is conceived in terms not only of the attributes of God but also of those of the deities. When the problem of evil in Akan thought is pushed to its logical limits, however, its philosophical nature is quite similar to that in Western philosophy and theology.

The problem of evil in Western philosophy arises out of the contradiction between God's attributes of omnipotence and goodness (benevolence) on the one hand and the existence of evil on the other hand. Thus, given the three propositions:

1. God is omnipotent,
2. God is wholly good,
3. evil exists.

(3) is considered to be incompatible with (1) and (2), individually or jointly. If God is omnipotent, then He can completely eliminate evil, since there are no limits to what an omnipotent being can do, and if God is wholly good or benevolent then He would be willing to eliminate evil. Yet evil exists. The existence of evil, it is argued in Western philosophy, implies that either God does not exist or if He does exist He is not omnipotent or not wholly good or both. Of course various attempts have been made by philosophers and theologians to explain the sources of evil in this world.

In Akan philosophy and theology God is conceived as omnipotent and wholly good. Yet the Akan thinkers do not appear to find these attributes of God incompatible with the fact of the existence of moral evil. One might suppose that the Akan thinkers are dodging the philosophical issue here, but this is not so. Rather, they locate the source of the problem of evil elsewhere than in the logic of the relationships between the attributes of God and the fact of existence of evil.

For the Akan, evil is not a creation of God; that would be inconsistent with the goodness of God. Akan thinkers generally believe that it was not God who created evil (*Nyame ambō bōne*). Then how is the existence of evil explained? According to them, there are two main sources of evil: the deities (*abosom,* including all supernatural forces such as magic forces, witches, etc.) and mankind's own will. About half a dozen assembled discussants were unanimous in asserting that "evil derives from evil spirits" (*bōne firi obonsam*). The deities are held either to be good and evil or to have powers of good and evil. Thus, unlike Onyame (God), they are not wholly good, and hence they are the authors of evil things. Although the deities were created by God, they are considered in Akan theology and cosmology to have independent existence of some sort; they operate independently of God and in accordance with their own desires and intentions.

Since the deities that constitute one source of evil in this world are held not to be wholly good, one might suppose that the problem of evil is thereby solved. Busia, for instance, thought that

> . . . the problem of evil so often discussed in Western philosophy and Christian theology does *not* arise in the African concept of deity. It is when a God who is not only all powerful and omniscient but also perfect and loving is postulated that the problem of the existence of evil becomes an intellectual and philosophical hurdle. The Supreme Being of the African is the Creator, the source of life, *but between Him and man lie many powers and principalities good and bad, gods, spirits, magical forces, witches to account for the strange happenings in the world.*

It is not clear what Busia means by "deity" here; perhaps he means the Supreme Being, God. If so, his view of the attributes of the Supreme Being—a view that implies some limitation on the Supreme Being as conceived in African thought—is disputable. Be that as it may, the view that the African concept of the Supreme Being does not give rise to the problem of evil is of course predicated on the assumption that the lesser spirits created by Him are conceived of as good *and* bad, so that the quandaries arising out of the conflict of omnipotence and perfect good-ness on the one hand and evil on the other hand cease to exist. But this conclusion is premature and unsatisfactory philosophically.

The immediate question that arises is this: Why should a wholly good God create a being that embodies in itself both good *and* evil pow-ers or dispositions? One possible answer may be that it was not God who created the evil powers or actions of a lesser spirit, but that these result from the operations of the independent will of the spirit itself. But this answer is not wholly sat-isfactory either. First, God, being a higher entity, can destroy the lesser spirits as well as the other powers and forces. Consequently, God has the power to eliminate or control the evil wills and actions of the lower beings such as the lesser spir-its and so to eliminate evil from the world. Sec-ond, since God is wholly good and eschews evil (*Nyame mpē bōne*), as an Akan proverb has it, he would not refrain from eliminating evil or con-trolling evil wills. Even if it were granted that God endowed the lesser spirits with independent wills, it might be expected that the wholly good God would be willing to intervene when he sees them using their wills to choose to act wrongly and so to cause evil. Would it have been wrong for God to intervene in the evil operations of the independent free wills of the lesser spirits in or-der to eliminate evil? But if he had done so, would he not have disrupted the free wills with which he endowed them? (These questions come up again in discussing mankind as a source of evil.) Thus, contrary to Busia's assertion, it is clear that the Akan concept of deity does gener-ate the philosophical problem of evil. Busia's as-sertion would be true only if a lesser spirit, held to be both good *and* bad, were considered as the supreme or ultimate spiritual being. But this, as we saw in Chapter 5, is not the case. It is Onyame who is the Supreme and Absolute Being.

The other source of evil, according to Akan thought, is human will. On this some of my dis-cussants advanced the following views:

Evil comes from man's character.
(*bōne fi onipa suban*)

In the view of this discussant, character deter-mines the nature of our actions; bad character gives rise to evil actions, and good character gives rise to good actions. The person with bad char-acter, he asserted, thinks evil, and it is such evil thoughts that translate or issue in morally evil ac-tions. According to him, it is impossible for evil to come from Onyame (God) because (1) On-yame is good (*Onyame ye*), and (2) our character, from which evil proceeds, is of our own making; what our character is, or will be, is our responsi-bility, not God's. In a discussion with a different group of three elders, two of them also blamed evil on human character, but the third one, criti-cizing the other two, asked: "Is it not *Onyame* who created the world and us and all that we are?" He answered his own question by saying: "If Onyame made us what we are, then he cre-ated, along with everything else, evil too." To this one of the others retorted: "It is surely *not* Onyame who tells or forces a person to go and rape, steal, and kill. It is the person's own desires and mind" (*n'aprēde ne n'adwen*). But the con-ception of the human source of moral evil was shared by two other discussants, both from dif-ferent communities. One of them maintained that "Onyame did not create evil; evil comes from man's own actions" (*Onyame ambō bōne; bōne firi onipa nneyēe*), and the other that "On-yame is not the cause of evil, but our own think-ing and deliberation" (*bōne mfi Onyame; efi yēn ankasa adwendwen mu*).

Arguing that God is not the author of evil, another discussant maintained that "evil comes from man's conscience" (*tiboa*). His position is that a human being has what is called *tiboa*, con-science (moral sense, that is, a sense of right and wrong), which enables one to see the difference (*nsoe*) between good and evil. Putting it bluntly, he said, "Man is not a beast (*aboa*) to fail to dis-tinguish between the good and evil." The com-parison between man and beast is intended as a distinction between moral sense and amoral sense on the one hand, and between rationality (in-telligence) and irrationality (nonintelligence) on the other hand. The implication is that it is only conscienceless, irrational beasts that cannot distinguish between good and evil. Since, according to this traditional thinker, our possession of *tiboa* enables (or, should enable) us to do correct moral thinking, evil stems from our inability to exercise the moral sense. But this argument is not persuasive. Having the ability to do correct moral thinking, or to distinguish between good and evil, does not necessarily imply possession of the moral will to carry out the implications of the distinction. This traditional wise man assumes that it does, but this assumption, I think, is mistaken. So that the statement "Evil comes from man's conscience" must perhaps be taken to mean that evil stems from the inability to exercise either our moral sense or our moral will.

In sum, the basic premise of the arguments of the Akan thinkers on the problem of evil is generally that God does not like evil (*Nyame mpɛ bōne*) and hence did not create it (*Nyame ambō bōne*). Evil, according to most of them, proceeds from man's character, conscience, desires, and thoughts—all of which suggest, within the Akan conceptual system, that evil stems from the exercise by the person of his or her own free will (*onipa ne pɛ*), as was in fact explicitly stated by a discussant.

It was made clear that the general nature of destiny (*nkrabea*) allows for the concept of human freedom, and therefore of choice, and that within the context of human actions—which are *not* to be considered as events—the concept of determinism is inapplicable. Thus, the view of the human source of moral evil appears to stem from a set of related concepts in the Akan metaphysical system.

This argument seems to me a potent one. Nevertheless, some difficult questions might be raised against it. For instance: Why did not God, if he is omnipotent and wholly good, make human beings such that they always choose the good and avoid the evil? Or, having endowed them with freedom of the will, why does God not intervene when he sees them using this freedom to choose the wrong thing and so to cause evil? Is God unable to control human will? Is he unable to control what he has created? And if he

is able, why does he not do so? Can the argument that evil results from the exercise of human free will really be sustained?

If God is omnipotent, then he certainly could have made human beings such that they always choose the good and avoid the evil, that he could also intervene in the event of human freedom of the will leading to evil, and that he could thus control human will. But if God had done all this, humans would act in a wholly determined way, without any choice whatever—a situation that would run counter to the *general* nature of the concept of destiny and the notion of human action as held by Akan thinkers. That would also have led to the subversion of rationality, which not only distinguishes human beings from beasts, but also enables human beings generally to judge before acting. The argument that God should have made humans such that they always choose the good implies that God should have made them nonrational and thus less human, wholly without the ability to choose. Thus, the subversion of rationality together with its concomitants of choice, deliberation, judgment, etc., constitutes a *reductio ad absurdum* of the view that the wholly good God should have created humans such that they always choose the good. The Akan thinkers, like thinkers in most other cultures, would rather have humankind endowed with rationality and conscience than to have them fashioned to behave like a beast. Hence, God's provision of rationality and freedom of the will and of choice is justified. If humans debase this provision, knowing that this would bring evil in its wake, then they, not their Creator, should be held responsible.

What if God made humans such that they use their rationality always to choose the good? Would they have been free under such circumstances? The answer must be no, inasmuch as the choice of the good would have been predetermined, which means that no choice ever existed.

This discussion shows that the problem of evil does indeed arise in Akan philosophy and theology. The Akan thinkers, although recognizing the existence of moral evil in the world, generally do not believe that this fact is inconsistent with the assertion that God is omnipotent and wholly good. Evil, according to them, is ultimately the result of the exercise by humans of their freedom of the will with which they were endowed by the Creator, *Ōbōadeē.*

Suggestions for Further Reading

See John L. Mackie, "Evil and Omnipotence," *Mind,* Vol. 64 (1955), 200–212, for a critical discussion of the free will defense in a Western theological context and Alvin Plantinga's *God, Freedom, and Evil* (New York: Harper & Row, 1974) and *God and Other Minds: A Study of the Rational Justification of Belief in God* (Ithaca, NY: Cornell University Press, 1967) for a defense of the free will defense and a discussion of the "Lucifer theory."

If you are interested in an overview of African thought, John S. Mbiti's *African Religion and Philosophy* (Garden City, NY: Doubleday, 1969) is an old standby. *African Philosophy: An Introduction* edited by Richard A. Wright (New York: University Press of America, 1984), provides a useful bibliography and a collection of essays on a wide variety of topics.

Those of you concerned with the issue of whether there "really" is an African philosophy as well as with problems that arise in trying to compare African and European philosophy will wish to consult Kwasi Wiredu's *Philosophy and African Culture* (London: Cambridge University Press, 1980) and Paulin J. Hountondji's *African Philosophy: Myth and Reality* (Bloomington, IN: Indiana University Press, 1983). For a recent collection of essays exploring the development of African philosophy and identifying four main trends (ethnophilosophy, professional philosophy, philosophic sagacity, and nationalist-ideological philosophy) see *African Philosophy: The Essential Readings,* edited by Tsenay Serequebertan (New York: Paragon House, 1991). Also Kwame Anthony Appiah's *In My Father's House: Africa in the Philosophy of Culture* (London: Methuen, 1992) is a thoughtful and careful reflection on a variety of issues surrounding African philosophy. See especially Chapter 6 for a careful consideration of rationality in a cross-cultural context.

10.4. Why Do Babies Suffer?

It is more difficult to deal with the theological problem of evil in the concrete than in the abstract. Abstractly we can always say things like, "Well, God allows evil because in the long run it is for the greater good." That sounds plausible. Less abstractly we can say, "God allows innocent babies to suffer because in the long run it is for their own good." That sounds less plausible, but still okay. Now imagine it is your baby who is terribly burned and suffers horribly. Suppose someone comes up to you and says, "Well, I know you are upset, but look on the bright side. God would not have allowed this to happen if it weren't for your own good and the good of your baby." You might seriously consider hitting someone who said that. I know I would. It sounds too uncaring.

The following selection was written by B. C. Johnson, a pen name for an author who wishes to remain anonymous. Johnson considers a concrete case and shows how all of the traditional theodicies sound rather hollow and inadequate as responses. We seem to be making excuses for God and allowing the divine to get away with behavior that we would not tolerate in our fellow human beings. This does not lead Johnson to conclude that God does not exist. But he does conclude that if God does exist, it is very unlikely that God is perfectly good.

Before you read this selection, make a list of all the various answers you can think of that explain why God permits a six-month-old baby to painfully burn to death.

Reading Questions

1. As you read, see if the answers on your list are discussed by Johnson and note what he has to say about them. If you think any of your answers are particularly good and Johnson's criticism of them unfair, indicate how you would respond to what Johnson has to say.

2. What have you learned about the theological problem of evil and the proposed solutions to it that you had not thought about before?

3. In the last few paragraphs, Johnson presents an argument that concludes, "It is unlikely that God is all good." Summarize this argument and indicate what you think is wrong with it. If you can find nothing wrong with it, do you agree with the conclusion? Why?

God and the Problem of Evil

B. C. JOHNSON

HERE IS A COMMON situation: a house catches on fire and a six-month-old baby is painfully burned to death. Could we possibly describe as "good" any person who had the power to save this child and yet refused to do so? God undoubtedly has this power and yet in many cases of this sort he has refused to help. Can we call God "good?" Are there adequate excuses for his behavior?

First, it will not do to claim that the baby will go to heaven. It was either necessary for the baby to suffer or it was not. If it was not, then it was wrong to allow it. The child's ascent to heaven does not change this fact. If it was necessary, the fact that the baby will go to heaven does not explain why it was necessary, and we are still left without an excuse for God's inaction.

It is not enough to say that the baby's painful death would in the long run have good results and therefore should have happened, otherwise God would not have permitted it. For if we know this to be true, then we know—just as God knows—that every action successfully performed must in the end be good and therefore the right thing to do, otherwise God would not have allowed it to happen. We could deliberately set houses ablaze to kill innocent people and if successful we would then know we had a duty to do it. A defense of God's goodness which takes as its foundation duties known only after the fact would result in a morality unworthy of the name. Furthermore, this argument does not explain why God allowed the child to burn to death. It merely claims that there is some reason discoverable in the long run. But the belief that such a reason is within our grasp must rest upon the additional belief that God is good. This is just to counter evidence against such a belief by assuming the belief to be true. It is not unlike a lawyer defending his client by claiming that the client is innocent and therefore the evidence against him must be misleading—that proof vindicating the defendant will be found in the long run. No jury of reasonable men and women would accept such

From The Atheist Debater's Handbook *by B.C. Johnson (Buffalo, NY: Prometheus Books), pp. 99–108. Copyright © 1981 by B. C. Johnson. Reprinted by permission of the publisher.*

a defense and the theist cannot expect a more favorable outcome.

The theist often claims that man has been given free will so that if he accidentally or purposefully causes fires, killing small children, it is his fault alone. Consider a bystander who had nothing to do with starting the fire but who refused to help even though he could have saved the child with no harm to himself. Could such a bystander be called good? Certainly not. If we would not consider a mortal human being good under these circumstances, what grounds could we possibly have for continuing to assert the goodness of an all-powerful God?

The suggestion is sometimes made that it is best for us to face disasters without assistance, otherwise we would become dependent on an outside power for aid. Should we then abolish modern medical care or do away with efficient fire departments? Are we not dependent on their help? Is it not the case that their presence transforms us into soft, dependent creatures? The vast majority are not physicians or firemen. These people help in their capacity as professional outside sources of aid in much the same way that we would expect God to be helpful. Theists refer to aid from firemen and physicians as cases of man helping himself. In reality, it is a tiny minority of men helping a great many. We can become just as dependent on them as we can on God. Now the existence of this kind of outside help is either wrong or right. If it is right, then God should assist those areas of the world which do not have this kind of help. In fact, throughout history, such help has not been available. If aid ought to have been provided, then God should have provided it. On the other hand, if it is wrong to provide this kind of assistance, then we should abolish the aid altogether. But we obviously do not believe it is wrong.

Similar considerations apply to the claim that if God interferes in disasters, he would destroy a considerable amount of moral urgency to make things right. Once again, note that such institutions as modern medicine and fire departments are relatively recent. They function irrespective of whether we as individuals feel any moral urgency to support them. To the extent that they help others, opportunities to feel moral urgency are destroyed because they reduce the number of cases which appeal to us for help. Since we have not always had such institutions, there must have been a time when there was greater moral urgency than there is now. If such a situation is morally desirable, then we should abolish modern medical care and fire departments. If the situation is not morally desirable, then God should have remedied it.

Besides this point, we should note that God is represented as one who tolerates disasters, such as infants burning to death, in order to create moral urgency. It follows that God approves of these disasters as a means to encourage the creation of moral urgency. Furthermore, if there were no such disasters occurring, God would have to see to it that they occur. If it so happened that we lived in a world in which babies never perished in burning houses, God would be morally obliged to take an active hand in setting fire to houses with infants in them. In fact, if the frequency of infant mortality due to fire should happen to fall below a level necessary for the creation of maximum moral urgency in our real world, God would be justified in setting a few fires of his own. This may well be happening right now, for there is no guarantee that the maximum number of infant deaths necessary for moral urgency are occurring.

All of this is of course absurd. If I see an opportunity to create otherwise nonexistent opportunities for moral urgency by burning an infant or two, then I should *not* do so. But if it is good to maximize moral urgency, then I *should* do so. Therefore, it is not good to maximize moral urgency. Plainly we do not in general believe that it is a good thing to maximize moral urgency. The fact that we approve of modern medical care and applaud medical advances is proof enough of this.

The theist may point out that in a world without suffering there would be no occasion for the production of such virtues as courage, sympathy, and the like. This may be true, but the atheist need not demand a world without suffering. He need only claim that there is suffering which is in excess of that needed for the production of various virtues. For example, God's active attempts to save six-month-old infants from fires would not in itself create a world without suffering. But no one could sincerely doubt that it would improve the world.

The two arguments against the previous theistic excuse apply here also. "Moral urgency" and "building virtue" are susceptible to the same criticisms. It is worthwhile to emphasize, however, that we encourage efforts to eliminate evils; we approve of efforts to promote peace, prevent famine, and wipe out disease. In other words, we do value a world with fewer or (if possible) no opportunities for the development of virtue (when "virtue" is understood to mean the reduction of suffering). If we produce such a world for succeeding generations, how will they develop virtues? Without war, disease, and famine, they will not be virtuous. Should we then cease our attempts to wipe out war, disease, and famine? If we do not believe that it is right to cease attempts at improving the world, then by implication we admit that virtue-building is not an excuse for God to permit disasters. For we admit that the development of virtue is no excuse for permitting disasters.

It might be said that God allows innocent people to suffer in order to deflate man's ego so that the latter will not be proud of his apparently deserved good fortune. But this excuse succumbs to the arguments used against the preceding excuses and we need discuss them no further.

Theists may claim that evil is a necessary by-product of the laws of nature and therefore it is irrational for God to interfere every time a disaster happens. Such a state of affairs would alter the whole causal order and we would then find it impossible to predict anything. But the death of a child caused by an electrical fire could have been prevented by a miracle and no one would ever have known. Only a minor alteration in electrical equipment would have been necessary. A very large disaster could have been avoided simply by producing in Hitler a miraculous heart attack—and no one would have known it was a miracle.

To argue that continued miraculous intervention by God would be wrong is like insisting that one should never use salt because ingesting five pounds of it would be fatal. No one is requesting that God interfere all of the time. He should, however, intervene to prevent especially horrible disasters. Of course, the question arises: where does one draw the line? Well, certainly the line should be drawn somewhere this side of infants burning to death. To argue that we do not know where the line should be drawn is no excuse for failing to interfere in those instances that would be called clear cases of evil.

It will not do to claim that evil exists as a necessary contrast to good so that we might know what good is. A very small amount of evil, such as a toothache, would allow that. It is not necessary to destroy innocent human beings.

The claim could be made that God has a "higher morality" by which his actions are to be judged. But it is a strange "higher morality" which claims that what we call "bad" is good and what we call "good" is bad. Such a morality can have no meaning to us. It would be like calling black "white" and white "black." In reply the theist may say that God is the wise Father and we are ignorant children. How can we judge God any more than a child is able to judge his parent? It is true that a child may be puzzled by his parents' conduct, but his basis for deciding that their conduct is nevertheless good would be the many instances of good behavior he has observed. Even so, this could be misleading. Hitler, by all accounts, loved animals and children of the proper race; but if Hitler had had a child, this offspring would hardly have been justified in arguing that his father was a good man. At any rate, God's "higher morality," being the opposite of ours, cannot offer any grounds for deciding that he is somehow good.

Perhaps the main problem with the solutions to the problem of evil we have thus far considered is that no matter how convincing they may be in the abstract, they are implausible in certain particular cases. Picture an infant dying in a burning house and then imagine God simply observing from afar. Perhaps God is reciting excuses in his own behalf. As the child succumbs to the smoke and flames, God may be pictured as saying: "Sorry, but if I helped you I would have considerable trouble deflating the ego of your parents. And don't forget I have to keep those laws of nature consistent. And anyway if you weren't dying in that fire, a lot of moral urgency would just go down the drain. Besides, I didn't start this fire, so you can't blame *me*."

It does no good to assert that God may not be all-powerful and thus not able to prevent evil. He can create a universe and yet is conveniently unable to do what the fire department can do—rescue a baby from a burning building. God should at least be as powerful as a man. A man, if he had been at the right place and time, could have killed Hitler. Was this beyond God's abilities? If God knew in 1910 how to produce polio vaccine and if he was able to communicate with somebody, he should have communicated this knowledge. He must be incredibly limited if he could not have managed this modest accomplishment. Such a God if not dead, is the next thing to it. And a person who believes in such a ghost of a God is practically an atheist. To call such a thing a god would be to strain the meaning of the word.

The theist, as usual, may retreat to faith. He may say that he has faith in God's goodness and therefore the Christian Deity's existence has not been disproved. "Faith" is here understood as being much like confidence in a friend's innocence despite the evidence against him. Now in order to have confidence in a friend one must know him well enough to justify faith in his goodness. We cannot have justifiable faith in the supreme goodness of strangers. Moreover, such confidence must come not just from a speaking acquaintance. The friend may continually assure us with his words that he is good but if he does not act like a good person, we would have no reason to trust him. A person who says he has faith in God's goodness is speaking as if he had known God for a long time and during that time had never seen Him do any serious evil. But we know that throughout history God has allowed numerous atrocities to occur. No one can have

justifiable faith in the goodness of such a God. This faith would have to be based on a close friendship wherein God was never found to do anything wrong. But a person would have to be blind and deaf to have had such a relationship with God. Suppose a friend of yours had always claimed to be good yet refused to help people when he was in a position to render aid. Could you have justifiable faith in his goodness?

You can of course say that you trust God anyway—that no arguments can undermine your faith. But this is just a statement describing how stubborn you are; it has no bearing whatsoever on the question of God's goodness.

The various excuses theists offer for why God has allowed evil to exist have been demonstrated to be inadequate. However, the conclusive objection to these excuses does not depend on their inadequacy.

First, we should note that every possible excuse making the actual world consistent with the existence of a good God could be used in reverse to make that same world consistent with an evil God. For example, we could say that God is evil and that he allows free will so that we can freely do evil things, which would make us more truly evil than we would be if forced to perform evil acts. Or we could say that natural disasters occur in order to make people more selfish and bitter, for most people tend to have a "me-first" attitude in a disaster (note, for example, stampedes to leave burning buildings). Even though some people achieve virtue from disasters, this outcome is necessary if persons are to react freely to disaster—necessary if the development of moral degeneracy is to continue freely. But, enough; the point is made. Every excuse we could provide to make the world consistent with a good God can be paralleled by an excuse to make the world consistent with an evil God. This is so because the world is a mixture of both good and bad.

Now there are only three possibilities concerning God's moral character. Considering the world as it actually is, we may believe: (*a*) that God is more likely to be all evil than he is to be all good; (*b*) that God is less likely to be all evil than he is to be all good; or (*c*) that God is equally as likely to be all evil as he is to be all good. In case (*a*) it would be admitted that God is unlikely to be all good. Case (*b*) cannot be true at all, since—as we have seen—the belief that God is all evil can be justified to precisely the same extent as the belief that God is all good. Case (*c*) leaves us with no reasonable excuses for a good God to permit evil. The reason is as follows: if an excuse is to be a reasonable excuse, the circumstances it identifies as excusing conditions must be actual. For example, if I run over a pedestrian and my excuse is that the brakes failed because someone tampered with them, then the facts had better bear this out. Otherwise the excuse will not hold. Now if case (*c*) is correct and, given the facts of the actual world, God is as likely to be all evil as he is to be all good, then these facts do not support the excuses which could be made for a good God permitting evil. Consider an analogous example. If my excuse for running over the pedestrian is that my brakes were tampered with, and if the actual facts lead us to believe that it is no more likely that they

were tampered with than that they were not, the excuse is no longer reasonable. To make good my excuse, I must show that it is a fact or at least highly probable that my brakes were tampered with—not that it is just a possibility. The same point holds for God. His excuse must not be a possible excuse, but an actual one. But case (*c*), in maintaining that it is just as likely that God is all evil as that he is all good, rules this out. For if case (*c*) is true, then the facts of the actual world do not make it any more likely that God is all good than that he is all evil. Therefore, they do not make it any more likely that his excuses are good than that they are not. But, as we have seen, good excuses have a higher probability of being true.

Cases (*a*) and (*c*) conclude that it is unlikely that God is all good, and case (*b*) cannot be true. Since these are the only possible cases, there is no escape from the conclusion that it is unlikely that God is all good. Thus the problem of evil triumphs over traditional theism.

Suggestions for Further Reading

Edward H. Madden and Peter H. Hare have written a book, *Evil and the Concept of God* (Springfield, IL: Charles C. Thomas, 1968) that goes even further than Johnson. They argue that theism is unable to make sense of the facts of evil and that this inability constitutes a good reason for rejecting belief in God. Richard Swineburne, in *The Existence of God* (Oxford: Clarendon Press, 1979) argues that evil does not count as evidence against God's existence.

Nelson Pike has edited a collection of readings pro and con with an excellent bibliography. See *God and Evil: Readings on the Theological Problem of Evil* (Englewood Cliffs, NJ: Prentice-Hall, 1964).

Video

Bridge at San Luis Rey (89 minutes, produced by New World Video) tells the story of a priest, deeply affected by the apparently chance deaths of five people who plunged to their deaths when a bridge broke. He investigates the pasts of each to see if he can discover some reason why God took their lives. See your Media Services Catalogue for more information.

10.5. Evil Cannot be Explained

There has been a variety of Christian responses to the problem of evil, although none of them has ever achieved the status of official dogma. One response, known as the "Augustinian theodicy," is named after the great Christian theologian Augustine of

Hippo (354–430). According to St. Augustine, God created a perfect world. Evil and sin originated in the disobedience of one of God's angels, Lucifer, who in turn tempted Adam and Eve to sin. They did so out of their own free will. God is not responsible for evil; human beings under the influence of fallen angels are responsible. So Augustine claims, "All evil is either sin or the punishment for sin."

Another major Christian response is known as the "Irenaean theodicy," named after St. Irenaeus (c. 130–c. 202). According to this theodicy, God created a good but not perfect world. Human beings are endowed with the capacity for great moral and spiritual development, but they are not perfect. In order for them to develop to their full extent, they must freely respond to whatever evils and temptations exist. In so doing, they have an opportunity to develop into "children of God." The Irenaean theodicy is sometimes called the "soul-making" defense because it argues, in effect, that God permits evil to happen so that humans have the opportunity to perfect their souls (moral and spiritual character).

Although these two theodicies are very different, both attempt to reconcile the existence of evil with the existence of an all-powerful and all-good God. A third major Christian response abandons that attempt. *Process theology* argues that God's power is limited. God is good and loving, but is unable to stop or prevent all evil. God suffers along with humans, working in and through the world and human action to bring about the best that is possible. But the best is not always free from pain and sorrow.

Jewish responses to the problem of evil, like the Christian responses, have been varied. Because of the history of Jewish persecution and suffering, the problem of evil has been particularly central to Jewish thought. The terrible, unspeakable suffering during the Holocaust in this century raised the problem of evil once again, for both Christian and Jew, in a most intense way. Some have tried to retain God's power and goodness by finding explanations that blame humans for such evils. But this Augustinian approach seems particularly harsh, especially in light of all the innocent people who were murdered. Others have questioned whether God is, in fact, perfectly good. Literary treatments often raise the cry of what we might call "a theodicy of protest." And still others have questioned whether God has the power to prevent all evil.

Emil Fachenheim (1916–) is a Jewish philosopher who teaches at the University of Toronto. He is a survivor of the Holocaust, one of the most horrific if not the most horrific instances of humanities' inhumanities. Arriving at Auschwitz, one of the most infamous concentration camps run by the Nazis, Jewish parents were asked to decide which of their children they wanted to send to forced labor, and which they wanted to send to the gas chamber! Lampshades were made by the Nazis out of the skins of their victims! The horror is unimaginable. How could anyone make sense of such evil? Fachenheim believes that the Holocaust resists both rational and theological explanations. Thought is paralyzed. Theodicies crumble. But life is not paralyzed. According to Jewish tradition, God gave 613 commandments. The Holocaust, according to Fachenheim, provides us with a new commandment, the 614th.—resist evil and fight to overcome it.

Reading Questions

1. What is the main point of Fachenheim's essay?
2. Why does he argue that seeking a purpose in Auschwitz is blasphemous, but seeking a response to it is appropriate?

3. What does Fachenheim mean by "the particularity of Auschwitz?"

4. What is the second *Shema Yisrael* ("Hear, Oh Israel")?

5. While Fachenheim states that no redeeming divine voice is heard at Auschwitz, a commanding voice is heard. What is the command?

6. Formulate an analytical and a critical question about this essay and answer them.

Jewish Faith and the Holocaust: A Fragment

EMIL FACHENHEIM

I

Within the past two centuries, three events have shaken and are still shaking Jewish religious existence—the Emancipation and its aftereffects, the Nazi Holocaust, and the rise of the first Jewish state in two thousand years—and of these, two have occurred in our own generation. From the point of view of Jewish religious existence, as from so many other points of view, the Holocaust is the most shattering. Doubtless the Emancipation and all its works have posed and continue to pose powerful challenges, with which Jewish thought has been wrestling all along—scientific agnosticism, secularism, assimilation, and the like. The Emancipation presents, however, a challenge *ab extra,* from without, and for all its well-demonstrated power to weaken and undermine Jewish religious existence, I have long been convinced that the challenge can be met, religiously and intellectually. The state of Israel, by contrast, is a challenge *ab intra,* from within—at least to much that Jewish existence has been throughout two millennia. But this challenge is positive—the fact that in one sense (if not in many others) a long exile has ended. That it represents a positive challenge was revealed during and immediately after the Six Day War, when biblical (i.e., preexilic) language suddenly came to life.

The Holocaust, too, challenges Jewish faith from within, but the negativity of its challenge is total, without light or relief. After the events associated with the name of Auschwitz, everything is shaken, nothing is safe.

To avoid Auschwitz, or to act as though it had never occurred, would be blasphemous. Yet how face it and be faithful to its victims? No precedent exists either within Jewish history or outside it. Even when a Jewish religious thinker barely begins to face Auschwitz, he perceives the possibility of a desperate choice between the faith of a millennial Jewish past, which has so far persisted through every trial, and faithfulness to the victims of the present. But at the edge of this abyss there must be a great pause, a lengthy silence, and an endurance.

II

Men shun the scandal of the particularity of Auschwitz. Germans link it with Dresden; American liberals, with Hiroshima. Christians deplore antisemitism-in-general, while Communists erect monuments to victims-of-Fascism-in-general, depriving the dead of Auschwitz of their Jewish identity even in death. Rather than face Auschwitz, men everywhere seek refuge in generalities, comfortable precisely because they are generalities. And such is the extent to which re-

From The Jewish Return to History *by Emil Fachenheim. Copyright © 1978 by Emil Fachenheim. Reprinted by permission of Georges Borchardt, Inc., for the author. Footnotes deleted.*

ality is shunned that no cries of protest are heard even when in the world community's own forum obscene comparisons are made between Israeli soldiers and Nazi murderers.

The Gentile world shuns Auschwitz because of the terror of Auschwitz—and because of real or imagined implication in the guilt for Auschwitz. But Jews shun Auschwitz as well. Only after many years did significant Jewish responses begin to appear. Little of real significance is being or can be said even now. Perhaps there should still be silence. It is certain, however, that the voices, now beginning to be heard, will grow ever louder and more numerous. For Jews now know that they must ever after remember Auschwitz, and be its witnesses to the world. Not to be a witness would be a betrayal. In the murder camps the victims often rebelled with no other hope than that one of them might escape to tell the tale. For Jews now to refrain from telling the tale would be unthinkable. Jewish faith still recalls the Exodus, Sinai, the two destructions of the Temple. A Judaism that survived at the price of ignoring Auschwitz would not deserve to survive.

It is because the world shrinks so fully from the truth that once a Jew begins to speak at all he must say the most obvious. Must he say that the death of a Jewish child at Auschwitz is no more lamentable than the death of a German child at Dresden? He must say it. And in saying it, he must also refuse to dissolve Auschwitz into suffering-in-general, even though he is almost sure to be considered a Jewish particularist who cares about Jews but not about mankind. Must he distinguish between the mass-killing at Hiroshima and that at Auschwitz? At the risk of being thought a sacrilegious quibbler, he must, with endless patience, forever repeat that Eichmann was moved by no such "rational" objective as victory when he diverted trains needed for military purposes in order to dispatch Jews to their death. He must add that there was no "irrational" objective either. Torquemada burned bodies in order to save souls. Eichmann sought to destroy both bodies and souls. Where else and at what other time have executioners ever separated those to be murdered now from those to be murdered

later to the strain of Viennese waltzes? Where else has human skin ever been made into lampshades, and human body-fat into soap—not by isolated perverts but under the direction of ordinary bureaucrats? Auschwitz is a unique descent into hell. It is an unprecedented celebration of evil. It is evil for evil's sake.

A Jew must bear witness to this truth. Nor may he conceal the fact that Jews in their particularity were the singled-out victims. Of course, they were by no means the sole victims. And a Jew would infinitely prefer to think that to the Nazis, Jews were merely a species of the genus "inferior race." This indeed was the theme of Allied wartime propaganda, and it is still perpetuated by liberals, Communists, and guilt-ridden Christian theologians. Indeed, "liberal"-minded Jews themselves perpetuate it. The superficial reason is that this view of Auschwitz unites victims of all races and creeds: it is "brotherly" propaganda. Under the surface, however, there broods at least in Jewish if not in some Gentile minds an idea horrible beyond all description. Would even Nazis have singled out Jews for such a terrible fate unless Jews had done *something* to bring it upon themselves? Most of the blame attaches to the murderers: must not at least some measure of blame attach to the victims as well? Such are the wounds that Nazism has inflicted on some Jewish minds. And such is the extent to which Nazism has defiled the world that, while it should have destroyed every vestige of antisemitism in every Gentile mind on earth, Auschwitz has, in some Gentile minds, actually increased it.

These wounds and this defilement can be confronted only with the truth. And the ineluctable truth is that Jews at Auschwitz were not a species of the genus "inferior race," but rather the prototype by which "inferior race" was defined. Not until the Nazi revolution had become an anti-Jewish revolution did it begin to succeed as a movement; and when all its other works came crashing down only one of its goals remained: the murder of Jews. This is the scandal that requires, of Germans, a ruthless examination of their whole history; of Christians, a pitiless reckoning with the history of Christian antisemitism; of the whole world, an inquiry into the grounds of its indifference for twelve long years. Resort to theories of suffering-in-general or persecution-in-general permits such investigations to be evaded.

Yet even where the quest for explanations is genuine there is not, and never will be, an adequate explanation. Auschwitz is the scandal of evil for evil's sake, an eruption of demonism without analogy; and the singling-out of Jews, ultimately, is an unparalleled expression of what the rabbis call groundless hate. This is the rock on which throughout eternity all rational explanations will crash and break apart.

How can a Jew respond to thus having been singled out, and to being singled out even now whenever he tries to bear witness? Resisting rational explanations, Auschwitz will forever resist religious explanations as well. Attempts to find rational causes succeed, at least up to a point, and the search for the religious, ideological, social, and economic factors leading to Auschwitz must be relentlessly pressed. In contrast, the search for a purpose in Auschwitz is foredoomed to total failure. Not that good men in their despair have not made the attempt. Good Orthodox Jews have resorted to the ancient "for our sins we are punished," but this recourse, unacceptable already to Job, is in this case all the more impossible. A good Christian theologian sees the purpose of Auschwitz as a divine reminder of the sufferings of Christ, but this testifies to a moving sense of desperation—and to an incredible lapse of theological judgment. A good Jewish secularist will connect the Holocaust with the rise of the state of Israel, but while to see a causal connection here is possible and necessary, to see a purpose is intolerable. A total and uncompromising sweep must be made of these and other explanations, all designed to give purpose to Auschwitz. No purpose, religious or non-religious, will ever be found in Auschwitz. The very attempt to find one is blasphemous.

Yet it is of the utmost importance to recognize that seeking a purpose is one thing, but seeking a response quite another. The first is wholly out of the question. The second is inescapable. Even after two decades any sort of adequate response

may as yet transcend the power of any Jew. But his faith, his destiny, his very survival will depend on whether, in the end, he will be able to respond.

How can a Jew begin to seek a response? Looking for precedents, he finds none either in Jewish or in non-Jewish history. Jewish (like Christian) martyrs have died for their faith, certain that God needs martyrs. Job suffered despite his faith, able to protest within the sphere of faith. Black Christians have died for their race, unshaken in a faith which was not at issue. The one million Jewish children murdered in the Nazi Holocaust died neither because of their faith, nor in spite of their faith, nor for reasons unrelated to faith. They were murdered because of the faith of their great-grandparents. Had these great-grandparents abandoned their Jewish faith, and failed to bring up Jewish children, then their fourth-generation descendants might have been among the Nazi executioners, but not among their Jewish victims. Like Abraham of old, European Jews some time in the mid-nineteenth century offered a human sacrifice, by the mere minimal commitment to the Jewish faith of bringing up Jewish children. But unlike Abraham they did not know what they were doing, and there was no reprieve. This is the brute fact which makes all comparisons odious or irrelevant. This is what makes Jewish religious existence today unique, without support from analogies anywhere in the past. This is the scandal of the particularity of Auschwitz which, once confronted by Jewish faith, threatens total despair.

I confess that it took me twenty years until I was able to look at this scandal, but when at length I did, I made what to me was, and still is, a momentous discovery: that while religious thinkers were vainly struggling for a response to Auschwitz, Jews throughout the world—rich and poor, learned and ignorant, religious and nonreligious—had to some degree been responding all along. For twelve long years Jews had been exposed to a murderous hate which was as groundless as it was implacable. For twelve long years the world had been lukewarm or indifferent, unconcerned over the prospect of a world without

Jews. For twelve long years the whole world had conspired to make Jews wish to cease to be Jews wherever, whenever, and in whatever way they could. Yet to this unprecedented invitation to group suicide, Jews responded with an expected will to live—with, under the circumstances, an incredible commitment to Jewish group survival.

In ordinary times, a commitment of this kind may be a mere mixture of nostalgia and vague loyalties not far removed from tribalism; and, unable to face Auschwitz, I had myself long viewed it as such, placing little value on a Jewish survival which was, or seemed to be, only survival for survival's sake. I was wrong, and even the shallowest Jewish survivalist philosophy of the postwar period was right by comparison. For in the age of Auschwitz a Jewish commitment to Jewish survival is in itself a monumental act of faithfulness, as well as a monumental, albeit as yet fragmentary, act of faith. Even to do no more than remain a Jew after Auschwitz is to confront the demons of Auschwitz in all their guises, and to bear witness against them. It is to believe that these demons cannot, will not, and must not prevail, and to stake on that belief one's own life and the lives of one's children, and of one's children's children. To be a Jew after Auschwitz is to have wrested hope—for the Jew and for the world—from the abyss of total despair. In the words of a speaker at a recent gathering of Bergen-Belsen survivors, the Jew after Auschwitz has a second *Shema Yisrael:* no second Auschwitz, no second Bergen-Belsen, no second Buchenwald—anywhere in the world, for anyone in the world!

What accounts for this commitment to Jewish existence when there might have been, and by every rule of human logic should have been, a terrified and demoralized flight from Jewish existence? Why, since Auschwitz, have all previous distinctions among Jews—between religious and secularist, Orthodox and liberal—diminished in importance, to be replaced by a new major distinction between Jews committed to Jewish survival, willing to be singled out and counted, and Jews in flight, who rationalize this flight as a rise to humanity-in-general? In my view nothing less will do than to say that a commanding Voice

speaks from Auschwitz, and that there are Jews who hear it and Jews who stop their ears.

The ultimate question is: where was God at Auschwitz? For years I sought refuge in Buber's image of an eclipse of God. This image, still meaningful in other respects, no longer seems to me applicable to Auschwitz. Most assuredly no *redeeming* Voice is heard from Auschwitz, or ever will be heard. However, a *commanding* Voice is being heard, and has, however faintly, been heard from the start. Religious Jews hear it, and they identify its source. Secularist Jews also hear it, even though perforce they leave it unidentified. At Auschwitz, Jews came face to face with absolute evil. They were and still are singled out by it, but in the midst of it they hear an absolute commandment: *Jews are forbidden to grant posthumous victories to Hitler.* They are commanded to survive as Jews, lest the Jewish people perish. They are commanded to remember the victims of Auschwitz, lest their memory perish. They are forbidden to despair of man and his world, and to escape into either cynicism or otherworldliness, lest they cooperate in delivering the world over to the forces of Auschwitz. Finally, they are forbidden to despair of the God of Israel, lest Judaism perish. A secularist Jew cannot make himself believe by a mere act of will, nor can he be commanded to do so; yet he can perform the commandment of Auschwitz. And a religious Jew who has stayed with his God may be forced into new, possibly revolutionary, relationships with him. One possibility, however, is wholly unthinkable. A Jew may not respond to Hitler's attempt to destroy Judaism by himself cooperating in its destruction. In ancient times, the unthinkable Jewish sin was idolatry. Today, it is to respond to Hitler by doing his work.

In the Midrash, God is, even in time of unrelieved tragedy, only "seemingly" powerless, for the Messiah is still expected. In Elie Wiesel's *Night,* God hangs on the gallows, and for the hero of Wiesel's *The Gates of the Forest,* a Messiah who is able to come, and yet at Auschwitz failed to come, is not to be conceived. Yet this same hero asserts that precisely because it is too late we are commanded to hope. He also says the Kad-

dish, "that solemn affirmation, filled with gran-
deur and serenity, by which man returns to God
His crown and His scepter." But how a Jew after

Auschwitz can return these to God is not yet
known. Nor is it yet known how God can receive
them. . . .

Suggestions for Further Reading

See John Hick's *Evil and the God of Love,* 2d ed. (New York: Harper & Row, 1978) for a
fine historical study of the problem. His *Philosophy of Religion,* 4th ed. (Prentice-Hall, 1990),
pp. 39–55, gives a clear and concise summary of the Augustinian, Irenaean, and process theodicies. For a more detailed treatment of process theology see David Griffin, *God, Power and
Evil: A Process Theodicy* (Philadelphia: Westminster Press, 1976) and Barry L. Whitney, *Evil
and the Process God* (New York: Mellen Press, 1985). For a literary treatment of the issue that
supports a "soul-making" theory, see L. Stafford Betty, *The Rich Man: A Galilean Chronicle*
(New York: St. Martin's Press, 1984). For an exchange of different viewpoints see *Encountering
Evil: Live Options in Theodicy,* edited by Stephen T. Davis (Atlanta: John Knox Press, 1981).
John Roth's opening essay reflects a Jewish "theodicy of protest" approach.

Jewish literature on the Holocaust and evil is extensive. See *Evil and Exile* by Elie Wiesel
and Philippe de Saint-Cheron (Notre Dame: University of Notre Dame Press, 1990); *Dimensions of the Holocaust* by Elie Wiesel, et al. (Evanston, IL: Northwestern University, 1977);
Jon D. Levenson, *Creation and the Persistence of Evil: The Jewish Drama of Divine Omnipotence*
(San Francisco: Harper & Row, 1988); Martin Buber, *Good and Evil* (New York: Charles Scribner's Sons, 1952); Richard L. Rubenstein, *After Auschwitz: Radical Theology and Contemporary Judaism* (New York: Bobbs-Merrill, 1966); and David Birnbaum, *God and Evil: A Unified
Theodicy/Theology/Philosophy* (Hoboken, NJ: Ktav Publishing House, 1989), for starters. Harold S. Kushner, in *When Bad Things Happen to Good People* (New York: Schocken Books, 1961),
presents a Jewish version of the limited God argument.

Videos

Nazi Concentration Camps (59 minutes, 1945 National Audio/Visual Center) is an official
film record of the Nazi death camps as filmed by allied Forces advancing into Germany at the
end of World War II.

Sophie's Choice (155 minutes, CBS/Fox Video, 1982) dramatizes the effect on one human
being of the Holocaust. Available from Films for the Humanities and Sciences are two films
dealing with the Holocaust, *The Life of Anne Frank* (25 minutes, 1989) and *The Suicide of A
Camp Survivor: The Case of Primo Levi* (72 minutes, 1993) and one dealing with anti-Semitism,
The Longest Hatred: The History of Anti-Semitism (150 minutes, 1993). All available from
Films for the Humanities and Sciences.

Triumph of Will (120 minutes, produced by Crown Movie Classics, 1934) records the Nazi
Party Congress held at Nuremberg in 1934. See *The Killing Fields* (142 minutes, produced by
Warner Brothers, 1984) for a chilling account of the atrocities committed by the Khmer Rouge
in Cambodia.

See your Media Services Catalogue for more information.

Chapter 11

Who Am I and Can I Survive Death?

HAVE YOU EVER THOUGHT about who you are? I don't mean what your name is or what your personality is like. I mean, have you ever thought about your fundamental identity? Have you ever wondered to what the word "I" refers?

You might want to say that the word "I" refers to your body. This would mean that you are your body, and I am my body. That seems simple enough. But notice the words "your body" or "my body." Why do we say "my" body as if the body were something the I possessed? This way of talking seems to imply that we make a distinction between ourselves and our bodies. And of course we can lose parts of our bodies or even have parts of them replaced without losing or replacing ourselves.

Maybe "I" doesn't refer to the body, but to something that goes on inside the body, like thoughts or sensations. So you are what you think, perceive, and feel. But we run into the same problem, don't we? After all, we speak of "my" thoughts, "my" perceptions, and "my" feelings. Also, these things are constantly changing, but is the "I" constantly changing? Are you a different person every time you have a different thought, feeling, or sensation?

If "I" does not refer to my body or my thoughts, perceptions, and feelings, maybe it refers to my mind. My mind is what has thoughts, perceptions, and feelings so you might say it possesses them. And since my mind tells my body what to do, you might even say that my body is possessed by my mind. Or, at least, my mind inhabits my body.

As the above bit of thinking about the question, "Who am I?" indicates, the discussion sooner or later leads one to talk about the mind and the body. This seems natural enough since we normally think of ourselves as human beings, and we commonly think of humans as having minds and bodies. But what precisely are the mind and the body, and how are they related to each other? These questions constitute what philosophers call the **mind-body problem.**

Generally speaking, the proposed solutions to the mind-body problem fall into two groups: dualistic and monistic. Dualistic theories hold that the mind and the body are two different substances. The mind is conscious, nonspatial, and private (only you have

441

direct access to your own mind). The body is unconscious, spatial, and public (it can be viewed by others). Now how do these two substances, so defined, relate?

One theory, usually associated with Descartes, is called **interactionism.** According to this theory mind and body causally interact in the sense that mental events (e.g., thoughts) can cause physical events (e.g., walking) and physical events (e.g., taking a sleeping pill) can cause mental events (e.g., feeling sleepy). This seems plausible enough at first, but the problem of how two substances so radically different can causally affect each other has led to considerable controversy as well as to the development of other theories.

Some dualists who reject the idea of causal interactionism subscribe to **parallelism.** The German philosopher Leibniz (1646–1716), for example, argued that there is a preestablished harmony between mental and physical events so that they run in parallel, like two clocks set to tick together. Mind and body appear to interact, but in fact they do not. A physical event occurs (e.g., a blow to the arm) and parallel to that event, but uncaused by it, a mental event (e.g., pain in the arm) occurs.

This seems somewhat fantastic, so other dualists have been led to yet a third theory called **epiphenomenalism.** According to this theory, mental events are by-products of physical events as smoke is a by-product of fire. This means that physical events cause mental events, but mental events cannot cause physical events. Mental events are just things that happen when certain brain activities take place. The brain activity is what is primary; the mental activity is secondary.

Monistic solutions to the mind-body problem deny that the mind and the body are two different substances. For example, *materialism* (see Section 7.5), or "physicalism," as it is sometimes called, holds that mental events are not significantly different from physical events. There is no such thing as a mental substance above and beyond the physical. There are several varieties of materialism, but a popular version, called the **identity theory,** proposes that mental events are identical with brain processes in much the same way as lightning flashes are identical with electrical discharges.

Where some versions of materialism attempt to reduce mind to matter, idealism (see Section 7.4) attempts to reduce matter to mind. If you recall the reading from Bishop Berkeley, you will see how such an argument might progress. Berkeley argues that since all we ever experience are sensations and since sensations are mental, matter is an unwarranted and unneeded inference. Only minds and mental events exist.

A third kind of monism is called the **double-aspect theory.** This view, argued by the Dutch philosopher Spinoza (1632–1677), proposes that we rethink what we mean by mind and body (matter). Instead of thinking of these as things or substances, we should think of them as qualities, characteristics, or aspects. There is one substance, Spinoza argued, that in itself is neither mental nor physical, but that has at least two different aspects or qualities called mind and body. A modern version of this theory was suggested by the famous British philosopher Bertrand Russell (1872–1970). Russell called his theory **neutral monism** and characterized it as the view that what exists is neither mental nor physical but neutral.

The question, "Who am I?" leads to questions about the nature of human beings, questions about what they are made of or what constitutes their being. But it also leads to other questions, in particular questions about what a person is. We must be careful to distinguish the concept of "person" from the concept "human being." Human being refers to a biological species, one to which we happen to belong. Person, on the other hand, is not a biological concept. We can bring out the distinction by pointing to the example of the space alien E.T. It would appear that E.T. is a person, but certainly not a human being in the biological sense. This distinction is central to much of the debate about abortion (see Section 5.2) since many claim that while a fetus belongs to the biological species human being, it is not a person, but only potentially a person. So another important issue the question, "Who am I?" leads to is the question, "What is a person?"

The question, "Who am I?" also leads to another issue, the issue of the identity of persons through time. Consider this puzzle: Are you the same person today as you were when you were five years old? If we mean by "same" a kind of strict identity such that if A is identical with B then A and B have the same properties the answer is obviously "no." You have a different set of properties today (such as size and age) than you did when you were five. If we mean by "same" similar, but not absolutely identical, then the answer is "yes." But is similarity good enough? If I am only similar to my former self, then I have changed. And if I have changed, how much have I changed? For example, does it make sense to hold the person I am today responsible for the act of stealing cookies at age five? If my mother suddenly discovered that I, not my sister, stole the cookies, and I lied about it, should she call me up and scold me many years later?

The question, "Who am I?" is deceptively simple. But, as we have seen, reflection on an answer leads to issues about the nature of human beings, about the existence of minds and bodies, about the relationship between minds and bodies, about how to define a person, and issues about personal identity through time. But these sorts of issues may seem awfully abstract and academic. "Are they of any practical consequence?" you might well ask. The answer is, "Yes." There is a host of moral questions such as abortion and euthanasia surrounding the issue of personhood. But there are also important questions about the possibility of life after death that are directly related to these abstract questions.

Have you ever wondered if there is life after death? Do we live on after the death of our bodies? Is there a heaven or hell? What about reincarnation? Can I move from one body to another? If I don't remember my past lives, how can I really claim they are *my* past lives? Is there an immortal soul? What is life like apart from the body? Does the idea of a resurrection of the body make any sense? Is it probable that at death I will just go to sleep and then wake up with a new body? Would it still be me if my body is different?

The problem of survival is closely related to the mind-body problem and the problem of personal identity. For example, if we define the person as a mental substance, then we might argue that our soul or mind survives death. If souls exist and if souls can live without bodies, then perhaps life after death consists of the **immortality of the soul**. And even if souls cannot live or at least not live for long without bodies, then maybe some sort of **reincarnation** is possible—souls moving from one body to another after the death of the last body. Conversely, if we identify the person with the body or some part of it like the brain, then it seems clear we do not survive death because it is evident that the body, including the brain, ceases to function at death and eventually decays. But as we shall see perhaps there are some kinds of materialism which are compatible with survival.

Or maybe you aren't your soul or body exclusively, but a combination of things—a mind, a body, a personality. If that combination could be recreated after the first combination died, could we not say that you survived death? The idea of a **resurrection of the body**, while open to a variety of interpretations, seems to indicate that life in a new body after the death of this one is possible.

But maybe death is too much of a trauma. Maybe the person cannot survive. If so, does that make life pointless? Is this life only worth living if there is some other life? Maybe this life is valuable in itself. Maybe living forever would get boring. Then again, maybe not.

11.1. You Are Your Mind

We return once again to Descartes, in particular to the last chapter of his *Meditations* (see Sections 8.2 and 9.3). Let me remind you of his argument so far. Descartes was concerned with proving representational realism true. That is, he wanted to show for certain that physical objects really do exist outside our minds. He began by using his method of doubt to show that all our beliefs about an external world based on our sensations can be doubted. Hence the most direct way to know the external world, namely, by sensation, is blocked by doubt. He then discovered that he could not doubt that he existed as a thinking thing as long as he was thinking because every time he doubts (thinks) that he exists he proves that he exists (thinks). So he found a certain foundation from which to begin. But he was trapped in his own mind. He sought a way out by showing that God exists. If he could prove that God exists, he could be certain that at least one thing outside his own mind exists. This he attempts in Meditation V with his famous argument from perfection.

Along the way Descartes also tried to establish a rule for distinguishing true ideas from false. Ideas that are clear and distinct are true. He also thought he discovered the cause of error. We can use our will to choose to believe things that our understanding does not completely grasp. Hence we can be confident that God is good and not the source of error. He also tried to show that material things are essentially different from mental things. Matter is extended in space and mind is not.

So Descartes believed he had established with absolute certainty the existence of his own mind as a mental substance and the existence of a perfectly good God. How did he get from there to a world made up of physical objects external to our minds? In the Meditation that follows Descartes makes that move.

He argues that physical objects outside his mind exist because there are only three possible causes of his perception of such objects:

1. his mind causes the perceptions,
2. God causes them, or
3. physical objects cause them.

We have, Descartes argues, a strong inclination to believe that (3) is true. If it were not true, then God who is perfectly good and who has given us this strong inclination would be a deceiver since it is neither evident nor certain that our mind causes our perceptions of physical objects or that God does. But since he has proved (at least to his satisfaction) that God is perfectly good, then it follows that God is not a deceiver, hence (3) is true.

Central to Descartes's view is a sharp distinction between the mind which is a non-physical substance (not extend in space and private) and objects outside the mind which are physical substances (extended in space and public). One of these outside objects is our own body. But unlike rocks (so far as we know), persons are a unique combination of the nonphysical (the mind) and the physical (the body). In addition, it appears that human minds (what they think) can cause their bodies (a physical substance) to act in certain ways.

The standard interpretation of Descartes is that he not only establishes a mind-body dualism, but he also supports a theory of interactionism. According to this theory, the mind and body can causally interact even though one is a mental substance and the other is a physical substance. Recently, some philosophers have questioned whether Descartes did in fact support interactionism. Descartes corresponded about this very issue with Princess Elisabeth of Bohemia in May and June of 1643. Elisabeth was puzzled about how interactive causation might happen since causation is a mechanical process requiring contact between bodies extended in space. But the mind is not extended in space and hence can have no contact with a physical body. So how do you raise your arm? Read this correspondence and decide for yourselves whether Descartes does support interactionism.

Reading Questions

1. What two reasons does Descartes give in support of the proposition that material objects *can* exist?

2. What is the difference between having a mental image and having a pure understanding? Is having a mental image essential to one's self? Why?

3. Why does Descartes think it is *probable* that physical objects exist?

4. Summarize in your own words the reasons Descartes gives which led him to believe physical objects exist outside his mind and the reasons which led him to doubt this belief?

5. What leads Descartes to conclude it is certain that he really is distinct from his body and can exist without it?

6. From what does it follow that physical objects exist?

7. How is Descartes "present in" his body and of what does his "whole self" consist?

8. How do the mind and body differ, according to Descartes?

9. How can dreaming be distinguished from waking? Do you agree or not? Why?

10. Do you think Descartes holds an interactionist theory? Why or why not?

Meditation VI

RENÉ DESCARTES

On the Existence of Material Objects and the Real Distinction of Mind from Body

IT REMAINS FOR ME to examine whether material objects exist. Insofar as they are the subject of pure mathematics, I now know at least that they can exist, because I grasp them clearly and distinctly. For God can undoubtedly make whatever I can grasp in this way, and I never judge that something is impossible for Him to make unless there would be a contradiction in my

From René Descartes's Meditations On First Philosophy, *trans. Ronald Rubin (Claremont, CA: Areté Press, 1986), pp. 40–53. Reprinted by permission of Areté Press.*

grasping the thing distinctly. Also, the fact that I find myself having mental images when I turn my attention to physical objects seems to imply that these objects really do exist. For, when I pay careful attention to what it is to have a mental image, it seems to me that it's just the application of my power of thought to a certain body which is immediately present to it and which must therefore exist.

To clarify this, I'll examine the difference between having a mental image and having a pure understanding. When I have a mental image of a triangle, for example, I don't just understand that it is a figure bounded by three lines; I also "look at" the lines as though they were present to my mind's eye. And this is what I call having a mental image. When I want to think of a chiliagon, I understand that it is a figure with a thousand sides as well as I understand that a triangle is a figure with three, but I can't imagine its sides or "look" at them as though they were present. Being accustomed to using images when I think about physical objects, I may confusedly picture some figure to myself, but this figure obviously is not a chiliagon—for it in no way differs from what I present to myself when thinking about a myriagon or any other many sided figure, and it doesn't help me to discern the properties that distinguish chiliagons from other polygons. If it's a pentagon that is in question, I can understand its shape, as I can that of the chiliagon, without the aid of mental images. But I can also get a mental image of the pentagon by directing my mind's eye to its five lines and to the area that they bound. And it's obvious to me that getting this mental image requires a special mental effort different from that needed for understanding—a special effort which clearly reveals the difference between having a mental image and having a pure understanding.

It also seems to me that my power of having mental images, being distinct from my power of understanding, is not essential to my self or, in other words, to my mind—for, if I were to lose this ability, I would surely remain the same thing that I now am. And it seems to follow that this ability depends on something distinct from me.

If we suppose that there is a body so associated with my mind that the mind can "look into" it at will, it's easy to understand how my mind might get mental images of physical objects by means of my body. If there were such a body, the mode of thinking that we call imagination would only differ from pure understanding in one way: when the mind understood something, it would turn "inward" and view an idea that it found in itself, but, when it had mental images, it would turn to the body and look at something there which resembled an idea that it had understood by itself or had grasped by sense. As I've said, then, it's easy to see how I get mental images, if we suppose that my body exists. And, since I don't have in mind any other equally plausible explanation of my ability to have mental images, I conjecture that physical objects probably do exist. But this conjecture is only probable. Despite my careful and thorough investigation, the distinct idea of bodily nature that I get from mental images does not seem to have anything in it from which the conclusion that physical objects exist validly follows.

Besides having a mental image of the bodily nature which is the subject-matter of pure mathematics, I have mental images of things which are not so distinct—things like colors, sounds, flavors, and pains. But I seem to grasp these things better by sense, from which they seem to come (with the aid of memory) to the understanding. Thus, to deal with these things more fully, I must examine the senses and see whether there is anything in the mode of awareness that I call sensation from which I can draw a conclusive argument for the existence of physical objects.

First, I'll remind myself of the things that I believed really to be as I perceived them and of the grounds for my belief. Next, I'll set out the grounds on which I later called this belief into doubt. And, finally, I'll consider what I ought to think now.

To begin with, I sensed that I had a head, hands, feet, and the other members that make up a human body. I viewed this body as part, or maybe even as all, of me. I sensed that it was influenced by other physical objects whose effects could be either beneficial or harmful. I judged these effects to be beneficial to the extent that I felt pleasant sensations and harmful to the extent that I felt pain. And, in addition to sensations of pain and pleasure, I sensed hunger, thirst, and other such desires—and also bodily inclinations towards cheerfulness, sadness, and other emotions. Outside me, I sensed, not just extension, shape, and motion, but also hardness, hotness, and other qualities detected by touch. I also sensed light, color, odor, taste, and sound— qualities by whose variation I distinguished such things as the sky, earth, and sea from one another.

In view of these ideas of qualities (which presented themselves to my thought and were all that I really sensed directly), I had some reason for believing that I sensed objects distinct from my thought—physical objects from which the ideas came. For I found that these ideas came to me independently of my desires so that, however much I tried, I couldn't sense an object when it wasn't present to an organ of sense or fail to sense one when it was present. And, since the ideas that I grasped by sense were much livelier, more explicit, and (in their own way) more distinct than those I deliberately created or found impressed in my memory, it seemed that these ideas could not have come from me and thus that they came from something else. Having no conception of these things other than that suggested by my sensory ideas, I could only think that the things resembled the ideas. Indeed, since I remembered using my senses before my reason, since I found the ideas that I created in myself to be less explicit than those grasped by sense, and since I found the ideas that I created to be composed largely of those that I had grasped by sense, I easily convinced myself that I didn't understand anything at all unless I had first sensed it.

I also had some reason for supposing that a certain physical object, which I viewed as belonging to me in a special way, was related to me more closely than any other. I couldn't be separated from it as I could from other physical objects; I felt all of my emotions and desires in it

and because of it; and I was aware of pains and pleasant feelings in it but in nothing else. I didn't know why sadness goes with the sensation of pain or why joy goes with sensory stimulation. I didn't know why the stomach twitchings that I call hunger warn me that I need to eat or why dryness in my throat warns me that I need to drink. Seeing no connection between stomach twitchings and the desire to eat or between the sensation of a pain-producing thing and the consequent awareness of sadness, I could only say that I had been taught the connection by nature. And nature seems also to have taught me everything else that I knew about the objects of sensation—for I convinced myself that the sensations came to me in a certain way before having found grounds on which to prove that they did.

But, since then, many experiences have shaken my faith in the senses. Towers that seemed round from a distance sometimes looked square from close up, and huge statues on pediments sometimes didn't look big when seen from the ground. In innumerable such cases, I found the judgments of the external senses to be wrong. And the same holds for the internal senses. What is felt more inwardly than pain? Yet I had heard that people with amputated arms and legs sometimes seem to feel pain in the missing limb, and it therefore didn't seem perfectly certain to me that the limb in which I feel a pain is always the one that hurts. And, to these grounds for doubt, I've recently added two that are very general: First, since I didn't believe myself to sense anything while awake that I couldn't also take myself to sense in a dream, and since I didn't believe that what I sense in sleep comes from objects outside me, I didn't see why I should believe what I sense while awake comes from such objects. Second, since I didn't yet know my creator (or, rather, since I supposed that I didn't know Him), I saw nothing to rule out my having been so designed by nature that I'm deceived even in what seems most obviously true to me.

And I could easily refute the reasoning by which I convinced myself of the reality of sensible things. Since my nature seemed to impel me towards many things which my reason rejected, I didn't believe that I ought to have much faith in nature's teachings. And, while my will didn't control my sense perceptions, I didn't believe it to follow that these perceptions came from outside me, since I thought that the ability to produce these ideas might be in me without my being aware of it.

Now that I've begun to know myself and my creator better, I still believe that I oughtn't blindly to accept everything that I seem to get from the senses. Yet I no longer believe that I ought to call it all into doubt.

In the first place, I know that everything that I clearly and distinctly understand can be made by God to be exactly as I understand it. The fact that I can clearly and distinctly understand one thing apart from another is therefore enough to make me certain that it is distinct from the other, since the things could be separated by God if not by something else. (I judge the things to be distinct regardless of the power needed to make them exist separately.) Accordingly, from the fact that I have gained knowledge of my existence without noticing anything about my nature or essence except that I am a thinking thing, I can rightly conclude that my essence consists solely in the fact that I am a thinking thing. It's possible (or, as I will say later, it's certain) that I have a body which is very tightly bound to me. But, on the one hand, I have a clear and distinct idea of myself insofar as I am just a thinking and unextended thing, and, on the other hand, I have a distinct idea of my body insofar as it is just an extended and unthinking thing. It's certain, then, that I am really distinct from my body and can exist without it.

In addition, I find in myself abilities for special modes of awareness, like the abilities to have mental images and to sense. I can clearly and distinctly conceive of my whole self as something that lacks these abilities, but I can't conceive of the abilities' existing without me, or without an understanding substance in which to reside. Since the conception of these abilities includes the conception of something that understands, I see that these abilities are distinct from me in the way that a thing's properties are distinct from the thing itself.

I recognize other abilities in me, like the ability to move around and to assume various postures. These abilities can't be understood to exist apart from a substance in which they reside any more than the abilities to imagine and sense, and they therefore cannot exist without such a substance. But it's obvious that, if these abilities do exist, the substance in which they reside must be a body or extended substance rather than an understanding one—for the clear and distinct conceptions of these abilities contain extension but not understanding.

There is also in me, however, a passive ability to sense—to receive and recognize ideas of sensible things. But, I wouldn't be able to put this ability to use if there weren't, either in me or in something else, an active power to produce or make sensory ideas. Since this active power doesn't presuppose understanding, and since it often produces ideas in me without my cooperation and even against my will, it cannot exist in me. Therefore, this power must exist in a substance distinct from me. And, for reasons that I've noted, this substance must contain, either formally or eminently, all the reality that is contained subjectively in the ideas that the power produces. Either this substance is a physical object (a thing of bodily nature which contains formally the reality that the idea contains subjectively), or it is God or one of His creations which is higher than a physical object (something which contains this reality eminently). But, since God isn't a deceiver, it's completely obvious that He doesn't send these ideas to me directly or by means of a creation which contains their reality eminently rather than formally. For, since He has not given me any ability to recognize that these ideas are sent by Him or by creations other than physical objects, and since He has given me a strong inclination to believe that the ideas come from physical objects, I see no way to avoid the conclusion that He deceives me if the ideas are sent to me by anything other than physical objects. It follows that physical objects exist. These objects may not exist exactly as I comprehend them by sense; in many ways, sensory comprehension is obscure and confused. But these objects must at least have in them everything that I clearly and distinctly understand them to have—every general property within the scope of pure mathematics.

But what about particular properties, such as the size and shape of the sun? And what about things that I understand less clearly than mathematical properties, like light, sound, and pain? These are open to doubt. But, since God isn't a deceiver, and since I therefore have the God-given ability to correct any falsity that may be in my beliefs, I have high hopes of finding the truth about even these things. There is undoubtedly some truth in everything I have been taught by nature—for, when I use the term "nature" in its general sense, I refer to God Himself or to the order that He has established in the created world, and, when I apply the term specifically to *my* nature, I refer to the collection of everything that God has given *me*.

Nature teaches me nothing more explicitly, however, than that I have a body which is hurt when I feel pain, which needs food or drink when I experience hunger or thirst, and so on. Accordingly, I ought not to doubt that there is some truth to this.

Through sensations like pain, hunger, and thirst, nature also teaches me that I am not present in my body in the way that a sailor is present in his ship. Rather, I am very tightly bound to my body and so "mixed up" with it that we form a single thing. If this weren't so, I—who am just a thinking thing—wouldn't feel pain when my body was injured; I would perceive the injury by pure understanding in the way that a sailor sees the leaks in his ship with his eyes. And, when my body needed food or drink, I would explicitly understand that the need existed without having the confused sensations of hunger and thirst. For the sensations of thirst, hunger, and pain are just confused modifications of thought arising from the union and "mixture" of mind and body.

Also, nature teaches me that there are other physical objects around my body—some that I ought to seek and others that I ought to avoid. From the fact that I sense things like colors, sounds, odors, flavors, temperatures, and hardnesses, I correctly infer that sense perceptions come from physical objects which vary as widely

(though perhaps not in the same way) as the perceptions do. And, from the fact that some of these perceptions are pleasant while others are unpleasant, I infer with certainty that my body—or, rather, my whole self which consists of a body and a mind—can be benefited and harmed by the physical objects around it.

There are many other things which I seem to have been taught by nature but which I have really accepted out of a habit of thoughtless judgment. These things may well be false. Among them are the judgments that a space is empty if nothing in it happens to affect my senses; that a hot physical object has something in it resembling my idea of heat; that a white or green thing has in it the same whiteness or greenness that I sense; that a bitter or sweet thing has in it the same flavor that I taste; that stars, towers, and other physical objects have the same size and shape that they present to my senses; and so on.

If I am to avoid accepting what is indistinct in these cases, I must more carefully explain my use of the phrase "taught by nature." In particular, I should say that I am now using the term "nature" in a narrower sense than when I took it to refer to the whole complex of what God has given me. This complex includes much having to do with my mind alone (such as my grasp of the fact that what is done cannot be undone and of the rest of what I know by the light of nature) which does not bear on what I am now saying. And the complex also includes much having to do with my body alone (such as its tendency to go downwards) with which I am not dealing now. I'm now using the term "nature" to refer only to what God has given me insofar as I am a composite of mind and body. It is this nature which teaches me to avoid that which occasions painful sensations, to seek that which occasions pleasant sensations, and so on. But this nature seems not to teach me to draw conclusions about external objects from sense perceptions without first having examined the matter with my understanding—for true knowledge of external things seems to belong to the mind alone, not to the composite of mind and body.

Thus, while a star has no more effect on my eye than a flame, this does not really produce a positive inclination to believe that the star is as small as the flame; for my youthful judgment about the size of the flame, I had no real grounds. And, while I feel heat when I approach a fire and pain when I draw nearer, I have absolutely no reason for believing that something in the fire resembles the heat, just as I have no reason for believing that something in the fire resembles the pain; I only have reason for believing that there is something or other in the fire which produces the feelings of heat and pain. And, although there may be nothing in a given region of space that affects my senses, it doesn't follow that there aren't any physical objects in that space. Rather I now see that, on these matters and others, I used to pervert the natural order of things. For, while nature has given sense perceptions to my mind for the sole purpose of indicating what is beneficial and what harmful to the composite of which my mind is a part, and while the perceptions are sufficiently clear and distinct for that purpose, I used these perceptions as standards for identifying the essence of physical objects—an essence which they only reveal obscurely and confusedly.

I've already explained how it can be that, despite God's goodness, my judgments can be false. But a new difficulty arises here—one having to do with the things that nature presents to me as desirable or undesirable and also with the errors that I seem to have found in my internal sensations. One of these errors seems to be committed, for example, when a man is fooled by some food's pleasant taste into eating poison hidden in that food. But surely, in this case, what the man's nature impels him to eat is the good tasting food, not the poison of which he knows nothing. We can draw no conclusion except that his nature isn't omniscient, and this conclusion isn't surprising. Since a man is a limited thing, he can only have limited perfections.

Still, we often err in cases in which nature does impel us. This happens, for example, when sick people want food or drink that would quickly harm them. To say that these people err as a result of the corruption of their nature does not solve the problem—for a sick man is no less

a creation of God than a well one, and it seems as absurd to suppose that God has given him a deceptive nature. A clock made of wheels and weights follows the natural laws just as precisely when it is poorly made and inaccurate as when it does everything that its maker wants. Thus, if I regard a human body as a machine made up of bones, nerves, muscles, veins, blood, and skin such that even without a mind it would do just what it does now (except for things that require a mind because they are controlled by the will), it's easy to see that what happens to a sick man is no less "natural" than what happens to a well one. For instance, if a body suffers from dropsy, it has a dry throat of the sort that regularly brings the sensation of thirst to the mind, the dryness disposes the nerves and other organs to drink, and the drinking makes the illness worse. But this is just as natural as when a similar dryness of throat moves a person who is perfectly healthy to take a drink which is beneficial. Bearing in mind my conception of a clock's use, I might say that an inaccurate clock departs from its nature, and, similarly, viewing the machine of the human body as designed for its usual motions, I can say that it drifts away from its nature if it has a dry throat when drinking will not help to maintain it. I should note, however, that the sense in which I am now using the term "nature" differs from that in which I used it before. For, as I have just used the term "nature," the nature of a man (or clock) is something that depends on my thinking of the difference between a sick and a well man (or of the difference between a poorly-made and a well-made clock)—something regarded as extrinsic to the things. But, when I used "nature" before, I referred to something which is *in* things and which therefore has some reality.

It may be that we just offer an extrinsic description of a body suffering from dropsy when, noting that it has a dry throat but doesn't need to drink, we say that its nature is corrupted. Still, the description is not purely extrinsic when we say that a composite or union of mind and body has a corrupted nature. There is a real fault in the composite's nature, for it is thirsty when drinking would be harmful. It therefore remains to be asked why God's goodness doesn't prevent *this* nature's being deceptive.

To begin the answer, I'll note that mind differs importantly from body in that body is by its nature divisible while mind is indivisible. When I think about my mind—or, in other words, about myself insofar as I am just a thinking thing—I can't distinguish any parts in me; I understand myself to be a single, unified thing. Although my whole mind seems united to my whole body, I know that cutting off a foot, arm, or other limb would not take anything away from my mind. The abilities to will, sense, understand, and so on can't be called parts, since it's one and the same mind that wills, senses, and understands. On the other hand, whenever I think of a physical or extended thing, I can mentally divide it, and I therefore understand that the object is divisible. This single fact would be enough to teach me that my mind and my body are distinct, if I hadn't already learned that in another way.

Next, I notice that the mind isn't directly affected by all parts of the body, but only by the brain—or maybe just by the small part of the brain containing the so-called "common sense." Whenever this part of the brain is in a given state, it presents the same thing to the mind, regardless of what is happening in the rest of the body (as is shown by innumerable experiments that I need not review here).

In addition, I notice that the nature of body is such that, if a first part can be moved by a second that is far away, the first part can be moved in exactly the same way by something between the first and second without the second part's being affected. For example, if A, B, C, and D are points on a cord, and if the first point (A) can be moved in a certain way by a pull on the last point (D), then A can be moved in the same way by a pull on one of the middle points (B or C) without D's being moved. Similarly, science teaches me that, when my foot hurts, the sensation of pain is produced by nerves distributed throughout the foot which extend like cords from there to the brain. When pulled in the foot, these nerves pull the central parts of the brain to which

they are attached, moving those parts in ways designated by nature to present the mind with the sensation of a pain "in the foot." But, since these nerves pass through the shins, thighs, hips, back, and neck on their way from foot to brain, it can happen that their being touched in the middle, rather than at the end in the foot, produces the same motion in the brain as when the foot is hurt and, hence, that the mind feels the same pain "in the foot." And the point holds for other sensations as well.

Finally, I notice that, since only one sensation can be produced by a given motion of the part of the brain that directly affects the mind, the best conceivable sensation for it to produce is the one that is most often useful for the maintenance of the healthy man. Experience teaches that all the sensations put in us by nature are of this sort and therefore that everything in our sensations testifies to God's power and goodness. For example, when the nerves in the foot are moved with unusual violence, the motion is communicated through the middle of the spine to the center of the brain, where it signals the mind to sense a pain "in the foot." This urges the mind to view the pain's cause as harmful to the foot and to do what it can to remove that cause. Of course, God could have so designed man's nature that the same motion of the brain presented something else to the mind, like the motion in the brain, or the motion in the foot, or a motion somewhere between the brain and foot. But no alternative to the way things are would be as conducive to the maintenance of the body. Similarly, when we need drink, the throat becomes dry, the dryness moves the nerves of the throat thereby moving the center of the brain, and the brain's movements cause the sensation of thirst in the mind. It's the sensation of thirst that is produced, because no information about our condition is more useful to us than that we need to get something to drink in order to remain healthy. And the same is true in other cases.

This makes it completely obvious that, despite God's immense goodness, the nature of man (whom we now view as a composite of mind and body) cannot fail to be deceptive. For, if something produces the movement usually associated with an injured foot in the nerve running from foot to brain or in the brain itself rather than in the foot, a pain is felt as if "in the foot." Here the senses are deceived by their nature. Since this motion in the brain must always bring the same sensation to mind, and since the motion's cause is something hurting the foot more often than something elsewhere, it's in accordance with reason that the motion always presents the mind a pain in the foot rather than elsewhere. And, if dryness of the throat arises, not (as usual) from drink's being conducive to the body's health, but (as happens in dropsy) from some other cause, it's much better that we are deceived when our bodies are sound. And the same holds for other cases.

In addition to helping me to be aware of the errors to which my nature is subject, these reflections help me readily to correct or avoid those errors. I know that sensory indications of what is good for my body are more often true than false; I can almost always examine a given thing with several senses; and I can also use my memory (which connects the present to the past) and my understanding (which has now examined all the causes of error). Hence, I need no longer fear that what the senses daily show me is unreal. I should reject the exaggerated doubts of the past few days as ridiculous. This is especially true of the chief ground for these doubts—namely, my inability to distinguish dreaming from being awake. For I now notice that dreaming and being awake are importantly different: the events in dreams are not linked by memory to the rest of my life like those that happen while I am awake. If, while I'm awake, someone were suddenly to appear and then immediately to disappear without my seeing where he came from or went to (as happens in dreams), I would justifiably judge that he was not a real man but a ghost—or, better, an apparition created in my brain. But, if I distinctly observe something's source, its place, and the time at which I learn about it, and if I grasp an unbroken connection between it and the rest of my life, I'm quite sure that it is something in my waking life rather than in a dream. And I ought not to have the slightest doubt about the reality of such things if I have examined them with all my senses, my memory, and my understanding without finding any conflicting evidence. For, from the fact that God is not a deceiver, it follows that I am not deceived in any case of this sort. Since the need to act does not always allow time for such a careful examination, however, we must admit the likelihood of men's erring about particular things and acknowledge the weakness of our nature.

Correspondence with Princess Elisabeth, Concerning the Union of Mind and Body

RENÉ DESCARTES

Elisabeth to Descartes

May 6-16, 1643

... ⟨I ASK⟩ YOU TO TELL ME how man's soul, being only a thinking substance, can determine animal spirits so as to cause voluntary actions. For every determination of movement seems to come about either by the propelling of the thing moved, by the manner in which it is propelled by that which moves it, or else by the quality and shape of the surface of the latter. Now contact is required for the first two conditions, and extension for the third. But you exclude extension entirely from the notion you have of the soul, and contact seems to me incompatible with something which is immaterial. Therefore I ask you for a more explicit definition of the soul than you give in your metaphysics, i.e., of its substance, apart from its action, thought. For even if we suppose that soul and thought are, like the attributes of God, inseparable, a thesis difficult enough anyway to establish [for the child] in the mother's womb and in fainting spells, still we can acquire a more perfect idea of them if we consider them separately. . . .

Descartes to Elisabeth

May 21, 1643

. . . [T]he question which your Highness raises seems to me one which can most reasonably be asked as a consequence of my published writings. For there are two aspects of the human soul upon which depends all knowledge we can have of its nature. One of these is that it thinks; the other, that, united to the body, it can act and suffer with the body. I said almost nothing of the latter aspect, for I was interested in expounding the first clearly. My principal objective was to establish the distinction between soul and body, and for that purpose only the first characteristic of the soul was useful, and the other would not have been at all helpful. But since your Highness sees so clearly, that no one can dissemble anything from you, I will try to explain how I conceive the union of the soul with the body, and how the soul has the power to move the body.

First, I hold that there are in us certain primitive notions, which are like the models on whose pattern we form all other knowledge. There are very few of these notions. After the most general—being, number, duration, etc., which apply to all that we could know—we have, specifically for body, only the notion of extension, from which are derived the notions of figure and motion. And for the soul alone, we have only the notion of thought, in which are included the conceptions of the understanding and the incli-

nations of the will. Finally, for soul and body together, we have only the notion of their union, from which are derived our notions of the power which the soul has to move the body, and of the body to act on the soul, to cause feelings and passions.

I believe too that all human knowledge consists in nothing else but in distinguishing these notions clearly and in attributing each of them correctly to the thing to which it applies. For when we want to explain some difficulty by means of a notion which is not appropriate to it, we cannot fail to be mistaken. Similarly we should err if we try to explain one of these notions in terms of another. For they are primitive, and each can be understood only in terms of itself. Now our senses have made the notions of extension, figure, and motion much more familiar than the others. Thus the main cause of our errors is that we ordinarily try to use these notions to explain things to which they are inappropriate, as when we want to use imagination to conceive of the nature of the soul, or, in trying to conceive the manner in which the soul moves the body, we think of it as similar to the way in which a body is moved by another body.

In the *Meditations,* which your Highness has so kindly read, I tried to explain the notions which belong to the soul only, distinguishing them from those which belong only to the body. Consequently the matter that I must next explain is the manner of conceiving those notions which apply to the union of the soul with the body, apart from those which belong only to body or only to the soul. In this regard it seems to me that what I wrote at the end of my *Replies to the Sixth Objections* could well be of use here. For we cannot expect to find these notions anywhere except in our soul, which contains all of them in itself, by its nature, but which does not always adequately distinguish them one from another, nor does it attribute them to the objects to which we should attribute them.

Thus I believe that we have in the past confused the notion of the power by which the soul acts in the body with that by which one body acts in another; and that we have attributed both of these, not to the soul, which we did not yet know, but to the different qualities of body, that is, to gravity, to heat, and to other qualities which we supposed to be real, that is, to have an existence distinct from that of body and therefore to be substances, even though we called them qualities. To conceive them we have sometimes used notions which are in us to know body and sometimes those which are in us to know the soul, according to whether that which we have attributed to them has been material or immaterial. For example, in supposing that gravity is a real quality, of which we have no other knowledge than that it has the power to move the body in which it is toward the center of the earth, we have no difficulty in conceiving how it moves this body nor how it is joined to it. We do not suppose that this occurs by any actual contact of one surface with another, but rather we experience in ourselves that we have a particular notion which enables us to understand this. Yet I hold that we misuse this notion in applying it to gravity (something which is not really distinct from body, as I hope to show in my *Physics*). For this notion has been given us to conceive the manner by which soul moves body. . . .

Elisabeth to Descartes

June 10–20, 1643

I must confess that . . . I find in myself all the causes of error which you mention in your letter, and I am unable to banish them entirely, because the life I am constrained to lead does not permit me enough time at my disposal to acquire a habit of meditation according to your rules. From time to time the interests of my House, which I must not neglect, or the conversations and amusements that I cannot evade, beset my feeble mind so strongly with annoyances and boredom that it becomes, for a long time thereafter, useless for anything else. This will serve, I hope, as an excuse for my stupidity in being unable to understand the idea by which we must judge how the soul (unextended and immaterial) can move the body, in terms of the notion which you previously had of gravity. Nor do I see why this power of moving a body toward the center of the earth,

which you once erroneously attributed to the body under the name of quality, should be likely to convince us that a body can be impelled by something immaterial. It is more likely that the demonstration of a contrary truth ⟨about gravity⟩, which you promise in your *Physics*, would strengthen our belief in the impossibility ⟨of soul moving body⟩; chiefly because our idea ⟨of gravity⟩ (which cannot claim the same perfection and objective reality as that of God) might have been invented out of ignorance of that which really moves these bodies toward the center ⟨of the earth⟩. And since no material cause is present to the senses, we would have attributed it to its opposite, the immaterial. Yet I have never been able to conceive of the immaterial except as a negation of matter with which it can have no communication.

I confess that it would be easier for me to concede matter and extension to the soul, than the capacity to move a body and to be moved, to an immaterial being. For if the first ⟨moving a body⟩ is brought about by ⟨transfer of⟩ information, it would be necessary that the ⟨animal⟩ spirits which cause movements be intelligent. But you do not attribute intelligence to anything corporeal. And even though in your *Meditations on Metaphysics* you show the possibility of the second ⟨body moving soul⟩, it is yet very difficult to understand how a soul, as you have described it, when it has the faculty and habit of reasoning, can lose all that because of some ⟨bodily⟩ vapors. And it is difficult also to understand how the soul, which is able to exist without the body, and has nothing in common with it, yet should be thus governed by the body. . . .

Descartes to Elisabeth

June 28, 1643

Madame,

I am very much obliged to your Highness because, after you have seen that I explained myself badly in my previous letters on the question it pleased you to ask me, you still accord me the patience to listen to me again on the same subject, and that you afford me the occasion to note the things which I omitted. The chief omissions seem to me to be the following. After I distinguished three types of ideas or primitive notions, each of which is known to us individually and not by a comparison of one with another, i.e., the notions we have of the soul, of the body, and that of the union of the soul with the body, I should have explained the differences in these three sorts of notions, and in the operations of the soul by which we come to have these notions, and I should explain the means by which we make each of these easy and familiar to ourselves. I should have explained also why I utilized the comparison with gravity, and I should have made clear that even though we might want to consider the soul as material (which we do when we conceive properly its union with the body) we do not thereby cease to know that it is separable from the body. These are, I think, all the problems that your Highness has set for me to deal with here.

First of all, then, I discern a great difference in these three sorts of notions, in that the soul cannot be conceived other than by the pure understanding; body (that is, extension, figure, and motion) may also be known by the understanding alone, but can be known much better by the understanding when it is aided by imagination. Finally, the notions which apply to the union of soul and body can be known only obscurely by the understanding alone, and no better by the understanding aided by the imagination; but they can be known very clearly by the senses: Hence it follows that those who never philosophize and who use only their senses do not doubt that the soul moves the body and that the body acts on the soul. But they consider the two as a single thing, that is, they consider the union of the two and to consider the union between two things is to consider them as one single thing. Metaphysical thoughts, which exercise only the pure understanding, are of use in rendering the notion of the soul familiar to us. The study of mathematics, which exercises in the main the imagination in the consideration of figures and motions, accustoms us to form very distinct notions of body. But it is by means of ordi-

nary life and conversations and in abstaining from meditation and from studying things which exercise the imagination, that one learns to conceive the union of soul and body.

I'm almost afraid that your Highness may think that I am not speaking seriously here, but that would be contrary to the respect I owe you, and which I shall never fail to pay. And I can say, truthfully, that the chief rule that I have always observed in my studies, and that which I think has been most useful to me in acquiring knowledge, has been that I have devoted only a very few hours each day to thoughts which occupy imagination, and a very few hours each year, to those which occupy the understanding alone, and I have given all the rest of my time to the relaxation of the senses and to the repose of my mind. I count here among the exercises of the imagination all serious conversations and everything to which we must pay attention. It is this which has led me to withdraw to the country. Even though in the busiest city in the world I could have as many hours to myself as I employ now in study, nonetheless I could not employ them so efficiently when my intellect would be tired by the attention that the bustle of life requires.

For that reason I take the liberty of expressing here to your Highness my true appreciation of your ability, among the affairs and cares which are never lacking to those who are at the same time of great mind and of great birth, to find leisure to attend to those meditations which are requisite to understanding fully the distinction between the soul and the body. But I am of the opinion that it was these meditations, rather than the thoughts which require less attention, which cause you to find some obscurity in the notion that we have of their union. It does not seem to me that the human mind is capable of conceiving very distinctly, and at the same time, both the distinction between mind and body, and their union. To do that, it is necessary to conceive them as a single thing and at the same time consider them as two things, which is self-contradictory.

In explaining this matter I assumed that your Highness had reasons which prove the distinction of the mind and body still very much in mind, and I did not at all intend to furnish you with reasons to put them aside, to represent to yourself the notion of the union which everyone experiences in himself without philosophizing; that is to say, that there is a single person who has at the same time a body and a thought which are of such a nature that this thought can move the body and can experience the events which happen to the body. Thus in an earlier letter when I used the comparison of gravity and other qualities which we imagine commonly to be united to bodies just as thought is united to ours, I did not bother much that the comparison was not quite apt, because these qualities are not real in the way that we suppose they are, because I thought that your Highness was already entirely persuaded that the soul is a substance distinct from the body.

But since your Highness remarks that it is easier to attribute matter and extension to soul than to attribute to it the capacity to move a body and to be moved by it, without being material itself, I would ask your Highness to feel free in attributing this matter and extension to the soul, for this is nothing else than to conceive it united to the body. And after having considered this and experienced the union in yourself it will be easy for you to consider that the matter which you have attributed to thought is not thought itself, and that the extension of matter is of a different nature from the extension of thought. For the first ⟨extension of matter⟩ is determined at a certain location, and excludes from that location every other corporeal extension, which the second ⟨extension of thought⟩ does not. Thus your Highness will be able to recover easily the knowledge of the ⟨distinction⟩ of the soul and body, even though she has considered their union.

Finally, although I believe it is quite necessary to have understood, once in one's life, the principles of metaphysics, because it is through them that we receive knowledge of God and of our soul, I believe too that it would be very harmful to devote one's understanding to meditations about these principles, because we cannot attend as well to the functions of imagination and the senses. It is better to be content with retaining in memory and in belief the conclusions that one has at one time drawn, and to employ the rest of the time that one has for study for thoughts in which the understanding acts with the imagination and the senses. . . .

Suggestions for Further Reading

Colin McGinn in *The Character of Mind* (Oxford: Oxford University Press, 1982) provides a concise introduction to the mind-body problem, as does Chapter 4 of *Philosophical Problems and Arguments: An Introduction* by James Cornman and Keith Lehrer (New York: Macmillan, 1982). John Beloff's *The Existence of Mind* (New York: Citadel, 1964) provides an examination of arguments for and against dualism. Don't forget to consult the articles in the *Encyclopedia of Philosophy* dealing with dualism and the mind-body problem. For a classic attack on mind-body dualism see *The Concept of Mind* by Gilbert Ryle (New York: Harper-Collins Publishers, 1949, especially the first chapter. For a classic defense see Curt Ducasse, "In Defense of Dualism," from *Dimensions of Mind*, edited by Sidney Hook (New York: University Press, 1960).

Video

The Mind-Body Problem, (30 minutes, produced by Julian Isaacs, Thinking Allowed Productions, 1988) argues that a materialistic view of mind is not compatible with the latest scientific evidence.

See your Media Services Catalogue for more information.

11.2. You Are an Embodied Self

Descartes's notion that the mind causally interacts with the body (see Section 11.1) has been criticized for a variety of reasons. One has to do with the mysterious nature of the suppposed causality. How can an immaterial substance that is nonspatial cause a material substance (the spatial body) to do anything? Causality requires some sort of contact. But how can this contact take place? This was the worry Princess Elisabeth expressed. It is closely related to the worry many philosophers have about libertarian notions of free will (Section 6.2). Libertarianism posits the self as a free causal agent. One advantage of Descartes's view is that it supports this notion. But problems arise when one tries to specify exactly how the self (mind) is itself not the effect of some other cause and, in addition, how the self can be a causal agent.

Another problem has to do with a physical law called "the conservation of energy." According to this law (well established in current physical theory), the amount of energy in the universe is constant. However, if minds can act on physical bodies, new energy is created every time the mind causes the body to act. So interactionism appears to stand in direct contradiction to known physical laws.

A more recent line of criticism derives from mounting evidence about the brain and how it operates. Many scientists and philosophers now believe that it is only a matter of time until we can explain human behavior in physical terms. The more we learn about the brain and how it works, the more it seems evident that so called "mental" states are totally dependent upon the way the brain functions. If we had never seen a computer and suddenly discovered one, we might suppose that it was operated by some little person inside. But as we learn more about the computer and how it works, we realize that there is no little person or self, inside. The computations it performs are due to a complex mechanical arrangement and a program which provides instructions. So too, the argument goes, is the human brain.

Another recent criticism of Descartes's notion of the self as mind does not focus on the issue of interactionism, but attacks the very idea of the self which underlies the theory of interaction. Cartesian dualism is a refined and sophisticated version of Plato's soul-body dualism. Both types of dualism have been immensely influential in Western culture. In fact, most of us were raised to believe in some kind of dualism. The very way we talk about ourselves, our minds, and our bodies reflects a dualistic viewpoint. We talk and think about our bodies as if they were shells or containers we just happen to inhabit. In other words, being in a body is not a necessary nor essential characteristic of who we are. But imagine a world in which we had no eyes, or ears, no sense of touch or smell or taste. What would such a world be like? "We would be very isolated," you might plausibly respond. Quite so. And isn't Descartes's mind quite isolated as well?

Eve Browning Cole (Professor of philosophy at the University of Minnesota, Duluth) summarizes, in the next selection, a critique of Descartes that stems from feminist philosophy. She argues that Descartes's procedure and his notion of the self pays insufficient attention to the fact that the self is embodied and exists in a network of relations with others. This fault has led to sexism insofar as it has reinforced a masculine notion of the self as autonomous, detached, and dominant over matter.

Reading Questions

1. What are some of the motivations, according to Cole, behind the philosophical discomfort with the physical body?

2. In what sense, according to Cole, is Descartes setting himself an artificial task?

3. Cole claims that if Descartes were working in collaboration with others, he could not easily entertain such radical doubts. Why?

4. What is the main point of the section entitled "The Uncertain Body?"

5. What is meant by "the relational self," and what difference would it have made if Descartes had begun his thought there?

6. In what sense is the concept of a radically isolated subject incoherent?

7. What does it mean to say, "the cartesian ego is quintessentially masculine" and to say "the relational self . . . is more aligned with feminine identity development?" What do you think about these two claims?

8. How is the "appearance obsession" related to Descartes's views about the relationship between mind and body according to Cole?

9. What does Cole mean by the "embodied self?"

10. In light of what Descartes says in his correspondence with Princess Elisabeth about the "union" of the soul and body as a primitive notion, do you think Cole is right when she criticizes Descartes for not sufficiently acknowledging the importance of the fact that the self is embodied? Why or why not?

Body, Mind and Gender

EVE BROWNING COLE

WE HAVE ALREADY had occasion to observe that much of Western philosophy has displayed a definite discomfort with the fact that human minds come in human *bodies,* that consciousness and the thought processes it underlies are embodied in more or less gross matter. It is not very difficult to understand some of the motivations behind this discomfort. For thoughts do not seem to be subject to the same limitations as ordinary physical objects; in imagination, I can accomplish things which seem to transcend the limits of space and time. Vivid memories defy the irrecoverability of the past, seeming to bring to life dead friends, bringing into the present past scenes, meals, and dreams. Dreams themselves are a powerful impetus toward regarding the mind as something more than or different from the physical "container" which it "inhabits" (though we shall soon see reasons to question these terms). And personal identity, the "I" who is the location of my consciousness, stretches back in time to embrace the child I was, the adolescent I became, and the woman I am now, even though in the physical sense I can only claim to be exactly what I now am (the past being no longer present).

Thus there are certain *prima facie* reasons for at least questioning how consciousness, thought, dreams, and identity relate to the physical world. But we will see that quite often philosophers have gone much further than questioning the relationship, to the extent of privileging the mental over the physical, derogating the physical and the human body along with it to a secondary ontological status, counseling efforts to transcend the body in order to apprehend truth, and even regarding the fact that mental events can cause physical events as a miracle performed by God on a daily basis! While this last, far from being a majority view, seems to have been instead a desperate expedient recommended only by one philosopher (Malebranche), it is symptomatic of something having gone badly wrong at the philosophical starting point.

Let us look more closely at the way in which the relation between body and mind, and the status of the body in the grand scheme of things, become problematic for philosophy. As our companion in this inquiry we will choose René Descartes—whose philosophical outlook, especially as represented in the designedly popular work *Meditations on First Philosophy* (published in 1641), proved enormously influential and remains a standard component of introductory studies of Western philosophy today.

Solitary Meditations, Radical Doubts

Descartes's work came at an extremely crucial juncture for Western philosophy. He entered a philosophical milieu still largely dominated by the medieval scholastic tradition, itself based heavily on a theologized and incomplete digestion of the legacy of the ancient Greeks. Studying with the Jesuits at the college of La Flèche, he received a "classical" and rather intellectually conservative education. Descartes made a radical break with this tradition, however, and set institutional philosophy off in a wholly new direction. Seeking to provide a philosophical method which would be accessible to all who possess common sense, providing a set of "rules for the direction of the mind" which would be so simple that "even women" would be able to follow them, his contributions to philosophy were revolutionary and of inestimable worth and influence. His contribution to the topic of this chapter, however, is highly problematic; and the difficulties he bequeathed to subsequent modern Western thought are enormous.

The full title of Descartes's *Meditations* is *Meditations on First Philosophy: In Which the Existence of God and the Distinction Between Mind and Body Are Demonstrated*. This full title is instructive as to how Descartes himself viewed his purpose in the work, which is often read in modern terms as a refutation of skepticism or an essay in foundationalism. By his own description, it is a work of *metaphysics*.

Descartes begins by confessing that he has long been aware that false beliefs have formed a part of his world view, and that a general and total mental "housecleaning" would need to be undertaken, in order to discover which of his views should be retained and which discarded. The procedure for this belief-testing, which he now proposes to undertake (since he is at present free "from every care" and "happily agitated by no passions") is that of *doubting*. He will attempt to cast doubt on each of his present beliefs; only those that survive the doubt ordeal will be retained. Rather than holding up individual beliefs for scrutiny, however, he proposes to address their general bases:

> . . . [I]t will not be requisite that I should examine each [belief] in particular, which would be an endless undertaking; for owing to the fact that the destruction of the foundations of necessity brings with it the downfall of the rest of the edifice, I shall only in the first place attack those principles upon which all my former opinions rested.

This project raises several interesting issues. First, Descartes is firmly committed to a *hierarchical* view of the structure of his belief system. The metaphor of the edifice of opinion, an ordered structure in which there is a top-down organization of architectural form, is an epistemological image to which we return in the next chapter when we discuss images of belief systems, and the power of the metaphors we choose to represent cognition.

But note also the extreme *solitude* of Descartes's project here. He is proposing to take apart and rebuild his entire belief structure in isolation from the rest of the world, and particularly from other human beings. The idea that an epistemological value test could reliably be applied in complete isolation from other knowers, that one's own relations of knowing the world could be tested through demolition and then rebuilt to stringent specifications entirely of one's own devising, is extraordinary. When we consider the contexts in which knowing takes place, in which knowledge is sought and constructed, few of these appear to be ones in which isolation is afforded or even desirable (we might think of archeological digs, science labs, classrooms, reading groups, research institutes, fact-finding missions to other countries, courtrooms, and other typical situations in which knowledge is found and formed in human minds; none is an individual-based project).

Thus Descartes is setting himself an *artificial* kind of task, in the dual sense that his knowledge-seeking environment is atypical and that the envisioned "new and improved" cognitive structure or edifice of opinion will be his *own* individual artifact.

But the solitariness of Descartes's project has also another implication/motivation. Only in radical isolation from the rest of the human social world can Descartes *fully* explore the reliability of his entire belief system. For if he were exploring in collaboration with others, if the meditations he undertakes were the work of a Cartesian task force, he would have to make concessions to the reliability of certain beliefs before the task force could begin its work. He would have to trust that the others were thinkers, perhaps even thinkers on a par with himself; that they were working with him rather than against him, that they could have and work toward a common goal, that their words could be understood, trusted, believed, taken more or less at face value. In other words, the Cartesian project could not motivate total doubt if it were not so solitary. The powerful skeptical doubts which Descartes is about to summon into existence will answer only to the call of an isolated individual human

mental voice. They are creatures of solitude. Descartes's individualistic starting point has lasting and dramatic effects on his total project and its overall outcomes.

The Uncertain Body

As the doubt program progresses, Descartes discards his trust in his senses as a source of reliable belief. Since (he reasons) the senses have deceived him in the past, it is advisable to suspend belief in sensory information for the duration of his meditations until he can uncover some justification for their occasional reliable operations.

But the senses have been the source of his belief that he is an embodied creature, that he exists in or as a physical organism, in addition to being an originator of thoughts. Thus he must suspend his belief in the existence of the embodied Descartes and conceive of himself only as a locus of thoughts and other mental events, possibly not embodied at all, possibly embodied very differently from the way he has always pictured and experienced himself:

> I shall . . . suppose, not that God who is supremely good and the fountain of truth, but some evil genius not less powerful than deceitful, has employed his whole energies in deceiving me; I shall consider that the heavens, the earth, colors, figures, sound, and all the other external things are nought but the illusions and dreams of which this genius has availed himself in order to lay traps for my credulity; I shall consider myself as having no hands, no eyes, no flesh, no blood, nor any senses, yet falsely believing myself to possess all these things; I shall remain obstinately attached to this idea. . . .

Descartes will conceive of "himself" as something independent of his body, and will discover in this incorporeal consciousness the one indubitable truth which will function for him as an Archimedean immovable point, from which his belief structure can be rebuilt. This point is the certain truth of his own existence.

Descartes has effectively divided himself, and his belief structure, into two components: the certain mind, the component in which he will repose confidence at least as to its existence, and the uncertain body, about whose reality he will remain in a state of doubt until complex argumentation proves a limited trustworthiness, a constricted and carefully policed reliability.

Armed with the certainty of his own existence (as an insular node of consciousness which may or may not be embodied), Descartes goes on to demonstrate the existence of God, the fact that God is neither a grand deceiver nor the kind of being who would tolerate such massive deception of his creatures, and finally infers that the senses' urgings toward belief are not in themselves so awfully unreliable after all.

But the body, on Descartes's showing, remains forever only a probability, never a certainty. Since certainty is the Cartesian Holy Grail, this means that the body is irredeemably a second-class citizen in the metaphysical scheme of things. First rank in Descartes's universe is held by "thinking things," nodes of consciousness that can through purely rational processes follow deductive argumentation to absolutely certain conclusions. The body cannot participate in this process with its own humble abilities, here conceived as sensation and perception; it either impedes the rational process or, tamed and disciplined, stands dumbly by and lets knowledge happen. Highest epistemological honors go to the elements of deductive reasoning processes: mathematical laws, logical principles, indubitable truths. These construct the knowable core of the world, and to them in human experience is superadded a "flesh" of more dubious nature: bodies, colors, touches, smells, and the entire organic contents of the universe.

This theme, the privileging of the mental over the physical, does not originate with Descartes by any means. It is familiar to readers of Plato, who describes the relationship of soul to body in vivid terms:

> . . . [W]hen the soul uses the instrumentality of the body for any inquiry, whether through sight or hearing or any other sense—because using the body implies using the senses—it is drawn away by the body into the realm of the variable, and loses its way and becomes confused and dizzy, as though it were fuddled, through contact with things of a similar nature. . . . But when it investigates by itself, it passes into the realm of the pure and everlasting and immortal and changeless. . . . [*Phaedo* 79c-d]

Here the body is cast in the role of a bad companion, bad company for the soul to keep, company that drags it down to its own level and impedes its effective functioning. A nonphysical form of knowing, in which the soul or mind operates "by itself," is much to be preferred.

Two features of this way of discussing the relation of mind to body, common to Plato and Descartes, should be noted. First, it is striking how easily both drop into the mode of thought in which a human being becomes not one but two, and two *different,* kinds of entity. There quickly emerges a kind of logical and metaphysical distance between mind and body, an alienation that provokes disagreement about what to believe, what to seek, how to behave. But secondly, this is not a disagreement among equals. The mind or soul is in Descartes's view the locus of certainty and value, in Plato's view the part of the human composite akin to the "pure" and "divine." Its relationship to the body is to be one of dominance; the body is to be subordinated and ruled.

An individual human being contains within the self, therefore, a fundamental power dialectic in which mind must triumph over body and must trumpet its victory in flourishes of "pure" rationality by means of which its soundness is demonstrated and ratified. Far from being an isolated peculiarity of a small handful of philosophers, moreover, this general dialectic is seen being set up and played out in many theaters of Western culture, from religion to popular morality, from Neoplatonism to existentialism. . . .

Feminist Critiques

We have already noted the extraordinary isolation of Descartes's metaphysical musings; he cuts off not only the instructions of his perceptive faculties, but also the entirety of his human social surroundings, to seek a certainty accessible only to the lone and insular conscious node "I." A feminist critique of Cartesian method might well begin with just this feature of his project.

The Cartesian ego, rather than being the ground for certainty and the Archimedean point which some philosophers have taken it to be, may in fact be the result of a mistaken abstraction. Feminist philosophers such as Caroline Whitbeck and Lorraine Cole have convincingly argued that a preferable starting point for understanding the contents of human consciousness is *the relational self*, the self presented as involved in and importantly constituted by its connectedness to others. Each of us at this moment is connected as it were by invisible threads to an indefinite number of specific other human beings. In some cases, these connections are relatively remote; for example, we are all members of the same species and have biological similarities. Similarity is a relationship; therefore we are all related. Western culture has not tended to place much weight on this species relationship, however, and in some notorious institutions such as chattel slavery the reality of the relationship has been implicitly or explicitly denied. In other cases, the relationships in which we now stand are of deep significance in defining who we are, how we think, and how we act.

Starting with the concept of the relational self would greatly have changed the course of Descartes's meditations. If other persons are not just colorful wallpaper the design of which I contemplate from inside a mental fishbowl but actually part of who I am, then distancing myself from them in thought and supposing that I am the only consciousness in the universe becomes, if not impossible, extremely illogical. What would I hope to accomplish? If on the other hand I begin by granting them mentality and humanity, I will proceed by considering the specific ways in which their contributions to my mental life are made.

Paula Gunn Allen writes that, in Native American cultures, the question "Who is your mother?" is another and more profound way of asking who one is. In asking, one is inquiring about one of the most significant parts of a person's identity, for the influence of the mother and the mother's contribution to the child's self is considerable. In much the same way, we might begin a metaphysics of the self by asking "To whom am I related? In what ways? What contributions to my consciousness are presently being made, and by whom?" Such a beginning acknowledges the fundamental importance of sociality in human existence.

Here it might be objected that Descartes's . . . methodological skepticism about the existence and reality of other minds remains a possible position even for a relational self. Haven't we merely sidestepped the skeptical possibility by granting the mentality and humanity of the others? Doesn't it really still seem possible that they are all phantasms, or robots, or results of direct C-fiber stimulation by a mad scientist on a distant planet?

Yes, skeptical possibilities remain and cannot be ruled out. But taking the standpoint of the relational self allows us to affirm that such possibilities *do not matter*. What matters is that relationships are granted metaphysical priority over isolated individuals, so that the embeddedness of the self in a social world becomes its primary reality. The exact nature of the individuals involved becomes a matter of secondary importance. I grant at the outset that others make constitutive contributions to my experience, and I to theirs. This mutual interrelation becomes the ground for any further inquiry rather than functioning as a more or less uncertain inductive conclusion. Thus, to return to the problem of other minds, we can see that the philosopher's uncertainty about the mentality of the "foreign body" at the bus stop is a symptom of a flawed starting point rather than a genuine puzzle attending our reflective lives. The philosopher's mistake is to begin from isolation and attempt to reason himself back into society; we in fact begin in society and this is not an accidental but a deep truth about us.

We might go even further and argue that the concept of a radically isolated subject as the seat of consciousness is simply incoherent. We do not begin to think and speak in solitude, but in concert with our culture and with the specific representatives of the culture in whose care we find ourselves. We form ourselves in a collective process that is ongoing; our thoughts are never entirely our own, intersubjectivity is basic, while individual subjectivity is secondary and an abstraction.

Some feminist philosophers have analyzed the isolation of the ego and the "fishbowl" syndrome of some philosophy of mind in terms of differences between masculine and feminine gender socialization. Developmental psychologists have suggested that the structure and dynamics of relationships with other human beings differ profoundly for traditionally socialized men and women. Due largely to the fact that, in most cultures and historical epochs, women function as the primary caregiver for children of both sexes while men enter into the life of the family in a more intermittent way, it is to be expected that male children will form their earliest sense of themselves by *distinguishing* themselves from their female caregiver, realizing that they are members of the group from which the (distant, absent, or intermittently present) male family members derive. Female children will form their sense of themselves by *identifying* with the female caregiver, realizing that they share with her membership in the group of female family members.

This early direction of the sense of self, either to distinguish oneself and differ from, or to identify oneself and resemble, leaves a lasting legacy in the child's heart and mind. The adult character which emerges from the socialization process is marked by the tendency toward either clear and stark ego boundaries (if male) or flexible and mobile ego boundaries (if female). A whole constellation of dispositions and traits goes alongside this basic distinction. The masculine ego, formed at a distance from its primary role exemplar, displays a lifelong tendency toward independence, distancing from others, and endless acts of "proving" the masculinity which it modeled, with some uncertainty, on the distant fellow *man*. The feminine ego, formed in close proximity to its primary role exemplar, has life-long tendencies toward identifying with others, reciprocating feelings, being dependent on others and relating to them easily even confusing its own needs with those of others—since it early on perceived that part of being a woman was to place others first, as a primary caregiver must frequently do.

This developmental thesis about gender identity, though impossible to demonstrate empirically and almost certainty *not* crossculturally or crossracially, offers a tempting explanation for the philosophical model of the isolated self we have traced in Descartes and seen lurking behind the problem of other minds. The Cartesian ego is quintessentially *masculine* in its solitary doubting program, in its self-confidence about its quest, in its ambition ("proving" itself all on its own resources), and in its uneasiness. . . .

By contrast, the relational self which some feminist philosophers have proposed as an alternative starting point for philosophy of mind, and for grounding our understanding of human experience generally, is more aligned with feminine identity development.

In addition to proposing that philosophers start from a conception of the human self as relational, as situated within a web of cultural and personal relationships which not only shape but do much to constitute its being and its thought, feminist philosophers have also criticized the Cartesian legacy for the relation between mind and body which it conveys.

We saw above that Descartes (and others) operate from a position that separates mind, self, consciousness, ego from the physical body these are said to "inhabit" or . . . "animate." In Descartes, the distinction is so drastic that mind and body are said to share no attributes whatsoever; they are oppositionally defined and thus, metaphysically speaking, mutually exclusive. Consciousness is nonphysical, nonextended, and inhabits an order of being completely distinct from that in which the body lives. The body is a machine, operated by the mind in the case of the human being, mindless and purely mechanical in the case of other animals.

This drastic dualism is vulnerable to criticism

from many different directions; feminist critics begin with the observation that in Western culture and throughout its history, we can observe a tendency to identity women with the natural, the physical, the bodily. Nature is personified as a female, a "mother"; women are portrayed as more closely linked to nature, less completely integrated into civilization and the cultural order, than men. Men are rational agents, makers of order and measure, controllers of history; women are emotional vessels, subjects of orders and measures, passive observers of history. No one describes this more clearly or more influentially for modern psychology than Sigmund Freud, who writes:

> The fact that women must be regarded as having little sense of justice is no doubt related to the predominance of envy in their mental life; for the demand for justice is a modification of envy and lays down the condition subject to which we can lay envy aside. We also regard women as weaker in their social interests and as having less capacity for sublimating their instincts than men.

Freud subsumes women into the domain of the natural, where instinct rules and justice is foreign.

Now, if man is to mind as woman is to body, as appears from much of the literature and iconography of Western culture throughout historical time, and if we adhere to a generally Cartesian view of the self as a purely mental entity, then the self of the woman becomes deeply problematic. Can women have Cartesian egos? Genuine selves? It would appear to be impossible if woman's essence is located in the domain of the bodily. Clearly some other and less dichotomously dualistic conception of the self must be sought.

The associations between woman and body in Western culture have had a decidedly negative aspect, which feminist critics have stressed. The reduction of a woman's value to the culturally inscribed value of a certain feminine appearance and protest against that reduction have been strong themes of feminist criticism for several decades. Nevertheless, the appearance obsession which women are encouraged to develop in our culture, according to which a more-or-less single standard of feminine beauty applies to all women, no matter their age, race, build, or life-style, is as strong as ever and, some argue, gaining strength. In addition now to being slim, youthful, cosmetically adorned to the correct degree, fashionably dressed, and as light-skinned as possible (with of course a healthy tan to indicate white-skinned class-privilege), women must ideally have "hard bodies" with muscle-definition acquired by hours of grueling workouts and aerobic routines. That this formula cannot be met by the poor, those who don't have the time to devote to the pursuit of beauty, or those whose bodies resist the mold for whatever reason, does not mean that the standard does not hold its pristine severity over all women's heads equally. (Sadly, the appearance obsession does seem to be extending to men as well, but still seems to pertain to them in lesser degree.)

In a recent classroom discussion of trends in advertising, one young female student spoke out with sincere enthusiasm: "I can't wait till I get older! I'm going to eat whatever I want, wear whatever I want, and just not care!" An older female student turned to her and said, "Why wait? It isn't any easier to look different at age fifty than at age twenty." This exchange was instructive in many ways. There was anger in the second woman's voice; she heard herself as older being dismissed somehow from the class of viable potential beauties. There was a strange assumption behind the first woman's statements, to the effect that until some unspecified age, women are under an obligation to eat and to dress in ways other than those they would choose if not constrained. And there was in the second speaker's choice of the word *different* to describe an undisciplined woman the implicit admission that the *norm,* what it means to be *non*different, is precisely the cultural ideal of the dieting and carefully dressed youthful appearance. But this is clearly false, as a simple glance at the immense variety of actual women's bodies in any real-life situation will immediately confirm. The so-called *norm* is in fact extremely rare. Yet an enormous amount of women's energy is devoted to its pursuit. Constant dieting, eating disorders such as anorexia and bulimia, compulsive exercising, and (not least of all) enormous cash investments in beauty and fashion, are all symptomatic of the power of the cultural ideal.

To connect with our previous discussion of the gendered distinction between mind and body, men generally do not in our culture tend to identify themselves and their worth as persons with the details of their physical bodies' appearances. While in recent years the standards of male attractiveness have undoubtedly become more exacting, men clearly feel more relaxed about not meeting these standards.

Let us summarize the contribution which the dualistic Platonic-Cartesian model of the self has made to our cultural conceptions of body and mind: (1) The body's relationship to the mind, in any given human being, is one of unruly bondage or servitude; mind properly dominates its body and directs its actions, while body properly obeys. (2) Mind's behavior and dispositions are, however, described in terms more appropriate to masculine gender identity (activity, ruling or hegemony, capacity for abstraction and objectivity, distanced contemplation, dispassionate analysis), while body's configurations tend toward feminine (passivity, subordination, unconscious physicality, sensuous and emotional implication, confusion). (3) Thus, while rationality becomes defined as a mostly masculine project, an adorned and disciplined physicality becomes the feminist project—leading to the contemporary obsession of middle-class women with weight and appearance generally. Women are given the cultural prescription to be docile bodies, adorned and available for participation in the rational schemes of the male-dominated social order. Thus the fact that in some basic respects the Cartesian ego is a masculine ego can be seen to have enormous reverberations throughout modern life. It is of no small significance to recognize that a certain outlook in the philosophy of mind provides a perfect recipe for male dominance and women's subordination.

Several important qualifications need to be made here, however. First, the neat gender di-

chotomy we have drawn in the ratio of proportion:

Male:Mind::Female:Body

does not appear to hold cross-racially. That is, nonwhite males in a white-dominated culture will be treated in much the same way as bodies are treated by minds in the Cartesian framework: They will be dominated, ruled, directed, used. Furthermore, white females will participate in this domination and rule, functioning as "minds" in a bureaucratic manner; and white women will benefit from skin privilege at the expense of the dominated nonwhite men and women. The nonwhite populations will be accorded *mental* attributes that correspond to the physical attributes of the body in the Cartesian scheme; they will be considered less than fully rational, emotional, "natural" or savage, sensuous, weak-willed, and so forth. So the factor of race does much to complicate a mind-body value map which takes *only* gender into account. This has led some feminist philosophers to hypothesize that *both* sexism and racism are more about power than they are about either sex or race.

A second qualification concerns the relationship between what, for want of a clearer word, we could call ideology and social reality. The rational man and the physical woman, intellectual masculinity and corporeal femininity, are creatures of ideology. This means that they are intensely value-laden concepts structuring culture and its expectations, rather than empirical generalizations drawn from observation of real women and real men. But ideology and reality touch one another at multiple points and reciprocally influence each other at these points of contact. It may be a strange-sounding philosophical thesis that rationality has been interpreted in terms defined as masculine, but it takes on a gruesomely real shape when a Berkeley philosophy professor announces to his classes that women can't do logic, or when another philosophy professor writes to the secretary of the American Philosophical Association that white women and black people of both sexes display analytical capabilities inferior to those of white men. This is ideology shaping social reality with a vengeance.

Believing that the drastic dualism of the traditional picture of body's relation to mind, along with the inbuilt evaluatively hierarchical model of dominance and subordination which gives the model its working directives, are both deeply flawed, feminist philosophers look for alternatives.

A beginning point is to conceive of the human self as intrinsically embodied: An *embodied self* can displace the only questionably embodied Cartesian ego, the uncomfortably body-trapped Platonic soul, as a foundation for further inquiry into the nature of human experience. To conceive of the self as essentially or intrinsically embodied means to acknowledge the centrality of the physical in human psychology and cognition, for one thing. It means opening the door to the possibility of a bodily wisdom, to revaluing the physical human being, in ways that promise both better metaphysical schemes and more ethical models for human interaction. Breaking down the valuational hierarchy between mind and body, attempting to think of them as woven and melded together into what constitutes who we are and who we ought to be, eliminates the perhaps primary internal oppression model of mind over body. As a culture, however, we have learned to think of the body, and of those primarily identified with it, in terms of scorn (even when those latter people are ourselves). We have learned to privilege the "rational" over the emotional (conceived as proceeding from physical sources), the basely corporeal, the manual and

tactile; to weigh technorationality over the mute testimony of nature and our own bodies. Those of us who are women have at times been encouraged to view our bodies with contempt when we perceive them as falling short of the beauty ideal or when we are addressed rudely in sexual terms by strangers. How can we begin to approach the relation of mind and body not as a *problem* but as a source of liberatory insight and joy?

French feminist philosophers, building on their national intellectual tradition, which placed the phenomenology of *lived experience* at center stage, have made exciting progress in constructing the basis for a liberatory philosophy of the body. They have argued that the dominant tradition in Western philosophy has made women's bodies problematic in two contradictory ways: In one way, woman and body are equated as essentially physical, and women's entire personalities become sexualized (think of the late Victorian habit of referring to women as a group with the phrase "the sex," as if men were "the nonsex"). In another direction, however, the sexualized woman is either ignored in philosophy, so complete is her subsumption under the rubric *Nature,* or she is philosophized about in male terms, and her (now highlighted in neon) sexuality is described in terms appropriate only to a certain specific cultural construction of *male* sexuality. She is thus obscured as a subject, discussed as an object.

This means that, for a genuinely liberatory philosophy of the body to be developed, women must reclaim in theory and in practice their own physicality, their own sexuality. . . .

Suggestions for Further Reading

Susan Bordo, *The Flight to Objectivity: Essays on Cartesianism and Culture* (Albany: SUNY Press, 1987) develops in more detail some of the ideas summarized here. Also see Lynda Lange, "Sexist Dualism: Its Material Sources in the Exploitation of Reproductive Labor," *Praxis International,* Volume 9 (1990), 400–407. Rosemary Radford Ruether has developed this line of criticism from a theological perspective in "Body-Soul and Subject-Object Dualism as the Model of Oppression" in *Liberation Theology: Human Hope Confronts Christian History and American Power* (New York: Paulist Press, 1972). Also Caroline Whitbeck develops a nondualistic viewpoint from a feminist perspective in "A Different Reality: Feminist Ontology" in *Women, Knowledge, and Reality: Explorations in Feminist Philosophy,* edited by Ann Garry and Marilyn Pearsall (Boston: Unwin Hyman, 1989). See *The Nature of the Self* by Risieri Frondizi

(Carbondale, Ill.: Southern Illinois University Press, 1953) for a critique of Descartes and the development of a relational and functionalistic view of the self.

11.3. There Is No Self

Buddhism developed in India around 500 B.C.E. (see Section 2.1) and quickly came into conflict with some of the basic ideas of Hindu philosophy. Among the areas of conflict was the issue of the existence of the self. Hinduism and Buddhism gave very different answers to the question, "Who am I?" Some Hindu philosophers answered, "You are the *Atman*," (for a discussion of the *Atman* see Section 7.3) and Buddhism responded with the assertion, "There is no *Atman*." This is called **anatta** (also *An-atman)* or the no-self doctrine.

In order to understand this teaching, we must back up a moment to another Buddhist teaching called **anicca** or impermanence. The doctrine of impermanence is a logical implication of the doctrine of dependent origination. If everything that exists is dependent on something else for its existence, (as the thesis of dependent origination holds) there can be no independently existing things. This amounts to a denial of the existence of substances since substances are usually thought of as independently existing things. And it is quite clear that some Indian philosophers regarded the *Atman* as an independently existing thing (for example, see Shankara in Section 7.3). The *Atman* is eternal and permanent.

If there are no substances and if everything is impermanent, it follows that what exists is in constant process. In contrast to Plato's essentialist metaphysics (Section 7.2), Buddhism teaches a process view of reality. There are no Forms or Essences, only ever-changing processes. Hence, according to Buddhist thought, we are wrong if we think of the *jiva* (individual soul or ego) as a permanent substance the way Plato did, or if we think of the *Atman* (Self) as a permanent substance the way some Hindu thinkers did. There is no soul, no ego, no Self, if we mean by any of those terms some independently existing substance or essence.

Please note that Buddhists are not denying that you or I exist. They are only denying a particular philosophical view about our natures, the view that the word "I" refers to some unchanging substance called the Self or soul. According to Buddhist philosophy, humans are made up of what they call the **"five aggregates."** These consist of physical form, sensation, conceptualization, dispositions to act, and consciousness. There is no substance over and above these aggregates.

"What," I hear you say, "I am nothing but a collection of elements! How disappointing." It seems so to those of us raised with the idea that what is most important about us is our souls. If we have no souls, then we have no value, or so our culture has taught us. But our cultural conditioning in this regard may blind us to the value of the Buddhist concept of **anatta.**

The no-self teaching had particular moral and religious value for Buddhism because once we are clear about the fact that there is no substantial self, we can be released from suffering and motivated to act with compassion. Suffering and selfishness arise from desiring things and clinging to them. But if there is no self, then selfish desiring and clinging amount to one vast illusion, a dream from which those who know the truth about the self can awake. However, to know the truth requires experiential knowledge based on meditation, not intellectual knowledge based on reading or thinking. What appears at first glance to be a negative doctrine becomes positive once its moral and religious implications are understood.

But what does all of this have to do with the mind/body problem? Unlike Western concerns, the problem that concerns Buddhists is how to overcome suffering. So the question, "Who am I?" inevitably leads them down a different path. Even so, it is interesting to note that of the five aggregates, all but the first one refer to what Western philosophers would call mental events. The mind-body problem can be stated in Buddhist terms, but it is not a problem about how two totally different substances can causally interact. Rather, it is a problem about how differing processes can causally affect each other. Since both mental processes and physical processes are dependent on each other, the sharp separation of totally different substances characteristic of dualism does not enter the picture. This does not mean that Buddhist philosophers faced no problems in working out the details of how the aggregates might be related, but the dualist and substantialist assumptions so characteristic of the mind-body problem in the West did not shape the problem for them.

Nevertheless, the Buddhist thesis of no-self is not without its parallels in the West. According to C. D. Broad (see his *The Mind and Its Place in Nature* published by Littlefield, Adams, 1960, p. 558) two theories about the self developed in Western philosophy. One he calls the Center theory. According to this theory, the unity of the mind is constituted by a center which is not identical with any of one's thoughts, feelings, or sensations, but thoughts, feelings, and sensations can be characterized as states of this center. This center or self, is thought of by Descartes as an immaterial substance. The other theory can be called either the Non-Center theory or the Bundle theory. According to this theory, there is no center (self) over and above mental events. All we are is a bundle of mental events, and our unity consists in the fact that these mental events are interrelated in certain characteristic ways. David Hume (Section 8.3) is often interpreted as holding the Bundle theory. According to Hume, when he examines his mental life, all he ever finds are a series of thoughts, feelings, and sensations. Hard as he looks, he can find no self or soul above and beyond his changing mental events. The self or soul is a fiction we construct in order to characterize the unity we feel binds these bundles together.

It is tempting to characterize the Buddhist idea of the no-self and the five aggregates as yet another version of the Bundle or Non-Center theory. And indeed it does seem to be related insofar as it denies there is a substantive, immaterial center of consciousness which has mental states but is not identical with such states. However, there is also a difference, at least a difference with the way Hume articulates the Bundle theory. The bundle Hume is concerned with is a purely mental bundle of thoughts, feelings, and sensations. The five aggregates the Buddhists speak of include more than this. We are not just a unified bundle of mental events, but a unified aggregate which includes our physical bodies as well.

I think it would be a mistake to attempt to interpret the no-self theory (at least as it is presented in the following selections) as yet another theory (like the Bundle theory) of the self. This so-called "theory" is not really a theory of the self, but a critique of the substantive theory. Its intention is not to create a new theory, but to show what is wrong with existing theories.

The first selection below comes from the *Digha Nikaya* and is attributed to the Buddha himself. It deals with teachings about the permanence and existence of the soul found in Hindu philosophy. Buddhist monks found themselves in debate with Hindus on these issues, and this selection instructs them on how they can argue with their opponents and thereby show their opponents' views about the soul to be false. It is the classic expression of the sorts of arguments refined and elaborated in latter Buddhism. Note that this selection ends with a statement about the afterlife. Clearly one advantage of the doctrine that there is a soul, is that one can explain life after death and reincarnation in terms of this soul persisting after the death of the body. But if there is no soul, what, if anything persists?

The second selection is the famous simile of the chariot found in the *Milindapanha*. It would seem that if there is no soul, then all kinds of absurd things follow. King Menander, a Greek who ruled northwestern India in the second century B.C.E., is quick to point out these absurdities when the Buddhist monk Nagasena denies that his personal name refers to a permanent individual substance. Nagasena counter-argues, using the King's own logic and the example of a chariot to show that the King himself believes there is no chariot above and beyond its parts, yet sees no problem in using the term "chariot" as a practical designation. So too is the word "I." It is just a convenient way of talking, a mere sound, without any reference to something substantial.

Reading Questions

1. What is wrong with maintaining that the soul is sentient (conscious)?
2. What is wrong with maintaining that the soul is not sentient?
3. What is wrong with maintaining that consciousness or sentience is a property or characteristic of the soul?
4. Since the notion of the soul and of surviving death are closely related, what must a Buddhist monk who rejects these theories of the soul believe about a perfected being who has died?
5. How does King Menander argue against Nagasena's assertion that the name "Nagasena" is only a practical designation and does not refer to any permanent individual?
6. How does Nagasena counter the King's argument?
7. Who do you think wins this debate, Nagasena or King Menander? Why?
8. What unanswered questions do these readings leave you with? Can you figure out how to answer them?

False Doctrines About the Soul and the Simile of the Chariot

False Doctrines About the Soul

AGAIN THE SOUL MAY BE thought of as sentient or insentient, or as neither one nor the other but having sentience as a property. If someone affirms that his soul is sentient you should ask, "Sentience is of three kinds; happy, sorrowful, and neutral. Which of these is your

From The Buddhist Tradition in India, China and Japan, *edited by Wm. Theodore De Bary. Copyright © 1969 by Wm. Theodore De Bary. Reprinted by permission of The Modern Library, a Division of Random House, Inc., pp. 20–23.*

soul?" For when you feel one sensation you don't feel the others. Moreover these sensations are impermanent, dependent on conditions, resulting from a cause or causes, perishable, transitory, vanishing, ceasing. If one experiences a happy sensation and thinks "This is my soul," when the happy sensation ceases he will think "My soul has departed." One who thinks thus looks on his soul as something impermanent in this life, a blend of happiness and sorrow with a beginning and end, and so this proposition is not acceptable.

If someone affirms that the soul is not sentient, you should ask, "If you have no sensation, can you say that you exist?" He cannot, and so this proposition is not acceptable.

And if someone affirms that the soul has sentience as a property you should ask, "If all sensations of every kind were to cease absolutely there would be no feelings whatever. Could you then say 'I exist'?" He could not, and so this proposition is not acceptable.

When a monk does not look on the soul as coming under any of these three categories . . . he refrains from such views and clings to nothing in the world; and not clinging he does not tremble, and not trembling he attains Nirvāna. He knows that rebirth is at an end, that his goal is reached, that he has accomplished what he set out to do, and that after this present world there is no other for him. It would be absurd to say of such a monk, with his heart set free, that he believes that the perfected being survives after death—or indeed that he does not survive, or that he does and yet does not, or that he neither does nor does not. Because the monk is free his state transcends all expression, predication, communication, and knowledge.

[From *Dīgha Nikāya*, pp. 2.64 ff]

The Simile of the Chariot

THEN KING MENANDER went up to the Venerable Nāgasena, greeted him respectfully, and sat down. Nāgasena replied to the greeting, and the King was pleased at heart. Then King Menander asked: "How is your reverence known, and what is your name?"

"I'm known as Nāgasena, your Majesty, that's what my fellow monks call me. But though my parents may have given me such a name . . . it's only a generally understood term, a practical designation. There is no question of a permanent individual implied in the use of the word."

"Listen, you five hundred Greeks and eighty thousand monks!" said King Menander. "This Nāgasena has just declared that there's no permanent individuality implied in his name!" Then, turning to Nāgasena, "If, Reverend Nāgasena, there is no permanent individuality, who gives you monks your robes and food, lodging and medicines? And who makes use of them? Who lives a life of righteousness, meditates, and reaches Nirvāna? Who destroys living beings, steals, fornicates, tells lies, or drinks spirits? . . . If what you say is true there's neither merit nor demerit, and no fruit or result of good or evil deeds. If someone were to kill you there would be no question of murder. And there would be no masters or teachers in the [Buddhist] Order and no ordinations. If your fellow monks call you Nāgasena, what then is Nāgasena? Would you say that your hair is Nāgasena?" "No, your Majesty."

"Or your nails, teeth, skin, or other parts of your body, or the outward form, or sensation, or perception, or the psychic constructions, or consciousness? Are any of these Nāgasena?" "No, your Majesty."

"Then are all these taken together Nāgasena?" "No, your Majesty."

"Or anything other than they?" "No, your Majesty."

"Then for all my asking I find no Nāgasena. Nāgasena is a mere sound! Surely what your Reverence has said is false!"

Then the Venerable Nāgasena addressed the King.

"Your Majesty, how did you come here—on foot, or in a vehicle?"

"In a chariot."

"Then tell me what is the chariot? Is the pole the chariot?" "No, your Reverence."

"Or the axle, wheels, frame, reins, yoke, spokes, or goad?" "None of these things is the chariot."

"Then all these separate parts taken together are the chariot?" "No, your Reverence."

"Then is the chariot something other than the separate parts?" "No, your Reverence."

"Then for all my asking, your Majesty, I can find no chariot. The chariot is a mere sound. What then is the chariot? Surely what your Majesty has said is false! There is no chariot! . . ."

When he had spoken the five hundred Greeks cried "Well done!" and said to the King, "Now, your Majesty, get out of that dilemma if you can!"

"What I said was not false," replied the King. "It's on account of all these various components, the pole, axle, wheels, and so on, that the vehicle is called a chariot. It's just a generally understood term, a practical designation."

"Well said, your Majesty! You know what the word 'chariot' means! And it's just the same with me. It's on account of the various components of my being that I'm known by the generally understood term, the practical designation Nāgasena."

[From *Milindapañha* (Trenckner ed.), pp. 25f.]

Suggestions for Further Reading

Chapter 12 on "The Nature of the Self" in John Koller's *Oriental Philosophies,* 2d ed., clearly explains the various views developed in later Buddhism and provides a good bibliography. A more detailed study is Paul J. Griffiths's *On Being Mindless: Buddhist Meditation and the Mind-Body Problem* (La Salle, IL: Open Court, 1986). The concluding chapter provides a concise summary of the major philosophical issues. See also Chapters 2 and 6 of Walpola Rahula's *What the Buddha Taught* (New York: Grove, 1959); and Joaquin Perez-Remon's *Self and Non-Self in Early Buddhism* (The Hague: Mouton, 1980); and Steven Collens's *Selfless Persons: Imagery and Thought in Theravada Buddhism* (London: Cambridge University Press, 1982). See "The No-Self Theory: Hume, Buddhism, and Personal Identity," *Philosophy East and West: A Quarterly of Comparative Philosophy,* Vol. 43, April 1993, 175–200, for a presentation of the view that the no-self theory is not a new theory of the self analogous to reductionism or versions of the Bundle theory.

Video

See *Mind as a Myth* (30 minutes, J. Krishnamurti, Thinking Allowed Productions), in which Krishnamurti argues, in Buddhist fashion, that the notion of the mind or self existing as an entity apart from our thoughts about it is mistaken.

See your Media Services Catalogue for more information.

11.4. You Are Not a Machine

Have you ever wondered whether computers can think? Of course, they can think in the sense that they can process information. But I mean really think, that is, can they be conscious? If they can, perhaps our brains are like complex computers, vastly intricate machines which can process information in such a way that consciousness is the result.

As I pointed out in the introduction to this chapter, one set of answers to the mind-body problem is called "monism" because it denies that humans are made up of two radically different things, minds and bodies. One version of monism, usually called "materialism" or "physicalism" claims that only bodies (matter) exist. The problem this answer must explain is why we have a conscious, mental life (thoughts, feelings, sensations) that appears to be nonphysical in nature. In attempting to solve this problem, various kinds of physicalistic theories have been proposed. I briefly mentioned the identity theory in the introduction. According to this theory, mental states are identical with brain states. When we think a certain kind of thought or dream a certain sort of dream, certain sorts of physical events are happening in various parts of our brain, which can be observed and studied by science (see Section 7.5 for one version of the identity theory). One problem with this theory is that mental states seem to have characteristics different from physical states. For one thing they are private while physical states are publically observable. For another, it appears unlikely that the same kind of brain state accompanies the same kind of thought or sensation. For example, I feel pain and you feel pain and the other day, Peanut, my fat blind cat, also felt pain when I accidently stepped on his tail. Now my brain and yours may be sufficiently alike so that our brain states might also be sufficiently alike. But the brain of my cat, and indeed the brains of many other animals are quite different and it seems unlikely that even though we might have similar mental states (e.g., feeling pain) we would have identical brain states. Also, for two things to be identical they must have identical properties. A brain state, being physical, is located in space. But where in space is my feeling of being sorry that I stepped on my cat's tail? Is it possible for a brain scientist to observe some kind of electrical event in my brain (a brain state) and read my thoughts? When I see Arthur the dog chasing Peanut the cat can some scientist looking at my brain activity see the same thing? Hardly!

Identity theorists have their answers to these sorts of questions, but these kinds of problems with the identity theory have led other materialists to develop a different sort of theory, a theory called **functionalism.**

According to this theory, the brain operates like a computer. Computers process information according to a program or set of instructions. The result is a visual image on a monitor. So too, the brain. It processes information according to a program or set of instructions, and the result is what we call mental states—thoughts, feelings, sensations, and so on. The set of instructions is called "software" in contrast to the "hardware" of the computer (the wiring in the computer which allows it to receive the software instructions and process information accordingly).

John Searle is Professor of Philosophy at the University of California, Berkeley. In the following selection, taken from the 1984 Reith Lectures, Searle argues that machines cannot think (be conscious) and thus, by implication, that functionalistic theories of mind fail. He offers what has become a classic example of a "thought" experiment in the field, the Chinese Room, in order to show that no matter how complex and sophisticated digital computers may become, they will never be able to produce consciousness and hence the human brain must be significantly unlike a computer since the brain can cause consciousness.

Central to Searle's argument is a distinction between syntax (the grammatical rules which govern the arrangement of words in a sentence) and semantics (the meaning a sentence has). Computers manipulate symbols according to syntax (a set of rules for their arrangement), but it does not follow that computers are aware of the meaning (semantics) of those symbols. If I only knew the syntax of Chinese, but not the semantics, could I be said to know Chinese?

Reading Questions

1. According to Searle, what causes mental processes?
2. According to Searle, what is the "strong artificial intelligence (AI)" view?
3. What is one consequence of the strong AI view?
4. Why is Searle's refutation of the strong AI view independent of developments in computer technology?
5. What does Searle mean when he says, "The mind is more than a syntax, it has a semantic?"
6. What is the point of Searle's example of the Chinese Room?
7. Describe the two types of response Searle has received to his argument and his counter-response.
8. What four conclusions does Searle draw and what are the premises on which they are based?
9. Has Searle made his case to your satisfaction, that is, has he proved to you that digital computers are, in principle, unable to think or have a mind like a human mind? Why or why not?

Can Computers Think?

JOHN SEARLE

. . . THOUGH WE DO NOT KNOW in detail how the brain functions, we do know enough to have an idea of the general relationships between brain processes and mental processes. Mental processes are caused by the behavior of elements of the brain. At the same time, they are realized in the structure that is made up of those elements. I think this answer is consistent with the standard biological approaches to biological phenomena. Indeed, it is a kind of commonsense answer to the question, given what we know about how the world works. However, it is very much a minority point of view. The prevailing view in philosophy, psychology, and artificial intelligence is one which emphasizes the analogies between the functioning of the human brain and the functioning of digital computers. According to the most extreme version of this view, the brain is just a digital computer and the mind is just a computer program. One could summarize this view—I call it "strong artificial intelligence," or "strong AI"—by saying that the mind is to the brain, as the program is to the computer hardware.

This view has the consequence that there is nothing essentially biological about the human mind. The brain just happens to be one of an indefinitely large number of different kinds of hardware computers that could sustain the programs which make up human intelligence. On this view, any physical system whatever that had the right program with the right inputs and outputs would have a mind in exactly the same sense that you and I have minds. So, for example, if you made a computer out of old beer cans powered by windmills; if it had the right program, it would have to have a mind. And the point is not that for all we know it might have thoughts and

Reprinted by permission of the author and Harvard University Press, from Minds, Brains and Science, *by John Searle, Cambridge, MA: Harvard University Press. Copyright © 1984 by John Searle.*

feelings, but rather that it must have thoughts and feelings, because that is all there is to having thoughts and feelings: implementing the right program.

Most people who hold this view think we have not yet designed programs which are minds. But there is pretty much general agreement among them that it's only a matter of time until computer scientists and workers in artificial intelligence design the appropriate hardware and programs which will be the equivalent of human brains and minds. These will be artificial brains and minds which are in every way the equivalent of human brains and minds.

Many people outside of the field of artificial intelligence are quite amazed to discover that anybody could believe such a view as this. So, before criticizing it, let me give you a few examples of the things that people in this field have actually said. Herbert Simon of Carnegie-Mellon University says that we already have machines that can literally think. There is no question of waiting for some future machine, because existing digital computers already have thoughts in exactly the same sense that you and I do. Well, fancy that! Philosophers have been worried for centuries about whether or not a machine could think, and now we discover that they already have such machines at Carnegie-Mellon. Simon's colleague Alan Newell claims that we have now discovered (and notice that Newell says "discovered" and not "hypothesized" or "considered the possibility," but we have *discovered*) that intelligence is just a matter of physical symbol manipulation; it has no essential connection with any specific kind of biological or physical wetware or hardware. Rather, any system whatever that is capable of manipulating physical symbols in the right way is capable of intelligence in the same literal sense as human intelligence of human beings. Both Simon and Newell, to their credit, emphasize that there is nothing metaphorical about these claims; they mean them quite literally. Freeman Dyson is quoted as having said that computers have an advantage over the rest of us when it comes to evolution. Since consciousness is just a matter of formal pro-

cesses, in computers these formal processes can go on in substances that are much better able to survive in a universe that is cooling off than beings like ourselves made of our wet and messy materials. Marvin Minsky of MIT says that the next generation of computers will be so intelligent that we will "be lucky if they are willing to keep us around the house as household pets." My all-time favorite in the literature of exaggerated claims on behalf of the digital computer is from John McCarthy, the inventor of the term "artificial intelligence." McCarthy says even "machines as simple as thermostats can be said to have beliefs." And indeed, according to him, almost any machine capable of problem-solving can be said to have beliefs. I admire McCarthy's courage. I once asked him: "What beliefs does your thermostat have?" And he said: "My thermostat has three beliefs—it's too hot in here, it's too cold in here, and it's just right in here." As a philosopher, I like all these claims for a simple reason. Unlike most philosophical theses, they are reasonably clear, and they admit of a simple and decisive refutation. It is this refutation that I am going to undertake in this chapter.

The nature of the refutation has nothing whatever to do with any particular stage of computer technology. It is important to emphasize this point because the temptation is always to think that the solution to our problems must wait on some as yet uncreated technological wonder. But in fact, the nature of the refutation is completely independent of any state of technology. It has to do with the very definition of a digital computer, with what a digital computer is.

It is essential to our conception of a digital computer that its operations can be specified purely formally; that is, we specify the steps in the operation of the computer in terms of abstract symbols—sequences of zeros and ones printed on a tape, for example. A typical computer "rule" will determine that when a machine is in a certain state and it has a certain symbol on its tape, then it will perform a certain operation such as erasing the symbol or printing another symbol and then enter another state such as moving the tape one square to the left. But the symbols have no meaning; they have no semantic content; they are not about anything. They have to be specified purely in terms of their formal or syntactical structure. The zeros and ones, for example, are just numerals; they don't even stand for numbers. Indeed, it is this feature of digital computers that makes them so powerful. One and the same type of hardware, if it is appropriately designed, can be used to run an indefinite range of different programs. And one and the same program can be run on an indefinite range of different types of hardwares.

But this feature of programs, that they are defined purely formally or syntactically, is fatal to the view that mental processes and program processes are identical. And the reason can be stated quite simply. There is more to having a mind than having formal or syntactical processes. Our internal mental states, by definition, have certain sorts of contents. If I am thinking about Kansas City or wishing that I had a cold beer to drink or wondering if there will be a fall in interest rates, in each case my mental state has a certain mental content in addition to whatever formal features it might have. That is, even if my thoughts occur to me in strings of symbols, there must be more to the thought than the abstract strings, because strings by themselves can't have any meaning. If my thoughts are to be *about* anything, then the strings must have a *meaning* which makes the thoughts about those things. In a word, the mind has more than a syntax, it has a semantics. The reason that no computer program can ever be a mind is simply that a computer program is only syntactical, and minds are more than syntactical. Minds are semantical, in the sense that they have more than a formal structure, they have a content.

To illustrate this point I have designed a certain thought-experiment. Imagine that a bunch of computer programmers have written a program that will enable a computer to simulate the understanding of Chinese. So, for example, if the computer is given a question in Chinese, it will match the question against its memory, or data base, and produce appropriate answers to the

questions in Chinese. Suppose for the sake of argument that the computer's answers are as good as those of a native Chinese speaker. Now then, does the computer, on the basis of this, understand Chinese, does it literally understand Chinese, in the way that Chinese speakers understand Chinese? Well, imagine that you are locked in a room, and in this room are several baskets full of Chinese symbols. Imagine that you (like me) do not understand a word of Chinese, but that you are given a rule book in English for manipulating these Chinese symbols. The rules specify the manipulations of the symbols purely formally, in terms of their syntax, not their semantics. So the rule might say: "Take a squiggle-squiggle sign out of basket number one and put it next to a squoggle-squoggle sign from basket number two." Now suppose that some other Chinese symbols are passed into the room, and that you are given further rules for passing back Chinese symbols out of the room. Suppose that unknown to you the symbols passed into the room are called "questions" by the people outside the room, and the symbols you pass back out of the room are called "answers to the questions." Suppose, furthermore, that the programmers are so good at designing the programs and that you are so good at manipulating the symbols, that very soon your answers are indistinguishable from those of a native Chinese speaker. There you are locked in your room shuffling your Chinese symbols and passing out Chinese symbols in response to incoming Chinese symbols. On the basis of the situation as I have described it, there is no way you could learn any Chinese simply by manipulating these formal symbols.

Now the point of the story is simply this: by virtue of implementing a formal computer program from the point of view of an outside observer, you behave exactly as if you understood Chinese, but all the same you don't understand a word of Chinese. But if going through the appropriate computer program for understanding Chinese is not enough to give *you* an understanding of Chinese, then it is not enough to give *any other digital computer* an understanding of Chinese. And again, the reason for this can be stated quite simply. If you don't understand Chinese, then no other computer could understand Chinese because no digital computer, just by virtue of running a program, has anything that you don't have. All that the computer has, as you have, is a formal program for manipulating uninterpreted Chinese symbols. To repeat, a computer has a syntax, but no semantics. The whole point of the parable of the Chinese room is to remind us of a fact that we knew all along. Understanding a language, or indeed, having mental states at all, involves more than just having a bunch of formal symbols. It involves having an interpretation, or a meaning attached to those symbols. And a digital computer, as defined, cannot have more than just formal symbols because the operation of the computer, as I said earlier, is defined in terms of its ability to implement programs. And these programs are purely formally specifiable—that is, they have no semantic content.

We can see the force of this argument if we contrast what it is like to be asked and to answer questions in English, and to be asked and to answer questions in some language where we have no knowledge of any of the meanings of the words. Imagine that in the Chinese room you are also given questions in English about such things as your age or your life history, and that you answer these questions. What is the difference between the Chinese case and the English case? Well again, if like me you understand no Chinese and you do understand English, then the difference is obvious. You understand the questions in English because they are expressed in symbols whose meanings are known to you. Similarly, when you give the answers in English you are producing symbols which are meaningful to you. But in the case of the Chinese, you have none of that. In the case of the Chinese, you simply manipulate formal symbols according to a computer program, and you attach no meaning to any of the elements.

Various replies have been suggested to this argument by workers in artificial intelligence and in psychology, as well as philosophy. They all have something in common; they are all inadequate. And there is an obvious reason why they have to be inadequate, since the argument rests on a very simple logical truth, namely, syntax alone is not sufficient for semantics, and digital computers insofar as they are computers have, by definition, a syntax alone.

I want to make this clear by considering a couple of the arguments that are often presented against me.

Some people attempt to answer the Chinese room example by saying that the whole system understands Chinese. The idea here is that though I, the person in the room manipulating the symbols do not understand Chinese, I am just the central processing unit of the computer system. They argue that it is the whole system, including the room, the baskets full of symbols and the ledgers containing the programs and perhaps other items as well, taken as a totality, that understands Chinese. But this is subject to exactly the same objection I made before. There is no way that the system can get from the syntax to the semantics. I, as the central processing unit have no way of figuring out what any of these symbols means; but then neither does the whole system.

Another common response is to imagine that we put the Chinese understanding program inside a robot. If the robot moved around and interacted causally with the world, wouldn't that be enough to guarantee that it understood Chinese? Once again the inexorability of the semantics-syntax distinction overcomes this maneuver. As long as we suppose that the robot has only a computer for a brain then, even though it might behave exactly as if it understood Chinese, it would still have no way of getting from the syntax to the semantics of Chinese. You can see this if you imagine that I am the computer. Inside a room in the robot's skull I shuffle symbols without knowing that some of them come in to me from television cameras attached to the robot's head and others go out to move the robot's arms and legs. As long as all I have is a formal computer program, I have no way of attaching any meaning to any of the symbols. And the fact that the robot is engaged in causal interactions with the outside world won't help me to attach any meaning to the symbols unless I have some way of finding out about that fact. Suppose the robot picks up a hamburger and this triggers the symbol for hamburger to come into the room. As long as all I have is the symbol with no knowledge of its causes or how it got there, I have no way of knowing what it means. The causal interactions between the robot and the rest of the world are irrelevant unless those causal interactions are represented in some mind or other. But there is no way they can be if all that the so-called mind consists of is a set of purely formal, syntactical operations.

It is important to see exactly what is claimed and what is not claimed by my argument. Suppose we ask the question that I mentioned at the beginning: "Could a machine think?" Well, in one sense, of course, we are all machines. We can construe the stuff inside our heads as a meat machine. And of course, we can all think. So, in one sense of "machine," namely that sense in which a machine is just a physical system which is capable of performing certain kinds of operations, in that sense, we are all machines, and we can think. So, trivially, there are machines that can think. But that wasn't the question that bothered us. So let's try a different formulation of it. Could an artefact think? Could a man-made machine think? Well, once again, it depends on the kind of artefact. Suppose we designed a machine that was molecule-for-molecule indistinguishable from a human being. Well then, if you can duplicate the causes, you can presumably duplicate the effects. So once again, the answer to that question is, in principle at least, trivially yes. If you could build a machine that had the same structure as a human being, then presumably that machine would be able to think. Indeed, it would be a surrogate human being. Well, let's try again.

The question isn't: "Can a machine think?" or: "Can an artefact think?" The question is: "Can a digital computer think?" But once again we have to be very careful in how we interpret the question. From a mathematical point of view, anything whatever can be described *as if* it were a digital computer. And that's because it can be described as instantiating or implementing a computer program. In an utterly trivial sense, the pen that is on the desk in front of me can be described as a digital computer. It just happens to have a very boring computer program. The program says: "Stay there." Now since in this sense, anything whatever is a digital computer, because anything whatever can be described as implementing a computer program, then once again, our question gets a trivial answer. Of course our brains are digital computers, since they implement any number of computer programs. And of course our brains can think. So once again, there is a trivial answer to the question. But that wasn't really the question we were trying to ask. The question we wanted to ask is this: "Can a digital computer, as defined, think?" That is to say: "Is instantiating or implementing the right computer program with the right inputs and outputs, sufficient for, or constitutive of, thinking?" And to this question, unlike its predecessors, the answer is clearly "no." And it is "no" for the reason that we have spelled out, namely, the computer program is defined purely syntactically. But thinking is more than just a matter of manipulating meaningless symbols, it involves meaningful semantic contents. These semantic contents are what we mean by "meaning."

It is important to emphasize again that we are not talking about a particular stage of computer technology. The argument has nothing to do with the forthcoming, amazing advances in computer science. It has nothing to do with the distinction between serial and parallel processes, or with the size of programs, or the speed of computer operations, or with computers that can interact causally with their environment, or even with the invention of robots. Technological progress is always grossly exaggerated, but even subtracting the exaggeration, the development of computers has been quite remarkable, and we can reasonably expect that even more remarkable progress will be made in the future. No doubt we will be much better able to simulate human behavior on computers than we can at present, and certainly much better than we have been able to in the past. The point I am making is that if we are talking about having mental states, having a mind, all of these simulations are simply irrelevant. It doesn't matter how good the technology is, or how rapid the calculations made by the computer are. If it really is a computer, its operations have to be defined syntactically, whereas consciousness, thoughts, feelings, emotions, and all the rest of it involve more than a syntax. Those features, by definition, the computer is unable to *duplicate* however powerful may be its ability to *simulate*. The key distinction here is between duplication and simulation. And no simulation by itself ever constitutes duplication.

What I have done so far is give a basis to the sense that those citations I began this talk with are really as preposterous as they seem. There is a puzzling question in this discussion though, and that is: "Why would anybody ever have thought that computers could think or have feelings and emotions and all the rest of it?" After all, we can do computer simulations of any process whatever that can be given a formal description. So, we can do a computer simulation of the flow of money in the British economy, or the pattern of power distribution in the Labour party. We can do computer simulation of rain storms in the home counties, or warehouse fires in East London. Now, in each of these cases, nobody supposes that the computer simulation is actually the real thing; no one supposes that a computer simulation of a storm will leave us all wet, or a computer simulation of a fire is likely to burn the house down. Why on earth would anyone in his right mind suppose a computer simulation of mental processes actually had mental processes? I don't really know the answer to that, since the idea seems to me, to put it frankly, quite crazy from the start. But I can make a couple of speculations.

First of all, where the mind is concerned, a lot of people are still tempted to some sort of behaviorism. They think if a system behaves as if it understood Chinese, then it really must understand Chinese. But we have already refuted this form of behaviorism with the Chinese room argument.

Another assumption made by many people is that the mind is not a part of the biological world, it is not a part of the world of nature. The strong artificial intelligence view relies on that in its conception that the mind is purely formal; that somehow or other, it cannot be treated as a concrete product of biological processes like any other biological product. There is in these discussions, in short, a kind of residual dualism. AI partisans believe that the mind is more than a part of the natural biological world; they believe that the mind is purely formally specifiable. The paradox of this is that the AI literature is filled with fulminations against some view called "dualism," but in fact, the whole thesis of strong AI rests on a kind of dualism. It rests on a rejection of the idea that the mind is just a natural biological phenomenon in the world like any other.

I want to conclude this chapter by putting together the thesis of the last chapter and the thesis of this one. Both of these theses can be stated very simply. And indeed, I am going to state them with perhaps excessive crudeness. But if we put them together I think we get a quite powerful conception of the relations of minds, brains and computers. And the argument has a very simple logical structure, so you can see whether it is valid or invalid. The first premise is:

1. *Brains cause minds*

Now, of course, that is really too crude. What we mean by that is that mental processes that we consider to constitute a mind are caused, entirely caused, by processes going on inside the brain. But let's be crude, let's just abbreviate that as three words—brains cause minds. And that is just a fact about how the world works. Now let's write proposition number two:

2. *Syntax is not sufficient for semantics*

That proposition is a conceptual truth. It just articulates our distinction between the notion of what is purely formal and what has content. Now, to these two propositions—that brains cause minds and that syntax is not sufficient for semantics—let's add a third and a fourth:

3. *Computer programs are entirely defined by their formal, or syntactical, structure*

That proposition, I take it, is true by definition; it is part of what we mean by the notion of a computer program.

4. *Minds have mental contents; specifically, they have semantic contents*

And that, I take it, is just an obvious fact about how our minds work. My thoughts, and beliefs, and desires are about something, or they refer to something, or they concern states of affairs in the world; and they do that because their content directs them at these states of affairs in the world. Now, from these four premises, we can draw our first conclusion; and it follows obviously from premises 2, 3 and 4:

CONCLUSION 1

No computer program by itself is sufficient to give a system a mind. Programs, in short, are not minds, and they are not by themselves sufficient for having minds.

Now, that is a very powerful conclusion, because it means that the project of trying to create minds solely by designing programs is doomed from the start. And it is important to re-emphasize that this has nothing to do with any particular state of technology or any particular state of the complexity of the program. This is a purely formal, or logical, result from a set of axioms which are agreed to by all (or nearly all) of the disputants concerned. That is, even most of the hardcore enthusiasts for artificial intelligence agree that in fact, as a matter of biology, brain processes cause mental states, and they agree that programs are defined purely formally. But if you put these conclusions together with certain other things that we know, then it follows immediately that the project of strong AI is incapable of fulfillment.

However, once we have got these axioms, let's see what else we can derive. Here is a second conclusion:

CONCLUSION 2

The way that brain functions cause minds cannot be solely in virtue of running a computer program.

And this second conclusion follows from conjoining the first premise together with our first conclusion. That is, from the fact that brains cause minds and that programs are not enough to do the job, it follows that the way that brains cause minds can't be solely by running a computer program. Now that also I think is an important result, because it has the consequence that the brain is not, or at least is not just, a digital computer. We saw earlier that anything can trivially be described as if it were a digital computer, and brains are no exception. But the importance of this conclusion is that the computational properties of the brain are simply not enough to explain its functioning to produce mental states. And indeed, that ought to seem a commonsense scientific conclusion to us anyway because all it does it remind us of the fact that brains are biological engines; their biology matters. It is not, as several people in artificial intelligence have claimed, just an irrelevant fact about the mind that it happens to be realized in human brains.

Now, from our first premise, we can also derive a third conclusion:

CONCLUSION 3

Anything else that caused minds would have to have causal powers at least equivalent to those of the brain.

And this third conclusion is a trivial consequence of our first premise. It is a bit like saying that if my petrol engine drives my car at seventy-five miles an hour, then any diesel engine that was capable of doing that would have to have a power output at least equivalent to that of my petrol engine. Of course, some other system might cause mental processes using entirely different chemical or biochemical features from those the brain in fact uses. It might turn out that there are beings on other planets, or in other solar systems, that have mental states and use an entirely different biochemistry from ours. Suppose that Martians arrived on earth and we concluded that they had mental states. But suppose that when their heads were opened up, it was discovered that all they had inside was green slime. Well still, the green slime, if it functioned to produce consciousness and all the rest of their mental life, would have to have causal powers equal to those of the human brain. But now, from our first conclusion, that programs are not enough, and our third conclusion, that any other system would have to have causal powers equal to the brain, conclusion four follows immediately:

CONCLUSION 4

For any artefact that we might build which had mental states equivalent to human mental states, the implementation of a computer program would not by itself be sufficient. Rather the artefact would have to have powers equivalent to the powers of the human brain.

The upshot of this discussion I believe is to remind us of something that we have known all along: namely, mental states are biological phenomena. Consciousness, intentionality, subjectivity and mental causation are all a part of our biological life history, along with growth, reproduction, the secretion of bile, and digestion.

Suggestions for Further Reading

For a clear and concise introductory account see Chapter 12 "Bodies and Minds" in Jeffrey Olen's *Persons and Their World: An Introduction to Philosophy* (New York: Random House, 1983). See Jerry Fodor's *Representations: Philosophical Essays on the Foundations of Cognitive Science* (Cambridge: MIT Press, 1983) for an exposition and defense of functionalism. Hubert L. Dreyfus's *What Computers Can't Do: The Limits of Artificial Intelligence* (New York: Harper & Row, 1979) sides with Searle in the debate over computers. Hans Moravec, *Mind Children: The Future of Robot and Human Intelligence* (Cambridge: Harvard University Press, 1988) argues that we are rapidly approaching a time when the boundaries between biological and postbiological intelligence will dissolve. For a collection of essays on the issues see (especially Part III) *Mindwaves: Thoughts on Intelligence, Identity and Consciousness* edited by Colin Blakemore and Susan Greenfield (Oxford: Basil Blackwell, 1987).

Videos

Mind Over Machine (30 minutes, produced by Hubert Dreyfus) and *Minds, Brains and Science* (30 minutes, produced by John Searle, both from Thinking Allowed Productions, 1988) argue against the analogy between the mind and a computer, supporting some of the ideas about consciousness that Descartes also endorsed.

See your Media Services Catalogue for more information.

11.5. You Are a Machine

You probably don't like to think of yourself as a machine. After all, a machine is a thing, a mere "it," while you are a "person." I know I don't normally think of myself as a machine, and, like you, I think of myself as something more than an impersonal thing. But what if we are "virtual" machines? That is, what if our conscious life is the result of imposing a particular pattern of rules (software) on fixed structures (hardware)?

Daniel C. Dennett, Professor of Philosophy at Tufts University and a leading advocate of the theory that the brain is just a very complex and sophisticated computer (hardware) and consciousness is the result of its programming (software), argues against Searle's claim that computers cannot think. In his book, *Consciousness Explained* (from which the following selection is taken), Dennett advances the thesis that human consciousness is a complex set of meme-effects in brains that can be understood as the result of the operations of a virtual machine. A meme is "a unit of cultural transmission, or a unit of imitation" (p. 202). Tunes, ideas, catch-phrases are all examples of memes. Our brain processes memes by creating "multiple drafts," that is, it operates by parallel, multitrack processes of interpreting and elaborating sensory input. What Dennett hopes to do is replace the "Cartesian theater" model of the self (a place or center where consciousness happens) with a "Center of Narrative Gravity" view of the self (a fictional central character we each create via a story or narrative—the character from whose point of view the story is told).

Dennett is convinced, and would like to convince you, that computers can be conscious in the same sense we are conscious, if they can pass the "Turing test." This test is named after its creator, Alan Turing, a brilliant mathematician and computer scientist, who proposed an operational test for deciding whether a computer can think. Turing argued that we can conclude a computer can think if it can regularly beat a human opponent in the "imitation game." Two "contestants," according to this "game" show, are hidden from a human judge. One is a human and the other is a computer. They can communicate with the judge by typing messages on computer terminals. Both the human and the computer try to convince the judge, by their responses to questions posed by the judge, that they are a human, conscious, thinker. If the judge cannot regularly spot the difference (pick out the computer responses from the human responses), the computer "wins" (is judged to have a mind!). If it quacks like a duck, it is a duck even if it doesn't look like one or walk like one or is made out of the same stuff.

Turing's test reflects a view called **behaviorism** which is a materialistic theory of the mind (see the introduction to this chapter). According to this theory, so-called mental events are the same thing as behaviors or dispositions to behave. Thus, if I have a pain in my leg, I am disposed (have a tendency) to say, "Ouch" and rub the spot where it hurts. My behavior or my disposition to behave in such a fashion is the same as "experiencing pain in my leg." If a computer behaves like a conscious mind in the Turing test, why not say it is conscious?

In fairness to Dennett, it should be noted that he does not subscribe to behaviorism. He is a functionalist (see last section) with respect to the mind/body issue. However, he does believe that if computer responses can pass the Turing test, then those who argue that machines cannot think must come up with some very convincing reasons why we should not think so.

Reading Questions

1. What is the main point Dennett makes?
2. How does Dennett respond to Searle's Chinese Room example?
3. Create a critical question about Dennett's argument and answer it.
4. Who has convinced you, Searle or Dennett? Why?

Consciousness Imagined

DANIEL C. DENNETT

1. Imagining a Conscious Robot

The phenomena of human consciousness have been explained in the preceding chapters in terms of the operations of a "virtual machine," a sort of evolved (and evolving) computer program that shapes the activities of the brain. There is no Cartesian Theater; there are just Multiple Drafts composed by processes of content fixation playing various semi-independent roles in the brain's larger economy of controlling a human body's journey through life. The astonishingly persistent conviction that there is a Cartesian Theater is the result of a variety of cognitive illusions that have now been exposed and explained. "Qualia" have been replaced by complex dispositional states of the brain, and the self (otherwise known as the Audience in the Cartesian Theater, the Central Meaner, or the Witness) turns out to be a valuable abstraction, a theorist's fiction rather than an internal observer or boss.

If the self is "just" the Center of Narrative Gravity, and if all the phenomena of human consciousness are explicable as "just" the activities of a virtual machine realized in the astronomically adjustable connections of a human brain, then, in principle, a suitably "programmed" robot, with a silicon-based computer brain, would be conscious, would have a self. More aptly, there would be a conscious self whose body was the robot and whose brian was the computer. This implication of my theory strikes some people as obvious and unobjectionable. "*Of course* we're machines! We're just very, very complicated, evolved machines made of organic molecules instead of metal and silicon, and we are conscious, so there can be conscious machines—us." For these readers, this implication was a foregone conclusion. What has proved to be interesting to them, I hope, are the variety of unobvious implications encountered along the way, in particular those that show how much of the commonsense Cartesian picture must be replaced as we learn more about the actual machinery of the brain.

Other people, however, find the implication that there could be, in principle, a conscious robot so incredible that it amounts in their eyes to the *reductio ad absurdum* of my theory. A friend of mine once responded to my theory with the following heartfelt admission: "But, Dan, I just can't imagine a conscious robot!" Some readers may be inclined to endorse his claim. They should resist the inclination, for he misspoke. His error was simple, but it draws attention to a fundamental confusion blocking progress on understanding consciousness. "You *know* that's false," I replied. "You've often imagined conscious robots. It's not that you can't imagine a conscious robot; it's that you can't imagine *how* a robot could be conscious."

Anyone who has seen R2D2 and C3PO in *Star Wars,* or listened to Hal in *2001,* has imagined a conscious robot (or a conscious computer—whether the system is up-and-about, like R2D2, or bedridden, like Hal, is not really that crucial to the task of imagination). It is literally child's play to imagine the stream of consciousness of an "inanimate" thing. Children do it all the time. Not only do teddy bears have inner lives, but so does the Little Engine That Could. Balsam trees stand silently in the woods, fearing the woodsman's ax but at the same time yearning to become a Christmas tree in some nice warm house, surrounded by happy children. Children's literature (to say nothing of television) is chock full of opportunities to imagine the conscious lives of such mere things. The artists who illustrate these fantasies usually help the children's imagination by drawing expressive faces on these phony agents, but it's not essential. Speaking—as Hal does—will serve about as well, in the absence of an expressive face, to secure the illusion that there is someone in there, that it is like something to be Hal, or a teddy bear, or a choo-choo train.

That's the rub, of course: These are all illusions—or so it seems. There are differences among them. It's obvious that no teddy bear is conscious, but it's really not obvious that no robot could be. What is obvious is just that it's hard to imagine how they could be. Since my friend found it hard to imagine *how* a robot could be conscious, he was reluctant to imagine a robot *to be* conscious—though he could easily have done so. There is all the difference in the world between these two feats of imagination, but people tend to confuse them. It is indeed mind-bogglingly difficult to imagine how the computer-brain of a robot could support consciousness. How *could* a complicated slew of information-processing events in a bunch of silicon chips amount to conscious experiences? But it's just as difficult to imagine how an organic human brain could support consciousness. How *could* a complicated slew of electrochemical interactions between billions of neurons amount to conscious experiences? And yet we readily imagine human beings to be conscious, even if we still can't imagine *how* this could be.

How could the brain be the seat of consciousness? This has usually been treated as a rhetorical question by philosophers, suggesting that an answer to it would be quite beyond human comprehension. A primary goal of this book has been to demolish that presumption. I have argued that you *can* imagine how all that complicated slew of activity in the brain amounts to conscious experience. My argument is straightforward: I have shown you how to do it. It turns out that the way to imagine this is to think of the brain as a computer of sorts. The concepts of computer science provide the crutches of imagination we need if we are to stumble across the *terra incog-*

nita between our phenomenology as we know it by "introspection" and our brains as science reveals them to us. By thinking of our brains as information-processing systems, we can gradually dispel the fog and pick our way across the great divide, discovering how it might be that our brains produce all the phenomena. There are many treacherous pitfalls to avoid—such inviting dead ends as the Central Meaner, "filling in," and "qualia," for instance—and no doubt there are still some residual confusions and outright errors in the sketch I have provided, but at least we can now see what a path would be like.

Some philosophers have declared, however, that crossing this divide is strictly impossible. Thomas Nagel (1974, 1986) has claimed that there is no getting to the subjective level of phenomenology from the objective level of physiology. More recently Colin McGinn has claimed that consciousness has a "hidden structure" that lies beyond both phenomenology and physiology, and while this hidden structure could bridge the gap, it is probably forever inaccessible to us.

> The kind of hidden structure I envisage would lie at neither of the levels suggested by Nagel: it would be situated somewhere between them. Neither phenomenological nor physical, this mediating level would not (by definition) be fashioned on the model of either side of the divide, and hence would not find itself unable to reach out to the other side. Its characterization would call for radical conceptual innovation (which I have argued is probably beyond us).

The "software" or "virtual machine" level of description I have exploited in this book is exactly the sort of mediating level McGinn describes: not explicitly physiological or mechanical and yet capable of providing the necessary bridges to the brain machinery on the one hand, while on the other hand not being explicitly phenomenological and yet capable of providing the necessary bridges to the world of content, the worlds of (hetero-)phenomenology. We've done it! We *have* imagined how a brain could produce conscious experience. Why does McGinn think it is beyond us to engage in this "radical conceptual innovation"? Does he subject the various software approaches to the mind to a rigorous and detailed analysis that demonstrates their futility? No. He doesn't examine them at all. He doesn't even try to imagine the intermediate level he posits; he just notes that it seems obvious to him that there is nothing to hope for from this quarter.

This spurious "obviousness" is a great obstacle to progress in understanding consciousness. It is the most natural thing in the world to think of consciousness as occurring in some sort of Cartesian Theater, and to suppose that there is nothing really wrong with thinking this way. This seems obvious until you look quite hard at what we might learn about the brain's activities, and begin trying to imagine, in detail, an alternative model. Then what happens is rather like the effect of learning how a stage magician performs a conjuring trick. Once we take a serious look backstage, we discover that we didn't actually see what we thought we saw onstage. The huge gap between phenomenology and physiology shrinks a bit; we see that some of the "obvious" features of phenomenology are not real at all: There is no filling in with figment; there are no intrinsic qualia; there is no central fount of meaning and action; there is no magic place where the understanding happens. In fact, there is no Cartesian Theater; the very distinction between onstage experiences and backstage processes loses its appeal. We still have plenty of amazing phenomena to explain, but a few of the most mindboggling special effects just don't exist at all, and hence require no explanation.

Once we make some progress on the difficult task, imagining how a brain produces the phenomena of consciousness, we get to make some slight adjustments in the easy task: imagining someone or something to be conscious. We may continue to think of this by positing a stream of consciousness of sorts, but we no longer endow that stream with all of its traditional properties. Now that the stream of consciousness has been reconceived as the operations of a virtual machine realized in the brain, it is no longer "obvi-

ous" that we are succumbing to an illusion when we imagine such a stream occurring in the computer brain of a robot, for instance.

McGinn invites his readers to join him in surrender: It's just impossible to imagine how software could make a robot conscious. Don't even try, he says. Other philosophers have fostered this attitude by devising thought experiments that "work" precisely because they dissuade the reader from trying to imagine, in detail, how software could accomplish this. Curiously, the two best known both involve allusions to China: Ned Block's (1978) Chinese Nation and John Searle's (1980, 1982, 1984, 1988) Chinese Room. Both thought experiments rely on the same misdirection of imagination, and since Searle's has been the more widely discussed, I will concentrate on it. Searle invites us to imagine him locked in a room, hand-simulating a giant AI program, which putatively understands Chinese. He stipulates that the program passes the Turing test, foiling all attempts by human interlocutors to distinguish it from a genuine understander of Chinese. It does not follow, he says, from this merely behavioral indistinguishability that there is any genuine understanding of Chinese, or any Chinese consciousness, in the Chinese Room. Searle, locked in the room and busily manipulating the symbol strings of the program according to the program, doesn't thereby gain any understanding of Chinese, and there is nothing else in the room that understands Chinese either (this is "just obvious," as Frank Jackson would say).

This thought experiment is supposed to prove the impossibility of what Searle calls "strong AI," the thesis that "the appropriately programmed digital computer with the right inputs and outputs would thereby have a mind in exactly the sense that human beings have minds" (Searle, 1988a). There has been a huge outpouring of reaction to Searle's many versions of this thought experiment over the last decade, and while philosophers and others have always found flaws in his thought experiment when it is considered as a logical argument, it is undeniable that its "conclusion" continues to seem "obvious" to many people. Why? Because people don't actually imagine the case in the detail that it requires.

Here is an informal experiment that will help us see if my diagnosis is correct. First, let's imagine a brief excerpt from the Chinese Room's winning dialogue with the judge in the Turing test. (For convenience, I've translated it from Chinese to English.)

Judge: Did you hear about the Irishman who found a magic lamp? When he rubbed it a genie appeared and granted him three wishes. "I'll have a pint of Guinness!" the Irishman replied, and immediately it appeared. The Irishman eagerly set to sipping and then gulping, but the level of Guinness in the glass was always magically restored. After a while the genie became impatient. "Well, what about your second wish?" he asked. Replied the Irishman between gulps, "Oh well, I guess I'll have another one of these!"

Chinese Room: Very funny. No, I hadn't heard it—but you know, I find ethnic jokes in bad taste. I laughed in spite of myself, but really, I think you should find other topics for us to discuss.

J: Fair enough, but I told you the joke because I want you to explain it to me.

CR: Boring! You should never explain jokes.

J: Nevertheless, this is my test question. Can you explain to me how and why the joke "works"?

CR: If you insist. You see, it depends on the assumption that the magically refilling glass will go on refilling forever, so the Irishman has all the stout he can ever drink. So he hardly has a reason for wanting a duplicate, but he is so stupid (that's the part I object to) or so besotted by the alcohol, that he doesn't recognize this, and so, unthinkingly endorsing his delight with his first wish come true, he asks for seconds. These background assumptions aren't true, of course, but just part of the ambient lore of joke-telling, in which we suspend our disbelief in magic, and so forth. By the way, we could imagine a somewhat labored continuation in which the Irishman turned out to be "right" in his second wish after all—perhaps he's planning to throw a big

party, and one glass won't refill fast enough to satisfy all his thirsty guests (and it's no use saving it up in advance . . . we all know how stale stout loses its taste). We tend not to think of such complications, which is part of the explanation of why jokes work. Is that enough?

This conversation is not dazzling, but let's suppose it was good enough to fool the judge. Now we are invited to imagine all these speeches by CR being composed by the giant program Searle is diligently hand-simulating. Hard to imagine? Of course, but since Searle stipulates that the program passes the Turing test, and since this level of conversational sophistication would surely be within its powers, unless we try to imagine the complexities of a program capable of generating this sort of conversation, we are not following directions. Of course we should also imagine that Searle hasn't any inkling of what he is doing in the Chinese Room: he just sees zeroes and ones that he manipulates according to the program. It is important, by the way, that Searle invites us to imagine that he manipulates inscrutable Chinese characters instead of zeroes and ones, for this may lull us into the (unwarranted) supposition that the giant program would work by somehow simply "matching up" the input Chinese characters with some output Chinese characters. No such program would work, of course—do CR's speeches in English "match up" with the judge's questions?

A program that could actually generate CR's speeches in response to J's questions might look something like this in action (viewed from the virtual-machine level, not from Searle's ground-floor level). On parsing the first words, "Did you hear about . . ." some of the program's joke-detecting demons were activated, which called up a host of strategies for dealing with fiction, "second intention" language, and the like, so when the words "magic lamp" came to be parsed, the program had already put a low priority on responses complaining that there were no such things as magic lamps. A variety of standard genie-joke narrative frames (Minsky, 1975) or scripts (Schank and Abelson, 1977) were activated, creating various expectations for continuations, but these were short-circuited, in effect, by the punch line, which invoked a more mundane script (the script for "asking for seconds"), and the unexpectedness of this was not lost on the program. . . . At the same time, demons sensitive to the negative connotations of ethnic-joke-telling were also alerted, eventually leading to the second theme of CR's first response. . . . And so forth, in vastly more detail than I have tried to sketch here.

That fact is that any program that could actually hold up its end in the conversation depicted would have to be an extraordinarily supple, sophisticated, and multilayered system, brimming with "world knowledge" and meta-knowledge and meta-meta-knowledge about its own responses, the likely responses of its interlocutor, its own "motivations" and the motivations of its interlocutor, and much, much more. Searle does not deny that programs can have all this structure, of course. He simply discourages us from attending to it. But if we are to do a good job imagining the case, we are not only entitled but obliged to imagine that the program Searle is hand-simulating has all this structure—and more, if only we can imagine it. But then it is no longer *obvious*, I trust, that there is no genuine understanding of the joke going on. *Maybe* the billions of actions of all those highly structured parts produce genuine understanding in the system after all. If your response to this hypothesis is that you haven't the faintest idea whether there would be genuine understanding in such a complex system, that is already enough to show that Searle's thought experiment depends, illicitly, on your imagining too simple a case, an irrelevant case, and drawing the "obvious" conclusion from it.

Here is how the misdirection occurs. We see clearly enough that if there were understanding in such a giant system, it would not be Searle's understanding (since he is just a cog in the machinery, oblivious to the context of what he is doing). We also see clearly that there is nothing remotely like genuine understanding in any hunk of programming small enough to imagine read-

ily—whatever it is, it's just a mindless routine for transforming symbol strings into other symbol strings according to some mechanical or syntactical recipe. Then comes the suppressed premise: Surely *more of the same,* no matter how much more, would never add up to genuine understanding. But why should anyone think this was true? Cartesian dualists would think so, because they think that even human brains are unable to accomplish understanding all by themselves; according to the Cartesian view, it takes an immaterial soul to pull off the miracle of understanding. If, on the other hand, we are materialists who are convinced that one way or another our brains are responsible on their own, without miraculous assistance, for our understanding, we must admit that genuine understanding is somehow achieved by a process composed of interactions between a host of subsystems none of which understand a thing by themselves. The argument that begins "this little bit of brain activity doesn't understand Chinese, and neither does this bigger bit of which it is a part . . ." is headed for the unwanted conclusion that even the activity of the whole brain is insufficient to account for understanding Chinese. It is *hard to imagine* how "just more of the same" could add up to understanding, but we have very good reason to believe that it does, so in this case, we should try harder, not give up.

How might we try harder? With the help of some handy concepts: the intermediate-level software concepts that were designed by computer scientists precisely to help us keep track of otherwise unimaginable complexities in large systems. At the intermediate levels we see many entities that are quite invisible at more microscopic levels, such as the "demons" alluded to above, to which a modicum of quasi-understanding is attributed. Then it becomes not so difficult to imagine how "more of the same" could amount to genuine understanding. All these demons and other entities are organized into a huge system, the activities of which organize themselves around its own Center of Narrative Gravity. Searle, laboring in the Chinese Room, does not understand Chinese, but he is not alone in the room. There is also the System, CR, and it is to *that* self that we should attribute any understanding of the joke.

This reply to Searle's example is what he calls the Systems Reply. It has been the standard reply of people in AI from the earliest outings of his thought experiment, more than a decade ago, but it is seldom appreciated by people outside of AI. Why not? Probably because they haven't learned how to imagine such a system. They just can't imagine how understanding could be a property that emerges from lots of distributed quasi-understanding in a large system. They certainly can't if they don't try, but how could they be helped along on this difficult exercise? Is it "cheating" to think of the software as composed of homunculi who quasi-understand, or is that just the right crutch to help the imagination make sense of astronomical complexity? Searle begs the question. He invites us to imagine that the giant program consists of some simple table-hookup architecture that directly matches Chinese character strings to others, as if such a pro-

gram could stand in, fairly, for any program at all. We have no business imaging such a simple program and assuming that *it* is the program Searle is simulating, since no such program could produce the sorts of results that would pass the Turing test, as advertised. . . .

Complexity does matter. If it didn't, there would be a much shorter argument against strong AI: "Hey, look at this hand calculator. It doesn't understand Chinese, and any conceivable computer is just a giant hand calculator, so no computer could understand Chinese. Q.E.D." When we factor in the complexity, as we must, we really have to factor it in—and not just pretend to factor it in. That is hard to do, but until we do, any intuitions we have about what is "obviously" not present are not to be trusted. Like Frank Jackson's case of Mary the color scientist, Searle's thought experiment yields a strong, clear conviction only when we fail to follow instructions. These intuition pumps are defective; they do not enhance but mislead our imaginations. . . .

Suggestions for Further Reading

See Daniel C. Dennett's *Brainstorms: Philosophical Essays on Mind and Psychology* (Boston: Bradford Books, 1978) for more information on Dennett's views. A. M. Turing's "Computing Machinery and Intelligence," in *Mind*, Vol. 59 (1950) is the classic statement of his views. See Christopher Evans's *The Micro Millennium* (New York: Viking Press, 1979) and Morton Hunt's *The Universe Within* (New York: Simon & Schuster, 1982) for opposing views on the issue of artificial intelligence. Marvin Minsky's *The Society of Mind* (New York: Simon and Schuster, 1986) supports some of Dennett's views. *Artificial Intelligence and Natural Man* by Margaret Boden (New York: Basic Books, 1977) is one of the best introductions to the AI field.

11.6. How Much Can I Change and Still Be Me?

I imagine most of you have seen Star Trek and watched Captain Kirk and the others get beamed into and out of the transporter room. Although it is unclear precisely how this machine works, it seems to dismantle the crew molecule by molecule and reassemble them molecule by molecule at a different location. Would you say that Captain Kirk and the others are the same people when they are reassembled? My guess is you would say, "Yes." But let's imagine that it doesn't quite work like that on the home trip. Let's say molecules can stand just so many transports so that, while they can be beamed from the transporter room to some planet, on the return trip the only thing beamed back is a molecule blueprint. Fresh atoms from the well-stocked transporter room's reservoirs are then used to re-create the crew according to the blueprint. Would you say that the crew are the same persons? This question might be a bit harder to answer because the atoms have been changed and only the blueprint kept the same. Is that enough to make them the same? (I owe this provocative example to Daniel C. Dennett, see the introduction to *The Mind's I*.)

Jeffry Olen, author of our next selection and Professor of philosophy at the University of Wisconsin at Stevens Point, connects the issues of what is a person, personal identity, and personal survival by discussing the interesting fictional case of John Badger and Joe Everglade who apparently and mysteriously change identities. He argues that the idea of one continuing person must also involve the idea of one continuing stream of consciousness. Can such continuity carry over from one body to another? Olen thinks so, provided we adopt a functionalist viewpoint. Just as different computers can process the same information and run the same programs, so we might imagine it is possible to survive in another body/brain (computer) as long as our personalities and memories (soft-ware) are preserved.

Reading Questions

You should be used to reading philosophy by now and answering specific questions about the texts. So let's try some more general analytical and critical questions (see Section 1.3) and see how it goes.

1. What are the main points Olen makes?
2. What are the key terms and how does he define them?
3. What are the basic assumptions Olen makes?
4. What sorts of arguments does he give to support his views?
5. Is what Olen writes clear? If not, why are you puzzled? Over which points?
6. Does Olen overlook any important aspects of the topic that you can think of?
7. Do you agree or disagree with what Olen says? Be specific and say why you agree or disagree.

Personal Identity and Life After Death

JEFFRY OLEN

It is Sunday night. After a long night of hard drinking, John Badger puts on his pajamas, lowers the heat in his Wisconsin home to fifty-five degrees and climbs into bed beneath two heavy blankets. Meanwhile, in Florida, Joe Everglade kisses his wife goodnight and goes to sleep.

The next morning, two very confused men wake up. One wakes up in Wisconsin, wondering where he is and why he is wearing pajamas, lying under two heavy blankets, yet shivering from the cold. He looks out the window and sees nothing but pine trees and snow. The room is totally un-

From Persons and Their World: An Introduction to Philosophy *by Jeffry Olen. Copyright © 1983 Random House, pp. 231–237; 239–240; 243–247. Reprinted by permission of McGraw-Hill Publishing Company.*

familiar. Where is his wife? How did he get to this cold, strange place? Why does he have such a terrible hangover? He tries to spring out of bed with his usual verve but feels an unaccustomed aching in his joints. Arthritis? He wanders unsurely through the house until he finds the bathroom. What he sees in the mirror causes him to spin around in sudden fear. But there is nobody behind him. Then the fear intensifies as he realizes that it was his reflection that had stared back at him. But it was the reflection of a man thirty years older than himself, with coarser features and a weather-beaten face.

In Florida, a man awakens with a young woman's arm around him. When she too awakens, she snuggles against him and wishes him good morning. "Who are you?" he asks. "What am I doing in your bed?" She just laughs, then tells him that he will have to hurry if he is going to get in his ten miles of jogging. From the bathroom she asks him about his coming day. None of the names or places she mentions connect with anything he can remember. He climbs out of bed, marveling at the ease with which he does so, and looks first out the window and then into the mirror over the dresser. The sun and swimming pool confound him. The handsome young man's reflection terrifies him.

Then the phone rings. The woman answers it. It is the man from Wisconsin. "What happened last night, Mary? How did I get here? How did I get to look this way?"

"Who is this?" she asks.

"Don't you recognize my voice, Mary?" But he knew that the voice was not his own. "It's Joe."

"Joe who?"

"Your husband."

She hangs up, believing it to be a crank call. When she returns to the bedroom, the man in her husband's robe asks how he got there from Wisconsin, and why he looks as he does.

Personal Identity

What happened in the above story? Who woke up in Joe Everglade's bed? Who woke up in John

Badger's? Which one is Mary's husband? Has Badger awakened with Everglade's memories and Everglade with Badger's? Or have Badger and Everglade somehow switched bodies? How are we to decide? What considerations are relevant?

To ask such questions is to raise the problem of *personal identity*. It is to ask what makes a person the same person he was the day before. It is to ask how we determine that we are dealing with the same person that we have dealt with in the past. It is to ask what constitutes personal identity over time. It is also to ask what we mean by the *same person*. And to answer this question, we must ask what we mean by the word "person."

Persons

In the previous chapter, we asked what a human being is. We asked what human beings are made of, what the nature of the human mind is, and whether human beings are part of nature or distinct from it.

To ask what a *person* is, however, is to ask a different question. Although we often use the terms "person" and "human being" interchangeably, they do not mean the same thing. If we do use them interchangeably, it is only because all the persons we know of are human beings, and because, as far as we know, whenever we are confronted with the same human being we are confronted with the same person.

But the notion of a human being is a *biological* notion. To identify something as a human being is to identify it as a member of *Homo sapiens*, a particular species of animal. It is a type of organism defined by certain physical characteristics.

The notion of a person, on the other hand, is *not* a biological one. Suppose, for instance, that we find life on another planet, and that this life is remarkably like our own. The creatures we discover communicate through a language as rich as our own, act according to moral principles, have a legal system, and engage in science and art. Suppose also that despite these cultural similarities, this form of life is biologically different from human life. In that case, these creatures would be persons, but not humans. Think, for example, of the alien in *E.T.* Since he is biologically different from us, he is not human. He is, however, a person.

What, then, is a person? Although philosophers disagree on this point, the following features are relatively noncontroversial.

First, a person is an intelligent, rational creature. Second, it is a creature capable of a peculiar sort of consciousness—self-consciousness. Third, it not only has beliefs, desires, and so forth, but it has beliefs *about* its beliefs, desires, and so forth. Fourth, it is a creature to which we ascribe moral responsibility. Persons are responsible for their actions in a way that other things are not. They are subject to moral praise and moral blame. Fifth, a person is a creature that we treat in certain ways. To treat something as a person is to treat it as a member of our own moral community. It is to grant it certain rights, both moral and legal. Sixth, a person is a creature capable of reciprocity. It is capable of treating us as members of the same moral community. Finally, a person is capable of verbal communication. It can communicate by means of a *language,* not just by barks, howls, and tail-wagging.

Since, as far as we know, only human beings meet the above conditions, only human beings are considered to be persons. But once we recognize that to be a person is not precisely the same thing that it is to be a human being, we also recognize that other creatures, such as the alien in *E.T.* is also a person. We also recognize that perhaps not all human beings are persons—human fetuses, for example, as some have argued. Certainly, in the American South before the end of the Civil War, slaves were not considered to be persons. We might also mention a remark of D'Artagnan, in Richard Lester's film version of *The Three Musketeers.* Posing as a French nobleman, he attempted to cross the English Channel with a companion. When a French official remarked that his pass was only for one person, D'Artagnan replied that he was only one person—his companion was a servant.

Moreover, once we recognize the distinction between human beings and persons, certain questions arise. Can one human being embody more than one person, either at the same time or successive times? In the example we introduced at the beginning of this chapter, has Badger's body become Everglade's and Everglade's Badger's? Can the person survive the death of the human being? Is there personal survival after the death of the body?

THE MEMORY CRITERION AND THE BODILY CRITERION

Concerning identity through time in general, two issues must be distinguished. First, we want to know how we can *tell* that something is the same thing we encountered previously. That is, we want to know what the *criteria* are for establishing identity through time. Second, we want to know what *makes* something the same thing it was previously. That is, we want to know what *constitutes* identity through time.

Although these issues are related, they are not the same, as the following example illustrates. We can *tell* that someone has a case of the flu by checking for certain symptoms, such as fever, lack of energy, and sore muscles. But having these symptoms does not *constitute* having a case of the flu. It is the presence of a flu virus—not the symptoms—that makes an illness a case of the flu.

We commonly use two criteria for establishing personal identity. The first is the *bodily criterion,* the second the *memory criterion.* How do we apply them?

We apply the bodily criterion in two ways. First, we go by physical resemblance. If I meet someone on the street who looks, walks, and sounds just like Mary, I assume that it is Mary. Since the body I see resembles Mary's body exactly, I assume that it is Mary. Since the body I see resembles Mary's body exactly, I assume that the person I see is Mary. But that method can sometimes fail us, as in the case of identical twins. In such cases, we can apply the bodily criterion in another way. If I can discover that there is a continuous line from one place and time to another that connects Mary's body to the body I now see, I can assume that I now see Mary. Suppose, for example, that Mary and I went to the beach together, and have been together all afternoon. In that case, I can say that the person I am now with is the person I began the day with.

There are, however, times when the bodily criterion is not available. If Mary and Jane are identical twins, and I run across one of them on the street, I may have to ask who it is. That is, I may have to rely on Mary's memory of who she is. And, if I want to make sure that I am not being fooled, I may ask a few questions. If Mary remembers things that I believe only Mary can remember, and if she remembers them as happening to *her,* and not to somebody else, then I can safely say that it really is Mary.

Generally, the bodily criterion and the memory criterion do not conflict, so we use whichever is more convenient. But what happens if they do conflict? That is what happened in our imagined story. According to the bodily criterion, each person awoke in his own bed, but with the memories of someone else. According to the memory criterion, each person awoke in the other's bed with the body of someone else. Which criterion should we take as decisive? Which is fundamental, the memory criterion or the bodily criterion?

THE CONSTITUTION OF PERSONAL IDENTITY

To ask the above questions is to ask what *constitutes* personal identity. What is it that makes me the same person I was yesterday? What makes the author of this book the same person as the baby born to Sam and Belle Olen in 1946? Answers to these questions will allow us to say which criterion is fundamental.

Perhaps the most widely discussed answer to our question comes from John Locke (1632–1704), whose discussion of the topic set the stage for all future discussions. According to Locke, the bodily criterion cannot be fundamental. Since the concept of a person is most importantly the concept of a conscious being who can be held morally and legally responsible for past actions, it is *continuity of consciousness* that constitutes personal identity. The bodily criterion is fundamental for establishing sameness of *animal,* but not sameness of *person.*

Suppose, for instance, that John Badger had been a professional thief. If the person who awoke in Badger's bed could never remember any of Badger's life as his own, but had only Everglade's memories and personality traits, while the man who awoke in Everglade's bed remembered all of Badger's crimes as his own, would we be justified in jailing the man who awoke in Badger's bed while letting the man who awoke in Everglade's go free? Locke would say no. The person who awoke in Badger's bed was not Badger.

If we agree that it is sameness of consciousness that constitutes personal identity, we must then ask what constitutes sameness of consciousness. Some philosophers have felt that it is sameness of *mind,* where the mind is thought of as a continuing nonphysical substance. Although Locke did not deny that minds are nonphysical, he did not believe that sameness of nonphysical substance is the same thing as sameness of consciousness. If we can conceive of persons switching *physical* bodies, we can also conceive of persons switching *non*physical ones.

Then what does Locke take to be crucial for personal identity? *Memory.* It is my memory of the events of Jeffrey Olen's life as happening to *me* that makes me the person those events happened to. It is my memory of his experiences as *mine* that makes them mine.

Although Locke's answer seems at first glance a reasonable one, many philosophers have considered it inadequate. One reason for rejecting Locke's answer is that we don't remember everything that happened to us. If I don't remember anything that happened to me during a certain period, does that mean that whoever existed "in" my body then was not me? Hardly.

Another reason for rejecting Locke's answer is that memory is not always accurate. We often sincerely claim to remember things that never happened. There is a difference, then, between *genuine* memory and *apparent* memory. What marks this difference is the *truth* of the memory claim. If what I claim to remember is not true, it cannot be a case of genuine memory.

But that means that memory cannot constitute personal identity. If I claim to remember certain experiences as being my experiences, that does not make them mine, because my claim may be a case of apparent memory. If it is a case of genuine memory, that is because it is true that the remembered experiences are mine. But the memory does not *make* them mine. Rather, the fact that they *are* mine makes it a case of genuine memory. So Locke has the situation backward. But if memory does not constitute personal identity, what does?

Some philosophers have claimed that, regardless of Locke's views, it *must* be sameness of mind, where the mind is thought of as a continuing nonphysical entity. This entity can be thought of as the self. It is what makes us who we are. As long as the same self continues to exist, the same person continues to exist. The major problem with this answer is that it assumes the truth of mind-body dualism, a position we found good reason to reject in the previous chapter. But apart from that, there is another problem.

In one of the most famous passages in the history of philosophy, David Hume (1711–1776) argued that there is no such self—for reasons that have nothing to do with the rejection of dualism. No matter how hard we try, Hume said, we cannot discover such a self. Turning inward and examining our own consciousness, we find only individual experiences—thoughts, recollections, images, and the like. Try as we might, we cannot find a continuing self. In that case, we are justified in believing only that there are *experiences*—not that there is a continuing *experiencer*. Put another way, we have no reason to believe that there is anything persisting through time that underlies or unifies these experiences. There are just the experiences themselves.

But if we accept this view, and still require a continuing nonphysical entity for personal identity, we are forced to the conclusion that there is no such thing as personal identity. We are left,

that is, with the position that the idea of a person existing through time is a mere fiction, however useful in daily life. And that is the position that Hume took. Instead of persons, he said, there are merely "bundles of ideas."

Thus, the view that personal identity requires sameness of mind can easily lead to the view that there is no personal identity. Since this conclusion seems manifestly false, we shall have to look elsewhere. But where?

THE PRIMACY OF THE BODILY CRITERION

If neither memory nor sameness of mind constitutes personal identity, perhaps we should accept the view that sameness of *body* does. Perhaps it is really the bodily criterion that is fundamental.

If we reflect on the problem faced by Locke's theory because of the distinction between genuine and apparent memory, it is tempting to accept the primacy of the bodily criterion. Once again, a sincere memory claim may be either genuine memory or apparent memory. How can we tell whether the claim that a previous experience was mine is genuine memory? By determining whether I was in the right place in the right time to have it. And how can we determine that? By the bodily criterion. If my *body* was there, then *I* was there. But that means that the memory criterion must rest on the bodily criterion. Also, accepting the primacy of the bodily criterion gets us around Hume's problem. The self that persists through and has the experiences I call mine is my physical body.

This answer also has the advantage of being in keeping with materialism, a view accepted in the previous chapter. If human beings are purely physical, then persons must also be purely physical, whatever differences there may be between the notion of a person and the notion of a human being. But if persons are purely physical, what makes me the same person I was yesterday is no different in kind from what makes my typewriter the same typewriter it was yesterday. In both cases, we are dealing with a physical object existing through time. In the latter case, as long as we have the same physical materials (allowing for change of ribbon, change of keys, and the like) arranged in the same way, we have the same typewriter. So it is with persons. As long as we have the same physical materials (allowing for such changes as the replacement of cells) arranged in the same way, we have the same person.

Although this answer is a tempting one, it is not entirely satisfactory. Suppose that we could manage a brain transplant from one body to another. If we switched two brains, so that all the memories and personality traits of the persons involved were also switched, wouldn't we conclude that the persons, as well as their brains, had switched bodies? When such operations are performed in science-fiction stories, they are described this way.

But this possibility does not defeat the view that the bodily criterion is fundamental. It just forces us to hold that the bodily criterion must be applied to the brain, rather than the entire body. Personal identity then becomes a matter of brain identity. Same brain, same person. Unfortunately, even with this change, our answer does not seem satisfactory. Locke still seems somehow right. Let us see why.

BADGER AND EVERGLADE RECONSIDERED

Returning to our tale of Badger and Everglade, we find that some troubling questions remain. If Mrs. Everglade continues to live with the man who awoke in her bed, might she not be committing adultery? Shouldn't she take in the man who awoke in Badger's bed? And, once again assuming that Badger was a professional thief, would justice really be served by jailing the man who awoke in his bed? However we answer these questions, one thing is certain—the two men would always feel that they had switched bodies. So, probably, would the people who knew them. Furthermore, whenever we read science-fiction stories describing such matters, we invariably accept them as stories of switched bodies. But if we

accept the bodily criterion as fundamental, we are accepting the impossible, and the two men in our story, Mrs. Everglade, and their friends are mistaken in their beliefs. How, then, are we to answer our questions?

If we are unsure, it is because such questions become very tricky at this point. Their trickiness seems to rest on two points. First, cases like the Badger-Everglade case do not happen in this world. Although we are prepared to accept them in science-fiction tales, we are totally unprepared to deal with them in real life.

Second, and this is a related point, we need some way of *explaining* such extraordinary occurrences. Unless we know how the memories of Badger and Everglade came to be reversed, we will be unable to decide the answers to our questions. In the movies, it is assumed that some nonphysical substance travels from one body to another, or that there has been a brain transplant of some sort. On these assumptions, we are of course willing to describe what happens as a change of body. This description seems to follow naturally from such explanations.

What explains what happened to Badger and Everglade? We can rule out change of nonphysical substance, because of what was said in the previous chapter and earlier in this chapter. If we explain what happened as the product of a brain switch, then the bodily criterion applied to the brain allows us to say that Badger and Everglade did awaken in each other's bed, and that Mrs. Everglade would be committing adultery should she live with the man who awoke in her bed.

Are there any other possible explanations? One that comes readily to mind is hypnotism. Suppose, then, that someone had hypnotized Badger and Everglade into believing that each was the other person. In that case, we should not say that there had been a body switch. Badger and Everglade awoke in their own beds, and a wave of the hypnotist's hand could demonstrate that to everyone concerned. Their memory claims are not genuine memories, but apparent ones.

But suppose it was not a case of hypnotism?

What then? At this point, many people are stumped. What else could it be? The strong temptation is to say nothing. Without a brain transplant or hypnotism or something of the sort, the case is impossible.

Suppose that we accept this conclusion. If we do, we may say the following: The memory criterion and the bodily criterion cannot really conflict. If the memories are genuine, and not apparent, then whenever I remember certain experiences as being mine, it is possible to establish that the same brain is involved in the original experiences and the memory of them. Consequently, the memory criterion and the bodily criterion are equally fundamental. The memory criterion is fundamental in the sense that consciousness determines what part of the body is central to personal identity. Because sameness of consciousness requires sameness of brain, we ultimately must apply the bodily criterion to the brain. But the bodily criterion is also fundamental, because we assume that some physical object—the brain—must remain the same if the person is to remain the same.

THE MEMORY CRITERION REVISITED

Although the answer given above is a tidy one, it may still seem unsatisfactory. Perhaps it is a cheap trick just to dismiss the Badger-Everglade case as mere fantasy and then ignore it. After all, if we can meaningfully describe such cases in books and films, don't we have to pay some attention to them? As long as we can imagine situations in which two persons can switch bodies without a brain transplant, don't we need a theory of personal identity to cover them?

Philosophers are divided on this point. Some think that a theory of personal identity has to account only for what can happen in this world, while others think it must account for whatever can happen in any conceivable world. Then again, some do not believe that there is any conceivable world in which two persons could change bodies without a brain switch, while there are others who are not sure that such things are impossible in the actual world.

Without trying to decide the matter, I can make the following suggestion for those who demand a theory of personal identity that does not rely on the assumption that genuine memory is tied to a particular brain.

In the previous chapter, I concluded that functionalism is the theory of mind most likely to be true. To have a mind, I said, is to embody a psychology. I also said that we don't merely move our bodies, but write poetry, caress the cheek of someone we love, and perform all sorts of human actions. I might have expressed this point by saying that we are not just human beings, but persons as well. What makes a human being a person? We are persons because we embody a psychology.

If that is true, then it may also be true that we are the persons we are because of the psychologies we embody. If it is a psychology that makes a human being a person, then it is a particular psychology that makes a particular human being a particular person. Sameness of psychology constitutes sameness of person. In that case, we can agree with this much of Locke's theory—it is continuity of consciousness that constitutes personal identity. But what is continuity of consciousness, if not memory?

An answer to this question is provided by the contemporary British philosopher Anthony Quinton. At any moment, we can isolate a number of mental states belonging to the same momentary consciousness. Right now, for instance, I am simultaneously aware of the sound and sight and feel of my typewriter, plus the feel and taste of my pipe, plus a variety of other things. Such *momentary* consciousnesses belong to a continuous *series*. Each one is linked to the one before it and the one following it by certain similarities and recollections. This series is my own *continuity* of consciousness, my own *stream* of consciousness. It is this stream of consciousness that makes me the same person I was yesterday.

If we accept Quinton's theory, we can then say that the memory criterion, not the bodily criterion, is fundamental. We can also say that, even if in this world continuity of consciousness requires sameness of brain, we can conceive of worlds in which it does not. To show this, let us offer another possible explanation of the Badger-Everglade situation.

Suppose a mad computer scientist has discovered a way to reprogram human beings. Suppose that he has found a way to make us the embodiment of any psychology he likes. Suppose further that he decided to experiment on Badger and Everglade, giving Badger Everglade's psychology and Everglade Badger's and that is why the events of our story occurred. With this explanation and the considerations of the previous paragraphs, we can conclude that Badger and Everglade did change bodies. By performing his experiment, the mad scientist has made it possible for a continuing stream of consciousness to pass from one body to another. He has, in effect, performed a body transplant.

Should we accept Quinton's theory? There seems to be no good reason not to. In fact, there are at least two good reasons for accepting it. First, it seems consistent with a functionalist theory of the mind. Second, it allows us to make sense of science-fiction stories while we continue to believe that in the real world to be the same person we were yesterday is to have the same brain.

Life After Death

Is it possible for the person to survive the death of the body? Is there a sense in which *we* can continue to live after our bodies have died? Can there be a personal life after death?

According to one popular conception of life after death, at the death of the body the soul leaves the body and travels to a realm known as heaven. Of course, this story must be taken as metaphorical. Does the soul literally leave the body? How? Out of the mouth? Ears? And how does it get to heaven? By turning left at Mars? Moreover, if the soul remains disembodied, how can it perceive anything? What does it use as sense organs? And if all souls remain disembodied, how can one soul recognize another? What is there to recognize?

As these questions might suggest, much of this popular story trades on a confusion. The soul is thought of as a translucent physical substance, much like Casper the ghost, through which other objects can pass as they do through air or water. But if the soul is *really* nonphysical, it can be nothing like that.

If this story is not to be taken literally, is there some version of it that we can admit as a possibility? Is there also the possibility of personal survival through reincarnation as it is often understood—the re-embodiment of the person without memory of the former embodiment?

MATERIALISM AND THE DISEMBODIED SOUL

So far, we have considered both the mind and the body as they relate to personal identity. Have we neglected the soul? It may seem that we have, but philosophers who discuss the mind-body question and personal identity generally use the terms "mind" and "soul" interchangeably. Is the practice legitimate, or is it a confusion?

The practice seems to be thoroughly legitimate. If the soul is thought to be the crucial element of the person, it is difficult to see how it could be anything but the mind. If it is our character traits, personality, thoughts, likes and dislikes, memories, and continuity of experience that makes us the persons we are, then they must belong to the soul. If they are taken to be crucial for one's personal identity, then it seems impossible to separate them from one's soul.

Moreover, people who accept some version of the popular conception of life after death noted above believe in certain continuities between earthly experiences and heavenly ones. In heaven, it is believed, we remember our earthly lives, we recognize friends and relatives, our personalities are like our earthly personalities, and we are judged by God for our actions on earth. But if we believe any of this, we must also believe that the soul cannot be separated from the mind.

If that is the case, it is difficult to accept the continued existence of a disembodied soul. Once we accept some form of materialism, we seem compelled to believe that the soul must be embodied. Does that rule out the possibility of any version of the popular story being true?

Some philosophers think that it does. Suppose, for instance, that the mind-brain identity theory is true. In that case, when the brain dies, so does the mind. Since the mind is the repository of memory and personality traits, it is identical with the soul. So when the brain dies, so does the soul.

This is a powerful argument, and it has convinced a number of people. On the other hand, it has also kept a number of people from accepting materialism of any sort. If it is felt that materialism and life after death are incompatible, and if one is firmly committed to the belief in life after death, then it is natural for one to reject materialism.

Is there a way of reconciling materialism and life after death? I think so.

Although it seems necessary that persons must be embodied, it does not seem necessary that the same person must be embodied by the same body. In our discussion of personal identity, we allowed that Badger and Everglade might have changed bodies, depending on our explanation of the story. Let us try a similar story.

Mary Brown is old and sick. She knows she will die within a couple of weeks. One morning she does die. At the same time, in some other world, a woman wakes up believing herself to be Mary. She looks around to find herself in a totally unfamiliar place. Someone is sitting next to her. This other woman looks exactly like Mary's mother, who died years earlier, and believes herself to be Mary's mother. Certainly, she knows everything about Mary that Mary's mother would know.

Before the woman believing herself to be Mary can speak, she notices some surprising things about herself. She no longer feels old or sick. Her pains are gone, and her mind is as sharp as ever. When she asks where she is, she is told heaven. She is also told that her husband, father, and numerous old friends are waiting to see her. All of them are indistinguishable from the persons they claim to be. Meanwhile, back on earth, Mary Brown is pronounced dead. Is this woman

in "heaven" really Mary Brown? How could we possibly explain the phenomenon?

Suppose we put the story in a religious context. Earlier, we saw that one possible explanation of the Badger-Everglade case is that some mad computer scientist had reprogrammed the two so that each embodied the psychology of the other. Suppose we replace the mad scientist with God, and say that God had kept a body in heaven for the purpose of embodying Mary's psychology when she died, and that the person believing herself to be Mary is the new embodiment of Mary's psychology. Would this count as a genuine case of life after death?

If we accept the Badger-Everglade story, appropriately explained, as a case of two persons switching bodies, there seems no reason to deny that Mary has continued to live "in" another body. But even if we are unsure of the Badger-Everglade case, we can approach Mary Brown's this way. What is it that we want to survive after death? Isn't it our memories, our consciousness of self, our personalities, our relations with others? What does it matter whether there is some nonphysical substance that survives? If that substance has no memories of a prior life, does not recognize the souls of others who were important in that earlier life, what comfort could such a continuing existence bring? In what sense would it be the survival of the *person*? How would it be significantly different from the return of the lifeless body to the soil?

If we assume that our story is a genuine case of personal survival of the death of the body, we may wonder about another point. Is it compatible with Christian belief? According to John Hick, a contemporary British philosopher who imagined a similar story, the answer is yes. In I Corinthians 15, Paul writes of the resurrection of the body—not of the physical body, but of some spiritual body. Although one *can* think of this spiritual body as a translucent ghostlike body that leaves the physical body at death, Hick offers another interpretation.

The human being, Hick says, becomes extinct at death. It is only through God's intervention that the spiritual body comes into existence. By the resurrection of this spiritual body, we are to understand a *recreation* or *reconstitution* of the person's body in heaven. But that is precisely what happened in our story.

Thus, a materialist view of the nature of human beings is not incompatible with the Christian view of life after death. Nor, for that matter, is it incompatible with the belief that the spiritual body is nonphysical. If we can make sense of the claim that there might be such things as nonphysical bodies, then there is no reason why a nonphysical body could not embody a psychology. Remember—according to functionalism, an abstract description such as a psychology is independent of any physical description. Just as we can play chess using almost anything as chess pieces, so can a psychology be embodied by almost anything, assuming that it is complex enough. So if there can be nonphysical bodies, there can be nonphysical persons. Of course, nothing said so far assures us that the Christian story—or any other story of life after death—is true. . . .

REINCARNATION

Much of what has been said so far does, however, rule out the possibility of reincarnation as commonly understood. If human beings are purely physical, then there is no nonphysical substance that is the person that can be reincarnated in another earthly body. Moreover, even if there were such a substance, it is difficult to see how its continued existence in another body could count as the reincarnation of a particular person, *if* there is no other continuity between the old life and the new one. Once again, personal survival requires some continuity of consciousness. It is not sameness of *stuff* that constitutes personal identity, but sameness of consciousness. This requirement is often overlooked by believers in reincarnation.

But suppose that there is some continuity of consciousness in reincarnation. Suppose that memories and the rest do continue in the next incarnation, but that they are not easily accessible. Suppose, that is, that the slate is not wiped completely clean, but that what is written on it is hard to recover. In that case, the passage of the soul into a new incarnation would count as personal survival *if* there were such a soul to begin with.

Assuming, again, that there is not, what can we say about the possibility of reincarnation? To conceive of such a possibility, we must conceive of some very complicated reprogramming by God or some mad scientist or whatever. I shall leave it to you to come up with such a story, but I shall say this much. There does not seem to be any good reason to think that any such story is remotely plausible, least of all true.

The Final Word?

In this chapter we looked at two closely related questions: What constitutes personal identity? And is it possible for a person to survive the death of her own body?

The answer to the second question depended on the first. If we had concluded that the basis of personal identity is sameness of body, then we would have been forced to conclude that life after death is impossible. And there did seem to be good reason to come to these conclusions. How, we asked, could we assure that any memory claim is a case of genuine memory? Our answer was this. In the cases likely to confront us in our daily lives, we must establish some physical continuity between the person who had the original experience and the person who claims to remember it.

But the problem with this answer is that it is too limited. Because we can imagine cases like the Everglade-Badger example, and because our science-fiction tales and religious traditions offer stories of personal continuity without bodily continuity, we can say the following. Regardless of what happens in our daily lives, our concept of a person is a concept of something that does not seem tied to a particular body. Rather, our concept of a person seems to be tied to a particular stream of consciousness. If there is one continuing stream of consciousness over time, then there is one continuing person. Our question, then, was whether we can give a coherent account of continuity of consciousness from one body to another.

The answer was yes. Using the computer analogy of the functionalist, we can explain such continuity in terms of programming. If it is possible to "program" another brain to have the same psychology as the brain I now have, then it is possible for me to change bodies. And if it is possible for me to change bodies, then it is also possible for me to survive the death of my body.

Suggestions For Further Reading

The Mind's I: Fantasies and Reflections on Self and Soul, edited by Douglas R. Hofstadter and Daniel C. Dennett (New York: Basic Books, 1981), provides a collection of stimulating articles probing the puzzles of personhood. A volume edited by Amelie Oksenberg Rorty, *The Identities of Persons* (Berkeley: University of California Press, 1976) will prove challenging as it takes you deeper into the mystery of personal identity. Also see Derek Parfit, *Reasons and Persons* (Oxford: Clarendon Press, 1984), for a revisionist view of the nature of persons and much more. John Hick, in his *Philosophy of Religion,* 4th ed. (Englewood Cliffs, NJ: Prentice-Hall, 1990), develops the replica theory in his presentation of what he takes to be a plausible philosophical account of the Christian idea of the resurrection.

11.7. What About Reincarnation?

Belief in reincarnation is widespread in India and many Asian countries, and it is becoming increasingly popular in the West, especially among those influenced by New Age thought. There are a lot of popular books and some scholarly ones published on the topic each year. Reports abound in the media of people who claim to recall past lives. Many have tried hypnotic regression in the hopes of remembering a previous life.

If there is such a thing as reincarnation, what reincarnates? Popular belief would answer that the soul does and would equate the soul with the person. However, as Olen suggests in the last reading (Section 11.6), if personal identity is constituted by our memory and if we cannot remember our previous lives, then in what meaningful sense can we claim that we are reincarnated? Of course, some people claim to have memories of previous lives. If they do, this would constitute good grounds (at least according to Olen) to suppose that they (their person) has survived. But most of us don't. What is to be said of those who don't remember?

Among some Indian philosophers it is thought the *jiva* (ego, individual self, individual soul) reincarnates. But what is this *jiva*? If it is an immaterial stuff that has no memories of previous experiences, in what sense can it be the same person? However, according to other Indian philosophers, you are not really identical with your *jiva*. The *jiva* is not the true Self, the *Atman* is, and the *Atman* does not reincarnate. In fact, it is by coming to the realization of our true Self that we escape the cycle of reincarnation.

Buddhism accepts the idea of rebirth, but rejects transmigration—the notion that a soul substance migrates from this life to the next life. The five aggregates (body, sensation, thought, dispositions, and consciousness) separate at death (see Section 11.3). My next life is the effect of actions performed in this life and previous lives. Personal identity through time does not consist of a soul substance, but of a continuity of Karma. And, as in Hinduism, the goal of life is to find release from Karma and the cycle of rebirth.

Many Buddhist and Hindu philosophers would find the desire for some sort of personal immortality, even in the form of reincarnation, to be quite selfish and wrong-headed. Real salvation does not lie in endless personal existence, but in escape from the illusion of the ego.

Ghose Aurobindo (1872–1950) was born in India and educated in England. At King's College, Cambridge, he was an outstanding student in Greek and Latin. He was imprisoned in 1908 for participating in an Indian nationalist movement and while in prison had a powerful religious experience. Upon his release, he settled in Pondicherry, India and began an ashram (religious community).

Sri Aurobindo, as he is usually called, rejected the world-negating aspects of ancient Indian philosophy. He also introduced the idea of evolution and argued that *Brahman* (see Section 7.3) first involutes (turns in upon itself), next becomes manifest as matter, and then progressively develops toward consciousness through the process of evolution. Human consciousness and personhood is the highest stage of evolution that *Brahman* has so far reached. But there is a higher stage to come, which he calls the "life divine." That stage of "Godhood" will radically transform social, cultural, and individual life.

In the next selection, Sri Aurobindo seeks to clear up some common misconceptions about reincarnation. He uses the term **Purusha** or Person instead of *Atman* (true Self), contrasting it with **Prakriti** or the totality of nature that is not **Purusha.**

Reading Questions

1. Do you agree with Aurobindo that what is attractive about the "cruder" notion of reincarnation is the idea that our personality passes from one body to another? Why or why not? Do you agree that the loss of memory is a major objection to this theory of personal reincarnation? Why or why not?

2. How does Aurobindo characterize the Buddhist view of reincarnation?

3. Why does "metempsychosis" better characterize the Vedantist view?

4. What have you learned about reincarnation that you did not know before?

5. If your personality and memories do not reincarnate, in what sense can we say that *you* reincarnate?

6. Do you believe in reincarnation or not? Why?

The Reincarnating Soul

SRI AUROBINDO

HUMAN THOUGHT IN the generality of men is no more than a rough and crude acceptance of unexamined ideas; it is a sleepy sentry and allows anything to pass the gates which seems to it decently garbed or wears a plausible appearance or can mumble anything that resembles some famil-

From Sri Aurobindo, The Problem of Rebirth, *1952, pp. 20–27. Reprinted by permission of the Sri Aurobindo Ashram.*

iar password. Especially is this so in subtle matters, those remote from the concrete facts of our physical life and environment. Even men who will reason carefully and acutely in ordinary matters and there consider vigilance against error an intellectual or a practical duty, are yet content with the most careless stumbling when they get upon higher and more difficult ground. Where precision and subtle thinking are most needed, there they are most impatient of it and averse to the labour demanded of them. Men can manage fine thought about palpable things, but to think subtly about the subtle is too great a strain on the grossness of our intellects; so we are content with making a dab at the truth, like the painter who threw his brush at his picture when he could not get the effect that he desired. We mistake the smudge that results for the perfect form of a verity.

It is not surprising then that men should be content to think crudely about such a matter as rebirth. Those who accept it, take it usually ready-made, either as a cut and dried theory or a crude dogma. The soul is reborn in a new body—that vague and almost meaningless assertion is for them sufficient. But what is the soul and what can possibly be meant by the rebirth of a soul? Well, it means reincarnation; the soul, whatever that may be, had got out of one case of flesh and is now getting into another case of flesh. It sounds simple—let us say, like the Djinn of the Arabian tale expanding out of and again compressing himself into his bottle or perhaps as a pillow is lugged out of one pillow-case and thrust into another. Or the soul fashions itself a body in the mother's womb and then occupies it, or else, let us say, puts off one robe of flesh and then puts on another. But what is it that thus "leaves" one body and "enters" into another? Is it another, a psychic body and subtle form, that enters into the gross corporeal form—the Purusha perhaps of the ancient image, no bigger than a man's thumb, or is it something in itself formless and impalpable that incarnates in the sense of becoming or assuming to the senses a palpable shape of bone and flesh?

In the ordinary, the vulgar conception there is no birth of a soul at all, but only the birth of a new body into the world occupied by an old personality unchanged from that which once left some now discarded physical frame. It is John Robinson who has gone out of the form of flesh he once occupied; it is John Robinson who tomorrow or some centuries hence will reincarnate in another form of flesh and resume the course of his terrestrial experiences with another name and in another environment. Achilles, let us say, is reborn as Alexander, the son of Philip, a Macedonian, conqueror not of Hector but of Darius, with a wider scope, with larger destinies; but it is still Achilles, it is the same personality that is reborn, only the bodily circumstances are different. It is this survival of the identical personality that attracts the European mind today in the theory of reincarnation. For it is the extinction or dissolution of the personality, of this mental, nervous and physical composite which I call myself that is hard to bear for the man enamoured of life, and it is the promise of its survival and physical reappearance that is the great lure. The one objection that really stands in the way of its acceptance is the obvious non-survival of memory. Memory is the man, says the modern psychologist, and what is the use of the survival of my personality, if I do not remember my past, if I am not aware of being the same person still and always? What is the utility? Where is the enjoyment?

The old Indian thinkers—I am not speaking of the popular belief which was crude enough and thought not at all about the matter—the old Buddhistic and Vedantist thinkers surveyed the whole field from a very different standpoint. They were not attached to the survival of the personality; they did not give to that survival the high name of immortality; they saw that personality being what it is, a constantly changing composite, the survival of an identical personality was a non-sense, a contradiction in terms. They perceived indeed that there is a continuity and they sought to discover what determines this continuity and whether the sense of identity which enters into it is an illusion or the representation of a fact, of a real truth, and, if the latter, then what that truth may be. The Buddhist denied any real identity. There is, he said, no self, no person; there is simply a continuous stream of energy in action like the continuous flowing of a river or the continuous burning of a flame. It is this continuity which creates in the mind the false sense of identity. I am not now the same person that I was a year ago, not even the same person that I was a moment ago, any more than the water flowing past yonder ghaut is the same water that flowed past it a few seconds ago; it is the persistence of the flow in the same channel that preserves the false appearance of identity. Obviously, then, there is no soul that reincarnates, but only Karma that persists in flowing continuously down the same apparently uninterrupted channel. It is Karma that incarnates; Karma creates the form of a constantly changing mentality and physical bodies that are, we may presume, the result of that changing composite of ideas and sensations which I call myself. The identical "I" is not, never was, never will be. Practically, so long as the error of personality persists, this does not make much difference and I can say in the language of ignorance that I am reborn in a new body; practically, I have to proceed on the basis of that error. But there is this important point gained that it is all an error and an error which can cease; the composite can be broken up for good without any fresh formation, the flame can be extinguished, the channel which called itself a river destroyed. And then there is non-being, there is cessation, there is the release of the error from itself.

The Vedantist comes to a different conclusion; he admits an identical, a self, a persistent immutable reality,—but other than my personality, other than this composite which I call myself. In the Katha Upanishad the question is raised in a very instructive fashion, quite apposite to the subject we have in hand. Nachiketas, sent by his father to the world of Death, thus questions Yama, the lord of that world: Of the man who has gone forward, who has passed away from us, some say that he is and others "this he is not"; which then is right? What is the truth of the great passage? Such is the form of the ques-

tion and at first sight it seems simply to raise the problem of immortality in the European sense of the word, the survival of the identical personality. But that is not what Nachiketas asks. He has already taken as the second of three boons offered to him by Yama the knowledge of the sacred Flame by which man crosses over hunger and thirst, leaves sorrow and fear far behind him and dwells in heaven securely rejoicing. Immortality in that sense he takes for granted as, already standing in that farther world, he must surely do. The knowledge he asks for involves the deeper, finer problem, of which Yama affirms that even the gods debated this of old and it is not easy to know, for subtle is the law of it; something survives that appears to be the same person, that descends into hell, that ascends into heaven, that returns upon the earth with a new body, but is it really the same person that thus survives? Can we really say of the man "He still is," or must we not rather say "This he no longer is?" Yama too in his answer speaks not at all of the survival of death, and he only gives a verse or two to a bare description of that constant rebirth which all serious thinkers admitted as a universally acknowledged truth. What he speaks of is the Self, the real Man, the Lord of all these changing appearances; without the knowledge of that Self the survival of the personality is not immortal life but a constant passing from death to death; he only who goes beyond personality to the real Person becomes the Immortal. Till then a man seems indeed to be born again and again by the force of his knowledge and works, name succeeds to name, form gives place to form, but there is no immortality.

Such then is the real question put and answered so divergently by the Buddhist and the Vedantin. There is a constant re-forming of personality in new bodies, but this personality is a mutable creation of force at its work streaming forward in Time and never for a moment the same, and the ego-sense that makes us cling to the life of the body and believe readily that it is the same idea and form, that it is John Robinson who is reborn as Sidi Hossain, is a creation of the mentality. Achilles was not reborn as Alexander but the stream of force in its works which created the momentarily changing mind and body of Achilles flowed on and created the momentarily changing mind and body of Alexander. Still, said the ancient Vedanta, there is yet something beyond this force in action, Master of it, one who makes it create for him new names and forms, and that is the Self, the Purusha, the Man, the Real Person. The ego-sense is only its distorted image reflected in the flowing stream of embodied mentality.

Is it then the Self that incarnates and reincarnates? But the Self is imperishable, immutable, unborn, undying. The Self is not born and does not exist in the body, rather the body is born and exists in the Self. For the Self is one everywhere— *in* all bodies, we say, but really it is not confined and parcelled out in different bodies except as the all-constituting ether seems to be formed into different objects and is in a sense in them. Rather all these bodies are in the Self; but that also is a figment of space-conception, and rather these bodies are only symbols and figures of itself created by it in its own consciousness. Even what we call the individual soul is greater than its body and not less, more subtle than it and therefore not confined by its grossness. At death it does not leave its form, but casts it off, so that a great departing Soul can say of this death in vigorous phrase, "I have spat out the body."

What then is it that we feel to inhabit the physical frame? What is it that the Soul draws out from the body when it casts off this partial physical robe which enveloped not it, but part of its members? What is it whose issuing out gives this wrench, this swift struggle and pain of parting, creates this sense of violent divorce? The answer does not help us much. It is the subtle or psychical frame which is tied to the physical by the heart-strings, by the cords of life-force, of nervous energy which have been woven into every physical fibre. This the Lord of the body draws out and the violent snapping or the rapid or tardy loosening of the life-cords, the exit of the connecting force constitutes the pain of death and its difficulty.

Let us then change the form of the question and ask rather what it is that reflects and accepts the mutable personality, since the Self is immutable? We have, in fact, an immutable Self, a real Person, lord of this ever-changing personality which, again, assumes ever-changing bodies, but the real Self knows itself always as above the mutation, watches and enjoys it, but is not involved in it. Through what does it enjoy the changes and feel them to be its own, even while knowing itself to be unaffected by them? The mind and ego-sense are only inferior instruments; there must be some more essential form of itself which the Real Man puts forth, puts in front of itself, as it were, and at the back of the changings to support and mirror them without being actually changed by them. This more essential form is the mental being or mental person which the Upanishads speak of as the mental leader of the life and body, *mano-mayaḥl prāṇla-Śarīra-neta*. It is that which maintains the ego-sense as a function in the mind and enables us to have the firm conception of continuous identity in Time as opposed to the timeless identity of the Self.

The changing personality is not this mental person; it is a composite of various stuff of Nature, a formation of Prakriti and is not at all the Purusha. And it is a very complex composite with many layers; there is a layer of physical, a layer of nervous, a layer of mental, even final stratum of supramental personality; and within these layers themselves there are strata within each stratum. The analysis of the successive couches of the earth is a simple matter compared with the analysis of this wonderful creation we call the personality. The mental being in resuming bodily life forms a new personality for its new terrestrial existence; it takes material from the common matter-stuff, life-stuff, mind-stuff of the physical world and during earthly life it is constantly absorbing fresh material, throwing out what is used up, changing its bodily, nervous and mental tissues. But this is all surface work; behind is the foundation of past experience held back from the physical memory so that the superficial consciousness may not be troubled or interfered with by the conscious burden of the past, but may concentrate on the work immediately in hand. Still that foundation of past experience is the bed-rock of personality; and it is more than that. It is our real fund on which we can always draw even apart from our present superficial commerce with our surroundings. That commerce adds to our gain, modifies the foundation for a subsequent existence.

Moreover, all this is, again, on the surface. It is only a small part of ourselves which lives and acts in the energies of our earthly existence. As behind the physical universe there are worlds of which ours is only a last result, so also within us there are worlds of our self-existence which throw out this external form of our being. The subconscient, the super-conscient are oceans from which and to which this river flows. Therefore to speak of ourselves as a soul reincarnating is to give altogether too simple an appearance to the miracle of our existence; it puts into too ready and too gross a formula the magic of the supreme Magician. There is not a definite psychic entity getting into a new case of flesh; there is a metempsychosis, a reinsouling, a rebirth of a new psychic personality as well as a birth of a new body. And behind is the Person, the unchanging entity, the Master who manipulates this complex material, the Artificer of this wondrous artifice.

This is the starting-point from which we have to proceed in considering the problem of rebirth. To view ourselves as such and such a personality getting into a new case of flesh is to stumble about in the ignorance, to confirm the error of the material mind and the senses. The body is a convenience, the personality is a constant formation for whose development action and experience are the instruments; but the Self by whose will and for whose delight all this is, is other than the body, other than the action and experience, other than the personality which they develop. To ignore it is to ignore the whole secret of our being.

Suggestions for Further Reading

See the article on Aurobindo in the *Encyclopedia of Philosophy* for more background information on his life and views. His major work, entitled *The Life Divine,* is available in many different editions. For a scientific study of reincarnation see Ian Stevenson's *Twenty Cases Suggestive of Reincarnation,* 2d ed. (Charlottesville: University of Virginia Press, 1974). Also see *Karma and Rebirth in Classical Indian Traditions,* edited by Wendy Doniger O'Flaherty (Berkeley: University of California Press, 1980), for a valuable collection of texts. See Michael A. Slote, "Existentialism and the Fear of Dying," *American Philosophical Quarterly* (Vol. 12) January 1975, 17–28, for an approach to the issue which does not focus on after-life theories, but on the very real knowledge we each have of our own deaths and the effect that has on how we live now.

Videos

In Search of Life After Death (24 minutes, Hartley Films, 1976) investigates "near death experiences" and assesses what evidence they might constitute for survival of death. Also by Hartley, *Life After Death* (32 minutes, 1970) explores ideas about survival and the reasons people have for supposing the belief is true.

Reincarnation: The Untrue Fact (39 minutes, produced by the Theosophical Society of America, 1990, distributed by Wishingwell) looks at evidence suggestive of reincarnation.

Postscript

Multiculturalism—
What Are Its Advantages?

IT SEEMS APPROPRIATE to conclude this collection of multicultural readings in philosophy by reflecting on why it is important to study philosophy from a multicultural perspective. We now have some experience with that perspective, and we should be in a better position to assess it. In my Preface I suggest that we are all enriched by diversity of viewpoints. But how are we enriched?

One answer may be that we are exposed to valuable ideas, good arguments, interesting concepts, and influential literature from traditions that would not otherwise be available to us. Just how valuable these voices, traditionally excluded from the literature commonly used to introduce students to philosophy, are you can judge for yourself after having heard some of them. However, that judgment may be difficult because our standards of value are shaped by a particular tradition that may have ignored culturally diverse voices in the past. We need to expand our horizons and thereby our standards of judgment in the course of listening to these diverse voices. My discussion of rationality in the first chapter reflects this need for expanded standards. Of course some may argue that there are no objective standards by which we can render judgments of comparative worth. Perhaps the most we can hope for is "solidarity" to use Richard Rorty's term (see Section 8.5). But if there are no objective standards then is there any particular reason to find other voices valuable other than we happen to decide to treat them that way? But is that good enough?

There may also be moral reasons for a multicultural approach, not the least of which is that justice would seem to demand that we recognize other cultures and traditions to be as valuable as our own, and thereby reverse the harm that has been done to the identity of the excluded, a harm which implies, by its very exclusion, that those "others" are not worth listening to.

But who are those "others"? A group can only be "other" with respect to some group which claims a kind of centrality. If this is "our" culture, the others are those from different cultures. But what is "our" culture? Who is this "our"? Too often the "our" has referred, in the United States at least, to the descendants of white Anglo-

European immigrants. But is that really "our" culture? Is not, has not, United States culture been diverse from the start? Have not the cultures of the indigenous peoples been themselves diverse? And with the coming of the conquering Europeans, have not the English, French, Spanish, Portuguese, Germans, and many others come? And have not the Russians, Polish, Scandinavians, Africans, Irish, Jews, Asians, Mexicans and still others come? And have not women been here all along? We are a diverse culture and perhaps, in the final analysis, one of the important benefits of reading philosophy in a multicultural context is that we will all come to recognize our diversity and thereby cease to think of "our" in terms of one cultural group.

The first selection below is from the last part of Charles Taylor's (Professor of Philosophy and Political Science at McGill University) essay "Multiculturalism and 'The Politics of Recognition.'" In the first part of his essay, Taylor compares two different types of liberal government. One type protects no particular culture, but insures the welfare and rights of all citizens. The other type nurtures a particular culture, yet also protects the basic welfare and rights of all citizens who do not conform to the prevailing culture. Taylor argues that the second type of liberal government is better than the first. Near the end of his essay, Taylor focuses on the topic of multiculturalism in education and notes that it is based on the demand that we all recognize the equal value of different cultures. He grapples with what sense can be made of this demand.

The second selection is by Susan Wolf, Professor of Philosophy at The Johns Hopkins University. She comments on Taylor's argument, pointing out that Taylor fails to see the unique situation of women and that he fails to recognize a second kind of harm that is done by excluding other cultural viewpoints, the harm that we fail to recognize who we really are.

Reading Questions

1. Summarize the main points of Taylor's essay in your own words.
2. Formulate a critical question about what Taylor says and answer it.
3. Why, according to Wolf, is the situation of women not fully parallel with the situation of members of unappreciated cultures? How does the failure of recognition of underprivileged groups compare to the failure of recognition of women?
4. What does Wolf find right about Taylor's argument?
5. What does Wolf find disturbing about Taylor's view that we treat the demand for recognition as a presumption?
6. According to Wolf, what is the significant good that results from having available and studying a multicultural literature?
7. Do you believe Wolf's claim is correct when she says that the most pressing reason for a multicultural curriculum is the fact that justice demands we recognize the multicultural nature of *our* community? Why or why not?
8. How do you think Taylor might respond to Wolf's criticism?

Multiculturalism and "The Politics of Recognition"

CHARLES TAYLOR

THE CHARGE I'M THINKING OF HERE is provoked by the claim sometimes made on behalf of "difference-blind" liberalism that it can offer a neutral ground on which people of all cultures can meet and coexist. On this view, it is necessary to make a certain number of distinctions—between what is public and what is private, for instance, or between politics and religion—and only then can one relegate the contentious differences to a sphere that does not impinge on the political.

But a controversy like that over Salman Rushdie's *Satanic Verses* shows how wrong this view is. For mainstream Islam, there is no question of separating politics and religion the way we have come to expect in Western liberal society. Liberalism is not a possible meeting ground for all cultures, but is the political expression of one range of cultures, and quite incompatible with other ranges. Moreover, as many Muslims are well aware, Western liberalism is not so much an expression of the secular, postreligious outlook that happens to be popular among liberal *intellectuals* as a more organic outgrowth of Christianity—at least as seen from the alternative vantage point of Islam. The division of church and state goes back to the earliest days of Christian civilization. The early forms of the separation were very different from ours, but the basis was laid for modern developments. The very term *secular* was originally part of the Christian vocabulary.

All this is to say that liberalism can't and shouldn't claim complete cultural neutrality. Liberalism is also a fighting creed. The hospitable variant I espouse, as well as the most rigid forms, has to draw the line. There will be variations when it comes to applying the schedule of rights, but not where incitement to assassination is concerned. But this should not be seen as a contradiction. Substantive distinctions of this kind are inescapable in politics, and at least the nonprocedural liberalism I was describing is fully ready to accept this.

But the controversy is nevertheless disturbing. It is so for the reason I mentioned above: that all societies are becoming increasingly multicultural, while at the same time becoming more porous. Indeed, these two developments go together. Their porousness means that they are more open to multinational migration; more of their members live the life of diaspora, whose center is elsewhere. In these circumstances, there is something awkward about replying simply, "This is not how we do things here." This reply must be made in cases like the Rushdie controversy, where "how we do things" covers issues such as the right to life and to freedom of speech. The awkwardness arises from the fact that there are substantial numbers of people who are citizens and also belong to the culture that calls into question our philosophical boundaries. The challenge is to deal with their sense of marginalization without compromising our basic political principles.

This brings us to the issue of multiculturalism as it is often debated today, which has a lot to do with the imposition of some cultures on others, and with the assumed superiority that powers this imposition. Western liberal societies are thought to be supremely guilty in this regard, partly because of their colonial past, and partly because of their marginalization of segments of their populations that stem from other cultures. It is in this context that the reply "this is not how we do things here" can seem crude and insensitive. Even if, in the nature of things, compromise is close to impossible here—one either forbids murder or allows it—the attitude presumed by the reply is seen as one of contempt. Often, in fact, this presumption is correct. Thus we arrive again at the issue of recognition.

Recognition of equal value was not what was at stake—at least in a strong sense—in the preceding section. There it was a question of whether cultural survival will be acknowledged as a legitimate goal, whether collective ends will be allowed as legitimate considerations in judicial review, or for other purposes of major social policy. The demand there was that we let cultures defend themselves, within reasonable bounds. But the further demand we are looking at here is that we all *recognize* the equal value of different cultures; that we not only let them survive, but acknowledge their *worth*.

What sense can be made of this demand? In a way, it has been operative in an unformulated state for some time. The politics of nationalism has been powered for well over a century in part by the sense that people have had of being despised or respected by others around them. Multinational societies can break up, in large part because of a lack of (perceived) recognition of the equal worth of one group by another. This is at present, I believe, the case in Canada—though my diagnosis will certainly be challenged by some. On the international scene, the tremendous sensitivity of certain supposedly closed societies to world opinion—as shown in their reactions to findings of, say, Amnesty International, or in their attempts through UNESCO to build a new world information order—attests to the importance of external recognition.

But all this is still *an sich*, not *für sich*, to use Hegelian jargon. The actors themselves are often the first to deny that they are moved by such considerations, and plead other factors, like inequality, exploitation, and injustice, as their motives. Very few Quebec independentists, for instance, can accept that what is mainly winning them their fight is a lack of recognition on the part of English Canada.

What is new, therefore, is that the demand for recognition is now explicit. And it has been made explicit, in the way I indicated above, by the spread of the idea that we are formed by recognition. We could say that, thanks to this idea, misrecognition has now graduated to the rank of a harm that can be hardheadedly enumerated along with the ones mentioned in the previous paragraph.

One of the key authors in this transition is undoubtedly the late Frantz Fanon, whose influential *Les Damnés de la Terre* (*The Wretched of the Earth*) argued that the major weapon of the colonizers was the imposition of their image of the colonized on the subjugated people. These latter, in order to be free, must first of all purge themselves of these depreciating self-images. Fanon recommended violence as the way to this freedom, matching the original violence of the alien imposition. Not all those who have drawn from Fanon have followed him in this, but the notion that there is a struggle for a changed self-image, which takes place both within the subjugated and against the dominator, has been very widely applied. The idea has become crucial to certain strands of feminism, and is also a very important element in the contemporary debate about multiculturalism.

The main locus of this debate is the world of education in a broad sense. One important focus is university humanities departments, where demands are made to alter, enlarge, or scrap the "canon" of accredited authors on the grounds that the one presently favored consists almost entirely of "dead white males." A greater place ought to be made for women, and for people of non-European races and cultures. A second focus is the secondary schools, where an attempt is being made, for instance, to develop Afrocentric curricula for pupils in mainly black schools.

The reason for these proposed changes is not, or not mainly, that all students may be missing something important through the exclusion of a certain gender or certain races or cultures, but rather that women and students from the excluded groups are given, either directly or by omission, a demeaning picture of themselves, as though all creativity and worth inhered in males of European provenance. Enlarging and changing the curriculum is therefore essential not so much in the name of a broader culture for everyone as in order to give due recognition to the hitherto excluded. The background premise of these demands is that recognition forges identity, particularly in its Fanonist application: dominant groups tend to entrench their hegemony by inculcating an image of inferiority in the subjugated. The struggle for freedom and equality must therefore pass through a revision of these images. Multicultural curricula are meant to help in this process of revision.

Although it is not often stated clearly, the logic behind some of these demands seems to depend upon a premise that we owe equal respect to all cultures. This emerges from the nature of the reproach made to the designers of traditional curricula. The claim is that the judgments of worth on which these latter were supposedly based were in fact corrupt, were marred by narrowness or insensitivity or, even worse, a desire to downgrade the excluded. The implication seems to be that absent these distorting factors, true judgments of value of different works would place all cultures more or less on the same footing. Of course, the attack could come from a more radical, neo-Nietzschean standpoint, which questions the very status of judgments of worth as such, but short of this extreme step (whose coherence I doubt), the presumption seems to be of equal worth.

I would like to maintain that there is something valid in this presumption, but that the presumption is by no means unproblematic, and involves something like an act of faith. As a presumption, the claim is that all human cultures that have animated whole societies over some considerable stretch of time have something important to say to all human beings. I have worded it in this way to exclude partial cultural milieux within a society, as well as short phases of a major culture. There is no reason to believe that, for instance, the different art forms of a given culture should all be of equal, or even of considerable, value; and every culture can go through phases of decadence.

But when I call this claim a "presumption," I mean that it is a starting hypothesis with which we ought to approach the study of any other culture. The validity of the claim has to be demonstrated concretely in the actual study of the culture. Indeed, for a culture sufficiently different from our own, we may have only the foggiest idea *ex ante* of in what its valuable contribution might consist. Because, for a sufficiently different culture, the very understanding of what it is to be of worth will be strange and unfamiliar to us. To approach, say, a raga with the presumptions of value implicit in the well-tempered clavier would be forever to miss the point. What has to happen is what Gadamer has called a "fusion of horizons." We learn to move in a broader horizon, within which what we have formerly taken for granted as the background to valuation can be situated as one possibility alongside the different background of the formerly unfamiliar culture. The "fusion of horizons" operates through our developing new vocabularies of comparison, by means of which we can articulate these contrasts. So that if and when we ultimately find substantive support for our initial presumption, it is on the basis of an understanding of what constitutes worth that we couldn't possibly have had at the beginning. We have reached the judgment partly through transforming our standards.

We might want to argue that we owe all cultures a presumption of this kind. I will explain later on what I think this claim might be based. From this point of view, withholding the presumption might be seen as the fruit merely of prejudice or of ill-will. It might even be tantamount to a denial of equal status. Something like this might lie behind the accusation leveled by supporters of multiculturalism against defenders of the traditional canon. Supposing that their reluctance to enlarge the canon comes from a mixture of prejudice and ill-will, the multiculturalists charge them with the arrogance of assuming their own superiority over formerly subject peoples.

This presumption would help explain why the demands of multiculturalism build on the already established principles of the politics of equal respect. If withholding the presumption is tantamount to a denial of equality, and if important consequences flow for people's identity from the absence of recognition, then a case can be made for insisting on the universalization of the presumption as a logical extension of the politics of dignity. Just as all must have equal civil rights, and equal voting rights, regardless of race or culture, so all should enjoy the presumption that their traditional culture has value. This extension, however logically it may seem to flow from the accepted norms of equal dignity, fits uneasily within them, as described in Section II, because it challenges the "difference-blindness" that was central to them. Yet it does indeed seem to flow from them, albeit uneasily.

I am not sure about the validity of demanding this presumption as a right. But we can leave this issue aside, because the demand made seems to be much stronger. The claim seems to be that a proper respect for equality requires more than a presumption that further study will make us see things this way, but actual judgments of equal worth applied to the customs and creations of these different cultures. Such judgments seem to be implicit in the demand that certain works be included in the canon, and in the implication that these works have not been included earlier only because of prejudice or ill-will or the desire to dominate. (Of course, the demand for inclusion is *logically* separable from a claim of equal worth. The demand could be: Include these because they're ours, even though they may well be inferior. But this is not how the people making the demand talk.)

But there is something very wrong with the demand in this form. It makes sense to demand as a matter of right that we approach the study of certain cultures with a presumption of their value, as described above. But it can't make sense to demand as a matter of right that we come up with a final concluding judgment that their value is great, or equal to others'. That is, if the judgment of value is to register something independent of our own wills and desires, it cannot be dictated by a principle of ethics. On examination, either we will find something of great value in culture C, or we will not. But it makes no more sense to demand that we do so than it does to demand that we find the earth round or flat, the temperature of the air hot or cold.

I have stated this rather flatly, when as everyone knows there is a vigorous controversy over the "objectivity" of judgments in this field, and whether there is a "truth of the matter" here, as there seems to be in natural science, or indeed, whether even in natural science "objectivity" is a mirage. I do not have space to address this here. . . . I don't have sympathy for these forms of subjectivism, which I think are shot through with confusion. But there seems to be some special confusion in invoking them in this context. The moral and political thrust of the complaint concerns unjustified judgments of inferior status allegedly made of nonhegemonic cultures. But if those judgments are ultimately a question of the human will, then the issue of justification falls away. One doesn't, properly speaking, make judgments that can be right or wrong; one expresses liking or dislike, one endorses or rejects another culture. But then the complaint must shift to address the refusal to endorse, and the validity or invalidity of judgments here has nothing to do with it.

Then, however, the act of declaring another culture's creations to be of worth and the act of declaring oneself on their side, even if their creations aren't all that impressive, become indistinguishable. The difference is only in the packaging. Yet the first is normally understood as a genuine expression of respect, the second often as unsufferable patronizing. The supposed beneficiaries of the politics of recognition, the people who might actually benefit from acknowledgment, make a crucial distinction between the two acts. They know that they want respect, not condescension. Any theory that wipes out the distinction seems at least *prima facie* to be distorting crucial facets of the reality it purports to deal with.

In fact, subjectivist, half-baked neo-Nietzschean theories are quite often invoked in this debate. Deriving frequently from Foucault or Derrida, they claim that all judgments of worth are based on standards that are ultimately imposed by and further entrench structures of power. It should be clear why these theories proliferate here. A favorable judgment on demand is nonsense, unless some such theories are valid. Moreover, the giving of such a judgment on demand is an act of breathtaking condescension. No one can really mean it as a genuine act of respect. It is more in the nature of a pretend act of respect given on the insistence of its supposed beneficiary. Objectively, such an act involves contempt for the latter's intelligence. To be an object of such an act of respect demeans. The proponents of neo-Nietzschean theories hope to escape this whole nexus of hypocrisy by turning the entire issue into one of power and counterpower. Then the question is no more one of respect, but of taking sides, of solidarity. But this is hardly a satisfactory solution, because in taking sides they miss the driving force of this kind of politics, which is precisely the search for recognition and respect.

Moreover, even if one could demand it of them, the last thing one wants at this stage from Eurocentered intellectuals is positive judgments of the worth of cultures that they have not intensively studied. For real judgments of worth suppose a fused horizon of standards, as we have seen; they suppose that we have been transformed by the study of the other, so that we are not simply judging by our original familiar standards. A favorable judgment made prematurely would be not only condescending but ethnocentric. It would praise the other for being like us.

Here is another severe problem with much of the politics of multiculturalism. The peremptory demand for favorable judgments of worth is paradoxically—perhaps one should say tragically—homogenizing. For it implies that we already have the standards to make such judgments. The standards we have, however, are those of North Atlantic civilization. And so the judgments implicitly and unconsciously will cram the others into our categories. For instance, we will think of their "artists" as creating "works," which we then can include in our canon. By implicitly invoking our standards to judge all civilizations and cultures, the politics of difference can end up making everyone the same.

In this form, the demand for equal recognition is unacceptable. But the story doesn't simply end there. The enemies of multiculturalism in the American academy have perceived this weakness, and have used this as an excuse to turn their backs on the problem. But this won't do. A response like that attributed to Bellow which I quoted above, to the effect that we will be glad to read the Zulu Tolstoy when he comes along, shows the depths of ethnocentricity. First, there is the implicit assumption that excellence has to take forms familiar to us: the Zulus should produce a *Tolstoy*. Second, we are assuming that their contribution is yet to be made (*when* the Zulus produce a Tolstoy . . .). These two assumptions obviously go hand in hand. If they have to produce our kind of excellence, then obviously their only hope lies in the future. Roger Kimball puts it more crudely: "The multiculturalists notwithstanding, the choice facing us today is not between a 'repressive' Western culture and a multicultural paradise, but between culture and barbarism. Civilization is not a gift, it is an achievement—a fragile achievement that needs constantly to be shored up and defended from besiegers inside and out."

There must be something midway between the inauthentic and homogenizing demand for recognition of equal worth, on the one hand, and the self-immurement within ethnocentric standards, on the other. There are other cultures, and we have to live together more and more, both on a world scale and commingled in each individual society.

What there is is the presumption of equal worth I described above: a stance we take in embarking on the study of the other. Perhaps we don't need to ask whether it's something that others can demand from us as a right. We might simply ask whether this is the way we ought to approach others.

Well, is it? How can this presumption be grounded? One ground that has been proposed is a religious one. Herder, for instance, had a view of divine providence, according to which all this variety of culture was not a mere accident but was meant to bring about a greater harmony. I can't rule out such a view. But merely on the human level, one could argue that it is reasonable to suppose that cultures that have provided the horizon of meaning for large numbers of human beings, of diverse characters and temperaments, over a long period of time—that have, in other words, articulated their sense of the good, the holy, the admirable—are almost certain to have something that deserves our admiration and respect, even if it is accompanied by much that we have to abhor and reject. Perhaps one could put it another way: it would take a supreme arrogance to discount this possibility *a priori*.

There is perhaps after all a moral issue here. We only need a sense of our own limited part in the whole human story to accept the presumption. It is only arrogance, or some analogous moral failing, that can deprive us of this. But what the presumption requires of us is not peremptory and inauthentic judgments of equal value, but a willingness to be open to comparative cultural study of the kind that must displace our horizons in the resulting fusions. What it requires above all is an admission that we are very far away from that ultimate horizon from which the relative worth of different cultures might be evident. This would mean breaking with an illusion that still holds many "multiculturalists"—as well as their most bitter opponents—in its grip.

Comment

SUSAN WOLF

OF THE MANY issues Charles Taylor's extraordinarily rich and stimulating essay raises, I have chosen to focus on the one he discusses last, and to explore, as Taylor does, the ways in which the politics of recognition properly bears on the issue of multicultural education. Before turning to this topic, though, I feel a need to remark on one of the paths not taken—namely, one that would have focused on specifically feminist concerns. Professor Taylor rightly notes the common historical and theoretical roots of the demand for recognition and of an appreciation of its importance that are evident in feminist as well as multicultural politics. But there are differences also, both in the harms suffered and in the ways to correct them. It would be a shame if, while acknowledging the importance of recognition, and specifically, the importance of recognizing difference, we failed to recognize the differences among different failures of recognition and among the harms that ensue from them.

The failures of recognition on which Professor Taylor primarily focuses are, first, a failure literally to recognize that the members of one or another minority or underprivileged group *have* a cultural identity with a distinctive set of traditions and practices and a distinctive intellectual and aesthetic history, and, second, a failure to recognize that this cultural identity is of deep importance and value. The harms most obvious in this context are, at the least, that the members of the unrecognized cultures will feel deracinated and empty, lacking the sources for a feeling of community and a basis for self-esteem, and, at the worst, that they will be threatened with the risk of cultural annihilation. The most obvious remedies involve publicizing, admiring, and explicitly preserving the cultural traditions and achievements of these groups, understood as traditions and achievements specifically belonging to the descendants of the relevant cultures.

The situation of women, however, is not fully parallel with that of members of unappreciated cultures. While the predominant demand for recognition in multicultural contexts is the demand to have one's culture and one's cultural identity recognized as such, to have one's identity *as* an African-American or Asian-American or Native American appreciated and respected, the question of whether and how significantly and with what meaning one wants to be recognized as a woman is itself a matter of deep contention. For clearly there is a sense in which women have been recognized as women—indeed, as "nothing but women"—for all too long, and the question of how to move beyond that specific, distorting type of recognition is problematic in part because there is not a clear, or a clearly desirable, separate cultural heritage by which to redefine and reinterpret what it is to have an identity as a woman.

Unlike the French Canadians, or perhaps to a lesser degree the Mormons, the Amish, or the Orthodox Jews living in the United States, women as a group are not remotely threatened with the risk of annihilation as a distinctly gendered group. Despite advances in biotechnology that make the option biologically possible, this particular harm is not one about which women need to worry. The predominant problem for women as women is not that the larger or more powerful sector of the community fails to notice or be interested in preserving women's gendered identity, but that this identity is put to the service of oppression and exploitation. The failures of recognition most evident in this context are, first, a failure to recognize women as individuals, with minds, interests, and talents of their own, who may be more or less uncomfortable with or indifferent to the roles their gender has assigned them, and, second, the failure to recognize the values and the skills involved in the activities traditionally associated with women and the ways in which experience with and attention to those activities may enhance rather than limit one's intellectual, artistic, and professional abilities in other contexts. . . .

Specifically, I want to consider, as Taylor has, the demand for the recognition of the diversity of cultures, and particularly the way this demand is expressing itself in the sphere of education. As Professor Taylor notes, the demand for equal respect for different cultures, or for members of and descendants of different cultures, has led to the demand that the contributions of these cultures be recognized—and recognized immediately—as equally valid and valuable. As Taylor also notes, this is a demand that, at least in its most frequent formulations, is internally inconsistent and so impossible to satisfy. For the demand that all cultures and the works they produce be evaluated as equally good is intertwined with a repudiation of all possible standards for evaluation, which would undermine the validity of judgments of equal worth as much as it undermines judgments of inferior worth. Taylor argues, rightly, I think, that the subjectivist strand in these arguments as ultimately destructive to the goals that the arguments are constructed to support. He argues rightly that, although subjectivism offers a quick and easy response to the demands for justifying a revision of the canon, it is a response that ultimately ends in contempt for the very practice of justification, for the vocabulary of critical appreciation, and for anything that could serve as a basis for authentic respect. Thus, he argues (rightly again) that it is a mistake to demand that works of every culture be evaluated, prior to inspection and appreciation, as equally good works, which equally display human accomplishment, and which make equal contributions to the world's store of beauty and brilliance.

Still, I find something oddly disturbing in Taylor's own view about what follows from this, and in his own proposal about what, if we are not to be subjectivists, we must understand the right to recognition legitimately to entail. Taylor suggests that recognition requires us to give all cultures the *presumption* that "[since they] have animated whole societies over some considerable stretch of time [they] have something important to say to all human beings." This would commit us to studying these cultures, to expanding our imaginations and opening our minds so as to put ourselves in a position to see what, if anything, is distinctively valuable in them. In time, when the presumption has paid off, we can shift our justification to one of equal or distinctive worth, for then and only then will we be in a position to understand and articulate what specific and distinctive values each culture has to offer.

It seems to me that this line of thought takes us in an unfortunate direction, that it leads us away from one of the crucial issues that the politics of recognition urges us to address. For at least one of the serious harms that a failure of recognition perpetuates has little to do with the question of whether the person or culture who goes unrecognized has anything important to say to all human beings. The need to correct those harms, therefore, does not depend on the presumption or the confirmation of the presumption that a particular culture is distinctively valuable to people outside the culture.

One way to bring out what I have in mind is by imagining, unrealistic as it may be, that the hypothetical Saul Bellow actually listens to Taylor and takes his remarks to heart. Presumably, when Bellow allegedly made that remark about Tolstoy and the Zulus, his underlying thought was that the canon that included Tolstoy and all those other dead white males simply represented the best of what world culture has to offer, the masterpieces of human civilization. Now it is pointed out to him that he is not in a position to make that claim—for he is barely acquainted with the achievements of Asian and African and nonwhite American civilization, and even insofar as he is acquainted with them, he is quite incompetent to assess them.

Were Bellow to accept the charge against him, he would thereby acknowledge that his remark had revealed an arrogance of enormous proportions, and that it reflected an outrageous failure of recognition. For in unthinkingly identifying the masterpieces of European culture with the masterpieces of human civilization, he was failing to recognize—failing even to see—all the human civilization that was not European.

We are to imagine that Bellow does accept the charge, that he now amends his understanding of the canon as representing, not the great works of civilization, but the great works of European civilization. What effect would this have? My own guess is that Bellow, or, if not Bellow, many of his colleagues, would cede the point without altering his views about what the curriculum should be. I imagine him replying, "Well, per-haps I was out of line in describing the canon as representing the achievements of the world. But if it doesn't represent the achievements of the world, at least it represents the achievements of *our* world, of *our* culture, and that's sufficient to justify it as the centerpiece of *our* curriculum."

But this response reveals a second failure of recognition, at least as intolerable as the first. For we must imagine Bellow to be addressing these remarks, at the very least, to his colleagues and students at the University of Chicago. And, elite as that institution is, we know that the group includes many who are not Europeans. He says, referring to white, European culture, "This is our culture." But the audience is not all white, and is not all descended from Europeans. What does he make of all those other bodies in the room?

It is not clear—perhaps it is not determinate—whether the sort of failure of recognition depicted here is better interpreted as a literal exclusion of African-Americans and others from the audience, as if to say, "When I speak of *our* culture, of course, I don't mean *yours*," or whether we should see it as a patronizing willingness to accept those outlying members of the University of Chicago community as honorary whites, honorary Europeans (and probably honorary males). Either way, this sort of failure of recognition is extremely pervasive in our educational institutions, and it constitutes a level of insult and damage in need of immediate remedy.

The insult portrayed here is an insult fundamentally to individuals and not to cultures. It consists either in ignoring the presence of these individuals in our community or in neglecting or belittling the importance of their cultural identities. Failing to respect the existence or importance of their distinctive histories, arts, and traditions, we fail to respect them as equals, whose interests and values have equal standing in our community.

This failure of respect, however, does not depend on any beliefs about the relative merit of one culture compared to another. Nor does the need to remedy it rest on the claim, presumed or confirmed, that African or Asian or Native American culture has anything particularly important to teach the world. It rests on the claim that African and Asian and Native American cultures are part of our culture, or rather, of the cultures of some of the groups that together constitute our community.

Every time I go to the library with my children, I am presented with an illustration of how generations past have failed to recognize the degree to which our community is multicultural, and of how the politics of recognition can lead, and indeed is leading, to a kind of social progress. My children tend to gravitate toward the section with folk stories and fairy tales. They love many of the same stories that I loved as a child — Rapunzel, the Frog Prince, the Musicians of Bremen — but their favorites also include tales from Africa, Asia, Eastern Europe, and Latin America that were unavailable to me when I was growing up.

Did my mother fail to recognize these books as ones I might enjoy? Did she push them back into the stacks, almost as a reflex, when she saw the illustrators' foreign styles or the slanted eyes or dark skin of the characters? Probably she would have, had these books been in the library. But before my mother's powers of recognition could be put to the test, I suspect that others had limited the selection. For the librarians had probably failed to recognize those books as they went through long lists and catalogues, deciding what to order. And the catalogues themselves probably reflected the decisions of editors and publishers who at an earlier stage had failed to recognize, in the manuscripts that were sent to them and in the authors they chose to cultivate and encourage, the potential to interest, please, and more generally reward that the retelling of these stories possessed.

Remarkable progress has been made in this area, I think, with remarkable results. Obviously, one important result is that African-American children, Asian-American children, and others can find books in the library expressing and illustrating traditions and legends to which they are more closely tied and books in which the characters look and speak more like they and their parents and grandparents do. Another is that

people with stories to tell and pictures to paint that express the traditions and the life of these cultures recognize that they have these things to offer and that there is an audience to receive them joyfully. Yet another is that *all* American children now have available to them a diversity of literary and artistic styles — and, simply, a diversity of stories — that could constitute the beginning of a truly multicultural heritage. When one child with this exposure encounters another, she neither expects him to be the same as she nor sees him as alien or foreign.

In fact, the storybooks and legends from these other lands and other cultures are as rewarding to me and my children as the German and French fairy tales with which the children's libraries of my generation were filled — they provide as much delight to the ear and the eye, and inspire the imagination as fully. But the value I want to emphasize in applauding this multicultural expansion of available folktales is not directly or primarily related to a comparative assessment of these stories' literary value. The most significant harm to which the previous failures of recognition in our libraries contributed was not that we were deprived access to some great folktales, as great as or even greater than the ones represented on the shelves. For there never was a shortage of great stories for children to read or a competition to determine which single story was the very best. The most significant good, or at least the one I wish to emphasize, is not that our stock of legends is now better or more comprehensive than before. It is, rather, that by having these books and by reading them, we come to recognize ourselves as a multicultural community and so to recognize and respect the members of that community in all our diversity.

How these considerations bear on the subject of university education — and, even more specifically, on the subject of revising the canon — is a complex matter, for the goals of a university education, the appropriate methods for achieving these goals, the responsibilities of public as opposed to private institutions, are all matters of controversy in relation to which discussions of the value of multiculturalism must be placed.

Surely, one goal of university education is to acquaint students with and teach students how to appreciate *great* literature, *great* art, *great* philosophy, and the *best* of scientific theory and method. With respect to this goal, the judgment that one artwork or idea or theory is objectively better than another, insofar as such judgments can intelligibly and sensibly be made, will be relevant to curriculum decisions independently of any consideration of the cultural traditions from which these works and thoughts stem. Evidently, it was with this goal in mind that Bellow allegedly made his offensive remark, and it is with this same goal in mind that Taylor's reply condemns it.

My aim has not been to dispute the propriety of this goal in education, or of Taylor's remarks about the implications that our newly developing recognition of non-Western, non-European, nonwhite cultures has for our ideas about how to attain it. Rather, it has been to point out that this is not, nor has it ever been, the only legitimate goal of education. Learning to think rigorously and creatively, to look and listen sensitively and with an open mind, have always been educational goals that are pursued through a variety of methods of which exposure to great works is but one. More to the point, learning to understand *ourselves, our* history, *our* environment, *our* language, *our* political system (and the history, culture, language, and politics of societies of particular interest or proximity to us), have always been goals whose justification and value are not disputed.

Until recently, perhaps, whites descended from Europe have not felt the need to sort out what reasons they (or we) had for wanting to study and to teach their literature and their history. The politics of recognition has increased their sensitivity to the fact that *their* literature might not be coextensive with great literature. Recognizing this gives us occasion to wonder what does explain and justify their interest in and commitment to studying Shakespeare, for example—is it his sheer objective, transcultural greatness or his importance in defining and shaping our literary and dramatic traditions? In the case of Shakespeare, I should think, there is no

need to choose. Both are perfectly good reasons for studying Shakespeare, for including Shakespeare in the curriculum. More generally, both *types* of reason that these singular reasons exemplify have their place in educational decision-making. Both forms of justification are affected by a conscientious recognition of cultural diversity.

Taylor, following Bellow's lead, is concerned with the first type of justification. He takes it for granted that one's reason for studying one culture rather than another must be that that culture is of particular objective importance, or that it has some especially valuable aesthetic or intellectual contribution to make. Taylor is right to note that the values reflected in this type of reason also give us reason to search the world over, with patience and with care, to find and learn to appreciate great human achievements, wherever they may be.

Taylor's reason for studying different cultures, then, is that over time these studies are very likely to "pay off" in terms of an enlarged understanding of the world and a heightened sensitivity to beauty. This is *a* reason for studying different cultures, to be sure, but it is not the only reason, nor, I think, is it the most pressing one.

My point in this essay is to acknowledge the legitimacy of the second type of justification, but to insist that in this context, at least as much as in the former one, there is a need for a conscientious recognition of cultural diversity. Indeed, in this context, we might even say that justice requires it.

There is nothing wrong with having a special interest in a culture because it is one's own, or because it is the culture of one's friend or one's spouse. Indeed, having a special communal interest in one's own communal culture and one's own communal history is part of what keeps the communal culture alive, part of what creates, reforms, and sustains that culture. But the politics of recognition has consequences for what is justified on these grounds that are at least as important as its consequences for what can be justified impartially. The politics of recognition urges us not just to make efforts to recognize the other more actively and accurately—to recognize those people and those cultures that occupy the world in addition to ourselves—it urges us also to take a closer, less selective look at who is sharing the cities, the libraries, the schools we call our own. There is nothing wrong with allotting a special place in the curriculum for the study of our history, our literature, our culture. But if we are to study our culture, we had better recognize who we, as a community, are.

Suggestions for Further Reading

Allan Bloom, in a controversial book, *The Closing of the American Mind* (New York: Simon & Schuster, 1987) claims that relativism and nonjudgmental openness and tolerance have come to characterize students in the university, and we have lost any shared visions of the public good while scrambling to accommodate the "goods" of diverse and demanding groups. Another book that has sparked considerable debate is *Illiberal Education: The Politics of Race and Sex On Campus* by Dinesh D'Souza (New York: The Free Press, 1991). D'Souza believes that multicultural activists have divided the university and the result is not a truly diverse community, but "balkanization." D'Souza's footnotes will provide a good guide to the extensive literature on this topic. Also see *Pluralism in a Democratic Society* edited by Melvin M. Tumin and Walter Plotch (New York: Praeger, 1977) for a series of essays growing out of a conference whose purpose was to arrive at a clear definition of cultural pluralism and to discover the best ways to teach and learn about cultural pluralism.

Beyond A Dream Deferred: Multicultural Education and the Politics of Excellence edited by Becky W. Thompson and Sangeeta Tyagi (University of Minnesota Press, 1993) includes case studies as well as general reflection covering a broad range of issues from feminist and ethnic studies to gay and lesbian concerns.

Appendix A

A Little Logic

LOGIC IS THE STUDY of the norms or rules that ought to guide our reasoning if we wish to think clearly. It is important to note that many philosophers think of logic as a *normative* study, not a *descriptive* study. It does not describe how, in fact, we reason. Cognitive psychology does that. Rather, logic seeks to discover the norms or rules by which we *ought* to reason if we wish to reason clearly and consistently.

I will consider three major aspects of logical reasoning. The first aspect deals with the analysis of arguments (breaking them into their parts), the second deals with the evaluation of arguments (distinguishing good ones from bad ones), and the third with the construction of arguments. The reason logic focuses on arguments is that we often express our reasoning by means of argumentation.

In the sections that follow, I am going to provide you with a lot of technical information about these three aspects in a condensed form, so you are going to have to read carefully and pay close attention. Be sure to answer the questions and do the exercises. Logical reasoning is a skill and, like all skills, is best learned by practice.

A.1. Analysis of Arguments

The first step in the analysis of arguments is recognizing an argument. The second step is distinguishing which statements are the premises and which the conclusion.

Statements (also called propositions) are sentences that assert something to be true or false. For example, "My name is Gary." Note that all statements are sentences, but not all sentences are statements. Thus the command, "Gary, get the ball!" is a sentence, but not a statement because it asserts nothing to be true (or false). Statements are the building blocks of arguments.

When you think of an argument, you probably think of a disagreement or a fight. In logic the word "argument" is used in a technical sense. It is an attempt to demonstrate that something is true by providing reasons in support of it. Hence an *argument* is a sequence of *statements* used to support, back up, give reasons for, or prove something. The supported statement is called the *conclusion*. The statement (there may be only one or there may be more than one) supporting the conclusion is called the *premise*.

Note that arguments are made up of statements. Note further that statements, when combined into an argument, are either premises or conclusions depending on the role they play in the argument. This indicates that arguments are not just a collection of any odd assortment or sequence of statements, but a collection in which the various statements are connected in a particular way. Consider these examples:

EXAMPLE A
1. Gary, get the ball.
2. Now throw it.
3. Was that a nice toss?
4. It certainly was.

EXAMPLE B
1. I have a fat, blind cat.
2. My cat fell into the pool.
3. Look, it's doing the backstroke!

EXAMPLE C
1. If I will study hard, then I probably will get a good grade.
2. I will study hard.
3. I probably will get a good grade.

Example C is an argument, but examples A and B are not arguments. See if you can figure out why. State the differences among these three examples that account for C being an argument while A and B are not.

When analyzing arguments, it is helpful to identify the conclusion first. Once that is done, the premises fall into place more easily. If you can find no conclusion, chances are you may not be dealing with an argument. However, arguments can be incomplete. Sometimes the conclusion is not stated, but only implied. In such cases you must supply it. Arguments also can be complex. Each premise may be supported by one or more subarguments. In such cases, the premises of the main argument are themselves conclusions of the subarguments. Or there may be several major arguments, each linked in that the conclusion of one becomes a premise for the next one and so on. It is not always possible to reduce arguments to simple premise and conclusion form. If you can so reduce arguments, it helps in both understanding them and evaluating them. If you cannot, then at least try to pick out the major points. Ask yourself, "What is the author trying to get me to believe, and why does he or she think I ought to believe it?"

The third step in analyzing arguments is to determine whether they are inductive or deductive.

Arguments come in two types: inductive and deductive. You have all probably heard of inductive and deductive arguments. Many of you also have been taught to think that inductive arguments move from specific cases to general cases and deductive arguments move from the general to the specific. This is certainly true of some kinds of deductive and inductive reasoning, but it is not true of all kinds. Hence, in logic, a more technical definition is used.

Logic arguments are classified as *inductive* if their conclusions provide information in addition to the information contained in the premises. Hence, if the premises are true, the conclusion may or may not be true. Example: "I conclude that all events have causes because every event observed so far has had a cause." What is the premise? What is the conclusion? If the premise is true, might the conclusion still be false? If so, this is an inductive argument.

Arguments are not always expressed with their premises stated first, their conclusion last, and each statement numbered. However, it is often helpful to rewrite them in this form so the connection between premises and conclusion can be more clearly seen. Thus:

1. Every event observed so far has had a cause. (Premise)
2. Therefore, all events have causes. (Conclusion)

An argument is called *deductive* if the conclusion is inferred solely from the information contained in the premises. In other words, the conclusion provides no new information. If the inference is successful, the deductive argument is said to be *valid*. This means that *if* its premises are true, its conclusion *must* be true. For example, suppose I argue that I am bound to die because all humans die and I am a human. What is the conclusion? Which statements are the premises? Does the conclusion provide new information? If the premises are true, must the conclusion be true? (If you are uncertain about the answers to these questions or any others in this section, bring them up in class and ask about them.)

The fourth step in analyzing arguments is to identify the kind of inductive or deductive argument with which you are dealing.

There are several kinds of inductive arguments. One common type is called a *generalization* because the conclusion generalizes beyond the cases reported in the premises. For example, I might argue from the link between smoking and cancer in 10,000 cases to the likelihood of such a link in most cases. Another common type is *analogy*. Analogical arguments try to persuade us that something will be true of one thing because of its similarity to another thing. For example, I might argue that the world is designed by some intelligent being because the world is *like* a machine and machines are designed by intelligent beings.

There are also several kinds of deductive arguments. I am going to list five common kinds of valid deductive arguments in symbolic form (there are also invalid deductive arguments, as we shall see shortly).

1. *Modus ponens* (MP)

$p \supset q$ p and q stand for any statement and $\supset$ stands for "If . . . then . . . ."
p $\therefore$ stands for "therefore" and the line marks the division between prem-
$\therefore q$ ises and conclusion.

This argument is read: "If p is true, then q is true. p is true. Therefore q is true." If we substitute the statement "I pay attention" for p and "I will learn logic" for q we get:

"If I pay attention, then I will learn logic."
"I am paying attention."
"Therefore, I will learn logic."

2. *Modus tollens* (MT)

$p \supset q$ $\sim$ stands for "not."
$\sim q$
$\therefore \sim p$

Read: "If p is true, then q is true. q is not true. Therefore p is not true." Using "I love logic" for p and "I love rock and roll" for q, read the *modus tollens* argument.

3. Hypothetical syllogism (HS)

$$p \supset q$$
$$q \supset r$$
$$\therefore p \supset r$$

Note how the conclusion links the first statement of the first premise with the last statement of the second premise. This simply makes explicit the link that is established via statement q. You can extend the premises in this sort of argument indefinitely as long as you link the preceding premise with the subsequent premise via a common statement. The statement will be the consequent of one premise and the antecedent of the next. Example: $p \supset q, q \supset r, r \supset s, s \supset t, t \supset u, u \supset v, v \supset w$. Therefore, $p \supset w$.

4. Disjunctive syllogism (DS)

$$p \vee q \quad \text{or} \quad p \vee q \quad \text{"} \vee \text{" stands for "or"}$$
$$\frac{\sim p}{\therefore q} \qquad \frac{\sim q}{\therefore p}$$

This can be read "Either p is true or q is true. p is not true. Therefore q is true." The "$\vee$" (or) is exclusive, hence *if* we know that one of the statements is false (as the second premise tells us) then we can conclude that the other one is true.

5. Dilemma (D)

$p \vee q$ "Either p is true or q is true."
$p \supset r$ "If p is true, then r is true."
$q \supset s$ "If q is true, then s is true."

$\therefore r \vee s$ "Therefore either r is true or s is true."

Note that the two statements of the first premise constitute the antecedents of the second and third premises respectively. Also note that the disjunctive conclusion uses the consequent statements of the second and third premises. This sort of argument is handy to use if you are arguing against someone's position and you wish to force him or her into a corner, so to speak (that is, show that he or she has two options, neither of which is desirable given his or her position).

All five of these are *valid forms* of deductive arguments. There are ways of proving that they are valid forms (that is, *if* their premises are true, their conclusions *must* be true), but I will not go into that here. If you are interested, you can check any standard textbook on logic (see suggested readings at the end of this appendix), and it will show you how to prove these forms valid.

Exercise I   Logic is a skill that needs to be practiced and applied. To see if you have understood this section on the analysis of arguments answer the following:

1. T or F   A premise is a statement supporting a conclusion.
2. T or F   "Are you happy?" is a statement.
3. T or F   The following group of sentences constitute an argument: "Bee-Bee exists because the grass is green, the sky is blue, and Maria loves Bob."
4. Is the following an argument? If so, what is the conclusion? "It is right, too, that philosophy should be called the science of truth; for a theoretical science ends in truth, as a practical science ends in action." (Aristotle)

5. Consider: "Every time I have been to the dentist in the past, it has hurt. Therefore, I am afraid that when I go tomorrow it will hurt." This is (a) inductive, (b) deductive, (c) a *modus ponens,* (d) an analogy, (e) not an argument.

6. Consider: "The brain is like a computer. Its structure is the hardware, and socialization is the software. Sensations are the input which it processes. Thus, just as the output of a computer is predictable once we know the hardware, software, and input, so the actions of the human being are predictable." This argument is (a) deductive, (b) a generalization, (c) an analogy, (d) inductive, (e) both c and d.

7. Consider: "Either the soul is aware or it is not. If it is, then it changes. If it is not aware, then it does not exist. Hence, either the soul changes or it does not exist." (a) The conclusion to this argument is the first sentence. (b) The first sentence is the first premise. (c) The conclusion is unstated. (d) This is not an argument, (e) This is a disjunctive syllogism.

8. T or F   If what is stated in question 7 is an argument, it is deductive.

9. Consider: "You have a choice of admitting that people are morally responsible for what they do or they are not morally responsible. After all, people are either free or they are not. If they are free, then they are morally responsible, but if they are not free, they are not." This argument is (a) an analogy, (b) a generalization, (c) a *modus ponens,* (d) a dilemma, (e) a hypothetical syllogism.

10. Confucius argued: "If words are not correctly used, then we will be deceived. If we are deceived, then dictators can rule. If words are not correctly used, dictators can rule." (a) The last sentence is the conclusion. (b) This is a hypothetical syllogism. (c) This is a *modus tollens.* (d) This is a deductive argument. (e) All except c.

11. Consider: "If reforming the medical care system works, then the president has shown good judgment. Reforming the medical system has worked. Therefore, the president has shown good judgment." This is (a) an inductive argument, (b) a *modus tollens,* (c) a *modus ponens,* (d) a dilemma, (e) a disjunctive syllogism.

12. Construct a disjunctive syllogism. Let p = Logic is fun, and q = Gumby exists.

13. Create an MT argument. Let p = I am unconscious. Use any statement you wish for q.

14. Construct an MP argument. Write it out using anything you wish for p and q.

Check your answers with the key provided at the end of Appendix A. If you missed a question, try to figure out your mistake. If you don't understand what you did wrong, bring it up in class.

A.2. Evaluation of Arguments and Definitions

After analyzing an argument, we need to evaluate it in order to determine whether it is a good one or a bad one. If it is a good one, we may have some confidence that its conclusion can be accepted. If it is a bad one, we ought to be suspicious of the conclusion.

Step 1: Check to see if the terms are adequately defined.

Arguments are made up of statements, but statements are made up of words. Some of these words are crucial to the argument and need to be adequately defined. Some philosophers maintain that definitions are not true or false; rather, they are more or less helpful. Their purpose is to draw boundaries and thereby distinguish one thing from another. If the boundaries are drawn in helpful ways, the definition is a good one. However, other philosophers have argued that good definitions express the essence of something. They tell us what something really is. If so, then definitions are more than just helpful in clarifying how we are using words. They truly express (or fail to express) the very essence of the thing being defined.

Here are some rules that you can use to evaluate definitions. A good definition should:

1. be clear and precise
2. be stated in positive form rather than negative form, if possible (e.g., it should not include a negation such as "not")
3. be noncircular
4. be broad enough to include all cases designated by actual usage
5. be narrow enough to exclude cases beyond the range of actual usage
6. state, if analytic, essential characteristics

Suppose we are discussing abortion and we begin to wonder whether the fetus is a human being. I assert that it is not, and you ask me to define what I mean by "human being." I present Aristotle's famous definition: "A human being is a rational animal."

Is this a good definition? Well, is it clear and precise? By clarity I mean is it free from ambiguity, and by precision I mean is it free from vagueness. *Ambiguity* refers to the fact that, since words mean different things, it is often not clear from the context which meaning is intended. For example, the word "animal" (according to Webster's dictionary) can mean: "1. a living organism capable of sensation and voluntary motion; 2. any creature other than man that is four-footed; 3. a brutish, debased or inhumane person." Now I think it is clear from the context that I am using the word "animal" in the first sense. Hence, in this context its meaning is not ambiguous.

Vagueness refers to the range of applicability of a term. For example, the word "bald" is vague because it is unclear how much hair must be missing before one qualifies for that title. One might argue that the word "rational" in Aristotle's definition is vague. A wide range of actions might be termed rational. Where does one draw the line? Is a computer "rational" because it can calculate? Further clarification of the meaning of rational in this connection must be provided.

The definition we are considering ("humans are rational animals") is stated in a positive form and hence meets the second criterion. I think you can easily see the reason for this rule. If I defined humans as "not frogs" that would not be very helpful because it fails to narrow the range of meaning very much. It should be noted, however, that in some cases negative definitions are the only kind possible. So God, it has been argued by some theologians, can only be defined negatively, that is, as not finite (infinite), not temporal (eternal), and so on.

The rule about circularity is obvious. It is not helpful to define a human being as "a being that is human." The definition ought to provide some useful information, not just repeat what is being defined (usually called the *definiendum*) in somewhat different terms. "Human beings are rational animals" does provide more information about what I consider human beings to be and hence is not circular.

When using rules 4 and 5 about broadness and narrowness, it is helpful to use a technique called *counterexample*. When checking a definition, see if you can think of a clear-cut example of the *definiendum* that is not covered by the proposed definition or a clear-cut example of something that fits the definition, but is not an example of the *definiendum*. For instance, if I had defined human beings as "two-legged animals" you might have argued that this is far too broad because birds are two-legged animals, yet they are not humans. Or you might have argued that the definition I have given (rational animal) is too narrow because people in comas, people who are mentally disturbed, or very small infants who are not "rational" are still normally regarded as human. This point is particularly relevant to our discussion about abortion. I clearly intended to exclude fetuses from the category "human" by my definition. But my definition may be so narrow that it excludes other things that normal usage includes. If it does, is it really helpful in advancing our thinking?

These rules about broadness and narrowness have their exceptions. Some definitions are *stipulative*. That is, they express a special usage for a term that differs from common usage. Technical definitions in science are often of this sort. Stipulated usage might be much broader or much narrower (usually the latter) than actual usage. This is perfectly acceptable if the parties to the discussion are aware that a stipulative definition is being used and agree to its use for the purposes at hand. So if, for the purposes of discussing abortion, we all agree to define humans as rational animals and hence exclude fetuses from that category, we can then go on to discuss other issues such as whether the fetuses, as *potential* humans, have rights that outweigh the rights of women to control their own reproductive processes.

In considering the last rule (number 6) about essential characteristics we must note that there are different kinds of definition. One kind, stipulative, I have just mentioned. Another kind, called *cluster* definition, states that something will be an example of the *definiendum* if it has most or all of a given set of characteristics. So, for instance, if I listed twenty-five characteristics of human being (rational and animal being only two of the twenty-five) and said anything that had *any sixteen* of them I was willing to call "human" I would be offering a cluster definition. If this is the case, rule number 6 would not apply because I would not be claiming that any one of the twenty-five was essential. However, there is another kind of definition called "analytic" or "essential" and in this case, rule number 6 does apply.

Someone offering an *analytic definition* is attempting to express the essence of the *definiendum*. According to Aristotle, this sort of definition expresses the *genus* or class to which the *definiendum* belongs and the *differentiae* or characteristics that distinguish it from other members of its genus. So, for example, "animal" is the genus or class and "rational" is the *differentia* or that trait distinguishing humans from other members of the class "animal."

To express the "essence" of something is to state its necessary *and* sufficient characteristics. To claim that rationality and animality are the *necessary* characteristics of being human is to claim that anyone without these characteristics is not a human being. To claim that they are *sufficient* is to assert that anything that has these characteristics is human. (Note: Something can be sufficient without being necessary and vice versa. A rock hitting a window is sufficient to break it, but not necessary since a baseball might do as well. Milk is necessary to make yogurt, but not sufficient. However, essential characteristics must be both necessary and sufficient.)

This rule is closely related to rules 4 and 5 and can be applied in a similar way by thinking about possible counterexamples. However, it is a bit different in that rules 4 and 5 have to do with the range of normal usage; this rule has to do with necessary and sufficient traits.

Let's consider a computer. It is not an animal and hence cannot be human according to my definition, if being an animal is a necessary condition. (Note: It is clear that being an animal by itself is not a sufficient condition since there are lots of animals that are not human.) But computers can perform rational functions. They can calculate and solve problems that are too complex for the human mind. If they are rational in some sense, does that make them human? Only if being rational by itself is a sufficient condition for being human. If something must be *both* rational and animal to be a human, then a computer, while qualifying on one count, fails to qualify on the other.

Often it is extremely difficult to express the essence of something (that is, to find a set of conditions that are both sufficient and necessary) and, in some cases, there may be no set of traits that are both sufficient and necessary. Also, as I indicated above, many philosophers question the whole idea of "essence" and deny that things have essential natures that can be expressed in definitions. Meaning is determined by use and context, they argue, not by fixed, unchanging essences.

Step 2: Check to see if the statements are clear and precise.

We need not linger long on this step. Just as words can be ambiguous and vague, so too can sentences. Check each of the premises and the conclusion to see whether the meaning is clear and precise. For example, if I asserted that this appendix contains 8,000 words, would you know whether it contains 8,000 different words or 8,000 words total? "This appendix contains 8,000 words" is ambiguous. It may mean different things, and it is not clear which is meant.

Step 3: Check to see if the premises are true.

Since the conclusion of an argument depends on the premises, if one or more of the premises is false, the argument as a whole is thereby weakened. Of course, in many cases, we are not in a position to know whether the premises are true. In such cases we might ask ourselves whether the premises are plausible (could they be true?) or suspend judgment, provided we are in a position to do so. I add this qualification just in case you decide to remain in a building after someone has shouted, "Fire!" because you cannot smell any smoke. I would suggest you leave, just to be on the safe side, even if you are not certain there is strong evidence to support the conclusion that the building is on fire. Of course, if you are visiting a mental hospital and a patient tells you to leave because extraterrestrials have just invaded the grounds, you might consider staying.

Step 4: Check to see whether the assumptions upon which the argument rests are plausible and warranted.

All arguments depend on theories and assumptions which are sometimes unstated. If these theories and assumptions are implausible or unwarranted, the argument is thereby weakened. If I try to persuade you to buy a rug made out of fireproof material to place in front of your fireplace, you might be inclined to do so knowing that sparks from fireplaces can cause fires. However, if I tried to persuade you to wear red underwear to ward off the "evil eye," you might be inclined to dismiss my argument because the assumptions on which it was based seem to you implausible.

Step 5: Check to see whether the premises are relevant to the conclusion.

We said above that one way of thinking about the connection between the premises and the conclusion is to think of the premises as supporting the conclusion. We might also express this relationship in terms of the conclusion following from the premises. Hence, we need to ask whether the conclusion follows from the information given in the premises. For example, does it follow from the fact that wars and famine reduce overpopulation that we ought to welcome them as blessings in disguise? Or does it follow from the fact that someone is male that he will be a good president? Does it follow that God exists because the Bible, Jesus, Muhammad, and the Qur'an have said so?

Step 6: If the argument is deductive, check to see if it is valid.

This rule applies only to deductive arguments since only those kinds of arguments are valid or invalid. A deductive argument is valid if its form is valid. Validity refers to the *form* of the argument, not its content. If its form is such that the conclusion must be true if the premises are true, then it is valid. Note: This does not say that the premises have to, in fact, be true. It just says that *if* they are true, then the conclusion must also be true. In fact, the premises may be false and the argument still valid. For example, the argument "If cows are purple, Gumby exists. Cows are purple. Therefore Gumby exists" is valid (MP), but all its premises are false.

A good way to check for validity is to see if the argument fits a standard valid form such as those we discussed in the last section (MP, MT, HS, DS, and D). There are all kinds of valid forms and other ways of checking. You may consult any standard textbook on logic for additional information.

There are also some forms of arguments that are known to be invalid. For example:
Fallacy of affirming the consequent

$p \supset q$

q

———

$\therefore p$

Fallacy of denying the antecedent

$p \supset q$

$\sim p$

———

$\therefore \sim q$

If the argument fits one of these forms, it is *invalid*. Again, check a logic text for more information on invalid forms and on why they are invalid.

Since validity has to do with form, not content, also check to see if the premises are true after checking for validity. If the argument is valid and the premises are true, the argument is called *sound*. If the premises are not true, the argument is *unsound* even if its form is valid.

Validity and soundness apply to deductive arguments only. Inductive arguments are either strong or weak, but never valid or invalid. Further, we should not say that arguments are true or false since only statements are true or false. Rather, arguments are called "valid or invalid, sound or unsound" if deductive, and "strong or weak" if inductive.

Step 7: Check to see whether the conclusion of an argument leads to an absurdity.

There is a type of argument known as *reductio ad absurdum* (reduction to absurdity). It takes the form of *modus tollens*. Let *p* be the conclusion of some argument. If *p* implies *q,* and if *q* is false or absurd, then *p* must also be absurd. This technique of evaluation will not tell you what is wrong with an argument, but it will tell you if something is fishy. For example, suppose I argued that thoughts are just electrical impulses in the brain because people without electrical activity in their brian are unconscious. You might try to show my reasoning wrong by arguing, "If thoughts are electrical impulses in the brain, then I should be able to read your thoughts by reading a graph that displays the electrical activity of your brain. But it is absurd to claim I can read your mind by reading an electrical graph. Therefore, thoughts are not identical with electrical impulses."

Note that your *reductio* does not tell us what is wrong with my argument, it only tells us that we should be suspicious of it. In fact, what is wrong with it would be revealed by the application of step 5. The conclusion that thoughts and electrical brain activity are identical does not follow from the premise that the absence of such activity is correlated with the absence of thought. Perhaps this premise shows that thought and electrical activity in the brain are related in some way, perhaps even that thought is somehow dependent on electrical activity in the brain, but it does not show that thought and such activity are one and the same thing.

Step 8: Check to see if the argument is an example of one of the common fallacies.

A *fallacy* is a bad argument and, by the application of the above steps, we have been checking for fallacies all along. There are *formal* fallacies such as the two I discussed under step 6, and there are *informal* fallacies. Any standard logic text includes a list of the most common fallacies and an explanation as to why they constitute faulty reasoning. I provide a very brief sample of some of the most common ones here.

1. Hasty generalization—This occurs when someone uses an example that is not typical to make a general point covering all causes. Example: "No one should drink alcohol in any amount, because my father drank alcohol, became an alcoholic, and died."

2. Begging the question—This occurs when someone assumes what they are trying to prove. Example: "God exists because the Bible says so and God wrote it."

3. Black and white—This bit of faulty reasoning occurs when someone falsely limits alternatives. Example: "Either we attack that country or we appease it and history shows appeasement is futile. Therefore, let it be war!"

4. Strawperson—This names the situation (all too common) of misconstruing the opponent's argument and refuting the misconstrual rather than the actual argument. Example: Pete argues that he is pro-choice because he believes women have the right to decide matters relating to their own bodies. Jack responds by arguing that Pete is pro-choice because he is in favor of murder. Since murder is wrong, Pete's pro-choice position is wrong. In fact, Pete's reason for being pro-choice is quite different from Jack's charge.

5. False analogy—This is a very common type of fallacy in which the alleged similarities either do not hold or are not relevant to the conclusion. Socrates, in a

dialogue with his friend Crito, argues that he must obey the laws of the state because the state is like his parents. Since the state has nurtured him as his parents have, he owes it respect and obedience. This argument has been criticized on the grounds that the analogy between the state and parents does not hold (states do not nurture in the same sense parents do) and even if it did, if one's parents gave you an unjust order it would be your moral obligation to disobey. Hence the similarity is irrelevant to the conclusion.

There is more to evaluating arguments than what I have covered here, but this is enough to get you started. A word of caution: Some people get so excited about their newfound critical tools that they go around picking arguments with people in order to refute them. Or they think that philosophy involves putting other people down and showing how stupid their reasoning is. The purpose of evaluating arguments is to improve our reasoning. Evaluation ought to be a constructive, not a negative process. If you find an argument that is bad, find out why, see if you can remove the defect, and construct a better one. Our reasoning can always stand improvement.

Exercise II   To see if you have understood how to evaluate arguments, answer the following questions and check your answers.

1. T or F   One would not be able to ask the question, "Are we having fun yet?" if the word "fun" were not vague.
2. T or F   In the definition "free will is voluntary choice," the genus is "choice."
3. T or F   In the definition "love is the feeling of intimacy and affection," the *differentiae* are intimacy and affection.
4. T or F   If "being loved by God" is a necessary condition of something being good, then nothing is good unless it is God-beloved.
5. T or F   If "being God-beloved" is a sufficient condition of goodness, then something that is not God-beloved might still be good.
6. "If Socrates should escape, then it is right to escape. It is not right to escape, therefore Socrates should not escape." This argument is (a) invalid, (b) a hasty generalization, (c) a fallacy of affirming the consequent, (d) valid, (e) both a and c.
7. John Calvin argues, "Since everything that God wills is fair and just for the very reason that He wills it, the terrible fate of the damned does not violate the principle of justice." This argument is an example of (a) begging the question, (b) strawperson, (c) hasty generalization, (d) black and white, (e) the fallacy of denying the antecedent.
8. "Either Jesus is the Son of God or he is a liar. He is not a liar. Therefore, he must be the Son of God." This is an example of (a) a strawperson, (b) black and white, (c) hasty generalization, (d) the fallacy of denying the antecedent, (e) begging the question.
9. With a friend, use the rules of a good definition and discuss whether Hobbes's definition, "Jealousy is love with fear that the love is not returned," is a good one.
10. Analyze and evaluate the following arguments, then compare your analysis

and evaluation with another student's and discuss how they differ. Remember, identify the conclusion first.

(a) "If there is life after death, then life is meaningful. If life is meaningful, then there is a reason for my life. If there is life after death, then there is reason for my life." (b) "There are two reasons why human beings are free. First, they experience freedom every time they make a choice that is voluntary and second, if humans were not free then our whole criminal justice system, which is based on the assumption that humans are responsible for their behavior, would make no sense."

A.3. Constructing Arguments

It is valuable to learn how to analyze and evaluate other people's arguments. People are always trying to persuade us of something. It helps to be able to follow their reasoning and evaluate it. But ultimately we want to become independent thinkers. We want to reason for ourselves and construct our own arguments. Logic can help us do that.

Constructing your own arguments requires more creativity than analyzing and evaluating what someone else has said. I can give you some hints that will help you build your own arguments, but in the final analysis you are the one who has to do the thinking. And thinking can be hard work. It takes time, concentration, and leisure to think an issue or a problem through to some kind of solution.

1. Start with your conclusion.

This seems odd advice. A conclusion should come at the end of the thought process, not at the beginning. In a sense it does and my advice supposes that you have already thought about an issue and reached some kind of tentative conclusion about what you think. For example, most of you have already thought about abortion or the death penalty or God's existence and formulated some beliefs about those issues. Start there, with what you already believe about some problem, and work backwards. For example, suppose you believe women should be treated as equal to men. State that as your conclusion and then look for your premises (I need to thank Richard Purtill, p. 219, for this example. See the list of suggested readings at the end of this appendix.)

2. Examine your reasons.

Why do you believe your conclusion? What has convinced you? List your reasons. These are your premises. State them as clearly and precisely as you can. For example, you think women ought to be treated as equal to men because there are no differences between men and women that justify unequal treatment. Further, it is unfair to treat people unequally unless such treatment is justified.

3. Use the appropriate argument type.

Cast your argument in premise and conclusion form using one of the standard types as a guideline. For example, if your conclusion is a generalization from specific cases, or if your reasons involve an analogy, and if your conclusion adds new information not contained in the premises, then you should state it as an inductive type of argument. If it is possible to state your argument in a valid deductive form, you may prefer that formulation since it presents a much more compelling argument. (Remember, in a valid deductive argument, the conclusion must be true if the premises are true but in an inductive argument, the premises may all be true and the conclusion might still be false.) Be sure to select one of the known valid forms as your blueprint.

It is sometimes helpful to substitute letters for the statements of your argument. This will help you see which statements are equivalent, and it will aid you in arranging the statements into a valid format. For instance, let's see if we can get the argument about equality into a deductively valid form. Let q = "Women should be treated as equal to men." Let p = "There are no differences between women and men that justify unequal treatment." We can now use *modus ponens* to create the following valid argument:

1. If there are no differences between women and men that justify unequal treatment, then women should be treated as equal to men. ($p \supset q$)
2. There are no differences between women and men that justify unequal treatment. (p)
3. Therefore, women should be treated as equal to men. (q)

Note that I have left out one of the reasons given above, namely that it is unfair to treat people unequally unless such treatment is justified. We could recast the argument in a more complex form to include this principle. Or as we develop our argument we might mention this as an assumption on which the argument is based. Presenting your argument in premise and conclusion form always involves some simplification. It is a shorthand way of stating things. However, stating it in this form has the advantage of clarity. You can always flesh things out and bring in the complications in the discussion of the argument.

Once you have your argument stated, evaluate it. Use the steps we discussed in the last section to examine your own argument. Play devil's advocate and try to expose its weaknesses. Then repair those weaknesses as you develop your argument.

4. Define your terms.

You do not have to define every word you use, but you do need to define key words that might be unclear. In our example, I think words like "men" and "women" and "differences" are clear enough. But what about "equal treatment"? That seems to be a key part of this argument and might well be vague or ambiguous. Our definition should try to remove any ambiguity or vagueness.

There are different ways of defining words, as we noted in the last section. Analytic definitions are particularly difficult to provide because of the need to state both the necessary and sufficient characteristics of the *definiendum*. It is easier to give a cluster type of definition in which you state what you take to be the most important (but not necessarily the essential) characteristics of the *definiendum*.

Suppose you think the main characteristics of equal treatment are impartial judgment, fair dealings, and balanced recompense. If you do, then these would be your defining characteristics. Anything exemplifying one or more of these traits would be an example of equal treatment.

Be sure to use the criteria of a good definition to check your own definitions. For instance, are the words "impartial," "fair," and "balanced" any less vague than the word "equal"? If you find problems, try to improve the definition. It is best to think of concrete examples (such as same pay for same work) and ask whether these constitute examples of equal treatment and why they do (or don't).

5. Support your premises and justify your assumptions.

Are your premises true? Sometimes your premises and assumptions will be widely accepted principles or facts that do not require support or further justification. Other times they will be controversial. Support controversial premises and assumptions with evidence and additional argumentation.

For example, the first premise (if there are no differences between women and men that justify unequal treatment, then women should be treated as equal to men) of the argument about equality seems uncontroversial. Most people would agree that if unequal treatment is not justified, it ought not to be practiced. However, you may wish to make explicit the assumption on which this premise is based. The assumption is that it is *unfair* to treat people unequally unless such treatment is justified. In other words, you are assuming, all things being equal, that equal treatment is better than unequal treatment. This is a value judgment that, I believe, most people would accept. But you need to make it explicit and, if someone should happen to challenge it, you would need to be prepared to support it by further argumentation.

Your second premise (there are no differences between women and men that justify unequal treatment) is controversial and therefore does require support. Most arguments that support inequality maintain that there are significant differences between men and women that do justify unequal treatment. How might you support the second premise? Well, you might make a list of all the differences that those who favor unequal treatment cite, such as: women are more emotional than men, men are stronger than women, men are better at math and science than women, and so on. The first thing you could do with such a list is sort the *real differences* from the *unreal* ones. For example, it is simply not true that women are more emotional than men. However, it is true that men are, generally speaking, physically stronger than women (at least with respect to upper body strength). Once you have your list of real differences, the key question you need to ask is, "Do these real differences *justify* unequal treatment?" To be more concrete, "Is it right to pay women less than men if they are physically weaker?" In seeking an answer to this question you will need to reintroduce the principle of fairness you have assumed.

Sometimes a good strategy is to assume the opposite of what you want to support and see where that leads (recall the *reductio* argument). Let's assume women should be paid less than men because they are weaker. Given the fairness principle, it follows that men who are weaker than other men and men who are weaker than women ought to be paid less. But this is absurd. Does a pay scale based on physical strength make any sense? This line of reasoning has uncovered a good general principle we can now use to examine other differences, namely, "If a given difference (x) is not used as a basis for unequal treatment of men, it is reasonable to conclude it should not be used as a basis for unequal treatment of women." You can now support the second premise by showing that all the real differences between men and women also exist among men, and if they are not used to justify unequal treatment among men, they should not be used to justify unequal treatment among women.

When supporting your premises and developing your argument it is always best to state the strongest objections to your position. If you can refute the best objections, you thereby strengthen your argument. If you cannot refute them, you had better reconsider your reasoning.

6. Use clear examples and illustrations.

Confusion often arises on the abstract level. Bring your reasoning back down to earth with concrete illustrations. Often, just trying to think up good illustrations reveals a mistake in reasoning or opens up a new line of argument. Notice how, in developing the equality argument, we moved back and forth between concrete examples and more general principles.

7. Keep your audience in mind.

We not only use logical reasoning to clarify our own thinking, to help us make decisions, and to arrive at solutions to problems, we also use it to persuade other people, defend ourselves, and refute other people's arguments. If your audience is another person, persuasive and rhetorical considerations are important. Don't overstate your case. Don't claim more than you can demonstrate. Qualify your conclusions appropriately. Be courteous. Emphasize areas of agreement. Appeal to generally accepted principles and definitions. Be clear and use concrete examples. Make it clear that you are interested in arriving at the most reasonable conclusion and that you are not interested in just scoring points.

Keep in mind that there are many different uses of argument. Often we use arguments to *persuade* others, and I have assumed such a context in the example I have given. But we also use arguments to *reconcile* seemingly opposed ideas. For example, philosophers have been much concerned with reconciling the principle of causation with the view that humans are free. And we use arguments to *dissolve* problems. Philosophers in this century, for example, have spent much time and effort trying to show that some philosophical problems, such as the relationship between the mind and the body, are pseudoproblems. When evaluating and constructing arguments it is important to keep in mind their purpose. Convincing others is only one of the many uses of argument.

Exercise III   Answer the following questions. Check your answers to see what you have learned about constructing arguments. If you get something wrong, see if you can determine your mistake.

1. If you were using the argument form called *modus ponens* and you knew the first premise was, "If the existence of God is a matter of faith, it cannot be proved," what would be the second premise?
2. If you were using the argument form called *modus tollens* and you knew the conclusion was, "God does not exist" and the second premise was, "Not everything that happens is good," what would the first premise be?
3. Suppose you were using the hypothetical syllogism to construct an argument that concludes, "If I think, then I exist." What might your first and second premises be like?
4. Suppose you were using the disjunctive syllogism to show that Zhuangzi was dreaming he was a butterfly. What might your first and second premises be like?
5. Give a definition of suffering.
6. Give a definition of happiness.
7. Give a definition of good.
8. Provide a concrete illustration of the principle, "We should not believe beyond the evidence."

9. Create an inductive argument using an analogy that concludes that God exists.
10. Create an argument in favor of the position that drugs ought to be legalized. Compare your argument with someone else's in the class. Discuss which one is better and why.

Suggestions for Further Reading

Irving M. Copi has written a standard and widely used book, *Introduction to Logic,* 7th ed. (New York: Macmillan, 1986), that will provide you with more detailed explanations and a wider range of exercises relating to the topics I have discussed in this appendix. Also see Robert Rafalko's *Logic for an Overcast Tuesday* (Belmont, CA: Wadsworth, 1990).

Chapter 1 of *A Logical Introduction to Philosophy* by Richard L. Purtill (Englewood Cliffs, NJ: Prentice-Hall, 1989) provides a useful discussion of analytic and cluster definitions. The last two chapters on analyzing and constructing philosophical arguments might also prove useful, provided you take the time to learn the logical notation and techniques he has developed in the body of the book.

Since reading, writing, and constructing philosophical arguments are closely related you can also benefit from looking at A. P. Martinich's *Philosophical Writing: An Introduction* (Englewood Cliffs, NJ: Prentice-Hall, 1989).

Answers to Exercise I

1. T
2. F
3. F
4. Yes. "Philosophy should be called the science of truth." There is a missing premise here, namely, "philosophy is a theoretical science."
5. a
6. e
7. b
8. T
9. d
10. e
11. c
12. Two forms are possible: (a) Logic is fun or Gumby exists. Logic is not fun, therefore Gumby exists. (b) Logic is fun or Gumby exists. Gumby does not exist, therefore logic is fun.
13. If I am unconscious then q (whatever you say), not q, therefore I am not unconscious.
14. Whatever the content, the form should be "If p then q," "p," therefore "q."

Answers to Exercise II

1. T
2. T
3. T

4. T
5. T
6. d
7. a
8. b

Answers to Exercise III

1. "The existence of God is a matter of faith."
2. "If God exists, everything that happens is good."
3. First: "If I think, I am alive." (You may use any statement you wish for the consequent; mine is only one example.) Second: "If I am alive, I exist."
4. First: "Either Zhuangzi is dreaming he is a butterfly or he is not." Second: "It is not the case that he is not dreaming that he is a butterfly."
5. Compare your definition to Spinoza's definition of suffering as the "transition from a more perfect to a less perfect state." Is your definition better or not? Why?
6. Compare your definition to Aristotle's definition of happiness as "living well and doing well." Is his better? Why or why not?
7. Compare your definition to Mill's definition of good as "mental and physical pleasure." Which do you think is better and why?
8. An owner of an airline who orders his planes to fly because he believes they are safe even though they have not been properly inspected.
9. Here is one example. Machines are ordered for a purpose by an intelligent designer. The universe is also arranged for a purpose, just like a machine. Hence it too must be intelligently designed, and the name for the designer is God.

Appendix B

Glossary

Absolute skepticism. (see **Skepticism**)

Advaita Vedanta. A school of Hindu philosophy founded by Shankara and teaching that reality is nondual (*advaita*).

Aesthetics. A subdivision of the field of axiology (value theory) which has to do with philosophical reflection on a range of concepts relevant to art, such as beauty, harmony, structure, plot, texture, narrative, fiction, composition, and so on.

Allah. The Muslim name for God. Allah is viewed as a unitary sovereign, creator God of infinite mercy and goodness whose will is absolute.

Analytic statements. Statements that are necessarily true by virtue of the meaning of the words. According to Hume, such statements are about the relations of ideas, and it is not possible for their negation to be true. They are the opposite of synthetic statements.

Anarchism. The political theory asserting that governments, by their very nature, are immoral and should not be formed. It is based on the idea that only the individual has ultimate moral authority.

Anatta (also Anatman). A Buddhist term meaning "no-self." It refers to the Buddhist doctrine that there is no *Atman*. It is the denial of the notion that there exists a substance which constitutes the human self or soul.

Anicca. A Buddhist term meaning "impermanence." According to this teaching there are no eternal substances, essences, or ideal Forms (as in Plato's theory of Forms).

A posteriori. Latin meaning "following from" or "after" and used to characterize reasoning based on sense experience and to identify human experience as the place from which ideas come. Knowledge that *follows from* or comes from experience is called *a posteriori*.

A priori. Latin meaning "prior to" or "before" and used to refer to reasoning based on reason (in contrast to sense experience) and to identify ideas as innate (acquired *prior* to sense experience) or as valid independent of experience. Mathematical knowledge is frequently characterized as *a priori* because its truth does not depend on sense experience.

Atheism. The belief that God does not exist.

Atman. Usually translated "Self." According to some schools of Hindu philosophy, it is pure consciousness or consciousness itself and constitutes the essence of all reality. It is to be distinguished from the ego, or individual self.

Axiology. A branch of philosophy concerned with developing a theory of value. Ethics (moral value) and aesthetics (artistic value) are two main subdivisions.

Behaviorism. The view that mental states are either equivalent to the behaviors of an organism or dispositions to behave.

Brahman. A Sanskrit term that can refer to the creator God or, as in Shankara, to the source and essence of all reality. Sometimes translated as "Godhead," a term that refers to the essence of the divine.

Categorical imperative. This concept refers to a command or law that is unconditional. Such a law instructs us to do something regardless of the consequences. According to Kant, this is the principle of all morality. Kant characterized it as the highest moral law and formulated it in several ways, one of which states that humans should be treated as ends, not means.

Classical liberalism. A political position that promotes individual sovereignty and the maximizing of freedom from state intervention.

Coherence theory of truth. (see **Truth**)

Common sense skepticism. (see **Skepticism**)

Compensatory justice. The sort of justice that demands the correct distribution of benefits to those who have suffered unfair hardship. Affirmative action programs are often justified on these grounds.

Correspondence theory of truth. (see **Truth**)

Cosmological argument. An *a posteriori* argument from the existence of the universe (cosmos) to God as the cause, creator, or explanation of the universe's existence.

Dao. A concept central to Chinese philosophy, usually translated as "The Way." It has a variety of meanings, but is often used to refer to the way of nature or the way reality functions.

De. A Chinese word meaning "excellence" or "power," often translated as "virtue."

Deism. A view of God that emphasizes God's remoteness from the creation. God is a first cause who starts the universe running according to natural laws and does not interfere in its operation.

Democracy. The political theory stating that the people are sovereign and have the right to rule.

Deontological. This term refers to ethical theories (such as Kant's) that stress the importance of the motive of doing one's duty as a determining factor in assessing the moral value of actions. It is the motive for, not the consequences of, actions that count.

Dependent origination. A Buddhist doctrine asserting that the existence of all things is conditioned by or dependent on the existence of other things.

Descriptive. This concept is usually contrasted with normative (what ought to be) and is used to refer to a type of reflection that seeks to describe the way in *fact* things are.

Determinism. The belief that every event has a cause in the sense that for every event there is a set of conditions such that if the conditions were repeated the event would be repeated.

Dharma. A Sanskrit term meaning "duty," also "teachings" or "doctrines." In Hindu philosophy, it is often used to refer to the moral law and order believed to be inherent in nature.

Direct realism. (see **Realism**)

Distributive justice. The fair distribution of benefits such as wealth, privileges, rights, and honor among the members of a society.

Divine command theory. A position holding that what makes an action morally right is the fact that God commands or wills it.

Doctrine of the mean. A Confucian concept referring to a universal moral order that consists in the harmony of all things. Also the title of a Confucian book developing this idea.

Double-aspect theory. The view that the mind and body are two different aspects of one substance, which is itself neither mental nor physical. (see **Neutral monism**)

Dualism. A metaphysical theory holding that two fundamentally different things, usually characterized as mind and matter (body), are real.

Egalitarianism. The view that all persons, just because they are persons, should share equally in all benefits and burdens.

Eightfold path. This term refers to the way of attaining enlightenment taught by Buddhism. This path consists of right views, right thought, right speech, right action, right livelihood, right effort, right mindfulness, and right concentration.

Empiricism. An epistemological theory holding that (1) knowledge derives from sense experience and (2) knowledge claims are verified by reference to sense experience.

Epiphenomenalism. This term refers to a theory that views mental events as by-products of physical events.

Epistemology. A branch of philosophy concerned with developing a theory of knowledge and truth.

Ethics. A subdivision of axiology concerned with the study of moral value.

Eudaimonia. This term is usually translated as "happiness" or "living well" and can be thought of as self-realization. The concept is used by Aristotle to refer to the final good or purpose of human action, namely, to realize or actualize essential human nature.

Existentialism. A philosophical movement that takes as its starting point reflection on the concrete existence of humans and what it means to be a human being living in the sort of world in which we actually live.

Fascism. The political view that the interests of the individual ought to be subordinated to the interests of the state. Usually associated with right-wing popular movements that celebrate military power and use the power of the state to suppress dissent.

Fatalism. The view that some or all events are predetermined by an impersonal force or power.

Five aggregates. These are physical form, sensation, conceptualization, dispositions to act, and consciousness. According to Buddhism, they constitute the processes that make up the individual.

Five Pillars of Islam. These are the five central practices of Islam: (1) witnessing that there is no God but Allah and that Muhammad is his Apostle, (2) *salat* or mandatory prayers, (3) *zakat* or mandatory alms, (4) fasting during the holy month of Ramadan, and (5) *hajj* or pilgrimage to Mecca.

Formal principle of justice. The principle stating that we ought to treat people fairly with respect to relevantly similar (or relevantly different) traits.

Forms. (see **Theory of Forms**)

Foundationalism. The claim that rationality and knowledge rest on a firm foundation of self-evident truths.

Four causes. Aristotle's theory that things which exist have four causes: an efficient cause or agency by which they are made, a material cause or stuff out of which they are made, a formal cause (the idea or essence) according to which they are made, and a final cause or purpose for which they are made.

Four Noble Truths. The name for the heart of the Buddha's teaching: (1) life is suffering, (2) the cause of suffering is craving, (3) suffering can be overcome, and (4) the Eightfold Path or the Middle Way of right understanding, thought, speech, action, livelihood, effort, mindfulness, and concentration is the way to attain release from suffering.

Functionalism. Used in the context of the debate about mind and body, functionalism holds that the human brain is analogous to a computer. A given brain state can be viewed as a mental state because it performs the appropriate function.

Hard determinism. The theory that every event has a cause and that this fact is incompatible with the existence of free will. Hence human beings should not be held morally responsible for their actions because it is impossible for them to do other than what they do.

Hedonism. A moral theory holding that the highest or greatest good is pleasure.

Idealism. A metaphysical theory holding that only ideas (minds and mental events) are real or that they are more real, valuable, and enduring than material things. In an ethical context, "idealistic" is sometimes used to refer to a person who lives by ideals or to a view based on principle.

Identity theory. The view that mental events are identical with brain events.

Immortality of the soul. The view that the soul, which constitutes the essence of a person, lives forever and can exist apart from a physical body.

Indirect realism. (see **Realism**)

Innate ideas. Refers to ideas we are born with. A concept used by rationalists to characterize the state of the human mind prior to sense experience.

Interactionism. The theory that the mind and body, though they are two distinct and different substances, nevertheless are able to causally affect one another.

Kalam. A name for an Arabic school of theology concerned with cosmological arguments for God's existence.

Karma. This term comes from a Sanskrit word meaning "action." It is often used to refer to the consequences of actions and the natural moral law that governs actions called the law of Karma ("You will reap what you sow.").

Karma yoga. This term refers to a practice that allegedly allows one to escape karmic consequences and hence to escape the cycle of reincarnation.

Laissez-faire capitalism. An economic theory based on the idea of a totally free market.

Law of Noncontradiction. A cannot be A and not A in the same respect and at the same time.

Li. A Confucian concept meaning order, ceremony, custom, and propriety.

Libertarianism. The theory that human choice is not caused (determined) by antecedent events. Human beings are free agents with the power to decide contrary to the influence of character and inclination. Hence, when deciding freely, humans can and should be held morally responsible. This term is also used in a political context to name a movement that supports the idea that the role of government ought to be severely restricted and individual freedom ought to be maximized.

Madhyamika. A school of Buddhist philosophy founded by Nagarjuna, which stresses the critical analysis of ideas, the inherent contradictoriness of all intellectual views, and the idea that truth is twofold.

Materialism. The metaphysical view holding that matter alone is real, also called physicalism. Negatively, it is the denial of the existence of immaterial, mental, and spiritual reality. Also used in an ethical context to refer to a value system that prizes material goods and possessions above other things.

Material principle of justice. This term refers to some specific trait upon which decisions of distribution, retribution, and compensation are made, for example, all those who work 25 years get a 10 percent bonus.

Mechanism. The view that the universe operates like a machine according to the law of cause and effect. The opposite of a teleological view.

Metaphysics. A major branch of philosophy which has traditionally been viewed as attempting to develop a theory of what is genuinely real.

Methodical skepticism. (see **Skepticism**)

Middle Way. This term is used in general to characterize Buddhist teaching and practice as a "middle" way between extremes. It also has a variety of specialized meanings, such as specific reference to the Fourth Noble Truth or the Eightfold Path.

Mind-body problem. The problem of defining what mind and body are and stating clearly how they are related.

Monism. A metaphysical theory holding that reality is one.

Moral absolutism. (see **Objectivism**)

Moral relativism. (see **Relativism**)

Moral skepticism. The position that doubts the existence of moral truth and the possibility of ethical knowledge.

Muslim. Literally it means "one who submits to Allah's will" and is used to refer to the members of the Islamic religion.

Naive realism. Same as direct realism. (see **Realism**)

Naiyayika. An Indian school of philosophy concerned with a whole range of philosophical issues, but most often associated with advancing a theory of knowledge called "Pramana." (See **Pramana**)

Naturalism. The view that the universe is a self-existing, self-regulating, homogeneous system.

Natural theology. (see **Theology**)

Neutral monism. The view that what exists is neither mental nor physical, but neutral with respect to these properties. (See **Double-aspect theory**)

Nirvana. A Buddhist term meaning "release from suffering." Attaining *nirvana* is thought to be the goal of life.

Normative. This concept, often contrasted with descriptive, is used to refer to a type of reflection that seeks to discover the way things *ought* to be. It has to with norms (rules for correct behavior).

Nyaya. A name for a school of Hindu philosophy that emphasizes logic and holds that there are four sources of knowledge: perception, inference, comparison, and testimony.

Objective idealism. The view that reality is a manifestation of an absolute mind.

Objectivism. A view holding that there is some permanent, transcultural, and transhistorical framework for determining rationality, knowledge, truth, reality, and moral value. The opposite of relativism.

Occam's razor. A principle advocated by William Occam that advises us not to multiply entities beyond necessity. That is, when inventing explanations for an event we should posit as existing only those things necessary to explain the event.

Ontological argument. An *a priori* argument for God's existence that attempts to deduce God's existence from a definition of God's nature.

Ontology. The study of being as such. A major subdivision of metaphysics.

Pantheism. The view that God is the infinite, unitary, and self-existing cause of all existence and is the same as nature.

Parallelism. The theory that mental and physical events parallel one another in a coordinated manner, but do not causally interact.

Paternalism. The view that one person or group knows what is in the best interests of others.

Philosophy. This word derives from the Greek word for "love of wisdom." It has been defined in a variety of ways, one of which is the notion that philosophy is the rational attempt to formulate, understand, and answer fundamental questions.

Philosophy of religion. The use of philosophical methods to study a variety of religious issues such as the relation of faith to reason, God's existence, life after death, and the nature of religious experience.

Pluralism. The metaphysical theory holding that there are many different realities and that they are not reducible to a single reality or to only two basic realities. Also used in a different context to refer to a society characterized by a variety of different cultural groups.

Positivism. A view holding that modern science and its methods are the sole trustworthy guide to the truth.

Pragmatic theory of truth. (see **Truth**)

Pragmatism. The name for a philosophical movement that developed in the United States, which stresses that, in determining both the meaning and truth of our beliefs, we must pay attention to their implications for our behavior.

Prajna. This word is often translated as "wisdom," "insight," or "knowledge." It is used by Buddhists to refer to direct insight into reality.

Prakriti. A Sanskrit term usually translated as "matter" or "nature." It refers to that which is not conscious.

Pramana. The means of knowledge developed in Indian philosophy: perception, inference, comparison (analogy), and reliable testimony.

Praxis. Reflection on the world and the social conditions of humans and action designed to change the conditions of oppression.

Predestination. The belief that some or all events (including the salvation of some people) are predetermined by a personal divine power.

Primary qualities. (see **Secondary qualities**)

Problem of evil. In the broad sense, it refers to the problem of explaining and making sense of evil. In the theological sense, it refers to the difficulty of reconciling the existence of evil with the existence of a perfectly good, all-powerful, creator God.

Problem of freedom and determinism. If all events are caused, how can human actions be free?

Problem of induction. The problem of providing a rational justification for inductive reasoning. Hume claimed we could not provide such a justification and so our trust in inductive reasoning was rooted in custom or habit, not reason.

Problem of one and many. Is reality fundamentally one thing or many things?

Process ontology. The view that change is a basic feature of reality and that all aspects of reality are interrelated.

Purusha. A Sanskrit term meaning "person," often used for a cosmic being from which the universe is derived.

Rationalism. An epistemological theory holding that all genuine knowledge derives from reason and is justified *a priori* (independent of sense experience). The opposite of empiricism.

Realism. The view that objects exist apart from a mind that knows them. *Representational or indirect* realism holds that sensations put us indirectly in touch with real objects which they represent; *direct* realism holds that we are directly in touch with physical objects via our senses.

Reincarnation. The view that souls or karmic effects can become attached to successive physical bodies and hence be reborn over and over again.

Relativism. A view found in both ethics and epistemology that denies the existence of objective, transcultural moral values and/or standards of rationality. The only moral values and standards of rationality that exist are relative to either individuals (*individual relativism*) or societies (*social relativism*).

Ren. A Confucian concept commonly translated as "benevolence" or "humaneness." It refers to the highest human virtue or excellence.

Representational realism. (see **Realism**)

Resurrection of the body. The view that after death a person is recreated and constitutes the same person who lived before death.

Retributive justice. A corrective distribution of burdens to persons who undeservedly enjoy benefits or to those who are guilty of failing to fulfill their responsibilities. Legal penalties for breaking the law are examples of the application of this principle.

Revealed theology. (see **Theology**)

Samsara. A Buddhist and Hindu concept referring to the life of suffering and the constant round of birth, death, and rebirth in which we are trapped.

Secondary qualities. The objects of the five senses (sounds, colors, odors, flavors, textures) are called secondary because they exist in the mind. *Primary qualities* (extension, figure, motion, rest, solidity, and number) are traits of physical objects that exist apart from the mind.

Shi'a. A branch of Islam that believes Allah gave the right to rule to the religious leaders (Imans).

Skepticism. An epistemological theory which, in its absolute form, contends that knowledge is not possible. *Common sense* skepticism and *methodical* skepticism are not so absolute. The former doubts some but not all knowledge claims and the latter uses doubt as a tool in the search for truth.

Social and political philosophy. The normative (as opposed to the descriptive) study of government, the state, and issues of social policy.

Social contract. A theory of political sovereignty claiming that the authority of government derives from a voluntary agreement among all the people of a society to form a political community and to obey the laws laid down by the government they collectively select.

Socialism. An economic system based on collective ownership of the means of production, rational economic planning, and the equal distribution of goods and services.

Socratic method. The method of critical analysis Socrates developed in an effort to uncover the essential qualities of various concepts.

Soft determinism. Also called compatibilism because, according to this theory, determinism (the fact that every event has a cause) is compatible with the existence of human freedom. Human beings can and should be held morally responsible for whatever they voluntarily do.

Solipsism. The view that only your own mind and thoughts exist; nothing besides them is really real.

Subjective idealism. The view that physical objects do not exist apart from their perception.

Sublation. Literally this word means "to carry or wipe away." Often used in logic for the activity of contradicting, negating, or correcting. The concept is used by Shankara in conjunction with the distinction between appearance and reality. Appearance is sublatable, but reality is not.

Substance ontology. A view holding that permanence is the basic feature of reality and that one or more substances exist independently in the sense that they would exist even if other things did not.

Sufism. A mystical movement in Islam which teaches that a direct and immediate experience of Allah is possible.

Sunni. A branch of Islam that believes Allah gave the right to rule to the whole community.

Synthetic statements. Statements whose truth value depends on the way the world is. According to Hume, they are about matters of fact, and it is possible for their negation to be true. They are the opposite of analytic statements.

Tabula rasa. The term means "blank tablet or slate." It is used by some empiricists to characterize the state of the human mind prior to sense experience. It stands in contrast with the concept of innate ideas.

Teleological argument. An *a posteriori* argument for God's existence, which begins with the premise that the world exhibits purposeful order and concludes that this order is the result of the actions of a divine intelligence.

Teleology. The word comes from the Greek *telos* (goal, purpose, or end) and *logos* (word, reason, study), hence, literally, "the study of ends or goals." It is often used to refer to the position that the universe has a goal, purpose, or final cause and that everything that happens contributes toward achieving that goal or outcome. In ethics, it is used to refer to those theories that stress that the consequences or outcomes of actions are what determines their moral value.

Theism. The view that God is the infinite, unitary, all-powerful, perfectly good, self-existent cause of all things and is a personal being who created the universe out of nothing and directs it according to teleological laws.

Theocracy. The political theory that holds that God is and ought to be the ruler of human societies and the government must rule according to God's laws.

Theodicy. In the broad sense, any proposed solution to the problem of evil. In the narrow sense, any solution to the problem of evil that reconciles the existence of evil with the existence of God.

Theology. The study of divine reality or God, sometimes divided into *natural theology,* which deals with possible knowledge about God based on the use of reason alone, and *revealed theology,* which claims knowledge about God based on special revelations.

Theory of forms. A Platonic theory claiming that forms or concepts constitute essences that exist in their own right, as entities independent of the world of appearances in which they may be manifest.

Totalitarianism. The political theory claiming that the state's entitlement to rule extends to all aspects of life and that the authority of the state is beyond question.

Truth. Three theorists have determined philosophical discussion: (1) the *pragmatic theory,* which holds that "p is true if and only if believing that p is true works," (2) the *correspondence theory,* which holds that "p is true if and only if p corresponds to the facts," and (3) the *coherence theory,* which holds that "p is true, if and only if p is logically implied by q, and q is true."

Utilitarianism. A moral theory holding that the value of an action resides in its utility or use for the production of pleasure or happiness.

Wakan Tanka. This is one of the names used by the Lakota Native Americans for the Supreme Being.

Wuwei. A Chinese word meaning "no action" and referring to acting unselfishly, naturally, and spontaneously.

Xiao. The Confucian virtue of familial love, loyalty, obedience, and piety.

Yi. The Confucian principle of rightness. Do what is good because it is good.

Yin and yang. A Chinese concept referring to the basic opposites that make up reality and are complementary. *Yin* is the passive and *yang* the active force.